SOCIAL PROBLEMS

Thirteenth Edition

D. STANLEY EITZEN
Colorado State University

MAXINE BACA ZINN
Michigan State University

KELLY EITZEN SMITH
University of Arizona, Drachman Institute

PEARSON

Boston   Columbus   Indianapolis   New York   San Francisco   Upper Saddle River
Amsterdam   Cape Town   Dubai   London   Madrid   Milan   Munich   Paris   Montreal   Toronto
Delhi   Mexico City   Sao Paulo   Sydney   Hong Kong   Seoul   Singapore   Taipei   Tokyo

Editor in Chief: *Dickson Musslewhite*
Publisher: *Charlyce Jones-Owen*
Editorial Assistant: *Maureen Diana*
Program Manager: *Beverly Fong*
Director of Marketing: *Brandy Dawson*
Senior Marketing Manager: *Maureen Prado Roberts*
Team Lead, Production: *Ann Marie McCarthy*
Production Project Manager: *Manuel Echevarria*
Director of Digital Media: *Brian Hyland*
Senior Media Project Manager: *Nikhil Bramhavar*

Media Production Manager: *Peggy Bliss*
Digital Media Editor: *Alison Lorber*
Art Director: *Anne Bonanno Nieglos*
Interior Designer: *Wanda España/Wee Design Group*
Cover Designer: *Studio Montage*
Cover Photo: *Jochen Tack/Alamy*
Full Service Project Manager: *Karen Berry/Laserwords*
Manufacturing Manager: *Mary Fischer*
Manufacturing Buyer: *Diane Peirano*
Printer: *Courier/Kendallville*

Credits and acknowledgments borrowed from other sources and reproduced, with permission, in this textbook appear on the appropriate page within text.

Library of Congress Cataloging-in-Publication Data

Eitzen, D. Stanley.
  Social problems / D. Stanley Eitzen, Colorado State University, Maxine Baca Zinn, Michigan State University, Kelly Eitzen Smith, University of Arizona. — Thirteenth Edition.
    pages cm
  Includes bibliographical references and index.
  ISBN 0-205-88188-2
  1. Social problems. 2. Social problems—United States. 3. Social structure—United States. 4. United States—Social conditions—1945–
I. Zinn, Maxine Baca. II. Smith, Kelly Eitzen. III. Title.
  HN17.5.E372 2013
  361.1—dc23

2013014676

10 9 8 7 6 5 4 3 2 1

Student Hardcover Edition:
ISBN 10:   0-205-88188-2
ISBN 13: 978-0-205-88188-8

Books á la Carte Edition:
ISBN 10:   0-205-88239-0
ISBN 13: 978-0-205-88239-7

PEARSON

www.pearsonhighered.com

BRIEF CONTENTS

CONTENTS

BOX FEATURES

PREFACE

Social Problems, Thirteenth Edition, examines inherently interesting subjects such as corporate crime, racism, sexism, urban decay, poverty, health care, the changing economy, the politics of drugs, antigovernment movements, and terrorism. The typical book on social problems describes these phenomena separately, using a variety of explanations. Students exposed to such a mélange of approaches might retain their interest in these problems, but they probably would complete the book with little grasp of how social problems are interrelated and society's role in their creation and perpetuation. This book is different. The approach is consistently sociological. There is a coherent framework from which to analyze and understand society's social problems.

The overarching goal in *Social Problems*, Thirteenth Edition, is to capture the imaginations of our readers. We want them not only to be interested in the topics but also to become enthusiastic about exploring the intricacies and mysteries of social life. We want them, moreover, to incorporate the sociological perspective (imagination) into their explanatory repertoire. The sociological perspective requires, at a minimum, acceptance of two fundamental assumptions. The first is that individuals are products of their social environment. Who they are, what they believe, what they strive for, and how they feel about themselves are all dependent on other people and on the society in which they live. The incorporation of the sociological perspective requires that we examine the structure of society to understand such social problems as racism, poverty, and crime. This method, however, runs counter to the typical explanations people offer for social ills. The choice is seen in an example supplied by Thomas Szasz:

> *Suppose that a person wishes to study slavery. How would he go about doing so? First, he might study slaves. He would then find that such persons are generally brutish, poor, and uneducated, and he might conclude that slavery is their "natural" or appropriate social status. . . . Another student "biased" by contempt for the institution of slavery might proceed differently. He would maintain that there can be no slave without a master holding him in bondage; and he would accordingly consider slavery a type of human relationship and, more generally, a social institution supported by custom, law, religion, and force. From this point of view, the study of masters is at least as relevant to the study of slavery as is the study of slaves. (Szasz 1970:123–124)*

Most of us, intuitively, would make the first type of study and reach a conclusion. This book, however, emphasizes the second type of study: looking at "masters" as well as "slaves." An observer cannot gain an adequate understanding of racism, crime, poverty, or other social problems by studying only bigots, criminals, and the poor. Therefore, we focus on the social structure to determine the underlying features of the social world in an effort to understand social problems.

Because the emphasis is on social structure, the reader is required to accept another fundamental assumption of the sociological perspective (see Eitzen, Baca Zinn, and Smith 2013). We refer to the adoption of a critical stance toward all social forms. Sociologists must ask these questions: How does the social system really work? Who has the power? Who benefits under the existing social arrangements, and who does not? We should also ask questions such as, Is the law neutral? Why are some drugs illegal and others, known to be harmful, legal? Why are so few organizations in the United States—which is characterized as a democracy—democratic? Is U.S. society a meritocratic one in which talent and effort combine to stratify people fairly? Questions such as these call into question existing myths, stereotypes, and official dogma. The critical examination of society demystifies and demythologizes. It sensitizes the individual to the inconsistencies present in society. But, most important, a critical stance toward social arrangements allows us to see their role in perpetuating social problems. In conclusion, the reader should be aware that we are not dispassionate observers of social problems.

Let us, then, briefly make our values more explicit. We oppose social arrangements that prevent people from developing to their full potential. That is, we reject political and social repression, educational elitism, institutional barriers to racial and sexual equality, economic exploitation, and official indifference to human suffering. Stating these feelings positively, we favor equality of opportunity, the right to dissent, social justice, an economic system that minimizes inequality, and a political system that maximizes citizen input in decisions and provides for an adequate healthcare system and acceptable living conditions for all people. Obviously, we believe that U.S. society as currently organized falls short of what we consider to be a good society. The problem areas of U.S. society are the subjects of this edition. So, too, are structural arrangements around the globe that harm people.

In 2001, the Colorado Commission on Higher Education (a state oversight commission appointed by the governor) commissioned a conservative watchdog group to evaluate teacher education programs in the state universities of Colorado. The report criticized the University of Colorado's School of Education for pushing an agenda that "indoctrinates" students in issues of race, class, gender, and sexual orientation. David Saxe, the principal investigator of the report, said, "More than any other reviewed institution, CU's teacher education programs are the most politically correct and stridently committed to the social justice model" (quoted in Curtin 2001:1B). Suffice it to say that our approach to social problems would also be castigated by Mr. Saxe, for we are absolutely committed to social justice; and this means, among other things, understanding how many social problems of U.S. society are rooted in the hierarchical arrangements based on class, race, gender, and sexuality.

NEW TO THIS EDITION

Since the last edition of *Social Problems* was published, certain events have shaken U.S. society, and important trends have become even more significant, making a major revision necessary. For example,

- The U.S. has ended its involvement in the Iraq war and is committed to do the same in Afghanistan. The U.S. budget for the military continues to rise. The terrorist threat remains with us, both from external and internal sources.
- World population continues to increase by about 76 million a year, almost all of the increase in poor countries. Put another way, 157 new people join the world's population every minute, 153 of them in developing countries.
- The U.S. population has moved past 300 million and will add another 120 million by 2050. At about 5 percent of the world's population, the United States has an enormous environmental footprint—emitting one-fourth of the world's greenhouse gases and using one-fourth of the world's resources.
- Non-Whites will be the numerical majority in the United States by 2042. Immigration increases racial/ethnic tensions in some parts of the nation.
- Politics in the United States has been more and more polarized, resulting in factions unwilling to compromise.
- The Supreme Court has ruled that money is a form of speech and therefore cannot be curtailed in politics. As a consequence, money from large organizations and wealthy individuals is swamping elections and making a mockery of democracy.

- Although some large cities in the United States are showing signs of vigor, many are troubled with growing dependent populations, shrinking job markets, increasing racial tensions, and declining economic resources to meet their problems.
- The economy continues its massive transformation from a manufacturing economy to one based on service/knowledge. This causes disruptions as some companies fail while others succeed. Globalization, with jobs and tasks moving outside the country, adds to the unemployment woes accompanying the economic transformation.
- The Great Recession hit in 2007 and caused havoc on Wall Street, Main Street, and in families. Unemployment rose precipitously. Wall Street tumbled. The value of housing dropped, causing bankruptcies and foreclosures. These economic difficulties continue.
- Government bailouts of the banks and recovery efforts such as an economic stimulus, plus the cost of conducting two wars, raised the national debt dramatically to $15.8 trillion by July 2012. This huge debt provided a rationale to limit government by reducing or eliminating social welfare programs.
- Obamacare has been upheld by the Supreme Court. The public is divided on this healthcare reform.

This thirteenth edition of *Social Problems* considers each of these important trends and events as well as others. Some of the topics new to this edition are:

- Gender inequality and the workplace
- The new racial demography
- How the U.S. ranks among industrialized nations in investing in and protecting children
- The effects of the Great Recession on families
- Financing the 2012 political campaigns
- The politics of Obamacare
- A critique of trickle-down economics
- The continuing influence of the Tea Party movement
- The Latino Paradox
- The effects of gridlock in Congress
- The declining flow of immigrants from Mexico to the United States
- Efforts at voter suppression in many states
- Emptying out of much of the Great Plains and Appalachia while other rural areas are booming with natural resource extraction
- The trend toward returning to urban density
- China's one-child policy
- The drug war on the U.S.–Mexico border
- The persistent problem of not enough jobs
- The Upper Big Branch and other mining disasters
- The discriminatory practices of banks in lending to African Americans and Latinos
- The role of inequality in the health of the public
- Twenty-first century warfare
- Legacy of the Iraq and Afghanistan wars

Six types of panels are included:

- Voices panels provide the personal views of those affected by a social problem.
- A Closer Look elaborates on a topic in detail.

- Social Problems in Global Perspective panels illustrate how other societies deal with a particular social problem. This global emphasis is also evident in panels and tables that compare the United States with other nations on such topics as crime/incarceration, medical care, and education.
- Social Policy panels look at policy issues and highlight social policies that work to alleviate particular social problems.
- Looking Toward the Future panels examine the trends concerning the social problems under consideration at the beginning of a new millennium.
- Speaking to Students panels address issues especially pertinent to college students.

Also included are:

- New MySocLab icons in the margins of the text highlight resources in Pearson's unique online resource that enhance the content within the text.
- End-of-chapter pedagogy includes Chapter Reviews and Key Terms.

In summary, this new edition of *Social Problems* improves on the earlier editions by focusing more deliberately on five themes: (1) the structural sources of social problems; (2) the role of the United States in global social problems; (3) the centrality of class, race, gender, sexuality, and disability as sources of division, inequality, and injustice; (4) the critical examination of society; and (5) solutions to social problems.

NOTE ON LANGUAGE USAGE

In writing this book, we have been especially sensitive to our use of language. Language is used to reflect and maintain the secondary status of social groups by defining them, diminishing them, trivializing them, or excluding them. For example, traditional English uses masculine words (man, mankind, he) to refer to people in general. Even in the ordering of masculine and feminine or of Whites and Blacks within the discussion, one category consistently preceding its counterpart subtly conveys the message that the one listed first is superior to the other. In short, our goal is to use language so that it does not create the impression that one social class, race, or gender is superior to any other.

The terms of reference for racial and ethnic categories are changing. Blacks increasingly use the term African American, and Hispanics often refer to themselves as Latinos. In *Social Problems*, Thirteenth Edition, we use both of these terms for each social category because they often are used interchangeably in popular and scholarly discourse.

Also, we try to avoid the use of America or American society when referring to the United States. America should be used only in reference to the entire Western Hemisphere: North, Central, and South America (and then, in the plural, Americas). Its use as a reference to only the United States implies that the other nations of the Western Hemisphere have no place in our frame of reference.

SUPPLEMENTS

Instructor's Manual and Test Bank Each chapter in the Instructor's Manual includes the following resources: Chapter Summary, Learning Objectives, Critical Thinking Questions, Activities for Classroom Participation, and Suggested Films.

Designed to make your lectures more effective and to save preparation time, this extensive resource gathers together useful activities and strategies for teaching your Social Problems course. Also included in this manual is a test bank of over 1,500 multiple-choice, true/false, and essay questions. The Instructor's Manual and Test Bank is available to adopters for download from the Pearson Instructors Resource Center at www.pearsonhighered.com.

MyTest This computerized software allows instructors to create their own personalized exams, to edit any or all of the existing test questions, and to add new questions. Other special features of this program include random generation of test questions, creation of alternate versions of the same test, scrambling question sequence, and test preview before printing. For easy access, this software is available within the instructor section of the MySocLab for *Social Problems*, Thirteenth Edition, or for download from the Pearson Instructors Resource Center at www .pearsonhighered.com.

PowerPoint Presentations The PowerPoint presentations for *Social Problems*, Thirteenth Edition, are informed by instructional and design theory. You have the option in every chapter of choosing from any of the following types of slides: Lecture, Line Art, and Image PowerPoints. The Lecture PowerPoint slides follow the chapter outline and feature images from the textbook integrated with the text. The Special Topics PowerPoint slides allow you to integrate rich supplementary material into your course with minimal preparation time. Additionally, all of the PowerPoints are uniquely designed to present concepts in a clear and succinct way. They are available to adopters for download from the Pearson Instructors Resource Center at www.pearsonhighered.com.

ACKNOWLEDGMENTS

We thank the following reviewers of the previous editions of *Social Problems* for their helpful comments:

Payton Andrews, Cape Fear Community College
Ernestine Avila, California State University, San Bernardino
Leonard Beeghley, University of Florida
Moshe ben Asher, California State University, Northridge
Deva Chopyak, Cosmunes River College
Jesse Goldstein, Baruch College
Jeanne Humble, Bluegrass Community & Technical College
Gary Hytrek, California State University, Long Beach
Dana Mayhew, Bristol Community College
Adrienne Trier-Bieniek, Western Michigan University

Special thanks to our friend and longtime user of *Social Problems*, Laurel Davis-Delano, Springfield College, for her careful and helpful critiques of previous editions. Maxine Baca Zinn thanks Paula Miller in the Department of Sociology, Michigan State University, for research assistance.

Finally, we especially want to thank our families for their ongoing support and inspiration.

D. Stanley Eitzen
Maxine Baca Zinn
Kelly Eitzen Smith

MYSOCLAB™

MySocLab is a state-of-the-art interactive and instructive solution for the Social Problems course, designed to be used as a supplement to a traditional lecture course or to completely administer an online course. MySocLab provides access to a wealth of resources all geared to meet the individual teaching and learning needs of every instructor and every student. Highlights of MySocLab include:

- MySocLab for *Social Problems* provides all the tools you need to engage every student before, during, and after class. An assignment calendar and gradebook allow you to assign specific activities with due dates and to measure your students' progress throughout the semester.
- The **Pearson eText** lets students access their textbook anytime, anywhere, and anyway they want, including *listening online*. The eText for *Social Problems* features integrated videos, Social Explorer activities, additional readings and interactive self-quizzes.
- A **Personalized Study Plan** for each student, based on Bloom's Taxonomy, arranges activities from those that require less complex thinking—like remembering and understanding—to more complex critical thinking—like applying and analyzing. This layered approach promotes better critical thinking skills, helping students succeed in the course and beyond.
- **Sociology in Focus** (www.sociologyinfocus.com) is a blog by sociologists for students that highlights a sociological perspective on current events, pop culture, and everyday life. Updated weekly, Sociology in Focus is a terrific way to bring current examples into the classroom.

NEW FEATURES OF MYSOCLAB

Three exciting new features of MySocLab are Social Explorer, MySocLibrary, and Core Concepts in Sociology Videos.

- **Social Explorer** activities connect with topics from the text, engaging students with data visualizations, comparisons of change over time, and data localized to their own communities.
- **MySocLibrary**, available in the Pearson eText, contains 200 classic and contemporary articles that enable students to explore the discipline more deeply. Multiple choice questions for each reading help students review what they've learned—and allow instructors to monitor their performance.
- **Video Series in Sociology** features sociologists in action, exploring important concepts in Sociology. Each video is accompanied by a short quiz.

MYSOCLAB AND SOCIAL PROBLEMS, THIRTEENTH EDITION

New to this edition are correlations to the many resources in MySocLab with topics within the each chapter. Icons are now included in the margins that connect resources and content, making the integration of MySocLab even more flexible and useful to instructors for making assignments and for engaging students by giving them the opportunity to explore important sociological concepts, and enhance their performance in this course.

MySocLab is available at no additional cost to the student when an access code card is packaged with a new text. It can also be purchased separately. Visit www.mysoclab.com for more information.

The test of our progress is not whether we add more to the abundance of those who have much, it is whether we provide enough for those who have too little.

—Franklin Delano Roosevelt,
Second Inaugural Address, 1937

The Sociological Approach to Social Problems

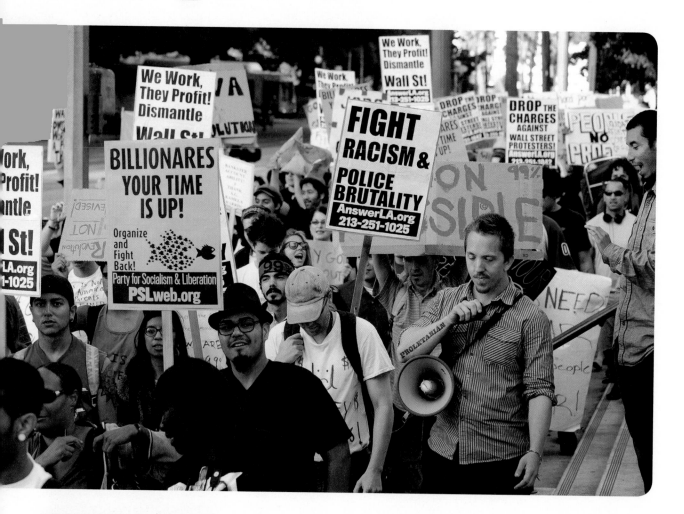

((• Listen to Chapter 1 on **MySocLab**

LEARNING OBJECTIVES

1.1 Understand how sociologists approach the study of social problems.

1.2 Explain the complex nature of defining a social problem.

1.3 Describe the two main types of social problems.

1.4 Explain and apply the sociological imagination to different social problems.

1.5 Compare/contrast the person-blame approach to social problems and the system-blame approach.

1.6 Understand the four basic research designs and research methods that sociologists use to study social problems.

The official population of the United States surpassed the 300 million mark at 7:46 a.m. EDT on October 17, 2006. In 2043, when the typical reader of this text is about 50 years old, it is estimated that the United States will have added another 100 million people, reaching 400 million. What will life in the United States be like when you reach middle age with that added 100 million? Will the problems of today be eliminated or reduced, or will they have worsened? Consider these issues:

Immigration and the browning of America. Immigration from Latin America and Asia is fueling the population growth. About half of the last 100 million Americans are immigrants and their U.S.-born children. Half of the next 100 million will be immigrants or their children. By 2042, the race/ethnicity mix will be such that non-Whites will surpass Whites as the numerical majority. The increasing numbers of non-Whites will likely fuel racial/ethnic unrest among them as they experience discrimination and low-paying, demeaning jobs and among the native-born, who fear that the low wages of recent immigrants either take away their jobs or keep their wages low. With the additional millions of immigrants added in the coming decades, previously White rural areas and small towns will begin to deal with the challenges of new ethnic and racial residents.

The graying of America. After 2030, one of five U.S. residents will be at least 65 (similar to the proportion in Florida today). The increase in the number of elderly will cause problems with funding Social Security and Medicare, placing a greater burden on the young to support the elderly through these programs. This divide between workers who support the old with payroll taxes will have a racial, as well as a generational, dimension because the workers will be increasingly people of color and the elderly overwhelmingly White (Harden, 2006).

The inequality gap. Today the wealth and income of the affluent grows rapidly while the income of workers languishes. The inequality gap now is at record levels, resulting in a diminished middle class. As the middle class is squeezed, the trend is for more downward mobility than upward mobility. As the inequality gap enlarges, will it result in greater social unrest, extreme political movements, more crime?

The increasing power of money to influence elections and public policy. A 2010 Supreme Court decision allows corporations and other organizations to spend unlimited amounts to elect or defeat political candidates. Individuals can also spend millions to further their candidates and causes. Add to this the influence of organizations through their lobbyists to influence policies. The consequence of this inverse relationship between money and power is obvious. Where, we might ask, is the voice of the poor heard? What happened to our democratic ideals?

Globalization and the transformation of the economy. The U.S. economy has undergone a dramatic shift from one dominated by manufacturing to one now characterized by service occupations and the collection, storage, and dissemination of information. As a result of this transformation, relatively well-paid employment in manufacturing products such as automobiles has dwindled and been replaced with jobs in lower-paying service industries. Most of the manufacturing is now done in foreign countries where U.S. corporations produce the same products but with cheaper labor, lower taxes, and fewer governmental controls. Some services, such as research, accounting, and call centers, have also been transferred to overseas companies to increase profits. Currently, these trends have negatively affected U.S. workers by making their jobs more insecure and reducing or eliminating their benefits.

In the coming decades, as 100 million people are added and new technologies enhancing globalization are developed, will the working conditions and standard of living of U.S. workers decline or be enhanced?

The plight of the poor. Nearly one in six Americans is poor: 46.2 million Americans were "officially" poor in 2010. The number of Americans without health insurance was 49.0 million. The numbers of those receiving food stamps were the highest on record. Emergency food requests and people seeking emergency shelter are increasing. The government considers those with incomes at or below 50 percent of the poverty level to be "severely poor." In 2010, 20.466 million Americans were in this category. Two factors lead to the speculation that the needs of the poor will not be met satisfactorily in the future. First, the trend is for the federal government to reduce "safety net" programs that help the poor, such as welfare to single mothers, nutrition programs, Head Start, and the like. Moreover, the national minimum wage was only $7.25 an hour in 2012, far below a living wage.

The environmental impact. Currently, the United States, at about 4.5 percent of the world's population, consumes one-fourth of the world's energy, most particularly oil, and is the world's greatest producer of greenhouse gases that result in global warming. More people leads to more traffic congestion, more suburban sprawl, and more landfills. Population growth means greater demand for food, water, fossil fuels, timber, and other resources. At present, land is being converted for development (housing, schools, shopping centers, roads) at about twice the rate of population growth. Adding another 100 million people with today's habits (large houses, gas-guzzling transportation, suburban sprawl, and the consumption of products designed to be obsolete) will lead to an ecological wasteland. But perhaps recognition of the negative environmental impacts of current usage patterns will lead to our reducing waste, finding alternative energy sources, making greater use of mass transit, increasing housing density, and finding other ways to sustain and even enhance the environment.

The numbers seeking refuge in homeless shelters has increased dramatically in recent years.

THE HEALTH OF WOMEN AND THEIR CHILDREN

International Comparisons

A few days before Mother's Day 2010, a global relief and development organization, Save the Children, published its "State of the World's Mothers," ranking forty-three developed nations and 117 countries in the developing world on ten measures related to the health of women and their children, their education, and their political status. Norway ranked number one as the best place to be a mother, and the United States ranked twenty-eighth. This was behind nearly all of the nations in Western and Central Europe and Scandinavia. The six indicators of mothers' well-being are lifetime risk of maternal mortality, percentage of women using modern contraception, percentage of births attended by skilled personnel, percentage of pregnant women with anemia, adult female literacy rate, and participation of women in national government. Among the factors affecting the placement of the United States were the following:

- The U.S. rate of lifetime maternal mortality was 1 in 4,800, compared to 1 in 47,600 for Ireland.
- The United States ranked eighth in under 5 mortality rate per 1,000 live births.
- The United States also lags in the political status of women. Only 17 percent of seats in the U.S. national government were held by women, compared to 39 percent of the national legislature in Norway.
- The United States has a female life expectancy of 81 years. Eighteen nations have a higher life expectancy for women, led by Japan with 86 years.
- The United States is the least generous of the forty-three More Developed Countries in terms of maternity leave benefits.

Source: State of the World's Mothers. 2010. Save the Children, London, UK (May).

At the global level, the earth is warming because of human activities, most prominently the use of oil and other carbons. Global warming will have disastrous effects during this century—coastal flooding, shifting agricultural patterns, violent weather, spread of tropical diseases, and loss of biodiversity, to name a few. The United States is the primary user of petrochemicals, and China will surpass it around 2025.

The growing global inequality. While the United States' population will increase by 100 million before midcentury, the world will grow by 50 percent, adding 3 billion (for a total of 9 billion) people. Almost all this growth will occur among the poorest nations. Today, an estimated 1.1 billion people are undernourished. Most do not have clean water and adequate sanitation. Half of the world's people live on less than $2 a day, one-sixth on less than $1 a day. Hundreds of millions are ravaged by diseases such as malaria, chronic diarrhea, Ebola, dengue, and parasites. At the other extreme, the richest nations live lavish lifestyles, consuming and wasting most of the world's resources. Multinational corporations profit from exploiting the resources and labor of the poorest countries. This gap between the fortunate few and the impoverished, desperate masses continues to widen.

The underdeveloped world, already in dire straits, will face enormous obstacles in providing the minimum of food, water, housing, and medical attention for their peoples as they add billions in population. The result will be ever-greater numbers of desperate people on this planet, making the world less safe. Unless the affluent nations and international organizations make structural changes to aid the underdeveloped countries, conflicts over scarce resources will increase, as will sectarian and tribal violence and acts of terrorism.

TABLE 1.1
How America Ranks Among Industrialized Countries in Investing in and Protecting Children

1st in gross domestic product
1st in number of billionaires
1st in number of persons incarcerated
1st in health expenditures
1st in student expenditures
1st in military technology
1st in defense expenditures
1st in military weapons exports
17th in reading scores
22nd in low birthweight rates
23rd in science scores
30th in infant mortality rates
31st in math scores
31st in the gap between the rich and the poor
Last in relative child poverty
Last in adolescent birth rates (ages 15 to 19)
Last in protecting our children against gun violence

Source: Children's Defense Fund. 2011. *State of America's Children*. Washington, DC, Children's Defense Fund, p. xiv.

An increasingly dangerous world. September 11, 2001, unleashed a chain of negative events. Those terrorist acts on the World Trade Center and the Pentagon caused death and destruction and redirected government policies. The United States responded with a war on Al-Qaeda in Afghanistan and a preemptive war on Iraq, presumably to squelch terrorism and spread democracy throughout the Middle East. To fight the war on terror, the United States suspended the civil rights of prisoners, including their protection from the use of techniques that many would define as torture, and spied on American citizens. Suicide bombers (the "guided missiles" of the militarily weak) have destabilized the Middle East and threaten terror worldwide. There is the growing threat of nuclear proliferation, with North Korea joining the nuclear club in 2006 and Iran threatening to join the club soon. As the world's population soars, with its consequent poverty, hunger, water shortages, disease, and political chaos, the United States will be increasingly unsafe. Will we face these incredible problems and find solutions? That is the ultimate question.

These issues highlight the social problems addressed in this book. Although the focus is on the dark side of social life, our hope is that readers will find this exploration intriguing, insightful, and useful (for a summary of social problems as experienced by children in the United States, see Table 1.1).

1.1 Understand how sociologists approach the study of social problems.

Explore on MySocLab Activity: Why Do Sociologists Study Social Problems?

HISTORY OF SOCIAL PROBLEMS THEORY

Typically, social problems have been thought of as social situations that a large number of observers felt were inappropriate and needed remedying. Early U.S. sociologists applied a medical model to the analysis of society to assess whether some pathology was present. Using what were presumed to be universal criteria of normality, sociologists commonly assumed that social problems resulted from "bad" people—maladjusted people who were abnormal because of mental deficiency, mental disorder, lack of education, or incomplete socialization. These social pathologists, because they assumed that the basic norms of society are universally held, viewed social problems as behaviors or social arrangements that disturb the moral order. For them, the moral order of U.S. society

"Where did we go wrong?"

Mischa Richter/The New Yorker Collection/Cartoonbank.com

defined such behaviors as alcoholism, suicide, theft, and murder as social problems. But this approach did not take into account the complexity inherent in a diverse society.

In a variation of the absolutist approach, sociologists in the 1920s and 1930s focused on the conditions of society that fostered problems. Societies undergoing rapid change from the processes of migration, urbanization, and industrialization were thought to have pockets of social disorganization. Certain areas of the cities undergoing the most rapid change, for example, were found to have disproportionately high rates of vice, crime, family breakdowns, and mental disorders.

In the past few decades, many sociologists have returned to a study of problem individuals—deviants who violate the expectations of society. The modern study of deviance developed in two directions. The first sought the sources of deviation within the social structure. Sociologists saw deviance as the result of conflict between the culturally prescribed goals of society (such as material success) and the obstacles to obtaining them that some groups of people face. The other, of relatively recent origin, has focused on the role of society in creating and sustaining deviance through labeling those people viewed as abnormal. Societal reactions are viewed as the key in determining what a social problem is and who is deviant.

Most recently, some sociologists have tried to alert others to the problematic nature of social problems themselves (see Spector and Kitsuse 1987). These theorists emphasize the **subjective nature of social problems**. They say that what is defined as a social problem differs by audience and by time. Pollution, for example, has not always been considered a social problem. This perspective also examines how particular phenomena come to be defined as social problems, focusing on how groups of people actively influence those definitions.

This brief description reveals several issues that must be addressed in looking at social problems. First, sociologists have difficulty agreeing on an adequate definition of social problems. Second, there is continuing debate over the unit of analysis: Is the focus of inquiry individuals or social systems? Related to the latter is the issue of numbers: How many people have to be affected before something is a social problem? In this regard, C. Wright Mills (1962) made an important distinction: If a situation such as unemployment is a problem for an individual or for scattered individuals, it is a "private trouble." But if unemployment is widespread, affecting large numbers of people in a region or the society, it is a "public issue" or a "social problem."

TOWARD A DEFINITION OF SOCIAL PROBLEMS

There is an **objective reality of social problems:** There are conditions in society (such as poverty and institutional racism) that induce material or psychic suffering for certain segments of the population; there are sociocultural phenomena that prevent a significant number of societal participants from developing and using their full potential; there are discrepancies between what a country such as the United States is supposed to stand for (equality of opportunity, justice, democracy) and the actual conditions in which many of its people live; and people are fouling their own nest through pollution and the indiscriminate use of natural resources (Eitzen 1984). This normative approach assumes that some kinds of actions are likely to be judged deleterious in any context. Therefore, one goal of this book is to identify, describe, and explain situations that are objective social problems.

There are several dangers, however, in defining social problems objectively. The most obvious is that subjectivity is always present. To identify a phenomenon as a problem implies that it falls short of some standard. But what standards are to be used? Will the standards of society suffice? In a pluralistic society such as the United States, there is no uniform set of guidelines. People from different social strata and other social locations (such as region, occupation, race, and age) differ in their perceptions of what a social problem is and, once defined, how it should be solved. Is marijuana use a social problem? Is pornography? Is the relatively high rate of military spending a social problem? Is abortion a social problem? There is little consensus in U.S. society on these and other issues. All social observers, then, must be aware of differing viewpoints and respect the perspectives of the social actors involved.

In looking for objective social problems, we must also guard against the tendency to accept the definitions of social problems provided by those in power. Because the powerful—the agencies of government, business, and the media—provide the statistical data (such as crime rates), they may define social reality in a way that manipulates public opinion, thereby controlling behaviors that threaten the status quo (and their power). The congruence of official biases and public opinion can be seen in several historical examples. Slavery, for instance, was not considered a social problem by the powerful in the South, but slave revolts were. In colonial New England, the persecution of witches was not a social problem, but the witches were (Szasz 1970). Likewise, racism was not a social problem of the Jim Crow South, but "pushy" Blacks were. From the standpoint of U.S. public opinion, dispossessing Native Americans of their lands was not a social problem, but the Native Americans who resisted were.

Thus, to consider as social problems only those occurrences so defined by the public is fraught with several related dangers. First, to do so may mean overlooking conditions that are detrimental to a relatively powerless segment of the society. In other words, deplorable conditions heaped on minority groups tend to be ignored as social problems by the people at large. If sociologists accept this definition of social problems as their sole criterion, they have clearly taken a position that supports existing inequities for minority groups.

Second, defining social problems exclusively through public opinion diverts attention from what may constitute the most important social problem: the existing social order (Liazos 1972). If defined only through public opinion, social problems are limited to behaviors and actions that disrupt the existing social order. From this perspective, social problems are manifestations of the behaviors of abnormal people, not of society; the inadequacies and inequalities perpetuated by the existing system are not questioned. The distribution of power, the system of justice, how children are educated—to name but a few aspects of the existing social order—are assumed to be proper by most of the public, when they may be social problems themselves.

By overlooking institutions as a source of social problems (and as problems themselves), observers disregard the role of the powerful in society. To focus exclusively on those who deviate—the prostitute, the delinquent, the drug addict, the criminal—excludes the unethical, illegal, and destructive actions of powerful individuals, groups, and institutions in U.S. society and ignores the covert institutional violence brought about by racist and sexist policies, unjust tax laws, inequitable systems of healthcare and justice, and exploitation by the corporate world (Liazos 1972).

TYPES OF SOCIAL PROBLEMS

1.3 Describe the two main types of social problems.

This book examines two main types of social problems: (1) acts and conditions that violate the norms and values present in society and (2) societally induced conditions that cause psychic and material suffering for any segment of the population.

Norm Violations

 Watch on **MySocLab Video:** Deviance and Inequality: Social-Conflict Analysis

Sociologists are interested in the discrepancy between social standards and reality for several reasons. First, this traditional approach directs attention to society's failures: the criminals, the mentally ill, the school dropouts, and the poor. Sociologists have many insights that explain the processes by which individuals experience differing pressures to engage in certain forms of **deviant behavior** (actions that violate the norms of a social organization) because of their location in the social structure (social class, occupation, age, race, and role) and in space (region, size of community, and type of neighborhood). A guiding assumption of our inquiry here, however, is that norm violators are symptoms of social problems, not the disease itself. In other words, most deviants are victims and should not be blamed entirely by society for their deviance; rather, the system they live in should be blamed. A description of the situations affecting deviants (such as the barriers to success faced by minority group members) helps explain why some categories of persons participate disproportionately in deviant behavior.

Another reason for the traditional focus on norm violation is that deviance is culturally defined and socially labeled. The sociologist is vitally interested in the social and cultural processes that label some acts and persons as deviant and others as normal. Because by definition some social problems are whatever the public determines, social problems are inherently relative. Certain behaviors are labeled as social problems, whereas other activities (which by some other criteria would be a social problem) are not. People on welfare, for example, are generally considered to constitute a social problem, but slumlords are not; people who hear God talking to them are considered schizophrenic, but people who talk to God are believed perfectly sane; murder is a social problem, but killing the enemy during wartime is rewarded with medals; a prostitute is punished, but the client is not; aliens entering the country illegally constitute a social problem and are punished, but their U.S. employers are not. The important insight here is that "deviance is not a property inherent in certain forms of behavior; it is a property conferred upon these forms by the audiences which directly or indirectly witness them" (Schur 1971:12). The members of society, especially the most powerful members, determine what is a social problem and what is not.

Powerful people play an important role in determining who gets the negative label and who does not. Because there is no absolute standard that informs citizens of what is deviant and what is not, our definition of deviance depends on which behaviors the law singles out for punishment. Because the law is an instrument of those in power, acts that are labeled deviant are so labeled because they conflict with the interests of those in power. Thus, to comprehend the labeling process, we must understand not only the norms and values of the society but also which interest groups hold the power (Quinney 1970).

Social Conditions

The second type of social problem emphasized in this text involves conditions that cause psychic and material suffering for some category of people in the United States. Here, the focus is on how the society operates and who benefits and who does not under existing arrangements. In other words, what is the bias of the system? How are societal rewards distributed? Do some categories of persons suffer or profit because of how schools are organized or juries selected, because of the seniority system used by industries, or because of how healthcare is delivered? These questions direct attention away from individuals who violate norms and toward society's institutions as the generators of social problems.

Social problems of this type generate individual psychic and material suffering. Thus, societal arrangements can be organized in a way that is unresponsive to many human needs.

When healthcare is maldistributed, when poverty persists for millions, when tax laws permit a business to write off 50 percent of a $100 luncheon but prohibit a truck driver from writing off a bologna sandwich, when government is run by the few for the benefit of the few, when businesses supposedly in competition fix prices to gouge the consumer, when the criminal justice system is biased against the poor and people of color, then society is permitting what is called **institutionalized deviance** (Doyle and Schindler 1974:13). Such a condition exists when the society and its formal organizations are not meeting the needs of individuals. But these conditions often escape criticism and are rarely identified as social problems. Instead, the focus has often been on individuals who vent their frustration in socially unacceptable ways. A major intent of this book is to view individual deviance as a consequence of institutionalized deviance.

In summary, here we consider **social problems** to be (1) societally induced conditions that cause psychic and material suffering for any segment of the population and (2) acts and conditions that violate the norms and values found in society. The distribution of power in society is the key to understanding these social problems. The powerless, because they are dominated by the powerful, are likely to be thwarted in achieving their basic needs (sustenance, security, self-esteem, and productivity). In contrast, the interests of the powerful are served because they control the mechanisms and institutions by which the perceptions of the public are shaped. By affecting public policy through reaffirming customs and through shaping the law and its enforcement, powerful interest groups are instrumental in designating (labeling) who is a problem (deviant) and who must be controlled. Our focus, then, is on the structure of society—especially on how power is distributed—rather than on "problem" individuals. Individual deviants are a manifestation of society's failure to meet their needs; the sources of crime, poverty, drug addiction, and racism are found in the laws and customs, the quality of life, the distribution of wealth and power, and the accepted practices of schools, governmental units, and corporations. As the primary source of social problems, society, not the individual deviant, must be restructured if social problems are to be solved. (See the panel titled "Social Problems in Global Perspective," which compares the United States with other nations on social problems).

Social Problems in Global Perspective

SOCIAL WELFARE STATES: A MIXTURE OF CAPITALISM AND SOCIALISM

The nations of Western Europe, Scandinavia, and Canada have generous welfare policies for their citizens, certainly much more generous than those available in the United States (the description here is general, characterizing all the nations to a degree, although there are variations among them). These nations are capitalistic, permitting private property and privately owned businesses, but to a much greater degree than in the United States these nations have publicly owned enterprises and some nationalization of industry, typically transportation, mineral resources, and utilities.

Most important, these nations provide an array of social services to meet the needs of their citizens that is much greater than in the United States. These services include a greater subsidy to the arts (symphony orchestras, art exhibitions, artists, auditoriums), more public spaces (parks, public squares, recreation facilities), more resources for public libraries, universal preschool education, free public education through college, universal health insurance, housing subsidies to help low-income families, paid leave for new parents (mother and father), the provision of safe government childcare facilities, extended unemployment benefits, paid vacations, and excellent retirement benefits, including paid long-term care if necessary.

These services are expensive, resulting in relatively high taxes, almost double the rate in the United States, but if you add to taxes the costs of private health insurance, medical care, the cost of private social services such as daycare, the total is more or less equal (Feagin, Feagin, and Baker 2006:483).

As a result of this extensive and universality of social services, the people in the social welfare states have several advantages over those living in the United States: longer life expectancy, lower infant and maternal mortality, greater literacy, less poverty and homelessness, lower rates of violent crime, a lower proportion of single-parent households, and a proportionately larger middle class.

Are the people in these countries less free than Americans? There is freedom of speech and freedom of the press in each of the nations. The governments in these countries, for the most part, permit greater individual freedom than is found in the United States for personal behaviors (greater acceptance of homosexuality, legalization of prostitution, few restrictions on abortion, and the like).

Is there a downside? These countries are not immune to economic problems such as recessions, high unemployment, and citizen unrest over high taxes. In the past few years, the governments in these countries have reduced some of their social programs, but they are still much more generous than the United States (which has also curbed its more meager welfare programs). Typically, government leaders in each of these countries have argued that more austere programs are needed to stimulate the economy and permit the government to pay its bills. These measures have been met with citizen protest, particularly from the labor unions, which are much stronger than in the United States. It will be interesting to see how reduction in the welfare state plays out. If the austerity measures hold, will the countries follow the U.S. example and become more unequal, experience increased social unrest, see a rise in social problems? Or, as conservatives argue, will more capitalism and less socialism make these nations more efficient and more prosperous?

1.4 Explain and apply the sociological imagination to different social problems.

👁 **Watch on MySocLab Video:** Applying the Sociological Perspective

THE SOCIOLOGICAL IMAGINATION

Sociology is the discipline that guides this inquiry into the sources and consequences of social problems. This scholarly discipline is the study of society and other social organizations, how they affect human behavior, and how these organizations are changed by human endeavors. C. Wright Mills (1916–1962), in his classic *The Sociological Imagination* (1959), wrote that the task of sociology is to realize that individual circumstances are inextricably linked to the structure of society. The **sociological imagination** involves several related components (Eitzen and Smith 2003:8):

- The sociological imagination is stimulated by a willingness to view the social world from the perspective of others.

- It involves moving away from thinking in terms of the individual and her or his problem and focusing rather on the social, economic, and historical circumstances that produce the problem. Put another way, the sociological imagination is the ability to see the societal patterns that influence individuals, families, groups, and organizations.
- Possessing a sociological imagination, one can shift from the examination of a single family to national budgets, from a poor person to national welfare policies, from an unemployed person to the societal shift from manufacturing to a service/ knowledge economy, from a single mother with a sick child to the high cost of healthcare for the uninsured, and from a homeless family to the lack of affordable housing.
- To develop a sociological imagination requires a detachment from the taken-for-granted assumptions about social life, and establishing a critical distance (Andersen and Taylor 2000:10–11). In other words, one must be willing to question the structural arrangements that shape social behavior.

When we have this imagination, we begin to see the solutions to social problems not in terms of changing problem people but of changing the structure of society.

SOCIAL STRUCTURE AS THE BASIC UNIT OF ANALYSIS

1.5 Compare/ contrast the person-blame approach to social problems and the system-blame approach.

There is a very strong tendency for individuals—laypeople, police officers, judges, lawmakers, and social scientists alike—to perceive social problems and prescribe remedies from an individualistic perspective. For example, they blame the individual for being poor, with no reference to the maldistribution of wealth, low-wage work, and other socially perpetuated disadvantages that blight many families generation after generation; they blame African Americans for their aggressive behavior, with no understanding of the limits placed on social mobility for African Americans by the social system; they blame dropouts for leaving school prematurely, with no understanding that the educational system fails to meet their needs. This type of thinking helps explain the reluctance of people in authority to provide adequate welfare, healthcare, and compensatory programs to help the disadvantaged.

The fundamental issue is whether social problems emanate from the pathologies of individuals (**person-blame**) or from the situations in which deviants are involved (**system-blame**), that is, whether deviants are the problem itself or only victims of it. The answer no doubt lies somewhere between the two extremes, but because the individual- or victim-blamers have held sway, we should examine their reasoning (Ryan 1976).

Person-Blame Approach versus System-Blame Approach

Let's begin by considering some victims, such as the children in a slum school who constantly fail. Why do they fail? The victim-blamer points to their **cultural deprivation**.* They do not do well in school because their families speak different dialects, because their parents are uneducated, because they have not been exposed to the educational

---

*Cultural deprivation is a loaded ethnocentric term applied by members of the majority to the culture of the minority group. It implies that the culture of the group in question is not only inferior but also deficient. The concept does remind us, however, that people can and do make invidious distinctions about cultures and subcultures. Furthermore, people act on these distinctions as if they were valid.

benefits available to middle-class children (such as visits to the zoo, computers in the home, extensive travel, attendance at cultural events, exposure to books). In other words, the defect is in the children and their families. System-blamers look elsewhere for the sources of failure. They ask, What is there about the schools that make slum children more likely to fail? The answer is found in the irrelevant curriculum, class-biased IQ tests, the tracking system, overcrowded classrooms, differential allocation of resources within the school district, and insensitive teachers, whose low expectations for poor children create a self-fulfilling prophecy.

Ex-convicts constitute another set of victims. Why is their **recidivism** rate (reinvolvement in crime) so high? The victim-blamer points to the faults of individual criminals: their greed, their feelings of aggression, their weak control of impulse, their lack of conscience. The system-blamer directs attention to very different sources: the penal system, the scarcity of employment for ex-criminals, and even the schools. For example, 20 to 30 percent of inmates are functionally illiterate; that is, they cannot meet minimum reading and writing demands in U.S. society, such as filling out job applications. Yet these people are expected to leave prison, find a job, and stay out of trouble. Illiterate ex-criminals face unemployment or at best the most menial jobs, with low wages, no job security, and no fringe benefits. System-blamers argue that first the schools and later the penal institutions have failed to provide these people with the minimum requirements for full participation in society. Moreover, lack of employment and the unwillingness of potential employers to train functional illiterates force many to return to crime to survive.

The inner-city poor are another set of victims. The conditions of the ghetto poor, especially African Americans, have deteriorated since the mid-1960s. Some observers believe that this deterioration is the result of the transplantation of a southern share-cropper culture (Lemann 1986), welfare programs (Murray 1984), and laziness. The more compelling system-blame argument, however, is made by William J. Wilson (1987). He claims that the ghetto poor endure because of the disappearance of hundreds of thousands of low-skill jobs, those mainly involving physical labor, in the past forty years or so. Wilson's contention, supported by research, is that the pathologies of the ghetto (such as teenage pregnancy, illegitimacy, welfare dependency, and crime) are fundamentally the consequence of too few jobs.

Why do some criminals commit crimes after they are released from prison? Is it entirely their fault, or are there social forces that limit their choices and lead them to continued criminal behavior?

The strong tendency to blame social problems on individuals rather than on the social system lies in how people tend to look at social problems. Most people define a social problem as behavior that deviates from the norms and standards of society. Because people do not ordinarily examine critically the way things are done in society, they tend to question the exceptions. The system not only is taken for granted but also has, for most people, an aura of sacredness because of the traditions and customs with which they associate it. Logically, then, those who deviate are the source of trouble. The obvious question observers ask is, Why do these people deviate from norms? Because most people view themselves as law-abiding, they feel that those who deviate do so because of some kind of unusual circumstance, such as accident, illness, personal defect, character flaw, or maladjustment (Ryan 1976:10–18). The flaw, then, is a function of the deviant, not of societal arrangements.

Interpreting social problems solely within a person-blame framework has serious consequences. First, because societal causes are not addressed, social problems remain in place (Davis-Delano 2009). Second, it frees the government, the economy, the system of stratification, the system of justice, and the educational system from any blame. Instead of focusing on the poor, what are those elements of society that keep poor people poor, such as segregated schools, unfair wages, not enough jobs, and the high cost of housing and healthcare?

This protection of the established order against criticism increases the difficulty of trying to change the dominant economic, social, and political institutions. A good example is the strategy social scientists use in studying the origins of poverty. Because the person-blamer studies the poor rather than the nonpoor, the system of inequality (buttressed by tax laws, welfare rules, and employment practices) goes unchallenged. A related consequence of the person-blame approach, then, is that the relatively well-off segments of society retain their advantages.

A social-control function of the person-blame approach is that troublesome individuals and groups are controlled in a publicly acceptable manner. Deviants—whether they are criminals, mentally ill, or social protesters—are incarcerated in prisons or mental hospitals and administered drugs or other forms of therapy. This approach not only directs blame at individuals and away from the system, but it also eliminates the problems (individuals).

A related consequence is how the problem is treated. A person-blame approach demands a person-change treatment program. If the cause of delinquency, for example, is defined as the result of personal pathology, then the solution must clearly lie in counseling, behavior modification, psychotherapy, drugs, or some other technique aimed at changing the individual deviant. The person-blame interpretation of social problems provides and legitimates the right to initiate person-change rather than system-change treatment programs. Under such a scheme, norms that are racist, sexist, or homophobic, for example, go unchallenged.

The person-blame ideology invites not only person-change treatment programs but also programs for person-control. The system-blamer would argue that this emphasis, too, treats the symptom rather than the disease.

A final consequence of a person-blame interpretation is that it reinforces social myths about the degree of control individuals have over their fate. It provides justification for a form of **social Darwinism**: that the placement of people in the stratification system is a function of their ability and effort. By this logic, the poor are poor because they are the dregs of society. In short, they deserve their fate, as do the successful in society. Thus, in this viewpoint, little sympathy exists for government programs to increase welfare to the poor. (See the insert on William Graham Sumner for an example of this ideology.)

Reasons for Focusing on the System-Blame Approach

We emphasize the system-blame approach in this book. We should recognize, however, that the system-blame orientation has dangers. First, it is only part of the truth. Social problems are highly complex phenomena that have both individual and systemic origins. Individuals, obviously, can be malicious and aggressive for purely psychological reasons. Clearly, society needs to be protected from some individuals. Moreover, some people require particular forms of therapy, remedial help, or special programs on an individual basis if they are to function normally. But much behavior that is labeled deviant is the end product of social conditions.

A second danger of a dogmatic system-blame orientation is that it presents a rigidly deterministic explanation of social problems. Taken too far, this position views individuals as robots controlled totally by their social environment. A balanced view

William Graham Sumner and Social Darwinism

William Graham Sumner (1840–1910), the sociologist who originated the concepts of folkways and mores, was a proponent of social Darwinism.

This doctrine, widely accepted among elites during the late nineteenth and early twentieth centuries, was a distorted version of Charles Darwin's theory of natural selection. From this viewpoint, success is the result of being superior. The rich are rich because they deserve to be. By this logic, the poor also deserve their fate because they are biological and social failures and therefore unable to succeed in the competitive struggle.

Social Darwinism justified not only ruthless competition but also the perpetuation of the status quo. Superior classes, it was believed, should dominate because their members were unusually intelligent and moral. The lower classes, on the other hand, were considered inferior and defective. Their pathology was manifested in suicide, madness, crime, and various forms of vice.

On the basis of this philosophy, Sumner opposed social reforms such as welfare to the poor because they rewarded the unfit and penalized the competent. Such reforms, he argued, would interfere with the normal workings of society, halting progress and perhaps even contributing to a regression to an earlier evolutionary stage.

acknowledges that human beings may choose between alternative courses of action. This issue raises the related question of the degree to which people are responsible for their behavior. An extreme system-blame approach absolves individuals from responsibility for their actions. To take such a stance would be to argue that society should never restrict deviants; this view invites anarchy.

Despite these problems with the system-blame approach, it is the guiding perspective of this book for three reasons. First, because average citizens, police officers, legislators, social scientists, and judges tend to interpret social problems from an individualistic perspective, a balance is needed. Moreover, as noted earlier, a strict person-blame perspective has many negative consequences, and citizens must recognize these negative effects of their ideology.

A second reason for using the system-blaming perspective is that the subject matter of sociology is not the individual—who is the special province of psychology—but society. Because sociologists focus on the social determinants of behavior, they must make a critical analysis of the social structure. An important ingredient of the sociological perspective is the development of a critical stance toward social arrangements. Thus, the sociologist looks behind the facades to determine the positive and negative consequences of social arrangements. The sociologist's persistent questions must be, Who benefits under these arrangements? Who does not? For this reason, there should be a close fit between the sociological approach and the system-blaming perspective.

A final reason for the use of the system-blame approach is that the institutional framework of society is the source of many social problems (such as racism, pollution, unequal distribution of healthcare, poverty, and war). An exclusive focus on the individual ignores the strains caused by the inequities of the system and its fundamental intransigence to change. A guiding assumption of this book is that because institutions are made by human beings (and therefore are not sacred), they should be changed whenever they do not meet the needs of the people they were created to serve.

Understand
the four basic research
designs and research
methods that sociologists
use to study social
problems.

View on
MySocLab Figure:
Steps in the Research
Process

SOCIOLOGICAL METHODS: THE CRAFT OF SOCIOLOGY

The analysis of social problems depends on reliable data and logical reasoning. These necessities are possible, but some problems must be acknowledged. Before we describe how sociologists gather reliable data and make valid conclusions, let us examine the kinds of questions sociologists ask and the two major obstacles sociologists face in obtaining answers to these questions.

Sociological Questions

To begin, sociologists try to ascertain the facts. For example, let's assume that we want to assess the degree to which the public education system provides equal educational opportunities for all youngsters. To determine this, we need to conduct an empirical investigation to find the facts concerning such items as the amount spent per pupil by school districts within each state and by each state. Within school districts we need to know the facts concerning the distribution of monies by neighborhood schools. Are these monies appropriated equally, regardless of the social class or racial composition of the school? Are curriculum offerings the same for girls and boys within a school? Are extra fees charged for participation in extracurricular activities, and does this affect the participation of children by social class?

Sociologists also may ask comparative questions—that is, how does the situation in one social context compare with that in another? Most commonly, these questions involve the comparison of one society with another. Examples here might be the comparisons among industrialized nations on infant mortality, poverty, murder, leisure time, or the mathematics scores of 16-year-olds.

A third type of question that a sociologist may ask is historical. Sociologists are interested in trends. What are the facts now concerning divorce, crime, and political participation, for example, and how have these patterns changed over time? Figure 1.1 provides an example of a trend over time by examining the earnings of men and women in the United States from 1959 to 2010. What accounts for the plateau of men's earnings from 1972 on and the gradual increase in the earnings of women during those years? While the gap between men and women has narrowed, why is the female-to-male ratio still so low? What kept this ratio stable at around 60 percent from 1959 to 1982?

The three types of sociological questions considered so far determine the way things are. But these types of questions are not enough. Sociologists go beyond the factual to ask why. Why have real wages (controlling for inflation) declined since 1973 in the United States? Why are the poor, poor? Why do birthrates decline with industrialization? Why is the United States the most violent (as measured by murder, rape, and assault rates) industrialized society?

Explore on
MySocLab Activity:
Sociological Theories

A **sociological theory** is a set of ideas that explains a range of human behavior and a variety of social and societal events. The late Michael Harrington said this regarding the necessity of theory: "The data of society are, for all practical purposes, infinite. You need criteria that will provisionally permit you to bring some order into that chaos of data and to distinguish between relevant and irrelevant factors" (Harrington 1985:1). Thus, theory not only helps us to explain social phenomena, but it also guides research.

Problems in Collecting Data

A fundamental problem with the sociological perspective is that bane of the social sciences—objectivity. We are all guilty of harboring stereotyped conceptions of such social categories as Muslims, hard hats, professors, gays and lesbians, fundamentalists, business tycoons, socialists, the rich, the poor, and jocks. Moreover, we interpret

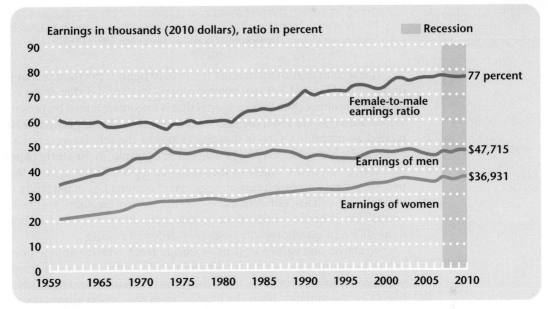

Earnings in thousands (2010 dollars), ratio in percent ⬛ Recession

77 percent

Female-to-male earnings ratio

$47,715

Earnings of men

$36,931

Earnings of women

FIGURE 1.1

Female-to-Male Earnings Ratio and Median Earnings of Full-Time, Year-Round Workers 15 Years and Older by Sex: 1960 to 2010

Data on earnings of full-time, year-round workers are not readily available before 1960.

Source: DeNavas-Walt, Carmen, Bernadette D. Proctor, and Jessica C. Smith. 2011. "Income, Poverty, and Health Insurance Coverage in the United States: 2010." U.S. Census Bureau, *Current Population Reports*, p. 60-239. Washington, D.C., U.S. Government Printing Office, p. 12.

events, material objects, and people's behavior through the perceptual filter of our religious and political beliefs. When fundamentalists oppose the use of certain books in school, when abortion is approved by a legislature, when the president advocates cutting billions from the federal budget by eliminating social services, or when the Supreme Court denies private schools the right to exclude certain racial groups, most of us rather easily take a position in the ensuing debate.

Sociologists are caught in a dilemma. On the one hand, they are members of society with beliefs, feelings, and biases. On the other hand, though, their professional task is to study society in a disciplined (scientific) way. This latter requirement is that scientist–scholars be dispassionate, objective observers. In short, if they take sides, they lose their status as scientists.

🔍 **View on MySocLab Figure:** The Debate Over Values in Sociological Research

This ideal of **value neutrality** (to be absolutely free of bias in research) can be attacked from three positions. The first is that scientists should not be morally indifferent to the implications of their research. Should we, for example, participate in research that shows how to manipulate people politically? Or should we be involved in finding out more efficient ways to get prisoners to reveal their secrets? Science has constructive and destructive potentials. Shouldn't we make value judgments in what we choose to investigate or not? (Gouldner 1962:212). Or, put another way, this time by the late historian Howard Zinn, explaining his style of classroom teaching:

> *I would start off my classes explaining to my students—because I didn't want to deceive them—that I would be taking stands on everything. They would hear my point of view in this course, that this would not be a neutral course. My point to them was that in fact it was impossible to be neutral. You Can't Be Neutral on a Moving Train [the title of Zinn's memoir] means that the world is already moving in certain directions. Things are*

*already happening. Wars are taking place. Children are going hungry. In a world like this—
already moving in certain, often terrible directions—to be neutral or to stand by is to col-
laborate with what is happening. (Quoted in Barsamian 1997:37–38)*

The second argument against the purely neutral position is that such a stance is
impossible. Howard Becker, among others, has argued that there is no dilemma—
because it is impossible to do research that is uncontaminated by personal and political
sympathies (Becker 1967; see also Gould 1998:19). This argument is based on several
related assumptions. One is that the values of the scholar–researcher enter into the
choices of what questions will be asked. For example, in the study of poverty, a critical
decision involves the object of the study—the poor or the system that tends to perpetuate poverty among a certain segment of society. Or, in the study of the problems
of youth, we can ask either of these questions: Why are some youths troublesome for
adults? Or, Why do adults make so much trouble for youths? In both illustrations,
quite different questions will yield very different results.

Similarly, our values lead us to decide from which vantage point we will gain
access to information about a particular social organization. If researchers want to
understand how a prison operates, they must determine whether they want a description from the inmates, from the guards, from the prison administrators, or from the
state board of corrections. Each view provides useful insights about a prison, but obviously a biased one. If they obtain data from more than one of these levels, researchers
are faced with making assessments of which is the more accurate view, clearly another
place in the research process where the values of the observers have an impact.

Perhaps the most important reason why the study of social phenomena cannot be
value free is that the type of problems researched and the strategies used tend either
to support the existing societal arrangements or to undermine them. Seen in this
way, social research of both types is political. Ironically, however, there is a strong
tendency to label only the research aimed at changing the system as political. By the
same token, whenever the research sides with the powerless, the implication is that
the hierarchical system is being questioned—thus, the charge that this type of research
is biased (Becker 1967:240, 242).

In summary, bias is inevitable in the study and analysis of social problems. The
choice of a research problem, the perspective from which one analyzes the problems, and the solutions proposed all reflect a bias that either supports the existing
social arrangements or does not. Moreover, unlike biologists, who can dispassionately
observe the behavior of sperm and the egg at conception, sociologists are participants
in the social life they seek to study and understand. As they study homelessness,
poor children, or urban blight, sociologists cannot escape from their own feelings
and values. They must, however, not let their feelings and values render their analysis invalid. In other words, research and reports of research must reflect reality, not
as the researcher might want it to be. Sociologists must display scientific integrity,
which requires recognizing biases in such a way that these biases do not invalidate the
findings (Berger 1963:5). When research is properly done in this spirit, an atheist can
study a religious sect, a pacifist can study the military-industrial complex, a divorced
person can study marriage, and a person who abhors the beliefs of the Ku Klux Klan
can study that organization and its members.

In addition to bias, people gather data and make generalizations about social
phenomena in a number of faulty ways. In a sense, everyone is a scientist seeking to
find valid generalizations to guide behavior and make sense of the world. But most
people are, in fact, very unscientific about the social world. The first problem, as we
have noted, is the problem of bias. The second is that people tend to generalize from

their experience. Not only is one's interpretation of things that happen to him or her subjective, but there also is a basic problem of sampling. The chances are that one's experience will be too idiosyncratic to allow for an accurate generalization. For example, if you and your friends agree that abortion is appropriate, that does not mean that other people in the society, even those of your age, will agree with you. Very likely, your friends are quite similar to you on such dimensions as socioeconomic status, race, religion, and geographic location.

Another instance of faulty sampling leading to faulty generalizations is when we make assumptions from a single case. An individual may argue that African Americans can succeed economically in this country as easily as Whites because she or he knows a wealthy African American. Similarly, you might argue that all Latinos are dumb because the one you know is in the slowest track in high school. This type of reasoning is especially fallacious because it blames the victim (Ryan 1976). The cause of poverty or crime or dropping out of school or scoring low on an IQ test is seen as a result of the flaw in the individual, ignoring the substantial impact of the economy or school.

Another typical way that we explain social behavior is to use some authority other than our senses. The Bible, for example, has been used by many people to support or condemn activities such as slavery, capital punishment, war, homosexuality, or monogamy (Spong 2005). The media provide other sources of authority for individuals. The media, however, are not always reliable sources of facts. Stories are often selected because they are unusually dramatic, giving the faulty impression of, for example, a crime wave or questionable air safety.

Our judgments and interpretations are also affected by prevailing myths and stereotypes. We just "know" certain things to be true, when they actually may be contradicted by scientific evidence. As examples, six common beliefs about the poor and racial minorities are presented and discussed.

1. *Most homeless people are disabled by drugs, mental disease, or physical afflictions.* The facts show, however, that the homeless, for the most part, are not "deficient and defective" but rather not much different than the nonhomeless. Most people are not homeless because of their individual flaws but because of structural arrangements and trends that result in extreme impoverishment and a shortage of affordable housing (Timmer, Eitzen, and Talley 1994).
2. *African American and Latino youth are more likely than White youth to smoke tobacco and be heavy binge drinkers of alcohol.* The facts belie this myth (Centers for Disease Control study, reported in McClam 2000).
3. *Welfare makes people dependent, lazy, and unmotivated.* Contrary to this image, however, the evidence is that most daughters of welfare recipients do not become welfare recipients as adults (Sklar 1993). Put another way, most women on welfare did not receive welfare as children (Center on Social Welfare and Law 1996).
4. *Welfare is given more generously to the poor than to the nonpoor.* Farm subsidies, tax deductibility for taxes and interest on homes, tax write-offs for business expenses, low-interest loans to students and victims of disasters, and pork-barrel projects are examples of government welfare and even the dependency of nonpoor people on government largesse. Most important, these government handouts to the nonpoor are significantly greater than the amounts given to the poor.
5. *There are more African Americans than Whites in poverty.* In 2010, 31.7 million Whites were below the poverty line, compared to 13.2 million Latinos, and 10.7 million African Americans.
6. *Unmarried women have babies to increase their welfare payments.* Three facts show that this belief of political conservatives is a myth (Males 1996): (a) From 1972 to

1996, the value of the average Aid to Families with Dependent Children (AFDC) check declined by 40 percent, yet the ratio of out-of-wedlock births rose in the same period by 140 percent; (b) states that have lower welfare benefits usually have more out-of-wedlock births than states with higher benefits; and (c) the teen out-of-wedlock birthrate in the United States is much higher than the rate in countries where welfare benefits are much more generous.

Conventional wisdom is not always wrong, but when it is, it can lead to faulty generalizations and bad public policy. Therefore, it is imperative to know the facts, rather than accept myths as real.

A similar problem occurs when we use aphorisms to explain social occurrences. The problem with this common tactic is that society supplies us with ready explanations that fit contradictory situations and are therefore useless. For instance, if we know a couple who are alike in religion, race, socioeconomic status, and political attitudes, that makes sense to us because "birds of a feather flock together." But the opposite situation also makes sense. If partners in a relationship are very different on a number of dimensions, we can explain this by the obvious explanation: "opposites attract." We use a number of other proverbs to explain behavior. The problem is that there is often a proverb or aphorism to explain the other extreme. These contradictory explanations are commonly used and, of course, explain nothing. The job of the sociologist is to specify under what conditions certain rates of social behaviors occur.

Sources of Data

Watch on MySocLab Video: Research Methodology

Sociologists do not use aphorisms to explain behavior, nor do they speculate based on faulty samples or authorities. Because we are part of the world that is to be explained, sociologists must obtain evidence that is beyond reproach. In addition to observing the canons of science scrupulously, four basic sources of data yield valid results for sociologists: survey research, experiments, observation, and existing data. We describe these techniques only briefly here.

Read on MySocLab Document: Sense and Nonsense About Surveys

Survey Research.   Sociologists are interested in obtaining information about people with certain social attributes. They may want to know how political beliefs and behaviors are influenced by differences in sex, race, ethnicity, religion, and social class. Or sociologists may wish to know whether religious attitudes are related to racial antipathy. They may want to determine whether poor people have different values from other people in society, the answer to which will have a tremendous impact on the ultimate solution to poverty. Or they may want to know whether voting patterns, work behaviors, or marital relationships vary by income level, educational attainment, or religious affiliation.

To answer these and similar questions, the sociologist may use personal interviews or written questionnaires to gather the data. The researcher may obtain information from all possible subjects or from a selected **sample** (a representative part of a population). Because the former method is often impractical, a random sample of subjects is selected from the larger population. If the sample is selected scientifically, a relatively small proportion can yield satisfactory results—that is, the inferences made from the sample will be reliable about the entire population. For example, a probability sample of only 2,000 from a total population of 1 million can provide data very close to what would be discovered if a survey were taken of the entire 1 million.

Typically with survey research, sociologists use sophisticated statistical techniques to control the contaminating effects of confounding **variables** to determine whether the findings could have occurred by chance, to determine whether variables are related, and to see whether such a relationship is a causal one. A variable is an attitude, behavior, or condition that can vary in magnitude and significance from case to case.

A special type of survey research, **longitudinal surveys**, has special promise. This type of research collects information about the same persons over many years and in doing so allows the observing researcher to "record the antecedents of current events and transitions" (Butz and Torrey 2006:1898). For example, the Panel Study of Income Dynamics at the University of Michigan has followed the same people for forty years, allowing the researchers to document the transitions from health to infirmity; from work to unemployment or retirement; and from singlehood to marriage, parenthood, divorce, and widowhood (Butz and Torrey 2006:1898).

- **Experiments.**   To understand the cause-and-effect relationship among a few variables, sociologists use controlled experiments. Let us assume, for example, that we want to test whether White students in interracial classrooms have more positive attitudes toward African Americans than Whites in segregated classrooms have toward them. Using the experimental method, the researcher would take a number of White students previously unexposed to Blacks in school and randomly assign a subset to an integrated classroom situation. Before actual contact with the Blacks, however, all the White students would be given a test of their racial attitudes. This pretest establishes a benchmark from which to measure any changes in attitudes. One group, the **control group**, continues school in segregated classrooms. (The control group is a group of subjects not exposed to the independent variable.) The other group, the **experimental group**, now has Blacks as classmates. (The experimental group is a group of subjects who are exposed to the independent variable.) Otherwise, the two groups are the same. Following a suitable period of time, the Whites in both groups are tested again for their racial attitudes. If this post-test reveals that the experimental group differs from the control group in racial attitudes (the **dependent variable**), then it is assumed that interracial contact (the **independent variable**) is the source of the change. (The dependent variable is a variable that is influenced by the effect of another variable. The independent variable is a variable that affects another variable.) As an example of a less-contrived experiment, a researcher can test the results of two different treatments on the subsequent behavior of juvenile delinquents. Delinquent boys who had been adjudicated by the courts can be randomly assigned to a boys' industrial school or a group home facility in the community. After release from incarceration, records are kept on the boys' subsequent behavior in school (grades, truancy, formal reprimands) and in the community (police contacts, work behavior). If the boys from the two groups differ appreciably, then we can say with assurance, because the boys were randomly assigned to each group, that the difference in treatment (the independent variable) was the source of the difference in behavior (the dependent variable).

- **Observation.**   Famed baseball great Yogi Berra once said in his unique way: "You can observe a lot by just watching." The researcher, without intervention, can observe as accurately as possible what occurs in a community, group, or social event. This type of procedure is especially helpful in understanding such social phenomena as the decision-making process, the stages of a riot, the attraction of cults for their members, or the depersonalization of patients in a nursing home. Case studies of entire communities have been very instrumental in the understanding of power structures and the complex interaction patterns in cities. Longtime participant observation studies of slum neighborhoods and gangs have been insightful in showing the social organization present in what the casual observer might think of as disorganized activity.

- **Existing Data.** The sociologist can also use existing data to test theories. The most common sources of information are the various agencies of the government. Data are provided for the nation, regions, states, communities, and census tracts on births, deaths, income, education, unemployment, business activity, health delivery systems, prison populations, military spending, poverty, migration, and the like. Important information can also be obtained from such sources as corporations, athletic teams and leagues, unions, and professional associations. Statistical techniques can be used with these data to describe populations and the effects of social variables on various dependent variables.

One goal of this book is to help the reader understand the social nature of social problems. Accepting the system-blame perspective is a necessary first step in efforts to restructure society along more humane lines. The job of social scientists in this endeavor should be to provide alternative social structures (based on theory and research) for those about which we complain. To do this job, social scientists must ask very different research questions from those posed in the past, and they must study not only the powerless but also the powerful.

ORGANIZATION OF THE BOOK

The organizing theme of this book is that many aspects of social problems are conditions resulting from cultural and social arrangements. It therefore begins by examining the fundamental organization of U.S. society. The remainder of Part One elaborates on the political economy of social problems, emphasizing the political and economic organization of society and its impact on social problems. The focus is on power because the powerful, by making and enforcing the laws, create and define deviance. They determine which behaviors will be rewarded and which ones punished. The powerful influence public opinion, and they can attempt to solve social problems or ignore them. Through policies for taxation and subsidies, the powerful determine the degree to which wealth is distributed in society. They also determine which group interests will be advanced and at whose expense.

The economy is equally important. The particular form of the economy establishes a distribution process not only for wealth but also for goods and services. In many important ways, Karl Marx was correct: The economy is the force that determines the form and substance of all other institutions—the church, school, family, and polity.

Critical scrutiny of the polity and the economy provides clues for the bias of society. It helps explain the upside-down qualities of society whereby the few benefit at the expense of the many; how reality gets defined in contested issues; how political and economic processes affect what is currently being done about social problems; and thus, why so many social policies fail.

Part Two focuses on the context of social problems in the United States. Chapter 3 examines world population and global inequality. Chapter 4 looks at environmental degradation globally and domestically. Chapter 5 focuses on two major population changes in the United States: the browning and the graying of America. The final chapter in Part Two provides a useful overview to social problems by focusing on the problems of location: urban, suburban, and rural.

Part Three examines a crucial element of U.S. social structure: the various manifestations of social inequality. It describes inequality based on wealth, race/ethnicity, gender, sexual orientation, and disability.

Part Four examines the impact of social structure on individuals. Deviant behavior is activity that violates the norms of an organization, community, or society. Consequently, deviance is culturally defined and socially labeled. Certain behaviors are also labeled as deviant because they conflict with the interests of the powerful in society. Public policy, then, reflects the values and interests of those in power and is codified into law. Members of society are also taught how to respond to deviants. The law and these structured responses to deviants are societal reactions that establish deviance in social roles; paradoxically, the degraded status that results from societal reactions reinforces the deviance that society seeks to control. Deviance, then, is fundamentally the result of social structure. We examine these processes in relation to two types of deviance: crime and drug use.

Part Five describes problems found within five representative institutions. Chapter 14 returns the focus to the economy and jobs. The number and types of jobs are undergoing a major shift with globalization and as society deindustrializes and moves toward a service economy. Although the resulting changes bring many opportunities, they also bring many problems, such as the widening gap between the haves and the have-nots and the emergence of a new form of poverty. Chapter 15 looks at the family-related problems of childcare, violence, and divorce. Chapter 16 illustrates how education, although necessary as the source for transmitting the necessary skills and shared understandings to each generation, is also a generator of social problems. Thus, it shows once again how social problems (in this case, inequality) originate in the basic structure of society. Chapter 17 focuses on the reasons for the high cost of healthcare in the United States and the effort to reform the healthcare system. National security, especially the threat of terrorism, is the final topic of Part Five.

The book concludes with a chapter that answers the question, What do we do about social problems? The solutions come from the bottom up—that is, people organize through human agency to change social structures (Eitzen and Stewart 2007). Solutions also come from the top down—social policies determined by the powerful (Eitzen and Sage 2007). Both of these forces and the interaction between the top and the bottom are the topics of the concluding chapter.

MySocLab   ✓ **Study** and **Review** on **MySocLab**

■ CHAPTER REVIEW

1. Historically, U.S. sociologists have viewed social problems in terms of social pathology: "Bad" people were assumed to be the sources of social problems because they disturbed the prevailing moral order in society.

2. In the 1920s and 1930s, sociologists focused on the conditions of society, such as the rapid changes accompanying urbanization and industrialization, as the sources of social problems.

3. More recently, many sociologists have returned to a study of problem individuals—deviants who violate the expectations of society. The modern study of deviance has developed in two directions. The first sought the sources of deviation within the social structure. The other, of relatively recent origin, has focused on the role of society in creating and sustaining deviance through labeling those viewed as abnormal. In this view, societal reactions are assumed to determine what a social problem is and who is deviant.

4. There is an objective reality to social problems; some conditions or situations do induce material and psychic suffering. There are several dangers, however, in defining social problems objectively. Subjectivity cannot be removed from the process. A standard must be selected, but in a pluralistic society, there are many standards. Moreover, social scientists not only disagree on what a social problem is but also cannot escape their own values in the study of social problems. Most important,

the objective approach to social problems entails acceptance of the definitions provided by the powerful. The acceptance of these definitions diverts attention away from the powerful and toward those the powerful wish to label negatively, thus deflecting observations away from what may constitute the most important social problem—the existing social order.

5. This book examines two types of social problems: (a) acts and conditions that violate the norms and values of society and (b) societally induced conditions that cause psychic and material suffering for any segment of the population. The key to understanding both types of social problems is the distribution of power.

6. The sociological imagination involves (a) a willingness to view the social world from the perspective of others; (b) focusing on the social, economic, and historical circumstances that influence families, groups, and organizations; (c) questioning the structural arrangements that shape social behavior; and (d) seeing the solutions to social problems in terms not of changing problem people but of changing the structure of society.

7. The focus is on the structure of society rather than on "problem" individuals. A guiding assumption of our inquiry is that norm violators are symptoms of social problems. These deviants are, for the most part, victims and should not be blamed entirely for their deviance; the system in which they live should also be blamed.

8. The person-blame approach, which we do not use, has serious consequences: (a) The social sources of social problems are ignored. (b) It frees the institutions of society from any blame and efforts to change them. (c) It controls "problem" people in ways that reinforce negative stereotypes. (d) It legitimates person-control programs. (e) It justifies the logic of social Darwinism, which holds that people are rich or poor because of their ability and effort or lack thereof.

9. The system-blame orientation also has dangers. Taken dogmatically, it presents a rigidly deterministic explanation for social problems, suggesting that people are merely robots controlled by their social environment.

10. Sociology depends on reliable data and logical reason. Although value neutrality is impossible in the social sciences, bias is minimized by the norms of science.

11. Sociologists use a variety of methods: surveys, experiments, observation, and the use of existing data sources.

■ KEY TERMS

Subjective nature of social problems. The idea that what is and what is not a social problem is a matter of definition. Thus, social problems vary by time and place.

Objective reality of social problems. The notion that societal conditions harm certain segments of the population and therefore are social problems.

Deviant behavior. Activity that violates the norms of a social organization.

Institutionalized deviance. When a society is organized in such a way as to disadvantage some of its members.

Social problems. Societally induced conditions that harm any segment of the population, and acts and conditions that violate the norms and values found in society.

Sociological imagination. C. Wright Mills's term emphasizing that individual troubles are inextricably linked to social forces.

Person-blame. The assumption that social problems result from the pathologies of individuals.

System-blame. The assumption that social problems result from social conditions.

Cultural deprivation. The assumption by the members of a group that the culture of some other group is not only inferior but also deficient. This term is usually applied by members of the majority to the culture of a minority group.

Recidivism. Reinvolvement in crime.

Social Darwinism. The belief that the place of people in the stratification system is a function of their ability and effort.

Sociological theory. A set of ideas that explains a range of human behavior and a variety of social and societal events.

Value neutrality. To be absolutely free of bias.

Sample. A representative part of a population.

Variable. An attitude, behavior, or condition that can vary in magnitude and significance from case to case.

Longitudinal survey. The collection of information about the same persons over many years.

Control group. The subjects not exposed to the independent variable.

Experimental group. The subjects exposed to the independent variable.

Dependent variable. The variable that is influenced by the effect of another variable.

Independent variable. A variable that affects another variable.

Wealth and Power: The Bias of the System

 Listen to Chapter 2 on **MySocLab**

LEARNING OBJECTIVES

2.1 Explain the mechanisms that promote monopolistic capitalism and the consequences of each on a capitalist society.

2.2 Describe how the U.S. government is biased in favor of the wealthy.

2.3 Explain the links between wealth, power, and the U.S. political system.

2.4 Demonstrate how corporations benefit from government actions.

The thesis of this book is that many of the problems of U.S. society result from the maldistribution of wealth and power. In essence, the state is not a neutral agent of the people but is biased in favor of those with wealth—the upper social classes and the largest corporations. The analysis shows that, contrary to popular belief, the U.S. system does not produce a society that is democratic, just, and equal in opportunity. Rather, we find that the United States is an upside-down society, with the few benefiting at the expense of the many. Finally, we see how our society itself is the source of social problems.

The study of social problems requires the critical examination of the structure of society. Some readers will find this approach uncomfortable, even unpatriotic. In this regard, introducing his critical analysis of the United States, political scientist Michael Parenti has said, and we agree,

> If the picture that emerges in the pages ahead is not pretty, this should not be taken as an attack on the United States, for this country and the American people are greater than the abuses perpetrated upon them by those who live for power and profit. To expose these abuses is not to denigrate the nation that is a victim of them. The greatness of a country is to be measured by something more than its rulers, its military budget, its instruments of dominance and destruction, and its profiteering giant corporations. A nation's greatness can be measured by its ability to create a society free of poverty, racism, sexism, imperialism, and social and environmental devastation, and by the democratic nature of its institutions. Albert Camus once said, "I would like to love my country and justice too." In fact, there is no better way to love one's country, no better way to strive for the fulfillment of its greatness, than to entertain critical ideas and engage in the pursuit of social justice at home and abroad. (1995:6)

This chapter is divided into three sections. The first describes the U.S. economy, with its concentration of corporate and private wealth. The second examines the political system and its links to the economic elites. The final section shows how the politicoeconomic system is biased in favor of those who are already advantaged.

U.S. ECONOMY: CONCENTRATION OF CORPORATE WEALTH

2.1 Explain the mechanisms that promote monopolistic capitalism and the consequences of each on a capitalist society.

The U.S. economy has always been based on the principles of capitalism; however, the present economy is far removed from a free enterprise system. The major discrepancy between the ideal system and the real one is that the U.S. economy is no longer based on competition among more-or-less equal private capitalists. It is now dominated by huge corporations that, contrary to classical economic theory, control demand rather than respond to the demands of the market. However well the economic system might once have worked, the increasing size and power of corporations disrupt it. This development calls into question what the appropriate economic form is for a post-industrial society.

Monopolistic Capitalism

Karl Marx, more than 130 years ago, when bigness was the exception, predicted that capitalism was doomed by several inherent contradictions that would produce a class of people bent on destroying it (see the insert on Karl Marx and "self-destruct" capitalism). The most significant of these contradictions for our purposes is the inevitability of monopolies. Marx hypothesized that free enterprise would result in some firms becoming bigger and bigger as they eliminate their opposition or absorb smaller competing firms. The ultimate result of this process is the existence of a monopoly in each

Karl Marx and Self-Destruct Capitalism

Karl Marx (1818–1883) was one of history's greatest social theorists. His ideas have fueled revolutionaries and revolutions. His writings have had an enormous impact on each of the social sciences. His intellectual contributions to sociology include (1) elaboration of the conflict model of society, (2) the theory of social change based on antagonisms between the social classes, (3) the insight that power originates primarily in economic production, and (4) concern with the social origins of alienation.

Marx believed that the basis of social order in every society is the production of economic goods. What is produced, how it is produced, and how it is exchanged determine the differences in people's wealth, power, and social status. Marx argued that because human beings must organize their activities to clothe, feed, and house themselves, every society is built on an economic base. The exact form this organization takes varies among societies and across time. The form that people chose to solve their basic economic problems would, according to Marx, eventually determine virtually everything in the social structure, including polity, family structure, education, and religion. In Marx's view, all these social institutions depend on the basic economy, and an analysis of society will always reveal its underlying economic arrangements.

Because it owns the means of production, the social class in power uses the noneconomic institutions to uphold its position. Thus, Marx believed that religion, the government, and the educational system are used by the powerful to maintain the status quo.

Marx argued that every economic system except socialism produces forces that eventually lead to a new economic form. In the feudal system, for example, the market and factory emerged but were incompatible with the feudal way of life. The market created a professional merchant class, and the factory created a proletariat. Thus, new inventions create a tension with the old institutions, and new social classes threaten to displace old ones. Conflict results, and society is rearranged with a new class structure and an alteration in the division of wealth and power based on a new economic form. Feudalism was replaced by capitalism; land ownership was replaced by factories and the ownership of capital.

Capitalism, Marx maintained, also carries the seeds of its own destruction. Capitalism will produce a class of oppressed people (the proletariat) bent on destroying it. The contradictions inherent in capitalism are (1) the inevitability of monopolies, which eliminate competition and gouge consumers and workers; (2) the lack of centralized planning, which results in overproduction of some goods and underproduction of others, encouraging economic crises such as inflation, slumps, and depressions; (3) demands for labor-saving machinery, which force unemployment and a more hostile proletariat; (4) that employers will tend to maximize profits by reducing labor expenses, thus creating a situation where workers will not have enough income to buy products, thus the contradiction of causing profits to fall; and (5) control of the state by the wealthy, the effect of which is passage of laws favoring themselves and thereby incurring more wrath from the proletariat. All these factors increase the probability that the proletariat will build class consciousness, which is the condition necessary to class conflict and the ushering in of a new economic system.

Sources: Robert J. Werlin. 1972. "Marxist Political Analysis." *Sociological Inquiry* 42 (Nos. 3–4): 157–181; Karl Marx. 1976. *Karl Marx: Selected Writings in Sociology and Social Philosophy* (T. B. Bottomore, Trans.). New York: McGraw-Hill, pp. 127–212. See also Michael Harrington. 1976. *The Twilight of Capitalism.* New York: Simon & Schuster.

of the various sectors of the economy. Monopolies, of course, are antithetical to the free enterprise system because they, not supply and demand, determine the price and the quality of the product.

For the most part, the evidence in U.S. society upholds Marx's prediction. Less than 1 percent of all corporations produce over 80 percent of the private-sector output. Most sectors of the U.S. economy are dominated by a few corporations. Instead of one corporation controlling an industry, the typical situation is domination by a small number of large firms. When four or fewer firms supply 50 percent or more of a particular market, a **shared monopoly** results, which performs much as a monopoly or cartel would. Most economists agree that above this level of concentration—a four-firm ratio of 50 percent—the economic costs of shared monopoly are most manifest. Government data show that a number of industries are highly concentrated (e.g., each of the following industries has four or fewer firms controlling at least 60 percent: light bulbs, breakfast cereals, milk supply, turbines/generators, aluminum, cigarettes, beer, chocolate/cocoa, photography equipment, trucks, cosmetics, film distribution, soft drinks, snack foods, guided missiles, and roasted coffee [Mokhiber 2010]).

This trend toward ever-greater concentration among the largest U.S. business concerns has accelerated because of two activities—mergers and interlocking directorates.

- **Megamergers.** There are thousands of mergers each year as giant corporations become even larger. Some of the largest mergers in U.S. history have occurred in recent years (for example, Time, Inc., and AOL joining with Warner Communications; Disney merging with Capital Cities/ABC; NBC merging with Comcast; United Airlines taking over Continental Airlines; the merger of Wells Fargo and First Interstate Banks; the merger of NationsBank and BankAmerica; Philip Morris taking over Miller Brewing; the AT&T buyout of Tele-Communications, Inc.; Citicorp merging with Travelers Group; Texaco buying out Getty Oil; Exxon merging with Mobil Oil; Exxon Mobil merging with XTO, and MCI World.Com's acquisition of Sprint). There have also been megamergers combining U.S. and foreign firms (for example, Daimler and Chrysler, British Petroleum and Amoco, and Deutsche Bank and Bankers Trust). The federal government encouraged these mergers by relaxing antitrust law enforcement on the grounds that efficient firms should not be hobbled.

  This trend toward megamergers has at least five negative consequences: (1) It increases the centralization of capital, which reduces competition and raises prices for consumers; (2) it increases the power of huge corporations over workers, unions, politicians, and governments; (3) it reduces the number of jobs (for example, when Citicorp and Travelers combined to make Citigroup, 10,400 jobs were eliminated; (4) it increases corporate debt; and (5) it is nonproductive. Elaborating on this last point, mergers and takeovers do not create new plants, products, or jobs. Rather, they create profits for chief executive officers, lawyers, accountants, brokers, bankers, and big investors.

- **Interlocking Directorates.** Another mechanism for the ever-greater concentration of the size and power of the largest corporations is **interlocking directorates**, the linkage between corporations that results when an individual serves on the board of directors of two companies (a **direct interlock**) or when two companies each have a director on the board of a third company (an **indirect interlock**). These arrangements have great potential to benefit the interlocked companies by reducing competition through the sharing of information and the coordination of policies.

In 1914, the Clayton Act made it illegal for a person to serve simultaneously on corporate boards of two companies that were in direct competition with each other. Financial institutions and indirect interlocks, however, were exempt. Moreover, the government has had difficulty determining what constitutes "direct competition." The result is that, despite the prohibition, over 90 percent of large U.S. corporations have some directors interlocked with other corporations. When directors are linked directly or indirectly, the potential exists for cohesiveness, common action, and unified power. Clearly, the principles of capitalism are compromised when this phenomenon occurs.

Despite the relative noncompetitiveness among the large corporations, many of them devote considerable efforts to convincing the public that the U.S. economy is competitive. Many advertisements depict the economy as an Adam Smith–style free market with competition among innumerable small competitors. This, however, is a myth. Competition does exist among the mom-and-pop stores, but they control only a minute portion of the nation's assets. The largest assets are located among the very large corporations, and competition there is minimal.

CASE STUDY   Media Monopolies

The media, through movies, television, radio, books, magazines, newspapers, and advertising, are major players in the creation of the culture, shaping what we think and do. The media play an influential role in a democracy because a democracy hinges on whether there is an informed electorate. The people need unbiased information and the push-and-pull of public debate if they are to be truly informed. These conditions become problematic, however, when the sources of information are increasingly concentrated in a few huge conglomerates guided only by commercial and bottom-line values. In 1983, fifty corporations controlled media in the United States. Now there are six —News Corporation, General Electric, Disney, Time Warner, CBS, and Viacom. Consider the range and scope of their media holdings:

- Viacom owns UPN, Paramount Pictures, DreamWorks, MTV, Nickelodeon, Nick at Nite, The Daily Show with Jon Stewart, TV Land, CMT, VH1, Movie Channel, Sundance Channel, Flick, Black Entertainment, and Comedy Central, to name a few of their holdings.
- CBS owns CBS News, CBS Radio, CBS Sports, CBS Films, Smithsonian TV, EcoMedia, Showtime, Simon and Schuster, MY Networks, and twenty-eight local TV stations.
- Some of Time Warner's holdings include *Time*, *People*, *Sports Illustrated*, *Fortune*, *Entertainment Weekly*, *Popular Science*, AOL, CompuServe, CNN, Cinemax, NASCAR.com, Warner Brothers Pictures, Warner Brothers Cable, TBS, TNT, Cartoon Network, HBO, The Movie Channel, and Court TV.
- A sample of News Corporation's media holdings includes Fox News, Fox Sports, Fox Business Network, National Geographic Channel, FX, 175 newspapers worldwide, Speed, Twentieth Century Fox, twenty-seven television stations in the United States, *New York Post*, *The Wall Street Journal*, *Weekly Standard*, *TV Guide*, *Barron's*, HarperCollins, ReganBooks, Zondervan Publishing, and My Space.
- Disney's media affiliates are ABC, ESPN, The Disney Channel, E! Entertainment, The History Channel, Disney Publishing, Hyperion Books, ABC Radio (seventy-three stations), Walt Disney Pictures, Miramax Films, Buena Vista Productions, and Pixar.
- Some of General Electric's media holdings are NBC, fourteen television stations in major markets, Telemundo, Universal Pictures, Universal Studios, CNBC, MSNBC, Bravo, USA Network, and A & E. In 2011 Comcast merged with NBC Universal, "marrying" the largest cable company and the biggest residential Internet service provider. The resulting merger owned fifty-two cable channels including the Golf channel, PBS Kids, E!, and the NBC network, plus twenty-seven local TV stations.

In addition to amusement parks, Disney has media holdings including ABC, ESPN, The Disney Channel, Hyperion Books, ABC radio, Walt Disney Pictures, Miramax Films, Buena Vista Productions, and Pixar.

In addition to these media giants, ten companies broadcast to two-thirds of the nation's radio audience. One of these, Clear Channel Communications, owns more than 850 radio stations, reaching 238 million listeners each month (Clear Channel 2012) (before the Telecommunications Act of 1996, which lifted ownership limits for radio stations, one company could not own more than forty stations nationwide). Clear Channel also owns forty-two television stations and a substantial number of billboards and other outdoor advertising.

Pearson Higher Education, the publisher of this text, is the world's largest publisher of college textbooks. College textbook publishing in the United States is dominated by Pearson, Thomson/Cengage, and McGraw-Hill.

In 1965, there were 860 owners of daily newspapers. Today there are fewer than 300. Many cities now have only one major newspaper. The most important newspapers are (1) the *New York Times*, which also owns the *Boston Globe* and fifteen other daily newspapers, as well as television and radio stations; (2) the *Washington Post* is also owner of Kaplan (one of the world's largest providers of educational services), TV stations in Detroit, Houston, Miami, Orlando, San Antonio, and Jacksonville, Slate, and Cable One; (3) News Corp (see above), the owner of the *Wall Street Journal*; and (4) Gannett, the owner of *USA Today*, major newspapers in Phoenix, Indianapolis, Cincinnati, Nashville, Louisville, Des Moines, and Detroit, plus twenty-three television stations.

These examples show the extent to which a few major corporations control what we see, hear, and read. What does it mean when the information and entertainment we receive are increasingly under monopolized control? First, the media help to define reality by determining what is important and, conversely, what is not. This shapes our understanding of what is a social problem. For instance, the evening news focuses much more on street crime, using a disproportionate number of images of people of color as perpetrators, than it does on white-collar and corporate crime.

Second, diverse opinions are rarely heard. Because a few media giants control the content and distribution of programming, smaller companies with distinctive viewpoints are increasingly rare. The content of talk radio, for example, leans heavily to the political right, as evidenced by the views of Rush Limbaugh, Glenn Beck, G. Gordon Liddy, Oliver North, Sean Hannity, Armstrong Williams, Michael Savage, Bob Grant, and Laura Ingraham. In a nation that is divided more or less equally politically, there are relatively few progressive voices on the radio. Conservatives, on the other hand, charge that the print media are biased toward the liberal position on political issues.

Third, reporting is sometimes compromised by conflict of interest. For example, did NBC, when it was owned by General Electric, report extensively on the long-term contamination of the Hudson River by a GE plant? Similarly, media corporations might shy away from news that is too critical of the government because of the corporation's political leanings, they do not want to offend customers, or they depend on government subsidies and favorable legislation.

Fourth, a media giant may, through its subsidiaries, push a political stance. For example, Clear Channel Communications, with 850 radio stations, used its considerable market power to drum up support for the war in Iraq. Following the 9/11 terrorist attacks, songs such as Cat Stevens's "Peace Train" and John Lennon's "Imagine" were blacklisted in the corporation's stations. The network sponsored pro-war rallies and a continuous barrage of uncritical comment (Marshall 2003). When one of the Dixie Chicks said that she was ashamed that President Bush came from Texas, Clear Channel Communications banned the Dixie Chicks' music from its country music stations (as did Cumulus Media).

Fifth, big stories (war, corruption, the economy, legislation) are often pushed aside in favor of "hot" stories, such as kidnappings and murders, and salacious stories about celebrities.

Finally, the messages we hear and see tend to focus on problem individuals rather than on problems with structural origins. Thus, the media pull us away from sociological interpretations—with critical consequences for social policy as we will see throughout this book.

Transnational Corporations

The thesis of the previous section is that there is a trend for corporations to increase in size, resulting eventually in huge enterprises that join with other large companies to form effective monopolies. This process of economic concentration provides the largest companies with enormous economic and political power. If, for example, we compare government budgets with gross corporate revenues, in 2009, the sales of Walmart, Royal Dutch Shell, and ExxonMobil each exceeded the gross domestic product of Indonesia (the fourth most populous country in the world). Combining these three transnational corporations, their sales revenues were more than the combined economies of the world's poorest 118 countries with a total population of more than 800 million.

View on MySocLab Figure: The Globalization of Capitalism: U.S. Ownership in Other Countries

Another trend—the globalization of the largest U.S. corporations—makes their power all the greater. This fact of international economic life has very important implications for social problems, both at home and abroad.

A number of U.S. corporations have substantial assets overseas, with the trend to increase these investments rapidly. In 2009, six of the top fifteen multinationals in sales were U.S.-based corporations (Forbes 2010). U.S. corporations are shifting more and more of their total assets outside the United States to increase profits. Resources necessary for manufacture and production tend to be cheaper in many other nations. Most significant, U.S. corporations increase their profits by moving their production facilities from high-wage situations to low-wage nonunion countries. Moreover, foreign production costs are lower because labor safety laws and environmental protection laws are much more lax than in the United States.

The consequences of this shift in production from the United States to other countries are significant. Most important is the reduction or even drying up of many semiskilled and unskilled jobs in the United States, increased welfare costs and increased discontent among people in the working class. (This problem of domestic job losses through overseas capital investments is discussed in detail in Chapter 14, where globalization, deindustrialization, capital flight, and outsourcing are considered.)

Another result of the twin processes of concentration and internationalization of corporations is the enormous power wielded by gigantic transnational corporations. In essence, the largest corporations control the world economy. Their decisions to build or not to build, to relocate a plant, or to start a new product or scrap an old one have tremendous impacts on the lives of ordinary citizens in the countries they operate from and invest in and on their disinvestment in U.S.-based operations.

Finally, transnational corporations tend to meddle in the internal affairs of other nations to protect their investments and maximize profits. These activities include attempts to overthrow governments considered unfriendly to corporate interests and payment of millions of dollars in bribes and political contributions to reactionary governments and conservative leaders in various countries.

Concentration of Wealth

View on MySocLab Figure: Distribution of Income and Wealth in the United States

The other discrepancy between free enterprise in its real and ideal states is the undue concentration of wealth among a few individuals and corporations. This imbalance makes a mockery of claims that capitalism rewards the efforts of all enterprising individuals.

- **Concentration of Corporate Wealth.** Wealth in the business community is centralized in a relatively few major corporations, and this concentration is increasing. In 2009, for example, the U.S. corporation with the most assets ($2.22 trillion) was Bank of America; the top corporation in sales—Walmart—had $408.2 billion in revenues; and the greatest producer of profits was Exxon-Mobil at $19.28 billion (Forbes 2010). The following examples show just how concentrated wealth is among the major U.S. corporations:

  - Less than 1 percent of all corporations account for over 80 percent of the total output of the private sector.
  - Of the 15,000 commercial U.S. banks, the largest fifty hold more than one-third of all assets.
  - One percent of all food corporations control 80 percent of all the industry's assets and about 90 percent of the profits.
  - Six transnational corporations ship 90 percent of the grain in the world market.

- **Concentration of Private Wealth and Income.** Capitalism generates inequality. Wealth is concentrated not only in the largest corporations but also among individuals and families. For example, in 2010, the two wealthiest were Bill Gates, head of software giant Microsoft, with an estimated fortune of $54 billion, and Warren Buffett of Berkshire Hathaway, with $45 billion.

  A few families are fabulously wealthy. The six heirs to the Walmart fortune, for example, were worth a combined $107 billion in mid-2012. Dividends from their Walmart stock add a cumulative total of $1 billion annually.

  The concentration of wealth is greatly skewed. Consider the following facts:

  - The combined net worth of the 400 richest Americans in 2011 was more than the total wealth of the bottom 185 million Americans.
  - In 2009 the richest 5 percent of U.S. households owned 63.5 percent of the nation's private wealth, the bottom 80 percent, collectively, held just 12.8 percent (Herbert

2011). There were 5.134 million millionaire households (excluding housing values), making the United States the nation with the most millionaires, followed by Japan (1.6 million), and China (1.4 million) (Becerra et al. 2012).

- The United States also had the largest number of ultra high net worth households (2,928), worth $100 million or more, and 363 billionaire households (Becerra et al. 2012).

The data on wealth always show more concentration than do income statistics, but the convergence of money among the few is still very dramatic when considering income. The share of the national income of the richest 20 percent of households was 50.2 percent, while the bottom 20 percent received only 3.3 percent of the nation's income in 2010. The data in Table 2.1 show that income inequality is increasing in U.S. society. Especially noteworthy is the sharp gain in the Gini index, which measures the magnitude of income concentration from 1970 to 2010. (See Table 2.1.) Comparing the U.S. Gini index with that of the developed countries in the OECD (Organization for Economic Cooperation and Development), the United States is by far the most unequal (Babones 2012). Examined another way, the Central Intelligence Agency ranked 140 nations on income inequality and found that the United States was ranked as 42nd most equal among the wealthy democracies with whom Americans compare themselves (Meyer 2012).

Another measure of this increasing gap is the difference in earnings between the heads of corporations and the workers in those corporations. In 1960, the average chief executive officer (CEO) of a Fortune 500 corporation was paid forty times more than the average worker. By 2011, it had risen dramatically to 380 times more (Pizzigati 2012). Put another way, over the past thirty years, CEO salaries have increased 127 times faster than worker salaries (Figueroa 2012). In 2011 the median salary of CEOs was $9.587 million. The typical American worker making the national average salary would have to work 233 years to equal that amount, and a minimum wage worker working full time would match the CEOs' salary in 636 years (Condon and Rexrode 2012). From another angle, assuming that typical CEO works a sixty-hour week, the pay would be $3,072.84 per hour, or $51.21 per minute. A minimum wage worker would have to work more than ten weeks to make what the median CEO earns in an

TABLE 2.1

Share of Aggregate Income by Each Fifth of Households, 1970, 1980, 1990, 2000, 2010

	Percentage Distribution of Aggregate Income					
Year	Lowest Fifth	Second Fifth	Third Fifth	Fourth Fifth	Highest Fifth	Gini* Index
2010	3.3	8.5	14.6	23.4	50.2	.469
2000	3.6	8.9	14.9	23.0	49.7	.460
1990	3.9	9.6	15.9	24.0	46.6	.428
1980	4.3	10.3	16.9	24.9	44.7	.403
1970	4.1	10.8	17.4	24.5	43.3	.394

*The income inequality of a population group is commonly measured using the Gini index. The Gini index ranges from 0, indicating perfect equality (i.e., all persons having equal shares of the aggregate income), to 1, indicating perfect inequality (i.e., where all of the income is received by only one recipient or one group of recipients and the rest have none). The increase in the Gini index for household income between 1970 and 2009 indicates a significant increase in income inequality.

Sources: U.S. Bureau of the Census, Current Population Surveys. Online. Available: http://www.census .gov/hhes/www/incineq.html. U.S. Census Bureau, Current Population Survey, 2009 and 2010 Annual Social and Economic Supplements.

hour. The average U.S. worker would have work nearly a month to make the CEOs' hourly salary (Borenstein 2012).

The inequality gap has risen dramatically for a number of reasons. The gain at the top reflects the increased tax benefits received by the affluent from changing tax laws. Another factor explaining this inequality gap is the changing job structure as the economy shifts from manufacturing to service and as U.S. jobs are exported (see Chapter 14). At the upper end, corporate executives added handsomely to their incomes while downsizing their domestic workforces. Congress has increased this upper-class feast by reducing taxes on capital gains (taxes on the profits from the sale of property) and by allowing the affluent to place as much of their income as they wish in special tax-deferred pay plans not available to the less well-to-do. Most significant were the tax cuts in 2001 and 2003. Since 2001, these cuts have resulted in over half a trillion dollars going to the richest 1 percent. To illustrate, in the 2008 tax year, households in the bottom 20 percent received $26 from these tax cuts while households in the top 1 percent received $50,495, and households in the top 0.1 percent received $266,151 in tax savings. See the "Social Policy" panel for more government policies that increase the inequality gap.

Social Policy

GOVERNMENT POLICIES EXACERBATE WEALTH INEQUALITY

Government policies have the power to expand or reduce the gap between the haves and the have-nots. Consider what we could do to lift up the underserved:

We could truly address the disgraceful truth that in this rich nation one in six children is raised in poverty and deprived of the healthy, fair start vital to equal opportunity. Now we have the resources to rebuild an aging and overburdened infrastructure—witnessed daily in power blackouts, collapsing sewers and aged water systems, overburdened airports, deferred toxic waste cleanups. Now we can redress the growing shortage of affordable housing and insure that every American has access to healthcare. (Borosage 2001:5)

All these actions are within our reach, but the decision makers have ruled them out, making the reduction of taxes paramount, which increases the inequality gap, already the most unequal by far among the industrialized nations. Here are some examples of how government policies enhance the advantages of the haves:

- Getting rid of the estate tax so that large fortunes can be passed on to the next generation.
- Reducing tax rates both on corporate profits and on unearned income such as dividends and capital gains so that the wealthy can more easily accumulate even more.
- Reducing tax rates on people with high incomes, shifting the burden to the payroll tax and other revenue sources that bear most heavily on people with lower incomes.
- On the spending side, cutting back on healthcare for the poor, on the quality of public education, and on state aid for higher education. This makes

it more difficult for people with low incomes to achieve upward mobility.

The affluent, by paying less in taxes, will, in effect, withdraw their support from programs that help those who are poor, those who do not have health insurance, and those who cannot afford decent housing. Former secretary of labor Robert Reich argues that what is really at issue here is the sorting of America, where our society is becoming more rigidly stratified. Reich says,

There's only one way to reverse the sorting mechanism. . . . We have to rededicate ourselves to strong public institutions that are indubitably public because they work well for everyone. Of course this means more money and higher performance standards. But it also requires a renewed public spiritedness—a we're-all-in-this-together patriotism that says it's good for Americans to transcend class, race, education, health, and fortune, and to participate together. (2000:64)

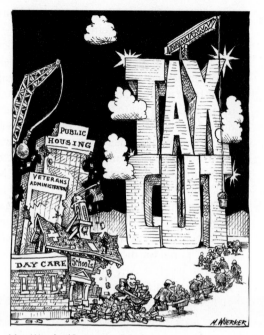

Matt Wuerker/Cartoonist Group

The recent tax policies have four major consequences. First, they exacerbate the unequal distribution of wealth in the United States, which is already the most unequal in the Western world. Second, the huge tax cuts occurred at the very time that the United States was conducting two costly wars in Iraq and Afghanistan and spending huge amounts to get the country out of the greatest economic disaster since the Great Depression. The result is a dramatic increase in the national debt. This leads to the third consequence: The ever-increasing debt is used to justify reductions in government spending for programs that help the less fortunate, and it weakens public institutions that benefit society. As the late political observer Molly Ivins has put it,

> The . . . reason it's dumb to cut taxes for the rich is the problem of social justice. We're already in trouble because the income gap between the rich and the rest of us keeps getting worse and worse. The rich buy their way out of our public institutions—schools, hospitals, parks—and then contribute money to politicians who let the public infrastructure go to hell. It doesn't work. (2003:39A)

Ivins points to the fourth negative consequence of the widening gap between the haves and the have-nots—the increasing political influence of the wealthy, which is the topic of the next section.

2.2 Describe how the U.S. government is biased in favor of the wealthy.

POLITICAL SYSTEM: LINKS BETWEEN WEALTH AND POWER

In many ways, the U.S. government represents the privileged few rather than the majority. Although the government appears democratic, with elections, political parties, and the right to dissent, the influence of wealth prevails. This influence is seen in the disproportionate rewards the few receive from the politicoeconomic system and in government decisions that consistently benefit them. Senator Bernie Sanders argues that the United States is, increasingly, an oligarchy. An **oligarchy** is a government ruled by the few. In

Sanders's words, "Oligarchy refers . . . to the fact that the decisions that shape our consciousness and affect our lives are made by a very small and powerful group of people" (Sanders 1994:B1). Other critics have taken this a step further, suggesting that the United States is a **plutocracy** (a government by or in the interest of the rich; e.g., Parenti 2008:27–39).

Government by Interest Groups

Watch on MySocLab Video: Politics in the United States

Democracy may be defined as a political system that is of, by, and for the people. It is a system under which the will of the majority prevails, there is equality before the law, and decisions are made to maximize the common good. The principles that define a democracy are violated by the rules of the Senate (see "A Closer Look: The Structure

A Closer Look

THE STRUCTURE OF THE SENATE AS A BARRIER TO DEMOCRACY

The U.S. Senate is designed to thwart popular will in at least two ways: the filibuster and the disproportionate power of small states.

The **filibuster** is a self-imposed rule of the Senate not found in the Constitution. It is the practice of holding the Senate floor to prevent a vote on a bill. In 1917 the Senate adopted a rule that allowed the Senate to end a debate with a two-thirds majority vote for "**cloture**." For the next fifty years, the Senate tried to invoke cloture but usually failed to gain the necessary two-thirds votes. Filibusters were used primarily by segregationists seeking to derail civil rights legislation. South Carolina's Strom Thurmond, for example, filibustered for 24 hours and 18 minutes (the all-time record) against the Civil Rights Act of 1957. The southern senators tried to stymie antilynching legislation in the Civil Rights Act of 1964, but failed when cloture was invoked after a fifty-seven-day filibuster. In 1975, the Senate reduced the number of votes required for cloture from two-thirds (67) to three-fifths (60). That is the rule now in place.

The political composition of the Senate in 2013 was 53 Democrats,

2 Independents who caucus with the Democrats, and 45 Republicans. Despite the public's election of a Democratic president in 2012 and adding enough Democrats to have a relatively large majority in the Senate, the Democrats have not been able to get legislation passed for two reasons: The Republicans often vote as a bloc to block the agenda of the Democrats and the difficulty in garnering 60 votes to defeat a filibuster. The use of the filibuster or the threat of a filibuster, once a relatively rare parliamentary move, has become commonplace. Since 2006, when Republicans became a minority in the Senate, there were almost 400 filibusters through the end of 2012.

The popular will is also thwarted in the Senate by the extraordinary power of small states (the following is from MacGillis 2009). For example, climate change legislation faces tough odds in the Senate because the states dominated by agriculture, coal, and oil, which are typically underpopulated states, are opposed. The coal state of Wyoming has a single vote in the House, compared to New York's 29 and

California's 53. In the Senate, however, each state has two, making Wyoming's senators equal in numerical weight to California's senators. North and South Dakota with a combined population of 1.4 million have twice as many senators as Florida (18.3 million), Texas (24.3 million), or Illinois (12.9 million). A few additional inequities with each state having two senators, regardless of population size:

- California is seventy times as large as the smallest state, Wyoming.
- The ten largest states have more than half the people in the United States, yet have only a fifth of the votes in the Senate.
- The twenty-one smallest states combined have fewer people than California, yet they have forty-two senators, while California has only two.

Although three small states (Vermont, Delaware, and Rhode Island) favor the Democrats, most of the states with small populations and large land areas are staunchly Republican. Thus, the Senate structure is not only unequal, it has a built-in bias. Is this what the founders of the United States had in mind when they wrote the Constitution?

of the Senate as a Barrier to Democracy"), and by special-interest groups, which by deals, propaganda, and the financial support of political candidates attempt to deflect the political process for their own benefit. Individuals, families, corporations, unions, professional associations, and various other organizations use a variety of means to obtain tax breaks, favors, subsidies, favorable rulings, and the like from Congress and its committees, regulatory agencies, and executive bureaucracies.

Special interests (e.g., National Rifle Association [NRA], the pharmaceutical industry, labor unions, dairy farmers) hire lobbyists to persuade legislators to vote for favorable legislation. At the national level, lobbying in 2011 was a $3.32 billion business and there were 12,655 registered lobbyists (which translated into twenty-three lobbyists for each member of Congress in 2011 (OpenSecrets.org 2012).

Interested parties lobby because there can be a significant payoff. In 2003 and 2004, for instance, 840 U.S. corporations lobbied Congress to change the tax laws enabling transnational companies to bring home their overseas earnings at a tax rate of 5.25 percent instead of 35 percent (the following is from Belsie 2009). They succeeded, accruing benefits through the new law—the American Jobs Creation Act of 2004. These benefits were stunning. For every dollar spent on lobbying for the tax break, corporations reaped a $220 benefit on their U.S. taxes—a 22,000 percent return on their investment. Those corporations spending more than $1 million on tax lobbying did even better—a 24,300 percent return. For example, Eli Lilly & Co. spent $8.52 million lobbying for this bill. It reaped more than $2 billion in return.

The argument supporting lobbying is that on various issues, there are lobbyists on both sides. Thus, it is argued, there is a balance of viewpoints that legislators weigh in their decision making. The evidence, however, does not support such a cheerful view. Of the top twenty organizations in spending to influence legislation, there is only one quasi-liberal group, the AARP. All of the rest speak for the top 1 percent of the income distribution (Kuttner 2012). The existence of lobbyists does not ensure that the national interest will be served, only that the interests of the powerful typically get their way. Who, for example, speaks for the interests of minority groups, the poor, the mentally challenged, children, renters, migrant workers—in short, who speaks for the relatively powerless? And if there is a voice for these people, does it match the clout of lobbyists backed by immense financial resources?

Financing of Political Campaigns

View on MySocLab Figure: Which Political Party Dominates?

Perhaps one of the most undemocratic features (at least in its consequences) of the U.S. political system is how political campaigns are financed. (See the "A Closer Look" panel for the other undemocratic features.) Campaigns are becoming increasingly expensive, with money needed to pay for staff, direct-mail operations, phone banks, computers, consultants, and media advertising. The cost of the presidential and congressional election in 2008 was $5.3 billion (up from $2.2 billion in 1996), including monies from the federal government, individuals, political parties, and organizations outside political parties. The 2012 election campaign cost more than $6 billion.

The cost of winning a seat in Congress is enormous. In 2010, the average winning House race cost $1.4 million, and the average winning Senate race cost almost $10 million. Computed another way, assuming a 40-hour work week, House members must raise, on average $367 an hour every week during their two-year term; Senators must come up with $815 an hour (Gilson 2012). Obviously, candidates must either be wealthy or accept money from various sources to finance their expensive campaigns.

'...with liberty and justice for sale.'

Clay Bennett/Washington Post Writers Group/Cartoonist Group

These costly campaigns favor incumbents, who have an easier time raising money than their opponents. The most favored recipients of political money are the chairs of powerful congressional committees.

Congress has attempted to curb the role of money in elections, but with little success. Donors and their lawyers have always found ways around the spending limit (*Economist* 2012). In 2002, it passed the Bipartisan Campaign Reform Act (also known as the McCain-Feingold law). This law limited the use of "soft money" in federal elections. Before this act was passed, individuals, corporations, unions, and other organizations were allowed to give unlimited amounts of money to political parties at the national, state, and local levels or to other private organizations that are technically independent of the candidates. Because this tactic was not covered by the election laws, the amounts raised were unlimited. This loophole was used by wealthy persons to contribute to the Republican and Democratic national parties (and indirectly to the presidential candidates).

McCain-Feingold did eliminate soft money in federal elections (buttressed by a favorable Supreme Court decision in 2003), but it did not limit the giving of large sums to affect election outcomes. A number of ways were employed to navigate the system and give large donations to build support among Democrat or Republican voters. The loophole used is called 527s, which are advocacy groups, tax exempt under Section 527 of the Internal Revenue Code, that finance political advertisements while not directly calling for the election or defeat of specific candidates (Dwyer 2004). Democrats, for example, created such organizations as the Media Fund and America Coming Together. Working through these organizations, billionaires George Soros and Peter Lewis pledged a total of $15 million, creating among other strategies the liberal Internet organization MoveOn.org. Republicans have set up comparable groups, such as the Leadership Forum, a fund-raising group headed by Washington lobbyists.

McCain-Feingold also limited maximum contributions to $2,300 per election cycle. While technically adhering to this limitation, corporate executives, lobbyists, and other insiders could maximize their political influence by a sophisticated system

A Closer Look

UNDEMOCRATIC ELECTIONS IN A DEMOCRACY?

A democracy is a political system that is of, by, and for the people. Democratic principles include (1) fair and open elections, (2) access by the people to accurate information, (3) accountability of the governors to the governed, (4) political equality among all citizens, and (5) due process of law. The United States claims to be a democracy. Is it?

The short answer is that the United States is a democracy in theory but not always in practice. We focus here on elections. Indian novelist Arundhati Roy has said this about elections: "I think it is dangerous to confuse the idea of democracy with elections. Just because you have elections doesn't mean you're a democratic country" (cited in Mickey Z 2006:7). Consider the following undemocratic practices in U.S. elections.

First, the writers of the Constitution framed what they considered a democracy, but they allowed voting only for White male property owners, which, of course, excluded women, Native Americans, Blacks, and renters. Senators were not popularly elected. Clearly, most of the governed had no power. The framers also set up the Electoral College, a device that gave the ultimate power of electing the president to the elite in each state and gave extraordinary power to the least populous states. Now most of these undemocratic principles have been overturned by amendments to the Constitution. But the Electoral College remains, allowing for a president to be elected with fewer votes than his or her opponent (e.g., George W. Bush was elected president in 2000 with 539,893 *fewer* votes than Al Gore). The Electoral College gives *all* electoral votes from a state to the winner in that state (e.g., in 2000 with nearly 3 million votes cast in Florida, George W. Bush won by a disputed margin of 537 votes and received all of Florida's 25 electoral votes, giving Bush a majority in the Electoral College). And, to top it all, an electoral vote in Wyoming (in 2004) corresponded to 167,081 persons, while an electoral vote in California represented 645,172 persons (because the number of electors is determined by the number of senators and representatives in that state, giving states with small populations disproportionate votes). In short, the Electoral College may or may not reflect the popular will. The winner-take-all system means that minorities may not be represented. Assume that a state has five districts, each electing a representative to the House of Representatives. If this state is predominantly Republican, it could have all five Republican representatives even though 40 percent (in this hypothetical case) are Democrats. Also, what if 30 percent of the state's citizens are Latino? It is possible that their voice will not be heard in Washington. Similarly, a city may have a seven-member city council elected at large by majority vote. The usual result is that not

of bundling—the pooling of a large number of contributions. This tactic is used by both political parties.

Another method to raise money is through contributions to a "foundation" or to a favorite charity. Through this loophole, donors could give unlimited contributions to a candidate. For example, during the 2008 campaign, four major defense contractors—Northrop Grumman, General Dynamics, Boeing, and Lockheed Martin—donated hundreds of thousands of dollars to the symphony orchestra in Johnstown, Pennsylvania. Why? Well, the orchestra is a favorite charity of Representative John Murtha, the chairman of the congressional committee that gives out lucrative defense contracts (Hernandez and Chen 2008). Similarly lobbyists can donate to favorite causes of the legislator, such as $336,224 that Representative James Clyburn received for his James E. Clyburn Research and Scholarship Foundation (Schouten and Overberg 2009). A fourth way to funnel special interest money legally is to honor members of Congress. In 2008 special interests donated one council member represents a poor section of the city.

Disenfranchisement also occurs when state legislatures under partisan control deliberately shape congressional districts (called **gerrymandering**) to increase their advantage. By moving the district boundaries (made all the easier these days with computers), the party in power can take an area that is overwhelmingly composed of their party members and move some of them to a neighboring area that is more evenly split. In this way, they can make both districts their districts. Thus, the system is rigged to help the party in power remain in power (Wang 2013). When a party wins an election, as the Republicans did in 2010, there is a probability that they will make changes in the election laws to benefit them. In anticipation of the 2012 election, Republican-dominated legislatures in thirty-eight states have pushed for measures to keep racial/ethnic minorities, the young, and the poor from voting. Similar to the use of literary tests and poll taxes in the

segregated South after the Civil War, these legislatures are erecting barriers to the fundamental right to vote (Jackson 2011). The targeted groups tend to vote for Democratic candidates. To stifle college students from voting, for example, states may not allow them to register if they have an out-of-state driver's license or they may schedule a primary vote during Spring Break. Under the guise of protecting from voter fraud (a very minor problem, at best), states may require a government-issued ID (driver's license or passport) in order to register. There are 21 million people in the U.S. without government IDs, typically the poor.

The two-party system that has emerged in the United States (political parties are not mentioned in the Constitution) is a major impediment to democracy. Corporations, special interests, and wealthy individuals sponsor both parties. The federal government subsidizes the two major parties, which keeps the strong parties strong and the weak parties weak. Third-party candidates are often excluded

from political debates because, it is argued, they have no chance of winning, a self-fulfilling prophecy. The election laws also make it difficult for third parties to get on the ballot. "How can U.S. elections be deemed truly democratic when only 'major' candidates are allowed to participate in televised debates and only those accepting inordinate amounts of cash from wealthy/corporate donors are considered 'major' candidates?" (Mickey Z 2006:7).

Finally, as shown in this chapter, money makes the difference in politics. The people get to vote between candidates selected by the wealthy (corporations, interest groups, or individuals), which means that voting does not always express the public will. As Mark Green says: "Because average voters pull levers but big donors pull strings, often public sentiment wants one thing while political elites deliver something else" (Green 2006:6). Thus, when public sentiment is at odds with the moneyed interests, the public often loses.

$35.8 million to honor legislators. A fifth source of money is the contributions to underwrite the expenses of political conventions. Although technically not a political contribution, the parties and candidates are beholden to the contributing corporations.

- **The Supreme Court Decision (*Citizens United v. Federal Election Commission*) in 2010.** As noted, while McCain-Feingold attempted to control spending, it was not always successful because of various ways to evade the law. With a Supreme Court decision in 2010, however, these efforts to get around McCain-Feingold were no longer necessary. By a landmark 5–4 decision the Supreme Court struck down the laws of twenty-two states and the federal government. It invalidated part of the McCain-Feingold campaign finance reform law that sought to limit corporate influence by ruling that the constitutional guarantee of free speech means that corporations, labor unions, and

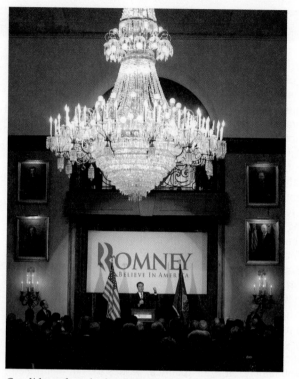

Candidates from both political parties hobnob with the rich and famous to finance their political campaigns.

other organizations can spend unlimited sums to help elect or defeat political candidates.* These organizations are still barred from making direct contributions to politicians, but they can now legally give unlimited amounts for ads to sway voters, as long as the ads are produced independently and not coordinated with a candidate's campaign. In effect, Exxon can spend millions to defeat an environmentalist candidate or Goldman Sachs could fund the entire cost of every congressional campaign in the United States (Alter 2010). As the *New York Times* editorialized: "The court's conservative majority has paved the way for corporations to use their vast treasuries to overwhelm elections and intimidate elected officials into doing their bidding" (*New York Times* 2010: para 1).

After the Supreme Court decision, individuals and groups were still limited to contributing $2,500 in the primary and another $2,500 in the general election directly to a candidate. But now individuals and groups could give unlimited amounts to an outside group (super PAC [political action committee]), if it is independent of a candidate. This "independence" has become a charade, however, since the super PACs are typically run by close political associates of the candidate. It is clear that

---

*It is important to point out that although labor unions have the same right as corporations to spend freely in elections, they are no match for the corporations. The Center for Responsive Politics provides the data from the 2007–2008 election cycle: (1) Corporations gave $1.964 billion in federal campaign contributions, compared to labor, which spent $74.8 million—a 15–1 disadvantage for labor (cited in Bybee 2010); and (2) business and corporate interests accounted for 70.8 percent of the total political contributions, while only 2.7 percent came from labor (cited in Chapin 2010).

In 2008, PhRMA, the pharmaceutical industry trade group, spent $200,000 on federal elections. After the Citizens United *decision, it spent $9.5 million.*

the contributions to a super PAC benefit the candidate just as if they were given directly to the candidate (Wertheimer 2012b). As evidence, the super PACs launch media blitz after media blitz in line with the political position of a candidate or attacking those of the candidate's opponent. The sources of these political donations can be kept secret.

This ruling has changed the political landscape. Small donors, who played a major role in the 2008 presidential election, have become irrelevant, being unable to match the treasuries of special interests and wealthy individuals. Super donors played a major role in the 2012 Republican presidential primaries, as two-thirds of the money for the candidates' super PACs came from mega-donors who contributed at least $500,000 (Schouten, Schnaars, and Korte 2012).

Money has been interpreted by a majority of the Supreme Court as a form of speech, and big money trumps small money. So the "speech" of the well-heeled is more important than the "speech" of ordinary citizens. For example, 196 donors provided about 80 percent of the money raised by super PACs in 2011. Commentator Ari Berman says the 2012 election was not defined by the 1 percent, but actually the superrich—the .0000063 percent (Berman 2012). Casino magnate Sheldon Adelson and his wife, for example, donated $52.2 million to groups favoring Republican candidates.

In sum, the super PACs corrupt democracy in two ways (Wertheimer 2012a). First, they allow a relatively few super-rich individuals and interest groups to have undue influence over the results of elections. For example, in the unsuccessful 2012 attempt to recall Republican Governor Scott Walker in Wisconsin, Walker won as his supporters outspent their opponents by 7.5 to 1. Ninety percent of that money came from out-of-state billionaires, business groups, and the National Rifle Association (Dreier 2012). Second, super PACs allow the ultra rich and wealthy interests to buy influence over government policy.

Future elections will likely be inundated by a flood of corporate spending. What will be the effects of this newly unleashed torrent of attack advertisements? Will the United States be a functioning democracy with this triumph of money equating with political power?

Candidate Selection Process

Closely related to the financing of campaigns is the process by which political candidates are nominated. Being wealthy or having access to wealth is essential for victory because of the enormous cost of the race. A few wealthy individuals can fund their own candidacy. For example, in 2010 Meg Whitman spent $138 million of her own money to run for governor of California. Typically, though, a serious candidate for high office must raise a considerable amount and most of this will represent a limited constituency—wealthy individuals and special interest groups.

Affluent individuals and the largest corporations influence candidate selection by giving financial aid to those candidates sympathetic with their views and withholding support from those whose views differ. The parties, then, are constrained to choose candidates with views congruent with the monied interests.

2.3 Explain the links between wealth, power, and the U.S. political system.

Read on
MySocLab Document:
The Power Elite

BIAS OF THE POLITICAL SYSTEM

Most people think of the machinery of government as a beneficial force promoting the common good, and it often is. But although the government can be organized for the benefit of the majority, it is not always neutral (Parenti 1978). The state regulates; it stifles opposition; it makes and enforces the law; it funnels information; it makes war on enemies (foreign and domestic); and its policies determine how resources are apportioned. In all these areas, the government is generally biased toward policies that benefit the business community. In short, power in the United States is concentrated in a **power elite**, and this elite uses its power for its own advantage.

Power in the United States is concentrated among people who control the government and the largest corporations. This assertion is based on the assumption that power is not an attribute of individuals but rather of social organizations. The elite in U.S. society are those people who occupy the power roles in society. The great political decisions are made by the president, the president's advisers, Cabinet members, members of regulatory agencies, the Federal Reserve Board, key members of Congress, and the Supreme Court. Individuals in these government command posts have the authority to make war, raise or lower interest rates, levy taxes, dam rivers, and institute or withhold national health insurance.

Formerly, economic activity was the result of many decisions made by individual entrepreneurs and the heads of small businesses. Now, a handful of companies have virtual control over the marketplace. Decisions made by the boards of directors and the managers of these huge corporations determine employment and production, consumption patterns, wages and prices, the extent of foreign trade, the rate at which natural resources are depleted, and the like.

The few thousand people who form this power elite tend to come from backgrounds of privilege and wealth. Although the very wealthy have a disproportionate impact on public policy, it would be a mistake, however, to equate personal wealth with power. Great power is manifested only through decision making in the very large corporations or in government. We have seen that this elite exercises great power. Decisions are made by the powerful, and these decisions tend to benefit the wealthy disproportionately. But the power elite is not formally organized; there is no conspiracy per se.

The interests of the powerful (and the wealthy) are served, nevertheless, through the way in which society is structured. This bias occurs in three ways: by the elite's influence over elected and appointed government officials at all levels, by the structure of the system, and by ideological control of the masses.

As noted earlier, the wealthy receive favorable treatment either by actually occupying positions of power or by exerting direct influence over those who do. Laws, court decisions, and administrative decisions tend to give them the advantage over middle-income earners and the poor.

More subtly, the power elite can get its way without actually being mobilized at all. The choices of decision makers are often limited by what are called **systemic imperatives**; that is, the institutions of society are patterned to produce prearranged results, regardless of the personalities of the decision makers. In other words, a bias pressures the government to do certain things and not to do other things. Inevitably, this bias favors the status quo, allowing people with power to continue to exercise it. No change is easier than change. The current political and economic systems have worked and generally are not subject to questions, let alone change. In this way, the laws, customs, and institutions of society resist change. Thus, the propertied and the wealthy benefit, while the propertyless and the poor remain disadvantaged. As Parenti has argued,

> The law does not exist as an abstraction. It gathers shape and substance from a context of power, within a real-life social structure. Like other institutions, the legal system is class-bound. The question is not whether the law should or should not be neutral, for as a product of its society, it cannot be neutral in purpose or effect. (1978:188)

In addition to the inertia of institutions, other systemic imperatives benefit the power elite and the wealthy. One such imperative is for the government to strive to provide an adequate defense against our enemies, which stifles any external threat to the status quo. Thus, Congress, the president, and the general public tend to support large appropriations for defense and homeland security, which in turn provide extraordinary profit to many corporations. In addition, the government protects U.S. transnational companies in their overseas operations so that they enjoy a healthy and profitable business climate. Domestic government policy also is shaped by the systemic imperative for stability. The government promotes domestic tranquility by squelching dissidents.

Power is the ability to get what one wants from someone else, by force, authority, manipulation, or persuasion. In Parenti's words, "The ability to control the definition of interests is the ability to define the agenda of issues, a capacity tantamount to winning battles without having to fight them" (Parenti 1978:41). U.S. schools, churches, and families possess this power. The schools, for instance, consciously teach youth that capitalism is the only correct economic system. This indoctrination to conservative values achieves a consensus among the citizenry concerning the status quo. Each of us comes to accept the present arrangements in society because they seem to be the only options that make sense. Thus, there is general agreement on what is right and wrong. In sum, the dominance of the wealthy is legitimized. Parenti observes, "The interests of an economically dominant class never stand naked. They are enshrouded in the flag, fortified by the law, protected by the police, nurtured by the media, taught by the schools, and blessed by the church" (Parenti 1978:84).

Finally, popular belief in democracy works to the advantage of the power elite, as Parenti has noted:

> As now constituted, elections serve as a great asset in consolidating the existing social order by propagating the appearances of popular rule. History demonstrates that the people might be moved to overthrow a tyrant who shows himself provocatively indifferent to their woes, but they are far less inclined to make war upon a state, even one dominated by the propertied class, if it preserves what Madison called "the spirit and form of popular government."

View on MySocLab Figure: Power in the United States: The Model Proposed by C. Wright Mills

Elections legitimate the rule of the propertied class by investing it with the moral authority of popular consent. By the magic of the ballot, class dominance becomes "democratic" governance. (1978:201)

CONSEQUENCES OF CONCENTRATED POWER

Who benefits from how power is concentrated in U.S. society? At times, almost everyone does; but often the decisions made tend to benefit the wealthy. Whenever the interests of the wealthy clash with those of other groups or even of the public at large, the interests of the former are served. Consider how the president and Congress deal with the problems of energy shortages, a huge national debt, inflation, or deflation. Who is asked to make the sacrifices? Where is the budget cut—are military expenditures reduced or are funds for food stamps slashed? When Congress considers tax reform, after the clouds of rhetoric recede, which groups benefit from the new legislation or from the laws that are left unchanged? When the economy was on the verge of collapse in 2008, who was bailed out by the government—the unemployed? The newly bankrupt? Those who lost their homes through foreclosure? No, the government spent many hundreds of billions of dollars to lift up the banks and insurance companies (some of which were perpetrators of the Great Recession). When a corporation is found guilty of fraud, violation of antitrust laws, or bribery, what are the penalties? How do they compare with the penalties for crimes committed by poor individuals? When there is an oil spill or other ecological disaster caused by a huge enterprise, what are the penalties? Who pays for the cleanup and the restoration of the environment? The answers to these questions are obvious: The wealthy benefit at the expense of the less well-to-do. In short, the government is an institution run by people—the rich and powerful or their agents—who seek to maintain their advantageous positions in society.

Two journalists, Donald Bartlett and James Steele, argue that there are two ways to get favorable treatment by Congress and the White House: Contribute generously to the right people and spend lavishly on lobbying (Bartlett and Steele 2000:40–42). If you do, you will get, for example, favorable tax rates, immunity from certain laws, government subsidies, and even a government bailout if needed. If you do not make generous political contributions and have lobbyists to make your case, then you will, according to Bartlett and Steele, pay a disproportionate share of taxes, pay higher prices for a range of products, be compelled to pay all of your debts, and you will see legislation for the social good weakened or killed. In essence, we have a political system where spending money for political purposes makes a huge difference, dividing Americans into the fortunate few and second-class citizens.

The bias of the system today is nothing new. Since the nation's founding, the government's policy has primarily favored the needs of the corporate system. The founding fathers were upper-class holders of wealth. The Constitution they wrote gave the power to people like themselves—White male property owners.

This bias continued throughout the nineteenth century as bankers, railroad entrepreneurs, and manufacturers joined the landed gentry as the power elite. The shift from local business to large-scale manufacturing during the last half of the nineteenth century saw a concomitant increase in governmental activity in the economy. Business was protected from competition by tariffs, public subsidies, price regulation, patents, and trademarks. When there was unrest by troubled miners, farmers, and laborers, the government invariably sided with the strong against the weak. Militia and federal troops were used to crush railroad strikes. Antitrust laws, although not used to stop the monopolistic practices of business, were invoked against labor unions.

During this time, approximately one billion acres of land in the public domain (almost half the present size of the United States) were given to private individuals and corporations. The railroads in particular were given huge tracts of land as a subsidy. These lands were and continue to be very rich in timber and natural resources. This active intervention by the government in the nation's economy during the nineteenth century was almost solely on the behalf of business.

The early twentieth century was a time of great government activity in the economy, which gave the appearance of restraining big business. However, the actual result of federal regulation of business was to increase the power of the largest corporations. The Interstate Commerce Commission, for instance, helped the railroads by establishing common rates instead of ruinous competition. Federal regulations in meat packing, drug manufacturing, banking, and mining weeded out the weaker cost-cutting competitors, leaving a few to control the markets at higher prices and higher profits. Even the actions of that great trustbuster, Teddy Roosevelt, were largely ceremonial. His major legislative proposals reflected the desires of corporation interests. Like other presidents before and since, he enjoyed close relations with big businessmen and invited them into his administration (Parenti 2008:57).

World War I intensified the government bias on behalf of business. Industry was converted to war production. Corporate interests became more actively involved in the councils of government. Government actions clearly favored business in labor disputes. The police and military were used against rebellious workers; strikes were treated as efforts to weaken the war effort and therefore as treasonous.

The New Deal is typically assumed to be a time when the needs of people impoverished by the Great Depression were paramount in government policies. But as Parenti has argued, the Franklin Roosevelt administration was more dedicated to business recovery rather than to social reform (Parenti 1980:74). Business was subsidized by credits, price supports, bank guarantees, stimulation of the housing industry, and the like. Welfare programs were instituted to aid people in dire circumstances, but even these humanitarian programs also worked to the benefit of the big business community. These programs were actually promoted by the business community because they reduced the threat of social unrest.

Two social scientists, Frances Fox Piven and Richard A. Cloward, in a historical assessment of government welfare programs, determined that the government institutes massive aid to the poor only when the poor constitute a threat (Piven and Cloward 1971). When large numbers of people are suddenly barred from their traditional occupations, they may begin to question the legitimacy of the system itself. Crime, riots, looting, and social movements aimed at changing existing social, political, and economic arrangements become more widespread. Under this threat, the government initiates or expands relief programs to defuse the social unrest. During the Great Depression, Piven and Cloward contend, the government remained aloof from the needs of the unemployed until there was a surge of political disorder. Added proof for Piven and Cloward's thesis is the contraction or even abolition of public assistance programs when stability is restored.

The historical trend for government to favor business over less powerful interests continues in current public policy. This bias is perhaps best seen in the aphorism enunciated by President Calvin Coolidge and repeated by subsequent presidents: "The business of America is business."

Subsidies to Big Business

A general principle applies to the government's relationship to big business: Business can conduct its affairs either undisturbed by or encouraged by government, whichever is of greater benefit to the business community. The government benefits the business community with hundreds of billions in subsidies annually. Corporations receive a wide range of favors, tax breaks, direct government subsidies to pay for advertising, research and training costs, and incentives to pursue overseas production and sales. The following are examples of governmental decisions that were beneficial to business.

((⸰ **Listen** on
MySocLab Audio: NPR:
Anheuser-Busch Takeover
Talk Shakes St. Louis

- State and local governments woo corporations with various subsidies, including tax breaks, low-interest loans, infrastructure improvements, and relatively cheap land. In 2006, for example, Mississippi offered Kia, the Korean automaker, $1 billion in incentives to build a plant (Georgia offered Kia $400 million). Similarly, to keep the New York Stock Exchange in New York City, the city and state of New York offered an incentive package worth more than $1 billion. Citizens for Tax Justice argued that when these subsidies occur, corporations manage to shield as much as two-thirds of their profits from state corporate income taxes. "The result: Money that could be spent on real economic development opportunities flows instead into the pockets of executives and the bill gets passed along to small taxpayers—local businesses and workers" (Singer 2006:6).
- Eleven days after the terrorist attacks of September 2001, Congress rushed through a $15 billion bailout of the airlines. Congress, however, did not provide any relief to the 140,000 fired airline workers or to the 2 million people employed by the hotel industry whose jobs were imperiled (Hightower 2002a).
- In 1996, instead of auctioning off the rights, Congress gave broadcasters spectrum rights to broadcast one channel of superhigh-resolution digital programs or several channels that could be used for digital interactive services or TV programs of high, but not superhigh, resolution, thus depriving the government of tens of billions of dollars (*New York Times* 2000:1).
- The government often funds research and develops new technologies (for example, the Internet) at public expense and turns them over to private corporations for their profit. This transfer occurs routinely with nuclear energy, synthetics, space communications, and pharmaceuticals
- Transnational corporations are permitted to set up tax havens overseas to make various intracompany transactions from a unit in one foreign country to another, thus legally sheltering them from U.S. taxes.
- In 2003 Congress passed the Medicare Prescription Bill. The pharmaceutical industry, using 675 lobbyists from 138 firms, nearly seven lobbyists for each senator, was successful in achieving favorable treatment in the legislation, including (1) a prohibition on the Medicare program from using its bargaining clout to directly negotiate deep drug-price discounts (one estimate is that prohibition will increase profits by $139 billion over eight years) and (2) a ban on the reimportation of prescription drugs from Canada, which cost about 50 percent less than in the United States (Public Citizen 2003).
- The more than $700 billion in government bailouts to the banks and financial firms in 2008 actually rewarded them for their reckless behaviors that led to the Great Recession (see Chapter 14).
- The government installs price supports on certain commodities, increasing the profits of those engaged in those industries and simultaneously costing consumers. For example, subsidies in agriculture were $15.4 billion in 2010. Farmers also received $5.7 billion in subsidies for ethanol, the fuel made from corn.

- The federal government directly subsidizes the shipping industry, railroads, airlines, and exporters of iron, steel, textiles, paper, and other products. Perhaps the best illustration of how business benefits from government policies are the benefits provided by the tax code. To illustrate: General Electric reported profits of $14.2 billion in 2010, $5.1 billion of which came from its U.S. operations. Although the top corporate tax rate is 35 percent, GE paid no U.S. taxes, actually receiving a refund of $3.2 billion.

Trickle-Down Solutions

Periodically, the government is faced with finding a way to stimulate the economy during an economic downturn. One solution is to spend federal monies through unemployment insurance, government jobs, infrastructure projects, and housing subsidies. In this way, the funds go directly to the people most hurt by shortages, unemployment, inadequate housing, and the like. Opponents of such plans contend that the subsidies should go directly to the wealthy in the form of tax reductions. Proponents of tax cuts argue that this will help the economy by encouraging companies to hire more workers, add to their inventories, and build new plants. Subsidizing the business class in this way, the advocates argue, benefits everyone. To provide subsidies to businesses rather than directly to needy individuals is based on the assumption that private profit maximizes the public good. In effect, proponents argue, because the government provides direct benefits to businesses and investors, the economic benefits indirectly trickle down to all.

Trickle-down solutions hurt the disadvantaged in at least two ways. First, reducing taxes on the wealthy increases the inequality gap between the "haves" and the "have-nots." In effect, the already fortunate become more fortunate, while the less fortunate trail ever further behind them. Moreover, reduced tax rates mean less revenue for the government. The result is a greater national debt, which then is used to justify cutting welfare programs. But, proponents of tax cuts believe that economic growth and revenues will result from them. The evidence, however, does not support this claim. Consider what has happened since the 2001 Bush tax cuts, the largest in U.S. history. The nonpartisan Congressional Research Service concluded in 2010 that the economy performed better in the time before the Bush tax cuts than after the tax cuts were enacted. Furthermore, the period from 2000 to 2007 was characterized by the weakest job growth since the Great Depression (Zakaria 2012; see also Bernstein 2012). The decade following the Bush tax cuts also saw a rapid rise in the federal debt.

There are at least two reasons government officials tend to opt for these trickle-down solutions. First, because government officials tend to come from the business class, they accept the conservative ideology, which says that what is good for business is good for the United States. The second reason for the pro-business choice is that government officials are more likely to hear arguments and receive contributions from the powerful. Because the weak, by definition, are not organized and they offer relatively little financially to political campaigns their voice is not heard or, if heard, not taken seriously in decision-making circles.

Although the government most often opts for trickle-down solutions, such plans are not very effective in fulfilling the promise that benefits will trickle down to the poor. The higher corporate profits generated by tax credits and other tax incentives do not necessarily mean that companies will increase wages or hire more workers. What is more likely is that corporations will increase dividends to the stockholders, which further increases the inequality gap. Job creation is also not guaranteed because companies may use their newly acquired wealth to purchase labor-saving devices. If so, then the government programs will actually have widened the gulf between the haves and the have-nots.

The Powerless Bear the Burden

Robert Hutchins, in his critique of U.S. governmental policy, characterized the basic principle guiding internal affairs as follows: "Domestic policy is conducted according to one infallible rule: The costs and burdens of whatever is done must be borne by those least able to bear them" (Hutchins 1976:4). The facts appear to justify this claim by Hutchins.

After the Great Recession hit in late 2007, federal and state governments had to reduce or eliminate programs. Where were the cuts made? Typically, social programs for the disadvantaged were targeted, not subsidies for businesses or tax breaks for homeowners. In the 2008–2009 school year, twenty-four states reduced their funding for early childhood education (mostly needed by children from low-income families). Low-income children's access to healthcare has also declined because of state budget cuts. So, too, were programs providing low-income families with temporary cash-assistance support, and childcare subsidies been reduced (Austin 2010). Public school education took the biggest hit with thirty-four states reducing school budgets in 2010 and twenty-one more seeking spending cuts in 2011–2012. The result is the laying off of large numbers of teachers; increasing class sizes; cutting electives such as music, art, and sports; eliminating summer school programs; and shortening the academic year.

When threatened by war, the government sometimes institutes a military draft. A careful analysis of the draft reveals that it is really a tax on the poor. During the height of the Vietnam War, for instance, only 10 percent of college men were drafted, although 40 percent of draft-age men were in college. Even for those educated young men who ended up in the armed services, there was a greater likelihood of their serving in noncombat jobs than for the non-college-educated. Thus, the chances of getting killed while in the service were about three times greater for the less educated than for the college educated (Zeitlin, Lutterman, and Russell 1977). Even more blatant was the practice that occurred legally during the Civil War. The law at that time allowed the affluent who were drafted to hire someone to take their place in the service.

In the Afghanistan and Iraq wars, the government decided not to have a draft but rely instead on volunteers. While patriotism was undoubtedly a factor in the decision of the volunteers to enlist, economic incentives (for example, enlistment bonus) to those from disadvantaged backgrounds was also a powerful motive. In effect, the battles were fought overwhelmingly by young men and women from the working and lower classes.

The poor, being powerless, can be made to absorb the costs of societal changes. In the nineteenth century, the poor did the backbreaking work that built the railroads and the cities. Today, they are the ones pushed out of their homes by urban renewal and the building of expressways, parks, and stadiums.

Following the devastation from Hurricane Katrina in Louisiana and Mississippi in 2005, priorities were set by decision makers as to where rebuilding should be initiated and where it should be delayed or ignored. In New Orleans, the bulk of the money spent first went to the business community and for repairing the Superdome (home field for the New Orleans Saints). Left behind were low-income families. Although Congress required that half of federal grant money help low-income people, some 90 percent of $1.7 billion in federal money spent in Mississippi went to repair condominiums for the affluent, rebuild casinos and hotels, and expand the Port of Gulfport (Eaton 2007).

Foreign Policy for Corporate Benefit

The operant principle here is that "foreign policy seems to be carried on in the light of the needs of the munitions makers, the Pentagon, the CIA, and the multinational corporations" (Hutchins 1976:4). For example, military goods are sold overseas for the profit of the arms merchants. Sometimes, arms are sold to both sides in a potential conflict, the argument being that if we did not sell them the arms, then someone else would, so we might as well make the profits.

The government has supported foreign governments that are supportive of U.S. multinational companies, regardless of how tyrannical these governments might be. The U.S. government has directly intervened in the domestic affairs of foreign governments to protect U.S. corporate interests and to prevent the rise of any government based on an alternative to the capitalist model (Parenti 2008:85). In Latin America, for example, since 1950 the United States has intervened militarily in Guatemala, the Dominican Republic, Chile, Uruguay, Nicaragua, Grenada, and Panama. As political scientist Michael Parenti characterizes it:

> Sometimes the sword has rushed in to protect the dollar, and sometimes the dollar has rushed in to enjoy the advantages won by the sword. To make the world safe for capitalism, the United States government has embarked on a global counter-revolutionary strategy, suppressing insurgent peasant and worker movements throughout Asia, Africa, and Latin America. But the interests of the corporate elites never stand naked; rather they are wrapped in the flag and coated with patriotic appearances. (1988:94)

Reprise: The Best Democracy Money Can Buy

Billions are spent on each federal election campaign. The consequence of this flood of money in elections is that it sabotages democracy in several ways. First, it makes it harder for government to solve social problems.

> How can we produce smart defense, environmental, and health policies if arms contractors, oil firms, and HMOs have a hammerlock over the committees charged with considering reforms? How can we adequately fund education and child care if special interests win special tax breaks that deplete public resources? (Green 2002:4)

Second, and related to the first, the have-nots of society are not represented among the decision makers. Moreover, because successful candidates must either be wealthy or be beholden to the wealthy, they are a different class of people from a different social world than most Americans.

> Since cash is the currency of elections, candidates troll for money where it is concentrated: in largely white, wealthy neighborhoods. . . . When a small, wealthy group in effect decides which candidates will have enough money to run a viable campaign, it is no great surprise that the agenda of policymakers is skewed toward its interests and not those of people of color and other underserved communities. (Gonzalez and Moore 2003:23A)

Third, the money chase creates part-time elected officials and full-time fundraisers. Not only is their time disproportionately spent in raising money, but their positions on policies become more and more in line with the politics of those who shower them with money.

Fourth, money diminishes the gap between the two major political parties because the candidates and parties seek and receive funds from the same corporate sources and wealthy individuals. Democrats in need of funds, even though they are more inclined than Republicans to support social programs and raising taxes, must temper these tendencies or lose their monetary support from wealthy interests. As Robert Reich has observed, "It is difficult to represent the little fellow when the big fellow pays the tab" (Reich 1989:A29).

Fifth, the money chase in politics discourages voting and civic participation (of the twenty-four Western democracies, the United States ranks twenty-third in voting turnout). In the 2000 presidential election, 49 percent of those who could have voted did not vote. This meant in effect that George W. Bush was elected by 24 percent of the electorate.

Sixth, big money in politics means than special interests get special access to the decision makers and receive special treatment from them.

In sum, the current politicoeconomic system is biased. It works for the benefit of the few at the expense of the many. Because the distribution of power and the organization of the economy give shape and impetus to the persistent social problems of U.S. society, the analysis of these problems requires a politicoeconomic approach.

MySocLab ✓ Study and Review on MySocLab

■ CHAPTER REVIEW

1. Although government sometimes works for the benefit of all, the state is not a neutral agent of the people but is biased in favor of the upper social classes and the largest corporations.

2. Marx's prediction that capitalism will result in an economy dominated by monopolies has been fulfilled in the United States. But rather than a single corporation dominating a sector of the economy, the United States has shared monopolies, whereby four or fewer corporations supply 50 percent or more of a particular market.

3. Economic power is concentrated in a few major corporations and banks. This concentration has been accomplished through mergers and interlocking directorates.

4. The inequality gap in the United States is the widest of all the industrialized nations. The gap continues to grow especially because of tax benefits for the affluent.

5. These tax policies, in addition to increasing the unequal distribution of wealth, increase the national debt, reduce government spending for programs to help the less fortunate, and weaken public institutions that benefit society. The widening gap increases the political influence of the wealthy.

6. The government tends to serve the interests of the wealthy because of the influence of interest groups and how political campaigns are financed.

7. Democracy is a political system that is of, by, and for the people. Democracy is undermined by special interests, which use money to deflect the political process for their own benefit.

8. The power elite in society (those who control the government and the largest corporations) tend to come from backgrounds of privilege and wealth. Their decisions tend to benefit the wealthy disproportionately. The power elite is not organized and conspiratorial, but the interests of the wealthy are served, nevertheless, by the way in which society is organized. This bias occurs through influence over elected and appointed officials, systemic imperatives, and ideological control of the masses.

9. Congress occasionally attempts to reduce the power of money over politics, but wealthy individuals, corporations, and interest groups find legal ways to avoid these constraints. In 2010 the Supreme Court ruled that individuals and organizations can give unlimited amounts to super PACs because money, in the Court's view, was a form of speech that is protected by the Constitution. This ruling has significant consequences for a democracy.

10. The government supports the bias of the system through its strategies to solve economic problems. The typical two-pronged approach is, on the one hand, to use trickle-down solutions, which give the business community and the wealthy

extraordinary advantages; and, on the other hand, to make the powerless bear the burden for solving social problems such as recessions and the growing national debt.

11. Business benefits from governmental actions through foreign policy decisions, which typically are used to protect and promote U.S. economic interests abroad.

12. The flood of money to support political parties and candidates sabotages democracy in several ways: (a) It makes it more difficult to solve social problems; (b) the interests of the have-nots are not served; (c) the money chase creates part-time legislators and full-time fundraisers; (d) money diminishes the gap between the two major parties because both seek and receive funds from the same corporate and individual sources; (e) it discourages voting and civic participation; and (f) big money in politics leads to a bias in the laws passed and the subsidies provided.

■ KEY TERMS

Shared monopoly. When four or fewer companies control 50 percent or more of an industry.

Interlocking directorate. The linkage between corporations that results when an individual serves on the board of directors of two companies (a **direct interlock**) or when two companies each have a director on the board of a third company (an **indirect interlock**).

Oligarchy. A political system that is ruled by a few.

Plutocracy. A government by or in the interest of the rich.

Democracy. A political system that is of, by, and for the people.

Filibuster. The Senate rule that allows a senator to hold the floor for an unlimited time as a strategy to prevent a vote.

Cloture. The vote needed to end a filibuster (currently 60 votes).

Gerrymander. The party in power shapes voting districts as a means to keep itself in power.

Power elite. People who occupy the power roles in society. They either are wealthy or represent the wealthy.

Systemic imperatives. The economic and social constraints on political decision makers that promote the status quo.

Power. The ability to get what one wants from someone else.

World Population and Global Inequality

 Listen to Chapter 3 on **MySocLab**

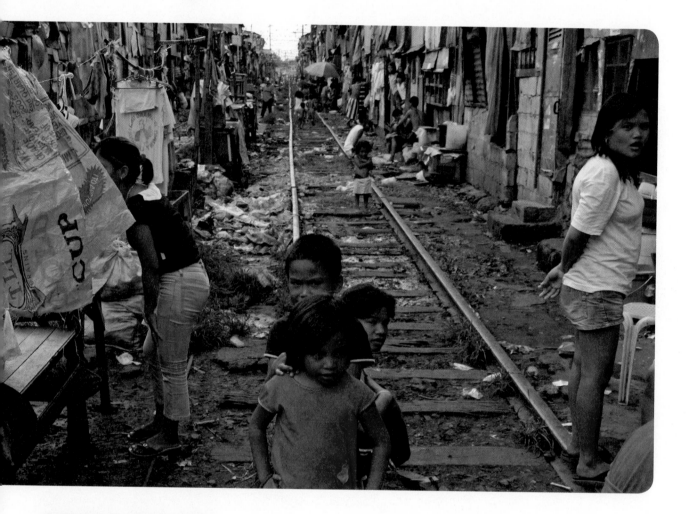

LEARNING OBJECTIVES

3.1 Understand the factors affecting world population growth.

3.2 Describe the extent of world poverty and the consequences of that poverty.

3.3 Explain the relationship between the United States and poor nations around the world.

3.4 Discuss how the U.S. and other wealthy nations can help impoverished countries.

The countries of the world vary widely in levels of material conditions. Some nations are disproportionately poor with rampant hunger, disease, and illiteracy. Other nations are exceptionally well off, with ample resources.

Here are some facts concerning the uneven distribution of the world's wealth:

- The richest 2 percent of adults own more than half of the world's household wealth.
- The poorest half of the world's adult population own barely 1 percent of global wealth.
- About 1.2 billion people live in wealthy countries and about 5.8 billion live in poor countries.
- In 2012 there were 1,226 billionaires worldwide. The top five countries in numbers of billionaires were the United States (425), followed by Russia (96), Mainland China (95), Germany (55), and India (48). Sub-Saharan Africa had only one billionaire (South Africa) (*Forbes* 2012).

The reasons for such global inequality include, as one might suspect, the degree of geographic isolation, climate, overpopulation, and natural resources. Another key determinant is the effect of power. The poor are poor, as we discuss, because they have been and continue to be dominated and exploited by powerful nations and corporations that have extracted their wealth and labor. This continuing domination of the weak by the powerful has resulted in an ever-widening gap between the rich and poor nations.

This chapter examines the plight of the poorest countries and the role of the richest—especially the United States—in maintaining global inequality. The first section focuses on world population growth, examining in particular the variables affecting why some nations have high growth and others do not.

The second part examines poverty throughout the world and the social problems generated by impoverishment, such as hunger, unhealthy living conditions, and economic/social chaos. The third part explores the relationship of the United States with the poor nations, historically through colonialism and currently through the impact of multinational corporations and official government policies.

WORLD POPULATION GROWTH

3.1 Understand the factors affecting world population growth.

View on **MySocLab Map:** Population Growth in Global Perspective

The number of people on this planet constitutes both a major problem and potential future calamity. The world population on October 31, 2011, reached an estimated 7.0 billion, and at its current rate of growth, the net addition annually is 82.9 million (the equivalent of adding the population of Iran every year). Put another way, the world has almost 1 million more people every four days (adding 227,252 more people each day)—all needing food, water, medicine, and homes for an average lifespan of 69 years (Whitty 2010:34). And, each new additional human being encroaches on the earth's environment, adding to the dangers of climate change, soil depletion, and limited fresh water. It is important to note in this regard that the burden here is on the developed nations. The average American's carbon footprint, for example, is twenty-three times bigger than that of the average Indian (Bauerlein and Jeffery 2010).

To put the population growth curve in perspective: It took all of human history (about 50,000 years) until about 1830 to reach the first billion. The next billion took 100 years (1930); the third billion, 30 years (1960); the fourth billion, 15 years (1995); the fifth billion, 12 years (1987); the sixth billion, 12 years (1999); the seventh billion, 13 years (2011), the eighth billion, 14 years (2025), and the ninth billion will take a projected 18 years (2043). Note that the momentum since the world reached 7 billion is slowing. It all depends on the fertility rate. For example, the United Nations projection of 9.1 billion in 2050 assumes a global fertility rate of 2.01 children per women in the years between 2045 and 2050. But half a child more and the world population would stabilize at 10.5 billion in 2055. Half a child less, and it stabilizes at 8 billion (Whitty 2010). Most significant, most of the current population growth occurs in the less-developed nations, where poverty, hunger, and infectious disease are already rampant. There is a strong inverse relationship between per capita GNP and population growth rates—the lower the per capita GNP, the higher the population growth. For example, the less-developed nations are expected to increase in population from 5.6 billion in 2009 to 8.2 billion in 2050, whereas the more developed countries are projected to grow from 1.2 billion to just 1.3 billion (Bremer et al. 2009). This is a consequence of **differential fertility** (differences in the average number of children born to a woman by social category). To illustrate, the fertility rate in the more developed countries in 2011 was 1.7, compared to 4.5 in the least developed countries (Population Reference Bureau 2011). These differences in **fertility rate** (the average number of births per woman) reveal a future world population that will be overwhelmingly from the developing countries. To illustrate, the natural increase (births minus deaths) in 2011 for the less developed countries was 81.1 million, compared to 1.9 million in the more developed countries (Population Reference Bureau 2011). (See Figure 3.1.)

The population growth rates in the poor countries make it difficult to provide the bare necessities of housing, fuel, food, and medical attention. Ironically, there is a relationship between poverty and fertility: The greater the proportion of a given population living in poverty, the higher is the fertility of that population. This relationship is not as irrational as it first appears. Poor parents want many children so that the children will help them economically and take care of them in their old age. Because so many children die, the parents must have a large number to ensure several surviving children. Large families make good economic sense to the poor because children are a major source of labor and income.

How do the nations of the world deal with the problems of expanding population? Basically, there are three ways to reduce fertility—through economic development, family-planning programs, and social change.

FIGURE 3.1

World Population Growth

Source: United Nations Population Division, World Population Prospects: The 2010 Revision, medium variant (2011).

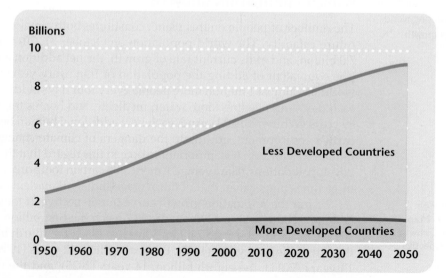

Demographic Transition

Read on
MySocLab Document:
Sixteen Impacts of
Population Growth

Historically, as nations have become more urban, industrialized, and modernized, their population growth has slowed appreciably. Countries appear to go through three stages in this process, which is known as the **modern demographic transition**. In the agricultural stage, both birth and death rates are high, resulting in a low population growth rate. In the transition stage, birthrates remain high, but the death rates decrease markedly because of access to more effective medicines, improved hygiene, safer water, and better diets. Many nations are presently in this stage, and the result for them is a population explosion. Much later in the process, as societies become more urban and traditional customs have less of a hold, birthrates decline, slowing the population growth and eventually stopping it altogether (as is now occurring in many nations of Europe and Japan). Figure 3.2 shows the population pyramids for less-developed countries where population growth is booming, and the more developed, where population growth is slow. Especially important to population growth is the "critical cohort" of those under age 20. There are more than 2 billion in this category in the developing countries. These young people will soon become parents (400 million are already between 15 and 19). What will be the fertility of this critical cohort? If the growth rate continues to slow, the demographic transition with its accompanying urbanization, medical advances, and the liberation of women from traditional gender roles will have worked.

The concept of a demographic transition is supported empirically. For example, birthrates in the developed world and the less developed world are down dramatically. Overall, due to increased urbanization, better access to contraceptives, and more women being educated, the global fertility rate has declined from an average of 4.92 children per woman in 1950 to 2.56 now. According to the United Nations, approximately 43 percent of the world's peoples live in countries at or below the

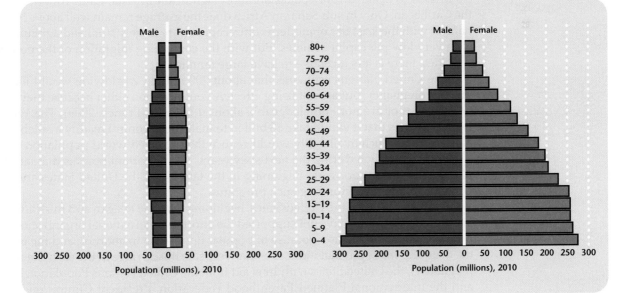

FIGURE 3.2

(a) More-Developed Countries Have Fewer Young People

(b) Less-Developed Countries Have More Young People

Source: UN Population Division, World Population Prospects: The 2008 Revision (2009).

replacement rate of 2.1. For example, not a single country in Europe is producing enough children to replace itself. To illustrate the extremes in fertility, Uganda has only moved slightly downward from a birth rate of 7.0 in 1960 to 6.5 in 2010. Iran, on the other hand, has experienced one of the most rapid fertility declines ever recorded—from an average of 7.7 births per woman in 1966 down to 1.7 today (Whitty 2010).

The problem, of course, is that the modern demographic transition experienced in Europe took about 200 years. With relatively high growth rates in the less-developed world plus a huge cohort in, or soon to be in, the child bearing category, this length of time is unacceptable because the planet cannot sustain the massive growth that will occur while the demographic transition runs its course. But the fertility rate is dropping more quickly than expected, even in the less-developed countries. For example, in sub-Saharan Africa, where the fertility rate is the highest, it has fallen from 6.7 children per woman in 1950 to 5.3 now. Worldwide, the use of contraception has risen from 10 percent of married women in the 1960s to 62 percent in 2009 (Bremer et al. 2009). The global fertility rate (2.56 in 2010) will continue to decline, but with so many women of childbearing age in the less-developed countries, the world's population is projected to increase by 2.4 million over the next 40 years to about 9.2 billion in 2050, when it will (theoretically) stabilize.

Family Planning

Beginning in the 1960s, international organizations such as the World Health Organization and UNICEF incorporated reproductive health into their missions. National governments, beginning with India in 1951, began to adopt family-planning policies (see the "Social Problems in Global Perspective" panel for a description of China's extreme family planning policy of one child per married couple). As a result, fertility rates have fallen. Worldwide, the average number of children per woman fell from 5.0 in 1950 to 2.5 in 2010. Declines are most significant in Asia, Latin America, and the Caribbean. Only in sub-Saharan Africa does the average remain well above 5. The nations with the least use of modern contraceptives are largely rural and agricultural with very low per capita incomes. But with the continuing migration of the poor to the cities, there is less incentive to have large families.

The United Nations estimates that about 200 million worldwide would like to prevent pregnancy, but are not using effective contraception either because they cannot afford it or are not knowledgeable about it (cited in Francis 2009). The World Bank estimates that it would take $8 billion to make birth control readily available on a global basis. Such availability would reduce the projected world population from 10 billion to 8 billion during the next sixty years. The important point is that family-planning programs do work. Beginning in the late 1960s, the United States and the United Nations began funding such programs.

Formal policies by the United States, beginning with the Reagan and Bush administrations (1980–1992), have not supported the efforts of international organizations to promote contraceptive use. Because of popular opposition to abortion and the use of the drug RU-486 (a pill that induces a relatively safe miscarriage in the early stages of pregnancy), the United States withdrew aid from the United Nations Population Fund and the International Planned Parenthood Federation. President Clinton reversed these policies, but President George W. Bush reinstated them in 2001. President Obama, however, restored U.S. funding for the United Nations Population Fund and rescinded the antifamily policy of the Bush administration (going back to President Reagan) that required all nongovernmental organizations that receive federal funds to refrain from performing abortions or citing abortion services offered by others.

Social Problems in Global Perspective

CHINA'S ONE-CHILD POLICY

In 1979 the successor to Chairman Mao, Deng Xiaoping, began a series of economic reforms leading to unprecedented economic growth (an average of 10 percent annually for thirty years), millions escaping poverty, a burgeoning middle class, and a modernizing of the nation's infrastructure and cities. Also in that year China initiated a one child per family policy to limit the population growth in the world's most populous nation.

The controversial policy worked. In 1970 the average Chinese woman had 5.8 children, now it is less than 2. It is estimated that it prevented 300 million births (the equivalent of the population of Europe). Even with this policy, China's population in 2012 was 1.34 billion, the largest in the world, followed by India's population of 1.22 billion. India, in contrast to China's one-child policy, encourages small family size through family planning (53 percent of married women use contraceptives), female literacy programs, and sterilization, which has reduced the birthrate over the past fifty years

from 6 births for each woman of childbearing age to 2.9. Still India grows by 48,000 every day and will surpass China as the world's largest population before 2030.

China's one-child policy is not universal within the country (*Economist* 2011) with about two-thirds required to have only one child (Wang 2012). It is aimed primarily at the ethnic Han Chinese living in urban areas (92 percent of Chinese are ethnic Hans). Also if both spouses are without siblings, or if their first born is a female, they may have two children.

The policy is implemented through incentives (Fitzpatrick 2009). Although the actual benefits for complying with the rule vary from place to place, they may include an extra month's salary each year until the child is 14, higher wages, interest-free loans, better housing, and the like. For those who have an extra child, there may be punishments such as a stiff fine, not receiving raises on the job, unemployment, or occasionally forcing the abortion of a fetus.

There are some significant consequences of this policy. On the positive side, it did limit population growth and this, in turn, aided the economic growth of the nation. But it gave rise to abortions, as parents wanted their only child to be a male (thus reinforcing the secondary status of females in society). This resulted in a skewed male/female ratio (normally 105 males per 100 females, became 120 males per 100 females). After more than thirty years of this policy, now there are fewer marriages because there are not enough potential brides. This also has an implication for manufacturing in China because the typical assembly line worker is a young woman, yet the numbers of young women are declining. A final consequence: Traditionally, elderly Chinese were dependent on the adult children for support and housing in their declining years. With several children, the burden was shared, but with the one-child policy, now there is only one child to take care of two aging parents.

Societal Changes

The third strategy to reduce population growth involves societal changes. Ingrained cultural values about the familial role of women and about children as evidence of the father's virility or as a hedge against poverty in old age must be changed.

Religious beliefs, such as the resistance of the Roman Catholic hierarchy and of fundamentalist Muslim regimes such as in Saudi Arabia to the use of contraceptives, are a great obstacle to population control. However, religion is not an insurmountable barrier. Despite the Catholic hierarchy's resistance to family planning, some nations with overwhelming Catholic majorities have extremely low birthrates. As examples, Italy had a fertility rate of 1.4 in 2011, Spain a rate of 1.4, and Chile had a 1.9 rate, each below the average of 2.11 needed to sustain a stable population. And some Muslim countries have instituted successful family planning. For example, in addition to Iran's fertility rate of 1.7, Syria, Bahrain, and the United Arab Emirates each had less

The World Bank estimates that about $8 billion would make birth control readily available globally.

than a 2.0 fertility rate in 2011. Perhaps the most significant social change needed to reduce fertility is to change the role of women. When women are isolated from activities outside the home, their worth depends largely on their ability to bear and rear children. Conversely, fertility rates drop when women gain opportunities and a voice in society (Sen 2000). Research has shown that increasing the education of women is one of the most effective ways to reduce birthrates. Educated women are more likely than uneducated women to marry later and use effective methods of family planning (*New York Times* 2002).

Read on MySocLab Document: Mate Selection and Marriage Around the World

Unplanned social change, such as economic hard times, also affects birthrates. Recent data show that economic difficulties for individual families in less-developed countries can cause couples to delay marriage and to be more likely to use contraceptives. When enough families are affected negatively by an economic downturn, the fertility rate can fall for a nation. This is opposite the usual relationship of declining birthrates accompanying long-term economic success (the demographic transition).

Thus, in the long run, the population problem may abate, perhaps even reducing economic inequality and altering the balance of power among nations. However, for those living now, their lives will be negatively affected by the current population growth in developing nations, environmental degradation, and the overwhelming poverty of billions.

> *Chaos is the increasingly real result of trying to support more than 6 billion people on this planet, spawning desperate mass migrations, wars over rights to fresh water, medical epidemics, bloody riots and crime waves nurtured in teeming shantytowns.*
>
> *The war on terrorism, too, cannot logically be divorced from the struggle for population sanity. Refugee camps and hopeless slums steadily churn out alienated, landless young men and women who are perfect cannon fodder for ambitious religious and political zealots. (Scheer 2002:1)*

3.2 Describe the extent of world poverty and the consequences of that poverty.

POVERTY

The World Bank defines poverty as living on less than $1.25 a day (adjusted for inflation) (the following data are from Chen and Ravallion 2012). Using this criterion, worldwide poverty is declining. Compared with 1981, the poverty rate has fallen from 52 percent of the world's population to 22 percent in 2008 (the most recent data available). This represents a decline from 1.94 billion people in 1981 to 1.29 billion. The progress is uneven in the developing world, however. There has been dramatic progress in East Asia where China alone reduced poverty for 662 million people from 1981 to 2008 and in South Asia where the poverty rate declined from 61 percent to 36 percent. Sub-Saharan Africa, though, had only a modest reduction from 51 percent to 47 percent. Despite these declines in poverty, the global inequality gap is enormous. This gap is found within nations. In Haiti, for example, the poorest 10 percent have only 0.7 percent of the nation's wealth (see the "Social Problems in Global Perspective" panel on Haiti). And this inequality gap is found among the nations, particularly nations in the northern hemisphere, which are relatively affluent, compared to the nations of the southern hemisphere, which are disproportionately poor.

The underdeveloped and developing nations are not only characterized by poverty, hunger, and misery but also by relative powerlessness because most of them were colonies and remain economically dependent on developed nations and transnational corporations, especially those of North America and Europe. These nations are also characterized by rapid population growth, high infant mortality, unsanitary living conditions, high rates of infectious diseases, low life expectancy, and high illiteracy. This section documents hunger, squalor, and marginality of life in these countries.

There is a striking maldistribution in **life chances** (the chances throughout one's life cycle to live and experience the good things in life) between those living in the developed and those in developing nations. The significance of worldwide poverty and its concentration in the developing-world nations cannot be overstated. The gap between the rich and poor countries is increasing, and the gap between the rich and poor in the poor countries is increasing. Those in absolute poverty suffer from disease, malnutrition, squalor, stigma, illiteracy, unemployment, and hopelessness. These deplorable conditions will likely lead to extreme solutions such as terrorist movements and government policies of military expansion.

Food and Hunger

The United Nations Food and Agricultural Organization maintains that the world's agriculture produces enough food to provide every person with at least 2,720 kilocalories every day for the world's population (cited in World Hunger Education Service 2011). Actually, if everyone adopted a vegetarian diet and no food was wasted, current production would feed 10 billion people, more than the projected population for 2050 (Bender and Smith 1997:5). Food production, however, is unevenly distributed, resulting in 925 million being malnourished (almost one in seven people) in 2010, about one in every three of the world's inhabitants being food insecure, and around 9 million people dying of malnutrition each year. How can we explain these chilling figures?

An obvious source of the problem is rapid population growth, which distorts the distribution system and strains the productive capacity of the various nations. The annual increase of 75 to 80 million people requires an enormous increase in grain production just to stay even. A number of factors are shrinking the productive land

Watch on MySocLab Video: Global Wealth and Poverty

Social Problems in Global Perspective

WHY IS HAITI SO POOR?

Persistent poverty in Haiti is historic and systemic. Consider the following reasons:

1. **Long history of violence.** When Columbus first landed on the island of Hispaniola, Arawak Indians inhabited the island. But the entire native population perished in about thirty years from newly introduced European diseases. To replace them, African slaves were imported by the Spaniards and by the French. The French established themselves on the western end (the Haitian third of the island) where they developed large sugar cane plantations. Haiti became the most productive French colony in the western hemisphere in sugar and coffee. But slavery was a cruel and violent system. By 1789 the French Revolution broke out. French colonies became restive. By now 30,000 whites, 40,000 mulattoes, and

500,000 slaves populated Haiti, and there were more and more slave revolts. Finally, by 1804 the slaves had thrown out their white masters and Haiti became the first independent black republic in the world. It was violent and loss of life was great. Sadly, the government of the new black republic of Haiti has ruled its own people by violence ever since.

2. **Government culture of corruption.** Almost every Haitian president since independence has seen his office as an opportunity for personal power and wealth. The same is true of lesser officials in government, so on the current scale of corruption, Haiti still ranks 183rd, with 185 being the worst. This means that revenues, taxes, duties, etc., as well as foreign loans and foreign aid vanish into the pockets of everyone who gains any kind of access before it can be spent to

finish public projects such as roads, schools, and medical programs that would benefit Haitian people. In recent decades the Haitian army and police have also been heavily involved in the lucrative illegal drug traffic.

3. **Isolation and vindictive ostracism.** Haiti became a small nation surrounded by largely English- and Spanish-speaking countries (the language of Haiti is Creole, a form of French). The United States refused even to recognize Haiti until 1862. The French, in the 1820s, threatened to re-invade Haiti and thus coerced the Haitians to pay the French an annual indemnity for the losses they incurred in the slave revolts that led to Haiti's independence in 1804. These payments were demanded by the French until 1888, which often took half of Haiti's annual GDP. And as long as this indemnity was not paid off, other European nations refused loans or aid. Haiti was treated as a pariah nation by the colonial powers.

throughout the world, in rich and poor countries alike. The earth loses 24 billion tons of topsoil each year. Irrigation systems that tap underground reserves are dropping water tables to dangerously low levels in many areas, causing the land to revert to dry-land farming. Air pollution and toxic chemicals have damaged some crops and water sources. The rising concentration of greenhouse gases (see Chapter 4) is changing the climates negatively. Each year millions of acres of productive land are converted to housing and roads. A growing number of people in developing countries are affluent enough to eat like Westerners; that is, they are eating more meat (Krugman 2008). The result is that a good deal of grain is diverted to feed livestock (it takes about 8 pounds of grain to produce a pound of beef; 6 pounds of grain to produce a pound of pork). Another important diversion of grains away from the food chain is the government subsidized conversion of crops into fuel (e.g., corn into ethanol).

Most significant, of course, is that almost all the population increase is occurring in regions and countries that are already poor. Because of low levels of economic development, the various levels of government, farmers, and others in these countries lack adequate money and credit for the machinery, fertilizer, pesticides, and technology necessary to increase crop production to meet the always increasing demand.

4. **Lack of education.** Slaves were never offered an education. Leaders among them emerged charismatically, but at independence less than 10 percent of the population could read or write. Most of those who were literate were the mulattoes. Thus they emerged as the ruling class, which also controlled more and more of the wealth in Haiti. In the 200 years since, the literacy rate has only increased to 30 percent. Thus, government and business, which require literacy, are restricted to a small minority that increasingly controls the power and wealth.

5. **Corporate exploitation of the poor.** Having obtained favorable deals with government and business interests in Haiti, foreign corporations (mostly U.S.) have negotiated highly profitable assembly plants in which they employ poor Haitians for wages as low as 10 to 14 cents an hour, assured by repressive Haitian dictators that no unions will be allowed, no human rights observers permitted, and other

such conditions. When Father Aristide, the first president in Haitian history to be elected by the poor in 1991, tried to increase the minimum wage to 25 cents an hour, he was overthrown in a coup by the Haitian army, which had been paid off by U.S. corporate interests. One example of corporate profits: A pharmaceutical company developed a blood plasma collection business in Haiti. Haitian poor could "sell" the plasma in a pint of their blood as often as once a week and "earn" as much as $295 a year. The pharmaceutical company then resold the plasma for seven times the price they had paid. Corporations involved in Haiti actively enlisted the support of the U.S. military as necessary to protect their interests. In 1915 Woodrow Wilson sent 2,000 U.S. marines into Haiti to occupy and take over the Haitian government to "bring stability to Haiti." They stayed until 1934.

6. **Few natural resources.** Haiti's terrain is mostly mountainous.

The once productive French sugar plantations on the central plain, river valleys, and coastal regions have long since deteriorated in fertility and erosion. Mountainsides have been denuded of trees by logging for export and firewood for daily use and are also badly eroded. Small bauxite deposits wait to be exploited, but otherwise Haiti has no mineral resources and must import all of its fossil energy fuels.

7. **Population pressures.** At the time of independence in 1804, the population of Haiti was less than 500,000. Today it is 10.1 million.

8. **Major natural disasters.** Haiti lies in "Hurricane Alley" and endures major storms. The devastating earthquake of 2010 reminded the world that Port-au-Prince, the capital, is built right over an active major earthquake-prone fault.

Source: Floyd G. Bartel. 2010. "Why Is Haiti So Poor?" Original essay, North Newton, Kansas (February 10).

The high cost of oil has an especially devastating effect on food production in poor nations. Food production in developing-world nations is also more adversely affected by natural disasters (floods and droughts) than it is in more affluent nations because these countries are less likely to have adequate flood control, irrigation systems, and storage facilities.

Another way to explain the food problem is to view it as a poverty problem. Food supplies are adequate, but people must have the resources to afford them. Because the poor cannot afford the available food, they go hungry. Although this view of poverty is correct, it has the effect of blaming the victims for their plight. To do so ignores the political and economic conditions that keep prices too high, make jobs difficult to obtain and poorly paid, and force too many people to compete for too few resources.

The major problem with food shortages is not food production, although that is exceedingly important, but the political economy of the world and of the individual nations. Economic and political structures thwart and distort the production and distribution of agricultural resources. (The following discussion is adapted from Lappe and Collins 1979, Lappe and Collins 1986, and Murdoch 1980.) The primary problem is inequality of control over productive resources. In each country in which hunger is a basic problem, most of the land is controlled by a small elite, and the rest of the population is squeezed onto small plots or marginal land or is landless. For example, although colonial rule ended in southern Africa decades ago, the small White minority still controls most of the arable land. The evidence is that when the few control most of the agriculture, production is less effective than when land is more equally apportioned among farmers. Yields per acre are less, land is underused, wealth produced is not reinvested but drained off for conspicuous consumption by the wealthy, and credit is monopolized. Most important, monopoly control of agricultural land is typically put into cash crops that have value as exports but neglect basic local needs.

Agriculture controlled by a few landowners and agribusiness interests results in investment decisions made on the basis of current profitability. If prices are good, producers breed livestock or plant crops to take advantage of the prices. This approach results in cycles of shortages and gluts. Small farmers, on the other hand, plant crops on the basis of local needs, not world prices.

The way food surpluses are handled in a world in which more than a billion people are chronically hungry is especially instructive. The grain surplus is handled by feeding more than a third of the world's production to animals. Crops are allowed to rot or are plowed under to keep prices high. Surplus milk is fed to pigs or even dumped to keep the price high. The notion of food scarcity is an obvious distortion when the major headaches of many agricultural experts around the world are how to reduce mountains of surplus and keep prices high.

From this point of view, then, the problem of food scarcity lies in the social organization of food production and distribution. The solution to hunger is to construct new forms of social organization capable of meeting the needs of the masses. The problem, though, goes beyond the boundaries of individual countries. The policies of the rich nations and multinational corporations are also responsible for the conditions that perpetuate poverty in the developing world. The United States, for example, supports the very conditions that promote hunger and poverty. The last section of this chapter documents this role.

Sickness and Disease

Chronic malnutrition, an obvious correlate of greater numbers of people and poverty, results in high infant mortality rates, shorter life expectancies, and a stunting of physical and mental capacities. Children are disproportionately the victims. We know that protein deficiency in infancy results in permanent brain damage. Vitamin deficiencies, of course, cause a number of diseases such as rickets, goiter, and anemia. Iron deficiency is a special problem for hungry children: Some 25 percent of men and 45 percent of women (60 percent for pregnant women) in developing countries are anemic, a condition of iron deficiency. Almost one-third of the world's people do not get enough iodine from food and water, causing goiters, dwarfism, and mental slowness (Kristof 2008).

Vitamin deficiencies make the individual more susceptible to influenza and other infectious diseases. Health in overpopulated areas is also affected by such problems as polluted water and air and inadequate sewage treatment.

Malnourishment also causes a low level of energy. Not only lack of food but also intestinal disorders commonly associated with poverty cause general lassitude in the afflicted.*

---

*Although low energy levels are a result of poverty, many persons have blamed poverty on an inherent lack of energy, or "drive," in the poor—a classic example of blaming the victim.

A Closer Look

THE BILL AND MELINDA GATES FOUNDATION'S WAR AGAINST MALARIA

Bill Gates, the cofounder of Microsoft, and his wife, Melinda, founded the Bill and Melinda Gates Foundation. The foundation is richly endowed with money from Bill Gates, the richest person in the United States, plus the bulk of the fortune of the second wealthiest person in the United States, Warren Buffett. In 2010, the foundation had an endowment of $37 billion.

The efforts of the foundation are directed at three main problems: global health, global development, and programs in the United States to improve education. We focus here on one part—the eradication of malaria, which the foundation,

working with other organizations, hopes to eradicate in the next decade.

Malaria is a disease of the developing world, mostly in sub-Saharan Africa and Asia. The disease is caused by a parasite transmitted by certain types of mosquitoes. More than 1 million African children have been saved from malaria since 2000, yet in 2011 some 781,000 people died from it with 85 percent children under 5 years old. Bill Gates feels that the corporate world is not working on the problem because the potential profits are few. "More money is being spent finding a cure

for baldness than developing drugs to combat malaria. The market does not drive scientists, thinkers, and governments to do the right things" (quoted in Gardner 2009). The Bill and Melinda Gates Foundation seeks to fill the void. It funds research to discover, develop, and clinically test malaria vaccines; it develops new malaria drugs that are more effective and affordable; it develops improved methods for malaria control (effective pesticides, insecticide-treated bed nets that protect against mosquitoes); it distributes insect nets and other protective gear; and it works to develop greater public awareness about malaria and advocate for effective research and control (Bill and Melinda Gates Foundation 2011).

The United Nations estimates that 1.1 million people do not have access to safe water and that 2.6 billion live in unsanitary squalor. This lack of a safe water supply and sanitation results in millions of cases of water-related diseases and more than 5 million deaths every year (De Souza, Williams, and Meyerson 2003). Polluted water, contaminated food, exposure to disease-carrying insects and animals, and unsanitary living conditions make the world's poor highly vulnerable to, among other diseases, chronic diarrhea, tuberculosis, malaria, Ebola, dengue, hepatitis, cholera, and parasites (see "A Closer Look"). More than half of the annual deaths in sub-Saharan Africa are caused by infectious and parasitic diseases. In addition to these diseases, one has emerged in the last thirty years or so with devastating effects—HIV.

HIV, the virus that causes AIDS, is transmitted through the exchange of bodily fluids, usually through sex, but also from contaminated needles, contact with tainted blood, or during birth for an infant born of an infected mother. Since the start of the AIDS **pandemic** (a worldwide epidemic) some three decades ago, 30 million have died. In 2010 an additional 34 million are living with HIV, two-thirds of them in sub-Saharan Africa. HIV/AIDS is the worst epidemic in human history, surpassing the Black Death that ravaged Europe in 1348, killing approximately 25 million. There is some hope. According to the United Nations, the global rate of new HIV infections fell by 25 percent from 2001 through 2009 (Healy and Maugh 2011).

The New Slavery

By conservative estimate, there are 27 million slaves in the world today, and the number is growing (this section is dependent largely on Bales 1999, 2000, Re 2002, and Cockburn 2009). Slavery today (the **new slavery**), just as slavery in other times, means the loss of freedom, the exploitation of people for profit, and the control of slaves through violence or its threat. But today's forms of slavery also differ from the past. First, slavery is no longer a lifelong condition, as the slave typically is freed after he or she is no longer useful (e.g., a prostitute who has AIDS). Second, sometimes individuals and families become slaves by choice—a choice forced by extreme poverty. The population explosion in the poorest nations has created a vast supply of potential workers who are desperate and vulnerable, conditions that sometimes translate into enslavement. Often the poor must place themselves in bondage to pay off a debt. Faced with a crisis (crop failure, illness), an individual borrows money, but having no other possessions uses his or her family's lives as collateral. The slave must work for the slaveholder until the slaveholder decides the debt is repaid. This situation is problematic because many slaveholders use false accounting or charge very high interest, making repayment forever out of reach. Sometimes the debt can be passed to subsequent generations, thus enslaving offspring. Debt bondage is most common in South Asia.

Impoverishment may also lead desperate parents to sell their children (often told that the children will have good jobs) to brokers who in turn sell them to slaveholders. This practice is common in Thailand as the conduit for young girls to end up as prostitutes in brothels against their will. The United Nations Children's Fund estimates that 200,000 children in West and Central Africa are sold into slavery annually by their parents. Most come from the poorest countries, such as Benin, Burkina Faso, or Mali, where up to 70 percent of the people live on less than $1 a day. Faced with grinding poverty, parents may sell their children to traders for as little as $15, in the hope that the children will find a better life. Girls end up as domestic workers or prostitutes while boys are forced to work on coffee or cocoa plantations or as fishermen. Sometimes poor young people with little prospect for success may deal directly with a broker who promises legitimate jobs, but once they are away from their homes, violence is used to take control of their lives.

There is an international traffic in slavery, involving forced migration, the smuggling of illegal immigrants, and criminal networks. At any one time, some 2.4 million people worldwide are victims of human trafficking (United Nations, quoted in Lederer 2012). The Central Intelligence Agency (CIA) estimates that 800,000

View on MySocLab Map: Prostitution in Global Perspective

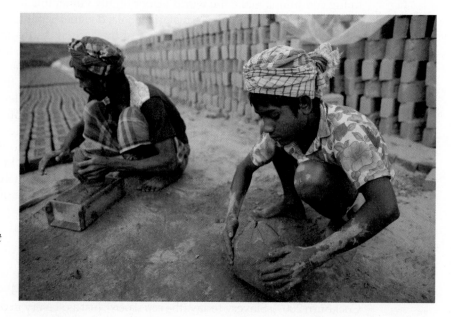

Often the poor must place themselves in debt bondage, using one's family as collateral, thus enslaving their children.

people are trafficked across national borders each year, not including millions trafficked within their own countries. At least 80 percent of the victims are female, up to half are minors, and 75 percent of all victims are trafficked into commercial sexual exploitation (Central Intelligence Agency 2012). These victims come from Asia, Africa, Latin America, Eastern Europe, and the nations of the former Soviet Union, where as many as two-thirds of women live in poverty. The anti-trafficking program at Johns Hopkins University estimates that 1 million undocumented immigrants are trapped in the United States in slavelike conditions (Bowe 2007). The State Department estimates that as many as 50,000 women and children (and a smaller number of men) are smuggled into the United States each year to be forced into prostitution, domestic service, or as bonded labor in factories and sweatshops. Immigrants pay as much as $50,000 (in debt bondage) to get smuggled into the United States with false promises of decent jobs. Once in this country, most find their passports are stolen, and they are forced to work as prostitutes or maids, on farms, or in sweatshops. They may be locked up, but even if not, they are trapped because they fear violence by the slaveholders, and they fear the police because they are illegals and because they are strangers in a strange land.

Concentration of Misery in Cities

In 1800, just 3 percent of the world's population lived in cities. In 1950, less than 30 percent were urban dwellers. In 2010, 50.5 percent of the world's population was urban. And, by 2050, when the planet's population reaches 9 to 10 billion, about 70 percent will likely live in cities, some of them **megacities** (an urban population of more than 10 million) (Bruinius 2010).

In 1950, only two cities qualified as "megacities." Today there are twenty-two, and by 2025 there will likely be another eight. Most of these huge urban places are in the developing countries of Asia, Africa, and Latin America (India, for example, has twenty-five of the 100 fastest growing cities worldwide). China provides another example of this rapid urbanization. In 1979 city dwellers represented just 10.6 percent of China's population. In 2012 the nation was 51.27 percent urban, with 160 cities of 1 million or more.

A major problem is that the infrastructure of cities in the developing world is overwhelmed by the exploding population growth (e.g., housing, schools, mass transportation, roads, sanitation, water treatment). A second problem is providing employment for their citizens. The special problem is to find employment for new immigrants to the cities—the farmers pushed off the land because of high rural density and the resulting poverty. The people who migrate to the cities are, for the most part, unprepared for life and work there. They do not possess mechanical skills; they are illiterate; they are steeped in tradition. The cities, too, are unprepared for them. Aside from the obvious problems of housing, schools, and sanitation, the cities of the developing nations do not have the industries that employ many workers. Because their citizens are usually poor, these countries are not good markets for products, so there is little internal demand for manufactured goods.

Another massive problem of the cities in the developing world is the mushrooming of squatter settlements ("shantytowns"), where 1 billion struggle to survive without clean water, sanitation, schools, and other infrastructure.

The immediate question for these immigrants is where to live. They have little choice but to create houses out of scraps (tin, plywood, paper) on land that does not belong to them (in streets, alleys, or ravines or on hillsides). Often they literally "live in shit" because the lack of sanitation forces excrement to pile up, creating serious health dangers (Montgomery 2009). Shantytowns are the fastest growing sections of cities of the developing countries.

How do squatters react to their deplorable situation? They are unemployed or work at the most menial of tasks. They are hungry. Their children remain illiterate. They suffer the indignities of being social outcasts. Will their alienation lead to terrorism and/or revolutionary activity? Some observers believe that for those experiencing abject poverty, the struggle is for the next meal, not for a redistribution of power. Others see the growing squatter settlements as breeding grounds for riots, terrorism, and radical political movements. The prospects for the cities of the developing countries are bleak. Their growth continues unabated. Unbelievable poverty and hunger are common. The inequality gap between the rich and poor is staggering. Jobs are scarce. Resources are limited and becoming more scarce as the number of inhabitants increases. The capital necessary for extensive economic development or for providing needed services is difficult to raise.

In sum, the high growth rates of cities, combined with the high concentration of people who are poor, unemployed, angry, hungry, and miserable, magnifies and intensifies other problems (such as racial and religious animosities, resource shortages, and pollution).

U.S. RELATIONS WITH THE DEVELOPING WORLD

3.3 Explain the relationship between the United States and poor nations around the world.

Read on
MySocLab Document:
The Uses of Global Poverty: How Economic Inequality Benefits the West

There is a huge gap between the rich and poor nations of the world. About 75 percent of the world's people live in the overpopulated and poverty-afflicted developing world, yet these nations produce only one-tenth of the world's industrial output and one-twelfth of its electric power output.

The nations of the developing world are underdeveloped for a number of reasons, including geography, climate, lack of arable land and minerals, and a history of continuous warfare; but the rich nations are also responsible. The developing world economies are largely the result of a history of colonialism and of economic domination by the developed nations in the postcolonial era.

As recently as 1914, approximately 70 percent of the world's population lived in a **colony** (a territory controlled by a powerful country that exploits the land and the people for its own benefit). As colonies of superpowers, their resources and labors were exploited. Leadership was imposed from outside. The local people were treated as primitive and backward. Crops were planted for the colonizer's benefit, not for the needs of the indigenous population. Raw materials were extracted for exports. The wealth thus created was concentrated in the hands of local elites and the colonizers. Population growth was encouraged because the colonizer needed a continuous supply of low-cost labor. Colonialism destroyed the cultural patterns of production and exchange by which these societies once met the needs of their peoples. Thriving industries that once served indigenous markets were destroyed. The capital generated by the natural wealth in these countries was not used to develop local factories, schools, sanitation systems, agricultural processing plants, or irrigation systems. Colonialism also promoted a two-class society by increasing land holdings among the few and landlessness among the many.

Although the process began centuries ago and ended, for the most part, since the 1960s, the legacy of colonialism continues to promote poverty today. In short, the heritage of colonialism that systematically promoted the self-interest of the colonizers and robbed and degraded the resources and the lives of the colonized continues. Vestigial attitudes, both within and outside these countries, and the continued dependency of developing nations on the industrialized superpowers, exacerbate their problems.

As a result, the gap between the developing world and the industrial nations continues to widen.

This section explores the relationship of the United States to the developing world, focusing on the economic mechanisms that maintain dependency and the political policies that promote problems within these countries.

View on
MySocLab Figure:
Distribution of Global
Income and Wealth

Transnational Corporations

Gigantic **transnational corporations**, most of which are U.S.-based, control the world economy. Their decisions to build or not to build, to relocate a plant, to begin marketing a new product, or to scrap an old one have a tremendous impact on the lives of ordinary citizens in the countries in which they operate and in which they invest.

In their desire to tap low-wage workers, the multinational corporations have tended to locate in poor countries. Although the poor countries should have benefited from this new industry (by, say, gaining a higher standard of living and access to modern technology), they have not for the most part. One reason is that the profits generated in these countries are mostly channeled back to the United States. Second, global companies do not have a great impact in easing the unemployment of the poor nations because they use advanced technology whenever feasible, which reduces the demand for jobs. Also, the corporations typically hire workers from a narrow segment of the population—young women.

The global corporations have enormous advantages over local competition when they move into an underdeveloped country. Foremost, they have access to the latest technology in information technology, machinery, or genetic engineering. Second, they receive better terms than local businesses when they borrow money. They are preferred customers because their credit is backed by their worldwide financial resources. Moreover, global banks and global corporations are, as noted in Chapter 2, closely tied through interlocking directorates and shared ownership. Thus, it is in the interest of these banks to give credit under favorable conditions to their corporate friends. Finally, the global corporations have an enormous advantage over local companies through their manipulation of the market, influence over local government officials, and their control of workers.

Two activities by transnationals are highly controversial because they have negative costs worldwide, especially to the inhabitants of developing nations—arms sales and the sale of products known to be harmful.

- **Arms Sales.**   The wealthy nations sell or give armaments to the poorer nations. Since the end of the Cold War, the United States has sold well over $100 billion worth of weapons abroad. In 2011, global arms sales by the United States totaled $46 billion. In that year, for the nineteenth straight year, the United States was the number one seller of arms abroad, accounting for 53 percent of all weapons sales, selling major conventional weapons to 62 countries (Astore 2012).

  The United States is actively engaged in promoting and financing weapons exports through 6,500 full-time government employees in the Defense, Commerce, and State Departments. These sales efforts are motivated by what was deemed to be in the national interests of the countries involved and by the profit to the manufacturers (in the United States, the multinationals most involved are Lockheed Martin, General Motors/Hughes, Northrop Grumman, General Electric, and Boeing). Not incidentally, the top ten arms-exporting companies give millions in political contributions (political action committees and soft money) during federal election campaigns.

There are several important negative consequences of these arms sales. First, they fan the flames of war. The United States sells weapons to countries actively engaged in military conflict. So rather than working to promote stability in already tense regions, the search for profits exacerbates the situation. Second, the United States has become an informal global shopping center for terrorists, mercenaries, and international criminals of all stripes (Bergman and Reynolds 2002). These gun sales are made through retail stores (not corporations), as the United States has such a lax system of controls over gun dealers and transactions at gun shows. September 11 and the subsequent war on terrorism have not changed U.S. gun control policies.

A third consequence is that arms sales can boomerang; that is, they can come back to haunt the seller (a phenomenon is known as "blowback"). For example, the United States has sold armaments to Iraq to aid in their fight with Iran, only to have those weapons used against its forces in the Gulf War in 1990 and the Iraq War of 2003 and beyond. Similarly, the United States aided the freedom fighters in Afghanistan as they fought the Soviets, only to have those weapons used later by Al-Qaeda and the Taliban against the United States after the terrorist attacks of September 11, 2001.

Fourth, the United States, in its zeal to contain or defeat regimes unfriendly to its interests, has sold arms to countries that are undemocratic and that violate human rights (Jackson 2011).

- **Corporate Sales That Endanger Life.** **Corporate dumping**, the exporting of goods that have either been banned or not approved for sale in the United States because they are dangerous, is a relatively common practice. Most often the greatest market for such unsafe products is among the poor in the developing world. These countries often do not bar hazardous products, and many of their poor citizens are illiterate and therefore tend to be unaware of the hazards involved with the use of such products.

  The United States and other industrialized nations continue to use the nations of the developing world as sources of profits as nations purchase these unhealthy products. For example, the Dalkon Shield intrauterine device was sold overseas in forty-two nations after the manufacturer, A. H. Robins, withdrew it from the U.S. market because of its danger to women. Similarly, after the Consumer Product Safety Commission forced children's garments with the fire retardant called tris phosphate off the domestic market because it was found to be carcinogenic, the manufacturer shipped several million garments overseas for sale.

  Chemical pesticides pollute water, degrade the soil, and destroy native wildlife and vegetation. The use of the most potent pesticides is banned in the United States. This ban, however, does not pertain to foreign sales: 25 percent of the pesticides exported by the United States are restricted or banned by the Environmental Protection Agency for domestic use.

  Another form of corporate dumping, in the literal sense of the word, is the practice of shipping toxic wastes produced in the United States to the developing world for disposal. This practice is attractive to U.S. corporations because the Environmental Protection Agency requires expensive disposal facilities, whereas the materials can be dumped in developing-world nations for a fraction of the cost. The host nations engage in such potentially dangerous transactions because they need the money.

  Some companies dump workplace hazards as well as hazardous products and waste materials in poor nations. Governmental regulations often require U.S. corporations to provide a reasonably safe environment for their workers. These requirements, such as not exposing workers to asbestos, lead, or other toxic substances, are often expensive to meet. Thus, many corporations move their manufacture (and unsafe working conditions) to a country with few or no restrictions. This move saves the companies money and increases their profits, but it disregards the health and safety of workers outside the United States.

Corporate dumping is undesirable for three reasons. First, and most obvious, it poses serious health hazards to the poor and uninformed consumers of the developing world. Second, the disregard of U.S. multinational corporations for their workers and their consumers in foreign lands contributes to anti-U.S. feelings in the host countries. Third, many types of corporate dumping have a boomerang effect; that is, some of the hazardous products sold abroad by U.S. companies are often returned to the United States and other developed nations, negatively affecting the health of the people in those countries. For example, the United States imports about one-fourth of its fruits and vegetables, and some of this produce is tainted with toxic chemical residues.

UNITED STATES IN THE GLOBAL VILLAGE

3.4 Discuss how the U.S. and other wealthy nations can help impoverished countries.

In the global economy, the fate of the world's poorest nations and the poor within these nations are of crucial importance to all nations. Huge gaps in income, education, and other measures of the quality of life make the world less safe. And, as the population growth surges in the developing world, the inequality gap will widen and the world will become less stable. Unless wealthy nations do more to help the poor nations catch up, the twenty-first century will witness Earth split into two very different planets, one inhabited by the fortunate few, and the other by poverty-stricken, desperate masses.

Watch on MySocLab Video: UN World Inequality

What can the wealthy nations do to help the impoverished nations? First, the affluent nations can pledge more resources targeted for development aid. The United Nations set a goal for the rich nations to give 0.7 percent of Gross National Income (GNI) to alleviate poverty in the poor nations. There are two major problems with this. First, the rich nations have failed to meet this obligation, giving instead around 0.2 to 0.4 percent, falling more than $100 billion short each year. Second, the type of aid often is not helpful. Rather than targeted to meet the needs of the poor, it is sometimes designed to meet the strategic and economic interests of the donor countries (for a nongovernmental approach to solving poverty, see the "Social Policy" panel); the aid benefits powerful domestic interest groups; and too little aid reaches those who most desperately need it (Shah 2009). For example, in 2008 the U.S. government spent $26 billion in foreign aid to address the plight of the world's poor. Much of this aid, however, was for armaments not humanitarian aid. In the case of Egypt, the United States gave $1.3 billion in 2008 to buy weapons; only $103 million for education, and $74 million for healthcare (O'Brien 2008).

The United States spends $700 billion a year on defense (see Chapter 18), which is $1.9 billion a day. What if the United States committed 10 percent of the annual military budget, combining it with the largesse of other wealthy nations, to eradicate diseases such as poliomyelitis and leprosy and reduce the spread of infectious diseases such as HIV/AIDS, malaria, and tuberculosis? How much would it take to give every child a basic level of literacy? The World Bank estimates that about $8 billion would make birth control readily available globally.

The wealthy nations can provide humanitarian aid to the developing nations with three provisos: (1) that it is truly humanitarian (such as technology, medical supplies, food, inoculation programs, family planning, agricultural equipment, sewage treatment systems, water treatment) and not military aid; (2) that the aid reaches the intended targets (those in need), not the well-off elites; and (3) that the governments in the impoverished nations have sensible plans for using the new resources, such as

Social Policy

ARE MICROLOANS THE ANSWER FOR THE WORLD'S POOR?

The 2006 Nobel Peace Prize was awarded to Muhammad Yunus, an economics professor from Bangladesh. Since the 1970s, Yunnis, through his Grameen Bank, has been offering very small loans (usually under $100) to the impoverished to start activities such as buying a dairy cow or a mobile phone that villagers can pay to use. Since then, the Bank has disbursed more than $5.3 billion to nearly 7 million borrowers who have no collateral. They pay a high interest rate (as much as 20 percent) to service these small loans, but 98 percent of the loans are paid off. Ninety-six percent of these loans are to women because traditionally banks in the developing world lend only to men.

This model for helping the world's poorest has attracted funds from various foundations (e.g., Michael and Susan Dell Foundation, Google.org, Bill and Melinda Gates Foundation) and from the World Bank, which grants loans of as little as $1,000 for enterprises such as brick making. Through these foundations, 91 million borrowers received microloans with loans totaling more than $70 billion by the end of 2009. The goal of the Microcredit Summit Campaign is to reach 175 million of the world's poorest families by 2015.

Without question, this microcredit movement has helped many poor women and their families, but there are problems. At the personal level, most borrowers do not climb out of poverty and many are trapped in a spiral of debt (Bajaj 2011). At the societal level, while microloans help some individuals and families, they do not have an impact on the poverty rate in the larger society (Bruck 2006:67; Cockburn 2009:9). Bangladesh and Bolivia, for example, have two of the most successful microcredit programs in the world, but they also remain two of the poorest countries of the world.

Two plans should be added to the microcredit program. At the microlevel, lending should be combined with other initiatives, such as education and healthcare. And foremost, the structural causes of poverty in these impoverished nations must be addressed. While small enterprises are good, what is needed are enterprises that hire workers. Moreover, the microloans initiative seeks solutions in the market and thus relieves government from their responsibilities for reducing poverty (Cockburn 2009:9). In the eyes of many, the market is a major source for the abject poverty in the world. Although microloans do help many individuals, they must be combined with structural societal reforms necessary to reduce overall poverty.

spending on health (e.g., the vaccination of children) and education, especially for women (Sen 1999).

How much commitment should the United States make to bringing poor nations up to a minimum standard? Many citizens, corporations, and politicians are indifferent to the plight of the poor, hungry, and sick far away. Many have misgivings about helping corrupt governments. Others are opposed to our support of family planning and the funding of abortion.

The ultimate interest of the United States is best served if there is peace and stability in the developing world. These goals can be accomplished only if population growth is slowed significantly, hunger and poverty are alleviated, and the extremes of inequality are reduced.

Explore on MySocLab Activity: Global Inequality: Chasing the American Dream: U.S. Immigration Patterns

If the United States and other developed nations do not take appropriate steps, human misery, acts of terrorism against affluent nations, tensions among neighbors, and wars—even nuclear war—will increase. The last factor becomes especially relevant given that a number of developing nations have nuclear bomb capabilities. Moreover, a number of developing-world countries have been alleged to have used chemical weapons. The ultimate question is whether the way these steps are implemented will help the developing world reduce its dependence on the more developed nations, the hunger and misery within their countries, and in the process, international tensions. We ignore the poor of the developing world at our peril.

■ CHAPTER REVIEW

1. The term *developing world* refers to the underdeveloped and developing nations where poverty, hunger, and misery are found disproportionately. These nations also are characterized by relative powerlessness, rapid population growth, high infant mortality, unsanitary living conditions, and high rates of illiteracy.

2. In late 2011, the world population reached 7 billion and was increasing by 82.9 million annually. About 99 percent of the population growth occurs in the developing world, where food, housing, healthcare, and employment are inadequate to meet present needs.

3. While world population is growing rapidly, the amount of productive land is shrinking in rich and poor countries alike because of the loss of topsoil, the lowering of water tables from irrigation and overgrazing, and pollution.

4. Within the nations experiencing the most rapid population growth, cities are growing much faster than are rural areas. The problems of survival for individuals and families are increased dramatically in cities: Food is too expensive, jobs are scarce and poorly paid, and sanitation problems increase the likelihood of disease. The concentration of the poor in the limited space of cities increases tensions and the probability of hostility.

5. There are three ways to reduce high fertility in the developing world: (a) economic development (modern demographic transition), (b) family-planning programs, and (c) social change, especially through the changing of traditional women's roles.

6. Poverty is a special problem of the developing world: 1.29 billion people have inadequate diets, high infant mortality, low life expectancy, and high rates of illiteracy. Poverty also contributes to high fertility.

7. Hunger is a worldwide problem, especially in the developing world, but even there food production is adequate to meet the needs of all of the people. The problem of hunger results from high prices, unequal distribution of food, overreliance on cash crops, and concentration of land ownership among very few people—all the consequences of the political economy in these nations and the world.

8. The developing world is underdeveloped for a number of reasons, the most important of which is a heritage of colonialism. Colonialism destroyed local industries and self-sufficient crop-growing patterns, drained off resources for the benefit of the colonizers, and promoted local elites through concentration of land ownership among the few. In the postcolonial era, the dependency of the developing world and its control by outside forces continue.

9. A huge worldwide problem, especially among the poor in the developing world, is HIV/AIDS. Since 1980 more than 60 million people have contracted this disease worldwide, with 30 million deaths.

10. It is estimated that there are 27 million slaves in the world. The new slavery is a consequence of extreme poverty, resulting in debt bondage and the sale of people to slaveholders.

11. The world economy is controlled by transnational corporations, the majority of which are based in the United States. Their power in the underdeveloped nations perpetuates the dependency of many developing-world nations on the United States.

12. Transnationals add to the tensions in developing-world countries through arms sales, corporate dumping of products known to be dangerous, and intervention in the domestic affairs of host countries.

13. The developed nations must work to alleviate the problems faced by the developing nations by increasing their financial commitment, by providing debt relief, and by working with international agencies to promote education and health programs. To do so is in our national interest.

■ KEY TERMS

Differential fertility. Differences in the average number of children born to a woman by social category.

Fertility rate. The average number of children born to each woman.

Modern demographic transition. A three-stage pattern of population change occurring as societies industrialize and urbanize, resulting ultimately in a low and stable population growth rate.

Life chances. The chances throughout one's life cycle to live and experience the good things in life.

Pandemic. A worldwide epidemic.

New slavery. The new slavery differs from traditional slavery in that it is, for the most part, not a lifelong condition and sometimes individuals and families become slaves by choice—a choice forced by extreme poverty.

Megacity. An urban agglomeration of more than 10 million people.

Colony. A territory controlled by a powerful country that exploits the land and the people for its own benefit.

Transnational corporation. A profit-oriented company engaged in business activities in more than one nation.

Corporate dumping. The exporting of goods that have either been banned or not approved for sale in the United States because they are dangerous.

Threats to the Environment

 Listen to **Chapter 4** on **MySocLab**

LEARNING OBJECTIVES

 Describe the nature and consequences of human-made threats to the environment.

4.2 Explain the role of the United States in the global war on the environment.

4.3 Describe the long-range international implications of and alternative solutions to threats to the environment.

Human societies have always altered their physical environments. They have used fire, cleared forests, tilled the soil, terraced hillsides, mined for mineral deposits, dammed rivers, polluted streams, and overgrazed grasslands. Since 1950 the pace and magnitude of the negative environmental impacts of human activities have increased and intensified. Especially significant are the extraordinary use of fossil fuels, the deforestation of the rain forests, the pumping of billions of tons of greenhouse gases into the air, the pollution of water by fertilizers, pesticides, and animal wastes, the emission of toxic chemicals, and the rapid erosion of topsoil. In effect, we human beings are fundamentally changing the planet in ways that are diminishing the planet's ability to sustain life.

As environmental problems are examined in this chapter, the discussion is guided by three facts. First, while some environmental problems are beyond human control (volcanoes, earthquakes, solar flares), *most are social in origin*. As a result, changing human behavior is the key to reducing or eliminating many of these environmental threats.

Second, the magnitude of environmental problems has become so great that the ultimate survival of the human species is in question. Third, although environmental problems may originate within a nation's borders, they usually have global consequences. Thus, this chapter examines human-made environmental problems at both the domestic and international levels. The first section describes the nature of these problems and their consequences. The second section examines the cultural and structural sources of environmental problems. The final section discusses some potential solutions.

4.1 Describe the nature and consequences of human-made threats to the environment.

WORLDWIDE ENVIRONMENTAL PROBLEMS

Earth's **biosphere** (the surface layer of the planet and the surrounding atmosphere) provides the land, air, water, and energy necessary to sustain life. This life-support system is a complex, interdependent one in which energy from the sun is converted into food. Three social forces are disturbing these **ecosystems** profoundly. First, the tremendous increase in population increases the demand for food, energy, minerals, and other products. With the world's population reaching over 7 billion and increasing by 6 to 7 million each month, the stresses on the environment mount (see Figure 4.1: World Population Estimates).

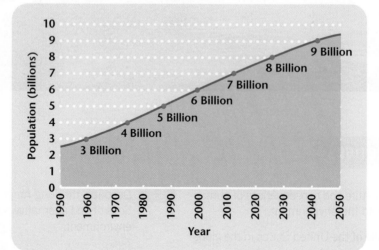

FIGURE 4.1

World Population Estimates, 1950–2050

Source: U.S. Census Bureau, International Data Base, June 2011 update. Public domain graph found at: www.census.gov/population/international/data/idb/worldpopgraph.php.

The second driving force contributing to the pressures on Earth's natural systems is growing inequality in income between the rich and poor (as discussed in Chapter 3). This inequality is a major source of environmental decline. Those at the top over-consume energy, raw materials, and manufactured goods, and for survival the poor must cut down trees, grow crops, fish, or graze livestock, often in ways that are harmful to the planet.

Consider the consumption patterns in the United States, with but 4.5 percent of the world's population:

- The United States consumes 25 percent of the world's fossil fuel. It burns 25 percent of the world's coal, 26 percent of the world's oil, and 27 percent of the world's natural gas (WorldWatch Institute 2012).
- Americans waste more food than most people eat in sub-Saharan Africa. Thirty-four million tons of food suitable for human consumption is wasted each year in the United States (Environmental Protection Agency 2011a).
- The United States consumes over 19 million barrels of petroleum each day, which is 22.5 percent of the total world consumption (U.S. Energy Information Administration 2011).
- Overall the United States ranks number two in greenhouse gas emissions (behind China). However, when taking into account the population in each country, the United States emits more CO_2 *per person* than any other industrialized nation (Rogers and Evans 2011).

The third driving force behind the environmental degradation of the planet is economic growth. This expansion of the global economy, although important for the jobs created and the products produced, has an environmental downside. Economic growth is powered by the accelerated extraction and consumption of fossil fuels, minerals, water, and timber. In turn, environmental damage increases proportionately. In the following sections we examine some of these serious environmental threats.

Degradation of the Land

View on MySocLab Figure: Endangered Wheat

Across the planet, a thin, three-foot layer of topsoil provides food crops for over 7 billion people and grazing for domesticated animals. This nutrient-rich topsoil, the source of food, fiber, and wood, is eroding at a faster rate than it can form. In fact, researchers estimate that we are losing about 1 percent of our topsoil every year (Paulson 2008). This topsoil is being depleted or lost because of careless husbandry and urbanization. Farmland is lost because of plowing marginal lands, leading to wind and water erosion. The fertility of farmland is lost because it is exhausted by overuse. It is also lost because of irrigation practices that poison the land with salt, a process called salinization. The overuse of irrigation also drains rivers and depletes aquifers faster than they can be replenished. The use of chemical fertilizers and pesticides kills helpful creatures, taints groundwater, and creates dead zones in the oceans (e.g., where the Mississippi River drains into the Gulf of Mexico).

In 2011 the Food and Agriculture Organization of the United Nations published a report that provides the first global assessment of the planet's land resources. According to the report, 25 percent of earth's land surfaces are "highly degraded," and another 8 percent are moderately degraded.

In addition to the degradation and loss of topsoil, productive land is lost through the growth of cities and urban sprawl. Consider these facts for the United States (Knickerbocker 2006):

- More area than the entire state of Georgia is now under pavement.
- Nearly 3,000 acres of farmland are converted to nonagricultural uses daily.

- Land is being converted for development at about twice the rate of population growth.
- When housing, shopping, schools, roads, and other uses are added up, each American occupies 20 percent more developed land than he or she did twenty years ago.

Destruction of the Tropical Rain Forests and Other Forms of Deforestation

Listen on **MySocLab Audio:** NPR: Amazon Rainforest Update

Tropical rain forests cover about 7 percent of Earth's dry land surface (about the same area as the forty-eight contiguous United States) and house about half of all species on Earth. About 1.9 billion acres of these forests remain in equatorial countries in the Caribbean, West Africa, Southeast Asia, and Latin America. These rich forests are rapidly being destroyed through the process of deforestation. For example, it is estimated that the island nation of Comoros (north of Madagascar) lost nearly 60 percent of its forests between 1990 and 2005. In this same period, Brazil led the world in losing 163,543 square miles of forest, which is roughly the size of California (Lindsey 2007). This massive destruction continues to occur because of economics, from the greed of developers to the desperation of poor peasants. Lumber, petroleum, and mining companies build roads into the jungles to extract their products and transport them to markets. Governments encourage the poor people to settle in these regions by building roads and offering land to settlers, who must clear it for farming. Cattle ranchers require vast expanses for their herds (five acres of pasture for each head). Land speculators clear huge areas for expected profits. The recovered land, however, is fragile, which leads to a cycle of further deforestation.

The sources of deforestation are not just local. The poverty of these nations (often the result of their colonial heritage), their indebtedness to wealthy nations, and the products needed by the wealthy nations are also responsible for the destruction of the tropical forests. China, the supplier of a third of the world's furniture, is the leading importer of illegally logged wood (Leslie 2008).

In the Cambodian rainforest, deforestation has occurred due to the demand for sassafras oil that is extracted from the roots of the rare Mreah Prew Phnom tree. While this oil is used to make some cosmetics, it is also a known ingredient in the recreational drug ecstasy. The organization Fauna and Flora International has uncovered illegal distilleries deep in the Cambodian mountains, and estimates there were at least seventy-five sassafras oil distilleries operating in 2006 (MacKinnon 2009).

U.S. corporations are also directly and indirectly involved in various aspects of rain forest destruction. These involve the timber companies such as Georgia-Pacific and Weyerhaeuser; mining companies such as Alcoa and Freeport McMoRan; oil companies such as Arco, Chevron, Exxon-Mobil, Conoco Phillips, and Unocal; paper companies such as Kimberly-Clark; and agricultural companies such as Chiquita.

The two major environmental consequences of this deforestation are climate change and the vanishing of species. The climate is affected in several related ways. As hundreds of thousands of forest acres are destroyed, rain patterns change. Huge areas once covered with plants, which give off moisture, are replaced by exposed, sandy soils. Also, the massive burning required to clear the land creates clouds of smoke that block the sun and lead to weather change. Thus, lush, green areas often become near deserts. The tropical forest in Brazil (the world's largest) has so much rainfall that it provides 20 percent of Earth's freshwater supply. What will be the long-range effects

The world's tropical rain forest is losing an area about half the size of Florida each year.

as this water supply dwindles? Just as important, forests absorb huge quantities of carbon dioxide through photosynthesis. Consequently, as forests are diminished so is Earth's capacity to absorb the gas most responsible for global warming. This diminished capacity to process carbon dioxide, changing it into oxygen, leads to changes in the climate and to desertification.

The second critical environmental consequence of deforestation is the loss of animal and plant species. Although these tropical forests cover only 7 percent of Earth's dry land surface, they are Earth's richest factory of life, containing more than half of the world's species of plants, insects, birds, and other animals. As the forests are cleared and burned, species become extinct.

Humanity benefits from nature's diversity in many ways. One important aspect is that exotic plants and animals are major sources of pharmaceuticals. For example, Squibb used the venom of the Brazilian pit viper to develop Capoten, a drug to lower high blood pressure. The yew, which grows in the Pacific Northwest, produces a potent chemical, taxol, which shows promise for curing certain forms of lung, breast, and ovarian cancer. Biotechnology provides the potential to improve agricultural crops by transferring genes from wild plants to domestic crops so that they can be drought resistant, repel insects, or create their own fertilizers naturally. By destroying the forests, we may be eliminating future solutions to disease and famine.

Environmental Pollution and Degradation

The following description of the various forms of pollution in industrial societies presents a glimpse of how humanity is fouling its nest.

- **Chemical Pollution.** Over 4 billion pounds of toxic chemicals are released by industry into the nation's environment each year (Scorecard 2011). These chemicals are found in food, used in detergents, fertilizers, pesticides, plastics, clothing, insulation, and

A crop duster sprays pesticides on a local farm. This is one source of chemical food contamination.

Watch on
MySocLab Slideshow:
Toxic Town

almost everything else. Some 202 of these chemicals, such as lead and mercury, harm children's brains and may be responsible for many developmental disabilities such as autism and attention deficit disorder (Laurance 2006).

The manufacture of chemicals requires disposing of the waste. Waste disposal, especially safe disposal of toxic chemicals, is a huge problem. These toxic chemicals are released into the air, water, land, underground, and public sewage either by accident or deliberately. Typically, corporations choose the cheapest means of disposal, which is to release the waste products into the air or water and to bury the materials in dump sites. In one infamous instance, over a number of years the Hooker Chemical and Plastics Corporation dumped 43.6 million pounds of eighty-two different chemical substances into Love Canal, New York, near Niagara Falls. Among the chemicals dumped were 200 tons of trichlorophenol, which contained an estimated 130 pounds of one of the most toxic and carcinogenic substances known—dioxin. Three ounces of this substance can kill more than a million people. (A variant of dioxin—Agent Orange—was used in the Vietnam War with extremely adverse results to vegetation and human life.) As a result of exposure to the various chemicals dumped at Love Canal, nearby residents had an unusual number of serious illnesses, a high incidence of miscarriages, and an unusual number of children born with birth defects.

The Love Canal dumpsite is only one of thousands of dangerous locations in the United States. The Environmental Protection Agency (EPA) places sites that pose the greatest risk to public health and the environment on the Superfund National Priorities List. Hurricane Katrina flooded three Superfund toxic waste sites in and around New Orleans, and this poses serious threats if any of their protective shields have been degraded (Eilperin 2005). As of January 2012, there are 1,297 sites on the Superfund National Priorities List (New Jersey tops the list with 112).

A movement known as **environmental justice** works to improve environments for communities and is especially alert to the injustices that occur when a particular segment of the population, such as the poor or minority groups, bears a disproportionate share of exposure to environmental hazards. This movement is a reaction against the overwhelming likelihood that toxic-producing plants and toxic waste dumps are located where poor people, especially people of color, live (when this pattern occurs, it is called **environmental racism**). "In Los Angeles more than 71 percent of African Americans live in highly polluted areas, compared to 24 percent of whites. Across the United States, black children are three times more likely to have hazardous levels of lead in their blood as a result of living near hazardous waste sites" (Oliver 2008:2). Robert Bullard, an expert on environmental racism, says that "Blacks and other economically disadvantaged groups are often concentrated in areas that expose them to high levels of toxic pollution: namely, urban industrial communities with elevated air and water pollution problems or rural areas with high levels of exposure to farm pesticides" (Bullard 2000:6–7).

U.S. corporations are also involved in global chemical pollution. They not only dump wastes into the oceans and the air, which of course can affect the people in other countries, but they also sell to other countries chemicals (such as pesticides) that are illegal to sell here because they are toxic. In addition, U.S. corporations have used other countries as dumpsites for their hazardous substances because the U.S. government outlawed indiscriminate dumping of toxic wastes in this country in 1975.

The nations of Western Europe and North America have relatively strict environmental laws, which is good for their inhabitants. These countries, however, transport roughly 2 million tons of toxic waste annually to poor nations that desperately need the cash.

Toxic wastes are also exported when U.S. multinational corporations move operations to countries with less stringent environmental laws. For example, the 2,000 foreign-owned (mostly by the United States) factories along the United States–Mexico border in Mexico (*maquiladoras*) have created environmental hazards on both sides of the border.

Another problem with toxic wastes is accidental spills from tankers, trucks, and trains as the wastes are transported. These spills number about 400 a year in the United States alone. When these incidents occur, the air, the groundwater, and the oceans may become polluted.

- **Solid Waste Pollution.** The United States discards 30 percent of the world's resources (Rogers 2005). As such, it is the largest producer of solid waste among the industrialized nations, both in absolute and per capita terms. According to the Environmental Protection Agency (2011b), in 2010 Americans generated 250 million tons of old food, glass, clothing, electronics, plastics, metals, textiles, rubber, wood, and paper. On average, each American produces 4.43 pounds of solid trash a day (up from 2.7 pounds in 1960). Approximately 34 percent of this trash is recycled, and the rest is incinerated or buried in landfills (see Figure 4.2).

The problem of what to do with solid waste is compounded by the increased amounts of waste that are contaminated with compounds and chemicals that do not appear in nature. These wastes pose new and unknown threats to human, animal, and plant life. One such health hazard is toxic sludge, a mix of human and industrial waste produced by wastewater treatment plants. About 4 million tons of sludge is dumped on farmland, golf courses, and parks as a form of fertilizer. Unless sludge is carefully treated and monitored, it can be tainted with *E. coli*, bacteria, viruses, heavy metals, solvents, and any combination of the thousands of chemicals used in U.S. industries. In 2010 a reservoir filled with toxic red sludge ruptured in western

FIGURE 4.2

Municipal Solid Waste
Disposal in the
United States

Source: U.S. Environmental Protection Agency (2011). "Municipal Solid Waste Generation, Recycling and Disposal in the United States: Facts and Figures for 2010." www.epa.gov/osw/nonhaz/municipal/pubs/msw_2010_factsheet.pdf.

A Closer Look

TECHNOLOGY AND TOXIC WASTE

The new technology found in most households in the developed world—personal computers, cell phones, televisions, and other electronic equipment—is laden with toxins that when thrown away will leach into groundwater or produce dioxins and other carcinogens when burned. The Environmental Protection Agency (2011b) estimates that there were 438 million new electronic products sold in the United States alone in 2009. What does this mean for the environment? Let's consider computers.

The computer revolution changes quickly, with each new generation having much more memory and being infinitely faster, yet available at a cheaper price than the original. As a result, millions of computers become obsolete every year. Thus, the disposal of personal computers and consumer electronics

("e-waste") is an enormous environmental problem.

- In 2009, in the United States an estimated 29.4 million computers were thrown away (an additional 18 million computers were recycled) (Environmental Protection Agency 2011b).
- Printed circuit boards and semiconductors contain cadmium, which is known to cause lung cancer and kidney damage with repeated exposure. In 2005, more than 2 million pounds of cadmium were discarded along with computers.
- The batteries and switches contain mercury. Mercury poisoning is known to cause chronic health problems from gum problems to nerve system damage. 400,000 pounds of mercury were discarded nationwide in 2005.

- Chromium is used as corrosion protection in computers and can cause respiratory tract irritation. In 2005, there were an estimated 1.2 million pounds of chromium in landfills.
- PVC (polyvinyl chloride) plastics are used on cables and housings, creating a potential waste of 250 million pounds per year.
- With the increased use of flat-panel monitors, it is estimated that 500 million defunct monitors were discarded by 2007, each of which contains phosphorus and 4 to 8 pounds of lead.

The problem is that only 38 percent of computers are recycled. The rest threaten the environment—here and abroad. Chances are that most of the obsolete computers will end up in the developing world—Africa, India, and China—where the poor, with little or no protection, are hired to extract items of value.

Hungary, releasing a 12-foot-high wall of sludge into nearby towns and rivers. The Hungarian government later imposed a fine on the aluminum plant responsible for the accident.

All landfills eventually leak seeping toxic residues into the groundwater. Many communities have contaminated drinking water and crops as a result. With the problem clearly becoming serious, some experimentation is now being conducted with landfills that have impermeable linings to prevent such pollution. (See the "A Closer Look" panel on how technology contributes to toxic waste pollution.)

There are several alternatives to dumping trash in landfills. One option has been to dump rubbish in the ocean. This practice has polluted beaches, poisoned fish, and hurt fisheries. As a result, international agreements and domestic legislation within various countries have curtailed this alternative. The environmentally preferred solutions are for the trash to be reprocessed to its original uses (paper, glass containers, metals) or converted into new products such as insulation.

The alternative most commonly selected is to incinerate the garbage (which disposes of 11.7 percent of the country's total waste). The burning of trash has two major benefits. It reduces the volume of garbage by almost 90 percent, and it can generate steam and electricity. The downside of burning trash, however, is significant. Incinerating plastics and other garbage releases toxic chemicals, including deadly dioxins and heavy-metal emissions, into the air. The residue (ash) is contaminated with lead and cadmium.

About 34 percent of solid waste is currently recycled, a positive environmental step. In fact, that rate has increased from just 10 percent in 1980. Another positive is the transforming of organic waste—paper, food scraps, and lawn clippings into compost, a product that invigorates agricultural soils. In 2010, over 19 million tons of yard trimmings were composted, representing almost a five-fold increase since 1990 (Environmental Protection Agency 2011b).

- **Water Pollution.** The major sources of water pollution are (1) industries, which pour into rivers, lakes, and oceans a vast array of contaminants such as lead, asbestos, detergents, solvents, acid, and ammonia; (2) farmers, whose pesticides, herbicides, fertilizers, and animal wastes drain into streams and lakes; (3) cities, which dispose of their wastes, including sewage, into rivers to end up downstream in another city's drinking water; and (4) oil spills, caused by tanker accidents and leaks in offshore drilling. These are problems throughout the world.

Watch on MySocLab Video: PBS FRONTLINE: Poisoned Waters

Water pollution is a most immediate problem in the less developed countries. Contaminated water in poor countries results in high death rates from cholera, typhoid, dysentery, and diarrhea. About 884 million people do not have access to safe drinking water, and if current trends continue 2.4 billion people will still be without access to basic sanitation by 2015 (World Water Assessment Programme 2009). More than 3 million die each year of easily preventable waterborne diseases such as diarrhea, dysentery, and cholera.

In the United States, the Mississippi River provides an example of the seriousness of water pollution. Greenpeace USA, an environmental organization, surveyed pollution in the Mississippi River and found that industries and municipalities along the river discharged billions of pounds of heavy metals and toxic chemicals into it. This dumping occurs along the 2,300 miles of the river; the worst pollution is concentrated along 150 miles in Louisiana, where 25 percent of the nation's chemical industry is located.

The EPA has a list of large toxic sites to be cleaned up with funds supplied by Congress. The largest of these Superfund sites is a 200-mile stretch of the upper Hudson

The Hudson River in New York remains one of the most polluted rivers in the United States.

River, where General Electric dumped 1.3 million pounds of polychlorinated biphenyls (PCBs) into the river over a thirty-year period. PCBs cause cancer in laboratory animals, and they are linked to premature births and developmental disorders. General Electric stopped the practice in 1977 when the federal government banned PCB use. More than three decades later, the New York State Health Department continues to advise women of childbearing age and children under age 15 not to eat any fish from the Hudson River and urges that no one eat any fish from the upper Hudson, where the cancer risk from such consumption is 700 times the EPA protection level. Between May and October 2009, Phase 1 of the Hudson River Dredging Project was completed, and 10 percent of the contaminated sediment was removed. The second phase of the cleanup began in 2011, with the goal of removing 2.4 million cubic yards of sediment. Thousands of pounds of PCBs remain in the sediment of the Hudson and continue to poison fish, wildlife, and humans.

- **Radiation Pollution.**   Human beings cannot escape radiation from natural sources such as cosmic rays and radioactive substances in Earth's crust. Technology has added greatly to these natural sources through the extensive use of x-rays for medical and dental uses, fallout from nuclear weapons testing and from nuclear accidents, and the use of nuclear energy as a source of energy.

     The dangers of radiation are evidenced to the extreme in the physical effects on the survivors of the atomic bombs at the end of World War II. These victims experienced physical disfigurement, stillbirths, infertility, and extremely high rates of cancer. A government study estimated that the radioactive fallout from Cold War nuclear weapons tests across the Earth probably caused at least 15,000 cancer deaths and 20,000 nonfatal cancers in U.S. residents born after 1951 (reported in Eisler 2002). In 1986, the most serious nuclear accident to date occurred at Chernobyl in the Soviet Union. The full consequences of this accident will not be known for years, but so far there have been numerous deaths in Russia, a large-scale increase in cancers and other illnesses, and widespread contamination of food and livestock as far away as Scandinavia and Western Europe. The most serious nuclear accident in the United States occurred with the near meltdown in Pennsylvania at Three Mile Island in 1979. Worldwide, the most recent example of a nuclear accident occurred in 2011 when a powerful earthquake and subsequent tsunami in Japan cause radiation leaks at the Fukushima Daiichi nuclear power station.

Less dramatic than nuclear accidents but lethal just the same have been the exposures to radiation by workers in nuclear plants and those living nearby. Thirty-two utility companies across the United States operate 104 commercial nuclear reactors, providing about 20 percent of the nation's electricity (second only to coal). Unlike coal, the electricity generated by nuclear energy does not produce carbon dioxide and other greenhouse gases. The problem involves the safe storage of nuclear waste. The generation of nuclear power creates radioactive by-products such as uranium mill tailings, used reactors, and the atomic waste itself. The safe storage of these materials is an enormous and perhaps impossible task because some remain radioactive for as long as 250,000 years. Neither the nuclear industry nor the government has a long-term solution for safe nuclear waste disposal.

The Hanford nuclear weapons plant in Washington State provides an example. For more than forty years, the U.S. government ran this facility, monitoring nuclear emissions but not notifying the workers or the 270,000 residents in the surrounding area of the dangers. It has now been revealed that the Hanford plant released over 400,000 curies of radioactive iodine into the atmosphere (a substance known to cause cancer). Similar situations have occurred at the weapons factories at Rocky Flats near Denver, Fernald near Cincinnati, and Savannah River in South Carolina, and at the testing sites for weapons in Nevada and other areas in the Southwest.

In 2012, U.S. federal regulators, signaling a renewed effort to use nuclear energy to cut the nation's reliance on fossil fuels, approved the first new nuclear plant in thirty years. It remains to be seen whether this will spark a renewed interest in expanding nuclear power in the United States.

- **Air Pollution.** According to the World Health Organization (2011), outdoor air pollution causes 1.3 million deaths per year worldwide. It is a major source of health

Hanford was the world's first full-scale nuclear reactor, built to produce plutonium for an atomic bomb during World War II.

problems such as respiratory ailments (asthma, bronchitis, and emphysema), cancer, impaired central nervous functioning, and cirrhosis of the liver. These problems are especially acute among people who work in or live near industrial plants in which waste chemicals are released into the air and among people who live in metropolitan areas where conditions such as temperature and topography tend to trap the pollutants near the ground (e.g., cities such as Mexico City, Los Angeles, and Denver).

In addition to air pollution from industry, automobiles emit five gases that have extremely serious consequences for the environment: carbon monoxide, carbon dioxide, nitrous oxide, chlorofluorocarbons, and ozone smog. The resulting greenhouse effect and the loss of ozone protection are topics discussed in the later section on climate change.

Fossil Fuel Dependence and Environmental Degradation

The Industrial Revolution involved, most fundamentally, the replacement of human and animal muscle by engines driven by fossil fuels. These fuels (coal, oil, natural gas) are also used for heating, cooking, and lighting. Considering just oil, the world consumes approximately 85 million barrels of oil a day. The United States is the greatest consumer of oil products, using approximately 19.2 million barrels of oil a day (22.6 percent of the world's daily consumption). The European Union is second at 13.7 million barrels, followed by China, Japan, and India (Central Intelligence Agency 2012). Carbon dioxide emissions from fossil fuels, the main villain among the greenhouse gases, have gone from almost nothing a hundred years ago to more than 4 metric tons of carbon per person each year. Each person in the United States, by the way, produces over 17 tons per year (Rogers and Evans 2011).

The worldwide demand for energy will rise sharply as the developing nations, where 99 percent of the world's population growth is taking place, industrialize and urbanize. People in the developing countries will be replacing traditional fuels such as wood and other organic wastes with electricity, coal, and oil. This likely trend has important consequences for the world and its inhabitants. First, the demand for fossil fuels has given extraordinary wealth to the elites in the nations of the Persian Gulf area, where most of the world's estimated petroleum reserves are located. Stability in this region is vital to U.S. interests because interruption in the flow of Persian Gulf oil will cause shortages and the price of other oil imports to rise dramatically, devastating the U.S. economy. In short, the maldistribution of the world's energy supply heightens world tensions.

Second, because most nations need to import oil, vast amounts are carried across the world's oceans in about 2,600 tankers. Along with offshore drilling, these voyages increase the probability of accidents that damage aquatic life, birds, and coastal habitats. Four examples of large-scale spills are the wreck of the *Amoco Cadiz* off the coast of France in 1978, spilling 68 million gallons of crude oil; the blowout of the Ixtoc I oil well, which poured 140 million gallons of oil into the Gulf of Mexico in 1979; the grounding of the *Exxon Valdez* in Alaska's Prince William Sound in 1989, which released 11 million gallons of crude oil into an ecologically sensitive region, contaminating 1,000 miles of coastline and destroying extraordinary amounts of fish and wildlife; and the April 2010 explosion of the Deepwater Horizon oil rig, operated by British Petroleum (BP). The BP oil spill killed eleven workers and leaked 185–205 million gallons of crude oil into the Gulf of Mexico. The oil slick killed marine life and devastated the coastal lands of Louisiana and the livelihoods of people who fish and shrimp in the Gulf (Ritchie, Gill, and Picou 2011).

The United States is the world's number one consumer of oil products.

Finally, and most important, the combustion of fossil fuels results in the emission of carbon dioxide, which appears to be related to climate change. The consequences of the present level of carbon dioxide emissions, plus the expected increase in the near future, may have disastrous consequences for Earth in the form of global warming.

Climate Change

Before the Industrial Revolution, forest fires, plant decomposition, and ordinary evaporation released carbon dioxide into the atmosphere, but in small enough amounts to be absorbed by growing plants and by the oceans without noticeable environmental effect. But in the past century or so, human activities—especially the reliance on fossil fuels, the use of chlorofluorocarbons to make plastic foam and as coolants in refrigerators and air conditioners, the destruction of the tropical rain forests—have increased the prevalence of dangerous gases beyond Earth's capacity to absorb them. The **greenhouse effect** occurs when these harmful gases accumulate in the atmosphere and act like the glass roof of a greenhouse. Sunlight reaches Earth's surface, and the gases trap the heat radiating from the ground. The results, according to the theory, are a warming of Earth, the melting of the polar ice caps, a significant changing of climate, droughts and megastorms, and the rapid spread of tropical diseases such as malaria, dengue fever, cholera, and encephalitis. Consider the following facts (Begley 2011):

- The earth has warmed by 2 degrees Fahrenheit in the last century.
- 2010 was the hottest year on earth.
- In the United States alone, nearly 1,000 tornadoes caused $9 billion in damage in 2010.
- A 2010 heat wave in Russia killed an estimated 15,000 people, while flooding in Australia and Pakistan killed over 2,000 people.

The issue of global warming and climate change is controversial, resulting in a divide between Democrats and Republicans. Seventy to seventy-five percent of self-identified

Watch on MySocLab Video: Environment and Society: World Climate Change

Listen on MySocLab Audio: NPR: Sources of Global Warming

Democrats believe humans are changing the climate, while the majority of Republicans (particularly Tea Party members) reject the scientific consensus (Klein 2011).

Scientists, on the other hand, do not debate that Earth is warmer or that carbon dioxide is emitted into the air in ever-increasing amounts, but they do differ on the relationship between the two facts. Some scientists are cautious, arguing that recent warming and dramatic climatic events are random and part of the natural year-to-year variations in weather. Their skepticism is fueled by a recent scandal in the scientific community. In late 2009, an anonymous computer hacker made public e-mails sent between climate scientists that seemed to indicate that data regarding global warming had been fabricated. Dubbed "Climategate" by the media, it fueled the debate over the extent and cause of global warming. See the "A Closer Look" panel for more information on Climategate.

On the other side of the debate, the majority of scientists are convinced that the magnitude of the greenhouse effect is great and accelerating and the cause is *human behavior*. China and the United States currently emit approximately 43 percent of the

A Closer Look

CLIMATEGATE

In 2007 the Intergovernmental Panel on Climate Change produced a report that claimed:

- Eleven of the previous twelve years (1995–2006) rank among the twelve warmest years on record since 1850.
- Sea levels are rising.
- Snow and ice are decreasing.
- Over the past fifty years, cold days, cold nights, and frosts have become less frequent.

Using data from a number of sources, the IPCC concluded that warming of the climate system is "unequivocal."

The issue of global warming has many critics, however. For example, meteorologist Mark Johnson writes, "I talk to many groups, large and small, about how AGW [Anthropogenic Global Warming] is just bad science. I tell them that study results are hand-picked and modified to fit a pre-determined conclusion" (Johnson 2009:1). Critics of global warming theory

have become even more outspoken since the incident in October 2009 dubbed "Climategate." A computer hacker posted more than a thousand e-mails from scientists at the Hadley Climatic Research Unit at Britain's University of East Anglia. The e-mails contain details regarding data gathering, and skeptics claim they are evidence of scientific fraud and misconduct. One particular e-mail cited most often refers to using a statistical "trick" to "hide the decline" in global temperatures. Although all of this is currently under investigation, a few items are clear. According to Jess Henig at Factcheck.org (Henig 2009:1):

- The messages, which span thirteen years, show a few scientists in a bad light. An investigation is underway, but there is still plenty of evidence that the earth is getting warmer and that humans are largely responsible.
- Some critics say the e-mails negate the conclusions of the 2007 report by the

Intergovernmental Panel on Climate Change, but the IPCC report relied on data from a large number of sources, of which CRU was only one.

- E-mails being cited as "smoking guns" have been misrepresented. For instance, one e-mail that refers to "hiding the decline" isn't talking about a decline in actual temperature as measured at weather stations. These have continued to rise, and 2009 may turn out to be the fifth warmest year ever recorded. The "decline" actually refers to a problem with recent data from tree rings.

Climategate seems to have had little influence on the world's understanding of global warming, as the U.N. Climate Change Conference proceeded as planned in December 2009. In advance of the conference "the national academies of thirteen nations issued a joint statement of their recommendations for combating climate change, in which they discussed the 'human forcing' of global warming and said that the need for action was 'indisputable' " (Henig 2009:4).

world's greenhouse gases. China's emissions are the highest in the world, but the United States still leads in carbon dioxide emissions per person. The average American is responsible for 17.67 tons per year, while the average Chinese is responsible for 5.83 tons (Rogers and Evans 2011).

4.2 Explain the role of the United States in the global war on the environment.

SOURCES OF U.S. ENVIRONMENTAL PROBLEMS

The United States has been blessed with an abundance of rich and varied resources (land, minerals, and water). Until recently, people in the United States were unconcerned with conservation because there seemed to be so vast a storehouse of resources that waste was not considered a problem. And as a result, Americans have disproportionately consumed the world's resources. For example, although they constitute 4.5 percent of the world's population, people in the United States use 25 percent of the world's oil output each year.

Although the perception of abundance may explain a tendency to be wasteful, it is only a partial and superficial answer. The underlying sources of our present environmental problems can be located in the culture and structure of U.S. society.

Cultural Sources

Watch on **MySocLab Video:** Sociology in Focus: Population, Urbanization, and Environment

Culture refers to the knowledge that the members of a social organization—in this case, a society—share. Shared ideas, values, beliefs, and understandings shape the behaviors, perceptions, and interpretations of the members of society. Although the United States is a multicultural society filled with diversity, some of the dominant ideologies of U.S. society have tended to legitimize or at least account for the wastefulness of Americans and their acceptance of pollution.

- **Cornucopia View of Nature.** Many Americans conceive of nature as a vast storehouse waiting only to be used by people. They regard the natural world as a bountiful preserve available to serve human needs. In this view, nature is something to be conquered and used; it is free and inexhaustible. This cornucopia view of nature is widespread and will likely persist as a justification for continuing abuse of the environment, even in an age of ecological consciousness. This view is complemented by an abundant faith in science and technology.

- **Faith in Technology.** Americans have historically sought to change and conquer nature. Damming rivers, cutting down timber, digging tunnels, plowing land, conquering space, and seeding clouds with silver nitrate are a few examples of this orientation to overcoming nature's obstacles rather than acquiescing to them.

  From this logic proceeds a faith in technology; a proper application of scientific knowledge can meet any challenge. If the air and water are polluted and if we are rapidly running out of petroleum, science will save us. We will find a substitute for the internal combustion engine, create plants that will "scrub" the air by using carbon dioxide as food, find new sources of energy, develop new methods of extracting minerals, or create new synthetics. Although this faith may yet be vindicated, we are beginning to realize that technology may not be the solution and may even be the source of the problem.

  Scientific breakthroughs and new technology have solved some problems and do aid in saving labor. But often, new technology creates unanticipated problems. Automobiles, for example, provide numerous benefits, but they also pollute the air and kill about 50,000 Americans each year. It is difficult to imagine life without electricity, but the generation of electricity pollutes the air (over half of the carbon emissions in the United States come from coal-burning electrical plants) and causes the thermal pollution of rivers. Insecticides and chemical fertilizers have performed miracles in agriculture but have polluted food and streams. Jet planes, while helping us in many ways, cause air pollution (one jet taking off emits the same amount of hydrocarbon as the exhausts from 10,000 automobiles). So our faith in science and technology has actually resulted in many environmental problems, yet ironically we must turn to science and new technologies to solve those same problems.

- **Growth Ethic.** Many Americans place a premium on progress and believe that something better is always attainable. This desire (which is encouraged by corporations and their advertisers) causes people to discard items that are still usable and to purchase new things. Thus, industry continues to turn out more products and to use up natural resources.

  Explore on MySocLab Activity: Problems of Place: The Southern Californian Sprawl

  The presumed value of progress has had a negative effect on contemporary U.S. life. Progress is typically defined to mean either growth or new technology. Community leaders typically want their cities to grow. Chambers of commerce want more industry and more people (and, incidentally, more consumers). The logic of capitalism is that every company needs to increase its profits from year to year. Thus, we all benefit if the gross national product increases each year. For all these things to grow as people wish, there must be a concomitant increase in population, products (and use of natural resources), electricity, highways, and waste. Continued growth will inevitably throw the tight ecological system out of balance, for there are limited supplies of air, water, and places to dump waste materials, and these supplies diminish as the population increases.

- **Materialism.** The U.S. belief in progress is translated at the individual level into consumption of material things as evidence of one's success. The U.S. economic system is predicated on the growth of private enterprises, which depend on increased demand for their products. If the population is more or less stable, then individuals can accomplish growth only through increased consumption. The function of the advertising industry is to create a need in individuals to buy a product that they would not buy otherwise. Consumption is also increased if products must be thrown away (such as nonreturnable bottles) or if they do not last very long. The policy of **planned obsolescence** (manufacturing and selling goods designed to wear out or to become out of fashion) by many U.S. companies accomplishes this goal of consumption very well, but it overlooks the problems of disposal as well as the unnecessary waste of materials.

- **Belief in Individualism.** Most people in the United States place great stress on personal achievement. They believe that hard work and initiative will bring individual success. The self-orientation (as opposed to collective-orientation) is, of course, related to capitalism. Through personal efforts, business acumen, and luck, the individual can (if successful) own property and see multiplying profits. Most Americans share this goal of great monetary success—the "American dream"—and believe that anyone can make it if he or she works hard enough. Curiously, people who are not successful commonly do not reject capitalism. Instead, they wait in the hope that their lot will improve or that their children will prosper under the system.

  The belief that private property and capitalism should not be restricted has led to several social problems: (1) unfair competition (monopolies, interlocking directorates, price fixing); (2) an entrepreneurial philosophy of caveat emptor ("let the buyer beware"), whose aim is profit with disregard for the welfare of the consumer; and (3) the current environmental crisis, due to people and corporations doing whatever is profitable while ignoring conservation of natural resources. Industrial pollution of air and water with refuse and agricultural spraying with pesticides that harm animal and human life are two examples of how individuals and corporations look out for themselves with little or no regard for the short-and long-range effects of their actions.

As long as people hold a narrow self-orientation rather than a group orientation, this crisis will steadily worsen. The use people make of their land, the water running through it, and the air above it has traditionally been theirs to decide because of the belief in the sanctity of private property. This belief has meant, in effect, that individuals have had the right to pave a pasture for a parking lot, to tear up a lemon grove for a housing development, to put down artificial turf for a football field, and to dump waste products into the ground, air, and water. Consequently, individual decisions have had the collective effect of taking millions of acres of arable land out of production permanently, polluting the air and water, and covering land where vegetation once grew with asphalt, concrete buildings, and Astroturf, even though green plants are the only source of oxygen.

In terms of solving environmental problems (especially climate change), a self-orientation is at odds with any lasting, sustainable solutions. Asking individuals to reduce their carbon footprint not for themselves, but for generations to come is contrary to the values of individualism.

In summary, traditional values of U.S. citizens lie at the heart of environmental problems. Americans want to conquer nature. They want to use nature for the good life, and this endeavor is never satisfied. Moreover, they want the freedom to do as they please and expect science and technology to solve any problems that arise.

Structural Sources

In addition to our cultural values, the structural arrangements in U.S. society reinforce the misuse of resources and abuses of the ecosystem.

- **Capitalist Economy.** The U.S. economic system of capitalism depends on profits. The quest for profits is never satisfied: Companies must grow; more assets and more sales translate into more profits. To maximize profits, owners must minimize costs. Among other things, this search for profits results in abusing the environment, resisting government efforts to curb such abuse, using corporate and advertising skills to increase the consumption of products (including built-in obsolescence), and to even denigrate the notion of global warming. For instance, according to the Union of Concerned Scientists, Exxon-Mobil, the world's largest oil company, funded forty-three ideological organizations nearly $16 million between 1998 and 2005 in an effort to mislead the public by discrediting the science behind global warming (2007).

  This last point needs elaboration. Profits require consumers; growing profits require overconsumption. Corporations use several mechanisms to generate the desire to purchase unnecessary products. Advertising generates hyper-consumerism by creating demand for products that potential consumers did not know they needed. Innovative packaging designs also help to sell products; the size, shape, and colors of the package and its display affect choices. Another common tactic is product differentiation whereby existing products (such as an automobile) are given cosmetic changes and presented to consumers as new. This planned obsolescence creates consumer demand as purchasers trade or throw away the "old" product for the "new."

The increased production that results from greater levels of consumption has three detrimental consequences for the environment: more pollution of air and water, depletion of resources, and a swelling of waste products (sewage, scrap, and junk).

Because the profit motive supersedes the concern for the environment, corporations are unwilling to comply with government regulations and to pay damages for ecological disasters such as oil spills. In addition, the possibility of solving environmental problems is further minimized under a capitalist system because jobs depend on business profits. Economic prosperity and growth mean jobs. Thus, most observers see only a narrow alternative between a safe environment and relatively full employment. The fate of many workers depends on whether companies are profitable. Solving environmental problems appears to be incompatible with capitalism unless ecological disasters occur.

- **Polity.** As discussed in Chapter 2, powerful interest groups fundamentally influence political decisions. This bias of the political system is readily seen in what has been government's relatively cozy relationship with large polluters: corporations. Typically, government intervention has had the effect of administering a symbolic slap on the wrist, and pollution of the environment has continued virtually unabated. The government has been ineffective in pushing the largest and most powerful corporations to do something unprofitable. For example, in 2011 President Obama overruled a proposed law by the Environmental Protection Agency that would have imposed stricter smog standards on corporations. The law was heavily opposed by business interests and is an example of how powerful interest groups can influence the system in their favor.

- **Demographic Patterns.** The population of the United States is generally concentrated in large metropolitan areas. Wherever people are concentrated, the problems of pollution are increased through the concentration of wastes. Where people are centralized, so too will be the emission of automobile exhausts, the effluence of factories, and the dumps for garbage and other human refuse.

  The location of cities is another source of environmental problems. Typically, cities have evolved where commerce would benefit the most. Because industry needs

Large cities like Los Angeles frequently have problems with air pollution.

plentiful water for production and waste disposal, cities tend to be located along lakes, rivers, and ocean bays. Industry's long-established pattern of using available water to dispose of its waste materials has caused rivers, such as the Missouri, Mississippi, and Ohio; lakes, such as Erie and Michigan; and bays like Chesapeake and New York to be badly polluted.

The ready availability of the automobile and the interstate highway system resulted in the development of suburbs. The growth of suburbs not only strained already burdened sewage facilities but also increased air pollution through increased use of the automobile. The greater the urban sprawl, the greater the existence of smog.

📖 Read on MySocLab Document: Dumping in Dixie: Race, Class, and the Politics of Place

System of Stratification.   One major focus of this book (and of Chapter 7, in particular) is how U.S. society victimizes the poor. Poor people and racial minorities are disproportionately exposed to the dangers of pollution, whether it takes the form of excessive noise, foul air, or toxic chemicals such as lead poisoning. These probabilities are called **environmental classism** and environmental racism. Another inequity is that the poor will have to pay disproportionately for efforts to eliminate pollution. That is, their jobs may be eliminated, their neighborhoods abandoned, and a greater proportion of their taxes required (through regressive taxes) to pay for environmental cleanups.

The bitter irony of the poor having to sacrifice the most to abate environmental problems is that it is the affluent who drive excessively, travel in jet planes, have large air-conditioned homes, consume large quantities of resources (conspicuous consumption), and have the most waste to dispose. Their demand increases economic demand and, concomitantly, industrial pollution.

This system of stratification also extends globally to the differences between countries, with the world's poorest people having the lowest carbon footprint, but suffering the most from climate change.

In summary, environmental problems in the United States stem from both cultural and structural sources. Thus, any proposed environmental solutions must take into account a multitude of factors.

SOLUTIONS TO THE ENVIRONMENTAL CRISES

4.3 Describe the long-range international implications of and alternative solutions to threats to the environment.

What can be done to change some of our most pressing environmental problems? In the 1970s, the public began to demand that something be done to address the fact that big cars, big cities, and big factories were harming our environment (Ruckelshaus 2010). As a result, on April 22, 1970, we celebrated the first Earth Day, and President Nixon created the Environmental Protection Agency to pass laws to clean up the air and water. Considerable progress has been made due to these early laws; however, some of the changes we face now require more than laws but a change in the public's mentality, a sense of responsibility for the entire planet (Ruckelshaus 2010).

Individual/Local Solutions

The needs of the group, community, society, and even the world must take precedence over those of the individual. The values people in the United States hold dear—such as growth and progress, capitalism, individualism, and the conquest of nature—will no longer be salient in a world of less space, endangered ecology, energy shortages, water shortages, and hunger. On an individual level, families can engage in behaviors such as recycling, composting, water-harvesting, reduction in energy use, and limiting their dependence on automobiles by choosing public transit (if available). While these individual actions are necessary and important, they are one small step in a much larger social problem. According to writer Joel Bleifuss, what is needed is a political movement that challenges the status quo by mobilizing large groups to use the ballot box to elect leaders who will change laws (2007). Thus we turn to broader societal-level solutions.

Societal-Level Solutions

At the societal level, the government must continue to enact comprehensive laws carrying severe criminal and civil penalties for harming the environment. At the corporate level, it means rigorous inspections of companies and prosecution of violators. Moreover, if penalized, these companies must not be allowed to pass the fines on to consumers through higher prices.

One obstacle to a comprehensive plan to curb pollution is our federal system of government, in which states and communities are free to set their own standards. In principle, this system makes sense because the people in an area should be the most knowledgeable about their situation. However, mining operations along Lake Superior cannot be allowed to dump tailings in the lake on the rationale that having to pay for recycling would reduce local employment levels. Similarly, air pollution is never limited to one locality; wind currents carry the pollutants beyond local borders and add to the cumulative effect on an entire region. Therefore, it seems imperative that the federal government establishes and enforces minimum standards for the entire country.

A rational plan to conserve energy, for example, could include government insistence on universal daylight saving time (it could even be extended to a two-hour difference, rather than one); strict enforcement of a relatively low speed limit (the 55 mph speed limit in 1983 saved an estimated 2.5 billion gallons of gasoline and diesel fuel [Mouawad and Romero 2005]); the use of governors on automobiles and thermostats; banning neon signs and other energy used in advertising; minimal use of outdoor lighting; and a reversal of the current policy that reduces rates for electricity and natural gas as the volume increases. For example, in 2011, President Obama set new fuel efficiency standards for 2017–2025 model cars and trucks. The new standard requires all new models to reach 54.5 miles per gallon, saving consumers money, reducing greenhouse gas pollution, and reducing America's need for oil.

Conserving energy will require not only individual alterations of lifestyles but also changes in the economic system. Under the current private enterprise system based on profits, corporations seek the profitable alternative rather than the conserving one. In the search for greater profits, we have shifted from railroads and mass transit (the most energy-efficient means of moving people and freight on land) to energy-inefficient cars, trucks, and planes. On the positive side, some U.S. city governments and planners have started to rethink how communities can be changed from communities based on urban sprawl and car dependence to connected, walkable, bikable, public-transit centered sustainable communities (see the "Looking Toward the Future" panel on transit-oriented development).

Some U.S. corporations are also leading the way in promoting conservation efforts. Thanks to "green" ideology becoming mainstream in the media (Davis Guggenheim's documentary of Al Gore's *An Inconvenient Truth* won an Academy Award and was one of the highest grossing documentaries of all time), numerous companies are making a concentrated effort to "go green." In 2011 *Newsweek* magazine ranked the 500 largest U.S. companies based on their environmental impact, their green policies, and

Looking Toward the Future

TRANSIT-ORIENTED DEVELOPMENT

In the last few years rising transportation costs, long commutes, congested roadways, and increasing pollution have led to a growing demand for public transportation options and cleaner, more walkable communities (Smith and Anderson 2010). In cities across the country there has been an unprecedented effort toward transit-oriented development to support this growing demand. Transit-oriented development (TOD) is defined as compact/dense development within walking distance (~1/2 mile) of public transportation. This development contains a mix of uses: housing types, jobs, shops, restaurants, and entertainment. The goal of transit-oriented development is walkable, sustainable communities for all ages and income levels. Some of the benefits of transit-oriented development include:

- Efficient use of land, energy, and resources
- Lower transportation costs for families
- Reduced dependence on foreign oil
- Less pollution
- Less traffic congestion
- Fewer car accidents
- Increased activity levels: walking/biking
- Increased property values
- Increased customers for local businesses
- Less crime: more "eyes on the streets"

As gas prices reach $4.00 per gallon, the demand for TOD accelerates. According to the Center for Neighborhood Technology (2012) less than one in three American communities (28 percent) is affordable for typical regional households when transportation costs are considered along with housing costs ("affordable" means that housing and transportation costs consume no more than 45 percent of income). The statistics are increasingly difficult to ignore: On average, households in auto-dependent neighborhoods spend 25 percent of their income on transportation, whereas households in walkable neighborhoods with good transit access and a mix of housing, jobs, and shops spend just 9 percent (Center for Transit-Oriented Development 2009).

their reputation among their peers and environmental experts. IBM earned the title of the "greenest company in America" thanks to its progressive environmental policies.

Can the United States continue to operate on an economic system that allows decisions about what to produce and how to produce it to be governed by profit rather than the common good? The heart of the capitalists' argument, going back to Adam Smith more than 200 years ago, is that decisions made on the basis of the entrepreneur's self-interest will also accomplish the needs of society most efficiently. This fundamental precept of capitalism is now challenged by the environmental crisis, the energy crisis, and the problems related to them. Can capitalism be amended to incorporate central planning regarding societal needs of a safe environment and plentiful resources? Perhaps it can. In the case of Hewlett-Packard, the company's recycling program has allowed HP to reclaim 1.7 billion pounds of e-waste over the past decade, including gold and copper, which it resells. In addition, reducing packaging material has paid off in reduced shipping costs (McGinn 2009). This shows that going green can result in company benefits.

Global-Level Solutions

Environmental problems are not confined within political borders. The world's inhabitants share the oceans, rivers, lakes, and air. If a corporation or a nation pollutes, the world's citizens are the victims. If the tropical forests are destroyed, we are all affected. If a country wastes finite resources or uses more than its proportionate share, the other nations are short-changed.

What should the nations of the world do about environmental crises? In 2011 world leaders met in Durban, South Africa, for the United Nations Climate Change Conference (called COP 17). The leaders meet annually to discuss reduction in their greenhouse gas emissions and efforts to hold the increase in global temperature below 2 degrees Celsius. For the first time, world governments committed to write a legally binding international treaty to reduce greenhouse gas emissions. The treaty will cover both developed and undeveloped countries and be in place in 2020. Government leaders will now begin the process of deciding what that treaty will look like and hope to have a document ready to sign by 2015.

The dangers posed by the future require solutions at many levels. At the physical level, global efforts must be directed to finding new sources of energy (e.g., fuel cells, solar, wind, biomass), methods to increase the amount of arable land, new types of food, better contraceptives, and relatively inexpensive ways to desalt seawater. At the social level, there must be changes in the structural conditions responsible for poverty, wasted resources, pollution, and the like. One such target would be to determine ways of overcoming the cultural habits (customs, values, beliefs) that reinforce high fertility, people's refusal to eat certain foods or to accept central planning, and the dependence on growth and technology. New forms of social organization, such as regional councils and world bodies, may be required to deal with social upheavals, economic dislocations, resource allocation, and pollution on a global scale. These new organizations will require great innovative thinking, for it is likely that the dominant modes of the present age not only are unworkable for the demands of an overpopulated planet but also are in large measure responsible for many of our present and future difficulties.

⊙ Watch on MySocLab Video: Looking Ahead: Toward a Sustainable Society and World

MySocLab ✓ Study and Review on MySocLab

■ CHAPTER REVIEW

1. Three social forces disturb Earth's biosphere profoundly: population growth, the overconsumption of energy and raw materials by rich countries, and global economic growth.
2. Although population growth (which occurs mostly in the developing countries) has adverse effects on the environment, the populations of rich countries are much more wasteful of Earth's resources and generate much more pollution.
3. The earth is losing productive land through degradation, erosion, and the growth of cities and urban sprawl.
4. Two major environmental consequences of deforestation are climate change and the vanishing of species.
5. Chemicals, solid waste disposal, and radiation pollute the land, water, and air.
6. The United States is the greatest consumer of oil products and produces more carbon dioxide per person than any other country.
7. The earth has warmed by 2 degrees Fahrenheit in the last century.
8. The cultural bases of the wasteful and environmentally destructive U.S. society are the dominant ideologies of (a) the cornucopia view of nature, (b) faith in technology, (c) the growth ethic, (d) materialism, and (e) the belief in individualism.
9. The structural bases for the misuse and abuse of the U.S. environment and resources are (a) the capitalist economy, (b) polity, (c) demographic patterns, and (d) the system of stratification.
10. Solutions to the environmental crisis must start with the individual, but progress into an energized political movement.

11. The government must play an active role and enact laws carrying criminal and civil penalties for harming the environment.
12. Some corporations are leading the way through progressive environmental policies.
13. At the latest United Nations Climate Change Conference, world leaders committed to writing an international treaty to reduce greenhouse gas emissions.
14. The dangers posed by these critical environmental problems require solutions at many levels: (a) at the physical level, we need discoveries and inventions of nonpolluting technologies and renewable resources; and (b) at the social level, we need changes in the structural conditions responsible for these problems and the creation of new forms of transnational social organizations.

■ KEY TERMS

Biosphere. The surface layer of the planet and the surrounding atmosphere.

Ecosystems. The mechanisms (plants, animals, and microorganisms) that supply people with the essentials of life.

Environmental justice. A movement to improve community environments by eliminating toxic hazards.

Environmental racism. The overwhelming likelihood that toxic-producing plants and toxic waste dumps are located where poor people, especially people of color, live.

Greenhouse effect. When gases accumulate in Earth's atmosphere and act like the glass roof of a greenhouse, allowing sunlight in but trapping the heat that is generated.

Culture. The knowledge (ideas, values, beliefs) that the members of a social organization share.

Planned obsolescence. The manufacture of consumer goods designed to wear out. Or existing products are given superficial changes and marketed as new, making the previous products outdated.

Environmental classism. The poor, because of dangerous jobs and residential segregation, are more exposed than the more well-to-do to environmental dangers.

Demographic Changes in the United States: The Browning and Graying of Society

((• Listen to Chapter 5 on **MySocLab**

LEARNING OBJECTIVES

5.1 Assess the historical settlement patterns that have occurred in the U.S.

5.2 Explain the facts versus myths of the changing racial landscape in America.

5.3 Explain the facts versus myths of the "graying of America."

5.4 Assess the potential consequences of the "graying of America."

5.5 Discuss how the elderly might cope with or respond to their devalued status in society.

Demography is the scientific study of a population—its current size, distribution, and composition as well as changes over time. That is the focus of this chapter, especially the two population shifts that are transforming U.S. society—one with external sources and the other internal. The first is the "new immigration." The racial landscape and rate of population growth are greatly affected as approximately 1 million immigrants annually, mostly Latino and Asian, set up permanent residence in the United States. The second population change is internal—the age of the population is rising rapidly. Both of these demographic transitions have profound implications for social problems, creating some and exacerbating others. The facts, myths, and consequences of these two demographic changes are the subjects of this chapter. We begin, though, with a brief demographic overview of the United States.

5.1 Assess the historical settlement patterns that have occurred in the U.S.

Watch on MySocLab Video: Demography: The Study of Population

PROFILE OF THE U.S. POPULATION

At the beginning of 2012, the population of the United States was approximately 313,000,000, the third highest in the world (behind China at 1.34 billion and India at 1.21 billion, and above Indonesia and Brazil). Unlike other developed nations, the population of United States continues to increase (at a rate of 1 percent per year) primarily because of the large influx of immigrants. The U.S. Census Bureau projects that the United States will have a population of 439 million by 2050 (Population Reference Bureau 2009). Following are some additional facts:

- In 2009, the average life expectancy at birth was 78 years (75.65 for males and 80.69 for females).
- Over four-fifths (83.7 percent) of Americans live in cities. Nine cities exceed 1 million residents: New York, Los Angeles, Chicago, Houston, Philadelphia, Phoenix, San Antonio, San Diego, and Dallas.
- The total fertility rate (the number of children a woman bears in her childbearing years) is 2.1, exactly at the replacement rate. This rate varies by race/ethnicity: Whites (1.8), Asian Americans (1.9), African Americans (1.9), and Latinos (2.9).
- One out of eight (12.9 percent) in the U.S. population is foreign born.
- The baby boom generation, roughly 76 million Americans born between 1946 and 1964, is the largest generation in U.S. history (at the crest of the boom, the total fertility rate was 3.8 children per woman). In 2011 they were 41 to 65 years old, and as they have done from the beginning, they are having an enormous impact on U.S. society. In 2011 the leading edge of the baby boomers was 65, adding, and for the next twenty years, an average of 10,000 additional people eligible for Medicare *each day*.
- Non-Whites are the majority in four states—California, Texas, New Mexico, and Hawaii—and the District of Columbia.
- Non-Whites make up about 37 percent of the U.S. population, compared to 20 percent in 1980.
- In 2011, for the first time, more than half (50.4 percent) of children younger than 1 were non-Whites.
- The number of Latinos in the United States is greater than the population of Canada.
- Google, Sun Microsystems, eBay, and Yahoo! are all companies founded or cofounded by immigrants.
- The boundary between Mexico and the United States has become perhaps the most militarized frontier between two nations at peace anywhere in the world (Massey 2006:2).

- There are approximately 6 million Muslims and 1.1 million Hindus in the United States.
- One in five householders is age 65 or older.

5.2 Explain the facts versus myths of the changing racial landscape in America.

NEW IMMIGRATION AND THE CHANGING RACIAL LANDSCAPE

Immigration, the permanent movement of people across political boundaries is shaking up society (parts of this chapter are taken from Eitzen, Baca Zinn, and Smith 2013, Chapter 8, and Baca Zinn, Eitzen, and Wells 2014, Chapter 5). The contemporary manifestation of this demographic force—the new immigration—is challenging the cultural hegemony of the White European tradition, creating incredible diversity in race, ethnicity, language, and culture; rapidly changing the racial landscape; and leading, often, to division and hostility.

Historically, immigration has been a major source of population growth and ethnic diversity in the United States. Immigration waves from northern and southern Europe, especially from 1850 to 1920, brought many millions of people, mostly Europeans, to America. In the 1920s the United States placed limits on the number of immigrants it would accept, the operating principle being that the new immigrants should resemble the old ones. The "national origins" rules were designed to limit severely the immigration of Eastern Europeans and to deny the entry of Asians.

The Immigration Act amendments of 1965 abandoned the quota system that had preserved the European character of the United States for nearly half a century. The new law encouraged a new wave of immigrants, only this time the migrants arrived not from northern Europe but from the Third World, especially Asia and Latin America. Put another way, 100 years ago Europeans were 90 percent of immigrants to the United States; now 90 percent of immigrants are from non-European countries. The result, obviously, is a dramatic alteration of the ethnic composition of the U.S. population. And the size of the contemporary immigrant wave has resulted in a visible and significant number of U.S. residents who are foreign born—40.0 million in 2010 (12.9 percent of the total population, up from 8 percent in 1990). (See Figure 5.1.) About 1 million immigrants enter the United States legally each year. Another 2.5 million people enter the United States illegally each year, but many return to their native countries either voluntarily or by force if caught by the Immigration and Naturalization Service. (See the "Social Policy" panel.) Although the number that enters clandestinely is impossible to determine, the Pew Hispanic Center estimated the unauthorized immigrant population at about 11.2 in March 2010 (down from 12 million in 2007) (Passel and Cohn 2011). Roughly 80 percent of these undocumented immigrants are Latino (and two-thirds of them are Mexicans).

Most unauthorized immigrants enter the United States by crossing the border with Mexico. The United States vigorously tries to stop illegal crossings of the Mexican border by the use of 17,000 Border Patrol agents who patrol in vehicles, on horses, and in boats, helicopters, and planes. Also, advanced technology such as reconnaissance drones, and seismic, magnetic, and infra-red sensors are employed to stem the flow of illegal immigration. Moreover, a third of the border has been fenced at great expense.

After a high of more than 1.6 million arrests of unauthorized immigrants in 2000, the number in 2011 was below 350,000 (*Economist* 2011). This significant drop in patrol arrests is because of heightened border control efforts, but just as important is the very slow U.S. economy and high unemployment, making jobs more uncertain and the diminished rewards not worth the risks for potential illegal immigrants (Jordan 2011).

View on MySocLab Figure: Projections of the Racial-Ethnic Makeup of the U.S. Population

View on MySocLab Figure: Countries of Origin of Unauthorized Immigrants to the United States

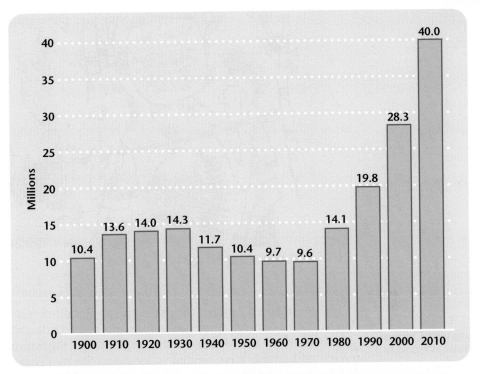

FIGURE 5.1

Foreign-Born Population:
1900–2010 (millions)

Source: U.S. Bureau of the Census.

Social Policy

THE UNINTENDED CONSEQUENCES OF RIGID POLICING OF THE BORDER

The U.S.–Mexican border is 1,989 miles in length. U.S. policy has been to increase the policing of this border, apprehending those who crossed illegally and sending them back to Mexico. Now Congress has authorized the building of a fence along this border. The cost to build and maintain this fence is an estimated $49 billion over the expected twenty-five-year life span of the fence.

Until the 1990s the border was patrolled but passage was relatively easy. In the early 1980s there were about 2,500 Border Patrol officers; now there are 12,000. The agency's annual budget has risen accordingly. The Border Patrol, in the last decade, has directed its efforts especially to areas where border

crossings were the easiest (around San Diego, California, and El Paso, Texas). As a result, the likelihood of successfully crossing the border has decreased dramatically. The Border Patrol has stopped millions of people from entering the United States illegally. These arrests are filmed and shown to the public, promoting ever-greater fears about the waves of Mexican workers flooding into the United States.

The increased emphasis on sealing the border has had two unintended consequences. First, it shifted the crossing routes to more remote but more dangerous areas. Using alternative routes has tripled the cost of getting across the border illegally and resulted in many people dying of thirst and exposure in

long foot marches across the desert. Second, and related to the first, those successful in crossing now tend to stay in the United States rather than move back and forth between the two countries.

In the past, many undocumented workers came to the United States, usually without their families, to follow the harvest or do other jobs for brief periods, and then returned to their families in Mexico. Now, with better policing, the migrants know that if they go back to Mexico, the odds are greater that they will not be able to return. This "seawall effect" keeps them here, and for that reason, they now arrive with their families and tend to stay. In other words, the increased militancy by the Border Patrol has had the effect of building a "wall" that, rather than keeping migrants out, actually keeps them in.

Mike Keefe/CAGLE CARTOONS

 Explore on
MySocLab Activity:
Demographic Changes:
Fifty Years in Brooklyn

The settlement patterns of this new migration differ from previous flows into the United States. Whereas previous immigrants settled primarily in the industrial states of the Northeast and Middle Atlantic regions or in the farming areas of the Midwest, recent immigrants have tended to locate on the two coasts and in the Southwest. Asians have tended to settle on the West Coast; Mexicans, although predominantly in the Southwest, are also scattered across the country, from urban Chicago to rural Kansas, as are other Latinos (e.g., Cubans in Florida and Puerto Ricans and Dominicans in New York).*

California is a harbinger of the demographic future of the United States. As recently as 1970, California was 80 percent White, but since then, it has been uniquely affected by immigration. The result is that Whites in California now are a numerical minority: In 2010 there were 14 million Latinos, 4.8 million Asians, and 15 million Whites. Latino children for the first time were a majority of California's under age 18 population.

Los Angeles has the largest population of Koreans outside Korea, the biggest concentration of Iranians in the Western world, and a huge Mexican population. The diverse population of southern California speaks 88 languages and dialects. One-fourth of California's schoolchildren are studying English as a foreign language. Greater Los Angeles has more than fifty foreign-language newspapers and television shows that broadcast in Spanish, Mandarin, Armenian, Japanese, Korean, and Vietnamese. For example, in one ZIP code—90706—lies Bellflower, where thirty-eight languages are spoken (Mohan and Simmons 2004).

For all this diversity, though, California, especially southern California, is becoming more and more Latino. California holds nearly half the U.S. Latino population and well over half the Mexican-origin population. Latinos are expected to surpass Whites in total California population by 2025. Similar concentrations of Latinos are found in Arizona and Texas. Historian David Kennedy argues that there is no precedent in U.S.

*Note well that there is a wide diversity among immigrant groups. For example, although there are over 3 million Latinos living in Florida, they come from several ethnic backgrounds: Cubans, Puerto Ricans, South Americans, Central Americans, Mexicans, and Dominicans.

history of one immigrant group having the size and concentration that the Mexican immigrant group has in the Southwest today (Kennedy 1996:68).

Immigration and Increasing Diversity

The United States is shifting from an Anglo-White society rooted in Western culture to a society with three large racial/ethnic minorities, each of them growing in size while the proportion of Whites declines. Five facts show the contours and magnitude of this demographic transformation.

- The non-White population is numerically significant, comprising more than one-third of the population (up from 15 percent in 1960). Four states have non-White majorities (California, Texas, New Mexico, and Hawaii). Minorities make up the majority in six of the nine U.S. cities with more than a million people—New York, Los Angeles, Chicago, Houston, Detroit, and Dallas.
- Racial minorities are increasing faster than the majority population. Although non-Whites are now more than one-third of the population, they account for half of all births nationally, and Whites are a minority of Americans age 3 and under. In eight states and the District of Columbia, minorities are the majority of students in pre-K and kindergarten (Meyerson 2011). Thus, by 2023 a majority of children (under 18) will be from a minority background (U.S. Census estimate, reported in Yen 2009); they will surpass Whites among working-age Americans by 2039, and by 2042 non-White minorities will exceed the White population in size (Roberts 2008).
- African Americans have lost their position as the most numerous racial minority. In 1990, for the first time, African Americans were less than half of all minorities. By 2000 Latinos outnumbered African Americans 42.7 million to 39.7 million. By 2010 Latinos outnumbered African Americans 50.4 to 37.7 million. By 2050 Latinos will comprise a projected 29 percent of the U.S. population, with African Americans at about 13 percent. This demographic transformation will make two common assumptions about race obsolete: that "race" is a "Black-and-White" issue, and that the United States is a "White" society.
- Immigration accounts for a large share (40 percent since 2000) of the nation's population growth. Today 12.9 percent of current U.S. residents are foreign born. The U.S. Census Bureau estimates that Latinos and Asians are growing more than ten times the pace of Whites (reported in El Nasser and Grant 2005). Immigration accounts for over a third of the current population growth directly and adds more indirectly, as first- (those foreign born) and second-generation (children of the foreign born) Americans have more children on average than the rest of the population.
- New patterns of immigration are changing the racial composition of society. Among the expanded population of first-generation immigrants, the Asian born now outnumber the European born, and those from Latin America, especially Mexicans, outnumber both. This contrasts sharply with what occurred as recently as the 1950s, when two-thirds of legal immigrants were from Europe and Canada. These trends signal a transformation from a White majority to a multiracial/multicultural society with the projected year of 2042 when Whites will become a "minority."

The pace of these changes is quickening. During the first decade of the twenty-first century, while the White population increased by 1.2 percent, the African American population rose by 11 percent, the Native American numbers increased by 15 percent, the Asians and Latino populations each increased by 43 percent.

Consequences of the New Immigration

The new immigration raises a number of questions. We consider three: (1) Do immigrants take jobs away from Americans? (2) Are immigrants a drain on society's resources? (3) Will the increasing proportion of non-Whites, fueled by immigration, lead to a blurring of racial lines or a heightening of tensions among the racial/ethnic groups?

- **Do Immigrants Take Jobs from U.S. Citizens?**   Recent immigrants from Mexico can earn five times the wage rate in the United States that they can earn in Mexico. This is the lure. Because most do not speak English and their skills are limited, they tend to work at low-wage occupations, such as gardeners, roofers, assemblers, custodians, restaurant help, maids, and migrant farm workers. The evidence is that immigrants do not have negative effects on the wages of most Americans, but they do on the low-wage/poorly skilled/poorly educated segment of workers. Harvard economist George J. Borjas, a long-time researcher of immigration, says that "the primary losers in this country are workers who do not have high school diplomas, particularly Blacks and native-born Hispanics" (cited in Henderson 2006).

    The wages of the lowest 15 percent of the workforce (typically, those with less than a high school degree) receive about 5 percent less in their paychecks because of competition from a large number of immigrants who are relatively uneducated, unskilled, and eager to work. See the "A Closer Look" panel for some positive benefits from undocumented workers.

A Closer Look

SOME SOCIETAL BENEFITS FROM UNDOCUMENTED WORKERS

The presence of 11 million illegal immigrants is a contentious issue in the United States. Most folks assume that these workers have negative consequences for society. Although there are some negative costs from undocumented workers (e.g., some native borns are hurt by the competition from illegal immigrants who are willing to work cheaply, the cost of educating their children, and the cost of emergency room care for uninsured migrants), they also bring major benefits to the overall economy (Streitland 2006).

- If there were no undocumented workers, a variety of industries would be disrupted. Employers in construction, hospitality, childcare, factories, food preparation, building maintenance, landscaping, and agriculture would have to attract new workers with higher wages. Wages for undereducated workers, retail prices at restaurants, and costs of food, housing, and many other goods and services would soar.
- Most undocumented immigrants contribute to Social Security but do not receive benefits, either because they used false papers to get payroll jobs or they returned to their native country.
- As society ages, there will be a continuous need for more workers, especially service workers. The Department of Labor estimates that in the next decade we will need 7.7 million more workers. Much of this demand will be for unskilled labor that has been met by undocumented workers (Zuckerman 2006).
- The 11 million undocumented immigrants are consumers, and although their household income is relatively low, collectively, they have considerable buying power. They pay rent, buy groceries and clothing, and take out loans for furniture, automobiles, and houses (Grow 2005). The estimated annual gross income of all U.S. workers born in Latin America, of both legal and illegal immigration status, was $450 billion in 2004. Approximately 93 percent of that amount is spent in the United States (from the Inter-American Development Bank, reported in Thornburgh 2006).

Mick Stevens/The New Yorker Collection/www.cartoonbank.com

Watch on
MySocLab Slideshow:
Immigrant Highway

This problem will increase in the future as the federal and state governments no longer provide welfare benefits to legal immigrants and most nonimmigrant welfare recipients are required to leave welfare and find work, adding several million workers to compete for relatively few jobs at the low end of the occupational scale.

Immigration is only partly responsible for this relationship between somewhat lower wages and undereducated workers. Also pushing wages lower are the shrinking manufacturing sector, the decline in union membership, the outsourcing of jobs, and the Great Recession, which has especially brought high unemployment to the construction industry, where so many new immigrants work (these are discussed in Chapter 14).

On the positive side, immigrants are more likely than the rest of the population to be self-employed and to start their own businesses, which in turn creates jobs and adds strength to local economies. Moreover, between 1990 and 2005 immigrants started one-fourth of all venture-backed public companies (Kotkin 2010).

Immigration stimulates economic growth in at least two additional ways. First, the immigrants buy products and services. Second, to the extent that cheap, low-skilled labor helps hold down prices, there is more demand for some services, leading to more economic growth and jobs. Cheaper labor by immigrants in restaurants encourages more consumers to dine more. Lower construction costs makes homes and home remodeling less expensive (Henderson 2006).

There is also a long-term gain from immigration. U.S. society, like much of the Western Europe is getting older (see the second half of this chapter). The birth rate is sinking and life spans are longer resulting soon in a population that is too old to work and pay its bills (Tucker 2010). Immigrants, who are usually young with growing families, will supply the needed demographic balance for a vibrant economy.

- **Are Immigrants a Drain on Society's Resources?** Immigrants pay a variety of taxes: income taxes, Social Security and Medicare taxes, and sales taxes. One study estimated that they pay $162 billion annually in federal, state, and local taxes (reported in West 2010). In the short run, however, immigrants consume more in public services and benefits than they pay in taxes. There are two reasons immigrants require more resources from the state than do nonimmigrant families. First, they have relatively large families, and these children go to public schools. Second, they pay less in taxes because they tend to earn low wages and have relatively little discretionary income.

In the long run, however, immigrants are a good investment for society. The Academy of Sciences study (Cassidy 1997) found that by the time a typical immigrant with a family dies, that immigrant and his or her children will have paid $80,000 more in taxes than they received in government benefits. The evidence is that immigrants are a fiscal burden for two decades or so, mainly because of educational costs. After that, the society benefits monetarily.

This conclusion fits at the national level: That is, most taxes paid by immigrants and income taxes withheld by the federal government are used in part to provide Social Security and healthcare benefits to the elderly. However, the state and local taxes paid by immigrants are relatively low, yet the services they consume (in particular, education) are disproportionately funded by state and local taxes. Immigration is a national problem, but one borne by the states. This unbalance is a source of growing hostility as evidenced by the anti-immigrant legislation in 2010 passed by the Arizona legislature.

Read on MySocLab Document: Mexican Americans and Immigrant Incorporation

There is also a global dimension to the economic benefits derived from immigrants. Most undocumented immigrants (i.e., those who entered the country illegally) are young, male, and Mexican. They leave their families in Mexico and work for months at a time as manual laborers in the United States. Typically, they send some of their earnings back to their families in Mexico—an aggregate $25 billion annually, according to the World Bank. As a source of foreign capital to Mexico, migrant remittances trail only oil, tourism, and illegal drugs.

- **Will the Increasing Proportion of Non-Whites Fueled by Immigration Lead to a Blurring of Racial Lines or a Heightening of Tensions among the Racial/Ethnic Groups?** The latest wave of immigration has taken place in a historical context that includes the restructuring of the U.S. economy (see Chapter 14) and an increasingly conservative political climate. New immigrants have always been seen as a threat to those already in place. The typical belief is that immigrants, because they will work for lower wages, drive down wages and take jobs away from those already settled here. These fears increase during economic hard times, when businesses downsize or when they outsource jobs, pay lower wages, and replace workers with technology as they adapt to the economic transformation. The hostility toward immigrants is also the result of the common belief that the new immigrants increase taxes because they require services (education, healthcare, and welfare) that cost much more than the taxes they produce.

Previous immigration waves were White, coming mostly from Ireland, England, Germany, Italy, and Eastern Europe. Today's immigrants, in sharp contrast, are coming from Latin America and Asia. They are non-White and have distinctly non-European cultures. When these racial and ethnic differences are added to economic fears, the mix is very volatile.

The situation is worsened further by where the new immigrants locate. Typically, they move where immigrants like themselves are already established. For example, 20 percent of the 90,000 Hmong in the United States live in Minnesota, mostly around Minneapolis–St. Paul. One in twelve Asian Indians lives in Illinois, primarily in the Chicago area. Approximately 40 percent of all Asian Americans live in California. This tendency of migrants to cluster geographically by race/ethnicity provides them with a network of friends and relatives who provide them with support. This pattern of clustering in certain areas also tends to increase the fear of nonimmigrants toward them. They fear that wages will be depressed and taxes will be greater because their new neighbors are relatively poor, tend to have children with special needs in school, and likely do not have health insurance.

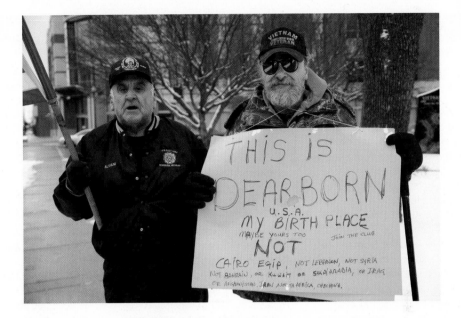

Some are angry with immigrants who they feel take their jobs and use state resources for their education and healthcare.

A second tendency is for new immigrants to locate where other poor people live for the obvious advantage of cheaper housing. A problem often arises when poor Whites live side by side with one or more racial minorities. Despite their common condition, tensions in such situations are heightened as groups disadvantaged by society often fight each other for relative advantage. The tensions between African Americans and Asian immigrants were evidenced, for example, during the South Los Angeles riots in 1992, when roughly 2,000 Korean-owned businesses were looted or damaged by fire.

The result of these factors is commonly an anti-immigrant backlash. Opinion polls taken over the past fifty years report consistently that Americans want to reduce immigration. Typically, these polls report that Americans believe that immigration in the past was a good thing for the country but that it no longer is.

The states with the most immigrants have the highest levels of anti-immigrant feeling. Several states have filed suit against the federal government, seeking reimbursement for the services provided to immigrants. Some twenty-two states have made English the official state language. Some states such as Arizona and Alabama have enacted laws that are punitive to recent emigrants (see the "Social Policy" panel). At the federal level, Congress passed a bill in late 2006 that authorized fencing a third of the 2,100-mile border between the United States and Mexico.

If present immigration patterns continue, by 2042 some one-third of the U.S. population will be post-1970 immigrants and their descendants and non-Whites will outnumber Whites. Under these circumstances of racial diversity, will the social meaning of ethnic and racial lines become increasingly blurred or more starkly defined? Will the people be pulling together or pulling apart? Will the gulf between affluent Whites and the disproportionately poor non-Whites be narrowed or widened? Will there be a de facto segregation as Whites who once lived and worked together with non-Whites move to White enclaves? Demographer William Frey has noted a "White flight" from high-immigration areas, a trend he fears may lead to the Balkanization of America (cited in Cassidy 1997:43). Is this our future?

Anti-immigration activists are becoming more numerous and vocal. The Southern Poverty Law Center says that tension over illegal immigration is contributing to a rise in hate groups and hate crimes across the nation. White supremacy groups are

Social Policy

ALABAMA'S IMMIGRATION LAW AND ITS CONSEQUENCES

Immigration policy concerning what to do about unauthorized immigrants is a hot-button political issue. It divides those who want to deport these migrants from those who want to resolve the problem by finding ways for them to gain work here legally. At the state level, six states—Arizona, Utah, Indiana, Alabama, Georgia, and South Carolina—had anti-immigrant laws that promoted racial profiling and discrimination and harassment of immigrants (*SPLC Report* 2012). Let's consider the Alabama law, which embodies the harshest provisions: (1) All residents of Alabama are required to show their legal papers for virtually every transaction with a state entity (e.g., to receive government-run municipal services such as water, get a construction permit, or check a book out of the library); (2) law enforcement officers are required to check the papers of residents that they think are undocumented, thus allowing officers to stop automobiles, question shoppers, and the like; (3) it is a crime for a lawyer to refuse to divulge information about his or her client to government immigration officials,

thus eliminating the attorney-client privilege; and (4) public schools are required to check the status of their students. A federal judge upheld the law in October 2011.

Consequences

The intent of Alabama's Immigration Law was to discourage unauthorized immigrants from moving into the state, and if there, to encourage them to leave. The law was successful in this regard as Latinos left the state in droves. Their leaving has some dire consequences for the state. The Center for American Progress estimates that for every 10,000 undocumented immigrants that stop working in the state, Alabama's economy will shrink by $40 million (reported in *Huffington Post* 2011). The state also takes an economic hit with the costs to implement and enforce the law. Moreover, Alabama will lose hundreds of millions in tax revenue. A report by the Center for Business and Economic Research at the University of Alabama argues that the new law would cause 70,000 to 140,000 undocumented

workers to lose jobs and would cost between $1.2 billion to $5.8 billion in the earnings of those immigrants as well as $56.7 million to $264.5 million in lost state income taxes and sales taxes (reported in *Fox News Latino* 2012). Those business activities that rely heavily on undocumented workers such as farming and construction lose revenues when their business slows, which also decreases state tax revenues, as well as harming small businesses.

Most important, this law (and similar ones from other states) is designed to intimidate vulnerable populations—most notably Latinos (Rosenthal 2011). It is another effort to oppress minority groups, an effort with a long history in Southern states. The Human Rights Watch Report argues that Alabama's law is grounded in discrimination, fosters a culture of fear, and denies basic rights to undocumented residents (reported in Hayes 2011). The U.S. Department of Justice has sued Alabama over this legislation. Alabama's attorney general has responded by arguing that the federal government has no legal right to infringe on a state's immigration policies. What do you think?

growing. Vigilante groups have organized to watch the borders. What brings the anti-immigration activists together is a generalized belief that their way of life is threatened by these newly arrived races/ethnicities.

Immigration and Agency

Immigration can be forced (e.g., the slave trade) or freely chosen. Immigration in this latter sense is clearly an act of **human agency** (rather than passively accepting structural constraints, people cope with, adapt to, and change their social situations to meet their needs). Most people in developing countries do not move. Others move, breaking with their extended family and leaving neighborhood and community ties, mostly to improve their economic situations or to flee repression.

Typically, new immigrants face hostility from their hosts, who, as we have seen, fear them as competitors or hate them because they are "different" or because they fear that they may be terrorists. In this latter instance, immigrants from Muslim countries have had to confront considerable hostility and suspicion since the terrorist acts of September 11, 2001. Recent immigrants also face language barriers as they seek jobs. Often, most especially for undocumented immigrants, their initial jobs are demeaning, poorly paid, and without benefits. How do they adapt to these often very difficult circumstances? Most commonly, immigrants move to a destination area where there is already a network of friends and relatives. These networks connect new immigrants with housing (often doubling up in very crowded but inexpensive conditions), jobs, and an informal welfare system (healthcare, pooling resources in difficult times). These mutual-aid efforts by immigrant communities have been used by immigrant networks throughout U.S. history, whether by Swedish settlers in Minnesota, Mennonite settlers in Kansas, Irish settlers in Boston, or Mexican or Vietnamese settlers now (Martin and Midgley 1999).

Watch on
MySocLab Video:
Latino Laborers

To overcome low wages, all able family members may work in the family enterprise or at different jobs and combine family resources. To overcome various manifestations of hostility by others, the immigrant community may become closer (the pejorative word is "clannish"), having as little interaction with outsiders as possible. Some may become involved in gangs for protection. Still others may move to assimilate as quickly as possible.

Effects of Immigration on Immigrants: Ethnic Identity or Assimilation?

Assimilation is the process by which individuals or groups adopt the culture of another group, losing their original identity. A principal indicator of assimilation is language. In 2000 slightly less than one in five Americans age 5 and older spoke a language other than English at home. Assuming the experience of earlier immigrants to the United States, it is likely that the shift to English usage will take three generations—from almost exclusive use by newcomers of their traditional language, to their children being bilingual, to their children's children (third-generation immigrants) being monolingual English speakers (Martin and Midgley 1999). According to the Pew Hispanic Center, in 2007, for example, 23 percent of adult first-generation Latinos said they could carry on a conversation very well in English, compared to 88 percent in the second generation and 94 percent in the third (reported in Gorman 2007).

If the past is a guide, the new immigrants will assimilate. But conditions now are different. An argument countering the assumption that the new immigrants will assimilate as did previous generations of immigrants is that the new immigrants are members of racial/ethnic groups, not Whites. The early waves of immigrants (post-1965) were mostly White Europeans. Over time these groups were absorbed into the "melting pot" of society's mainstream because jobs were relatively plentiful and they did not face racial antipathy. Today's immigrants, however, face a different reality. A commonly held assumption (the reasoning of the culture of poverty—see Chapter 7) is that when new immigrants do not assimilate easily or if they continue to be poor, it is their fault. Thus, blame for many social problems and resistance to assimilation is placed on the immigrants, thereby "ignoring the impact of larger forces, such as racism and the economic order, that limit opportunities for success and present barriers to assimilation" (Pyke 2008:212).

The current political mood is to eliminate affirmative action (as California did in 1997) and to reduce or eliminate social programs that help level the playing field so that minorities would have a fair chance to succeed. Some legislation is especially punitive toward recent immigrants, particularly the undocumented. Such public policies make it more difficult for new immigrants to assimilate than did their predecessors, should they wish to do so.

Another factor facing this generation of immigrants is that they enter the United States during a critical economic transformation and, since 2007, an economic crisis in which the middle class is shrinking and the working class faces difficult economic hurdles (see Chapter 14). A possible result is that the new immigrants, different in physical characteristics, language, and culture, will become scapegoats for the difficulties that so many face (Powers 2007). Moreover, their opportunities for advancement will be limited by the new economic realities.

The issue of immigrant adaptation to the host society is complex, depending on a number of variables. Zhou (1997) described a number of these critical variables, including the immigrant generation (i.e., first or second), their level in the ethnic hierarchy at the point of arrival, what stratum of U.S. society absorbs them, and the degree to which they are part of a family network.

Immigrants who move to the United States permanently have four options regarding assimilation. Many try to blend into the United States as quickly as possible. Others resist the new ways by either developing an adversarial stance toward the dominant society or resisting acculturation by focusing more intensely on the social capital (i.e., social networks) created through ethnic ties (Portes and Zhou 1993). The fourth alternative is to move toward a bicultural pattern (Buriel and De Ment 1997). That is, immigrants adopt some patterns similar to those found in the host society and retain some from their heritage. Although this concept of a bicultural pattern appears to focus on culture, the retention or abandonment of the ethnic ways depends on structural variables (Kibria 1997:207). These variables include the socioeconomic resources of the ethnic community, the extent of continued immigration from the sending society, the linkages between the ethnic community and the sending society, and the obstacles to obtaining equal opportunity in the new society.

In sum, the new immigration, occurring at a time of economic uncertainty and reduced governmental services, is having three pronounced effects that will accelerate in the foreseeable future: (1) an increased bifurcation between the haves and the have-nots, (2) increased racial diversity, and (3) a heightened tension among the racial and ethnic groups.

5.3 Explain the facts versus myths of the "graying of America."

THE AGING SOCIETY

The population of the United States is experiencing a pronounced change in its age structure—it has become older and is on the verge of becoming much older. In 1900 about one in twenty-five residents of the United States was 65 years and older. By 1950 it was about one in twelve. In 2000 one in eight was 65 and older, and by 2030, it will likely be around one in five, with more people over 65 than under age 18. In effect, by 2030, when most of today's college students will be around 50, there will be more grandparents than grandchildren. The Senior Boom is coming, and it will transform in many ways. Consider, for example, that beginning January 1, 2011, every single day for the next nineteen years more than 10,000 members of the **baby boom generation** (the bulge in the population born from 1948 to 1964) will reach the age of 65. As a result, the number of senior citizens will increase from 13 percent in 2010 to 20 percent in 2030. This dramatic increase will affect families as more seniors live with their adult children and as more children are parented by their grandparents. And it will affect politics as the elderly will likely vote as a bloc on issues in their interest such as Medicare and Social Security.

This section is divided into two parts: (1) a demographic description of the aged category now and in the future and (2) the implications of an aging society for social problems.

Demographic Trends

Until the twentieth century high **fertility** (birthrate) and high **mortality** (death rate) kept the United States a youthful nation. During the last century, however, the birthrate fell (except for during the post–World War II period, which was an anomaly), resulting in fewer children as a proportion of the total population. Most important, greater longevity because of advances in medical technology (everything from beta-blockers for reducing hypertension to organ transplants) has increased the life expectancy of Americans. The average life expectancy in 1900 was 49 years, and in 2011 it was 78.

So, essentially in 130 years (from 1900 to 2030), people age 65 and older will have shifted from one out of twenty Americans to one in five. The surge in the number of elderly during the next few decades is the consequence of three demographic forces: a continued low fertility rate, ever-greater life expectancy rates, and the baby boom generation (the 75 million born between 1946 and 1964, representing 70 percent more people than were born during the preceding two decades) reaching old age, beginning in 2011 and ending in 2030. (See Figure 5.2 showing the population pyramids for 2000 and 2050. Each shows the changing age structure as the baby boom group moves toward old age.)

Hidden within these statistics is another important fact about the old—they are getting older. In 1950, there were 600,000 in this category of 85 and older (the "old old") compared to 5.7 million in 2008, a ninefold increase. In 2030 there will be an estimated 8,500,000 (12 percent of the elderly) age 85 and over (see Figure 5.3). By 2050 this number is expected to be 19.0 million or 23 percent of all elderly Americans. In 1950 there were 2,300 Americans age 100 and older (15 per 1 million population). In 2010 there were some 71,991 (230 per 1 million population, reflecting the continued advances in medicine and nutrition) (Census Bureau, reported in *Janus Report* 2011:4). It is expected that the number of centenarians will increase to about 1 million by the middle of the twenty-first century. Children born today have a fifty-fifty chance of reaching 100 years of age.

Demographic Portrait of the Current Elderly Population

📖 **Read** on MySocLab Document: Facts and Fictions About an Aging America

Sex Ratio. Older women outnumber older men by a ratio of 3 to 2. As age increases, the disparity becomes greater—for those age 85 and older, there are about five women to every two men. By age 100 and older, four in five are women.

A combination of biological advantages for women and social reasons explains this difference. The secondary status of women in U.S. society has provided them with extra longevity. Traditional gender roles have demanded that men be engaged in the more stressful, demanding, and dangerous occupations. It will be interesting to note whether there are any effects on female longevity as women receive a more equal share of all types of jobs. Meanwhile, though, the current situation creates problems for the majority of elderly women, who are often widows and have low incomes.

Elderly women are more likely than men to live alone as widows. This is the result of two factors: the greater longevity of women and the social norm for men to marry younger women. Thus, to the extent that isolation is a problem of the aged, it

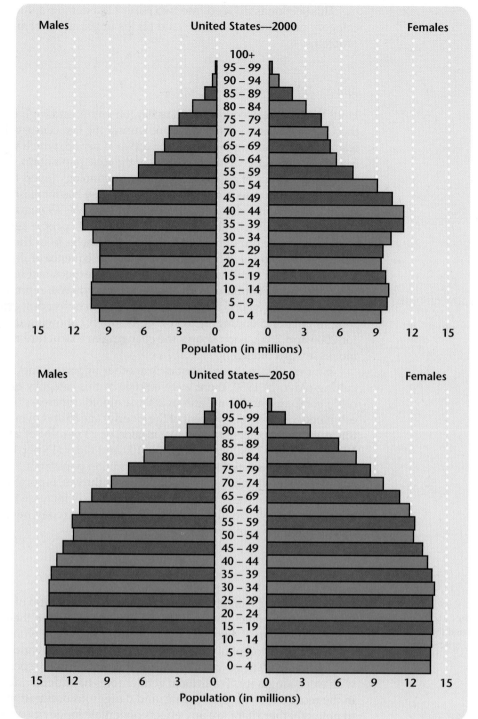

FIGURE 5.2

Age-Sex Structure of the United States in Years 2000 and 2050

Source: Shrestha, Laura B., and Elayne J. Heisler, 2011. The Changing Demographic Profile of the United States, Washington, DC: Congressional Research Service, 7-5700 (March 31). www.crs.gov.

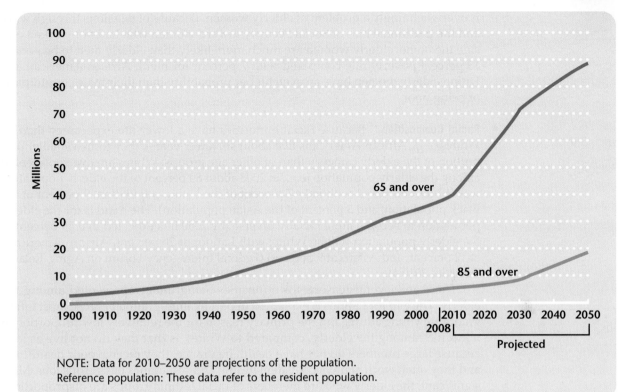

FIGURE 5.3

Population Age 65 and Over and Age 85 and Over, Selected Years 1900–2008 and Projected 2010–2050

Source: Federal Interagency Forum on Aging-Related Statistics. Older Americans 2010. Washington, DC: U.S. Government Printing Office, July 2010, p. 2.

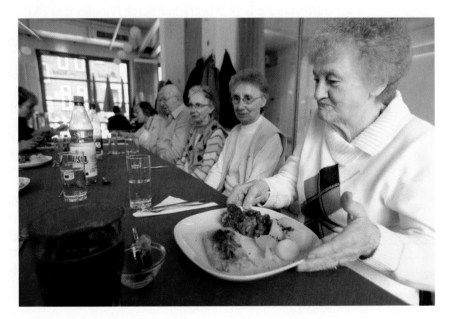

The elderly are disproportionately White and female.

is overwhelmingly a problem of elderly women. Because of pensions through work and the traditional bias of Social Security toward women who had not worked outside the home, elderly women are much more likely than elderly men to be poor (a 13 percent poverty rate compared with 7 percent for men). African American and Latino elderly women have an even higher probability than their male counterparts of being poor.

- **Racial Composition.**   Because racial minorities have a lower life expectancy than do Whites (e.g., African Americans live about six fewer years), they form a smaller proportion of the elderly category than of other age groups. Whites are overrepresented among the elderly population (e.g., in 2008 about 80 percent of the elderly population was White, compared with only 7 percent of the Latino population, 9 percent of the Black population, and 3 percent of the Asian population). The trend is for the elderly population to become more racially diverse (by 2050 it is expected that 59 percent of the elderly population will be White, with Latinos at 20 percent, African Americans at 12 percent, and Asians at 9 percent) (Federal Interagency Forum on Aging-Related Statistics 2010:4).

   There are several reasons for minorities being underrepresented among the elderly. The gap for Latinos is explained in part by immigration because most immigrants are young adults. But the primary reason for the relatively low proportion of minorities among the elderly, compared to Whites, is that they do not live as long because large numbers do not have health insurance, they receive poor healthcare, and they often work at physically demanding and sometimes dangerous jobs. Most significant, the elderly who are members of racial/ethnic groups are disproportionately poor.

- **Longevity.**   At the founding of the United States, life expectancy at birth was about 35 years. By 1900 life expectancy had increased to 47 years. In 2010 it was 78.7 years. This average masks some differences: (1) Women live longer than men (their life expectancy is 81.1, compared to 76.2 for men), and (2) there are racial gaps that show little sign of closing. For instance, the life expectancy for White females is 81.3 and for White males it is 78.5 years; for Black females it is 78.0 and for Black males it is 71.8. An interesting anomaly is the so-called "Latino Paradox." According to the Centers for Disease Control, on average, Latinos outlive Whites by 2.5 years and African Americans by 7.7 years despite their generally lower incomes and educational levels, their lower probability of having health insurance, and that they go to physicians less often than Whites. Despite these predictors of greater mortality, Latinos have lower rates of heart disease, cancer, and stroke than Whites. There are several possible reasons for this contradiction: (1) Immigrants who come to the United States are healthier, (2) Latinos have more exercise throughout their lives, (3) their diets are healthier, and (4) Latinos have close-knit families (Wright and Blackburn 2010).

- **Geographic Distribution.**   Some states and communities have disproportionately more older residents. One-fourth of all elderly Americans live in three states (California, Florida, and New York). Many rural states have a relatively high proportion of elderly, as these states experience a large outmigration of young people. Most elderly remain in their communities after retirement ("aging in place"), but those who move tend to migrate to the favorable climate found in the Sun Belt states (Florida, California, Arizona, Nevada, and Texas). Those who migrate are not representative of the elderly.

They tend to be younger and more affluent than those who stay in their home communities. Thus, they benefit their new communities by broadening the tax base through home ownership, strong purchasing power, and not burdening the local job market. The communities they left in the Snow Belt are negatively affected. The elderly who remain are disproportionately older and poorer and require more public assistance from a lower community tax base.

- **Wealth, Income, and Cumulative Advantage or Disadvantage.** For obvious reasons, the wealth accrued over a lifetime of work affects the quality of life during retirement. The economically challenged will continue to struggle with the exigencies of life after retirement, whereas those with economic advantage retain it in their later years. This changed for the relatively affluent, however, with the bursting of the economic bubble in 2007. Prior to the Great Recession, recent retirees, in general, had personal resources—education, income, and assets—unknown to previous cohorts. They benefited from a sharp rise in the stock market during the 1990s and extraordinary gains in real estate markets in the previous three decades, which ultimately they passed on to their fortunate heirs. Yet, many elderly missed out on the boom. They did not own a home or have enough assets to invest. But the boom did not last, which is discussed in greater detail in Chapter 14, presenting difficulties for many of the previously affluent.

  Home equity is most significant in having a reasonable net worth. In this regard, those who are currently in the old category had an advantage because their home purchases in the 1950s and 1960s were much cheaper in interest and mortgage payments relative to wages than were homes bought in the 1970s, 1980s, and 1990s. However, in the three years after the housing bubble burst, homes had lost $11 trillion in value. Moreover, the stock market lost over $7 trillion in value, with mutual funds dropping 38 percent. Investments in retirement savings (401(k)s) lost more than $1 trillion, and over an eighteen-month period, the investments in public pension plans lost a combined $1.3 trillion (Byrnes and Palmeri 2009). As a result, many who thought they had more than enough saved for retirement found that they did not. Many had to postpone retirement, remaining in the labor force indefinitely. Of course, although losing money, many of the affluent old remained comfortably affluent.

  Elderly members of a racial or ethnic minority are disproportionately poor. This relative lack of resources for racial minorities translates into a reduced likelihood, compared to Whites, of their receiving adequate healthcare and, when needed, living in nursing homes with full-time skilled nursing care under a physician's supervision.

  Elderly married couples tend to have greater net worth than elderly singles. Households maintained by unmarried elderly males have a greater net worth than households maintained by unmarried elderly women. Similarly, White married-couple households with a householder age 65 or older will likely have higher family incomes than racial minority married couples.

  Personal income is usually reduced by one-third to one-half after retirement. The important point is that those groups with advantage before becoming old maintain their economic advantage in old age—and the poor get poorer.

  Typically, we assume that economic inequality narrows after age 65, when benefit programs replace work as principal income sources. This is not the case as the inequalities from income and privilege tend to be magnified among elderly people. People who are initially advantaged, for example, are more likely than their less fortunate counterparts to receive good educations and obtain good jobs with better health and pension benefits, which lead to higher savings and better postretirement benefit incomes.

Most noteworthy, the government is partly responsible for these skewed advantages to the affluent. The relatively affluent are encouraged by the government, because of tax incentives, to invest in retirement income programs such as IRAs (individual retirement accounts), Keogh plans, or other tax-deferred programs. Thus, the already advantaged are given preferential tax treatment, which amounts to tax subsidization, thereby increasing their economic advantage over the disadvantaged after age 65.

In 2010, 9 percent of people age 65 and older were poor. This proportion is lower than the overall poverty rate because Social Security benefits are indexed for inflation. This poverty rate, below the nation's poverty rate of 15.1 percent, is perceived typically as a success. However, over 3.52 million elderly were poor in 2010, and more than that were in the "economically vulnerable" category—that is, they have incomes above the poverty line but below 150 percent of the official poverty rate.

The elderly spend about 20 percent of their incomes on healthcare, with the poor elderly spending about 35 percent of their incomes on healthcare. Roughly half of the incomes of the poor elderly goes for food. Thus, they are especially affected by inflation at the grocery store. The only recourse for the poor in inflationary times, when their incomes do not increase with spiraling costs, is either to eat less or to eat cheaper, less nutritious food.

The elderly poor spend about 20 percent of their incomes on energy for heat and electricity, both of which increase with inflation. Those on fixed incomes are likewise negatively affected by inflationary increases in the cost of rents, taxes, and healthcare. The last is a special burden for the old who are poor. Health costs for the elderly are almost four times those for people under age 65. The result is that the elderly poor tend to live in substandard housing, receive inadequate medical care, and have improper diets.

If the poor and the old are doubly cursed, then the elderly poor who are members of a racial or ethnic minority group experience a triple disadvantage. Individual and institutional sources of discrimination coalesce to make these people's lives especially miserable and problematic. The higher probability of older African Americans being poor is a direct consequence of their relatively low status throughout life. With average incomes only about 60 percent those of Whites, they have little chance to build a nest egg to supplement their pension incomes. African Americans are also more likely than Whites to have worked at jobs that did not provide retirement benefits and that did not qualify for Social Security (prior to 1974, for example, only 80 percent of elderly Blacks received some Social Security benefits, compared with 90 percent of older Whites). If they have worked at jobs qualifying for Social Security, minority members usually are eligible only for lower benefits because of their lower wages.

These related problems reflect the discrimination in the job market and unfair legislation. Clearly, equity in Social Security benefits will not occur until racial minorities and Whites experience similar work careers and compensation.

After a lifetime of lower earnings and receiving small or no pensions, elderly minorities must live in substandard housing. They are much more likely than elderly Whites to live in deteriorated housing with inadequate plumbing, heating, and sewage disposal. Similarly, the minority elderly suffer more health problems than do the majority elderly. For instance, among all minority elderly the prevalence of chronic disabilities is twice as high as among the White elderly.

5.4 Assess the potential consequences of the "graying of America."

PROBLEMS OF AN AGING SOCIETY

We focus on three problems inherent in our aging society: (1) inadequate income from pensions or Social Security, (2) the high cost of elderly healthcare, and (3) abuse of the elderly.

Social Security

Since the introduction of Social Security in the 1930s, this program has been a significant aid to the elderly. Social Security has reduced poverty significantly among the elderly—from 35.2 percent in 1959 to 9 percent in 2010. Social Security also provides life insurance benefits to the survivors in cases of the death of a breadwinner and disability payments when a wage earner is unable to work. Most fundamentally, through Social Security, society takes responsibility for the welfare of its elderly and people with disabilities.

Despite its considerable strengths, the Social Security program has several serious problems that place a disproportionate burden on certain categories of the elderly and on some portions of the workers paying into the program.

An immediate problem is that not all workers are covered by Social Security. Some groups of workers are unable to participate because they work for states with alternative retirement programs. Also, legislation has specifically exempted certain occupations (such as agricultural workers) from the Social Security program.

For workers who are eligible for Social Security, there are wide disparities in the benefits received. The amount of benefits depends on the length of time workers have paid into the Social Security program and the amount of wages on which they paid a Social Security tax. In other words, low-paid workers receive low benefits at retirement. Thus, 30 percent of the elderly who depend almost exclusively on Social Security benefits are still below the poverty line despite these benefits. These elderly typically are people who have been relatively poor during their working years or are widows.

On the surface, the Social Security system is gender neutral. Benefits are based purely on employment history, earnings, and family composition. This puts many women at a disadvantage since they are paid less on average and they work fewer years because of staying at home with younger children. Some of the disadvantages for women are:

- Social Security recognizes only paid work. The benefits for spouses (typically wives) who did not work in the labor force are 50 percent of the working spouse's benefits.
- Social Security benefits are based on the number of years worked and the amount earned from wages. Because women are in the workforce fewer years than men (mostly because they take time off to bear and care for children, eleven years on average) and because women generally earn less than men, women will receive smaller retirement benefits than men (Cawthorne and Gross 2008).
- A divorced woman receives half of her former husband's benefit if the couple was married at least ten years. If the divorce occurs before being married ten years, then she receives nothing.
- Where wife and husband are both employed, the wife will receive Social Security benefits for her work only if her benefits exceed those earned by her husband. If she collects a benefit based on her own wages, she loses the 50 percent spouse's payment for which her husband's payroll taxes paid.

- A woman who is widowed will not receive any Social Security benefits until age 60 unless she has a child under 16 or an older disabled child or she herself is disabled.

The Social Security system is financed through taxes on wages and salaries. From a payroll tax of 2 percent on the first $3,000 of earnings when it began in the 1930s, the rate has increased substantially over the years. The 2012 rate was 10.4 percent on the first $110,100 (the cap rises with inflation) of earnings, with the cost being split between the worker (4.2 percent) and the employer (6.2 percent), but most economists agree that the burden of the tax is on the employee because employers finance their share by paying their employees that much less.

The method of financing Social Security is not equitable because it disproportionately disadvantages lower-income wage earners. In other words, it is a **regressive tax:** It takes a larger percentage from people with the lowest incomes. The Social Security tax has the following negative features:

- It is levied at a constant rate (everyone, rich and poor, pays the same rate).
- It starts with the first dollar of earned income, offering no allowances or exemptions for the very poor.
- It applies only to wages and salaries, thus exempting income typical for the wealthy, such as interest, dividends, rents, and capital gains from the sale of property.
- It is imposed up to a ceiling ($110,100 in 2012). Thus, in effect, in 2012 a worker making $110,100 and an executive or a professional athlete making a $5 million salary paid exactly the same Social Security tax.

An overarching problem is facing Social Security—how to finance it in the future. Three demographic factors make financing the program problematic. The first is that more people are living to age 65, and the second is that people live much longer after reaching 65 than in earlier generations. Average life spans are fifteen years longer than they were when Social Security was created in 1935. The obvious consequence of this greater longevity is that the Social Security system pays out more and more to an ever-expanding pool of elderly who live longer and longer.

The third demographic factor working against the system is a skewed **dependency ratio** (the proportion of the population who are workers compared to the proportion not working). Social Security is financed by a tax on workers and their employers. In 1950 there were 16 workers for each person on Social Security; in 1970 there were 3.7 workers; in 2000 there were 3.2; and in 2030 there will be 2.1 workers for each person receiving benefits. At present, the Social Security Administration collects more in taxes than it pays out, with the surplus going into a trust fund. But as people live longer and the baby boomers reach retirement, this system will no longer support itself. Estimates vary, but sometime around 2018 the system will begin paying out more than it collects, and after 2042 it will be able to pay out only about 70 cents of each dollar of promised benefits (Zuckerman 2000). See the "Social Problems in Global Perspective" panel for the problems facing the developed nations as they become disproportionately old.

To deal with this pending crisis in funding Social Security, Congress will have to either raise Social Security taxes, use other revenues, or cut benefits. Other options include raising the age of eligibility (starting in 2000 and continuing to 2022, the age for receiving full benefits will gradually rise from 65 to 67). Raising the eligibility age is unfair to certain groups: African American males, for example, live nearly eight years less than White males, meaning that relatively few would receive benefits if the retirement age were raised to 70. Blue-collar workers also die earlier than professionals. A lifelong mine worker, for example, has only a fifty-fifty chance of reaching

Social Problems in Global Perspective

THE DEVELOPED WORLD TURNS GRAY

Over the next several decades, the nations in the developed world will experience an unprecedented growth in the number of their elderly and an unprecedented decline in the number of their youths. Peter Peterson, author of *Gray Dawn: How the Coming Age Wave Will Transform America and the World*, calls this demographic transformation the "Floridization of the Developed World" (Peterson 1999). In effect, today's Florida with its concentration of seniors (about one in five) is a demographic benchmark that every developed nation will reach and exceed, as did Italy in 2003, Japan in 2005, and Germany in 2006. France and Britain will exceed it in 2016, the United States in 2021, and Canada in 2023. In today's developed world, the elderly population is 14 percent, but by the year 2030, it will reach 25 percent.

This demographic shift has several consequences. First, as the proportion of the elderly population grows beyond 20 percent in a society, coupled with a corresponding fertility rate that does not replace itself (below 2.11), the working-age population will shrink. Japan, for example, suffered a 25 percent decline in its working-age population from 2000 to 2010.

Second, the shrinking of the working-age population means that productivity will decline and taxes and/or debts will rise to pay for the enormous burden of pensions and healthcare for the elderly. Or, alternatively, governments will have to reduce benefits to the elderly significantly, causing political upheavals.

Third, unless their fertility rates turn up, the total populations of Western Europe and Japan will shrink to about one-half of their current size by the end of the twenty-first century. The developing nations will continue to grow rapidly until leveling off around 2050, resulting in an ever-enlarging population gap between the developed and developing worlds and increasing resentment by the latter over the disproportionate resource use by an ever-smaller developed world.

Fourth, worker shortages will increase the demand for immigrant laborers, bringing diversity in religion, language, and customs. This diversity increases the possibility of racial and ethnic conflicts, as we are seeing, for example, in Germany, France, and Norway. Moreover, the increasing inequality gap between the new immigrants who arrive at the bottom of society's stratification system and those who are privileged will increase the possibility of clashes between the haves and the have-nots.

age 65. Another plan is the reduction or elimination of the cost of living adjustment (COLA), which allows the payments to keep pace with inflation. This proposal hurts the poor most because it is regressive. Another strategy is to tax Social Security benefits as income, which would protect the poor because they pay little, if any, federal income tax. Another solution that is popular with the Republican Party is to privatize Social Security. Generally, this would allow each individual to invest part of his or her Social Security taxes in the stock market. This plan would be beneficial when the stock market goes up, but it also makes retirement savings vulnerable to stock market declines. Imagine the consequences if Social Security had been privatized prior to the Great Recession.

Paying for Healthcare

Most older people are in reasonably good health. Of all age groups, however, the elderly are the most affected by ill health. Health problems escalate especially from age 75 onward, as the degenerative processes of aging accelerate. Consider the following facts:

- Although the elderly comprise only about 13 percent of the population presently, they consume more than one-third of all healthcare in the United States.

- Seniors are four times as likely as the nonelderly to be hospitalized. When hospitalized, they stay an average of about three days longer than the nonelderly.
- The medical expenses of the elderly are three times greater than those of middle-aged adults, yet their incomes are typically much less.
- The elderly account for more than one-third of all spending for prescription drugs.
- One in eight who are at least 65 years old has Alzheimer's disease. By 2030 the number will have doubled to one in four due to the aging of the population (Hyman 2008). The incidence of Alzheimer's disease, the leading cause of dementia in old age, rises sharply with advancing age—from one in ten people over the age of 65 to almost a fifty-fifty chance of getting the disease after age 85.
- Osteoarthritis, the degeneration of protective tissues around the body's joints, afflicts about half of those age 65 and older.
- The cost of long-term care is prohibitive. The average annual cost of a year in a nursing home in 2011 ranged from a low of $54,264 in Louisiana to a high of $119,355 in New York State (Genworth Financial 2011).

Read on MySocLab Document: Care Options for Older Mexican Americans: Issues Affecting Health and Long-Term Care Service Needs

Fidelity Investments estimates that a 65-year-old couple retiring in 2006 needed about $200,000 to cover health costs that were not covered by Medicare. That estimate does not include the cost of over-the-counter drugs, dental services, or long-term care (cited in Block 2006). Because Medicare does not pay for most long-term care, long-term care insurance is expensive, and Medicaid will help only after the patient's resources are exhausted, resulting in many elderly spending their last years impoverished.

Medicare, begun in 1965, is the federal health insurance program for those 65 and older. Everyone is automatically entitled to hospital insurance, home health care, and hospice care through this program (known as Medicare Part A). The supplemental medical insurance program (known as Medicare Part B) helps pay for doctor bills, outpatient services, diagnostic tests, physical therapy, and medical supplies. People may enroll in this program by paying a relatively modest monthly fee. Overall, Medicare is financed by payroll taxes, premiums paid by recipients, and a government subsidy.

There are three major problems with Medicare. First, it is insufficiently financed by the government. Second, from the perspective of the elderly, only about half of their health care bills are paid through the program, leaving many with substantial costs. The affluent elderly are not hurt because they can purchase supplemental health insurance. The poor are not hurt because they are also covered by Medicaid, a separate program financed by federal and state taxes that pays for the healthcare of indigent persons. The near poor, however, do not qualify for Medicaid, and they cannot afford additional health insurance.

A third problem with Medicare is that physicians feel the program underpays them for their services. As a result, many physicians limit the number of Medicare patients they will serve, some even refusing to serve any Medicare patients. Thus, some elderly have difficulty finding a physician.

Elder Abuse

- **Problems of the Institutionalized Elderly.** The data indicate that at any one time, between 4 and 5 percent of people age 65 and older are confined to nursing homes and other extended-care facilities. This low figure is misleading, however. It does not mean that only 4 to 5 percent of the aged ever will be confined to a nursing home. At age 65, a person may have no need for such a facility, but at 85 it may be a necessity.

The residents of nursing homes are typically age 75 and older, female, and White. Conspicuously absent are racial minorities.

The economically advantaged elderly are not as likely as their less wealthy age cohorts to be institutionalized, and if institutionalized, they are apt to be in private nursing homes and to receive better care. Kosberg (1976) compared nursing homes for private residents with those for welfare recipients and found the former decidedly superior in staffing, freedom, pleasantness of surroundings, cleanliness, patient communication, and meals. Kosberg found that homes for the affluent old tend to provide **therapeutic care** (the approach that focuses on meeting the needs of patients and on treatment), whereas homes housing welfare recipients tend to provide **custodial care** (the approach in a health facility that focuses on meeting the needs of the institution rather than those of the residents). This distinction is an important difference because custodial residents tend to receive less satisfactory care than do therapeutic residents. This has implications for the federal law stating that nursing home residents must use all their savings before receiving Medicaid. Because nursing home care costs are very high, and less than 8 percent of Americans have private insurance for lengthy care, long-term care results in many residents' spending themselves into poverty, at which time Medicaid will take over the financial payments. Previous research indicates that the shift to Medicaid results in a change from therapeutic care to custodial care.

There are two extreme points of view concerning the functions of nursing homes. One view is that such homes are necessary places for the elderly who need extensive healthcare. Obviously, such facilities are needed for people who have Alzheimer's disease and for people who have been paralyzed by strokes or are bedridden. The opposing view sees nursing homes as dumping grounds or repositories for getting rid of people who represent what we do not want to be or see. Whatever one's views on these institutions, one fact is pertinent: Although many nursing homes provide good environments for their residents, there are serious problems in others. There are no federal standards that nursing homes must meet for the health and safety of their residents. The standards are left to the individual states, and they vary in their standards and rigor in enforcing them.

Common problems in nursing homes with a custodial style are the overuse and misuse of drugs. Drugs can be used for a host of therapeutic reasons, but one common use is not healthful—drugging an individual to control behavior. The use of tranquilizers, for example, keeps people from complaining and from asking for service. This procedure minimizes disturbances, thereby requiring fewer personnel and thus increasing profits. Of course, the quality of life for the residents is diminished, and even their lives may be broken.

The nursing home business is big business. Two factors make the profit potential especially great: (1) The elderly population is growing at a 2 percent annual rate, and (2) the federal and state governments pay for much of the care. One consequence of these factors is the proliferation of private nursing homes (about 75 percent are private) organized to generate profits. Many of these facilities provide excellent care for their clients, but others have shown that their interest in profit exceeds their interest in clients.

Not all nursing homes are unnecessary, and not all owners and personnel are greedy and uncaring. Many older people benefit from a sheltered environment, and doubtless many of the 17,000 nursing homes in the United States are resident oriented and provide adequate—perhaps even superior—services to their clients.

But we must also acknowledge that there are widespread abuses in U.S. nursing homes. The danger, of course, is the profit motive—the less money that nursing homes spend on care such as living space, staff, food, heat in the winter and air conditioning in the summer, and recreational equipment, the more profit for the company and its shareholders.

What is the effect of institutionalization on the residents? Obviously, it will vary according to the facilities and treatment philosophy of a particular nursing home. But all care institutions (including prisons, mental hospitals, hospitals, and nursing homes) must be wary of depersonalizing individual clients. In the name of efficiency, people eat the same food at the same time, wear the same type of clothing, perform the same chores in the prescribed manner, watch the movies provided them, and live in rooms with identical dimensions and decor. The widespread use of tranquilizers compounds this depersonalization. The result is that docility and similarity abound, which makes management happy but obviously overlooks the individual needs of the elderly residents.

- **Noninstitutionalized Care of the Elderly by Their Children.** Two demographic trends mentioned earlier—the decline in fertility and an increased life expectancy—increase the likelihood of elderly parents living with their adult children. These trends result in a **beanpole family structure**—a vertical, four-generation family structure. There are three tiers of parent–child relations, two sets of grandparent–grandchild ties, and linkage between great-grandparent and grandchild (Bengston, Rosenthal, and Burton 1990:264).

  A variation of the beanpole family structure is the three-generation household, called the **sandwich family structure**, where parents care for their parents and their children.

  Families make the decision for the elderly to live with their children for a variety of reasons. Regardless of the reason, the new living arrangement may be satisfactory or it may be difficult because the elderly or their children or both may resent the lack of privacy and the erosion of independence, or there may be disagreement over disparate lifestyles.

  With this trend for more and more children assuming a caretaker role of their elderly parents, there is an increased likelihood of elder abuse. This abuse can take the following forms:

  - *Physical abuse:* hitting, slapping, shoving, and use of physical restraints, as well as the withholding of personal care, food, medicine, adequate medical attention, and the like.
  - *Psychological abuse:* verbal assaults, threats, fear, and isolation.
  - *Drug abuse:* encouragement by doctors and families to take too many drugs, which serves the families by keeping the elderly manageable.
  - *Financial exploitation:* theft or misuse of money and other personal property owned by the elderly.
  - *Violation of rights:* forcing a parent into a nursing home, for instance.

  For the most part, accurate information on how many elderly people are subjected to these abusive acts is impossible to obtain. The elderly victims are in a double-bind situation that traps them in an abusive situation in which they feel that they cannot notify the authorities. The abuser, by providing needed financial support to the dependent elderly, controls the situation. The elderly victim thus is unlikely to report the abuse for lack of alternative living arrangements. As a result, as many as five out of six cases of elder abuse go unreported (National Center on Elder Abuse 1998). Contributing to underreported elder abuse, many mistreated elders are homebound and isolated, and thus are unlikely to be seen at banks, senior centers, hospitals, health programs, and police stations (Wolf 2000:8).

Despite these problems with underreporting, Rosalie Wolf (2000), summarizing the findings from community surveys, found that 4 to 6 percent of older adults report experiencing incidents of domestic elder abuse, neglect, and financial exploitation. With about 35 million Americans 65 and older, a middle estimate of 5 percent yields an estimated 1,750,000 who are victims of some form of abuse.

The problem seems to occur in situations in which adult children are overwhelmed by the role of taking care of their parent or parents. The emotional, physical, and financial costs of caregiving can be enormous. Hospital and other medical costs are extremely expensive for the elderly because they are more prone to illness. There are obvious additional food and housekeeping costs. Furthermore, the timing of the additional financial burdens may be especially difficult for caretakers because it is likely to coincide with higher expenses for their children (college, wedding, helping them buy their first home).

Parents living with their adult children cause stress and resentment in a number of other ways as well. The household is more crowded, causing, for example, different sleeping arrangements, overcrowded bathrooms, and shortages of hot water. The caretaking responsibility is likely to be assumed by the wife, and she may resent the elders' presence because of the extra work, the intrusion into her privacy, and the excessive demands on her time. Of course, as parents age and disabilities become more pronounced, the care they need can become overwhelming. The wife may be especially hostile to the parents because she is losing the freedom she expected to have once her children were gone—freedom to travel, go back to school, or take a job. But with elderly parents to restrain her, she is back to the parental role.

Parents living with an adult child can cause special problems when they have not resolved their problems from an earlier time. The parents may continue to treat their adult child as a child, taking over or trying to take over the decision-making role. Or the hostile feelings generated when the child was an adolescent return to haunt both parties. Clearly, there is tension when the behaviors and values of the adult child do not coincide with those of the elderly parent. They may differ on political issues, religious issues, how the grandchildren should be raised, and what television programs to watch.

> The adult child may also resent parents living in his or her home because the adult child feels forced into the situation. Perhaps the other siblings live in different communities, and so the parents, no longer able to live alone, move in with the child living in their community. The hostile feelings increase if the adult child feels that other relatives are not sharing the burden, at least financially. This emphasis on the elderly causing stress among caregivers blames the victim. (Pillemer 1993:246–247)

Despite this disclaimer, the stress generated between the elderly and their caregivers is a major source of abuse. Stresses and tensions between the generations are inevitable. For some families, such a situation results in actual physical and mental abuse of the elderly. The psychological and social factors related to child and spouse abuse are also pertinent for the abuse of the elderly. One additional catalyst that must be considered is the **ageism** prevalent in society. Ageism promotes an atmosphere in which the elderly are devalued, negatively stereotyped, and discriminated against.

To the extent that older people accept these negative definitions of the aged, they may view abusive treatment as deserved or at least unavoidable. Similarly, if their children accept tenets of ageism, they are likely to assume that the elderly deserve their mistreatment.

5.5 Discuss how the elderly might cope with or respond to their devalued status in society.

Watch on MySocLab Slideshow: Aging and the Elderly

RESPONSES BY THE ELDERLY

People at age 65 today have twenty, thirty, or forty years more of life ahead of them. Some are financially secure, and many will be relatively healthy throughout their remaining years. Elderly people who are healthy and financially secure have opportunities to enjoy travel, leisure activities, social involvement, and other pursuits that make their lives full and meaningful.

But being old is a difficult stage in life for many. People who were once attractive, active, and powerful may no longer be so. They no longer are "tethered to society through a series of institutions—school, work, family, church, community—that structured [their] lives, defined [their] place in the world, and gave shape to [their] identity" (Rubin 2006:93). Their lives, once organized around pursuing goals, seem empty and meaningless. Some experience debilitating diseases that cause constant pain, restrict their freedom, and rob them of their vitality. Others are isolated in nursing homes or because they lost a spouse and their children live at a distance. Some elderly are poor and live lives of desperation and hopelessness, with inflation eating away their meager resources.

The elderly possess a devalued status in U.S. society. Being considered old by society and by oneself is a catalyst that provokes the individual to respond in characteristic ways. But—and this is the crucial sociological point—the elderly are reacting

"He's angry about getting old."

Frank Cotham/The New Yorker Collection/Cartoonbank

to socially structured inequalities and socially constructed definitions, not to age as such. In a different cultural setting in which status increases with age, observers might find different personality types and responses.

Some researchers have argued that senior citizens respond to the aging process by retreating from relationships, organizations, and society (called **disengagement**). This behavior is considered normal and even satisfying for the individual because withdrawal brings a release from societal pressures to compete, perform, and conform. Other researchers have quarreled with disengagement theory, arguing that many elderly people are involved in a wide range of activities.

Most elderly people do remain active until health problems curtail their mobility. Some 60 percent of people over 80 continue to live independently (Rubin 2006:90). A striking number of them are becoming more politically active in an attempt to change some of the social conditions especially harmful for them. Senior citizens are more politically active (voting, volunteering) than other age groups in society. Faced with common problems, many join in a collective effort to make a difference. Several national organizations are dedicated to political action that will benefit the elderly, including the American Association for Retired Persons (AARP), which, having over 40 million members, is the nation's largest special-interest organization; the National Committee to Preserve Social Security and Medicare; the National Council of Senior Citizens; the National Council on Aging (a confederation of some 1,400 public and private social welfare agencies); the National Caucus on Black Aged; and the Gerontological Society. Collectively, these organizations have many millions of members. They work through lobbyists, mailing campaigns, phone banks, advertising, and other processes to improve the lot of the elderly in U.S. society.

Just how effective these organizations are or will be is unknown. But as the elderly continue to increase in proportion, their sphere of influence is likely to increase as well. Currently, the elderly account for around 20 percent of the voting public. By 2038 seniors are projected to make up more than one-third of the electorate. Elderly citizens could be a significant voting bloc if they developed an age consciousness and voted alike. Politicians from states with a high concentration of elderly people are increasingly aware of their potential voting power, and legislation more sympathetic to the needs of the elderly may be forthcoming. It is probably only a matter of time before the elderly focus their concerns and become an effective pressure group that demands equity.

MySocLab ✔ **Study** and **Review** on **MySocLab**

■ CHAPTER REVIEW

1. A major demographic force in U.S. society is massive immigration. This immigration (adding about 1 million immigrants annually) differs from previous waves because the immigrants come primarily from Latin America and Asia rather than Europe.

2. Racial and ethnic diversity ("the browning of America") is increasing with the influx of immigrants and differential fertility (i.e., immigrant groups having a higher fertility rate than other groups).

3. The two fastest growing minorities are Latinos and Asian Americans.

4. The reaction of Americans to the new immigrants is typically negative. This reaction is based on two myths: (a) immigrants take jobs away from those

already here, and (b) immigrants are a drain on society's resources.

5. Immigrants face a dilemma: Do they fit into their new society, or do they retain the traditions of the society they left? Immigrants in the past, for the most part, assimilated. But conditions are different for the new immigrants: (a) They are members of racial/ethnic groups, not Whites; (b) the current political mood is to eliminate affirmative action programs and welfare programs; and (c) they have entered during difficult economic times brought about by the economic transformation.

6. The second major demographic shift is toward an aging society ("the graying of America").

7. The proportion of the U.S. population age 65 and older is growing. In this category, women outnumber men, and minorities are underrepresented. Although the elderly as a category are not disproportionately poor, the elderly who are women, minorities, or who live alone are disproportionately poor.

8. The Social Security program is the only source of income for about one-half of retired people and a major source of income for 80 percent of the elderly. The key problem is how this program will be financed in the future.

9. The Social Security program is biased in several ways: (a) Some workers are not included, (b) people with low career earnings receive fewer benefits, (c) women (homemakers, divorced, and widowed) are disadvantaged, and (d) the tax is regressive.

10. Medicare is the health insurance program for almost everyone age 65 and older. The program is insufficiently financed: (a) From the perspective of the elderly, the program does not pay enough of the medical expenses, and (b) the program is too expensive for the government to finance adequately.

11. At any one time, only about 5 percent of people age 65 and older are confined in nursing homes. These homes have important functions for those needing their services, but abuses are associated with some of these operations: Residents are given custodial care, drugged, and provided with inadequate nutrition.

12. As many as 1.5 million elderly people in the United States are physically abused by relatives annually. Most commonly, abuse occurs when adult children are overwhelmed by the role of taking care of their parents. Elder abuse also occurs in about one-third of the nation's nursing homes, according to government studies.

13. The elderly may respond to their devalued status in several characteristic ways. They may withdraw from social relationships; they may continue to act as they have throughout their adult lives; or they may become politically active to change the laws, customs, and social structures that disadvantage them.

14. The numbers and proportion of the elderly in the U.S. population will increase. This aging population will create a difficult burden for the young, who, through taxes, will be required to finance pension plans and other assistance for the elderly. If the gap between the needs of the elderly and the benefits they receive widens, political activity and age consciousness among older people are likely to increase.

■ KEY TERMS

Demography. The study of population.

Human agency. People are agents and actors who cope with, adapt to, and change social structures to meet their needs.

Assimilation. The process by which individuals or groups adopt the culture of another group, losing their original identity.

Baby boom generation. The people born in the fifteen-year period following World War II, when an extraordinary number of babies were born in the United States.

Fertility. Birthrate.

Mortality. Death rate.

Regressive tax. Taxing at a set percentage, which takes a larger proportion of the wealth from the poor than from the nonpoor.

Dependency ratio. The proportion of the population who work compared to the proportion who do not work.

Therapeutic care. The approach in a health facility that focuses on meeting the needs of residents.

Custodial care. The approach in a health facility that focuses on meeting the needs of the institution, resulting in poor-quality care for the patients.

Beanpole family structure. A family structure in which the number of living generations within linkages increases, but there is an intragenerational contraction in the number of members within each generation.

Sandwich family structure. Where parents care for both their parents and their children simultaneously.

Ageism. The devaluation of and the discrimination against the elderly.

Disengagement. The response by some people to the aging process of retreating from relationships, organizations, and society.

Problems of Place: Urban, Suburban, and Rural

((• Listen to Chapter 6 on MySocLab

LEARNING OBJECTIVES

6.1 Identify social problems that are tied to inner cities in the United States.

6.2 Identify social problems that are tied to suburban areas in the United States.

6.3 Discuss the social problems that are tied to rural areas in the United States.

The United States is an urban nation, with 83 percent of its people living in metropolitan areas and the remaining residing in rural communities and in open areas. This chapter examines the social problems of place: the problems unique to cities, to suburbs, and to rural areas.

URBAN PROBLEMS

6.1 Identify social problems that are tied to inner cities in the United States.

Some observers argue that although American cities in the past had problems, they are on the rebound as neighborhoods are revitalized, formerly abandoned downtowns are rebuilt with financial services and other businesses moving back, and it is becoming fashionable to live in the urban core. But although there are successes, many cities of the United States are in trouble. And, these troubles have been magnified by the Great Recession, which brought in its wake, declining sales tax revenue, falling real estate values, increased debt, and high social costs such as schools, pensions, and repairing the infrastructure (Fineman 2009:29). The focus of this section is on the grim reality for many cities in the United States.

Explore on MySocLab Activity: Urban Profile: Philadelphia

No other industrial nation has allowed the kind of decline and deterioration facing U.S. urban centers. Most of the social and economic problems discussed in this book are primarily concentrated and have their severest consequences in the city, particularly the largest cities (three out of ten Americans live in eight metropolitan areas with populations of 5 million or more). It is in this locale, more than any other, that many of these problems are expanding and intensifying. In this sense, place is crucial to understanding U.S. social problems.

Watch on MySocLab Video: Urbanization: The Growth of Cities

Urban poverty is especially acute and contributes to and is associated with a host of other city problems. These problems include a decaying infrastructure, a shortage of affordable housing, homelessness, inadequate public transit, pollution, lack of healthcare, failing public school systems, drugs, gangs, and crime.

Urban Job Loss

View on MySocLab Figure: Urban Growth and Urban Flight

About one-third of the jobs in major U.S. metropolitan areas are with corporations that export goods and services outside the metro area. These are the highest paying jobs with the best benefit packages, in such industries as aerospace, defense, international trade, oil refining, computer software and hardware development, pharmaceuticals, and entertainment. These export jobs create a second type of employment in metropolitan areas—regional-serving jobs. About a quarter of jobs in most metropolitan areas are regional serving—in finance, real estate, utilities, media, and other professional services. These jobs generally pay less than export jobs but still represent good employment opportunities. The remainder of jobs in metropolitan areas serve the local area. The best of these include schoolteachers, police officers, firefighters, other municipal employees, and neighborhood doctors and lawyers. The worst include low-wage, insecure, temporary, part-time, dead-end work with few or no benefits in retail, clerical, custodial, food service, and private security work. The "good" jobs are leaving or, in the case of business expansion and new jobs, not locating in the central city or in the older, closer suburbs; thus they are farther and farther away from the growing proportion of poor and minority people in the city.

Race and class, as well as the fear of crime, play into the corporate motivation to move to the fringes of urban areas. The perception of many corporations and their employees is that the central city is unsafe and has a large minority workforce. Sears's relocation from the Sears Tower in downtown Chicago to Hoffman Estates, 37 miles to the northwest, is a prime example of this perception. The move allows Sears to hire more highly educated workers, mostly White, who live near the 1.9-million-square-foot campus-style complex. The state of Illinois used taxpayer dollars to subsidize Sears's relocation with lowered land costs, infrastructure and expressway improvements, and tax abatements.

In addition to the jobs that cities have lost to the suburbs, there has been a net loss of good-paying and well-benefited jobs in the wider U.S. economy. These economic changes and their impact on U.S. society are discussed in detail in Chapter 14.

Particularly as the business of the old industrial cities of the northeastern and midwestern United States shifted from manufacturing to legal, financial, real estate, and other service work, the worst of the local-serving jobs, the jobs of low-skill workers, were hit hard. Especially affected were people of color in the inner city. As a result of the exodus of jobs away from the city and the deindustrialization of the economy, unemployment is high in the central cities. This theme is elaborated in Chapter 14.

Add to the loss of urban jobs from the transformation of the economy and through capital flight (companies moving to low-wage locales either within or outside the United States) the economic ravages of the Great Recession, where companies cut payrolls and consumers spent less. As a result, urban areas were especially hard hit. According to the Bureau of Labor Statistics, at the end of 2009 when the official U.S. unemployment rate was 10 percent, seventeen urban areas recorded jobless rates of at least 15 percent. Of the cities with 1 million or more, Detroit had the highest rate at 15.4 percent (U.S. Department of Labor 2010).

Disinvestment

Systematic patterns of investment and disinvestment have hurt U.S. cities. Banks, savings and loans, and insurance companies have redlined cities and metropolitan areas—literally drawing red lines on the map and making loans and providing insurance on one side of the line and not on the other. **Redlining** refers to the practice of not providing loans or insurance in what are deemed undesirable areas. These areas are almost always made up of high concentrations of poor minorities and located in the central cities. They are the communities that suffer the consequences of the disinvestment that denies loans to home buyers, small-business entrepreneurs, and neighborhood real estate developers.

The patterns of disinvestment and investment that have resulted from redlining in U.S. metropolitan areas have discriminated by both race and place.

- **Race.** Studies (of Atlanta, Detroit, Denver, for example) find consistently that African Americans have greater difficulty than Whites in receiving mortgage credit from banks and savings and loans. And, when approved for loans, they tend to pay a higher interest rate than Whites. These predatory lending practices also occur for automobile insurance where higher premiums are charged in low-income, minority neighborhoods, which are located near the downtown, than in middle-income, White neighborhoods away from the central core. Insurance rates are based on accident rates, and these rates are higher downtown than elsewhere—hence, the higher rates for those living nearby. Most downtown traffic, however, is not by residents but by people who live outside the city but shop or work downtown. The consequence is that the poor pay more.

- **Place.** Patterns of lending also discriminate with regard to location. Suburbs receive a much greater and disproportionate share of loans compared to the central city. This discrimination, of course, is clearly related to the patterns of disinvestment and investment based on race described previously because suburban areas are predominantly White, but inner-city neighborhoods are often African American or Latino.

City dollars, central city capital, regularly go to the suburbs. Bank deposits made by inner-city residents in city banks are more likely to be used for home and business loans in the suburbs than in the cities, where the need for capital is so apparent.

This sort of redlining, discrimination, and disinvestment ultimately leads to a self-fulfilling prophecy of decline in inner-city neighborhoods. When banks disinvest in a neighborhood, residents and small businesses cannot maintain their homes and property. Without loans, small businesses often fail, and the jobs, goods, and services they provide are lost to the neighborhood. Indeed, often the banks themselves are among the businesses that physically leave the community. Disinvestment by banks, savings and loans, and insurance companies also discourages other private investors and government agencies from investing in poor and minority neighborhoods.

The racist myth in the United States is that Black inner-city neighborhoods are run down because Blacks lack pride and other middle-class values. In reality, they lack capital, not pride and good values. This capital is denied to them and to their communities by primarily White-controlled financial institutions.

Federal Abandonment

Over the past three decades, the federal government has also made huge cuts in dollars and services for the central cities. Federal aid to cities has been systematically cut since the Reagan administration. Cuts have been made in the federal revenue sharing program, welfare, medical aid, subsidized housing, and essential social services. Successful urban programs—for public works, economic development, job training, housing, schools, and health and nutrition—have been systematically cut. In addition, most states, because of federal cutbacks, have reduced various forms of public assistance to the poor. Facing their fiscal crisis alone and with a shrinking tax base (because businesses have left), cities have had to cut services or raise taxes, with most doing both. Raising taxes while closing schools, hospitals, and police and fire stations, laying off municipal employees, neglecting health and housing codes, cutting public transit, and postponing infrastructure maintenance and improvements had the effect of encouraging more businesses, industry, jobs, and middle-class residents to leave the city. This movement, of course, only deepens the budgetary crisis of the downward-spiraling cities. And as urban government downsizes, the poor and working-class residents of the city are left to compete for the dwindling resources and services still available.

As the central cities lose population, jobs, and businesses, they also lose political clout in state legislatures, while the suburbs gain power, resulting in policies more favorable to the suburbs than to the central cities where fewer Americans live and relatively few of them vote. Moreover, central cities, with their relatively high concentrations of racial and ethnic minorities tend to favor Democrats, whereas people in the suburbs are more likely to be Republicans. Thus, Republicans are not motivated to fund the cities' needs, whereas Democrats are.

Urban Poverty

Poverty is a problem in many central cities, especially in the nation's largest cities. Within cities, poverty and especially child poverty is concentrated in particular urban neighborhoods. There has been not only an increase in poverty in central cities but also an increase in poverty in **central city poverty areas** (neighborhoods in which at least one in five households live below the poverty line are designated by the federal government as poverty areas). There has also been an increase in the poverty concentrated in **high-poverty areas** in U.S. cities—areas where at least two in five households, or 40 percent of households, fall below the official poverty line. Urban public housing developments are most likely to fall into this category.

People of color are also more likely to be concentrated in poverty areas in the city and much more likely to be among the poorest of the poor. Matching the high rates of Black and Latino central-city poverty are high rates of residential segregation. Actually, even the extremely high levels of segregation reflected in census-tract data underestimate racial separation and isolation. Racial segregation is even more severe when smaller units, such as immediate neighborhoods and blocks, are analyzed. High levels of segregation in housing also lead to segregation in schools, churches, and other neighborhood institutions.

Read on MySocLab Document: Fences and Neighbors: Segregation in 21st-Century America

This means that not only are the urban poor a growing proportion of all poor people in the United States but also that a growing proportion of the urban poor are racially segregated in poverty and high-poverty areas in the central city. Racial segregation contributes to and perpetuates poverty because it isolates poor people from the educational and economic opportunities they need. The schools in racially segregated, poor Black communities in the inner city are separate but not equal. The poor people living in the poorest, racially segregated, central-city neighborhoods are disconnected—both socially and physically—from urban labor markets. As a consequence of this "American apartheid," urban African Americans and Latinos are disproportionately unemployed and uneducated. Also, as poverty is more concentrated in inner cities, crime and violence proliferate. The poor may adopt violence as a survival strategy, which escalates violence even further. The structural analysis employed in our analysis focuses on social conditions, not immoral people. This focus allows us to understand that social conditions and policies of abandonment create racial impoverishment in U.S. inner cities.

Urban Housing Crisis

There are two sources of the current urban housing crisis—the lack of decent, affordable housing for the poor and the bursting of the housing bubble—leading to the Great Recession.

- **The Lack of Affordable Housing.** The government defines housing as "unaffordable" if it costs more than 30 percent of a family's monthly income. The demand for low-income and affordable housing in U.S. cities far exceeds the supply. For example, in 2009 there was a shortfall of almost 3.5 million housing units for the poorest households (Markee 2011). Moreover, 70 percent of low-income renter households were spending more than half their income on rent, *and this was before the current economic crisis* (Wardrip 2009:1). The sources of this gap include trends in the urban housing market that affect both the affordability of existing housing and the number of low-income units.

  One factor reducing housing affordability and the supply of low-income housing units in urban areas is that private developers and builders tend to invest only in middle-class and luxury housing, where the market provides the highest margins. This private real estate investment includes both condo conversion and gentrification.

  Condominium conversion involves taking rental units and turning them into apartments for sale. This process often displaces people who cannot afford a down

More than 70 percent of low-income renter households spend more than one-half of their income on rent.

payment and do not qualify for a home mortgage, which more affluent residents who can and do. **Gentrification** is the redevelopment of poor neighborhoods (run-down properties, warehouses, cheap apartments) into middle-class and upscale condominiums, townhouses, single-family dwellings, lofts, and apartments. Often, the original residents are displaced because they are unable to afford the increased rents, purchase prices, and property taxes based on the neighborhoods' rising property values.

The redevelopment of the downtown areas in many U.S. cities during the past two decades has also led to the loss of significant numbers of low-income housing units. As the economy moved from manufacturing to services, many big-city downtowns were remade as financial, real estate, legal, and retail centers. Building often boomed on the fringes of the old downtown areas and in the process destroyed most of the SROs (single-room occupancy hotels) in many cities. SROs had historically provided housing for economically marginal single persons in the city. Although apartments were small, and occupants often had to share a bathroom or a kitchen or both, the units were affordable and available for this part of the urban population. Now the SRO has become a thing of the past.

Slumlords have also contributed to the housing shortage in the inner city. **Slumlording** occurs when landlords buy properties in poor neighborhoods and have no intention of investing in their upkeep and maintenance. While neglecting these properties, slumlords collect as much rent as they can from their poor tenants. Or, with gentrification, the slumlords sell their deteriorated dwellings at a profit.

Another urban housing market phenomenon that adds to the housing crisis in some cities is **warehousing**. Here urban real estate speculators withhold apartments from the housing market. Speculators purchase buildings and gradually empty them by not renewing the rents. They hold the property until developers on the edges of gentrifying areas become interested and purchase them for considerably more than their original cost. Developers are especially attracted to warehoused apartments, which spare them the trouble of getting rid of poor and working-class tenants who will not be able to afford the newly gentrified property.

Read on
MySocLab Document:
Life and Death in the
City: Neighborhoods
in Context

All the forces in the urban housing market that have led to the shrinking supply of affordable and low-income housing have been met with, or encouraged by, failing government housing policies.

As early as the 1960s, federally financed urban renewal projects were bulldozing low-income housing in poor and working-class neighborhoods. In theory, federal urban renewal funds were meant for the rehabilitation and redevelopment of decaying urban neighborhoods. In practice, what usually happened was quite different. Cities applied for the federal funds and, when they received them, used their legal powers of eminent domain and other powers granted them under both federal and state urban renewal legislation to declare an area to be blighted. Once so designated, all structures in the area were eliminated. Often, this was done to facilitate the development of large public projects such as airports, colleges or universities, medical centers, or even private commercial projects on the now available land. The second phase of federal urban renewal was to include replacement housing for people who lost their homes or apartments and neighborhood. For the most part, however, funds were never appropriated for this phase, and urban renewal projects reduced the supply of low-income housing. Much of the housing stock lost was in fact blighted, but for many people, it was at least an affordable place to live.

Beginning with the Reagan administration, there have been over three decades of federal divestment in affordable housing infrastructure and programs. (For a survey of diminished government efforts to aid affordable housing, see Western Regional Advocacy Project 2010). The budget cutbacks during the Reagan and Bush administrations slashed federal housing funds by 70 percent. New construction of low-income housing by the Department of Housing and Urban Development (HUD), the federal agency responsible for the creation and maintenance of low-income housing in American cities, decreased by 90 percent. Congress and the Clinton administration decreased the HUD budget again in 1995—this time by 25 percent. For the first time in twenty years, funding for the construction of new public housing units was cut. For the first time, there was no increase in the number of available Section 8 certificates (certificates that subsidize tenants who live at or below the poverty line and who pay 30 percent of their incomes toward rent). Congress and the president also slashed funds for the maintenance and rehabilitation of existing public housing, thereby ensuring its further deterioration. They also repealed the long-standing federal one-for-one replacement rule, which required that a new unit of public housing be built before any old unit could be demolished. The Republican Congress and President Clinton endorsed these changes in public and subsidized housing at a time when the housing needs of the poorest households in U.S. cities were at an all-time high. Under President George W. Bush, HUD reduced the rent subsidies under Section 8. This affected 1.9 million of the most vulnerable urban residents. During the Obama administration, the constraints of budget shortfalls during the Great Recession, an increasing federal debt, and resistance by Tea Party Republicans led Congress to continue slashing the budget for low-income housing. Congress in 2011, for example, slashed the federal housing budget by $3.8 billion (a 9.2 percent reduction). The programs hit hardest were public housing repair, production of affordable homes, and housing assistance for seniors and people with disabilities.

These recent cutbacks in public housing in the United States come on top of an already meager public housing sector. When compared to the industrial democracies of Europe, for example, U.S. public housing makes up a small share of the total housing stock. In Germany, France, the Netherlands, and the Scandinavian countries, urban public housing often accounts for as much as 40 percent or more of all housing. In the

United States, only 1.3 percent of the housing stock is publicly owned. Throughout Europe there has been a more widespread recognition that the private housing market—housing for profit—will not adequately house all parts of the population. Therefore, a larger share of the housing stock, as compared to the United States, has been provided by the not-for-profit or public sector. In European social democracies, public housing has been for middle-class as well as for poor and working-class residents. In U.S. cities, public housing has been the housing of last resort for the poorest of the poor only. And only one-fifth of the poor live in government-subsidized housing of any kind, be it public housing run by local government, privately owned developments subsidized by HUD, or private apartments where tenants pay rent with government vouchers.

U.S. housing policies have also contributed to the **jobs/housing mismatch**. What little affordable low-income housing there is in U.S. metropolitan areas is kept out of the suburbs and urban fringe. The suburbs and edge cities have used legal, political, and economic means to prevent this kind of housing from being built in their communities. The problem with this is that job growth occurs on the remotest edges of metropolitan areas. Thus, people who need the jobs the most, the poor in the central city, are the farthest from them. The jobs are located where the inner-city poor cannot afford to live, or discrimination prevents their living there. The poor are also the least likely to be able to afford to own cars, and public transit systems rarely extend to the urban fringe.

The jobs/housing mismatch is a form of **spatial apartheid**. Jobs and job growth occur in one place, populated by relatively affluent Whites, whereas poor African Americans and Latinos are restricted to another place.

Trends in the urban housing market together with failed housing policies have had, and continue to have, predictable consequences for a growing number of urban households. One consequence is that more and more households are experiencing a rent squeeze. In 2010 some 53 percent of *all* tenants paid rents that exceeded the federal government's definition of affordable housing—not more than 30 percent of household income. More than one-quarter of all renters now devote more than half their income to rent. When the demand for low-cost housing exceeds the supply, the cost of low-cost rents rises, as it also does when gentrification upscales areas that once housed the poor and the near poor. When urban residents, particularly poor urban residents, have to pay more for housing, they have less money available for food, transportation, education, and healthcare.

When so much of an economically marginal family's budget is devoted to housing, a crisis such as a medical emergency or sudden unemployment often means that they are evicted from their homes, resulting in homelessness. All of the problems were exacerbated during the Great Recession (see Chapter 14). Homelessness is most concentrated in big cities, with families with children as the fastest-growing segment of the nation's homeless people.

- **The Bursting of the Housing Bubble.** The decade prior to 2007 was characterized by a housing frenzy—a housing boom with a surge in home/condominium buying, escalating housing values, and "flipping" (buying a home to be sold quickly for a profit). In the process, people took on mortgages that were too large, making them vulnerable to a downturn in housing values. People on the economic margins wanted in on the action and because of their questionable credit were given subprime loans, which on the surface offered no-money down loans with what appeared to be low interest rates. These "low" rates were low for a brief time, after which the "adjustable rate clause" (found in the fine print of the loan contract) was enforced. The resulting mortgage payments were beyond the reach for many.

Add to this mix the reckless and irresponsible deal making on Wall Street involving an intricate, intertwined system of loan brokers, mortgage lenders, hedge funds, and other predators. These forces converged in late 2007, creating a "perfect storm" of economic devastation. It began when subprime borrowers began defaulting on their mortgages, sending housing prices tumbling (Gandel and Lim 2008). Banks and brokerages that had borrowed money to increase their leverage failed or were sold for bargain rates. Credit dried up. Business slowed, causing companies to lay off workers by the tens of thousands. The newly unemployed had difficulty meeting their mortgage payments, causing the rate of foreclosures and bankruptcies to soar. By 2009 some 1.5 million homes owned through subprime loans were lost through foreclosures. Many home owners found that they owed more on their mortgages than what their homes were worth. In 2009 alone, there were 3.5 million foreclosure-related filings, up from 2.3 million in 2008.

Decaying Infrastructure

Read on
MySocLab Document:
Death of a Neighborhood

The fiscal crisis of the cities has also affected them physically. The urban infrastructure is crumbling. Old water mains regularly erupt in the winter. Streets are marred with potholes. Clogged and overburdened expressways deteriorate. Sewer systems are decaying and overstressed. Public transit stations, subway tunnels, and rail and trolley tracks all make mass transportation less efficient as years go by without needed maintenance. The U.S. Department of Transportation has rated 40 percent of all U.S. bridges, many in the oldest cities, as structurally deficient or functionally obsolete.

Spending on infrastructure is only about 2.5 percent of the federal budget. Governments in countries such as Germany, Japan, and the Netherlands invest public dollars in the urban infrastructure at a rate three to four times that of the United States. As a result of the U.S. government's failure to spend adequately on the infrastructure of the nation's cities, people are increasing endangered because of inadequate waste treatment, tainted water, leaking gas lines, structurally unsound bridges, and the like.

View on
MySocLab Figure:
A Global Boom: Cities with over One Million Residents

Many economists now believe that investing public dollars in a job creation program to rebuild the nation's infrastructure and a much needed and expanded mass transit system are the best way to spur economic growth and productivity.

Transportation, Pollution, and the Environment

Watch on
MySocLab Video:
ABC Nightline: Getting Out of Gridlock

The urban transportation system in the United States, again in contrast to most European cities, is dominated by the private automobile. Since 1970 the number of vehicles has increased more than twice as fast as population growth, with only a slight gain in road capacity. The consequences of this attachment to the automobile are enormous:

- Traffic jams are getting much worse. The annual amount of time the average commuter lost was 34 hours in 2009 because of traffic congestion; in Chicago and Washington, DC, drivers were idle an average of 70 hours a year (White 2011). In total, Americans waste 1.9 billion gallons of gasoline in traffic on congested roads (Stoller 2011).
- The vehicles we drive release over 1.7 billion metric tons of greenhouse gases into the atmosphere annually. Each gallon of gasoline burned creates 20 pounds of carbon dioxide (6 to 9 tons a year per typical vehicle) (U.S. Department of Energy n.d.).
- The development of the auto-dependent urban transportation system contributes to the suburbanization and deconcentration of metropolitan areas. Highways,

interstates, expressways, and cars helped to gut the central cities, taking away middle-class taxpayers, jobs, business, and retail and commercial activity.

Between 1945 and 1970 cities, states, and the federal government spent $156 billion constructing hundreds of thousands of miles of roads, but only 16 miles of subway were built in the entire country during the same time period (Liazos 1982). This subsidization of the automobile by the government continues, as 82 percent of federal transportation funds go to highways, and only 18 cents of every transportation dollar supports mass transit. Similarly, the federal government has subsidized air travel, with the building and expansion of airports, air traffic control, and security. Meanwhile, Amtrak and energy-efficient, city-friendly public transit systems are left behind (Jackson 2010).

The reliance on the private automobile at the expense of mass public transportation also further disadvantages the urban poor. Unable to afford owning and operating cars, they must rely on an underfunded and often undependable public transit system with limited service. Because most jobs are amid the malls, office parks, and construction in the suburbs, inner-city residents have difficulty finding the transportation to work there.

- **Other Environmental Threats in the Central City.** The air is not the only source of the environmental pollution concentrated in urban areas. Illegal dumping, lead paint poisoning, and abandoned hazardous waste sites also plague the central city. Research shows that communities that are low-income neighborhoods, especially those populated by people of color, bear a disproportionate burden of environmental hazards (when the victims are the poor, it is called **environmental classism;** when those exposed to environmental hazards are racial minorities, it is called **environmental racism**). For example, according to the Centers for Disease Control, 12 percent of U.S. children have been diagnosed with asthma at some point in their lives, but the rate is 34 percent for Puerto Rican children and 25 percent for African American children. This asthma epidemic is connected to air pollution from diesel engines and power plants, both of which tend to be concentrated in lower-income urban neighborhoods (Kehrl 2004).

As poor minority communities are illegally dumped on and find themselves on top of more and more toxic and hazardous wastes, waste management corporations scramble to locate their incinerators and disposal facilities in these neighborhoods. This often places these impoverished communities in the position of choosing between at least some kind of economic development and their collective health.

Health and Healthcare

Health and healthcare problems in U.S. society are discussed at length in Chapter 17. But here, these problems in urban locations deserve special attention because some health and healthcare problems are more concentrated in large cities.

Because poverty is concentrated in the central city, so are the diseases associated with it. Poor people in the city get tuberculosis and other diseases almost unheard of among the suburban middle class. Poor city dwellers are much more likely to die of cancer. Chronic conditions such as diabetes often go untreated. Many of the urban poor, without health insurance of any kind, cannot afford to burden their families with the huge debt that lifesaving technologies would bring.

Infant mortality rates are highest in poor minority neighborhoods in the inner city and are as high as or higher than in many developing world countries. African American infants are four times more likely to die from low birth weight than White infants. Many poor inner-city children who survive their first year are then threatened by such diseases as measles, tetanus, polio, tuberculosis, diphtheria, and whooping cough because they have not received adequate inoculations.

Another health problem adding to the burden of public hospitals is AIDS. The Centers for Disease Control and Prevention (CDC) confirms that the incidence of AIDS and the costs of caring for people with AIDS are highest and most concentrated in central cities, where gay men and intravenous drug users are overrepresented.

Many poor and working-class central-city residents have seen their small neighborhood or community hospitals close under the pressure of rising costs. For many of these hospitals, the number of indigent nonpaying patients became too high a proportion of their total number. More than one in ten U.S. hospitals is now routinely refusing to treat these people.

This means that more and more central-city residents are unable to find any medical care in private for-profit or private not-for-profit hospitals and clinics. Increasingly, they have only one alternative—the large, underfunded, understaffed, underequipped public hospitals that cannot legally deny them care. The problem is threefold (Orenstein 2001). First, the number of patient visits is rising. Second, the number of emergency departments is declining, increasing the load for those remaining emergency rooms, as the average annual patient volume is rising. Third, and related to the second, the number of hospital beds is declining while the nation's population is rising. One obvious reason for the decline in hospital beds is the closing of public hospitals in cities, which leaves the poor in increasing jeopardy.

Thus, facilities are being overwhelmed by the number of patients and the cost of treating them. Because they are unable to afford doctor visits or are unable to find doctors who will accept the lower fees of Medicaid (the state and federal government's insurance program for the poor), patients are coming to the emergency room sicker and in need of more costly care. But the urban public hospitals are less and less able to provide adequate care. As a result, urban public hospitals are forced to practice **triage**—treating the most urgent emergencies first. Other patients must wait for treatment, sometimes for days.

Many private hospitals that have remained open have done so by cutting high-cost services for the indigent. Many have closed emergency rooms and trauma units. High-risk obstetrical care, as well as drug and alcohol abuse treatment programs, also have been shut down. As private hospitals in the city abdicate these high-cost services, more of them must be taken over by public hospitals, increasing their burden with more patients and higher costs.

In short, the increasing number of uninsured and underinsured people seeking healthcare in the emergency rooms of public hospitals, the lack of federal government support for these hospitals, and the inability of city governments caught in a budgetary crisis to fund them, all ensure that without major reforms, urban health and healthcare can only deteriorate further.

Urban Schools

Public schools in the United States are separate and unequal. The more affluent middle class has moved to the suburbs, where their children attend virtually all-White schools; or if they have remained in the city and can afford it, they send their children to private schools. The less affluent and racial minorities are left in the city's public schools.

Urban schools are class segregated. With poverty becoming more geographically concentrated, poor children typically go to school with other poor children. Most significant, the amount of money spent on the education of the children attending city schools pales in comparison to what is spent on each student in the more affluent suburbs. This imbalance results from the heavy reliance on local property taxes to finance public schooling in the United States.

As suburbanization robs the city's tax base, the city becomes less able to adequately fund public education. Consequently, suburban schools, when compared to inner-city schools, are more likely to have smaller class sizes, more computers, a better library, special programs for the gifted and the disabled, and state-of-the-art equipment and facilities. Chapter 16 provides the details and the consequences of these severe inequities. As a preview, we note that the results of all of this inequity are predictable: lower standardized test scores and high dropout rates in many urban school districts. Already disadvantaged inner-city students are further disadvantaged.

Crime, Drugs, and Gangs

Watch on MySocLab Video: ABC Nightline: MS-13 Gang Life

The problems of crime and drugs in the United States are discussed in Chapters 12 and 13. These problems also have a special relation to urban areas. In the United States, crime has become a euphemism for cities. More specifically, there is a media and popular identification of crime, and the drugs and gangs assumed to be related to it, with the inner city. And because crime is also a code word for race, it comes to be associated in both media and popular accounts primarily with young African American males in the inner city.

Admittedly, the FBI's *Uniform Crime Report* and the U.S. Justice Department's National Crime Survey have shown for some time that poor minority males in the inner city have the highest arrest rates for serious felony offenses and are, along with other members of poor minority inner-city communities, the most likely to be victims of street crimes.

As we have seen, the cities have been gutted by job loss, disinvestment by corporations and banks, and a declining tax base that negatively affects schools and hospitals. Cities have increasing concentrations of poverty, rising unemployment and low-wage employment, and a dwindling supply of decent and affordable housing. All these conditions are related to street crime (F. Hagan 1994). And because the inner cities, mostly populated by racial and ethnic minorities, are especially vulnerable to these conditions, street crime is concentrated there, especially among inner-city youth and young adults.

In late 2009 the jobless rate for 16- to 24-year-old Black men was 34.5 percent, more than three times the rate for the entire population. Moreover, research finds evidence of discrimination (summarized in Haynes 2009):

- Lower-income White teens are more likely to find work than upper-income Black teens.
- Black men are less likely to receive a call back or job offer than equally qualified White men.
- Black men with a clean record fare no better than White men just released from prison in finding a job.

These young people are "disconnected youth" with nothing constructive to do. Many turn to hustling, "doing what they can—much of it illegal—to get along" (Herbert 2003b:2). They engage in an alternate or **informal economy** (alternative economic activities) to ensure their survival. An important part of this informal economy is criminal, much of it involving drugs. In effect, street crime becomes their work (Hagedorn 1998). Participation in drug rings can spell money, status, and survival. That the socioeconomic conditions in the inner city make it an ideal location for the illegal drug economy has not been lost on the people who control international drug trafficking. The gangs that provide members with meaningful social relationships and status in the barren, isolated inner city and with protection from other sources of violence in their communities can also ensure survival with specialized stolen property, drug, and weapons sales (Hagedorn 1998).

Official U.S. drug policy has deleterious effects on inner-city communities as well. By criminalizing them, the official strategy is to eliminate drugs and their negative consequences by arresting, prosecuting, convicting, and imprisoning drug users, buyers, and sellers. This "war on drugs" actually escalates drug selling, use, and addiction and magnifies the negative consequences that go with them (see Chapter 13). Criminalization increases drug prices and profits, thus making the drug trade more attractive. Sellers thus work to recruit more users and addicts. Because their drugs are illegal and expensive, users and addicts may have to steal or sell drugs to afford their own habits.

Besides failing as a drug-control strategy, the war on drugs is not being waged fairly. Although the official claim is one of zero tolerance, pursuing all users, buyers, and sellers no matter who or where they are, the war is racist and focused on young African American males in poor inner-city neighborhoods (see Chapter 12). One in three Black males is now under the supervision of the criminal justice system—on probation or parole, in jail or prison, or under pretrial release (a rate eight times higher than for White men). In many cities, and in many inner-city neighborhoods, this proportion is much higher. This only serves to marginalize further the already highly marginal poor Black inner-city residents, with ripple effects throughout Black families, schools, and communities.

- **Fear of Crime in the City.** Fear of crime is often exaggerated in comparison to the reality of, or actual potential for, criminal victimization. Often the fear is not of crime at all. What people identify as a fear of crime is often a fear of people of cultural and racial groups different than their own. Nonetheless, such misdirected fear of crime is often a significant factor in central-city decline. If people, corporations, retailers, and small businesses will not stay in or move to the city because they believe it is not safe, then the process of urban decline cannot be turned around. A self-fulfilling prophecy of central-city decline sets in. Because of the belief that the city is crime-ridden and unsafe, people, businesses, and jobs leave the city, thereby helping make it more crime prone and unsafe and further removing the possibility that the businesses and jobs that could begin to change the socioeconomic conditions that produce crime will go there in the future.

6.2 Identify social problems that are tied to suburban areas in the United States.

SUBURBAN PROBLEMS

For over fifty years, there has been a dramatic population shift in the United States—people moving from cities to the suburbs. Although this shift had begun in some metropolitan areas at the turn of the century or even earlier, it accelerated and became the dominant demographic trend in almost every major U.S. metropolitan area after 1950. As a result of this exodus, more Americans now live in the suburbs than in cities, rural areas, and small towns combined.

Although some middle-class Blacks have moved to the suburbs, those who move to the suburbs are predominantly upper-middle-class, middle-class, and, to a lesser extent, working-class Whites. This process of **White flight** continues to increase both class and race segregation. As suburbs grow and become essentially middle class and White, shrinking central cities are left with a greater proportion of their remaining population who are poor and minority, a trend heightened by the huge number of immigrants, mostly Latino and Asian, moving to U.S. cities. The suburbanization of the United States has meant the geographic separation of classes and races, particularly of middle-class Whites from poor African Americans. Today, very high levels of racial segregation persist in most major U.S. metropolitan areas. Even when Blacks leave the city, they are often resegregated in Black suburbs or in Black neighborhoods in White suburbs.

Middle-class Whites move to the suburbs for a better place to raise their children, better schools, and less crime, or as Eric Klinenberg has put it, moving to the suburbs was and is motivated often by the "search for sanctuary, security and class segregation" (Klinenberg 2004:40). Race plays a part in these motives. "A better place to raise children" often meant a neighborhood with few or no African Americans or Latinos. "Better schools" often meant virtually all-White schools not under court order to desegregate. And "crime" was synonymous with inner-city Blacks for many suburbanites. Those people moving to the suburbs were also attracted to the open space and the prospect of an unattached, single-family dwelling with a yard. This prospect was made more attainable by generally lower real estate costs and lower property tax rates outside the city.

Suburban Sprawl

Suburbanization is not a naturally occurring phenomenon. The suburbs were encouraged, supported, and directly subsidized by the federal government, and they profited large developers and corporations. The history of suburbanization in the United States, as Kenneth Jackson (1985), Peter Dreier (2000), and Daniel Lazare (2001) make clear, shows that federal government policies and spending shaped consumer choices that pushed people out of the cities and pulled them into the suburbs. The federal government financed the construction of the interstate highway and expressway system, which opened the suburbs to speculation and development and connected them to the city, where many suburbanites still worked. Housing policies implemented by the FHA (Federal Housing Authority) and VA (Veterans Administration), offering low-cost government-insured mortgages—reserved, for the most part, for Whites and the suburbs—facilitated the population shift. The government subsidizes home ownership by permitting taxes and mortgage interest to be tax deductible (a savings to homeowners of about $131 billion in 2010) (Kocieniewski 2010). Housing policies that allow local suburban governments to refuse public and subsidized housing in their communities have also encouraged the White middle class to reside where there is less affordable housing and few poor and minority residents. Cheap fossil fuels and low fuel taxes (such taxes are five to ten times higher in Europe than in the United States) have supported both suburbanization and the extreme dependency of American metropolitan areas on automobiles (discussed later). Also, policies set by Congress earmark these taxes to be spent on road building rather than mass transit. And local governments have set more favorable property tax rates to lure people, businesses, and jobs to the suburbs. Suburban municipalities added to their growth by providing commercial property tax waivers and other inducements to entice business to move there.

More than one-fourth of all cities with a population of between 100,000 and 400,000 are suburbs. The rapid growth of the suburbs has led to a new city form called "boomburgs." A **boomburg** is defined as a suburban city that has at least 100,000 people and has experienced double-digit growth every decade since it became defined by the Census Bureau as urban (2,500 or more). These cities have strip developments, office parks, and "big-box" retailers such as Home Depot and Best Buy with large parking lots.

The deconcentration of U.S. metropolitan areas is proceeding beyond the suburbs to what are being called "urban villages" or "edge cities" or "exurbs" even more remote from the central cities, sometimes as far as 40 miles from the central business district. These residential areas on the edge of metropolitan areas experienced rapid growth until the Great Recession hit in late 2007. High gas prices discouraging long commutes and the negative effects of the bursting of the housing bubble led many back toward the cities and renting. Thus, the end of the exurban explosion (Yen 2012).

The addition of new highways and beltways around and through metropolitan areas typically opens up new land for development of tract homes and strip malls at a rate about twice that of population growth. Such **suburban sprawl** (low-density, automobile-dependent development) absorbs more than 2 million acres of open space each year. It also results in slow commutes, traffic congestion, polluted air, over-crowded schools, automobile dependency, and visual blight (a similar look, whether on the outskirts of Phoenix, Omaha, or Detroit, composed of fast-food franchises, Walmarts, drive-through banks, tract housing architecture, and the like). Following are some facts associated with sprawl:

- Farmland around Denver is falling to sprawl at a rate of 90,000 acres a year.
- About 3.3 million Americans commute more than 50 miles each way to work.
- The greater Los Angeles metropolitan area continues to spread, especially 60 to 70 miles east toward the desert.
- Grass (most of it in suburban lawns) is the largest irrigated crop in the United States.

The effects of suburbanization and sprawl are enormous. First, there are environmental effects such as the disruption of wildlife habitats, the altering of rivers and streams, and pollution. In 2011 there were 246 million vehicles in the United States. According to the Department of Energy, these vehicles annually release over 1.7 billion metric tons of greenhouse gases into the atmosphere, contributing to climate change (reported in www.fueleconomy.gov n.d.). The autoculture of the suburbs shares considerable blame for this pollution.

A second consequence of suburbanization is, as mentioned earlier, that as the more affluent leave cities for the suburbs, they take their spending and their taxes with them, leaving businesses less profitable and city governments strapped for the funds to provide adequate services. This stress on the city is exacerbated by concentrating poverty in the cities—the homeless, new immigrants, the working poor, the elderly, and people with disabilities. This is further compounded by the movement of jobs from the cities to the suburbs.

Third, the economic costs of all this suburbanization, deconcentration, and sprawl are extremely high. Each time metropolitan areas spread out, new highways, streets, bridges, sewers, police and fire stations, and schools must be built. Much of this cost is covered by government with the public's tax dollars. Meanwhile, taxpayers in the cities and older suburbs watch their infrastructures, public transit, and schools deteriorate, even though it is almost always less costly to repair and maintain old infrastructure than to build new. See the "Looking Toward the Future" panel.

Finally, there are some health concerns. People who live in sprawling suburbs are much more likely to drive to school, to work, or to the store than are people living in densely populated cities and neighborhoods. As a result of less exercise, suburbanites have higher blood pressure and weigh an average of six pounds more than their counterparts in more walkable locales. Research also shows that people making long commutes are at a higher risk for high blood pressure, sleep deprivation, and depression (Longman 2001). They have more frequent disputes with their coworkers and families. They suffer more frequent and more serious illnesses, and they are more likely to experience premature deaths (Frank 2001).

Looking Toward the Future

RIGHTING THE URBAN–SUBURBAN IMBALANCE

Typically, there are huge disparities between cities and their suburbs. Businesses (and their property taxes) have left cities for the suburbs. People, usually relatively prosperous, have moved their residences (and their property taxes) from the city to the suburbs. Shopping areas have been built in the suburbs, taking customers and their sales taxes from the cities and causing many central-city businesses to close, with the subsequent loss of jobs.

Thus, with a few exceptions, the central cities of the United States have struggled financially, resulting in a decaying infrastructure, a decline in services, and inadequately financed schools. City residents, especially racial/ethnic minorities, have declining job opportunities and deal face-to-face with crime and drugs. But as the central cities decline, the suburbs prosper. The suburbs have incorporated into separate municipalities and school districts. The enlarged tax bases have provided for state-of-the-art schools, fire and police protection, parks, and other amenities. The result is a decaying central city, ringed by a series of growing, prosperous governmental entities separate from the city. In effect, the cities "remain woebegone, in part because so much of their potential taxable wealth lies in the suburbs, beyond their reach" (Traub 2003:17).

Do the suburbs and their residents owe anything to the central cities and, if so, should there be any redress for the inequities? Many suburbanites work in the central cities, thus depending on the city for adequate streets, subway systems, police protection, sanitation, and the like, but at no cost to them in taxes. Moreover, suburbanites are free riders when they use the amenities of the cities such as parks, zoos, symphony orchestras, museums, professional sports teams, and urban universities. One solution is a commuter tax of, say, 3 percent of income generated in the city. The mayor of New York City, for example, could say "to all those doctors and bankers in Westchester, 'we've given you a beautifully refurbished Grand Central Terminal, and we've given you Broadway and Central Park and subways without graffiti, and we're paying to protect you from terrorists; give us a mite out of your adjusted gross, for God's sake'" (Traub 2003:18). This idea seems fair enough, but it is almost universally rejected (an exception is Kansas City, Missouri, which taxes workers who commute from Kansas suburbs to work there).

Better yet would be the political integration of cities with their suburbs. Such integration is the only fair way for central cities to have their share of the wealth in metropolitan areas. Moreover, regional governments could better manage regional problems such as pollution control, safe water, police and fire protection, equality of educational opportunity, and efficient public transportation. Will these changes happen? Will the advantaged give up some of their advantages to achieve fairness, or will they continue to abuse this unequal but symbiotic relationship?

Automobile Dependency

As auto dependency causes sprawls and decentralizes urban areas, a vicious cycle of more cars and highways sets in. More automobiles traveling greater distances to the suburbs increases traffic congestion. This, in turn, leads to the construction of more and bigger highways, which encourages even more cars, further decentralizing metropolitan areas.

The decentralization that comes with auto transportation has destroyed the landscape and encouraged the spread of commercial strips, shopping malls, and multilane roads and streets. The shopping areas are spread out so that suburban residents cannot walk to a store, as is possible in high-density cities. Instead they must use an automobile.

Urban sprawl, with its reliance on the automobile, has also led to environmental pollution and a waste of natural resources, as noted above.

Social Isolation in the Suburbs

Moving to the suburbs is a move away from diversity and toward homogenization (Eitzen 2004). The suburbs are disproportionately White and relatively affluent. Suburbanites leave immigrants, racial minorities, poor people, and the homeless for life near people like themselves. More than 6 million households are situated in gated communities where the residents are walled off physically and socially from "others."

The physical arrangements of suburbs are especially socially isolating. Rather than walking to the corner grocery or nearby shop and visiting with the clerks and their neighbors, suburbanites drive somewhere away from their immediate neighborhood to shop among strangers. Or they may not leave their home at all, working, shopping, banking, and paying bills by computer. For suburban teenagers and children, almost everything is away—friends, practice fields, music lessons, jobs, schools, and the malls, resulting in a disconnect from those nearby. Suburban neighborhoods in particular are devoid of meeting places. In effect, the suburbs often suffer from a lack of community—and connection.

Transforming the Suburbs: The End of Sprawl?

The collapse of the housing market brought about by the Great Recession and relatively high gasoline prices have resulted in some changes in the suburbs. More and more people are reconsidering the wisdom of living so far from work in homes they can no longer afford.

Social Policy

THE FUTURE: RETURN TO URBAN DENSITY?

Urban sprawl with its attendant dependence on the automobile leads to a series of serious problems, among them: loss of agricultural land, dependence on foreign oil, and environmental crises such as air pollution and climate change. These are problems now. What about 2050 when today's college students will be in their 50s and 60s? By 2050 the United States will likely add 100 million people, requiring many millions of houses and many billions of square feet of office and other non-residential space (Harkinson 2010). If the United States continues its present patterns, suburbs will replace open space the size of New Mexico by 2050. If we build more freeways and add more cars, by mid-century Americans will drive 7 trillion miles per year—twice the mileage now.

Are there any alternatives? Some plans get at the edge of the problem such as more fuel-efficient cars, more mass transit, and replacing gasoline with cleaner burning natural gas for energy. A more focused approach to the "metastasizing, car-dependent sprawl" is urban density (that is, squeezing more people into cities and inner suburbs). High-rise apartments/condominiums are energy efficient as the layers of walls, ceilings, and floors provide excellent insulation. Urbanites do not drive much; they rely on mass transit and much of what they need in goods and services is within walking distance. Travel to work can be by bicycle, bus, subway, or train. Bicycling, by the way, is common in European cities, most notably Amsterdam, and it is on the rise now in U.S. cities (bike use is up 39 percent nationally since 2001) (Adler 2011).

A second alternative is to redesign urban and suburban communities (a movement called the "New Urbanism"). The new urbanism involves a comprehensive plan based on the old Main Street model, which is a web of pedestrian-friendly streets surrounding a mass-transit-served downtown center. This type of urban space features a diversity of uses such as homes, shops, restaurants, fitness gyms, entertainment centers, libraries, civic buildings, schools, and public spaces such as plazas, greens, parks, and squares closely connected so they are walkable or bikable (Pierce 2011). The key is to design these communities for people, not cars. In doing so, society saves open space, reduces car dependence and pollution, and strengthens community ties (*National Geographic* n.d.).

With housing values plummeting in the suburbs while neighborhoods close to downtown have held the value, there is a move back closer to the urban core. Homes close to urban centers or that have convenient access to mass transit are especially desirable (Penalver 2008).

Builders/developers of new suburban areas are changing their philosophy. Instead of isolated bedroom communities, with no core, they are building whole communities. Instead of strip malls and big box stores that people drive to, there will be community centers with shops, schools, and services nearby. These neighborhoods promote walking. Instead of building single-family homes exclusively, builders are providing a mix of residential styles (see the "Social Policy" panel).

These trends have the added benefits of saving energy, reducing traffic congestion, and cutting air pollution.

6.3 Discuss the social problems that are tied to rural areas in the United States.

RURAL PROBLEMS

By **rural**, we refer to the nonmetropolitan population that resides in small towns and the open countryside, an area encompassing 80 percent of the nation's land area. Much of this country is emptying out, especially the Great Plains and Appalachia, with the share of people in rural areas falling to 16 percent in 2010, down from the previous low of 20 percent in 2000. In 1910, 72 percent of the population lived in rural America.

More than one-third of all counties lost population since the 2010 census as jobs dried up and young adults left. Indicative of the rural decline is that the U.S. Postal Service plans to close thousands of branches in rural areas. And Delta Airlines, for example, ended flight service to twenty-four small airports in 2011 (Yen 2011). Rural counties growing in population did so because of jobs, such as the boom in natural gas, oil, and coal extraction in North Dakota, Montana, Pennsylvania, and Texas. Growing rural counties were those near metropolitan areas and those popular with retirees because of attractions such as lakes, deserts, and mountains. This section examines a variety of social problems faced by rural communities. But first, let's demythologize rural communities. To begin, contrary to common stereotypes, rural areas are not always alike. Typically, the image of rural areas is of family farms in

The economic boom has been both a blessing and a curse to the towns in the Bakken shale region of North Dakota.

farming communities in the Midwest, but retirement communities, Native American reservations, resort areas, and natural resource extraction industries are also found in rural areas (Flora et al. 1992).

Second, rural communities have changed dramatically in the last fifty years or so. In the past, rural areas were relatively homogeneous and self-sufficient, with a strong sense of common identity. The lives of people centered in their communities for schools, churches, banks, jobs, stores, and services.

But times have changed and, with them, so too the essence of rural life. Automobiles have made it possible to live in one town, work in another, and shop in a third. Schools have consolidated, with children from a wider area and even more than one town attending, lessening the attachment to one's community. Work, once focused on a single activity such as farming, ranching, mining, or lumbering, has broadened to, for example, making furniture, producing mobile homes, factory farming (replacing family farming), and massive food processing. Thus, work roles, once similar throughout the community, have become very different. Many of these communities, once comprising people similar in ethnicity, religion, and culture, have faced the influx of new neighbors, many of whom were recent immigrants, especially Latinos, with different customs and religious beliefs. The effect of these changes has been to lessen the bonds and common identity among rural residents in most contemporary rural communities.

Third, poverty is a greater problem in rural America than in the cities. Of the fifty counties with the highest child-poverty rates, forty-eight are in rural America (Pierre 2004:30).

Poverty

The poverty rate is highest in central cities, followed in order by rural and suburban (see Table 6.1). There are important differences between the rural and urban poor. The rural poor have some advantages over the urban poor (low-cost housing, raising their own food) and many disadvantages (low-paid work, higher prices for most products, lack of public transportation, fewer social services, and fewer welfare benefits).

Poverty rates in rural America are higher for racial and ethnic groups than for Whites, reflecting a historical legacy that has left rural areas with concentrated minority populations in certain areas. The highest concentration of U.S. poverty exists in four nonmetropolitan pockets: the Appalachian mountain region, where the poor are predominantly White; the old Southern cotton belt from the Carolinas to the Louisiana Delta, where the poor are mostly African American; the Rio Grande Valley/Texas Gulf Coast, where the poor are largely Latino; and the Southwest and upper Plains states, where Native Americans are concentrated in and around reservations. Indicating these patterns, ten states in 2010 (all from the South and Southwest) had child poverty

TABLE 6.1
Poverty Rates by Place 2010

	Poverty Rate
Central Cities	19.7%
Suburbs	11.8%
Nonmetropolitan areas	16.5%

Source: DeNavas-Walt, Carmen, Bernadette D. Proctor, and Jessica C. Smith, 2011. "Income, Poverty, and Health Insurance Coverage in the United States: 2010." *Current Population Reports*, P60-239 (September), p. 15.

A Closer Look

THE POOREST COMMUNITY IN THE UNITED STATES

There are about 1,450 **colonias** (shantytown settlements of Latino immigrants), home to an estimated 500,000, located along the Texas–Mexico border in South Texas (South Texas Colonia Initiative 2010). As described by the Attorney General of Texas, Greg Abbott: "Colonias are substandard housing developments, often found along the Texas–Mexico border, where residents lack basic services such as drinking water, sewage treatment, and paved roads" (Abbott 2009: para 1). Moreover, "these areas have become a geographic, social and economic state of isolation for thousands of families. Theirs is a daily reminder of the debilitating effects of poverty, lack of education, social isolation and critical need for essential health and human services" (Texas Health and Human Services Commission 2003).

Among places with 1,000 households or more, a colonia called Cameron Park is the poorest spot in the United States. Cameron Park, an unincorporated community of 6,000, is near Brownsville, Texas. It has the lowest per capita income of any location in the United States, $4,103 a year, and only about 20 percent of its residents are high school graduates.

Like other colonias, its housing is composed of shacks, trailers, campers, and run-down houses. Along with the decrepit housing, there are inadequate sewers, filthy conditions (roaches, rats, stagnant water), and terrible roads.

According to local officials and scholars, colonias were condemned to poverty at birth. Starting in the 1950s, developers snapped up low-lying, agriculturally worthless land along the border. They divided it into plots and sold it to the growing population of migrant workers allowed into the United States during and after World War II. . . . Lots were sold without access to water, sewers or electricity. Immigrant purchasers could buy land cheaply, but they did not receive title until it had been paid off. If they missed a payment, the developer could repossess the land, evict the buyer and sell it anew. For years the colonias grew, unfettered by state laws or local ordinances. They were filthy, frequently flooded and forgotten. Some were on the edge of cities, but the cities wanted no part of them, seeing them as a potential financial drain. . . . That

left Texas colonias in the hands of county governments, which, lacking the power to enact ordinances, were outgunned by Texas developers and real estate agents. (Hockstader 2002:29)

The economy has made the situation worse for the inhabitants of Cameron Park and the other colonias. The drought has meant fewer agricultural jobs. The textile industry that employed many (at relatively low wages) disintegrated as Levi's, Haggar, and Horace Small factories closed. Meanwhile the North American Free Trade Agreement (NAFTA) triggered a population boom, outpacing the supply of affordable housing.

Recently, there have been governmental efforts to fix substandard living conditions. The Texas Legislature has passed laws intended to remedy the conditions in existing colonias and to prevent new colonias (Abbott 2009). Moreover the legislature has authorized up to $175 million in state bonds to build or improve roads and drainage. And the U.S. Department of Housing and Urban Development now offers low-cost financing to build homes. Moreover, developers must provide basic infrastructure (water, sewer, roads, and drainage). Despite the laudable attempts, colonias still remain wretched places.

rates above 25 percent, and eleven states had child poverty rates between 20 and 24 percent (Kids Count 2011). (See the "A Closer Look" panel for a description of the poorest place in the United States.)

Rural minorities are especially vulnerable to poverty. To a large extent, poverty among rural minorities is rooted in societal-level forces that work against those of lower-class origins and non-Whites.

Jobs in Rural Areas

Historically, the work of rural people has centered on the resources of the land, whether through farming, mining, or forestry. These industries experience boom and bust cycles as the costs go up and down, depending on foreign competition, decline in prices because of too much production and discoveries of new deposits, or high prices because of scarcity. New technologies reduce the number of workers required for production. Employment in these activities peaked in the early 1900s, and, except for pockets of activity, been declining ever since.

Income in rural areas is lower than in metropolitan areas. In 2010, for example, the median household income in rural America was $40,287, compared to the median household income in central cities of $44,049, and $56,140 in the suburbs (DeNavas-Walt, Proctor, and Smith 2011).

- **Farming.**   Around 1800, 95 percent of Americans made their full-time living from agriculture. A hundred years ago it was 45 percent, and by the turn of the twenty-first century, it was less than 2 percent. The United States still has agriculture, but it is mostly large-scale agribusiness, as 1 percent of farmers account for more than half of all farm income. The demise of the family farm is the result of market forces. Competition from global markets required producing more per acre. The demands of national retail chains such as Walmart and McDonald's (Schlosser 2001) require standardization and huge outputs.

  This is accomplished with the latest and very expensive machinery, the cost of which is justified by farming huge areas, squeezing out the smaller farmers. Large-scale, homogenized production is profitable. In addition to harvesting crops (corn, soybeans, wheat, potatoes, vegetables, fruit), factory farms produce pigs, cattle, turkeys, chickens, and even catfish. Work is mechanized as much as possible, reducing the number of workers required.

  The implications of the demise of small-scale farms are several. The first and obvious consequence is that former farmers must find a new occupation, and the opportunities are few in rural America. Second, many, especially young people, are forced to leave the community for nonagricultural jobs (the average age of farmers was 57 in 2010). For every farmer under the age of 25, there are five who are 75 or older (Bryan 2012). Third, with the loss of people and their resources, many local communities decline in importance and function. This decline is exacerbated when the factory farms in a region are owned by outside corporations because the profits leave the area. Fourth, rural communities have become increasingly stratified with a few large-scale farmers at the top, small farmers barely getting by, and farm workers at the bottom making very meager wages without benefits.

Watch on
MySocLab Slideshow:
Auto Industry Layoffs

- **Manufacturing.**   Contrary to the common assumption, manufacturing in rural areas employs nearly twice as many workers as does farming. Some rural areas have industries tied to their agricultural base, such as textile mills and apparel manufacturing near the cotton growing in the South. But these industries have faded dramatically because of global competition. So mills have closed and manufacturers such as Levi's have moved their operations outside the United States to countries where labor and supplies are cheaper.

  Other industries have been attracted to rural areas, where land is relatively cheap and there is a supply of nonunionized labor willing to work for wages lower than in urban/suburban areas. So, for example, production of agricultural machinery, recreational vehicles, and parts supplies for the automotive industry has moved into rural areas. The problem is that these industries may leave at any moment because of economic misfortune or in search of workers willing to work for lower wages and benefits.

  A particular industrial form—meatpacking—has transformed some rural areas. Corporations such as Tyson, ConAgra, and Cargill have built slaughterhouses in remote towns across the rural Great Plains. In southwestern Kansas, for example, meatpacking operations in places such as Garden City, Dodge City, and Liberal have made these towns rural boomtowns and Kansas the biggest beef-packing state in the United States. The work in these plants is routinized, deskilled, and dangerous. The workers are primarily immigrants from Southeast Asia, Mexico, and Central America, thus transforming the racial/ethnic composition and cultural life of once homogeneous areas.

- **Extraction of Natural Resources.**   Historically, there have been boom and bust cycles for towns and rural areas with lucrative natural resources such as gold, silver, copper, coal, and oil shale were discovered and eventually depleted or the price no longer made it practical to continue. Today there is a tremendous oil boom in some rural areas brought about by the new technologies of horizontal drilling and hydraulic fracturing. Consider the Bakken oil formation, 640 square miles of oil, holding an estimated 34 billion barrels. The location is mainly in the northwest seventeen counties of North Dakota, and small parts of eastern Montana, and Saskatchewan, Canada. Williston, North Dakota, is located in the middle of the Bakken bonanza. Here is what has happened in Williston from the recent boom times (Johnson 2012). The once-stable population has risen from 12,000 in 2000 to at least 30,000 now. The agricultural base has been superseded by land speculation and oil-dominated activities (e.g., land that recently sold for $500 an acre now sells for $200,000 or more an acre). Unemployment is basically nonexistent as McDonald's pays a minimum of $15 an hour and jobs in the oil fields may start at over $100,000 a year for 80-hour work weeks. As a result, the average household income has increased by 130 percent over the last decade. The boom has increased greatly tax revenues for the local and state coffers.

    But while economic opportunities are plentiful, there is also a large downside to this oil boom (the following is from Johnson 2012; Holeywell 2011; and Schactman 2012). Most of the people moving in are men and this has led to a rise in crime (assaults, rape, prostitution). The Williston police department is overwhelmed with the increase in crime, increased traffic accidents, and alcohol/drug related incidents. The population surge has strained public resources for schools, medical facilities, wastewater treatment, fire fighting equipment, and roads. The cost of living has risen with the higher incomes. The cost of food, lumber, and other goods has soared. Housing, in particular, has skyrocketed. For example, a small one-bedroom apartment, which not long ago rented for less than $500 a month, now costs $2,000 (if you can find one).

    The dark side of the economic boom is just not the strains on the economics and infrastructure of the communities affected. The bigger issue is the loss felt by locals of their sense of community. The pace and rhythm of an economy based on agriculture has been replaced by rapid changes brought about by easy money, outside corporations, oil rigs, truck traffic, housing construction, and environmental problems. The people moving in are often quite different from the locals in race/ethnicity, occupational skills, and interests. They are strangers in a community once populated solely by friends and extended families with so many things in common. What does all of this mean for the sense of community that the locals once felt?

- **Recreation/Leisure.**   Rural areas with natural amenities—mountains, lakes, pleasant climates—have encouraged development and jobs, while the conditions best suited for agriculture—flat terrain and humid summers—have been left out. In some of these areas, mining or timber industries once flourished, then experienced economic decline. But with the coming of tourism, winter and summer resorts, and the building of vacation homes, these areas have been reborn. Jobs have been created in the building trades and in service areas. The jobs in the service sector tend to be lower wage, sometimes part time, with little opportunity for advancement and few benefits. These jobs are highly volatile because of the seasonality of tourism and second-home residency.

When amenity-based development occurs, the cost of living increases. Moreover, many low-paid workers cannot afford to live in the amenity-based communities and must commute from more affordable locations, sometimes at considerable distance. Similar to the situation in the slaughterhouse towns, the influx of newcomers and massive development into these once pristine areas often create a culture clash as traditional and newcomer values collide.

Environment

At least four environmental problems involve rural America. First, there is the continued reduction in the land devoted to farming and ranching. This lost land is covered subsequently with concrete, asphalt, and buildings. Covering the land, and consequently destroying its flora, intensifies global warming.

Second, there are several problems involving water. Most significant, massive irrigation takes water from the underground aquifers much faster than it can be replenished. For example, the Ogallala aquifer provides 30 percent of groundwater used for irrigation in the United States. This aquifer, which stretches 800 miles north to south and 400 miles east to west under the Great Plains, was first tapped in 1912. Its early use was from wells 50 feet deep or less with windmills as the primary mechanism for drawing the water. Now wells are sometimes 500 feet deep with pumps that allow a flow rate of 1,000 gallons a minute. Consequently, the Ogallala aquifer is now only one-third its original capacity. The overuse of water from the Ogallala and other aquifers will result in the loss of land for farming and increased desertification of the land.

Related to the draining of the aquifers by farmers is another problem with the water supply: entrepreneurs buying agricultural land not for farming or ranching but primarily for the water beneath it (Cook 2002; Hightower 2002b). For example, Cadiz, Inc., owns 20,000 acres in the Mojave Desert. It proposes to pump some 20 billion gallons of water to cities in Southern California. Similarly, land owned by T. Boone Pickens is above the Ogallala aquifer in the Texas Panhandle. He has been authorized by Texas to pump and sell up to 65 billion gallons of water a year, sending it by pipeline to San Antonio and Dallas. This privatization of water for profit—substituting private interest for public interest—will hasten the loss of water, this most precious of resources, for all of us.

A third environmental problem is a consequence of the use of pesticides, herbicides, and chemical fertilizers to maximize crop production. These chemicals are a serious health danger to agricultural workers. Also, these chemicals drain from the fields into streams, rivers, and lakes, raising the levels of nitrates and other poisons to dangerous levels. So, too, with the chemicals that seep into private and municipal wells destined for human consumption.

Factory farms present serious air and water pollution. A single hog operation may involve as many as 20,000 pigs, which produce an awful stench and problems with waste products from these animals (Johnson and Kuppig 2004). So, too, with cattle.

There is some evidence that the location of large-scale factory farms involves *environmental racism*. For example, a study found that reductions in community quality of life attributed to large-scale hog operations were more likely to be found in counties that are disproportionately Black than White (Stretesky, Johnston, and Arney 2003:231).

Healthcare and Delivery

This section is divided into two parts: disparities in health status comparing rural with metropolitan areas and the relatively inadequate medical infrastructure in rural America.

Residents in rural areas have greater health difficulties than those in metropolitan areas (Morton 2003):

- Death rates for children and young adults (ages 1 to 24 years) are higher.
- Death rates from unintentional injuries are higher.
- Death rates from motor vehicle traffic-related injuries are higher.
- Suicide rates for males are higher.
- Age-adjusted death rates for heart diseases, strokes, diabetes, nutritional deficiencies, and digestive organ cancers are higher.

Among the reasons for these disparities are the relatively old population in non-metropolitan areas, the more dangerous nature of work, the relatively high rate of uninsured, and exposure to pesticides, herbicides, and other dangerous chemicals. Most significant is the lack of medical help available in rural areas.

The medical infrastructure includes hospitals, public health departments, and emergency medical services. In each instance, the medical infrastructure is inadequate or sometimes nonexistent in rural America. Many rural hospitals have closed for financial reasons due to a low tax base and due to the relatively high proportion of Medicare and Medicaid patients that are underfinanced by federal and state governments. As hospitals close, patients must seek help but must travel greater distances for care. With fewer emergency rooms, more accident victims will die for lack of timely treatment.

Added to the weak healthcare infrastructure in rural areas is the difficulty in recruiting healthcare professionals. Only 9 percent of physicians practice in rural areas. There is also a shortage of dentists, pharmacists, and registered nurses (Bailey 2009). With low patient volume, relatively low income, and poor access to hospitals and the latest diagnostic tools, most physicians locate in the more lucrative metropolitan areas.

Small-Town Decline

Traditionally, social life in rural America centered on three local institutions—the town, the school, and the church. Of these, only the church remains. Schools have consolidated into much larger districts with schools located between towns they represent.

Rural towns once were the commercial and social hubs for the people living in the region. People shopped and banked there. They went there to have their hair cut or styled. They ate at the family-owned restaurants. They went to town on Saturday nights to shop, visit with friends, or engage in some form of recreation. The town gave the people its identity and sense of community. But this dynamic has changed. Local banks have been acquired by large corporations. Many local residents now work outside the community. They and others now eat in restaurants owned by corporations and do their shopping at the Walmarts, Home Depots, and supermarkets in larger towns many miles away. Combined with shopping on the Internet, the competition from these low-cost businesses caused many local businesses to shut down, in effect bringing about the closing of "Main Street" and the sense of community that binds residents in a rural area together.

Crime and Illicit Drugs

Statistically, rural areas are safer places than metropolitan areas. The data show consistently that rural crime rates are lower than in the central cities and their suburbs.

Rural dwellers are involved in illicit drugs (consumption, production, and trans-shipment), just as are their counterparts in central cities and suburbs (the following is from a study funded by the Drug Enforcement Administration, reported in Hazelden Foundation 2003):

- Eighth-graders in rural America are 83 percent more likely than those in urban areas to use crack cocaine, 43 percent more likely to smoke marijuana, and 29 percent more likely to drink alcohol.
- Tenth-graders in rural areas use drugs, except for Ecstasy and marijuana, at higher rates than tenth-graders in urban areas.
- Twelfth-graders in rural America use cocaine, amphetamines, inhalants, alcohol, cigarettes, and smokeless tobacco at higher rates than their urban counterparts.
- Adults in rural areas and large urban areas abuse alcohol and other drugs at about the same rates.

Also, most of the marijuana is grown in rural areas. By some measures it is the number one cash crop in the United States. Methamphetamine, in particular, is a rural drug phenomenon in production (clandestine laboratories) and consumption.

The arrest rate for drug offenses in rural America is lower than found in metropolitan areas by a factor of four (Mann, Rickey, Pittiway, and Weisheit n.d.). There are several reasons for this anomaly. Rural law enforcement agencies have fewer resources and relatively large areas to patrol. It is easier to hide clandestine activities in remote residences than in high-density areas of the city where neighbors are more likely to detect unusual odors and irregular activities. Covert operations, a common device to break urban drug rings, are difficult in rural areas because everyone knows the local police and is wary of strangers. Finally, because rural inhabitants, including police personnel, know everyone, there is a tendency to handle first offenses informally rather than in the criminal justice system.

The focus of this chapter has been on the social significance of geographical location and the social problems found there, whether in urban centers, bordering these centers in suburbs, or in rural areas. In effect, where one lives is a social location because the immediate environment affects social behavior—patterns of social interaction, population density, services available, employment opportunities, tax base, public transportation, and the like. The next five chapters center on other forms of social location as they influence social behavior and as they are the bases for social problems: poverty, race/ethnicity, gender, sexual orientation, and physical ability/disability.

■ CHAPTER REVIEW

1. Many social problems in the United States, including poverty, homelessness, decaying infrastructure, inadequate public transit, pollution, failure to deliver health services to all social classes, failing public schools, drugs, gangs, racism, and crime, are concentrated in large cities.

2. Through the process of suburbanization and metropolitan deconcentration, the central cities have lost people, jobs, industry, business, and their tax base. Central cities have also lost jobs in the transformation from a manufacturing to a service economy.

3. Beginning in the 1950s U.S. business and financial and lending institutions have tended to (a) disinvest in cities and invest in suburbs and (b) disinvest in Black and Latino neighborhoods and invest in White communities. This pattern of disinvestment

is directly responsible for urban neighborhood and central city decline.

4. The declining quality of life in U.S. big cities is reflected in increasing and intensifying poverty, the lack of affordable housing, homelessness, decaying infrastructure, inadequate public transit, pollution, health problems and the lack of access to adequate healthcare, underfunded and failing schools, crime, drugs, and gangs.

5. Urban poverty has been increasing and becoming more concentrated in particular areas in the central city. The poor have also been getting poorer, especially the minority poor. African Americans and Latinos are more likely than Whites in the city to be poor, and Blacks are much more likely to live in highly segregated neighborhoods that are also high-poverty areas.

6. Both the urban housing market and government-subsidized and public housing have failed to provide enough decent and affordable shelter in U.S. cities. The results are a dwindling supply of low-income housing and increasing urban homelessness.

7. The lack of public investment in the urban infrastructure has begun to significantly limit growth and productivity in the U.S. economy.

8. An automobile-dependent transportation system has polluted U.S. cities and promoted urban sprawl.

9. Poor and minority communities in the inner city are the site of a disproportionate amount of illegal dumping and toxic and hazardous waste (environmental classism and environmental racism).

10. Residents of poor and minority inner-city neighborhoods suffer most from lack of access to adequate healthcare as private hospitals in cities close their doors to under- and uninsured patients.

11. Because U.S. public education is funded primarily with local property taxes, gross inequalities exist between suburban and city schools.

12. When opportunities in the formal and legal economy are not forthcoming, young minority males turn to the informal economy for survival. Much of the informal economy is illegal, involving property crime, drug trafficking, and certain gang activities.

13. More Americans live in the suburbs than in cities and rural areas (including small towns) combined.

14. The suburbanization of the United States has meant the geographic separation of classes and races, particularly of middle-class Whites from poor African Americans.

15. Suburbs have been encouraged, supported, and directly subsidized by the federal government. Among these federal policies: the interstate highway system with beltways around cities, low-cost mortgages, tax breaks for homeowners, and low fuel taxes.

16. The physical arrangements of the suburbs are socially isolating. There are gated communities, fences between neighbors, and the necessity of driving away from the neighborhood to shop, work, and engage in leisure activities.

17. Rural poverty is higher and more persistent in rural areas than in metropolitan areas.

18. Employment in rural areas was once centered on resources of the land—farming, mining, and forestry. This situation has changed with the demise of small farms, replaced by large enterprises, the shift to factory farm operations. Manufacturing enterprises now employ many rural dwellers but at low pay and with few benefits, and workers live with the fear that businesses might move to other localities where wages are lower.

19. There are four environmental problems in rural America: (a) arable land is being lost to the suburbs; (b) irrigation is depleting aquifers faster than they can be recharged; (c) there is massive use of chemicals in farming; and (d) factory farms create serious pollution of the air, land, and water.

20. Rural residents have greater health difficulties than their urban counterparts. Two of the reasons for this disparity are a lack of medical personnel and inadequate health facilities.

21. Small towns are declining as commercial and social hubs. Many residents now work outside the community. They shop and seek entertainment elsewhere. The cumulative effects are the closing of local businesses and a loss of a sense of community.

22. Rural areas are safer than metropolitan areas, but rural crime rates are trending up. Comparing rural and urban residents on drug use, rural teenagers are more likely than urban teenagers to consume illicit drugs. Adults in both rural and urban settings use drugs at about the same rate.

■ KEY TERMS

Redlining. When banks, savings and loans, government agencies, and insurance companies refuse to make home and small-business loans and insure property in poor and minority neighborhoods.

Central city poverty areas. Neighborhoods in which at least one in five households live below the poverty line.

High-poverty areas. Neighborhoods where at least two in five households live below the poverty line.

Gentrification. The redevelopment of poor and working-class urban neighborhoods into middle- and upper-middle-class enclaves; often involves displacement of original residents.

Slumlording. Landlords buy properties in poor neighborhoods for rent income. They do not maintain these properties because to do so would lower their profits.

Warehousing. The withholding of apartments from the housing market by speculators who hope to sell them at a profit to developers.

Jobs/housing mismatch. The inability of central-city residents most in need of decent jobs to reach them on the urban fringe because (1) they cannot afford to operate a private automobile, and (2) the public transportation system is inadequate; moving to the urban fringe is not an option because of housing costs and racial segregation. To the extent that jobs and job growth occur in one place—affluent and White areas—and poor Blacks or Latinos are restricted to another, this "mismatch" is a form of spatial apartheid.

Spatial apartheid. The physical separation of Whites and nonwhites with Whites located where jobs and job growth are found and nonwhites located where they are not.

Environmental classism. When the poor in metropolitan areas are disproportionately exposed to toxic wastes.

Environmental racism. The tendency for minority areas in cities and metropolitan areas to be the targets of a disproportionate share of illegal dumping and the sites where most toxic and hazardous waste is disposed; these communities also suffer, as compared to more affluent White communities, from lax enforcement of environmental regulations and laws.

Triage. The practice in understaffed and underfinanced public hospitals of treating the most urgent emergencies first, thereby delaying the treatment of other cases.

Informal economy. When opportunities are not present in the regular legal economy, people in poor inner-city neighborhoods often turn to this alternate economic exchange and activity for survival; much of the informal economy is illegal activity involving crime and drug trafficking.

White flight. The movement of predominantly upper-middle-class, middle-class, and working-class Whites from the central cities to the suburbs.

Boomburg. A suburban city of at least 100,000 that has experienced double-digit growth each decade since it became urban.

Suburban sprawl. Low-density, automobile-dependent development outside the central city.

Rural. The nonmetropolitan population that resides in small cities and the open countryside.

Colonias. Shantytown settlements of Latino immigrants.

Poverty

 Listen to **Chapter 7** on **MySocLab**

LEARNING OBJECTIVES

7.1 Understand the extent of poverty in America.

7.2 Explain the myths and misperceptions about poor people.

7.3 Compare/contrast the various explanations for poverty: individual, cultural, and structural.

7.4 Explain the costs to society of having a significant portion of the population living in poverty.

7.5 Describe how poverty might be eliminated in the U.S. and what programs are needed to adequately address the needs of the poor population.

Many people in the world envy the United States. It is blessed with great natural resources, the most advanced technology known, and a very high standard of living. Despite these advantages, a significant portion of U.S. residents live in a condition of **poverty** (with a standard of living below the minimum needed for the maintenance of adequate diet, health, and shelter). Many millions are ill-fed, ill-clothed, and ill-housed. These same millions are discriminated against in the schools, in the courts, and in the job market, and discrimination has the effect of trapping many of the poor in that condition. The so-called American dream is just that for millions of people—a dream that will not be realized.

This chapter is descriptive, theoretical, and practical. On the descriptive level, we examine the facts of poverty—how many poor there are in the United States, where the poor are located, and what it means to be poor. Theoretically, we look at the various explanations for poverty—individual, cultural, and structural. On the practical level, we explore what might be done to eliminate extreme poverty.

There are two underlying themes in this chapter. The first theme is that most of the poor are impoverished for structural reasons, not personal ones, as is commonly believed. That is, the essence of poverty is inequality—in money and in opportunity. The second theme is important when we take up the possible solutions to this social problem: The United States has the resources to eliminate poverty if it would give that problem a high enough priority.

7.1 Understand the extent of poverty in America.

EXTENT OF POVERTY

What separates the poor from the non-poor? In a continuum, there is no absolute standard for poverty. The line separating the poor from the non-poor is necessarily arbitrary. Originally developed in the 1960s by the Social Security Administration (SSA), the **official poverty line, or poverty threshold**, is based on the minimal amount of money required for a subsistence level of life. To determine the poverty line, the SSA computed the cost of a basic, nutritionally adequate diet and multiplied that figure by three. This multiplier is based on a government research finding that in 1955, poor people spent one-third of their income on food. Since then, the poverty level has been readjusted annually by the Consumer Price Index to account for inflation. Using this official standard (the weighted average poverty thresholds are $11,139 for one person, $17,374 for a family of three, and $22,319 for a family of four), 15.1 percent of Americans (46.2 million) were poor in 2010 (DeNavas-Walt, Proctor, and Smith 2011). This is the largest number of people in poverty in the fifty-two years for which poverty estimates have been published (see Figure 7.1).

The official poverty line is not only arbitrary, but it also minimizes the extent of poverty in the United States. Critics point out that the government measure does not keep up with inflation, that housing costs now take up a much larger portion of the family budget than food, and that the poverty line ignores differences in health insurance coverage and the medical care needs of individual families.

Furthermore, a "one-size-fits-all" standard is not an adequate measure of poverty because there is a wide variation in the cost of living by locality. For example, a 2004 study found that for a family to be able to afford rent and utilities on a typical two-bedroom apartment, they would need an hourly wage of $22.83 in the District of Columbia, $20.93 in Massachusetts, $14.93 in Arizona, and $9.63 in Arkansas (Associated Press 2004b). Obviously, these figures are far above the federal minimum hourly wage of $7.25.

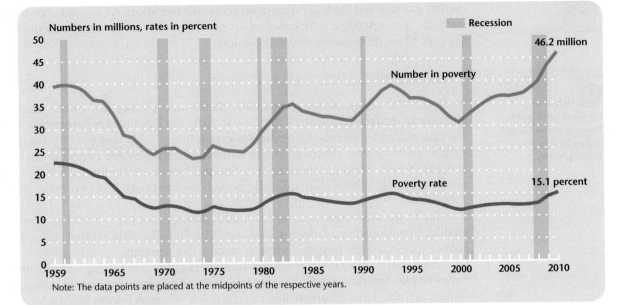

FIGURE 7.1

Number in Poverty and Poverty Rate: 1959 to 2010

Source: DeNavas-Walt, Carmen, Bernadette D. Proctor, and Jessica C. Smith. 2011. "Income, Poverty, and Health Insurance Coverage in the United States: 2010." U.S. Census Bureau, Current Population Reports, P60-239. U.S. Government Printing Office, Washington, D.C., [Figure 4, page 14].

In 2010, in order to address these issues, an Interagency Technical Working Group began developing suggestions and guidelines for a Supplemental Poverty Measure (SPM). The SPM is a more complicated measure of poverty that takes into account expenses such as food, clothing, shelter, and utilities (for details on the SPM see Short 2011). The SPM is not intended to replace the official poverty measure, but instead it will supplement the measure and be published yearly by the Census Bureau to provide a more complete picture of poverty in the United States. Recall that, according to the official poverty measure, in 2010 46.2 million (15.1 percent) of the U.S. population was poor. Using the SPM, this number increases to 49.1 million, or 16.0 percent.

Exact figures on the number of poor are difficult to determine. A major difficulty is that the poor are most likely to be missed by the U.S. census. People most likely overlooked in the census live in high-density urban areas where several families may be crowded into one apartment or in rural areas where some homes are inaccessible and where some workers follow the harvest from place to place and therefore have no permanent home. Transients of any kind may be missed by the census. Also, there are several million immigrants in this country illegally who avoid the census. The inescapable conclusion is that the proportion of the poor in the United States is underestimated because the poor tend to be invisible, even to the government. The Census Bureau estimated, for example, that it missed 3.4 million people, largely members of minority groups and the homeless, in the 2000 census.

Despite these difficulties and underestimates of the poverty population, the official government data are the best available to provide information about the poor. In the following sections we examine the facts of poverty using the official poverty measure. The statistics for the following sections are taken from DeNavas-Walt, Proctor, and Smith 2011 unless otherwise noted (the most recent available at the time of this writing). In December 2007, the United States experienced a collapse in the housing market that marked the beginning of an economic recession. As a result, many of the statistics demonstrate a worsening of economic conditions across the country. See Chapter 14 for more on the Great Recession.

Racial/Ethnic Minorities

View on MySocLab Figure: Poverty in the United States, by Age and Race-Ethnicity

Income in the United States is unequally distributed by race (for data on race and other social characteristics, see Table 7.1). In 2010, the U.S. Census Bureau found that the median family income for Asian American households was $64,308, compared with $54,620 for non-Hispanic White households, $37,759 for Latino households, and $32,068 for African American households. Not surprisingly, then, 9.9 percent of non-Hispanic Whites were officially poor, compared with 27.4 percent of African Americans.

Due to the after-effects of the economic recession, for every racial category real median income declined between 2009 and 2010. Statistics indicate that Asian households experienced the largest decline in income (3.4 percent).

These summary statistics mask the differences within each racial/ethnic category. For example, Americans of Cuban descent, many of whom were middle-class professionals in Cuba, have relatively low poverty rates, whereas Puerto Ricans, Mexicans, and Central Americans have disproportionately high poverty rates. Similarly, Japanese Americans are much less likely to be poor than Asians from Cambodia, Laos, and Vietnam.

TABLE 7.1
Selected Demographics of the Poverty Population, 2010

	Number in Poverty	Percent in Poverty
All people	46.2 million	15.1%
Race/Ethnicity		
White, not Hispanic	19.6 million	9.9%
Black	10.7 million	27.4%
Asian	1.7 million	12.1%
Hispanic	13.2 million	26.6%
Age		
Under 18 years	16.4 million	22.0%
Over 65	3.5 million	9.0%
Nativity		
Native born	38.6 million	14.4%
Foreign born	7.6 million	19.9%
Type of Family		
Married-couple	3.6 million	6.2%
Female-householder, no husband present	4.7 million	31.6%
Male-householder, no wife present	880,000	15.8%

Source: DeNavas-Walt, Carmen, Bernadette D. Proctor, and Jessica C. Smith. 2011. "Income, Poverty, and Health Insurance Coverage in the United States: 2010." U.S. Census Bureau, Current Population Reports, P60-239. U.S. Government Printing Office, Washington, D.C., table 4, pages 15–16.

In 2010, 7.6 million of the foreign-born individuals in the United States (19.9 percent of the foreign born) were poor. Of these poor foreign born, 44.0 percent were naturalized citizens and the remaining were noncitizens. Their poverty rates of 11.3 and 26.7 percent, respectively, indicate that those individuals who became citizens had significantly lower rates of poverty. These official statistics do not include the 6 to 10 million undocumented workers and their families who enter the United States illegally.

Gender

Women are more likely than men to be poor. This is a consequence of the prevailing institutional sexism in society. There is a dual labor market, with women found disproportionately in lower-paying jobs with fewer benefits. Thus, the female-to-male earnings ratio was 0.77 in 2010 (i.e., women earned 77 cents for every dollar earned by men). The relatively high frequency of divorce and the large number of never-married women with children, coupled with the cost of childcare, housing, and medical care, have resulted in high numbers of female-headed families (with no husband present) being poor (31.6 percent, compared to 6.2 percent for married-couple families and 15.8 percent for male-headed families with no wife present). This trend has been called the **feminization of poverty**, a term that implies that the large proportion of poor women is a relatively new phenomenon in U.S. society. However, this obscures the fact that women have always been more economically vulnerable than men, especially older women and women of color. But when women's poverty was mainly limited to these groups, their economic deprivation was mostly invisible. The plight of women's poverty became a visible problem when the numbers of White women in poverty increased rapidly in the past decade or so with rising marital disruption. Even with the growing numbers of poor White women, the term *feminization of poverty* implies that all women are at risk, when actually the probability of economic deprivation is much greater for certain categories of women. The issue, then, is not only gender by itself but class and race as well.

Age

The nation's poverty rate was 15.1 percent in 2010, but the rate was 22.0 percent for children under age 18 (see Table 7.1). The younger the child is, the greater the probability of living in poverty, with the rate being 25.3 percent for children under age 6. Children living in families with a female head of household, no husband present, had a poverty rate of 46.9 percent, a rate more than four times that for their counterparts in married-couple families (11.6 percent).

Place

View on
MySocLab Figure:
Patterns of Poverty

Poverty is not randomly distributed geographically; it tends to cluster in certain places. Regionally, the area with the highest poverty in 2010 was the South (16.9 percent).

There are 386 counties in the United States where more than 20 percent of the people live below the poverty line, called **persistent poverty counties** (U.S. Department of Agriculture 2012). These counties are overwhelmingly rural, with especially high numbers in counties such as Shannon in South Dakota, where the Pine Ridge reservation is located, and Starr in Texas, which is predominantly Hispanic.

Explore on
MySocLab Activity:
Next Door to
Greatness: Poverty
in Cambridge, MA

In addition to persistent poverty counties, the population in **extreme-poverty neighborhoods** is on the rise (areas where 40 percent of individuals live below the poverty line). It is interesting to note that compared to 2000, residents of extreme-poverty neighborhoods in 2005–2009 were more likely to be White, native-born, homeowners, and high school or college graduates (Kneebone et al. 2011). This spatial concentration of poverty has multiple implications:

1. Limited educational opportunities: Neighborhood schools with a high concentration of poor students means a lower tax base to support local schools, fewer resources, lower retention rates, and greater risk of failure as measured by standardized tests (Kneebone et al. 2011).
2. A reduction in services and elimination of local jobs as businesses relocate to areas where residents have more discretionary income.
3. Increased burden on local police, hospitals, and other services.
4. Declining neighborhood conditions results in a lowering of home values and lowered asset building for residents.
5. A higher incidence of poor physical health and mental health outcomes.

Poverty is greatest among those who do not have an established residence. People in this classification are typically the homeless and migrant workers. In 2012, the Department of Housing and Urban Development reported that there were approximately 636,000 homeless people across the country. The 2007–2009 economic recession has also resulted in an increase in the "doubled up" population (people who live with friends, family, or other nonrelatives for economic reasons). This population increased by more than 50 percent from 2005–2010 (National Alliance to End Homelessness 2012).

The other category, migrant workers, is believed to comprise about 3 million adults and children who are seasonal farm laborers working for low wages and no benefits. It is estimated that over half of all farm workers live below the official poverty line and that this percentage has not changed since the 1960s. Hispanics are overrepresented in this occupation.

Neighborhoods like this one in Detroit, Michigan, have been hard-hit by the economic recession.

The New Poor

In the past two decades, millions of blue-collar workers have lost their jobs as plants have closed and companies have moved in search of cheaper labor, or as workers have been replaced by robots or other forms of automation (see Chapter 14). Almost half of these newly unemployed were longtime workers (workers who had held their previous jobs at least three years). In January 2010, the United States hit an all-time high unemployment rate of 10 percent (Bureau of Labor Statistics 2010). Hardest hit was the state of Michigan (14.6 percent), as a result of the collapse of the auto industry, and Nevada (13 percent), as a result of the housing and construction bust. As of June 2012, the unemployment rate has declined from 2010 to 8.2 percent.

These **new poor** are quite different from the **old poor**. The old poor—that is, the poor of other generations—had hopes of breaking out of poverty; if they did not break out themselves, at least they believed their children would. This hope was based on a rapidly expanding economy. There were jobs for immigrants, farmers, and high school dropouts because of the needs of mass production. The new poor, however, are much more trapped in poverty. A generation ago, those who were unskilled and uneducated could usually find work and could even do quite well financially if the workplace was unionized. But now these workers are displaced or misplaced. Hard physical labor is rarely needed in a high-tech society. This phenomenon undercuts the efforts of the working class, especially Blacks, Hispanics, and other minorities who face the additional burden of institutional racism.

The Working Poor

Having a job is not necessarily a path out of poverty. U.S. census data show that over 2.6 million full-time workers were below the poverty line in 2010, as were another 8.0 million workers who worked at least part of the year. Despite working, these people remain poor because they hold menial, dead-end jobs that have no benefits and pay the minimum wage or below. In July 2009 the federal minimum wage was increased to $7.25 an hour. This adds up to roughly $14,500 (before taxes) for full-time work (falling almost $3,000 short of the poverty threshold for a family of three).

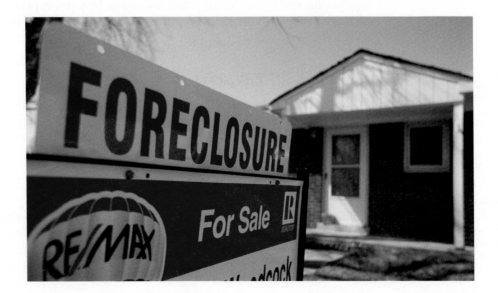

Since December 2007, the number of foreclosures in the United States has skyrocketed.

The lot of the **working poor** is similar to that of the nonworking poor on some dimensions and worse on others. They do society's dirty work for low pay and few if any benefits. They live in substandard housing, and their children go to underfinanced public schools. They are poor, but unlike the nonworking poor, they are not eligible for many government supports such as subsidized housing, medical care (Medicaid), and food stamps.

The Near Poor

The **near poor** are people with family incomes at or above the poverty threshold but below 125 percent of the threshold (e.g., with the official poverty line at $17,374 for a family of three, 125 percent of that number is $21,718). In 2010, 19.8 percent of the population was near poor, a significant portion of those being under the age of 18. The 2007 recession brought into focus the vulnerability of the near poor. The near poor are one accident, one illness, one job loss away from severe poverty, as indicated by the number of home foreclosures in 2008. Home foreclosure filings topped 3 million in 2008, up 81 percent from 2007 and 225 percent from 2006 (Armour 2009).

The Severely Poor

Watch on MySocLab Video: Witnesses to Hunger

Use of the official poverty line designates all people below it as poor, whether they are a few dollars short or far below that threshold. In reality, most impoverished individuals and families have incomes considerably below the poverty threshold. In 2010, for example, the average dollar amount needed to raise a poor family out of poverty was $9,244 (i.e., the average family needed $9,244 *additional* income just to reach the poverty threshold). For poor individuals not in families, the average income deficit was $6,225, and for poor women in female-headed households, the average income deficit was $9,742.

Listen on MySocLab Audio: NPR: A Few Small Steps to Homelessness

In 2010, 6.7 percent of the population (over 20 million Americans) was **severely poor** (i.e., living at or below half the poverty line). The number of severely poor has significantly increased since 1979. This upsurge in the truly destitute occurred because (1) many of the severely poor live in rural areas that have prospered less than other regions, (2) a decline in marriage resulted in a substantial increase in single mothers and unattached men, and (3) public assistance benefits, especially in the South, have steadily declined since 1980. We return to the explanations for poverty later in this chapter.

MYTHS ABOUT POVERTY

7.2 Explain the myths and misperceptions about poor people.

What should be the government's role in caring for its less-fortunate citizens? Much of the debate on this important issue among politicians and citizens is based on erroneous assumptions and misperceptions. Those myths and misperceptions are refuted in this section.

Just "Get a Job"

Listen on MySocLab Audio: NPR: Low-Wage America

A job is not necessarily the ticket out of poverty for many people: 10.6 million poor people worked in 2010, and 2.6 million of them worked full time but were still under the poverty threshold. They hold menial, dead-end jobs that have no benefits and pay the minimum wage (many actually less than the minimum wage). Today a full-time

A Closer Look

THE HOUSING AND TRANSPORTATION AFFORDABILITY INDEX

Housing costs factored as a percent of income has widely been utilized as a measure of affordability. Traditionally, a home is considered affordable when the costs consume no more than 30 percent of household income. In 2006, the Center for Neighborhood Technology and its partner, the Center for Transit Oriented Development, developed what they call the "Housing and Transportation Affordability Index" to measure home affordability in conjunction with transportation, as these two factors together make up the largest expenses for most households.

According to the Center for Neighborhood Technology, less than one in three American communities (28 percent) is affordable when transportation costs are considered along with housing costs ("affordable" means that housing and transportation costs consume no more than 45 percent of income) (2012). Rising gas prices, insurance costs, and car maintenance result in ever-increasing burdens on families, especially those who are already "house-poor," spending a significant portion of their income on housing.

As of 2012, the Housing and Transportation Index includes over 180,000 neighborhoods, and can be accessed at http://htaindex.cnt .org. On the site, individuals can check whether their area is affordable. The Index shows the impact that transportation costs in different locations have on a household's economic bottom line. For example, in Los Angeles, California, 46 percent of neighborhoods are considered "affordable" using the conventional measure of affordability (note that this means that in 54 percent of neighborhoods housing costs are more than 30 percent of household income). When taking transportation into account, 21 percent of neighborhoods in the Los Angeles metro area are unaffordable (see maps below).

Affordability: Housing costs as percent of area median income

Area Median Income = $58,987
Source: H+T Index, 2005–09

☐ 0 to 30%
◼ Greater than or equal to 30% (unaffordable)
☐ Data not available

Affordability: Housing and transportation costs as percent of area median income

Area Median Income = $58,987
Source: H+T Index, 2005–09

☐ 0 to 45%
◼ Greater than or equal to 45% (unaffordable)
☐ Data not available

Source: http://www.cnt.org/repository/2012-Fact-Sheet-LA.pdf.

minimum-wage worker earns roughly 83 percent of the poverty level for a family of three (in 1968 a family of three with one minimum-wage earner had a standard of living 17 percent *above* the poverty line). The main increase in the number of poor since 1979 has been among the working poor. This increase is the result of declining wages, higher numbers of working women who head households, a low federal minimum hourly wage, and an increase in housing costs. See "A Closer Look: The Housing and Transportation Affordability Index" for a review of the two biggest household expenses for families.

According to a 2012 report by the National Low Income Housing Coalition, there is not a single state in the country where it is possible to work forty hours per week at minimum wage and afford a two-bedroom apartment at Fair Market Rent. Figure 7.2 demonstrates the hourly wage needed by state to afford a two-bedroom unit.

Welfare Dependency

Read on MySocLab Document: The End of Welfare as We Know It: An Overview of the PRWORA

In 1996 Congress passed the **Personal Responsibility and Work Opportunity Reconciliation Act (PRWORA)** that reformed the welfare system (formally known as "Aid to Families with Dependent Children," or AFDC). This new law encompassed the following:

- It shifted welfare programs from the federal government to the states.
- It mandated that welfare recipients find work within two years.

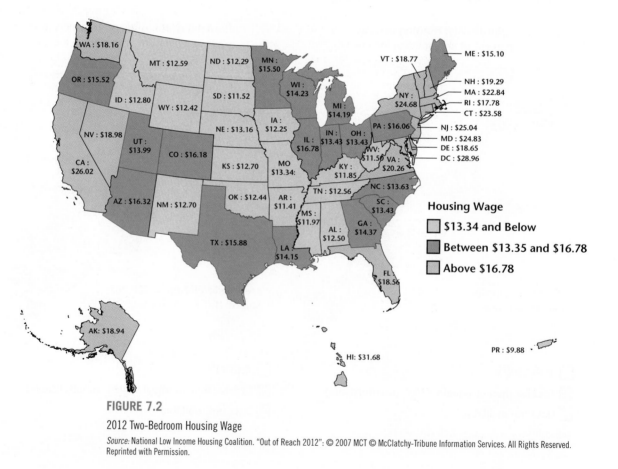

FIGURE 7.2

2012 Two-Bedroom Housing Wage

Source: National Low Income Housing Coalition. "Out of Reach 2012": © 2007 MCT © McClatchy-Tribune Information Services. All Rights Reserved. Reprinted with Permission.

- It limited welfare assistance to five years.
- It cut various federal assistance programs targeted for the poor by $54.5 billion over six years.

Thus, this law made assistance to the poor temporary (the new name "Temporary Assistance for Needy Families" or TANF, reflects this) and cut monies to supplemental programs such as food assistance and child nutrition. The assumption by policymakers was that welfare was too generous, making it easier to stay on welfare than to work, and welfare was believed to encourage unmarried women to have children.

We should recognize some facts about government welfare before the 1996 welfare reform (O'Hare 1996:11). First, welfare accounted for about one-fourth of the income of poor adults; nearly half of the income received by poor adults came from some form of work activity. Second, about three-fourths of the poor received some form of noncash benefit (Medicaid, food stamps, or housing assistance), but only about 40 percent received cash welfare payments. Third, the welfare population changes—that is, people move in and out of poverty every year (Rodgers 2006). Fourth, although the pre-reform welfare system was much more generous than now, it was inadequate to meet the needs of the poor. The average poor family of three on welfare had an annual income much below the poverty line. For example, in 1995, the *maximum* monthly cash benefit for a family of three under the old welfare system ranged from $120 in Mississippi to $712 in Hawaii, a level far below the poverty threshold (Rodgers 2006).

The new TANF system was put into place to promote employment over cash assistance to the poor and get people (i.e., single mothers) off welfare. Proponents of the system say that it has worked because the welfare rolls have decreased significantly. For example, in 1996, the last year under the old AFDC welfare system, 4.43 million families received assistance nationwide. In 2010, the TANF caseload was 1.86 million (Albelda 2012). The problem is, of course, how do you measure success? According

"I would share my cookies, but I'm afraid I'll set up a cycle of dependency."

Barbara Smaller/The New Yorker Collection/www.cartoonbank.com

to Randy Albelda, a decrease in the welfare rolls does not mean that the system is working. In fact, a comparison of poor families in 1996 to families in 2006 shows that while they are relying more on earnings than in the past, their average earnings have not increased much while government support has dropped off, leaving them with fewer resources and struggling to make it (2012).

Concerning the larger picture about government welfare programs, there is a fundamental misunderstanding by the U.S. public about where most governmental benefits are directed. We tend to assume that government monies and services go mostly to the poor (**welfare**), when in fact the greatest amount of government aid goes to the non-poor (**wealthfare**). Most (about three-fourths) of the federal outlays for human resources go to the non-poor, such as to all children in public education programs and to most of the elderly through Social Security Retirement and Medicare.

The upside-down welfare system, with aid mainly helping the already affluent, is also accomplished by two hidden welfare systems. The first is through tax loopholes (called **tax expenditures**). Through these legal mechanisms, the government officially permits certain individuals and corporations to pay lower taxes or no taxes at all. For illustration, one of the biggest tax expenditure programs is the money that homeowners deduct from their taxes for real estate taxes and interest on their mortgages, a total of approximately $76 billion in 2006 (mortgage interest is deductible on mortgages up to $1 million). Ironically, although less than one-fourth of low-income Americans receive federal housing subsidies, more than three-quarters of Americans, many living in mansions, get housing aid from Washington.

The second hidden welfare system to the non-poor is in the form of direct subsidies and credit to assist corporations, banks, agribusiness, and defense industries. Some examples include the savings and loan bailout, agribusiness subsidies, media subsidies, timber subsidies, aviation subsidies, mining subsidies, and tax avoidance by transnational corporations. These subsidy programs to wealthy and corporate interests amount to many times more than welfare assistance to the poor. Ironically, when Congress passed the sweeping welfare reforms of 1996, it did not consider the welfare programs for the non-poor.

The Poor Get Special Advantages

The common belief is that the poor get a number of handouts for which other Americans have to work—food stamps, Medicaid, and housing subsidies. As we have seen, these subsidies amount to much less than the more affluent receive, and recent legislation has reduced them even more. Most significant, the *poor pay more than the non-poor for many services*. This, along with earning low wages and paying a large proportion of their income for housing, helps to explain why some have such difficulty getting out of poverty.

The urban poor find that their money does not go as far in the inner city. Food and commodities, for example, cost more because supermarkets, discount stores, outlet malls, and warehouse clubs have bypassed inner-city neighborhoods. Because many inner-city residents do not have transportation to get to the supermarkets and warehouse stores, they must buy from nearby stores, giving those businesses monopoly powers (a similar situation to those poor in rural communities). In this and other ways, the poor pay more. Consider the following:

- Hospitals routinely charge more (sometimes twice as much or more) for services to patients without health insurance compared to those covered by a health plan (Ehrenreich 2004; S.E.I.U. 2005).

- Check-cashing centers, largely located in poor neighborhoods, prey on customers without bank accounts. They often charge 10 percent of the check's value, so a person cashing a $300 check will leave with only $270 (Ehrenreich 2006).
- There is a new trend in WIC (women, infants, and children)-only grocery stores that cater to low-income families. These stores are for participants of the Special Supplemental Nutrition Program for Women, Infants, and Children, and they accept only WIC vouchers as payment, not cash. State officials show prices are 10 to 20 percent higher in the WIC-only stores (Pear 2004).
- The "payday loan" industry offers an advance on a person's paycheck at high interest rates, a devastating financial obligation for those strapped for cash. Nationwide, the number of payday lending outlets has risen 11,000 percent since 1990 (Jeffery 2006). Initially, the payday loan industry was able to impose interest rates as high as 400 percent, a practice that has been somewhat curtailed as some states have stepped in and passed interest rate caps on the industry. These caps, however, still allow the payday loan industry to take advantage of those desperate for cash at interest rates anywhere from 17 to 60 percent. For those states without regulation, interest rates are much higher.
- Women, minorities, and lower-income borrowers are more likely than others to take out high-cost, subprime mortgages (Kirchhoff 2005).

The conclusion is obvious: Rather than receiving special advantages, the poor pay more for commodities and services in absolute terms, and they pay a much larger proportion of their incomes than the non-poor for comparable items. Similarly, when the poor pay sales taxes on the items they purchase, the tax takes more of their resources than it does from the non-poor, making it a **regressive tax**. Thus, efforts to move federal programs to the states will cost the poor more because state and local taxes tend to be regressive. Barbara Ehrenreich sums it up this way:

> So let's have a little less talk about how the poor should learn to manage their money, and a little more attention to all the ways that money is being systematically siphoned off. Yes, certain kinds of advice would be helpful: skip the pay-day loans and rent-to-pay furniture, for example. But we need laws in more states to stop predatory practices like $50 charges for check cashing. Also, think what some microcredit could do to move families from motels and shelters to apartments. And did I mention a living wage? If you're rich, you might want to stay that way. It's a whole lot cheaper than being poor. (2006:2)

CAUSES OF POVERTY

7.3 Compare/contrast the various explanations for poverty: individual, cultural, and structural.

Everyone in the United States has heard of the "American dream," the dream of upward mobility and economic success that is available to all. Yet, the statistics reveal that for the majority, upward mobility really is just a dream. According to the Pew Charitable Trusts (2012), 43 percent of Americans raised in the bottom income quintile remain stuck there as adults, and 70 percent remain below the middle. The same is true for those raised at the top of the wealth ladder, the majority will stay there. In fact, only 4 percent of those born in the bottom fifth income tier end up in the top tier. Who or what is to blame for poverty and lack of upward mobility? There are two very different answers to this question. One is that the poor are in that condition because of some deficiency: Either they are biologically inferior or their culture fails them by promoting character traits that impede their progress in society. The other response places the blame on the structure of society: Some people are poor because society has failed to provide equality in educational opportunity, because institutions discriminate against minorities, because private industry has failed to provide enough jobs, because automation has made some jobs obsolete, and so forth. In this view, society has worked in such a way as to trap certain people and their offspring in a condition of poverty.

Deficiency Theories

- **Innate Inferiority.** In 1882, the British philosopher and sociologist Herbert Spencer came to the United States to promote a theory later known as **social Darwinism** (see Chapter 1). He argued that the poor were poor because they were unfit. Spencer believed that as societies evolve, the strong will flourish and the weak will eventually die out. He felt that the government should stay out of the way of this progression and even went so far as to say that the government should not help the poor in any way, as that would impede the natural progression of evolution. Any type of government aid would just encourage laziness and slow down the elimination process.

  Social Darwinism has generally lacked support in the scientific community for fifty years, although it has continued to provide a rationale for the thinking of many individuals. In the last forty years, the concept has resurfaced in the work of three scientists. They suggest that the poor are in that condition because they do not measure up to the more well-to-do in intellectual endowment.

  Arthur Jensen, professor emeritus of educational psychology at the University of California, has argued that there is a strong possibility that African Americans are less well endowed mentally than Whites. From his review of the research on IQ, he found that approximately 80 percent of IQ is inherited, and the remaining 20 percent is attributable to environment. Because African Americans differ significantly from Whites in achievement on IQ tests and in school, Jensen claimed that it is reasonable to hypothesize that the sources of these differences are genetic as well as environmental (Jensen 1969, 1980).

  The late Richard Herrnstein, a Harvard psychologist, agreed with Jensen that intelligence is largely inherited. He went one step further, positing the formation of hereditary castes based on intelligence (Herrnstein 1971, 1973). For Herrnstein, social stratification by inborn differences occurs because (1) mental ability is inherited and (2) success (prestige of job and earnings) depends on mental ability. Thus, a **meritocracy** (social classification by ability) develops through the sorting process. This reasoning assumes that people who are close in mental ability are more likely to marry and reproduce, thereby ensuring castes by level of intelligence. According to this thesis, "in times to come, as technology advances, the tendency to be unemployed may run in the genes of a family about as certainly as bad teeth do now" (Herrnstein 1971:63). This is another way of saying that the bright people are in the upper classes and the dregs are at the bottom. The social Darwinists justify inequality just as it was years ago.

  Charles Murray, along with Herrnstein, wrote *The Bell Curve* (Herrnstein and Murray 1994), the latest major revival of social Darwinism. Using data from the National Longitudinal Study of Youth, they argued that wealth and other positive social outcomes are increasingly distributed across society according to intelligence (as measured by IQ tests), rather than social background. Although their work has come under fire in the scientific community, arguments regarding the role of biological inferiority continue to surface. For example, in 2005 Lawrence Summers (president of Harvard University at the time) made a speech regarding the underrepresentation of women in science. In his speech, he claimed that girls are less likely than boys to get the highest scores on standardized math and science tests and that a possible explanation for that is genetic differences between the sexes (Davidson 2005). Notwithstanding the flaws in the logic and in the evidence used by biological deficiency theorists (for excellent critiques of the Herrnstein and Murray work, see Gould 1994; Herman 1994; Reed 1994; and *Contemporary Sociology* 1995), we must consider the implications of their biological determinism for dealing with the problem of poverty.

First, biological determinism is a classic example of **blaming the victim**. The individual poor person is blamed instead of inferior schools, culturally biased IQ tests, low wages, corporate downsizing, or social barriers of race, religion, or nationality. By blaming the victim, this thesis claims a relationship between lack of success and lack of intelligence. This relationship is spurious because it ignores the advantages and disadvantages of ascribed status.

The Jensen-Herrnstein-Murray thesis divides people in the United States by appealing to bigots. It provides "scientific justification" for their beliefs in the racial superiority of some groups and the inferiority of others. By implication, it legitimates segregation and unequal treatment of so-called inferiors. The goal of integration and the fragile principle of egalitarianism are seriously threatened to the degree that members of the scientific community give this thesis credence or prominence.

Another serious implication of the biological determinism argument is the explicit validation of the IQ test as a legitimate measure of intelligence. The IQ test attempts to measure innate potential, but this measurement is impossible because the testing process must inevitably reflect some of the skills that develop during the individual's lifetime. For the most part, intelligence tests measure educability—that is, the prediction of conventional school achievement. Achievement in school is, of course, also associated with a cluster of other factors, most notably socioeconomic status.

Thus, the Jensen-Herrnstein-Murray thesis overlooks the important contribution of social class to achievement on IQ tests. This oversight is crucial because most social scientists feel that these tests are biased in favor of those who have had a middle- and upper-class environment and experience. IQ tests discriminate against the poor in many ways. They discriminate obviously in the language that is used, in the instructions that are given, and in the experiences they assume the subjects have had. The discrimination can also be more subtle. For minorities, the race of the person administering the test influences the results. Another less well-known fact about IQ tests is that in many cases they provide a **self-fulfilling prophecy**. IQ scores on the low or high end of the spectrum can influence the way a child is treated from that moment on. If a child is seen as "bright" or "slow," the child will be treated as such by his or her teachers. The kind of education the child receives as a result of that testing thus influences his or her future IQ.

Another implication is the belief that poverty is inevitable. The survival-of-the-fittest capitalist ideology is reinforced, justifying discrimination against the poor and continued privilege for the advantaged. Inequality is rationalized so that little will be done to aid its victims. Herrnstein and Murray in *The Bell Curve* argue that public policies to ameliorate poverty are a waste of time and resources. "Programs designed to alter the natural dominance of the 'cognitive elite' are useless, the book argues, because the genes of the subordinate castes invariably doom them to failure" (Muwakkil 1994:22). The acceptance of this thesis, then, has obvious consequences for what policy decisions will be made or not made in dealing with poverty. If their view prevails, then welfare programs will be abolished, as will programs such as Head Start.

Programs targeting poor children such as Head Start claim to result in numerous positive outcomes like higher graduation rates and lower rates of delinquency.

This raises the serious question: Is intelligence immutable, or is there the possibility of boosting cognitive development? A number of studies have shown that programs such as Head Start raise scores among poor children by as much as nine points. These results, however, fade out entirely by the sixth grade. Heckman (2006) argued that critics of Head Start are missing the larger picture. In other studies of early preschool intervention programs (similar to Head Start), participants have other successful outcomes, such as higher high school graduation rates, higher percentages of home ownership, lower rates of receipt of welfare assistance as adults, and fewer out-of-wedlock births. Consider the following examples:

- The Abecedarian Project conducted at the University of North Carolina studied high-risk children from 111 families. The study followed these families and children up to age 21 and found that those high-risk children who received high-quality, intense preschooling earned significantly higher scores on intellectual and academic measures as young adults, attained more years of total education, were more likely to attend a four-year college, and showed a reduction in teen pregnancy. They conclude that "the positive findings from this study have important policy implications. They show that a high-quality child care program can have a lasting impact on the academic performance of children from poverty backgrounds" (Campbell et al. 2002:55).
- In Ypsilanti, Michigan, high-risk African American children were randomly divided into two groups. Similar to the Abecedarian Project, one group received a high-quality, active-learning program as 3- and 4-year-olds. The other group received no preschool education. The two groups were compared when they were age 27, with these results:

By age 27, those who had received the preschool education had half as many arrests as the comparison group. Four times as many were earning $2,000 or more a month. Three times as many owned their own homes. One-third more had graduated from high school on *schedule. One-fourth fewer of them needed welfare as adults. And they had one-third fewer children born out of wedlock. (Beck 1995:7B)*

- Researchers at the University of Wisconsin studied 989 poor children, all born in 1980, who enrolled in the Chicago Child Parent Center Program no later than age 4 and were taught an average of 2.5 hours a day for eighteen months (reported in Steinberg 2001). The students were tracked until age 20. Comparing these students with 550 other poor children from the same neighborhoods, few of whom attended any preschool, researchers found that (1) fewer graduates of the Chicago program had been arrested for juvenile crimes, (2) more graduates of the program also graduated from high school, and (3) the Chicago program children were much less likely to be assigned to special education classes or to repeat a grade.

Recall that Herrnstein and Murray in *The Bell Curve* (1994) argued that public policies to ameliorate poverty are a waste of time and resources because of the biological inferiority of the poor. These examples indicate otherwise.

- **Cultural Inferiority.** One prominent explanation of poverty, called the **culture-of-poverty hypothesis**, contends that the poor are qualitatively different in values and lifestyles from the rest of society and that these cultural differences explain continued poverty. In other words, the poor, in adapting to their deprived condition, are found to be more permissive in raising their children, less verbal, more fatalistic, less likely to defer gratification, and less likely to be interested in formal education than the well-to-do. Most important is the contention that this deviant cultural pattern is transmitted from generation to generation. Thus, there is a strong implication that poverty is perpetuated by defects in the lifestyle of the poor. These ideas were behind the welfare reform of 1996. Welfare recipients were seen as individuals who needed to learn to value work, stop being "dependent," and stop transmitting deviant values to their children. From this view, the poor have a subculture with values that differ radically from values of the other social classes.

    Edward Banfield, an eminent political scientist, has argued that the difference between the poor and the non-poor is cultural—the poor have a present-time orientation, whereas the non-poor have a future-time orientation (Banfield 1977). He does not see the present-time orientation of the poor as an adaptation to the hopelessness of their situation. If poverty itself was to be eliminated, the former poor would probably continue to prefer instant gratification, be immoral by middle-class standards, and so on.

    A modern example of the culture-of-poverty position can be found in comments made by Lieutenant Governor Andre Bauer, who was running for governor of South Carolina in 2010. In a town hall meeting with state lawmakers and residents, he compared government assistance to feeding stray animals. He said:

    My grandmother was not a highly educated woman but she told me as a small child to quit feeding stray animals. You know why? Because they breed. You're facilitating the problem if you give an animal or a person ample food supply. They will reproduce, especially ones that don't think too much further than that. And so what you've got to do is you've got to curtail that type of behavior. They don't know any better. (Quoted in Cary 2010:1)

Bauer went on to say that the government is rewarding bad behavior by giving money to people who don't have to do anything for it (as previously mentioned, opinions similar to this were the driving force behind the welfare reform of 1996).

    Critics of the culture-of-poverty hypothesis argue that this hypothesis is just another way of blaming the victim rather than focusing on the structural conditions that foster certain behaviors. Furthermore, research shows that the poor do not abandon the dominant values of the society but, rather, retain them while simultaneously holding an alternative set of values focused on day-to-day survival. This alternative set is a result of *adaptation* to the conditions of their environment.

Most Americans believe that poverty is a combination of biological and cultural factors. Judith Chafel reviewed a number of studies on the beliefs of Americans and found that they "view economic privation as a self-inflicted condition, emanating more from personal factors (e.g., effort, ability) than external-structural ones (e.g., an unfavorable labor market, racism). Poverty is seen as inevitable, necessary, and just" (Chafel 1997:434). A 2005 study by Adeola confirms these findings: Even though Americans seem to perceive that the government spends too little on the poor, they also tend to blame poverty on the poor themselves. However, the 2007–2009 economic recession may have an effect on people's attitudes toward poverty as more and more people find themselves vulnerable in a struggling economy. In this case, individuals might turn to structural theories to explain poverty.

Structural Theories

In contrast to blaming the biological or cultural deficiencies of the poor, the structural theory states that how society is organized creates poverty and makes certain kinds of people especially vulnerable to being poor.

- **Institutional Discrimination.** Michael Harrington, whose book *The Other America* was instrumental in sparking the federal government's war on poverty, has said, "The real explanation of why the poor are where they are is that they made the mistake of being born to the wrong parents, in the wrong section of the country, in the wrong industry, or in the wrong racial or ethnic groups" (Harrington 1963:21). This is another way of saying that the structural conditions of society are to blame for poverty, not the poor. When the customary ways of doing things, prevailing attitudes and expectations, and accepted structural arrangements work to the disadvantage of the poor, it is called **institutional discrimination**. Let us look at several examples of how the poor are trapped by this type of discrimination.

Most good jobs require a college degree, but the poor cannot afford to send their children to college. Scholarships go to the best-performing students. Children of the poor often do not perform well in school. This underperformance by poor children results from the lack of enriched preschool programs for them and low expectations for them among teachers and administrators. This attitude is reflected in the system of tracking by ability as measured on class-biased examinations. Problems in learning and test taking may also arise because English is their second language. Because poverty is often concentrated geographically and schools are funded primarily by the wealth of their district, children of the poor typically attend inadequately financed schools. All these acts result in a self-fulfilling prophecy—the poor are not expected to do well in school, and they do not. Because they are failures as measured by objective indicators (such as the disproportionately high number of dropouts and discipline problems and the small proportion who desire to go to college), the school feels justified in its discrimination toward the children of the poor.

Another job-related trap for the poor is the way low-end jobs are paid. As previously mentioned, if working full time at the federal minimum wage of $7.25 per hour, you will not be able to afford a two-bedroom apartment at Fair Market Rent in any state in the country (National Low Income Housing Coalition 2012).

The poor are also trapped because they get sick more often and stay sick longer than the well-to-do. The reasons, of course, are that they cannot afford preventive medicine, proper diets, and proper medical attention when ill. The high incidence of sickness among the poor means either that they will be fired from their jobs or that they will not receive money for the days missed from work (unlike the well-to-do, who usually have jobs with such fringe benefits as sick leave and paid medical insurance). Not receiving a paycheck for extended periods means that the poor will have even less money for proper health care, thereby ensuring an even higher incidence of sickness. Thus, there is a vicious cycle of poverty. The poor tend to remain poor, and their children tend to perpetuate the cycle.

The traditional organization of schools and jobs in U.S. society has limited the opportunities of racial minorities and women. The next two chapters describe at length how these two groups are systematically disadvantaged by the prevailing laws, customs, and expectations of society, so we will only summarize the structural barriers that they face. Racial minorities are deprived of equal opportunities for education, jobs, and income. As a result, African Americans, for example, are half as likely to be wealthy and twice as likely to be poor as Whites. They are also twice as likely as Whites to be unemployed. Structuralists argue that these differences are not the result of flaws in African Americans but rather of historical and current discrimination in communities, schools, banks, and the work world. Similarly, women typically work at less prestigious jobs than do men and, when working at equal-status jobs, receive less pay and have fewer chances for advancement. These differences are not the result of innate gender differences but of personal, social, and societal barriers to equality based on gender.

- **Political Economy of Society.** The basic tenet of capitalism—who gets what is determined by private profit rather than collective need—explains the persistence of poverty. The primacy of maximizing profit works to promote poverty in several ways. First, employers are constrained to pay their workers the least amount possible in wages and benefits. Only a portion of the wealth created by the laborers is distributed to them; the rest goes to the owners for investment and profit. Therefore, employers must keep wages low. That they are successful is demonstrated by the millions of people *who worked full-time but were below the poverty line.*

  A second way that the primacy of profit promotes poverty is by maintaining a surplus of undereducated and desperate laborers who will work for very low wages. A large supply of these marginal people (such as minorities, women, and undocumented workers) aids the ownership class by depressing the wages for all workers in good times and provides the obvious category of people to be laid off from work in economic downturns.

  A third impact of the primacy of profits in capitalism is that employers make investment decisions without regard for their employees (potential or actual). If costs can be reduced, employers will purchase new technologies to replace workers (such as robots to replace assembly line workers). Similarly, owners may shut down a plant and shift their operations to a foreign country where wages are significantly lower.

  In sum, the fundamental assumption of capitalism is individual gain without regard for what the resulting behaviors may mean for other people. The capitalist system, then, should not be accepted as a neutral framework within which goods are produced and distributed but rather as an economic system that perpetuates inequality. This is the basic tenet of the Occupy Wall Street movement, whose protesters embraced the slogan "We are the 99 percent." The implication is that the capitalist system in the United States has resulted in the country being controlled by a 1 percent elite group with enormous political and economic power. The system does not allow for equal opportunity, but instead is characterized by wealth disparity and limited social mobility for the vast majority of citizens.

A number of political factors complement the workings of the economy to perpetuate poverty. Political decisions made to fight inflation with high interest rates, for example, hurt several industries, particularly automobiles and home construction, causing high unemployment.

The powerful in society also use their political clout to keep society unequal. For example, they resist efforts to raise the minimum wage, and they seek to reduce or eliminate government programs to help the poor. Clearly, the affluent in a capitalist society will resist efforts to redistribute their wealth to the disadvantaged. Their political efforts are, rather, to increase their benefits at the expense of the poor and the powerless.

In summary, the structural explanation of poverty rests on the assumption that the way society is organized perpetuates poverty, not the characteristics of poor people. The reality is that the causes of poverty are very complicated, as is evident by the diversity of the poverty population. In his ethnography of the working poor, David Shipler noted,

> In reality, people do not fit easily into myths or anti-myths, of course. The working individuals in this book are neither helpless nor omnipotent, but stand on various points along the spectrum between polar opposites of personal and societal responsibility. Each person's life is the mixed product of bad choices and bad fortune, of roads not taken and roads cut off by the accident of birth or circumstance. It is difficult to find someone whose poverty is not somehow related to his or her unwise behavior—to drop out of school, to have a baby out of wedlock, to do drugs, to be chronically late to work. And it is difficult to find behavior that is not somehow related to the inherited conditions of being poorly parented, poorly educated, poorly housed in neighborhoods from which no distant horizon of possibility can be seen. (2004:6–7)

Whether the causes of poverty are personal, structural, or a combination of both, 46.2 million individuals live below the federal poverty threshold, and the costs to society are enormous.

The Occupy Wall Street Movement opposes wealth and power disparity.

7.4 Explain the costs to society of having a significant portion of the population living in poverty.

👁 **Watch on MySocLab Video:** Consequences of Poverty

COSTS OF POVERTY

The concentration of poverty in certain areas has been linked to important outcomes such as crime and delinquency, educational problems, psychological distress, and health problems (U.S. Department of Housing and Urban Development 2012). The poor and those just above the poverty line generally receive inferior educations, live in substandard housing, are disproportionately exposed to toxic chemicals, are malnourished, and have health problems (see "A Closer Look: It's a Disaster for the Poor"). Let's further examine some of the consequences and economic costs of poverty.

A Closer Look

IT'S A DISASTER FOR THE POOR

Poverty and Vulnerability

Most people are aware of some of the effects of poverty, like the poor are less likely to have healthcare and more likely to suffer from illness. What is less obvious are the other vulnerabilities that result from being poor. The following examples demonstrate that socioeconomic status can make a real life-and-death difference:

- When the *Titanic* was rammed by an iceberg in 1912, 3 percent of female first-class passengers were killed; 16 percent of female second-class passengers were killed; and 45 percent of female third-class passengers were killed. In this case, the higher the economic status of the individual, the greater the probability of survival.
- The United Nations has determined a "disaster risk index" for countries that shows a direct correlation between vulnerability and poverty. Being poor greatly affects the risk of being a victim in an earthquake, a tropical cyclone, and a flood (United Nations 2004). This relationship appears to be largely the effect of the quality and structural soundness of housing.

Obviously, housing that is the least expensive may also be the least structurally sound and most vulnerable.

- In August 2005, Hurricane Katrina devastated the city of New Orleans. A close look at the numbers indicates that New Orleans was in trouble long before the hurricane. The Lower Ninth Ward of New Orleans was one of the most heavily damaged areas of the city. The residents of the Ninth Ward were 99 percent Black with a median household income of $19,918. Most important, 32 percent of residents in the Lower Ninth Ward had no vehicle in which to evacuate (Wagner and Edwards 2007).
- An Associated Press analysis of government data on industrial air pollution shows that Black Americans are 79 percent more likely than Whites to live in neighborhoods where industrial pollution is suspected of posing the greatest health danger. Residents in neighborhoods with the highest pollution scores also tend to be poorer, less educated, and more often unemployed (Pace 2005).
- Research has shown that lower socioeconomic status is

correlated with unsafe conditions that make the poor vulnerable to death by fire. These conditions may include absent or defective smoke detectors, use of space heaters, overcrowding, less fire-resistant housing, and electrical or heating malfunctions in poor households. Analyzing data from all large U.S. metropolitan counties, Hannon and Shai (2003) found that a high proportion of African Americans combined with low income appears to be associated with extremely high fire-death rates. They concluded: "It appears that the disadvantages associated with institutional racism (physical segregation and social isolation) exacerbate the problems of low income in relation to fire deaths" (2003:134).

- In July 1995, Chicago suffered a weeklong heat wave; temperatures soared, and 739 people died. In *Heat Wave*, sociologist Eric Klinenberg demonstrated how the patterns of mortality from this disaster reflect the inequalities that divide Chicago. Most of those who died were elderly, and most lived alone. In addition, most of the Blacks who died lived in severely impoverished conditions in areas with high population decline and abandoned housing stock.

Family Problems

Poverty damages families. Poor couples are twice as likely to divorce as more affluent couples. Jobless people are three to four times less likely to marry than those with jobs. Two-thirds of teenagers who give birth come from poor or low-income families, and their children are more likely to be poor (Zimmerman 2008).

Health Problems

According to the U.S. Census Bureau, in 2010, 49.9 million people (7.3 million children) had no private or public health insurance. About 15.3 million Hispanics, 8.1 million African Americans, and 23.1 million non-Hispanic Whites were uninsured. "When uninsured people get sick, they are less likely to seek medical attention until they are really sick and it is more expensive to treat them. Then, if they were not poor already, medical bills can push them into poverty. So poverty helps make people sick, and being sick helps make people poor" (Oppenheim and MacGregor 2006:2). Further, the uninsured may use emergency medical services in place of a regular doctor, as hospitals are required to render treatment regardless of insurance or ability to pay.

The infant mortality rate in some poor urban neighborhoods exceeds the rate in developing countries. The United States has a higher infant mortality rate than most other industrialized countries. Reflecting the disproportionate number of African Americans in poverty, infants born to African American mothers are twice as likely to die before their first birthday than infants of White mothers (Children's Defense Fund 2012).

Problems in School

In addition to health problems, children in the poorest families are six times as likely as their affluent counterparts to drop out of high school. Poor children experience less qualified teachers, fewer school resources and inadequate education facilities (see Chapter 16). Living in a neighborhood with a high poverty rate translates to graduation rates as much as 20 percentage points lower than those in more advantaged communities (Children's Defense Fund 2012). Marian Wright Edelman, president and founder of the Children's Defense Fund, aptly stated,

> Forty years after President Johnson declared a War on Poverty and signed the Civil Rights Act of 1964 into law, 50 years after Brown v. Board of Education, 108 years after Plessy v. Ferguson, and 141 years after President Lincoln's Emancipation Proclamation, a Black child still lacks a fair chance to live, learn, thrive, and contribute in America. Our nation's doors of economic and educational opportunity still have not opened to all of God's children who are Black, Brown, White, Native and Asian American, and poor. (Children's Defense Fund 2004:1)

Economic Costs

What are the consequences for society if a significant proportion of the populace is poor? In economic terms, the cost is very high. Holzer and colleagues (2007) examined these economic costs in detail and estimated that the costs to the United States associated with childhood poverty total about $500 billion per year. These costs are the inevitable consequence of reduced productivity and economic output by the poor, increased criminal behavior, and poor health.

> Most arguments for reducing poverty in the U.S., especially among children, rest on a moral case for doing so—one that emphasizes the unfairness of child poverty, and how it runs counter to our national creed of equal opportunity for all. But there is also an economic case for reducing child poverty. When children grow up in poverty, they are somewhat more likely than non-poor children to have low earnings as adults, which in turn reflects lower workforce productivity. They are also somewhat more likely to engage in crime (though that's not the case for the vast majority) and to have poor health later in life. Their reduced productive activity generates a direct loss of goods and services to the U.S. economy. (Holzer et al. 2007:1)

If poverty were eliminated through jobs that pay a living wage and adequate monetary assistance to the permanently disabled or elderly, the entire society would prosper from the increased purchasing power and the larger tax base. But economic considerations, though important, are not as crucial as humanitarian ones. A nation that can afford it must, if it calls itself civilized, eliminate the physical and psychological misery associated with poverty.

ELIMINATION OF POVERTY

7.5 Describe how poverty might be eliminated in the U.S. and what programs are needed to adequately address the needs of the poor population.

📖 **Read** on **MySocLab Document:** The Compassion Gap in American Poverty Policy

Must some portion of U.S. society live in poverty? Is there a way to get everyone above the poverty level to a level at which they are not deprived of the basics of adequate nutrition, healthcare, and housing? The remainder of this chapter enumerates some assumptions that appear basic to achieving such a goal.

Assumption 1: Poverty is a social problem and the source of other social problems; therefore, it must be eliminated. As presented in the previous section, poverty is correlated with crime, teenage pregnancy, divorce, poor health, and a host of societal problems. The costs to society are too extensive to ignore.

Assumption 2: Poverty can be eliminated in the United States. The United States could reduce its defense budget ($712.7 billion for fiscal year 2009), by many billions of dollars without threatening national security. The United States spends more than the next ten biggest defense spenders combined, most of whom are U.S. allies (see Figure 7.3). In fact, the United States accounts for 41 percent of the world's total military spending, followed distantly by China (8.2 percent of the world's spending). We could spend $200 billion less a year and still be number one militarily. The resulting savings, called the Peace Dividend, could be committed to bringing people in the United States above the poverty line.

Assumption 3: Poverty is caused by a lack of resources, not a deviant value system. Basic to a program designed to eliminate poverty is the identification of what keeps some people in a condition of poverty. Is it lack of money and power or the maintenance of deviant values and lifestyles? This question is fundamental because the answer determines the method for eliminating poverty. The culture-of-poverty proponents would address non-middle-class traits. The target would be the poor themselves, and the goal would be to make them more socially acceptable (for example, the welfare reform of 1996). Developing the social competence of the poor—not changing the system—would bring an end to poverty. This approach treats the symptom, not the disease. The disease can be cured only by attacking its sources within the society—the structural arrangements that maintain inequality.

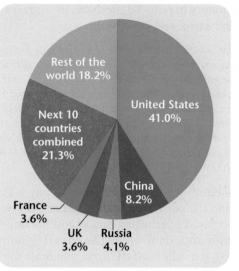

FIGURE 7.3

Global Military Spending

Source: SIPRI Military Expenditures Database 2012, http://milexdata .sipri.org.

Assumption 4: Poverty cannot be eliminated by the private sector of the economy. Assuming that private enterprises will not engage in unprofitable activities, we can assume also that private enterprise efforts will never by themselves eliminate poverty. In other words, private profit will tend to subvert the human needs that are of public concern; businesses will not provide jobs that they consider unnecessary or not immediately profitable, nor will they voluntarily stop activities that are profitable (e.g., renting deteriorated housing because the unimproved land may increase in value, or charging exorbitant interest rates to the poor, or lobbying to keep certain occupational categories outside minimum-wage restrictions, or moving their operations to another state or nation where wages are lower).

Conventional wisdom, however, suggests that private business is the answer because it will generate new and better-paying jobs. This solution simply will not work because the new poor, as noted earlier, differ dramatically from the old poor. Some of the new poor are workers who have been displaced by robots, computers, and other labor-saving devices. The jobs of others have moved—from the urban core to the suburbs, to other regions of the country, or to other countries, or have been lost due to the recession. The jobs were lost because of rational business decisions. In short, the private sector, with its emphasis on profit (and therefore efficiency), will not generate the new jobs needed to eliminate poverty.

Assumption 5: Poverty will not be eliminated by a rising economy. A common assumption is that a growing economy will help everyone—"a rising tide lifts all boats." This assumption has some validity, as evidenced by the very robust economy of the late 1990s, when unemployment dipped to 4 percent, jobs were plentiful, and wages for the bottom segment of the population shifted upward. But even in this untroubled economic time period, the lot of the poor did not improve much. Actually, affordable housing became even more of a problem because much low-cost housing was gentrified (refurbished for upscale renters) or demolished for office buildings or other uses irrelevant to the poor. Even in the best of times, the conditions of poverty limit and deny. Cities with low tax bases do not provide the needed social services such as pre- and postnatal healthcare and good schools. During the boom times of the 1990s, the federal government cut programs for the poor such as Head Start, Food Stamps, and

Aid to Families with Dependent Children (AFDC). Employers do not have jobs with decent wages and benefits, even in good times, for those with inadequate education and training.

Assumption 6: Volunteer help from well-meaning individuals, groups, and organizations will not eliminate poverty. In 1988, presidential candidate George H. W. Bush called for "a thousand points of light" as the solution to social problems such as poverty. Bush meant that charities and volunteers are the answers, not big government. At one level, this makes good sense. That is, churches and private organizations can and do provide food for the hungry, shelters for the homeless, and emergency care for the victims of natural disasters.

There are two problems with leaving poverty to charities. The first is that since 1980, the money received by charities and the number of adults volunteering their services to charities has declined. These declines occurred at a time of increasing need by the poor. The second problem is that because this plan is voluntary, the poor in many communities will be denied adequate food, clothing, healthcare, and shelter. Only a national program will ensure that the needs of every poor person are met.

In 2001, President George W. Bush proposed a variation on his father's "thousand points of light." This was for the federal government to provide funds to religious organizations that help the needy ("faith-based initiative"). In effect, the plan proposed to allow religious charities that serve the poor to compete for $8 billion annually in government funds (Benedetto 2001). Although laudable in many respects, given the important contributions by religious charities such as Catholic Charities and the Salvation Army, there are several problems with the plan. First, there is the danger that the churches will use federal resources to try to win converts to their religion, clearly an unconstitutional activity. Second, the government may bypass religious organizations that are not Christian or otherwise mainstream (e.g., Moslems, Buddhists,

In 2001, former President George W. Bush proposed a faith-based initiative, where religious charities could compete for federal money to serve the poor.

Scientologists), thereby missing important clusters of poor people. A third objection is that the White House might funnel funds on a political basis rather than according to need, such as to Catholic organizations to win the Catholic vote. Finally, this plan misses the essence of a federal plan to solve the poverty crisis across the United States (J. Jackson 2001).

Assumption 7: Poverty is a national problem and must be attacked with massive, nation-wide programs financed largely and organized by the federal government. Poverty must be addressed at the federal level to ensure that the poor throughout the nation will receive equal benefits and services. Poverty must be attacked nationally to deal with the structural problems that cause poverty (e.g., the changing economy that results in too few jobs, declining real wages for all but the top 20 percent, uneven resources for education, and a healthcare delivery system that misses or overlooks so many). Because many politicians believe that relatively high welfare benefits attract poor people from other states and because many states are in a fiscal crisis, there is a current trend to reduce welfare benefits at the state level. This is why poverty must be handled at the national level to ensure that the programs are funded uniformly.

MySocLab ✓ Study and Review on MySocLab

■ CHAPTER REVIEW

1. According to the government's arbitrary dividing line (which minimizes the actual extent of poverty), 15.1 percent of the U.S. population (2010) is officially poor. Disproportionately represented in this category are African Americans, Hispanics, children, and women (especially female heads of families; DeNavas-Walt, Proctor, and Smith 2011). The current poverty numbers are the highest they have been in the fifty-two years since poverty estimates have been published.

2. In 2010, 10.6 million poor people worked but remained under the poverty threshold. There is not a single state in the country where it is possible to work forty hours per week at minimum wage and afford a two-bedroom apartment.

3. In 1996, the federal welfare program was reformed. Assistance programs to the poor were drastically cut, time limits were set for welfare recipients, and recipients were required to find work within two years.

4. Families under the new welfare system (TANF) have fewer resources and struggle to make it, even though most are working.

5. Most governmental assistance is targeted to the affluent rather than the poor. Tax expenditures and other subsidies provide enormous benefits to the already affluent, which further redistributes the nation's wealth upward.

6. Rather than the poor receiving special advantages, research shows that the poor pay more than the non-poor for many services.

7. One explanation for poverty is that the poor themselves are in some way deficient. The innate inferiority hypothesis, for example, is a variant of social Darwinism promoted by Arthur Jensen and Richard Herrnstein. This hypothesis states that certain categories of people are disadvantaged because they are less well-endowed mentally.

8. Another position that blames the poor for their condition is the culture-of-poverty hypothesis. This hypothesis contends that the poor are qualitatively different in values and lifestyles from the affluent and that these differences explain their poverty and the poverty of their children.

9. Critics of the culture-of-poverty and the innate inferiority hypotheses charge that in blaming the victim, both theories ignore how social conditions trap individuals and groups in poverty.

10. In contrast to blaming biological or cultural deficiencies of the poor, structural theories focus on how society is organized in a way that creates poverty and makes certain people vulnerable to being poor.

11. Poverty is correlated with crime, teenage pregnancy, divorce, poor health, and a host of societal problems. For society as a whole, the economic costs of poverty reach the billions.

12. The elimination of poverty requires (a) a commitment to accomplish that goal; (b) a program based on the assumption that poverty results from a lack of resources rather than from a deviant value system; (c) recognition that poverty cannot be eliminated by the private sector of the economy, by a rising economy alone, or by charitable individuals or groups; and (d) recognition that poverty is a national problem and must be attacked by massive, nationwide programs largely financed and organized by the federal government.

■ KEY TERMS

Poverty. Standard of living below the minimum needed for the maintenance of adequate diet, health, and shelter.

Official poverty line, or poverty threshold. Arbitrary line computed by multiplying the cost of a basic nutritionally adequate diet by three.

Feminization of poverty. Viewed erroneously as a trend for contemporary women to be more economically vulnerable than men. This view obscures the fact that women have always been poorer than men, especially older women and women of color.

Persistent poverty counties. Counties in the United States where more than 20 percent of the people live below the poverty line.

Extreme-poverty neighborhoods. Areas in the United States where more than 40 percent of the people live below the poverty line.

New poor. Poor who are displaced by new technologies or whose jobs have moved away to the suburbs, to other regions of the country, or out of the country. They have less hope of escaping poverty than did the old poor.

Old poor. Poor of an earlier generation, who had hopes of breaking out of poverty because unskilled and semi-skilled jobs were plentiful.

Working poor. People who work but remain below the poverty threshold.

Near poor. People whose incomes are above the poverty threshold but below 125 percent of that threshold.

Severely poor. People whose cash incomes are at half the poverty line or less.

Personal Responsibility and Work Opportunity Reconciliation Act (PRWORA). In 1996, Congress passed this act, which reformed the welfare system. PRWORA shifted welfare programs from the federal government to the states; mandated that welfare recipients find work within two years; limited welfare assistance to five years; and cut various federal assistance programs targeted for the poor by $54.5 billion over six years.

Welfare. Government monies and services provided to the poor.

Wealthfare. Government subsidies to the non-poor.

Tax expenditures. Legal tax loopholes that allow the affluent to escape paying certain taxes and therefore to receive a subsidy (e.g., the tax deduction to homeowners).

Regressive tax. Tax rate that remains the same for all people, rich or poor. The result is that poor people pay a larger proportion of their wealth than do affluent people.

Social Darwinism. Belief that the place of people in the social stratification system is a function of their ability and effort.

Meritocracy. Social classification based on ability.

Blaming the victim. Belief that some individuals are poor, criminals, or school dropouts because they have a flaw within them, which ignores the social factors affecting their behaviors.

Self-fulfilling prophecy. Event that occurs because it is predicted. That is, the prophecy is fulfilled because people alter their behavior to conform to the prediction.

Culture-of-poverty hypothesis. View that the poor are qualitatively different in values and lifestyles from the rest of society and that these cultural differences explain continued poverty.

Institutional discrimination. When the social arrangements and accepted ways of doing things in society disadvantage minority groups.

Racial and Ethnic Inequality

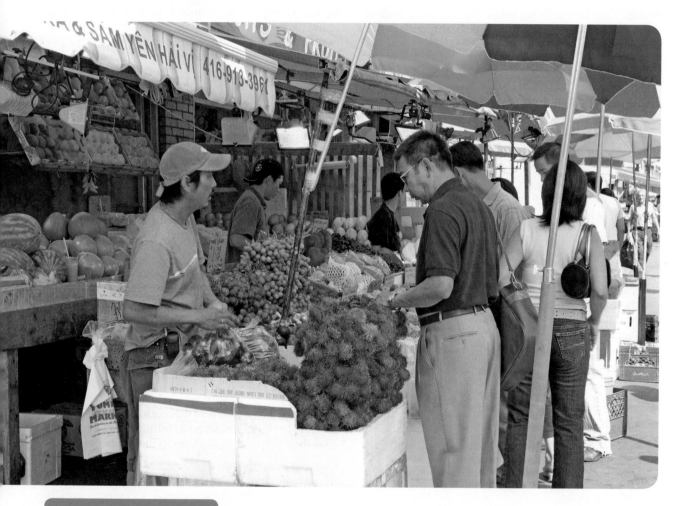

(((Listen to **Chapter 8** on **MySocLab**

LEARNING OBJECTIVES

8.1 Understand how race is a socially (not biologically) defined category.

8.2 Give a brief historical overview of four nonassimilated racial/ethnic groups: African Americans, Latinos, Asian Americans, and Native Americans.

8.3 Discuss racial inequality from different theoretical perspectives: deficiency theories,

bias theories, and structural discrimination theories.

8.4 Examine the role of public policy in both reducing racial bias and continuing racial bias in contemporary society.

8.5 Discuss and give examples of the growing racial strife in the United States.

Since its beginning, the United States has been a nation with a "race problem." Today, racial divisions are changing, but they are not disappearing. Three milestones reveal the extent of population change in the nation: (1) By 2001, more than half of the largest cities had more Blacks, Latinos, Asian Americans, and other minorities than Whites (Camarillo 2010). (2) In 2012, for the first time in history, over half of newborn children belonged to a racial or ethnic group. (3) Today, one in three U.S. residents is a minority. The United States is moving from being predominantly White to being a global society of diverse racial and ethnic peoples. Does this mean that the United States is becoming integrated and moving beyond racial disparities? Many people think that race no longer matters in the way it once did. After all, President Barack Obama, a Black man, holds the nation's highest office. Furthermore, people of color are visible in public positions. While these changes are important, they do not signal a post-racial society. This chapter examines why race continues to be important in the twenty-first century and what social problems accompany today's racial divisions.

8.1 Understand how race is a socially (not biologically) defined category.

 Watch on MySocLab Video: Racial Stereotypes and Discrimination

Read on MySocLab Document: Racial Stratification and Education in the United States: Why Inequality Persists

HOW TO THINK ABOUT RACIAL AND ETHNIC INEQUALITY

Why are some groups dominant and others subordinate? The basic reason is power—power derived from superior numbers, technology, weapons, property, or economic resources. Those holding superior power in a society—the **dominant group**—establish a system of inequality by dominating less powerful groups. This system of inequality is then maintained by power. The terms *dominant group* and *minority group* describe power differences regardless of the size of the groups.

Racial inequalities produce opportunities for some and oppression for others. The word *oppression* comes from a Latin word meaning "to crush," and thus racial oppression means keeping people of color down—that is, crushing them physically and in many other ways (Feagin 2006:8). Racial oppression reaches far back into the past of the United States. Racial inequalities are institutionalized in the structure of society leading to unequal outcomes for different racial and ethnic groups.

Racial stratification offers better occupational opportunities, income, and education to White people. These patterns are found throughout the world even as societies become more racially and ethnically diverse. Today, many racially defined people are becoming even more marginalized by global restructuring (discussed in Chapter 14), which includes sweatshops that employ people of color, new fiscal policies imposed on developing countries, and disruptions of national and local economies that force people to migrate in search of better jobs and better lives. Racial inequalities shape social relations around the world.

This chapter examines racial inequality from several vantage points. First, we outline the important features of racial and ethnic groups. We then profile four racial minority groups: African Americans, Latinos, Asian Americans, and Native Americans. Next, we examine explanations of racial inequality, followed by a look at its effect on Blacks and Hispanics in terms of income, jobs, education, and health. Finally, the chapter turns to contemporary trends in racial and ethnic relations.

The theme of the chapter is that racial problems have structural foundations. Our society remains structured along the lines of race, ethnicity, and color. Blatant forms of racism from the past have given way to new, more subtle practices. With the growth of racially defined minority groups, racial disparities persist even though they are sometimes hidden from view (Higginbotham and Andersen 2012; Lewis et al. 2004). In this chapter we show that race is a powerful force in shaping our institutions. This means that minority groups lack the same opportunities as everyone else. Keep in mind that minorities are not to blame for the race problem. Instead, the cause lies in our race-based system of social rights and resources. Keep in mind that our emphasis on racial inequality does not mean that minorities are passive victims of oppression. Their histories are filled with human agency and for centuries, racial minorities in the United States have fought against oppression, both as individuals and in groups.

RACIAL AND ETHNIC MINORITIES

8.2 Give a brief historical overview of four nonassimilated racial/ethnic groups: African Americans, Latinos, Asian Americans, and Native Americans.

Racial categories are a basis of power relations and group position. Size is not crucial in determining whether a group is the most powerful. A numerical minority may in fact have more political representation than the majority, as is the case in South Africa. Thus, the most important characteristic of a **minority group** is that it is dominated by a more powerful group.

Determining who is a minority is largely a matter of history, politics, and judgment—both social and political. Population characteristics other than race and ethnicity—such as age, gender, or religious preference—are sometimes used to designate minority status. However, race and ethnicity are the characteristics used most often to define the minority and majority populations in contemporary U.S. society (O'Hare 1992:5).

Sociologists agree that race is socially constructed. This means that some groups are racially defined, even though races per se, do not exist. What does exist is the *idea* that races are distinct biological categories. Races are thought to be physically distinguishable populations that share a common ancestry. But despite the common belief, social scientists now reject the biological concept of race. Scientific examination of the human genome finds no genetic differences between the so-called races. Fossil and DNA evidence show that humans are all one race, evolved in the last 100,000 years from the same small number of tribes that migrated from Africa and colonized the world (American Sociological Association 2003; Angier 2000; Bean et al. 2004; Feldman 2010; Mukhopadhyay and Henze 2003). Although there is no such thing as biological race, races are real insofar as they are *socially defined*. In other words, racial categories *operate* as if they are real. Racial categories are a mechanism for sorting people in society. They structure and segregate our neighborhoods, our schools, our churches, and our relationships (Higginbotham and Andersen 2009).

Listen on MySocLab Audio: NPR: A Revealing History of a Multiracial America

Racial classification in the United States is based on a Black–White dichotomy—that is, the construction of two opposing categories into which all people fit. However, social definitions of race have changed throughout the nation's history. At different points in the past, "race has taken on different meanings. Many of the people considered White and thought of as the majority group are descendants of immigrants who at one time were believed to be racially distinct from native-born White Americans, the majority of whom were Protestants" (Higginbotham and Andersen 2009:41). Racial categories vary in different parts of the country and around the world. Someone classified as "Black" in the United States might be considered "White" in Brazil and "Colored" (a category distinguished from both Black and White) in South Africa (Bamshad and Olson 2003:80). In the United States, a Black–White color line has always been complicated by regional racial divides. Today, the rapidly growing presence of Latino and Asian immigrants and the resurgence of Native American identification have changed the meaning and boundaries of racial categories. Their non-White status marks them as "other" and denies them many opportunities (Lewis, Kryson, and Harris 2004:5; Pyke 2004:55). Skin color complicates racial differences because it is a basis of ranking that favors lighter skin over darker skin. Both within and across racial and ethnic groups, lighter-skinned people have more advantages than those with darker skin (Burton et al. 2010). Global events also complicate the color lines. Before the events of 9/11, Middle Easterners and Muslim Americans were relatively invisible. The post 9/11 backlash created a new minority group. Arabs and Muslims are grouped together even though not all Muslims are Arabs and not all Arabs are Muslims. Nevertheless, many Americans have imagined that the United States is engaged with a Muslim or Arab enemy who is fundamentally different and dangerous (Bakalian and Bozorgmehr 2011; Beinin 2010).

Racial Categories

In Chapter 5, we discussed current immigration patterns that are reshaping the U.S. racial landscape. Immigration from Asia, Latin America, and the Caribbean is also changing the character of race and ethnic relations. Sociologists use the term **racial formation** to mean that society is continually creating and transforming racial categories (Omi and Winant 1994:55). For example, groups once self-defined by their ethnic backgrounds such as Mexican Americans and Japanese Americans are racialized as "Hispanics" and "Asian Americans." Middle Easterners coming from such countries as Syria, Lebanon, Egypt, and Iran are commonly grouped together and called "Arabs."

The U.S. government has changed its racial categories over time. For the first time in census 2000, people were allowed to record themselves in more than one racial category and this continued with the 2010 census. About 3 percent of people identify themselves as mixed-race (U.S. Census Bureau 2010). We can expect that the use of the mixed-race or multiracial option will grow, especially among the younger population. Marrying across racial lines is on the increase, as attitudes toward interracial unions become more tolerant. Thirteen percent of U.S. marriages now involve someone of a different race (Lee and Bean 2004:228). Already, children are much more likely than adults to identify themselves as multiracial. Four percent of the population under age 18 were identified in more than one racial category in the 2000 census, twice the percentage for adults (Kent et al. 2001:6; Prewitt 2003:39).

While the Census Bureau has begun to capture the complex mix of racial groups present in the United States, it used a confusing classification for Hispanics. According to the 2000 U.S. guidelines, Hispanics were considered to be an ethnic group, not a race. People who identified their ethnicity as Hispanic could also indicate a racial background by choosing "some other race." The Census Bureau acknowledges that the distinction between race and ethnicity is flawed. The 2010 census changed the Hispanic origin question to more clearly distinguish Hispanics by adding the sentence "For this census, Hispanic origins are not races" (Humes, Jones, and Ramirez 2011:12). In reality, Hispanics *are racialized* in the United States. Although classified as an ethnic group, "Hispanic" encompasses a range of ethnic groups. At the same time, although Hispanics are not officially defined as a race, they are *socially defined* in racial terms. In other words, the dominant society treats them as racially inferior. When any group comes to be thought of as a race, this means the group has become racialized (Taylor 2009:4). Hispanics are treated as a racial group, and many identify themselves as belonging to a distinctive racial category.

View on
MySocLab Figure:
Projections of the Racial-
Ethnic Makeup of the U.S.
Population

Despite the past and present racialization of people of color, common thinking about race is flawed. We tend to see race through a Black and White lens, thereby neglecting other rapidly growing racial groups. At the same time, we think of Whites, the dominant group, as raceless, or having no race at all (McIntosh 1992:79). In this view, Whiteness is the natural or normal condition. It is racially unmarked and immune to investigation. This is a false picture of race. In reality, the racial order shapes the lives of all people, even Whites who are advantaged by the system. (See the "Speaking to Students" panel titled "Got Privilege? Studying What It Means to Be White.") Just as social classes exist in relation to each other, "races" are labeled and judged *in relation to other races*. The categories "Black" and "Hispanic" are meaningful only insofar as they are set apart from, and in distinction to, "White." This point is particularly obvious when people are referred to as "non-White," a word that ignores the differences in experiences among people of color (Lucal 1996:246). Race is not simply a matter of two opposite categories but of power relations between dominant and subordinate groups (Weber 2010).

Speaking to Students

GOT PRIVILEGE? STUDYING WHAT IT MEANS TO BE WHITE

What does it mean to be "White"? Surprisingly, the answer to this question is not as simple as it may seem. Whiteness is not biological, nor is it determined solely by skin color or other physical attributes. Instead, whiteness is socially constructed, a product of micro and macro social forces and interactions across time. These forces work together to create the boundaries for the unique racial location we call White. Although all of those who identify or are identified as White live within the boundaries of this racial location, the concept of Whiteness does not imply that everyone who is White will have identical experiences. Historical and demographic location, class, gender and sexuality, among other things, shape what it means to be White.

Over the past thirty years, a new field has begun to emerge that studies the social constructions and boundaries of Whiteness, which is called "Critical Whiteness Studies (CWS)." This field has begun to piece together historical and contemporary data and narratives to determine who was considered to be "White" at different historical periods and why. In addition, CWS examines how these racial determinations granted individuals privilege based on whether they were perceived to be White.

One of clearest texts in showing how White privilege operates is Peggy McIntosh's "Unpacking the Invisible Knapsack" (1992). By privilege, she means "an invisible package of unearned assets that [Whites] can count on cashing in each day, but about which [Whites were] 'meant,' to remain oblivious. White privilege is like an invisible weightless knapsack."*

*Working Paper 189, "White Privilege and Male Privilege: A Personal Account of Coming to See Correspondences through Work in Women's Studies" (1988), by Peggy McIntosh.

At the heart of her argument is a focus on Whiteness as a system, not an individual identification. What this means is that White people reap certain benefits based on the fact that the system is set up to accommodate them, regardless of whether they themselves directly support racist practices or ideologies. These privileges allow Whites as a whole greater access to society's resources than people of color and leave less than an equal share of resources for those who are not similarly privileged.

As a student, you may be asking yourself "What, if anything, does this have to do with me?" If you are White, you may feel that you did not receive any special treatment just because of your skin color. You may have had to overcome obstacles that were placed in your path due to your class, gender, or sexuality. It may be especially difficult for you to accept your privilege

Ethnic Groups and Their Differences

How is race different from ethnicity? Whereas race is used for socially marking groups on the basis of presumed physical differences, ethnicity allows for a broader range of affiliation. **Ethnic groups** are distinctive on the basis of national origin, language, religion, and culture.

Ethnic groups have long been present in the United States. Since colonial times, Germans, Italians, Poles, Irish, and other groups have arrived with their own languages, religions, and culture.

Both race and ethnicity are historical bases for inequality in that they are constructed in a hierarchy from "superior" to "inferior." In the United States, some immigrants were viewed as belonging to an inferior race. For example, Jews were once racialized and later reconstructed as White (Brodkin 2009). Nevertheless, race and ethnicity have differed in how they incorporated groups into society. Race was the social construction setting people of color apart from European immigrant groups (Takaki 1993:10). Groups identified as races came into contact with the dominant

in comparison with other people of color who you perceive as not having had to overcome such obstacles. Recognizing White privilege does not mean that across the board, in every scenario, Whites always have it better than people of color. Just as there is White privilege, there are also privileges that come with being from the upper class, or possessing masculinity and/or heterosexuality. What it does mean is that you have been privileged in the area of race.

David Roediger's *Wages of Whiteness: Race and the Making of the American Working Class* (1991) is a great example of how White working class men, although not having access to the privileges of the upper class, utilized White privilege to their benefit. In this work, Roediger argues that constructions of Whiteness were at the heart of the establishment of the working class. White workers used race to separate themselves from workers of color and to rally other White workers, including White ethnics. This gave them enough power to receive certain benefits as a group, including higher wages and better

jobs that were not accessible to other workers.

Another book that highlights the interplay between different categories of social location is Ruth Frankenburg's *White Women, Race Matters: The Social Construction of Whiteness* (1993). The primary focus of this book is to show how Whiteness is constructed via gender and sexuality. Frankenburg provides numerous examples to detail how White women's experience of race differs from White men's, especially within sexual relationships. For example, she shows how White women who were in relationships with men of color were often seen as "supersexual" beings in ways they would not have been if they were a White man choosing to date a woman of color. Although White women have to overcome barriers created by their gender and sexuality, Frankenburg notes it is still important to recognize the fact that they are at the same time able to maintain their racial privilege.

Fortunately, there is a growing movement to examine White privilege. There are small steps we all can take to assist in this process.

Becoming aware of the different ways "Whiteness" affects you and those around you is the first step toward fighting against White privilege and for racial equality. If you are White, another step you can take is to attempt to forego the benefits heaped upon you by Whiteness. This will be difficult, especially in the beginning, since you may be unaware of many of these benefits. Tim Wise, in his book *White Like Me: Reflections on Race from a Privileged Son*, outlines a number of practical strategies that can be used to help tear down White privilege. These include "refus[ing] to shop at institutions with a pattern or history of discrimination," and "refer[ing] to white people with a racial designation when discussing them so as to stop normalizing whites as synonymous with human beings, people, or Americans."**

**Wise, Tim. 2008. *White Like Me: Reflections on Race from a Privileged Son*. Brooklyn, NY: Soft Skull Press, p. 118.

Source: Paula Miller, Department of Sociology, Michigan State University, 2010. This essay was written expressly for *Social Problems*, 12th Edition.

majority through force and state-sanctioned discrimination in work that was unfree and offered little opportunity for upward mobility. In contrast, European ethnics migrated to the United States voluntarily to enhance their status or to market their skills in a land of opportunity. They came with hope and sometimes with resources to provide a foundation for their upward mobility. Unlike racial groups, most had the option of returning if they found the conditions here unsatisfactory. The voluntary immigrants came to the United States and suffered discrimination in employment, housing, and other areas. Clashes between Germans, Irish, Italians, Poles, and other European groups during the nineteenth and early twentieth centuries are well documented. But most European immigrants and their descendants—who accounted for four-fifths of the U.S. population in 1900—eventually achieved full participation in U.S. society (Pollard and O'Hare 1999:5).

Over time, White ethnic groups were incorporated into society while keeping their cultures alive in their families and communities. Sociologists call this "optional ethnicity" (Waters 1996), that is, the ability to choose whether to identify with a group of origin and which cultural traits to keep. This option is possible for some White groups, but generally not for people of color who remain different from the dominant society because racial discrimination sets them apart from others.

Today globalization and transnational migration are changing the landscape of countries throughout the world. In the United States some groups have given up their ethnic customs, while others remain distinctive. As European countries struggle with political and economic integration, people may no longer identify as Italian, but as Lombardians, Sicilians, or Romans (Wali 1992:6). "The arrival of large numbers of people from the Middle East, East Asia, and Africa—many European countries now have minority ethnic populations of around 10 percent—is pushing aside old concepts of what it means to be French, or German, or Swedish" (Richburg 2004:17). Expanding communications networks and the increased social interaction that has resulted from immigration have not suppressed ethnic conflicts. In the last decade of the twentieth century, ethnic and religious differences led to massacres of ethnic Tutsis by Hutus in Rwanda; full-scale war involving Serb, Bosnian, Albanian, and other ethnic groups in the Balkans; and violence against ethnic Chinese in Indonesia (Pollard and O'Hare 1999:5). Across Europe today, anti-immigrant racism is on the rise. Growing fears of a mounting foreign influx are fueling political movements to stop racism.

Racial and Ethnic Groups in the United States

View on
MySocLab Map:
The Concentration of
Hispanics or Latinos,
African Americans, and
Asian Americans

In the United States, race and ethnicity both serve to mark groups as different. Groups *labeled as races* by the wider society are bound together by their common social and economic conditions. As a result, they develop distinctive cultural or ethnic characteristics. Today, we often refer to them as **racial-ethnic groups** (or racially defined ethnic groups). The term *racial-ethnic group* refers to groups that are socially subordinated and remain culturally distinct within U.S. society. It is meant to include (1) the systematic discrimination of socially constructed racial groups and (2) their distinctive cultural arrangements. The categories of *African American*, *Latino*, *Asian American*, and *Native American* have been constructed as both racially and culturally distinct. Each group has a distinctive culture, shares a common heritage, and has developed a common identity within a larger society that subordinates it. The racial characteristics of these groups define their place in society.

Terms of reference are also changing, and the changes are contested both within groups as well as between them. For example, *Blacks* continue to debate the merits

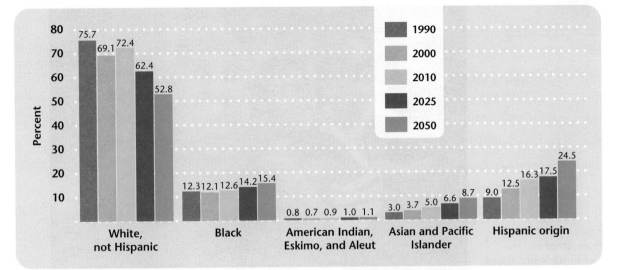

FIGURE 8.1

Percent of the Population, by Race and Hispanic Origin, 1990, 2000, 2010, 2025, and 2050

Sources: U.S. Bureau of the Census. 1997. "Population of the United States: 1997." Current Population Reports. Series P23-194. Washington, DC: U.S. Government Printing Office, p. 9. U.S. Bureau of the Census accessed online: www.census.gov/population/www/cen2000.

of the term *African American*, whereas *Latinos* disagree on the label *Hispanic*. In this chapter, we use such terms interchangeably because they are currently used in both popular and scholarly discourse.

Although European ethnics have moved into the mainstream of society, racially defined peoples have remained in a subordinate status. Native Americans, African Americans, Latinos, and Asians have not been assimilated. Continuing racial discrimination sets them apart from others. (See Figure 8.1 for the percentage of the U.S. population by race in selected years.)

- **African Americans.** In 2010, African Americans were 13 percent of the population (U.S. Census Bureau 2010). Before 1990, virtually all African Americans descended from people who were brought involuntarily to the United States before the slave trade ended in the nineteenth century. They entered the southern states to provide free labor to plantations, and as late as 1890, 90 percent of all Blacks lived in the South, 80 percent as rural dwellers. In the South, they endured harsh and violent conditions under slavery, an institution that would have consequences for centuries to come. During the nineteenth century, the political storm over slavery almost destroyed the nation. Although Blacks left the South in large numbers after 1890, within northern cities they also encountered prejudice, discrimination, and segregation that exposed them to unusually high concentrations of poverty and other social problems (Massey and Denton 1993:7; Takaki 1993:7). African Americans have a distinctive history of slavery and oppression.

  In the past two decades, the Black population in the United States has changed due to immigration from Africa and the Caribbean. In fact, more Blacks are coming from Africa than during the slave trade. About 50,000 legal immigrants arrive annually, and more have migrated here than in nearly the entire preceding centuries (Roberts 2005:A1, 2010). Black immigration from Africa and the Caribbean is making the population more diverse and posing unique challenges to today's Black

Recent immigration from Africa and the Caribbean has increased the cultural diversity of "African Americans."

immigrants (Shaw-Taylor 2009). Black immigration is also changing what it means to be Black. It has sparked a new debate about the "African American." It ignores the enormous linguistic, physical, and cultural diversity of the peoples of Africa. The term *Black* is also problematic in that it risks conflating people of African descent who were brought here as slaves with recent immigrants from Africa and the Caribbean (Mukhopadhyay and Henze 2003:675). In fact, the experiences of today's immigrants are markedly different from those who have descended as slaves.

- **Latinos.** As we saw in Chapter 5, the U.S. Latino population has now surpassed the African American population to become the nation's largest minority. In many respects, the Latino population is the driving force of this society's racial and ethnic transformation (Saenz 2004:29). In 2010, Hispanics or Latinos made up 16 percent of the total U.S. population (U.S. Census Bureau 2010). Although Hispanics are the largest minority, they are a varied collection of ethnic groups. Two-thirds (65 percent) of all Hispanic Americans are Chicanos or Mexican Americans, 9.2 percent are Puerto Ricans, 3.5 percent are Cubans, and 6.6 percent are "other Hispanic or Latino" (U.S. Census Bureau 2010).

  The *Hispanic* category was created by federal statisticians to provide data on people of Mexican, Cuban, Puerto Rican, and other Hispanic origins in the United States. The term was chosen as a label that could be applied to all people from the Spanish-speaking countries of Latin America and from Spain. Because the population is so diverse, there is no precise definition of group membership. Even the term *Latino*, which many prefer, is a new invention. Latinos tend to view themselves more by their ethnicity, meaning their national origins, language, and customs (Navarro 2012). While Latinos are often viewed as immigrants, the majority (63 percent) of the population was born in the United States. The rapid growth of the Hispanic population in recent years came from births, not immigration (Roberts 2010; Saenz 2010).

  The national origins of Latinos are diverse, and so is the timing of their arrival in the United States. As a result, Mexicans, Puerto Ricans, Cubans, and other Latino groups have distinctive histories that set them apart from each other. Cubans arrived largely in the period between 1960 and 1980; Mexicans originally became part of the United States in 1848, with the forcible annexation of much of what is now the Southwest and the Treaty of Guadalupe Hidalgo. Other Mexicans have been migrating continuously since 1890. Puerto Ricans came under U.S. control in 1898 and obtained citizenship in 1917; Salvadorans and Guatemalans have been migrating to the United States in substantial numbers during the past two decades.

As a result of these different histories, Hispanics are found in many legal and social statuses—from fifth-generation Americans to new immigrants, from affluent and well-educated to poor and unschooled. Such diversity means that there is no "Hispanic" population in the sense that there is a Black population. Hispanics do not have a common history. They do not compose a single community. Rather, they are collection of groups with different national origins, languages, racial identifications, and socioeconomic statuses. Saying that someone is Hispanic or Latino reveals little about attitudes, behaviors, beliefs, race, religion, class, or legal situation in the United States (Massey 1993).

Despite these differences, Latinos in the United States have a long history of discrimination by governments controlled by non-Hispanic Whites. Mexican Americans in the Southwest lost property and political rights as Anglos moved into the region in the 1800s. As late as the 1940s, local ordinances in some Texas cities blocked Mexican Americans from owning real estate or voting. Also, Mexican Americans were required to attend segregated public schools in many jurisdictions before 1950 (Pollard and O'Hare 1999:6).

• **Asian Americans.** Asian Americans are another rapidly growing minority group in the country. In 2010, Asian Americans made up about 4.8 percent of the U.S. population (Humes, Jones, and Ramirez 2011). Asians are now the largest group of new immigrants in the United States. In 2010, 36 percent of new immigrants were Asian compared with 32 percent for Hispanics (Pew Research Center 2012).

Like the Hispanic Latino population, the Asian population in the United States is extremely diverse, giving rise to the term *Pan-Asian*, which encompasses immigrants from Asian and Pacific Island countries and native-born citizens descended from those ethnic groups (Lott and Felt 1991:6). Until recently, immigrants who arrived in the United States from Asian countries did not think of themselves as Asians, or even as Chinese, Japanese, Korean, and so forth, but rather as people from Toisan, Hoeping, or some other district in Guangdong Province in China or from Hiroshima, Yamaguchik, or some other locale. It was not until the late 1960s, with the advent of the Asian American movement, that a Pan-Asian consciousness was formed (Espiritu 1996:51).

The largest Asian American groups in the United States are Chinese (22 percent), Filipinos (17 percent), Japanese (5 percent), Vietnamese (11 percent), Koreans (10 percent), and Asian Indians (19 percent) (U.S. Census Bureau 2010). There also are Laotians, Kampucheans, Thais, Pakistanis, Indonesians, Hmong, and Samoans (Lee 1998:15).

The characteristics of Asians vary according to their national origins and time of entry into the United States. Most come from recent immigrant families, but many Asian Americans can trace their family's American history back more than 150 years. From the earliest days of their arrival, dominant attitudes emphasized their "racial foreignness" (Chang 2010). Discrimination and anti-Asian laws prevented them from becoming genuine U.S. citizens. For example, the 1879 California Constitution barred the hiring of Chinese workers, and the federal Chinese Exclusion Act of 1882 halted the entry of most Chinese immigrants until 1943. Americans of Japanese ancestry were interned in camps during World War II by an executive order signed by President Franklin D. Roosevelt. Not until 1952 were Japanese immigrants granted the right to become naturalized U.S. citizens (Pollard and O'Hare 1999:6–7).

Whereas most of the pre–World War II Asian immigrants were peasants, recent immigrants vary considerably by education and social class. On the one hand, many arrived as educated middle-class professionals with highly valued skills and some knowledge of English. Others, such as the Indochinese, arrived as uneducated, impoverished refugees. These differences are reflected in the differences in income and poverty level by ethnic category. Asian Americans taken together have higher average incomes than do other groups in the United States. Although a large segment of this population is financially well off, many are poor. Asian Americans are seen as "the model minority," a well-educated and upwardly mobile group. But this stereotype is misleading. Not only is it used to blame other racial minorities for their own inequality, but it also ignores both the history of discrimination against Asians and their wide differences. Even the term *Asian American* masks great diversity.

- **Native Americans.** Once thought to be destined for extinction, today the Native American or American Indian population is larger than it has been for centuries. Now at 2 percent of the total U.S. population (U.S. Census Bureau 2010), Native Americans have more autonomy and are more self-sufficient than at any time since the last century (Snipp 1996:390). Nevertheless, the population remains barred from full participation in U.S. society.

  The tribes located in North America were and are extremely heterogeneous, with major differences in physical characteristics, language, and social organization. As many as 7 million indigenous people lived in North America when the Europeans arrived. The conquest made them "Indians." By 1890, they were reduced to less than 250,000 by disease, warfare, and, in some cases, genocide. In the first half of the nineteenth century, the U.S. government forced Native Americans from their homelands. Those forced migrations accelerated after President Andrew Jackson signed the Indian Removal Act of 1830. Many tribes then lived on marginal land that was reserved for them.

  The current political and economic status of Native Americans is the result of the process that forced them into U.S. society. Many factors led to the disparities we now observe between Native Americans and others, including the appropriation of Indian land for the gain of White settlers, the mismanagement by the Bureau of Indian Affairs of resources found on native lands, and the underinvestment by the general government in Native American education and healthcare (Adamson 2009).

  Important changes have occurred in the social and economic well-being of the Native American population from 1960 to the present. At the time of the 1970 census, Native Americans were the poorest group in the United States, with incomes well below those of the Black population. By 1980, despite poverty rates as high as 60 percent on many Indian reservations, poverty among Native Americans had declined. At the end of the twentieth century, Native Americans were better off than they were in the 1900s. Over the past few decades, Native Americans have made important gains in cutting poverty rates and increasing their educational levels. Yet even with these gains, Native Americans are nowhere near parity with White Americans. Today, Native Americans have a poverty rate of almost 27 percent, twice the White poverty rate (Muhammad 2009). Native peoples rank at the bottom of most U.S. socioeconomic indicators, with the lowest levels of life expectancy, per capita income, employment, and education (Harjo 1996; Muhammad 2009; Pollard and O'Hare 1999; Thornton 1996).

Although the conditions prevailing on many reservations resemble conditions in the developing world, a renaissance has occurred in Native American communities. In cities, modern pan-Indian organizations have been successful in making the presence of Native Americans known to the larger community and have mobilized to meet the needs of their people (Snipp 1996:390). A college-educated Native American middle class has emerged, Native American business ownership has increased, and some tribes are creating good jobs for their members (Fost 1991:26).

To summarize this section, the combined population of the four racial minority groups now accounts for 30 percent of the total U.S. population. New waves of immigration from non-European countries, high birthrates among these groups, and a relatively young age structure account for the rapid increase in minorities. By the middle of the twenty-first century, today's minorities will comprise nearly one-half of the U.S. population. (See Figure 8.1 for population projections through 2050.) African Americans, Latinos, Asian Americans, and Native Americans are different in many respects. Each group encounters different forms of exclusion. Nevertheless, as racial minorities, they remain at the lowest rungs of society.

EXPLANATIONS OF RACIAL AND ETHNIC INEQUALITY

8.3 Discuss racial inequality from different theoretical perspectives: deficiency theories, bias theories, and structural discrimination theories.

Why have some racial and ethnic groups been consistently disadvantaged? Three types of theories have been used to explain why some groups are treated differently: deficiency theories, bias theories, and structural discrimination theories.

Deficiency Theories

A number of analysts have argued that some groups are disadvantaged because they *are* inferior. That is, when compared with the majority, they are deficient in some important way. There are two variations of **deficiency theories**.

- **Biological Deficiency.** This classical explanation for racial inferiority maintains that group inferiority is the result of flawed genetic—and therefore hereditary—traits. This is the position of Arthur Jensen, Richard Herrnstein, and Charles Murray (as discussed in Chapter 7). *The Bell Curve* (Herrnstein and Murray 1994) is the latest in a long series of works claiming that Blacks are genetically inferior to Whites and that this inferiority explains differences in the social success of racial groups. Despite the media attention given the work of these and other theorists, there is no definitive evidence for the thesis that racial groups differ in intelligence. Biological deficiency theories are generally not accepted in the scientific community (see *Contemporary Sociology* 1995).

- **Cultural Deficiency.** Many explanations of racial subordination center on group-specific cultural traits handed down from generation to generation. According to this explanation, the cultures and behaviors of minority groups are dysfunctional when compared to those of the dominant group. In addition, these groups remain at the bottom because they fail to take advantage of the opportunities in society (Brown and Wellman 2005:188). From this perspective, minorities are disadvantaged because of their group-specific heritage and customs. Cultural deficiency was the basis of Daniel Patrick Moynihan's famous 1967 report, which charged that the "tangle of pathology" within Black ghettos was rooted in the deterioration of the Negro family (U.S. Department of Labor 1965). High rates of divorce, female-headed households, out-of-wedlock births, and welfare dependency were said to be the residues of slavery and discrimination, a complex web of pathological patterns passed down through the generations. The Moynihan report was widely criticized for being a classic case of "blaming the victim." It finds the problem within Blacks, not in the structure of society.

For over four decades, many social scientists strongly opposed cultural explanations. However, the culture of poverty is now back on the sociological agenda, this time using new definitions of culture and arguing that culture and social conditions work together to produce poverty and racial inequality (Small, Harding, and Lamont 2010; Wilson 2010). Still, the old cultural approach dominates in popular thought. Today, much of the public discussion about race and poverty rests on false assumptions about deficient minorities (Bonilla-Silva 2003; di Leonardo 1992; Reed 1990). Family "breakdown" is still used to explain African American problems, whereas a backward culture is said to produce Latino problems. Today's immigrant debates use culture to generate fear. For example, in his book, *Who Are We? The Challenges to American Identity* (2004), Samuel P. Huntington argues that a culture alien to Anglo-Saxon ways makes unchecked Latino immigration a threat to U.S. society.

Bias Theories

The deficiency theories blame minorities for their plight. **Bias theories**, on the other hand, blame the members of the dominant group. They blame individuals who hold *prejudiced attitudes* toward minorities. Gunnar Myrdal, for example, argued in his classic book, *An American Dilemma*, that prejudiced attitudes toward an entire group of people are the problem (Myrdal 1944). This argument reduces racism to the "prejudiced" acts of individual White Americans (Brown and Wellman 2005:189).

Many sociologists have argued that prejudiced attitudes are not the essence of racism. For example, David Wellman (1977) has challenged the notion that the hostile attitudes of White Americans, especially lower-class Whites, are the major cause of racism. Instead, he shows that many unprejudiced White people defend the traditional social arrangements that negatively affect minorities. Research by Lawrence Bobo (2009) shows that although prejudice has declined, most White Americans are still unwilling to support social practices and policies to address racial inequalities. Unbiased people fight to preserve the status quo by favoring, for example, the seniority system in occupations, or they oppose affirmative action, quota systems, busing to achieve racial balance, and open enrollment in higher education.

Today, we live in an era when laws to protect citizens from racial discrimination are firmly in place. The new conventional wisdom views racism as a remnant of the past, the result of individual White bigotry, which is diminishing (Brown and Wellman 2005). The focus strictly on prejudice is inaccurate because it concentrates on the bigots and ignores the structural foundation of racism. The determining feature of dominant-minority relations is not prejudice but differential systems of privilege and disadvantage. "The subordination of people of color is functional to the operation of American society as we know it and the color of one's skin is a primary determinant of people's position in the social structure" (Wellman 1977:35). Even if active dislike of minorities ceases, "persistent social patterns can endure over time, affecting whom we marry, where we live, what we believe and do, and so forth" (Elliot and Pais 2006:300).

Thus, institutional and individual racism generate privilege for Whites. Discrimination provides the privileged with disproportionate advantages in the social, economic, and political spheres. Racist acts, in this view, not only are based on hatred, stereotyped conceptions, or prejudgment but also are rational responses to the struggle over scarce resources by individuals acting to preserve their own advantage.

Structural Discrimination Theories

Deficiency and bias theories focus, incorrectly, on individuals: the first on minority flaws and the second on the flawed attitudes of the majority. Both kinds of theory ignore the social system that oppresses minorities. Michael Parenti has criticized those who ignore the system as victim blamers: "Focusing on the poor and ignoring the system of power, privilege, and profit which makes them poor is a little like blaming the corpse for the murder" (Parenti 1978:24). The alternative view is that racial inequality is not fundamentally a matter of what is in people's heads, not a matter of their private individual intentions, but rather a matter of public institutions and practices that create racism or keep it alive. **Structural discrimination theories** move away from thinking about "racism-in-the-head" toward understanding "racism-in-the-world" (Lichtenberg 1992:5).

Watch on MySocLab Video: Prejudice and Stereotypes

Many sociologists have examined race as a structural force that permeates every aspect of life. Those who use this framework make a distinction between individual racism and institutional racism (Carmichael and Hamilton 1967). **Individual racism** is related to prejudice. It consists of individual behavior that harms other individuals or their property. **Institutional racism** is structural. It comprises more than attitudes or behavior. It is structural, that is, *a complex pattern of racial advantage built into the structure of society*—a system of power and privilege that advantages some groups over others (Higginbotham and Andersen 2009:78). Because institutional racism views inequality as part of society's structure, individuals and groups discriminate, regardless of whether they are bigots. These individuals and groups operate within a social milieu that ensures racial dominance. The social milieu includes laws, customs, religious beliefs, and the stable arrangements and practices through which things get done in society.

Institutional or structural racism is not about beliefs. It is not only about actions directed at those considered racially different (meaning those not considered White). According to Howard Winant:

> . . . *structural racism is about the accretion of inequality and injustice in practice; it's about the way things work, regardless of the reasons why, it's about outcomes, not intentions or beliefs. So, if vast inequalities in wealth persist across racial lines, for example, they may persist not because White people presently intend to impoverish Black or Brown people; they may persist because of years and years of some people doing better than others do. Inequality accumulates; injustice becomes normal; they come to be taken for granted.* (2009:58)

While there are different structural theories of racial inequality, they all agree on the following points. First, history is important in determining present conditions and affecting resistance to change. Historically, institutions defined and enforced norms and role relationships that were racially distinct. The United States was founded and its institutions established when Blacks were slaves, uneducated, and different culturally from the dominant Whites (Patterson 2007:58). From the beginning, Blacks were considered inferior (the original Constitution, for example, counted a slave as three-fifths of a person). Religious beliefs buttressed this notion of the inferiority of Blacks and justified the differential allocation of privileges and sanctions in society.

Second, discrimination can occur without conscious bigotry. Everyday practices reinforce racial discrimination and deprivation. Although the actions of individual bigots are unmistakably racist, many other actions (choosing to live in a suburban neighborhood, sending one's children to a private school, or opposing government intervention in hiring policies) also maintain racial dominance (Bonilla-Silva 1996:475). With or without malicious intent, racial discrimination is the "normal" outcome of the system. Even if racism-in-the-head disappeared, racism-in-the-world would not, because it is the *system* that disadvantages (Lichtenberg 1992).

Finally, institutional discrimination is reinforced because institutions are interrelated. The exclusion of minorities from the upper levels of education, for example, is likely to affect their opportunities in other institutions (type of job, level of remuneration). Similarly, poor children will probably receive an inferior education, be propertyless, suffer from bad health, and be treated unjustly by the criminal justice system. These inequities are cumulative.

Institutional derogation occurs when minority groups and their members are made to seem inferior or to possess negative stereotypes through legitimate means by the powerful in society. The portrayal of minority group members in the media (movies, television, newspapers, and magazines) is often derogatory. For example, many studies depict Black men disproportionately as drug users, criminals, lower class, and "pathological" (Muwakkil 1998b:18). Such stereotypes are "controlling images" that define perceptions of minorities (Collins 1990). If we based our perceptions of minority populations on media images, we would have considerably skewed views. The media also provide us with explanations and interpretations intended to help us make sense of our society, including its multiracial composition. The ideas that pervade today's mass media obscure pervasive racial inequality. Instead we are bombarded by depictions of race relations that suggest discriminatory racial barriers have been dismantled and that the United States has become a truly color-blind nation (Gallagher 2010; Weber 2010). Color-blind racism is the belief that ignoring race and racial differences will produce racial equality (Bonilla-Silva 2009; Gallagher 2010). (See the "A Closer Look" panel on racial framing in the news.)

Why is U.S. society organized along racial lines? Sociologists have a long-standing debate over the relative importance of race and class in shaping systems of racial inequality. Those emphasizing class contend that the economy and class system are what produce racial inequality (see the discussion of the underclass later in the chapter). Some scholars argue that modern race relations are produced by world capitalism. Using the labor of non-White peoples began as a means for White owners to accumulate profits. This perspective contends that capitalism as a system of class exploitation has shaped race and racism in the United States and the world (Bonacich 1992).

Other structural theories point to race itself as a primary shaper of inequality. For example, racial-formation theory explains the sociohistorical process by which racial categories are created. This theory proposes that the United States is organized along racial lines from top to bottom—a racial state composed of institutions and policies to support and justify racial stratification (Omi and Winant 1986, 1994). Another theory, called *systemic racism*, also argues that race itself explains racial inequality. Systemic racism includes a diverse assortment of racism practices: the unjustly gained economic and political power of Whites, the continuing resource inequalities, and the White-racism ideologies, attitudes, and institutions created to preserve White advantages and power. Systemic racism is both structural and interpersonal. "At the macrolevel, large-scale institutions . . . routinely perpetuate racial subordination and inequalities. These institutions are created and re-created by routine actions at the microlevel by individuals" (Feagin 2000:16). Systemic racism is far more than a matter of individual bigotry, for it has been from the beginning a mental, social, and ideological reality (Feagin 2006:xiii).

Watch on
MySocLab Video:
Racial Stereotypes and Discrimination

Read on
MySocLab Document:
The Great American Football Ritual: Reproducing Race, Class, and Gender Inequality

A Closer Look

RACIAL FRAMING IN THE NEWS

Mass communication shapes our perception of racial and other minorities. Professional journalism practices for "getting out the news" in a 24/7 cycle and unmediated communication such as social networks, blogs, and texting allow biases about minorities to go unperceived and unchallenged.

The structure or *framing* of a news story can convey calculated, attention-grabbing, and unintentional biases. Think of framing as contextualizing a message by the choice and placement of words in the text. A headline or subhead frames what comes after.

What does each headline about new U.S. Census data signify in this example? **"Fewer White Babies"** or **"More Non-White Babies."** Does the wording suggest there is some sort of competition among races? Who would seem more advantaged or disadvantaged by the outcome?

The choice of picture illustrations also frame the census story. Think about a picture of a Black infant or another non-White race infant. Choosing a Black child's image reinforces the notion that race is mostly a Black issue. Images are important for framing not only because they can contradict the text, but also, as this case shows, they can give a false *color* to the story. Can you think of other examples like these?

More overt, yet stealthy, framing biases affecting minorities may also slip through media. *Dog-whistle* political speech uses ambiguous-seeming terms, also known as "code words," directed toward an audience that can "hear" their specific meaning. The voter ID controversy is a recent example. Liberals might bring to mind the term "poll tax," whereas conservatives frame it as a remedy for voting fraud. The coded racial subtext is clear to each audience. Can you think of more examples of coded speech?

When tragic events such as the Rodney King and Trayvon Martin cases ignite widespread public interest, we say they present "teachable moments" and "a good time to discuss race." This underscores the lack of frank discussion in both the media and a public that will not stray from their comfort zone. How minority journalists handle issues of race may influence their careers. Day-to-day or episodic stories are narrowly framed "offender-focused" rather than are the thematic stories that frame general minority issues, or "defender" stories.

News media expert Shanto Iyengar has studied how the framing of crime reports shapes viewers' attributions of responsibility. He finds that when television news provides viewers with a collective or contextual frame of reference for crime (thematic framing), viewers are more likely to attribute responsibility (both in terms of responsibility for causing the problem and curing the problem) to societal factors. After watching a thematic report, people cited unemployment and racial discrimination as potential causes of crime and recommended improved educational opportunities for the poor as an appropriate remedy (Iyengar 2010:273).

Why does the United States have this tremendous degree of racial inequality even though most White people are not "racist"? According to sociologist Eduardo Bonilla-Silva (2009:176), racial inequality exists because it benefits members of the dominant race.

8.4 Examine the role of public policy in both reducing racial bias and continuing racial bias in contemporary society.

DISCRIMINATION AGAINST AFRICAN AMERICANS AND LATINOS: CONTINUITY AND CHANGE

The treatment of Blacks and Hispanics has been disgraceful throughout American history. Through public policies and everyday practices, they have been denied the opportunities that should be open to all people. Since World War II, however, under pressure from civil rights advocates, the government has led the way in breaking down many discriminatory practices. Community organizing, civil rights legislation, landmark court decisions, and rising education have advanced the cause of racial equality. By the close of the twentieth century, many well-educated people of color had climbed into the middle class. They have taken advantage of fair-housing legislation and moved to the suburbs looking for better schools, safer streets, and better services. Yet having "made it" in the United States does not shield people of color from discrimination. Studies of public accommodation have found that in stores, bars, restaurants, and theaters, middle-class Blacks are ignored or treated with hostility (Feagin and Sikes 1994). No matter how affluent or influential, Blacks and other dark-skinned people are vulnerable to "microinsults" such as being followed around in stores (Bonilla-Silva 2003; Muwakkil 1998a).

Substantial growth of the minority middle class has not erased the problem of segregation. A class divide now characterizes minority communities across the country. As some successful people of color have become richer, many more unsuccessful ones have been marginalized. To be sure, much progress is evident in some areas. But in others, racial injustice remains deeply entrenched and is worsening (Lewis et al. 2004; Warren 2011).

Racism was clearly present in the aftermath of Hurricane Katrina, the costliest natural disaster ever to hit the United States. For days, the world watched as federal officials moved slowly to assist those stranded and dying in flooded houses and over-crowded shelters in New Orleans and the Gulf Coast areas. What was exposed was not just a broken levee but race and class divides both familiar and yet new. Even media commentators raised the reasonable question of whether the fact that a majority of those hardest hit in New Orleans were low-income Black residents had affected the slowness of the federal government response (DeParle 2007:163; Feagin 2006). The most comprehensive survey of Hurricane Katrina survivors found that both race and class played important roles in shaping response to the disaster (Elliot and Pais 2006). The evacuation plan was based on people driving out, yet 35 percent of Black households did not have a car, compared to 15 percent of White households. The Lower Ninth Ward, very poor and almost entirely Black, was one of the most heavily damaged areas of the city, while Whites disproportionately lived in more affluent higher areas less likely to suffer flooding (DeParle 2007).

The present segregation of African Americans cannot be dismissed as wrongs committed in the past. U.S. neighborhoods were sharply segregated in the 1990s (Massey and Denton 1993). Today, U.S. neighborhoods remain segregated. Although residential segregation is declining, it is not disappearing. Despite some progress toward integration in the last decade of the twentieth century, neighborhood segregation is a key feature of the U.S. social landscape. African Americans, in particular, continue to live in segregated neighborhoods in exceptionally high numbers (Farley and Squires 2012). Levels of Hispanic segregation have also risen (Rugh and Massey 2010). Residential segregation deprives minorities of economic and educational opportunities.

Income

The average income for White families and households is greater than the average income for those of Blacks and Hispanics. Racial income disparities have remained unchanged over time. In 2010, the median income of Black households was about $35,000, the median income of White households was about $55,000, and the median income of Hispanic households was about $41,000 (U.S. Census Bureau 2010). Even though the median household income for Blacks is still below that of Hispanics, per-person income for Hispanics is actually lower because Hispanics tend to have larger households (see Figure 8.2).

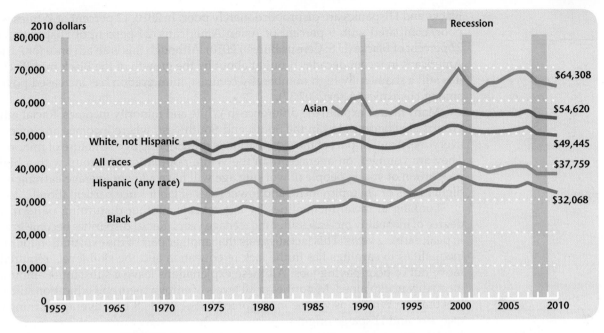

FIGURE 8.2

Real Median Household Income by Race and Hispanic Origin: 1967–2010

Note: Median household income data are not available prior to 1967.

Source: Carmen DeNavas-Walt, Bernadette D. Proctor, and Jessica C. Smith. 2011. U.S. Census Bureau, Current Population Reports, P60-239, *Income, Poverty, and Health Insurance Coverage in the United States: 2010.* Washington, DC: U.S. Government Printing Office, p. 8.

Read on MySocLab Document: Doubly Divided: The Racial Wealth Gap

Although the racial income gap is wide, the racial *wealth gap* is even wider. White families are generally wealthier than Black or Latino families (Collins, Leondar-Wright, and Sklar 1999). *Wealth* is the sum of important assets a family owns. It includes home ownership, pension funds, savings accounts, and investments. Many of these resources are inherited across generations. White families generally have greater resources for their children and bequeath them as assets at death. Sociologists call this "the cost of being Black" (Oliver and Shapiro 1995). The wealth gaps between Whites and minorities have grown to their widest levels in a quarter of a century. The recession and uneven recovery have erased decades of minority gains, leaving Whites with twenty times the net worth of Black households and eighteen times that of Hispanic households (National Latino Congresso 2011; Pew Research Center 2011).

One important indicator of a family's wealth is home ownership. Paying off a home mortgage is the way most people build net worth over their lifetimes. But because racial minorities encounter discrimination in their efforts to buy, finance, or insure a home, a great race gap remains (Farley and Squires 2012:360). Fewer than half of Blacks and Latinos and fewer than 60 percent of Asian Americans and Native Americans own their own homes, compared to three-quarters of Whites. Rampant racial discrimination prevails in the housing market, even after forty years of federal housing laws (Briggs 2005; Crowley 2002:25; Leondar-Wright et al. 2005:11).

Not only are poverty rates of minority groups higher than for Whites, but recent studies find rising numbers of African Americans and Latinos living in high-poverty neighborhoods (Cawthorne 2011). Although most poor people are White,

Blacks and Hispanics are disproportionately poor. In 2010, 12 percent of Whites were poor, compared with 9 percent of Asian Americans, 24 percent of Hispanics, and 27 percent of Blacks (U.S. Census Bureau 2010). Although this is an advance for African Americans in recent decades brought about by the growth of the Black middle class, it is still a shamefully high number. By contrast, immigration has increased poverty among Hispanics (Alter 2007:37).

Many factors explain the difference in White and minority incomes. Racial-ethnic groups are concentrated in the South and Southwest, where incomes are lower for everyone. Another part of the explanation is the differing age structure of minorities. They are younger, on average, than the White population. A group with a higher proportion of young people of working age will have a lower average earning level, higher rates of unemployment, and lower rates of labor force participation.

Looking at racial inequalities by age reveals another disturbing pattern. The degree of inequality increases after the teenage years. Racial disparities become greater in peak earning years. This fact suggests that another part of the explanation for racial inequalities in earnings lies in the lack of education and the skill levels required to move out of poor-paying jobs. All these explanations leave a substantial amount of inequality unexplained. Minorities at all levels of employment and education still earn less than do Whites, as we see in Chapter 14. (See Table 8.1 for average earnings by race, sex, and Hispanic origin.)

Education

In 1954, the Supreme Court outlawed segregation in the schools. Yet the landmark *Brown v. Board of Education* ruling did not end segregation. In fact, U.S. schools are now more racially segregated than ever before. Since the decades of the 1980s and 1990s, school resegregation has continued to grow in all parts of the country. More than a

TABLE 8.1

Mean Personal Income by Race-Ethnicity, Sex, and Education (2010)

		Educational Attainment			
		No High School	High School or Equivalent	Some College	Bachelor's Degree or Higher
White	Male	14,184	33,188	39,154	80,088
	Female	7,221	19,070	24,707	45,440
Black	Male	9,336	22,039	28,205	55,485
	Female	7,281	16,662	23,095	45,196
Asian	Male	11,115	25,510	27,543	72,062
	Female	7,877	16,883	19,355	42,709
Hispanic	Male	15,613	25,018	30,357	57,930
	Female	6,948	14,836	20,265	39,246
Totals	Male	13,254	31,222	37,308	77,624
	Female	7,216	18,582	24,216	45,143

Source: U.S. Census Bureau (2011). "Current Population Survey, Annual Social and Economic Supplement," Table generated at url: http://www.census.gov/hhes/www/cpstc/cps_table_creator.html.

third of African Americans and Hispanics attend schools with a minority enrollment of 90 to 100 percent (Darling-Hammond 2010). This is class as well as race segregation, both from Whites and from middle-class students (Darling-Hammond, 2010; Orfield and Lee 2012:331).

The 2010 high school graduation rate for Whites was 87 percent compared with 85 for Asian Americans, 81 percent for African Americans, and 62 percent for Hispanics (U.S. Census Bureau 2010). This is a growing problem because today 70 percent of jobs are knowledge-work jobs requiring high levels of literacy and specialized skills beyond high school (Darling-Hammond 2010).

What explains the minority education gap? Some educators blame children and their families for lack of effort, poor child-rearing, or a culture of "opposition" that causes underperformance among Black and Latino students. However, research points to larger social conditions:

> Educational outcomes for students of color are much more a function of their unequal access to key educational resources, including skilled teachers and a high-quality curriculum than they are a function of race. These disparities reinforce the wide inequalities in income among families, with the most resources being spent on children from the wealthiest communities and the fewest on the children of the poor, especially in high-minority communities. (Darling-Hammond 2010:300)

Minority participation in higher education has risen since the 1960s. College campuses are far more diverse than they were a century ago (Rothstein 2007:129). Nevertheless, there are large racial gaps in college enrollment and earned bachelor's degrees. In 2010, 13 percent of Hispanic 25- to 29-year-olds had gained a bachelor's degree compared with 19 percent of Blacks, 53 percent of Asian Americans, and 39 percent of Whites in that age group (Helliker 2011). Although many colleges actively recruit students of color, many factors contribute to low retention rates. Even when they reach college, students of color often confront a range of discriminatory barriers. Studies have consistently found that they are more alienated than White students and drop out more often than White students. Discrimination by Whites on and off campus is a recurring problem (Feagin 2000:170).

All these disparities translate into economic inequalities. Yet education alone is not the answer. Even with a college degree, African Americans and Latinos have higher unemployment rates than their White counterparts. This is compounded by the reality that education does not pay equally. Minority membership, regardless of the level of education, is underpaid compared with Whites of similar education. A highly educated White man still makes more money than anyone else. (See Table 8.1.)

Unemployment

African Americans and Latinos are more likely than Whites to be unemployed. For the last three decades, unemployment among Black workers has been twice that of White workers, with Latinos in between. In 2011, the unemployment rate for Latinos was 11 percent, compared with 15 percent for African Americans and 8 percent for Whites. Minority teenagers had an even harder time. The unemployment rate among Black teens was 37 percent; for Latinos, it was 30 percent; and for Whites, it was 21 percent (U.S. Bureau of Labor Statistics 2012a).

These government rates are misleading because they count as employed the almost 6 million people who work part time because they cannot find full-time jobs, and these rates also do not count as unemployed the discouraged workers, numbering more than 1 million, who have given up their search for work.

Type of Employment

African Americans and Latinos have always been an important component of the U.S. labor force. However, their job prospects are different from those of other people in the United States. Although no longer barred from particular occupations, as they were in the past, many occupations remain largely segregated by race and ethnicity (Moya and Marcus 2010:64). Minorities are more likely to work in low-skilled occupations and less likely to work in managerial or professional occupations (see Table 8.2). Black and Latino workers are more likely to be in jobs with pay too low to lift a family of four above the poverty line (Leondar-Wright et al. 2005:9). Sociological research shows that race is related to workplace recruitment, hiring, firing, job levels, pay scales, promotion, and degree of autonomy on the job. Seemingly neutral practices can advantage some groups and adversely affect others (American Sociological Association 2003; Shulman 2007).

Immigrants generally work in the lowest rungs of the low-wage workforce. They are more likely than natives to be food-preparation workers, sewing machine operators, parking lot attendants, housekeepers, waiters, private household cleaners, food-processing workers, agricultural workers, elevator operators, janitors, operators, fabricators, and laborers (Shulman 2007:101). Although Blacks, Hispanics, and Native Americans are in the least rewarding jobs, and many face discrimination in hiring and promotion, the occupational status of minorities improved slowly during the last decade. Still, huge gaps remain. As more minorities enter high-status work, they are confronting new discrimination practices in the form of "job ceilings" that keep them out of executive suites and boardrooms (Higginbotham 1994).

Globalization and shifts in the U.S. economy have diminished work opportunities across the land (see Chapter 14). The nation's job crisis has been catastrophic for African American and Latinos. High unemployment rates have affected minority communities much like a depression and threatened the viability of many Black communities. In 2009, joblessness for 16- to 24-year-old Black men reached Great Depression proportions with a rate of 34 percent—more than three times the rate for the general U.S. population (Ehrenreich and Muhammad 2009; Haynes 2009).

TABLE 8.2
Selected Labor Force Characteristics by Sex, Race, and Ethnicity (2011)

		Total %	Black %	Hispanic %	Asian %	White %
In civilian labor force	Men	70.5	64.2	76.5	73.2	71.3
	Women	58.1	59.1	55.9	56.8	58
Unemployed	Men	9.4	17.8	11.2	6.8	8.3
	Women	8.5	14.1	11.8	7.3	7.5
Occupations						
Management and professional	Men	34.4	23.5	15.6	49.1	34.9
	Women	41.5	34.1	25.2	44.4	42.3
Sales and service	Men	31.5	40.3	36.5	31.3	30.4
	Women	52.5	58.8	63	48.1	51.7
Skilled and unskilled manual	Men	34.1	36.2	47.9	19.6	34.7
	Women	6	7.1	11.8	7.5	6

Source: Bureau of Labor Statistics (2011). "Current Population Survey, Household Data Annual Averages," Tables 4, 5, and 10. Can be accessed from http://www.bls.gov/cps/tables.htm.

Because African Americans and Latinos established successful niches in civil service, they are also being replaced by government downsizing (American Sociological Association 2003). The new economy will be increasingly made up of people of color. If they continue to be denied equal access to higher-paying jobs, the entire society will be at risk for poverty and other problems associated with economic inequality.

Health

We have seen that minorities in the United States occupy lower rungs than Whites in the workforce. In addition, they have high rates of unemployment, and less wealth. These conditions translate into limited access to healthcare, greater stress, shorter life spans, and higher rates of disease for minorities (Moya and Marcus 2010:70). Hispanics are the most likely to be without health coverage. Thirty percent of Hispanics, 18 percent of African Americans, 15 percent of Asian Americans, and 13 percent of Whites were not covered by private or government medical insurance in 2010 (U.S. Census Bureau 2010). Hispanics born outside the United States were almost twice as likely to lack health insurance as their U.S.-born counterparts. Many are unfamiliar with the U.S. healthcare system, and a few are illegal immigrants who are afraid to seek medical assistance (del Pinal and Singer 1997:37; Folbre and Center for Popular Economics 2000).

Racial discrimination affects health in other ways as well. For example, chemical plants and toxic waste dumps are often located in or near minority communities. **Environmental racism** is the disproportionate exposure of some racial groups to environmental toxic substances. Race is the strongest predictor of hazardous waste facility location in the country. Even before Hurricane Katrina struck in 2005, New Orleans was already struggling with environmental assaults that ranged from floodwaters to toxic debris. People of color were most vulnerable to these assaults. Katrina was among the deadliest and most devastating disasters in U.S. history. Although public attention has focused on rebuilding the Gulf Coast, a lesser known crisis of lethal debris lingers, left over from hurricane damage (Bullard and Wright 2009). Nationally, three out of five African Americans and Latinos live in communities with abandoned toxic waste sites because of land use, housing patterns, and infrastructure development (Bullard 2007:87).

The health disadvantages of living in impoverished neighborhoods cannot be overstated. Those living in "high-opportunity" neighborhoods, which are typically White, can expect to live up to twenty years longer than residents of a "low-opportunity" neighborhood in the same city. Researchers at the Health Policy Institute of the Joint Center for Political and Economic Studies in Washington, DC, claim that zip code is more important than genetic code in determining a person's health (Coffey 2011:A2).

Racial disparities are found in access to healthcare and in treatment of serious diseases. Minorities receive lower-quality healthcare than Whites, even when their insurance and income are the same, because of racial prejudice and difference in the quality of health plans (Brown and Wellman 2005:191; Stolberg 2002). On virtually every measure of health, African Americans and Latinos are disadvantaged, as revealed in the following selected facts:

- Compared to the general population, Blacks and Hispanics are less likely to have a consistent source of medical care and more likely to use emergency rooms as a primary source of care. Compared to Whites, Hispanics had a 700 percent higher rate of visits to community health centers but a 35 percent lower rate of visits to physicians' offices. Compared to Whites, Blacks had a 550 percent higher rate of visits to community health centers but a 48 percent lower rate of visits to physicians' offices (Forrest and Whelan 2000).

- Native American women are 1.9 times as likely to die from cervical cancer compared to White women, and African Americans were 1.5 times as likely as Whites to have high blood pressure (National Conference of State Legislatures 2009).
- HIV/AIDS has had a devastating impact on minorities in the United States. Racial-ethnic minorities accounted for almost 71 percent of newly diagnosed cases of HIV infection in 2010. Over 80 percent of children born with HIV infection belong to minority groups (U.S. Department of Health and Human Services 2012).

8.5 Discuss and give examples of the growing racial strife in the United States.

CONTEMPORARY TRENDS AND ISSUES IN U.S. RACIAL AND ETHNIC RELATIONS

Racial diversity presents new social conditions that reflect differences in group power and access to social resources. Three major trends reveal old and new forms of racial inequality: racial strife, economic polarization of minorities, and a national shift in U.S. racial policies. These trends are occurring in a global context, closely associated with macrosocial forces around the world.

Ongoing Racial Strife

Watch on
MySocLab Video:
The Social Meaning of
Race and Ethnicity

Although the social dynamics of race are changing, the United States is still plagued by racial divisions. The growing immigrant and minority presence together with the nation's economic crisis are adding *new* tensions in society.

Anti-Hispanic sentiment increased steadily during the last two decades, producing restrictive immigration laws and policies such as Arizona's 2010 legislation requiring immigrants to carry proof of their legal status and to show IDs to police officers who suspect they may be illegally in the United States (Martin and Midgley 2010; Navarro 2011). Alabama, too, has enacted new legislation governing the treatment of illegal immigrants. Among other provisions, the law requires schools to determine students' immigration status (Reeves 2011). Arizona abolished ethnic studies programs throughout the state and books authored by Mexican Americans and Native Americans are banned in Tucson (Rodriguez 2012).

Anti-immigration movements often translate into hate-related activities. Another effect of the increasing anti-immigration sentiment in the nation is the surge in incidents of vigilantism—unauthorized attempts by ordinary citizens to enforce immigration laws. Some private citizens are increasingly taking the law into their own hands to stem the perceived "flood" of illegal immigrants into the country (National Council of La Raza 1999; Southern Poverty Law Center (SPLC) 2006, 2007). We now see new expressions of anti-Muslim/anti-Arab racism. Like old-fashioned forms of bigotry and hate crimes, this racism is also fueled by misbeliefs about minorities (Blauner 2001:191).

Instead of moving society "beyond race," the historic election of the first African American president has thrust some incidents of racial conflict onto center stage. Prominent Democrats such as former President Carter have publicly speculated that race—and by implication racism—is behind some of the attacks on President Obama at venues ranging from town hall meetings to the floor of Congress, as well as the "birther" movement's rumors about the president's birthplace.

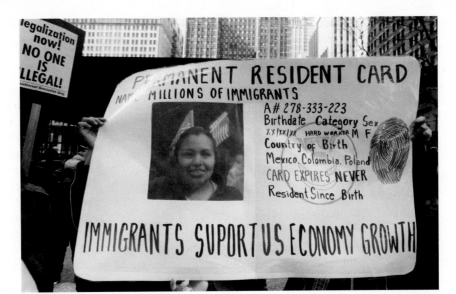

Perceptions that immigrants are taking jobs from Anglos increase racial tensions.

More Racially Based Groups and Activities

The Southern Poverty Law Center (SPLC) documented 1,000 hate groups in forty-eight states and the District of Columbia in 2010, a number that has swelled by 66 percent since 2000 (Potok 2011). Hate groups include White supremacist groups with such diverse elements as the Ku Klux Klan, neo-Confederate groups (those describing Southern culture as fundamentally White), Nazi-identified parties, and skinheads. Many groups use the Internet to spread their literature to young people. As a result, more than half of all hate crimes are now committed by young people ages 15 to 24. In addition to racist websites, cyber extremism flourishes in e-mail and in discussion groups and chat rooms (*Intelligence Report* 2001:47). Racism is also fueled by the proliferation of cable TV hosts who spread and legitimize extremist propaganda. The rise in racial extremism is driven by the country's changing racial composition and economic difficulties.

Read on
MySocLab Document:
Explaining and Eliminating
Racial Profiling

Profiling and Maltreatment.   Racial disparities in the criminal justice system have drawn scrutiny in recent years as the number of people in prison has increased fivefold since 1980. Most of those incarcerated are Black and Latino men (Ledger 2009:51; Moya and Marcus 2010:71). Racial minority individuals in lower-class communities are more likely to be stopped, interrogated, arrested, and prosecuted (Bonilla-Silva 2003; Warren et al. 2006). The past three decades have seen "numerous cases of race-related police brutality and misconduct, and official acknowledgements of systematic racial profiling" (Lewis et al. 2004:95). *Racial profiling* is the use of race and ethnicity as clues to criminality and potential terrorism. According to the Federal Bureau of Justice Statistics, in 2005 Black drivers were twice as likely to be arrested during traffic stops, whereas Latino drivers were more likely than Black or White drivers to receive a ticket (Robinson 2007). Racial profiling on the highways has become so prevalent that a term has emerged to explain it: "DWB—driving while Black" (Bonilla-Silva 2003). Since September 11, Arab Americans, Muslims, and other Middle Easterners have been the targets of threats, gunshots, firebombs, and other forms of vigilante violence (Fahim 2003). Fear of terrorism has provoked a rash of hate crimes and a national debate about the official use of profiling—that is, the use of race and ethnicity as clues to criminality and potential terrorism.

- **Campus Racial Tensions.**   Recent headlines about racism on college campuses have surprised many people because educational institutions are formally integrated. Yet campus racism is very much alive. Over the past few years, students of color have reported a dramatic increase in acts of racial discrimination, intolerance, hate crimes, and insensitivity among different cultures at institutions of higher education. Hateful and racially insensitive incidents have occurred on some of the most prestigious campuses in the country (NAACP 2009). According to the U.S. Department of Education and watchdog and advocacy groups, every year more than half a million college students are targets of bias-driven slurs or physical assaults. Every day, at least one hate crime occurs on a college campus, and every minute, a college student somewhere sees or hears racist, sexist, homophobic, or otherwise biased words or images. These problems are not isolated or unusual events. Instead, they reflect trends in the wider society.

Social and Economic Isolation in U.S. Inner Cities

The notion of a troubled "underclass," locked in U.S. inner cities by a deficient culture, is commonly used to explain racial poverty. According to this reasoning, broken families and bad lifestyles prevent minorities from taking advantage of the opportunities created by antidiscrimination laws. However, like the older cultural deficiency models we discussed earlier, this explanation is wrong on many counts. It relies heavily on behavioral traits to explain poverty. It blames the victims for conditions that are actually rooted in social structure. Social and economic changes have removed jobs and resources from inner-city residents. This reality is a better explanation of poverty among African Americans.

Inner cities are beset with a disproportionate share of social problems.

Social Policy

REDUCING THE RISK OF FUTURE DISASTERS FOR URBAN AFRICAN AMERICANS

African Americans not only have the highest levels of poverty in the country, but they are also the group that is most residentially segregated from and least likely to intermarry with Whites. Surveys also continue to reveal that many non-Black Americans express high levels of social distance (the degree to which people desire close or remote social relations with members of other groups) from African Americans. Given their limited social and economic resources, along with their geographic isolation, poor urban African Americans—especially children and the elderly—are disproportionately vulnerable to being left behind during a crisis situation.

What measures need to be taken to improve the social and economic position of African Americans and to avoid future disasters such as the recent one in New Orleans?

- Skills-development, employment, and health-maintenance programs need to be targeted to and strengthened for African Americans.
- Funding and access to education—including Head Start—should be increased for African Americans to bolster their social and economic well-being and competitiveness in the labor market.
- Additional policies, resources, and investment are needed to promote the development and

relocation of businesses (and thus jobs) to African American urban neighborhoods.
- Government agencies responsible for responding to natural disasters need to factor into their planning the economic and geographic isolation of African Americans—especially the African American urban poor.

Aggressive actions are needed to erase the marginalization of African Americans that Hurricane Katrina exposed. The failure to take such actions will have enormous economic and social costs—not just for African Americans, but for a society living with a disjuncture between its ideals and the reality of continued stratification along the color line.

Source: Rogelio Saenz, "The Social and Economic Isolation of Urban African Americans." Population Reference Bureau (2007):3–4. Reprinted with permission from the Population Reference Bureau.

Hurricane Katrina exposed relationships between racial disparities and emergency preparedness in the northern Gulf Coast. But disparities between Blacks and Whites are not unique to New Orleans. In large cities across the nation, African Americans are much more likely than Whites to live in communities that are geographically and economically isolated from the economic opportunities, services, and institutions that families need to succeed. Without jobs, cars, or phones, inner-city residents are utterly vulnerable to urban disaster. (See the "Social Policy" panel on reducing the risk of future disasters for African Americans.) This social entrapment can be explained *structurally*. In his classic studies of African American poverty at the end of the twentieth century, sociologist William J. Wilson found that the problems of the inner city are due to transformations of the larger economy and to the class structure of ghetto neighborhoods (1987, 1996). The movement of middle-class Black professionals from the inner city has left behind a concentration of the most disadvantaged segments of the Black urban population. Wilson's research reveals how crime, family dissolution, and welfare are connected to the structural removal of work from the inner city. The Black inner city is not destroying itself by its own culture; rather, it is being destroyed by economic forces.

Rising poverty rates among Latinos have led many policymakers and media analysts to conclude that Latinos have joined inner-city African Americans to form a hopeless underclass. This view of minority impoverishment is inaccurate. Although changes in the U.S. economy have hit Latinos hard because of their low educational attainment and their labor market position, structural unemployment has different effects on the many diverse Latino barrios across the nation (Moore and Pinderhughes 1994). The loss of jobs in Rust Belt cities has left many Puerto Ricans living in a bleak ghetto economy. Mexicans living in the Southwest, where low-paying jobs remain, have not suffered the same degree of economic dislocation. Despite high levels of poverty, Latino communities do not fit the conventional portrait of the underclass.

A structural analysis of concentrated poverty does not deny that inner cities are beset with a disproportionate share of social problems. As poverty is more concentrated in inner cities, crime and violence proliferate. The poor may adopt violence as a survival strategy, which escalates violence even further (Massey 1996). As Wilson explains, ". . . Structural conditions provide the context within which cultural responses to chronic economic and racial subordination are developed" (Wilson 2010:61). A structural analysis focuses on social conditions, not immoral people.

Racial Policies in the New Century

The 1960s civil rights movement legalized race-specific remedies to end racial bias. Government policies based on race overturned segregation laws, opened voting booths, created new job opportunities, and brought hopes of racial justice for people of color. As long as it appeared that conditions were improving, government policies to end racial injustice remained in place.

But by the 1980s, the United States had become a very different society from the one in which civil rights legislation was enacted. Economic restructuring brought new dislocations to both Whites and minorities. As racial minorities became an ever larger share of the U.S. population, racial matters grew more politicized. Many Whites began to feel uncomfortable with race-conscious policies in schools and the workplace. The social climate fostered an imaginary White disadvantage, said to be caused by affirmative action and multiculturalism. Although there is no empirical evidence for White disadvantage, a powerful conservative movement is producing new debates about the fairness of racial policies. A new form of racism has emerged. Color-blind racism is the belief that race no longer matters in people's experiences (Gallagher 2012).

Color-blindness is the basis for the current downsizing of policies related to affirmative action, school desegregation, and voting rights. Growing racial populations are controlled through many different forms of discrimination, including employment practices, neighborhood and school segregation, and other inequalities discussed in this chapter. In addition, the demise of the welfare state and the retreat from healthcare and other forms of social responsibility have caused minorities to lose ground. Finally, international systems of dominance (global capitalism and geopolitical relations) are producing still more racial inequalities in the United States (Allen and Chung 2000:802; Barlow 2008). Despite claims of color-blindness, race remains a building-block of U.S. society, a marker of difference, and a rationale for stratification (Kaplan 2011).

Explore on MySocLab Activity: Improvement Is Better than Assistance? Race, Spending, and Patterns of Inequality

While racism is a tool for exclusion, it is also the basis for political mobilization. Since the country was founded, people of color have struggled for social change. All racially defined groups have rich histories of resistance, community building, and social protest. Racial projects are organized efforts to distribute social and economic resources along racial lines (Omi and Winant 1994). Through social movements, groups organize and act to bring about social change. Despite the new racial climate, the struggle against racism continues. Multiracial organizations composed of racial ethnic *and* White antiracist activists continue to work at national and local levels to fight and eradicate racist prejudices and institutional racism.

■ CHAPTER REVIEW

1. Racial and ethnic stratification are basic features of U.S. society. They are also found throughout the world and are an important feature of globalization. Patterns of inequality are built into normal practices. They exclude people from full and equal participation in society's institutions. Racial and ethnic stratification exist because they benefit certain segments of society.

2. The concept of race is a social invention. It is not biologically significant. Racial groups are set apart and singled out for unequal treatment.

3. An ethnic group is culturally distinct in race, religion, or national origin. The group has a distinctive culture. Some ethnic groups such as Jews, Poles, and Italians have distinguishing cultural characteristics that stem from religion and national origin. Because racial groups also have distinctive cultural characteristics, they are referred to as *racial-ethnic* groups.

4. Minority racial and ethnic groups are systematically disadvantaged by society's institutions. Both race and ethnicity are traditional bases for social inequality, although there are historical and contemporary differences in the societal placement of racial-ethnic groups and White ethnic groups in this society.

5. Racial-ethnic groups are socially subordinated and remain culturally distinct within U.S. society. African Americans, Latinos, Asian Americans, and Native Americans are constructed as both racially and culturally distinct. Each group has a distinctive culture, shares a common history, and has developed a common identity within a larger society that subordinates it.

6. Deficiency theories view minority group members as unequal because they lack some important feature common among the majority. These deficiencies may be biological (such as low intelligence) or cultural (such as the culture of poverty).

7. Bias theories place the blame for inequality on the prejudiced attitudes of the members of the dominant group. These theories, however, do not explain the discriminatory acts of the unprejudiced, which are aimed at preserving privilege.

8. Structural theories argue that inequality is the result of external constraints in society rather than cultural features of minority groups. There are four main features of institutional discrimination: (a) forces of history shape present conditions; (b) discrimination can occur without conscious bigotry; (c) institutional discrimination is less visible than are individual acts of discrimination; and (d) discrimination is reinforced by the interrelationships among the institutions of society.

9. Civil rights legislation improved the status of some racial-ethnic groups, yet the overall position of Blacks and Latinos relative to Whites has not improved. Large gaps remain in work, earnings, and education. Global and economic transformations have contributed to the persistent poverty in U.S. urban centers.

10. The racial demography of the United States is changing dramatically. Immigration and high birthrates among minorities are making the United States a multiracial, multicultural society. These trends are also creating racial anxiety and racial conflict.

11. Public policy has shifted from race-conscious remedies to a color-blind climate that is dismantling historic civil rights reforms.

■ KEY TERMS

Dominant group. Group assigning subordinate status to minority groups.

Racial stratification. System of inequality in which race is the major criterion for rank and rewards.

Minority group. Subordinate group in society.

Racial formation. Sociohistorical process by which races are continually being shaped and transformed.

Ethnic groups. Groups characterized by culturally distinctive characteristics based on race, religion, or national origin.

Racial-ethnic group. Group labeled as a "race" by the wider society and bound together by members' common social and economic conditions, resulting in distinctive cultural and ethnic characteristics.

Deficiency theories. Explanations that view the secondary status of minorities as the result of their own behaviors and cultural traits.

Bias theories. Explanations that blame the prejudiced attitudes of majority members for the secondary status of minorities.

Structural discrimination theories. Explanations that focus on the institutionalized patterns of discrimination as the sources of the secondary status of minorities.

Individual racism. Overt acts by individuals that harm members of another race.

Institutional racism. Established and customary social arrangements that exclude on the basis of race.

Environmental racism. The disproportionate exposure of some racial groups to toxic substances.

Color-blindness. Idea that race no longer matters in explaining inequality or in policymaking because racism has been overcome.

Gender Inequality

((⋅ Listen to **Chapter 9** on **MySocLab**

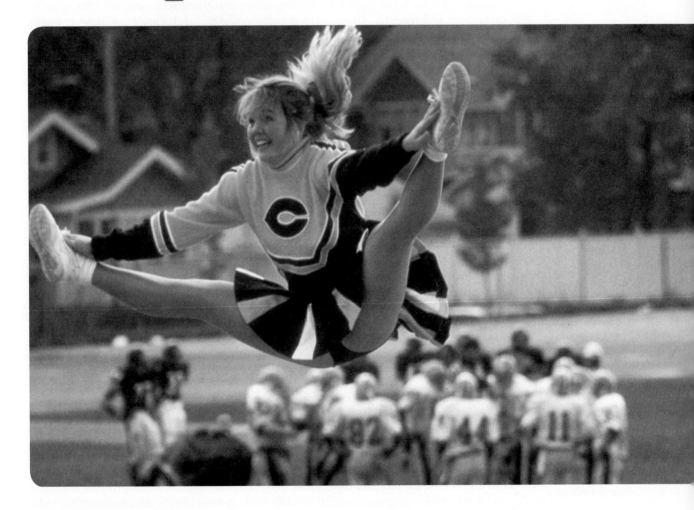

LEARNING OBJECTIVES

9.1 Compare the nature versus nurture arguments regarding gender differences in behavior.

9.2 Understand how the socialization process molds individuals into gendered beings.

9.3 Explain how institutions reinforce gender inequality.

9.4 Explain the factors that contribute to the earnings gap between women and men.

9.5 Discuss the social and individual costs of gender inequality.

9.6 Understand the three stages of feminism.

Every society treats women and men differently. Today, there is no nation where women and men are equals. Worldwide, women perform an estimated 60 percent of the work, yet they earn only 10 percent of the income and own only 10 percent of the land. Two-thirds of the world's illiterate are women. Despite massive political changes and economic progress in countries throughout the world, women continue to be the victims of abuse and discrimination. Even where women have made important strides in politics and the professions, women's overall progress remains uneven.

This chapter examines the social basis of gender inequality. We show how gender disparity and its problems are built into the larger world we inhabit. From the macrolevel of the global economy, through the institutions of society, to interpersonal relations, gender is the basis for dividing labor, assigning roles, and allocating social rewards. Until recently, these differences seemed natural. However, new research shows that gender is not natural at all. Instead, "women" and "men" are social creations. To emphasize this point, sociologists distinguish between *sex* and *gender*. **Sex** refers to the biological differences between females and males. **Gender** refers to the social and cultural patterns attached to women and men. Both sex and gender organize social life throughout the world.

Gender is not only about women. Men often think of themselves as "genderless," as if gender did not matter in the daily experience of their lives. Yet, from birth through old age, men are also **gendered**. This "gendering process, the transformation of biological males into socially interacting men, is a central experience for men" (Kimmel and Messner 2007:xvi). In the big picture, gender divisions make women and men unequal. But we cannot understand the gender system, or women's and men's experiences, by looking at gender alone; gender operates together with other power systems such as race, class, and sexual orientation. These overlapping categories produce different gender experiences for women and men of different races and classes. Nevertheless, the gender system denies women and men the full range of human and social possibilities. Gender inequalities produce social problems. In this chapter we examine gender stratification in U.S. society at both structural and interpersonal levels of social organization. We take a **feminist approach** (one in support of women's equality); the theme of this chapter is that social factors make women unequal to men.

9.1 Compare the nature versus nurture arguments regarding gender differences in behavior.

 Watch on **MySocLab Slideshow:** Gender Stratification

WOMEN AND MEN ARE DIFFERENTIATED AND RANKED

Gender stratification refers to the hierarchical placement of the sexes that gives women unequal power, opportunities, and resources. Although there is worldwide variation in women's and men's roles, gender inequality exists in most parts of the world. Every society has certain ideas about what women and men should be like as well as ways of producing people who are much like these expectations.

Scientists have competing explanations for gender differences. Biological models argue that innate biological differences between males and females produce different social behaviors. Anthropological models look at masculinity and femininity crossculturally, stressing the variations in women's and men's roles. Sociologists treat gender as a social creation deeply embedded in society.

Is Gender Biological or Social?

We know that there *are* biological differences between the two sexes. Debates about gender differences often fall back on "nature vs. nurture" arguments. The nurture camp argues that most differences are socially constructed. The opposing camp claims that differences between women and men are rooted in evolution. In 2005, Larry

Summers, then president of Harvard University, caused a storm by suggesting that innate ability could be a reason there were so few women in the top positions in mathematics, engineering, and the physical sciences. Biological explanations are persistent in some fields of science (Lorber 2011) and in the media (Barnett and Rivers 2004). Is the popular biological explanation correct? Are men "hardwired" to dominate women? To answer this question, let us first review the evidence for each position.

- **Biological Bases for Gender Roles.** Males and females are different from the moment of conception. Chromosomal and reproductive differences make males and females physically different. Hormonal differences in the sexes are also significant. The male hormones (androgens) and female hormones (estrogens) direct the process of sex differentiation from about six weeks after conception throughout life. They make males taller, heavier, and more muscular. At puberty, they trigger the production of secondary sexual characteristics. In males, these include body and facial hair, a deeper voice, broader shoulders, and a muscular body. In females, puberty brings pubic hair, menstruation, the ability to lactate, prominent breasts, and relatively broad hips. Actually, males and females have both sets of hormones. The relative proportion of androgens and estrogens gives a person masculine or feminine physical traits.

  These hormonal differences may explain in part why males tend to be more active, aggressive, and dominant than females. However, there are only slight differences in the levels of hormones between girls and boys in childhood. Yet researchers find differences in aggression between young girls and boys (Fausto-Sterling 1992).

  Biological differences between women and men are only averages. They are often influenced by other factors. For example, although men are on the average larger than women, body size is influenced by diet and physical activity, which in turn may be influenced by culture, class, and race. The all-or-none categorizing of gender traits is misleading because there is considerable overlap in the distribution of traits possessed by women and men. Although most men are stronger than most women, many women are stronger than many men. And although males are on the average more aggressive than females, the differences among males and among females are greater than the differences between males and females (Barnett and Rivers 2004; Basow 1996:81). Furthermore, gender is constantly changing. Femininity and masculinity are not uniformly shaped from genetic makeup. Instead, they are molded differently (1) from one culture to another, (2) within any one culture over time, (3) over the course of all women's and men's lives, and (4) between and among different groups of women and men, depending on class, race, ethnicity, and sexuality (Kimmel 1992:166).

- **The Social Bases for Gender Roles.** Cross-cultural evidence shows a wide variation of behaviors for the sexes. Table 9.1 provides some interesting cross-cultural data from 185 societies on the division of labor by sex. This table shows that for the majority of activities, societies are not uniform in their gendered division of labor. Even activities requiring strength, presumably a male trait, are not strictly apportioned to males. In fact, activities such as burden bearing and water carrying are done by females more than by males. Even an activity such as house building is not exclusively male. Although there is a wide variety in the social roles assigned to women and men, their roles seldom vary "randomly" (O'Kelly 1980:41). Despite the widespread cultural variation in women's and men's activities, every known society makes gender a major category for organizing social life. This is the social construction of gender. It is a sociological perspective that calls on social rather than biological differences to show how all societies transform biological females and males into socially interacting women and men (Andersen 2011).

TABLE 9.1
Sex Allocation of Selected Technological Activities in 185 Societies

Activity	Number of Societies in Which the Activity Is Performed by:					
	Males Exclusively	Males Usually	Both Sexes Equally	Females Usually	Females Exclusively	Percent Male
Smelting of ores	37	0	0	0	0	100.0
Hunting Large Land Fauna	139	5	0	0	0	99.3
Boat building	84	3	3	0	1	96.6
Mining and quarrying	31	1	2	0	1	93.7
Land clearing	95	34	6	3	1	90.5
Fishing	83	45	8	5	2	86.7
Tending Large Animals	54	24	14	3	3	82.4
House building	105	30	14	9	20	77.4
Generation of fire	40	6	16	4	20	62.3
Preparation of skins	39	4	2	5	31	54.6
Crop planting	27	35	33	26	20	54.4
Manufacture of leather products	35	3	2	5	29	53.2
Crop tending	22	23	24	30	32	44.6
Milking	15	2	8	2	21	43.8
Burden Carrying	18	12	46	34	36	39.3
Loom weaving	24	0	6	8	50	32.5
Fuel gathering	25	12	12	23	94	27.2
Manufacture of clothing	16	4	11	13	78	22.4
Pottery making	14	5	6	6	74	21.1
Dairy production	4	0	0	0	24	14.3
Cooking	0	2	2	63	117	8.3
Preparation of Vegetal Foods	3	1	4	21	145	5.7

Source: Adapted from "Factors in the Division of Labor by Sex: A Cross-cultural Analysis" by George P. Murdock and Caterina Provost, *Ethnology*, Vol. 12, no. 2 (April 1973), p. 207. Copyright by University of Pittsburgh. Reprinted by permission.

Gender and Power

Watch on MySocLab Video: Michael Kimmel: How Gender Became "Visible" to Sociologists

Gender differences are social creations that are embedded in society. The term **gendered institutions** means that entire institutions are patterned by gender (Acker 1992; Lorber 2005). Everywhere we look—the global economy, politics, corporate life, family life—men are in power. But men are not uniformly dominant. Some men have great power over other men. In fact, most men do not feel powerful; most feel powerless, trapped in stifling old roles and unable to changes their lives in ways they want (Kimmel 1992:171).

Nevertheless, socially defined differences between women and men legitimate **male dominance**, which refers to the beliefs, meanings, and placement that value men over women and that institutionalize male control of socially valued resources. **Patriarchy** is the term used for forms of social organization in which men are dominant over women.

Like race and class, "gender is a multilevel system of differences and disadvantages that includes socioeconomic arrangements and widely held cultural beliefs at the macrolevel, ways of behaving in relation to others and the interactional level, and acquired traits and identities at the individual level" (Ridgeway 1997:219). Gender inequality is tied to other inequalities such as race, class, and sexuality to sort women and men differently. These inequalities also work together to produce differences *among women* and differences *among men*. Some women derive benefits from their race, their class, or their sexuality while they are simultaneously restricted by gender. Such women are subordinated by patriarchy, yet race, class, and sexuality intersect to create for them privileged opportunities and ways of living (Baca Zinn, Hondagneu-Sotelo, and Messner 2010). For example, men are encouraged to behave in "masculine" fashion to prove that they are not gay (Connell 1992). In defining masculinity as the negation of homosexuality, **compulsory heterosexuality** is an important component of the gender system. Compulsory heterosexuality inflicts negative sanctions on those who are homosexual or bisexual. This system of sexuality shapes the gender system by discouraging attachment with members of the same sex. This enforces the dichotomy of "opposite" sexes. **Sexuality** is also a form of inequality in its own right because it grants privileges to those in heterosexual relationships. Like race, class, and gender, sexual identities are socially constructed categories. Sexuality is a way of organizing the social world on the basis of sexual identity and is a key linking process in the matrix of domination structured along the lines of race, class, and gender (Messner 1996:223).

Is male dominance universal? Scholars once claimed that all societies exhibit some forms of patriarchy in marriage and family forms, in division of labor, and in society at large (Ortner 1974; Rosaldo 1974). Today, most gender scholars depart from this view. Instead, they think that while sex differentiation is found in all societies, it does not always indicate low female status (Rogers 1978; Shapiro 1981). Male dominance is not homogeneous. Instead, it varies from society to society.

We should keep in mind that although gender stratification makes women subordinate to men, they are not simply the passive victims of patriarchy. Like other oppressed groups, women find ways to resist domination. Through personal and political struggles, they act in their own behalf, often changing the social conditions that subordinate them.

Watch on
MySocLab Video:
Gender and Inequality

What Causes Gender Inequality?

To explain gender and power, sociologists turn to social conditions. Structural thinking treats gender inequality as the outcome of male control over socially valued resources and opportunities. There are several models of gender inequality. Most of them focus on the divisions of labor and power between women and men and the different value placed on their work. This idea originated in the work of Friedrich Engels and Karl Marx. They wrote that industrialism and the shift to a capitalist economy widened the gap between the power and value of men and women. As production moved out of the home, the gendered division of labor left men with the greater share of economic and other forms of power (Chafetz 1997; Sapiro 1999:67).

Macrostructural theories explain gender inequality as an outcome of how women and men are tied to the economic structure of society (Neilson 1990:215). These theories say that women's economic role in society is a primary determinant of their overall status (Dunn 1996). The division between domestic and public spheres of activity gives men and women different positions of advantage and disadvantage. Their roles in the labor force and in the family are interdependent. Regardless of whether they work outside the home, women do the vast majority of childcare and household labor. Men are freed from these responsibilities. Women's reproductive roles and their responsibilities for domestic labor limit their association with the resources that are highly valued (Ridgeway 1997; Rosaldo 1980). Men's economic obligations in the public sphere ensure them control of highly valued resources and give rise to male privilege.

In capitalist societies, the domestic–public split is even more significant because highly valued goods and services are exchanged in the public, not the domestic, sphere. Women's domestic labor, although important for survival, ranks low in prestige and power because it does not produce exchangeable commodities (Sacks 1974). Because of the connections between the class relations of production (capitalism) and the hierarchical gender relations of its society (patriarchy) (Eisenstein 1979), the United States is a **capitalist patriarchy** where male supremacy keeps women in subordinate roles at work and in the home.

Socialization versus Structure: Two Approaches to Gender Inequality

To understand gender inequality, we must distinguish between (1) a gender roles approach and (2) a gender structure approach. The **gender roles approach** emphasizes traits that individuals acquire during the course of socialization, such as independent or dependent behaviors and ways of relating. The **gender structure approach** emphasizes factors that are external to individuals, such as the social structures and social interactions that reward women and men differently. These approaches differ in how they view the sexes, in how they explain the causes and effects of sexism, and in the solutions they suggest for ending inequality. Understanding sexism requires both the individual and the structural approaches. Although gender roles are learned by individuals, and produce differences in the personalities and behaviors of women and men, gender stratification is maintained by societal forces. This chapter emphasizes *social structure* as the cause of inequality.

9.2 Understand how the socialization process molds individuals into gendered beings.

LEARNING GENDER

The most complex, demanding, and all-involving role that a member of society must learn to play is that of female or male. "Casting" for one's gender role takes place immediately at birth, after a quick biological inspection; and the role of "female" or "male" is assigned. It is an assignment that will last one's entire lifetime and affect virtually everything one ever does. A large part of the next twenty years or so will be spent gradually learning and perfecting one's assigned sex role (David and Brannon 1980:117).

Sociologists use the term *gender socialization* to describe how we learn gender. Understanding socialization is important not only to explaining gender, but to explain gender inequality (Martin 2005:457). From infancy through early childhood and beyond, children learn what is expected of boys and girls, and they learn to behave according to those expectations.

The traits associated with conventional gender roles are those valued by the dominant society. Keep in mind that gender is not the same in all classes and races. However, most research on gender socialization reflects primarily the experience of White middle-class people—those who are most often the research subjects of these studies. How gender is learned depends on a variety of social conditions affecting the socialization practices of girls and boys. Still, society molds boys and girls along different lines.

Watch on MySocLab Video: Gender Socialization

Children at Home

Girls and boys are perceived and treated differently from the moment of birth. Their access to clothes, toys, books, playmates, and expressions of emotion are severely limited by gender (Martin 2005:457). Parents and "congratulations" greeting cards describe newborn daughters as "sweet," whereas boys are immediately described as "strong" and "hardy." Cards sent to parents depict ribbons, hearts, and flowers for girls, but mobiles, sports equipment, and vehicles for boys. Newborn greeting cards thus project an early gender scheme that introduces two "classes" of babies: one decorative, the other physically active and bringing greater joy (Valian 1998:19–20).

Children learn at a very early age what it means to be a boy or girl in our society. One of the strongest influences on gender role development in children occurs within the family setting, with parents passing on both overtly and covertly their own beliefs about gender (Witt 1997:254). From the time their children are babies, parents treat sons and daughters differently, dressing infants in gender-specific colors and giving them gender-differentiated toys. Color-coded differences reveal a relentless gender segregation with "little girls becoming adamantly attached to pink" (Sandler 2009). Parents expect different behaviors from boys and girls (Thorne 1993; Witt 1997). Although both mothers and fathers contribute to the gender stereotyping of their children, fathers have been found to reinforce gender stereotyping more often than mothers (Campenni 1999; Idle, Wood, and Desmarias 1993; Valian 1998; Witt 1997).

In addition to the parents' active role in reinforcing society's gender demands, a subtler message is emitted from picture books for preschool children. A classic sociological study of award-winning children's books conducted forty years ago found the following characteristics (Weitzman et al. 1972):

- Females were virtually invisible. The ratio of male pictures to female pictures was 11:1. The ratio of male to female animals was 95:1.
- The activities of boys and girls varied greatly. Boys were active in outdoor activities, whereas girls were passive and most often found indoors. The activity of the girls typically was that of some service for boys.
- Adult men and women (role models) were very different. Men led, women followed. Females were passive and males active. Not one woman in these books had a job or profession; they were always mothers and wives.

We have seen improvements in how girls and women are portrayed. Females are no longer invisible, they are as likely as males to be included in the books, and they have roles beyond their family roles. In many respects, however, gendered messages in children's books still exist (Crabb and Bielawski 1994). An update of the classic Weitzman study found that although the majority of female characters were portrayed as dependent and submissive, male characters were commonly portrayed as being independent and creative (Oskamp, Kaufman, and Wolterbeek 1996). Recent studies have found that despite some improvement, women and girls are still underrepresented in book titles and as central characters (McCabe et al. 2011; Nilges and Spencer 2002).

Gendered socialization is found even where gender roles are changing and socialization is becoming more flexible or androgynous. **Androgyny** refers to the combination of feminine and masculine characteristics in the same individual. Are girls more androgynous than boys? If so, what explains the difference? And what difference does androgyny make in an individual's overall well-being? Research has found that fathers who display the most traditional attitudes about gender transmit their ideas onto their sons more so than onto their daughters, whereas mothers who tend to have more liberal attitudes do not transmit their attitudes onto their daughters more than their sons. Consequently, "when the sons establish their own families, they will be more likely than the daughters to transmit traditional attitudes to their own sons" (Kulik 2002:456). Other researchers have also found that whereas adolescent girls tend to be more supportive of egalitarian gender roles than their parents (especially their fathers), adolescent boys follow their fathers' resistance to changes in traditional male roles. Therefore, it is predictable that males would be less likely than females to develop androgynous characteristics (Burt and Scott 2002). In a study of child-care books and parenting websites, sociologist Karen Martin found some evidence of gender-neutral child rearing. But she also found that children's nonconformity to gender roles is still viewed as problematic because it is linked with homosexuality (Martin 2005).

Gender identities affect individuals' well-being in various ways. Witt (1997) found that parents who foster androgynous attitudes and behaviors in their children ultimately cause their girls and boys to have high self-esteem and self-worth. Androgynous individuals appear to be able to more effectively manage stress and practice good health (Edwards and Hamilton 2004), and androgynous college students report having better relationships with their parents (Guastello and Guastello 2003:664).

Children at Play

Children teach each other to behave according to cultural expectations. Same-sex peers exert a profound influence on how gender is learned. In a classic study of children's play groups, Janet Lever (1976) discovered how children stress particular social skills and capabilities for boys and others for girls. Her research among fifth-graders (most of whom were White and middle class) found that boys, more than girls, (1) played outdoors, (2) played in larger groups, (3) played in age-heterogeneous groups, (4) were less likely to play in games dominated by the opposite sex, (5) played more competitive games, and (6) played in games that lasted longer.

Barrie Thorne's (1993) study of gender play in multiracial school settings found that boys control more space, more often violate girls' activities, and treat girls as contaminating. According to Thorne, these common ritualized interactions reflect larger structures of male dominance. In reality, the fun and games of everyday schoolchildren are *power play*, a complex social process involving both gender separation and togetherness. Children's power play changes with age, ethnicity, race, class, and social context. In her analysis of how children themselves construct gender in their daily play, Thorne shifted the focus from individual to *social relations*:

> The social construction of gender is an active and ongoing process. . . . Gender categories, gender identities, gender divisions, and gender-based groups, gender meanings—all are produced actively and collaboratively, in everyday life. When kids maneuver to form same-gender groups on the playground or organize a kickball game as "boys-against-the-girls," they produce a sense of gender as dichotomy and opposition. And when girls and boys work cooperatively on a classroom project, they actively undermine a sense of gender as opposition. This emphasis on action and activity, and on everyday social interactions that are sometimes contradictory, provides an antidote to the view of children as passively socialized. Gender is not something one passively "is" or "has." (1993:4–5)

Subsequent research on fourth-grade children in schoolyards supports Thorne's conclusions about gendered interaction in schoolyards. Boyle and her colleagues (Boyle, Marshall, and Robeson 2003) found a great deal of intragender variation in the schoolyard, with girls in particular engaging in many different activities. They also found that boys are more easily accepted into play with girls than is the case when girls try to play with a group of boys and that boys tend to use more space in the schoolyard and are more likely to violate girls' space and games than the reverse.

Toys play a major part in gender socialization. Toys entertain children; they also teach them particular skills and encourage them to explore a variety of roles they may one day occupy as adults. Like clothing, kids' toy stores and departments are sharply divided into girls' and boys' sections. Toys for boys tend to encourage exploration, manipulation, invention, construction, competition, and aggression. In contrast, girls' toys typically rate high on manipulability, creativity, nurturance, and attractiveness. Playing with gendered toys may encourage different skills in girls and boys (Renzetti and Curran 2003:89–92).

Girls are often involved in cross-gender or neutral toy behavior. Girls are often encouraged by both parents to branch out and play with neutral toys some of the time, but boys tend not to be given this same encouragement (Campenni 1999; England, 2010). While we may be seeing some changes in play and socialization of girls, the same does not appear true for boys. Studies have also found that messages transmitted to children from advertisements affect their toy use and that the effects are different for boys and girls. Research finds that the messages in commercials have stronger effects on boys than on girls (Pike and Jennings 2005).

Although girls are now encouraged to engage in activities such as playing video games, traditional gender stereotypes still underlie this pastime. Research finds that girls tend to become less stereotypical in their play as they age—choosing more neutral toys, sports, and computer games (while boys remain masculine in their play) (Orenstein 2008).

Dichotomous gender experiences may be more characteristic of White middle-class children than of children of other races. An important study on Black adolescent girls by Joyce Ladner has shown that Black girls develop in a more independent fashion (Ladner 1971). Other research has also found that among African Americans, both girls and boys are expected to be nurturant and expressive emotionally as well as independent, confident, and assertive (McAdoo 1988; Stack 1990). Recent studies examining whether or not the socialization of Black children is more gender-neutral than that in other groups is inconsistent. Most scholars now say there is too much variation in any group to make generalizations (Hill and Sprague 1999; M. Smith 2001).

Formal Education

In 1972, Congress outlawed gender discrimination in public schools through Title IX of the Educational Amendments Act. More than four decades later, schools continue to be powerful agents of socialization. Studies by the American Association of University Women (AAUW 1992, 1999) have offered compelling evidence that two decades after the passage of Title IX, girls and boys are not receiving the same education.

Recent media discussions of the "boy crisis" in U.S. schools portray young men as marginalized, while girls are taking over the schools. But many studies find that "over the past three decades, boys' test scores are mostly up, more boys are going to college, and more are getting bachelor's degrees" (Matthews 2006:A01; Von Drehle 2007). Although males do drop out of school more often than females, the trend is most pronounced among minorities and boys from low-income homes (Barnett and Rivers 2004; Matthews 2006). The "boy crisis" is an issue of race and class disadvantage, not one of gender difference.

Schools shortchange girls in every dimension of education. Let us examine the following areas: curriculum, teacher–student interactions, sports, and female role models.

- **Curriculum.** Schools are charged with the responsibility of equipping students to study subjects (e.g., reading, writing, mathematics, and history) known collectively as the formal curriculum. But schools also teach students particular social, political, and economic values that constitute the so-called hidden curriculum operating alongside the more formal one. Both formal and informal curricula are powerful shapers of gender (Booher-Jennings 2008; Renzetti and Curran 2003:109).

  Numerous studies find gender differences in the curriculum students are exposed to. For example, girls are more likely to participate in biological sciences and boys in the physical sciences (Adamuti-Trache and Andres 2008; Sadker 2002). In math, although girls and boys tend to take the same number of math courses, there are differences in what courses they take. Girls are more likely to end their math courses after a second algebra course; in fact, girls now outnumber boys in taking algebra and geometry. But boys are more likely to take trigonometry and calculus, which give them an advantage in higher level math skills (AAUW 1999; Andersen 2011).

  Although girls on the average receive higher grades in high school than boys, they tend to score lower on some standardized tests, which are particularly important because such tests scores are used to make decisions on the awarding of college scholarships and admissions. Schools ignore topics that matter in students' lives. The "evaded curriculum" is a term coined in the AAUW Report to refer to matters central to the lives of students that are touched on only briefly, if at all, in most schools. Students receive inadequate education on sexuality, teen pregnancy, the AIDS crisis, and the increase of sexually transmitted diseases among adolescents. According to the AAUW report, gender bias also affects males. Three out of four boys currently report that they were the targets of sexual harassment in schools—usually of taunts challenging their masculinity. In addition, although girls receive lower test grades, boys often receive lower overall course grades.

- **Teacher–Student Interactions.** Even when girls and boys are in the same classrooms, boys are given preferential treatment. Girls receive less attention and different types of attention from classroom teachers.

  Since the 1980s, educational reforms have been in place to foster gender equity in the schools. Teachers are advised to encourage cooperative cross-sex learning, to monitor their own (teacher) behavior to be sure that they reward male and female students equally, and to actively familiarize students with gender-atypical roles by assigning them specific duties as leaders, recording secretary, and so on (Lockheed 1985; cited in Giele 1988).

  Despite the fact that many teachers are trying to interact with their students in nongendered ways, studies show that they nonetheless continue to do so. In her study of third-grade classes, Garrahy (2001) found that although the teachers were claiming to be gender neutral, they often interacted differently with boys in the classroom. Spencer and Toleman (2003) found that the teachers spent more time with the male students when they were working independently and in small groups; perhaps most troubling, the students normalized and naturalized these gender differences. Unfortunately, despite the increasing awareness of gender inequality within schools, new teachers are not adequately being taught about gender equity issues.

Many forms of gender bias exist in education. For example, girls receive less attention and different types of attention from classroom teachers.

- **Sports.** Sports in U.S. high schools and colleges have historically been almost exclusively a male preserve (this section is dependent on Sage and Eitzen 2013). The truth of this observation is clearly evident if one compares by sex the number of participants, facilities, support of school administrations, and financial support.

  Such disparities have been based on the traditional assumptions that competitive sport is basically a masculine activity and that the proper roles of girls and women are as spectators and cheerleaders. What is the impact on a society that encourages its boys and young men to participate in sports while expecting its girls and young women to be spectators and cheerleaders? Sports reinforce societal expectations for males and females. Males are to be dominant and aggressive—the doers—while females are expected to be passive supporters of men, attaining status through the efforts of their menfolk.

  An important consequence of this traditional view is that approximately half of the population has been denied access to all that sport has to offer (physical conditioning, enjoyment, teamwork, goal attainment, ego enhancement, social status, and competitiveness). School administrators, school boards, and citizens of local communities have long assumed that sports participation has general educational value. If so, then girls and women should also be allowed to receive the benefits.

  In 1972, passage of Title IX of the Educational Amendments Act required that schools receiving federal funds must provide equal opportunities for males and females. Despite considerable opposition by school administrators, athletic directors, and school boards, major changes occurred over time because of this federal legislation. More monies were spent on women's sports; better facilities and equipment were provided; and women were gradually accepted as athletes. The most significant result was an increase in female participation. The number of high school girls participating in interscholastic sports increased from 300,000 in 1971 to 3.173 million in 2011. By the 2011 school year, 42 percent of all high school participants were female, and the number of sports available to them was more than double the number available in 1970. Similar growth patterns occurred in colleges and universities (Acosta and Carpenter 2012).

At the intercollegiate level, on the positive side, budgets for women's sports improved dramatically, from less than 1 percent of the men's budgets and no athletic scholarships in 1970 to 38 percent of the men's budgets and 33 percent of the scholarship budgets in 2008. Despite this marked improvement, women athletes remain underfunded. In Division 1 colleges and universities, women account for 53 percent of the college student population. But female athletes receive only 45 percent of participation opportunities, 34 percent of total money spent on total athletic scholarship dollars, and 32 percent of recruiting dollars. This inequality is reinforced by unequal media attention, the scheduling of games (men's games are always the featured games), and the increasing lack of women in positions of power. One ironic consequence of Title IX has been that as opportunities for female athletes increased and programs expanded, the opportunities for women as coaches and administrators diminished. In the early 1970s, most coaches of women's intercollegiate teams were women. By 2008, 46 percent of women's team coaches were women (Lopiano 2008). Females who aspire to coaching and athletic administration have fewer opportunities than males; girls and women see fewer women as role models in such positions. Thus, even with federal legislation mandating gender equality, male dominance is maintained.

- **Female Role Models.** The work that women and men do in the schools supports gender inequality. The pattern is the familiar one found in hospitals, business offices, and throughout the work world: Women occupy the bottom rungs while men have the more powerful positions. Women make up a large percentage of the nation's classroom teachers but a much smaller percentage of school district superintendents. In 2010, women comprised 80 percent of all elementary school teachers, more than half of all secondary school teachers (54 percent), and 61 percent of all school administrators (U.S. Bureau of Labor Statistics 2012b).

  Women are more likely to enroll in college than men. Since 1996, women have earned more bachelor's degrees than men. But women are far from equal in faculty and administrative ranks (Malveaux 2011). As the level of education increases, the proportion of women teachers declines. Even after four decades of attention to gender equity, women have not achieved the same status as men. Women are less likely than men to be employed as full-time tenure track faculty members, less likely to hold tenured or full professor positions, and comprise about a quarter of all college and university presidents (Curtis 2011).

  In the 2010 academic year (more than twenty years after the Office of Civil Rights issued guidelines spelling out the obligations of colleges and universities in the development of affirmative action programs), women represented only 42 percent of full-time faculty. Furthermore, they remained overwhelmingly in the lower faculty ranks, where faculty are much less likely to hold tenure. In 2010, women comprised 30 percent of full professors, 41 percent of associate professors, 48 percent of assistant professors, and 54 percent of instructors/lecturers. Twenty-six percent of college presidents are women (Cook and Kim 2012; National Center for Education Statistics 2010).

Socialization as Blaming the Victim

The discussion so far demonstrates that gender differences are learned. This does not mean that socialization alone explains women's place in society. In fact, a socialization approach can be misused in such a way that it blames women themselves for sex inequality. This is the critique offered by Linda Peterson and Elaine Enarson (1974).

Many years ago, they developed the argument that socialization diverts attention from structured inequality: "Misuse of the concept of socialization plays directly into the Blaming the Victim ideology; by focusing on the victim, responsibility for 'the woman problem' rests not in the social system with its sex-structured distribution of inequality, but in socialized sex differences and sex roles" (1974:8).

Not only is the cause of the problem displaced, but also so are the solutions. "Rather than directing efforts toward radical social change, the solution seems to be to change women themselves, perhaps through exhortation ('If we want to be liberated, we'll have to act more aggressive'). . . . Or, for example, changing children's literature and mothers' child-rearing practice" (8).

This issue raises a critical question: If the socialization perspective is limited and perhaps biased, what is a better way of analyzing gender inequality? To answer this question, let us look at how male dominance affects our society.

9.3 Explain how institutions reinforce gender inequality.

REINFORCING MALE DOMINANCE

Male dominance is both a force that socializes and a force that structures the social world. It exists at all levels of society, from interpersonal relations to larger institutions.

Language

Language perpetuates male dominance by ignoring, trivializing, and sexualizing women. Use of the pronoun *he* when the sex of the person is unspecified and of the generic term *mankind* to refer to humanity in general are obvious examples of how the English language ignores women. Common sayings such as "that's women's work" (as opposed to "that's men's work!"), jokes about female drivers, and phrases such as *women and children first* or *wine, women, and song* are trivializing. Women, more than men, are commonly referred to in terms that have sexual connotations. Terms referring to men (*studs, jocks*) that do have sexual meanings imply power and success, whereas terms applied to women (*broads, bimbos, hos*) imply promiscuity or subordination. In fact, the term *promiscuous* is usually applied only to women, although its literal meaning applies to either sex (Richmond-Abbott 1992:93). Research shows that there are many derogatory terms for women, but there are few for men generically (Sapiro 1999:329). Not only are there fewer derogatory terms that refer to men, but often such terms are considered derogatory because they invoke the images of women. "Some of the more common derogatory terms applied to men such as *bastard*, *motherfucker*, and *son of a bitch* actually degrade women in their role as mothers" (Romaine 1999:99). (See the "A Closer Look" panel on the use of animal terms to denigrate women.)

Interpersonal Behavior

Gender inequality is different than other forms of inequality because individuals on both sides of the power divide (that is women and men) interact very frequently (in the home, in the workplace, and in other role relations). Consequently, gender inequalities can be reproduced and resisted in everyday interactions (Ridgeway and Smith-Lovin 1999:191). New research even finds gender differences in Internet social networking.

Sociologists have done extensive research on the ways in which women and men interact, with particular attention being paid to communication styles. This research has found that in mixed-sex groups, men talk more, show more visual dominance, and

A Closer Look

"BITCHES," "BUNNIES," AND "BIDDIES"

How Animal Metaphors Degrade, Sexualize, and Denigrate Women

Many of the most derogatory words used to refer to women in our society share something in common: They use animal imagery to degrade women. For instance, women are frequently ridiculed as "bitches" and "shrews." Examining the definitions of these words makes their deeper meanings clear: The word *bitch* is defined as "the female of the dog, wolf, fox, etc." and second as "a lewd, or promiscuous woman" (*Webster's New World Dictionary* 1991:143), and a *shrew* is defined as "a scolding, nagging, evil-tempered woman" (*Webster's New World Dictionary* 1991:1243).

Why have such words that originally referred to animals come to be used as common slurs against women? To answer this question, we must address the positioning of animals in our society. In brief, humans are perceived as being distinct from and superior to other animals. This belief has left animals vulnerable to widespread abuse at human hands. This widespread abuse is possible because animals are considered property and are generally treated as commodities. Equating women (and other marginalized groups) with animals through language simultaneously degrades them as "less-than-human" (read as "less-than-men") and reinforces our society's devaluation of their lives.

Animal metaphors are also used to refer to privileged groups of men, but such references are certainly fewer in number (as are derogatory terms toward men in general) and tend to invoke the image of strong, virile, and more revered animals, such as tigers and bulls. In contrast, women

are compared to smaller, domesticated/dominated animals (such as cats or "chicks"), or to animals that are hunted as prey (such as foxes; Romaine 1999:101; Weatherall 2002:26). The use of specific animal metaphors therefore both illustrates and reinforces the power differentials between men and women in society. As Lakoff explained,

> English (like other languages) has many words describing women who are interested in power, presupposing the inappropriateness of that attitude. *Shrew* and *bitch* are among the more polite. There are no equivalents for men. There are words presupposing negative connotations for men who do not dominate "their" women, *henpecked* and *pussy-whipped* among them. There is no female equivalent. (2003:162; emphasis in original)

Not only are women who seek power commonly vilified as animals, but also the terms used to refer to men who fail to invoke their power against women likewise appeal to images of women as animals. Women are said to "henpeck," "pussywhip," and consequently emasculate and thus dehumanize men.

These animal metaphors not only serve to degrade individuals, but some also objectify and sexualize women: referring to a woman as a "pussy" or a "piece of tail" are clear illustrations. Often this sexualization is intertwined with the imagery of the hunt, whereby the (heterosexual) man is viewed as the predator and the woman/animal his prey. Is it a coincidence that the most infamous corporate symbol of the sexualization

of women—the Playboy bunny—is an animal, and a popularly hunted animal at that? The reverse is also true: Hunted animals are frequently referred to in ways that conjure up sexualized images of women. For instance, a study of sport hunting magazines details instances where bird decoys were referred to as "Barbie hens," deer antlers were referred to as "big 'uns," and the use of the feminine pronoun "she" to refer to hunted animals was commonplace (Kalof, Fitzgerald, and Baralt 2004).

In addition to the use of animal metaphors to degrade and sexualize women, animals and women who do not conform to society's demands and standards are also referred to using the same terms. For instance, the term *maiden* refers to a horse who has not won a race, but it is also used to refer to an unmarried woman (Romaine 1999:92). Animals and women who are perceived as being "past their prime" and whose bodies no longer neatly conform to the needs of society are referred to using the same terms, such as "biddy": "The hen ('biddy') who offers neither desirable flesh nor continued profitable egg production is regarded as 'spent'—and discarded. No longer sexually attractive or able to reproduce, the human 'old biddy' too has outlived her usefulness" (Dunayer 1995:13).

At first glance these linguistic metaphors may appear to be harmless. However, they not only reflect the current place of women and animals in society relative to men, but they also serve to subtly reinforce it. Therefore, these metaphors, and what they represent, warrant further examination and critique.

Source: Amy Fitzgerald, Department of Sociology, Michigan State University, 2004. This essay was written expressly for *Social Problems*, 10th edition.

interrupt more, whereas women display more tentative and polite speech patterns (Ridgeway and Smith-Lovin 1999).

Various forms of nonverbal communication also sustain male dominance. Men take up more space than do women and also touch women without permission more than women touch men. Women, on the other hand, engage in more eye contact, smile more, and generally exhibit behavior associated with low status. These behaviors show how gender is continually being created in various kinds of social interaction. Candace West and Don Zimmerman (1987) call this "doing gender." It involves following the rules and behaviors expected of us as males or females. We "do gender" because if we do not, we are judged incompetent as men and women. Gender is something we create in interaction, not something we are (Risman 1998:6).

Producing gender through interaction is becoming a lively sociological topic. Instead of treating gender only as identity, or a socialization, or stratification, this perspective emphasizes gender as dynamic *practices*—what people say and do as they engage in social interaction (Martin 2003; Ridgeway 1997). In this view, gender is a system of action in which gendered practices are learned and enacted in all social settings throughout an individual's life. Gender is enacted in school, families, workplaces houses of worship, and social movements. "In time, like riding a bicycle, gendering practices become almost automatic" (Martin 2003:325).

Mass Media

Much of the information we receive about the world around us comes not from direct experience but from the mass media—radio, television, newspapers, magazines, and the Internet. Although media are often blamed for the problems of modern society, they are not monolithic and do not present us with a simple message. The media have tremendous power. They can distort women's images and they can bring about change as well (Sapiro 1999:224). Women are still underrepresented on op-ed pages, on Sunday chat shows, and as experts in news stories (Pollitt 2010). Studies show that women journalists' role in newsrooms is shrinking even though women predominate in undergraduate and graduate journalism programs and have for decades (Lauer 2002). In magazines, women's portrayal has become less monolithic since the 1980s. With the rise of feminism, many magazines devoted attention to women's achievements. Alongside these new magazines, many "ladies" magazines continue to define the lives of women in terms of men—husbands or lovers.

One network news program is now anchored by a woman (Diane Sawyer), while "Rachel Maddow rules on cable" (Pollitt 2010). Still, women are underrepresented in television newsrooms. In 2011, women made up 39 percent of the television news workforce, whereas the percentage of women news directors in television was at 28 (Radio-Television Digital News Association 2012).

Studies have continually demonstrated that highly stereotyped behavior characterizes both children's and adult programming as well as commercials. Male role models are provided in greater numbers than are female, with the exception of daytime soap operas, in which men and women are equally represented. Prime-time television is distorted: Men represent 59 percent of prime time television characters, while women represent only 24 percent of prime time television characters (Lauzen 2011).

Images of women on entertainment television have changed greatly in recent decades. A report by the National Commission on Working Women found increasing diversity of characters portraying working women as television's most significant improvement. In many serials, women do play strong and intelligent roles, but in just as many shows, men are still the major characters and women are cast as glamorous objects, scheming villains, or servants. And for every contemporary show that includes positive images of women, there are numerous other shows in which women are sidekicks to men, sexual objects, or helpless imbeciles (Andersen 2011:62).

Television commercials have long presented the sexes in stereotyped ways. Women appear less frequently in ads than men, are much more likely to be seen in the home than in work settings, and are much more likely to appear in ads for food, home, and beauty/clothing products. Men are less likely to be shown cooking. Cleaning, shopping, or washing dishes. When men are shown in the context of family life, they are usually engaged in activities stereotypically associated with men—in cars or mowing the lawn. Moreover, they are usually seen with boys, not girls, and rarely with infants (Andersen 2011:621). In the past decade, however, the potential buying power of working women has caused the advertising industry to modify women's image. Working women have become targets of advertising campaigns. But most advertising aimed at career women sends the message that they should be superwomen—managing multiple roles of wife, mother, and career woman, and being glamorous as well. Such multifarious expectations are not imposed on men.

The advertising aimed at "the new woman" places additional stresses on women and at the same time upholds male privilege. Television commercials that show women breezing in from their jobs to sort the laundry or pop dinner in the oven reinforce the notion that it is all right for a woman to pursue a career as long as she can still handle the housework.

Religion

Most U.S. religions follow a typical pattern. The clergy is male, while the vast majority of worshipers are women (Paulson 2000). Despite important differences in religious doctrines, there are common views about gender. Among these are the beliefs that (1) women and men have different missions and different standards of behavior, and (2) although women and men are equal in the eyes of the deity, women are to some degree subordinated to men (Sapiro 1999:219; Thomas 2007). Limiting discussion to the Judeo-Christian heritage, let us examine some teachings from the Old and New Testaments regarding the place of women. The Old Testament established male supremacy in many ways. Images of God are male. Females were second to males because Eve was created from Adam's rib. According to the scriptures, only a male could divorce a spouse. A woman who was not a virgin at marriage could be stoned to death. Girls could be purchased for marriage. Employers were enjoined to pay women only three-fifths the wages of men: "If a male from 20 to 60 years of age, the equivalent is 50 shekels of silver by the sanctuary weight; if it is a female, the equivalent is 30 shekels" (Leviticus 27:3–4). As Gilman (1971) notes:

> The Old Testament devotes inordinate space to the listing of long lines of male descent to the point where it would seem that for centuries women "begat" nothing but male offspring. Although there are heroines in the Old Testament—Judith, Esther and the like—it's clear that they functioned like the heroines of Greek drama and later of French: as counterweights in the imaginations of certain sensitive men to the degraded position of women in actual life. The true spirit of the tradition was unabashedly revealed in the prayer men recited every day in the synagogue: "Blessed art Thou, O Lord . . . for not making me a woman." (51)

The New Testament retained the tradition of male dominance. Jesus was the son of a male God, not of Mary, who remained a virgin. All the disciples were male. The great leader of the early church, the Apostle Paul, was especially adamant in arguing for the primacy of males over females. According to Paul, "the husband is supreme over his wife," "woman was created for man's sake," and "women should not teach nor usurp authority over the man, but to be silent." Contemporary religious thought reflects this heritage. In 1998, the Southern Baptist Convention, the nation's biggest Protestant denomination, amended its statement of beliefs to include a declaration that "a woman shall submit herself graciously to her husband's leadership and a husband should provide for, protect and lead his family." Some denominations limit or even forbid women from decision making. Others allow women to vote but limit their participation in leadership roles.

There are, however, many indications of change. Throughout the West, women are more involved in churches and religious life (Paulson 2000; Thomas 2007; Van Biema 2004). The National Council of Churches seeks to end sexist language and to use "inclusive language" in the Revised Standard Version of the Bible. Terms such as *man, mankind, brothers, sons, churchmen*, and *laymen* would be replaced by neutral terms that include reference to female gender. But these terms, although helpful, do not address a fundamental theological cause: "When God is perceived as a male, then expecting a male voice interpreting the word of God naturally follows" (Zelizer 2004:11A).

The percentage of female seminary students has exploded in the past few decades. Yet women make up only 17 percent of the nation's clergy (U.S. Bureau of Labor Statistics 2012b). Across the United States, women clergy are struggling for equal rights, bumping up against what many call a "stained glass ceiling." Today, half of all religious denominations in the United States ordain women. At the same time, the formal rules and practices discriminate against women. In denominations that ordain women and those that do not, women often fill the same jobs: leading small churches, directing special church programs, preaching, and evangelizing (Van Biema 2004). Despite the opposition of organized religion, many women are making advances within established churches and leaving their mark on the ministerial profession.

The Law

That the law has been discriminatory against women is beyond dispute. We need only recall that women were denied the right to vote prior to the passage of the Nineteenth Amendment.

During the past four decades, legal reforms and public policy changes have attempted to place women and men on more equal footing. Some laws that focus on employment include the 1963 Equal Pay Act, Title VII of the 1964 Civil Rights Act, and the 1978 Pregnancy Discrimination Act. The 1972 Educational Amendments Act calls for gender equality in education. Other reforms have provided the framework for important institutional changes. For example, sexist discrimination in the granting of credit has been ruled illegal, and discrimination against pregnant women in the workforce is now prohibited by the law. Affirmative action (which is now under assault) remedied some kinds of gender discrimination in employment. Sexist discrimination in housing is prohibited, and the gendered requirements in the airline industry have been eliminated. Such laws now provide a basis for the equal treatment of women and men. But the force of these new laws depends on how well they are enforced and how they are interpreted in the courts when they are disputed.

Legal discrimination remains in a number of areas. There are still hundreds of sections of the U.S. legal code and of state laws that are riddled with sex bias or sex-based terminology, in conflict with the ideal of equal rights for women (Benokraitis and Feagin 1995:24). State laws vary considerably concerning property ownership by spouses, welfare benefits, and the legal status of homemakers.

Today, many legal reforms are threatened by recent Supreme Court decisions in the areas of abortion and affirmative action. For example, the right to abortion became the law of the land in the *Roe v. Wade* decision of 1973. *Roe v. Wade* was a major breakthrough for women, giving them the choice to control their bodies. But in 1989 and 1992, the Supreme Court narrowed women's rights by imposing restrictions on abortion. *Roe v. Wade* is still on the books, but the Supreme Court has returned the nation to a pre-*Roe v. Wade* patchwork of state regulations. Forty-nine states now have restrictions that make it more difficult for women to obtain abortions.

Politics

Women's political participation has always been different from that of men. Women received the right to vote in 1920, when the Nineteenth Amendment was ratified. Although women make up a very small percentage of officeholders, 1992 was a turning point for women in politics. Controversies such as Anita Hill's harassment allegations, the abortion rights battle, and the lack of representation at all levels of politics propelled women into the political arena. In 1992, Congress experienced its biggest influx of women (and minorities) in history. Subsequent elections have increased the number of women in our national legislature. But ninety years after the first woman was elected to Congress, women still hold fewer than a fifth of all national seats. They do only slightly better at the state level (Dokoupil 2011). As of 2012, seventeen U.S. senators are women, and seventy-three women are in the House of Representatives (Center for Women in Politics 2012). (See Table 9.2 for the percentages of U.S. women in elective office.) If Congress were representative of the nation, the Senate would have fifty-one women and the House 222 (Sklar 2004).

The United States lags behind other countries in the number of women elected officials.

TABLE 9.2
Percentages of Women in Elective Offices

Year	U.S. Congress	Statewide Elective	State Legislatures
1979	3.0%	11.0%	10.0%
1981	4.0%	11.0%	12.0%
1983	4.0%	11.0%	13.0%
1985	5.0%	14.0%	15.0%
1987	5.0%	14.0%	16.0%
1989	5.0%	14.0%	17.0%
1991	6.0%	18.0%	18.0%
1993	10.1%	22.2%	20.5%
1995	10.3%	25.9%	20.6%
1997	11.0%	25.4%	21.6%
1999	12.1%	27.6%	22.4%
2001	13.6%	27.6%	22.4%
2003	13.6%	26.0%	22.4%
2004	13.8%	26.0%	22.5%
2005	15.0%	25.7%	22.7%
2006	15.0%	25.1%	22.8%
2007	16.1%	24.1%	23.5%
2008	16.5%	23.2%	23.7%
2009	16.8%	22.6%	24.3%
2010	16.8%	22.5%	24.5%
2011	16.4%	21.8%	23.5%
2012	16.8%	23.3%	23.7%

Source: Center for Women in Politics. 2012. "Current Numbers of Women Office Holders," url: http://www.cawp.rutgers.edu/fast_facts/levels_of_office/Current_Numbers.php.

The gender gap in our nation's capital is scandalous. In Washington, DC's less visible workforce of professional staff employees, women hold 60 percent of the jobs, but they are nowhere equal to men. Congress has two classes of personal staff employees: highly paid men who hold most of the power and lower-paid women who are relegated to clerical and support staff. Many answer the phones and write letters to constituents—invisible labor that is crucial to their boss's reelection.

Women had a major place in the 2008 presidential election, with Hillary Clinton in the Democratic primary and Sarah Palin as the Republican nominee for vice president. Although neither candidate was elected to office, their campaigns sparked a national debate about women's access to political power. Globally, women are making substantial gains in politics. The United States has just over 16 percent female lawmakers in Congress. Although some facets of the gender gap appear to be narrowing, as Nancy Pelosi was sworn in as the first female speaker of the House of Representatives, sixty-five countries do better than the United States when it comes to women serving in national legislatures. For example, in Norway, 37 percent of lawmakers are women. In Sweden it is 45 percent (Nye 2012; Wheatcroft 2007). Furthermore, women have served as heads of state in nations such as Canada, France, Germany, the United Kingdom, Turkey, Pakistan, Chile, South Korea, and Liberia (Falk 2008). In the 200-year history of the United States, there has never been a female president or vice president (just two vice-presidential candidates). Today, there are only three female justices on the U.S. Supreme Court.

The gender gap refers to measurable differences in the way women and men vote and view political issues. Voting studies of national elections since 1980 demonstrate that women often vote differently from men, especially on issues of economics, social welfare, and war and peace (Renzetti and Curran 2003:229).

STRUCTURED GENDER INEQUALITY

9.4 Explain the factors that contribute to the earnings gap between women and men.

In this section of the chapter, we focus on the contemporary workplace because its patterns of segregation are among "the most tenacious problems in U.S. society" (Williams 1992:235). In fact, the United States has one of the highest levels of workplace gender inequality in the industrial world (Kimmel 2004:186). The workplace distributes women and men in different settings, assigns them different duties, and rewards them unequally.

Occupational Distribution

Explore on MySocLab Activity: Sex and Occupation

The new economy, discussed in Chapter 14, has changed both women's and men's employment rates. Increasingly, it is viewed as "normal" for adult women and men, regardless of parental status, to be employed (Bianchi 1995:110). Women's labor force participation rates have grown at a faster pace than men's in recent decades. Between 1970 and the early 1990s, women's numbers in the labor force increased twice as fast as those of men. (See the labor force participation rates for men and women in Figure 9.1.) At present, women's rate of labor force participation is holding steadily, while men's is declining. In 2010, 58 percent of women over 16 were in the labor force, compared with 71 percent of men. Today, as in the past, women's employment rates vary by race. African American women have had a long history of high workforce participation rates. In 2004, they edged ahead of other women. By 2011, they participated in the labor force at a rate of 59 percent; 58 percent of White women were in the labor force in 2011, compared with 56 percent of Hispanic women (U.S. Bureau of Labor Statistics 2012b). (See the labor force participation for women by race in Table 9.3.)

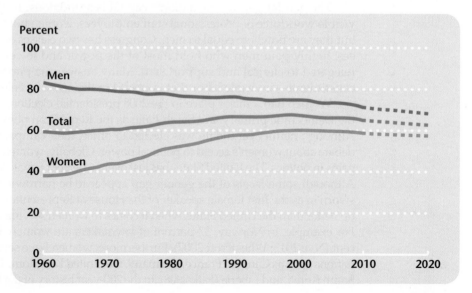

FIGURE 9.1

Labor Force Participation Rate by Sex, 1960–2010, and Projected 2020

Source: Toossi Mitra. 2012. "Labor Force Projections to 2020: A More Slowly Growing Workforce." *Monthly Labor Review.* Online: www.bls.gov/opub/mlr/2012/01/art3full.pdf.

TABLE 9.3
Percent Labor Force Participation Rates for Women, by Race, Selected Years and Projected 2020

Year	Black	White	Hispanic	Asian
1975	48.8	45.9	n/a	n/a
1986	56.9	55.4	50.1	57.0
1990	58.3	57.4	53.1	57.4
1996	60.4	59.8	53.4	58.8
2000	63.1	59.5	57.5	59.2
2006	61.5	59.3	56.1	57.6
2010	59.9	58.5	56.5	57.0
2016	63.1	58.8	57.8	58.7
2020	57.9	56.9	56.1	56.1

Source: U.S. Bureau of Labor Statistics. 2007. "Table 3: Employment Projections." Can be accessed at: http://www.bls.gov/emp/emplab05.htm. U.S. Bureau of Labor Statistics. 2011. "Table 3.3: Civilian Labor Force Participation Rates by Age, Gender, Race and Ethnicity, 1990, 2000, 2010, and Projected 2020." Can be accessed at: http://www.bls.gov/emp/ep_table_303.htm.

The increase in women's participation in the U.S. labor force is one of the most important social trends of the past century. Today's working woman may be any age. She may be any race. She may be a nurse or a secretary or a factory worker or a department store clerk or a public school teacher. Or she may be—although it is much less common—a physician or the president of a corporation or the head of a school system. Hers may be the familiar face seen daily behind the counter at the neighborhood coffee shop, or she may work virtually unseen, mopping floors at midnight in an empty office building.

Although the increase in women's labor force participation rates has been a social revolution, women have not achieved equality in the workplace. Some occupations have changed more than others and there has been little change in how traditionally female jobs are viewed and rewarded (England 2010). The typical female worker is a wage earner in clerical, service, manufacturing, or some technical job that pays poorly and gives her little control over her work. The largest share of women work in "service" and "sales and office" jobs. (See Table 9.4 for a listing of the twenty leading occupations for women.)

Since 1980, women have taken 80 percent of the new jobs created in the economy. Economic restructuring has altered the gender distribution of the labor force through changes in demands for jobs that women and men typically fill. For example, declines in manufacturing employment as well as automation and information technology have reduced the demands for jobs filled by men. Women, on the other hand, are overrepresented in economic sectors such as education and healthcare. The two occupations projected to grow most rapidly between now and 2018—registered nurses and home health aides—are typically filled by women (Folbre 2010).

Gender segregation refers to the pattern whereby women and men are situated in different jobs throughout the labor force (Andersen 2011:128). The overall degree of gender stratification has not changed much since 1900. Women and men are still concentrated in different occupations (Charles and Grusky 2005; Dubeck and Dunn 2002; England 2010).

Media reports of women's gains in traditionally male jobs are often misleading. In blue-collar work, for example, gains look dramatic at first glance, with the number

TABLE 9.4
Twenty Leading
Occupations of Employed
Women 2010 Annual
Averages (employment
in thousands)

Occupation	Total Employed Women	Total Employed (Men and Women)	Percent Women	Women's Median Weekly Earnings
Total, 16 years and older (all employed women)	65,638	139,064	47.2%	$669
Secretaries and administrative assistants	2,962	3,082	96.1	657
Registered nurses	2,590	2,843	91.1	1,039
Elementary and middle school teachers	2,301	2,813	81.8	931
Cashiers	2,291	3,109	73.7	366
Retail salespersons	1,705	3,286	51.9	421
Nursing, psychiatric, and home health aides	1,700	1,928	88.2	427
Waiters and waitresses	1,470	2,067	71.1	381
First-line supervisors/ managers of retail sales workers	1,375	3,132	43.9	578
Customer service representatives	1,263	1,896	66.6	586
Maids and housekeeping cleaners	1,252	1,407	89.0	376
Receptionists and information clerks	1,187	1,281	92.7	529
Childcare workers	1,181	1,247	94.7	398
Bookkeeping, accounting, and auditing clerks	1,179	1,297	90.9	628
First-line supervisors/ managers of office and administrative support	1,035	1,507	68.7	726
Managers, all others	1,014	2,898	35.0	1,045
Accountants and auditors	989	1,646	60.1	953
Teacher assistants	893	966	92.4	485
Personal and home care aides	838	973	86.1	405
Office clerks, general	837	994	84.2	597
Cooks	790	1,951	40.5	381

Source: Department of Labor. 2011. "20 Leading Occupations of Employed Women," url: http://www.dol.gov/wb/factsheets/20lead2010.htm.

of women in blue-collar jobs rising by 80 percent in the 1970s. But the increase was so high because women had been virtually excluded from these occupations until then. Women's entry into skilled blue-collar work such as construction and automaking was limited by the very slow growth in those jobs (Amott 1993:76). In 2010, only 1.8 percent of automotive service technicians and mechanics, 2 percent of construction workers, and 0.8 percent of tool and die makers were women. The years from 1970 to 1990 found more women in the fields of law, medicine, journalism, and higher education. Today, women fill 51 percent of all management positions (up from 19 percent in 1972). Still, there are fewer women than men in prestige jobs. In 2010, only 32 percent of lawyers and 35 percent of physicians and surgeons were women (U.S. Bureau of Labor Statistics 2012b).

Although women have made inroads in the high-paying and high-prestige professions, not all have fared equally. White women were the major beneficiaries of the new opportunities. There has been an occupational "trickle down" effect, as White women improved their occupational status by moving into male-dominated professions such as law and medicine, and African American women moved into the female-dominated jobs, such as social work and teaching, vacated by White women. This improvement for White women was related to federal civil rights legislation, particularly the requirement that firms receiving federal contracts comply with affirmative action guidelines (Amott 1993:76).

The Earnings Gap

Although women's labor force participation rates have risen, the gap between women's and men's earnings has remained relatively constant for three decades. Women workers earn less than men even when they work in similar occupations and have the same levels of education.

View on MySocLab Figure: The Gender Gap in Pay

The pay gap between women and men has narrowed. It hovered between 70 and 74 percent throughout the 1990s. In 2010, women earned 81 cents for every dollar men earned. Closing the wage gap has been slow, amounting to less than half a cent per year! "At this rate, 87 more years could go by before women and men reach parity" (Sklar 2004).

For women of color, earnings discrimination is even greater. Women's incomes are lower than men's in every racial group. Among women and men working year-round and full-time in 2010, White women earned 79 percent of White men's earnings; Black women earned 93 percent of Black men's earnings; Hispanic women earned 90 percent of Hispanic men's earnings (U.S. Bureau of Labor Statistics 2012b; see Figure 9.2). The earnings gap affects the well-being of women and their families. If women earned the same as men, their annual family incomes would rise by $4,000 and poverty rates would be cut in half. Their lost earnings could have bought a home, educated their children, and been set aside for retirement (Greim 1998; Love 1998; The Wage Gap 2003).

The earnings gap persists for several reasons:

- Women are concentrated in lower-paying occupations.
- Women enter the labor force at different and lower-paying levels than men.
- Women as a group have less education and experience than men; therefore, they are paid less than men.
- Women tend to work less overtime than men.

These conditions explain only part of the earnings gap between women and men. They do not explain why female workers earn less than male workers with the same

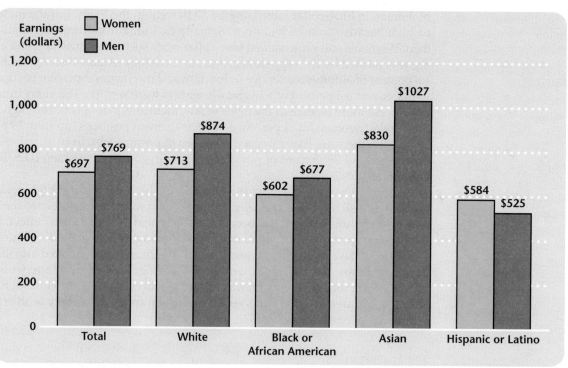

FIGURE 9.2

Median Usual Weekly Earnings of Full-Time Wage and Salary Workers, by Sex, Race, and Hispanic or Latino Ethnicity, 2012

Source: U.S. Department of Labor, Bureau of Labor Statistics, "TED: The Editor's Desk" (April 19, 2012), p. 1. http://www.dol.gov/cgi-bin/print.p1/opub.

educational level, work histories, skills, and work experience. Men with professional degrees may expect to earn almost $2 million more than their female counterparts (Sklar 2004). Study after study finds that if women were men with the same credentials, they would earn substantially more. Research on the income gap has found that women's and men's credentials explain some differences, but experience accounts for only one-third of the wage gap. The largest part of the wage gap is caused by sex discrimination in the labor market that blocks women's access to the better-paying jobs through hiring, promotion, and simply paying women less than men in any job (Dunn 1996; *ISR Newsletter* 1982; Leinwand 1999).

Intersection of Race and Gender in the Workplace

There are important racial differences in the occupational concentration of women and men. Women of color make up over 14 percent of the U.S. workforce (U.S. Bureau of Labor Statistics 2012b). They are the most segregated group in the workplace—concentrated at the bottom of the work hierarchy, in low-paying jobs with few fringe benefits, poor working conditions, high turnover, and little chance of advancement. Mexican American women, for example, are concentrated in secretarial, cashier, and janitorial jobs; Central American women in jobs as household cleaners, janitors, and textile machine operators; Filipinas as nurses, nurses' aides, and cashiers; and Black women as nurses aides, cashiers, and secretaries (Andersen 2011; Reskin 1999). White women are a privileged group in the workplace compared with women of color. A much larger share of White women (41 percent) than Black women (33 percent) or

Latinas (24 percent) held managerial and professional specialty jobs (U.S. Bureau of Labor Statistics 2012b).

Workplace inequality, then, is patterned by both gender and race—and also by social class and other group characteristics. One's placement in a job hierarchy as well as the rewards one receives depends on how these characteristics "combine" (Dubeck and Dunn 2002:48). Earnings for all workers are lowest in those areas of the labor market where women of color predominate.

How Workplace Inequality Operates

Watch on MySocLab Video: Women in the Workplace

Why are women unequal in the workplace? Several theories are used to explain job segregation and ongoing wage inequality. Some focus on individuals, others focus on structural conditions, and others call on interactional processes to explain women's disadvantages in the workplace.

Popular explanations for gender differentials point to women themselves. They claim that women's socialization, their education, and the "choices" they make to take time out of the workforce to have children produce different work experiences for men and women. *Human capital theory*, for example, rests on the individual characteristics that workers bring to their jobs. Of course, time in the workplace, education, and experience all play a part. But the reality is far more complex. Research finds that woman's individual characteristics, or their human capital, explains only a small part of employment inequality (Ridgeway 1997:224). Research shows that ideas and practices about gender are embedded in workplace structures. This means that the workplace itself produces gender disparities (Acker 1990; Martin 2003; Williams 1995). Let us examine the organization of the labor force that disadvantage women and advantage men.

Dual labor market theory centers on the labor market itself. The labor market is divided into two separate segments, with different characteristics, different roles, and different rewards. The primary segment is characterized by stability, high wages, promotion ladders, opportunities for advancement, good working conditions, and provisions for job security. The secondary market is characterized by low wages, fewer or no promotion ladders, poor working conditions, and little provision for job security. Women's work tends to fall in the secondary segment. For example, clerical work, the largest single occupation for women, has many of the characteristics associated with the secondary segment.

To understand women's disadvantages, we must look at structural arrangements that women confront in the workplace. A classic study by Rosabeth Kanter (1977), *Men and Women of the Corporation*, found that organizational location is more important than gender in shaping workers' behavior. Although women and men behave differently at work, Kanter demonstrated that the differences were created by organizational locations. Workers in low-mobility or blocked situations (regardless of their sex) tended to limit their aspirations, seek satisfaction in activities outside work, dream of escape, and create sociable peer groups in which interpersonal relationships take over other aspects of work. Kanter argued that "when women seem to be less motivated or committed, it is probably because their jobs carry less opportunity" (Kanter 1977:159).

Many features of work itself block women's advancement. For example, some structural explanations call on gender segregation, per se, in which women and men are concentrated in occupational categories based on gender. Much research in this tradition has explained why job segregation and wage inequality persist even as women have flooded the workforce and moved into "male" jobs. Sociologists Barbara Reskin and Patricia Roos (1990) studied eleven once-male-dominated fields that had become integrated between 1979 and 1988: book editing, pharmacy, public relations, bank management, systems analysis, insurance sales, real-estate sales, insurance adjusting and examining, bartending, baking, and typesetting and composition. Reskin and Roos found that women gained entry into these fields only *after* earnings and upward mobility in each of these fields declined; that is, salaries had gone down, prestige had diminished, or the work had become more like "women's work" (Kroeger 1994:50). Furthermore, in each of these occupations, women specialized in lower-status specialties, in different and less desirable work settings, and in lower-paid industries. Reskin and Roos call this process *ghettoization*. Some occupations changed their sex-typing completely, whereas some became resegregated by race as well as gender (Amott 1993:80; Reskin and Roos 1990).

Many fields that have opened up to women no longer have the economic or social status they once possessed. Their structures now have two tiers: (1) higher-paying, higher-ranking jobs with more authority and (2) lower-paying, more routinized jobs with less authority. Women are concentrated in the new, more routinized sectors of professional employment, but the upper tier of relatively autonomous work continues to be male dominated, with only token increases in female employment (Carter and Carter 1981). For example, women's entry into three prestige professions—medicine, college teaching, and law—has been accompanied by organizational changes. In medicine, hospital-based practice has grown as more women have entered the profession. Women doctors are more likely than men to be found in hospital-based practice, which provides less autonomy than the more traditional office-based practice. In college teaching, many women are employed in two-year colleges, where heavy teaching loads leave little time or energy for writing and publishing—the keys to academic career advancement. And in law, women's advancement to prestigious positions is being eroded by the growth of the legal clinic, where much legal work is routinized.

Many organizational features block women's advancement. In the white-collar workforce, the well-documented phenomenon of women going just so far—and no further—in their occupations and professions is called the **glass ceiling**. This refers to the invisible barriers that limit women's mobility despite their motivation and capacity for positions of power and prestige (Lorber 1994:227). In contrast, men who enter female-dominated professions generally encounter *structural advantages*, a "glass escalator," which tends to enhance their careers (Williams 1992).

Many of the old discriminatory patterns are difficult to change. In the professions, for example, sponsor–protégé systems and informal interactions among colleagues limit women's mobility. Sponsorship is important in training personnel and ensuring leadership continuity. Women are less likely to be acceptable as protégés. Furthermore, their sex status limits or excludes their involvement in the buddy system or the old-boy network (Epstein 1970). Such informal interactions continually re-create gender inequality. *Interactional theories* also explain why gender is such a major force in the labor process. Taken-for-granted interactions block women's progress even in new work settings with no prior history of gender differences. Women's inequality occurs as people use common sense ideas about gender in relating to others. According to Ridgeway, the gendered structures of work that are responsible for women's and men's outcomes are enacted and maintained through an interlocking web of *social relations* among workers, all of whom draw on gender to guide their workplace interactions (Ridgeway 2011:119).

Individual, structural, and interactional explanations of women's workplace inequality rest on *social processes* rather than outright discrimination. But it is important to recognize that outright discrimination can be found in the workplace. For example,

Explore on
MySocLab Activity:
Power Dynamics in the
Workforce: The Case of
Sexual Harassment

sexual harassment affects women in all types of jobs. Sexual harassment can include unwanted leers, comments, suggestions, or physical contact of a sexual nature as well as unwelcome requests for sexual favors. Some research finds that sexual harassment is prevalent in male-dominated jobs in which women are new hires because it is a way for male workers to dominate and control women who should be their equals.

Gender in the Global Economy

Gender relations in the United States and the world are linked to the global economy. Private businesses make investment decisions that affect the lives of women and men all around the world. In their search for profit, transnational corporations turn to developing nations where women and children prove a cheap work force. The demand for less expensive labor has produced a global system of production with a strong gendered component. The international division of labor affects both men and women. As manufacturing jobs switch to low-wage economies, men are often displaced. The *global assembly line* uses the labor of women, many of them young, single, and from poor rural areas. Women workers of particular classes/castes and races from poor countries provide a cheap labor supply for the manufacture of commodities distributed in the richer industrial nations.

The global economy is altering gender relations around the world by bringing women into the public sphere (Walby 2000). While this presents new opportunities for women, the disruption of male dominance can also result in the reaffirmation of local gender hierarchies through right-wing militia movements, religious revivalism, and other forms of masculine fundamentalism (Connell 1998). In addition, old forms of women's exploitation and abuse are being replaced by new forms of control. For example, women's work in the sex industry is now as an important part of globalization. The worldwide expansion of the sex club industry is closely linked to organized crime and the trafficking of women and girls across national boundaries (Jeffries 2008).

THE COSTS AND CONSEQUENCES OF SEXISM

9.5 Discuss the social and individual costs of gender inequality.

Who Benefits?

Clearly, gender inequality enters all aspects of social life in the United States and globally. This inequality is profitable to certain segments of the economy, and it also gives privileges to individual men.

Transnational corporations derive extra profits from paying women less than men. Women's segregation in low-paying jobs produces higher profits for some economic sectors—namely, those where most workers are women. Women who are sole breadwinners and those who are in the workforce on a temporary basis have always been a source of exploitable labor. These women provide a significant proportion of the marginal labor force capitalists need to draw on during upswings in the business cycle and to release during downswings (Edwards, Reich, and Weisskopf 1978:333).

Gender inequality is suited to the needs of the economy in other ways as well. The U.S. economy must accumulate capital and maintain labor power. This requires that all workers be physically and emotionally maintained. Who provides the daily maintenance that enable workers to be a part of the labor force? Women! They maintain workers through the unpaid work they do caring for home, children, and elders. Their caregiving keeps the economy going, and it also provides privileges for individual men at women's expense.

The Social and Individual Costs

Gender inequality benefits certain segments of society. Nevertheless, society at large and individual women and men pay a high price for inequality. Sexism diminishes the quality of life for all people. Our society is deprived of half of its resources when women are denied full and equal participation in its institutions. If women are systematically kept from jobs requiring leadership, creativity, and productivity, the economy suffers. The pool of talent consisting of half the population will continue to be underutilized.

Women's inequality also produces suffering for millions. We have seen that individual women pay a heavy price for economic discrimination. Their children pay as well. The poverty caused by gender inequality is one of the most pressing social problems facing the United States in the new century. Adult women's chances of living in poverty are still higher than men's at every age. As we saw in Chapter 7, this phenomenon is called the *feminization of poverty* (Pearce 1978). Economist Nancy Folbre points out that the highest risk of poverty comes from being female and having children—which helps explain the high rates of both female and child poverty in the United States. Folbre calls this trend the "pauperization of motherhood" (Folbre 1985; cited in Albelda and Tilly 1997:23). Of course, sexism produces suffering around the world. Some women are persecuted simply because they are women.

Sexism also denies *men* the potential for full human development because gender segregation denies employment opportunities to men who wish to enter such fields as nursing, grade-school teaching, or secretarial work. Eradicating sexism would benefit such males. It would benefit all males who have been forced into stereotypic male behaviors. In learning to be men, boys express their masculinity through physical courage, toughness, competitiveness, and aggression. Expressions typically associated with femininity, such as gentleness, expressiveness, and responsiveness, are seen as undesirable for males. Rigid gender norms make men pay a price for their masculinity.

Male inexpressiveness can hinder communication between husbands and wives, between fathers and children; it has been called "a tragedy of American society" (Balswick and Peck 1971). Certainly, it is a tragedy for the man himself, crippled by an inability to show the best part of a human being—his warm and tender feelings for other people (Balswick and Collier 1976:59).

9.6 Understand the three stages of feminism.

Watch on MySocLab Video: Feminism

FIGHTING THE SYSTEM

Feminist Movements in the United States

Gender inequality in this society has led to feminist social movements. Three stages of feminism have been aimed at overcoming sex discrimination. The first stage grew from the abolition movement of the 1830s. Working to abolish slavery, women found that they could not function as equals with their male abolitionist friends. They became convinced that women's freedom was as important as freedom from slavery. In July 1848, the first convention in history devoted to issues of women's position and rights was held at Seneca Falls, New York. Participants in the Seneca Falls convention approved a declaration of independence, asserting that men and women are created equal and that they are endowed with certain inalienable rights.

During the Civil War, feminists for the most part turned their attention to the emancipation of Blacks. After the war and the ratification of the Thirteenth Amendment abolishing slavery, feminists were divided between those seeking far-ranging economic, religious, and social reforms and those seeking voting rights for women. The second stage of feminism gave priority to women's suffrage. The women's suffrage amendment, introduced into every session of Congress from 1878 on, was ratified on August 26, 1920—nearly three-quarters of a century after the demand for women's suffrage had been made at the Seneca Falls convention. From 1920 until the 1960s, feminism was dormant. "So much energy had been expended in achieving the right to vote that the women's movement virtually collapsed from exhaustion" (Hole and Levine 1979:554).

Feminism was reawakened in the 1960s. Social movements aimed at inequalities gave rise to an important branch of contemporary feminism. The civil rights movement and other protest movements of the 1960s spread the ideology of equality. But like the early feminists, women involved in political protest movements found that male dominance characterized even movements seeking social equality. Finding injustice in freedom movements, they broadened their protest to such far-reaching concerns as healthcare, family life, and relationships between the sexes. Another strand of contemporary feminism emerged among professional women who discovered sex discrimination in earnings and advancement. Formal organizations such as the National Organization for Women evolved, seeking legislation to overcome sex discrimination (Freeman 1979).

These two branches of contemporary feminism gave rise to a feminist consciousness among millions of U.S. women. As a consequence, during the 1960s and early 1970s, many changes occurred in the roles of women and men. However, periods of recession, high unemployment, and inflation in the late 1970s fed a backlash against feminism. The contemporary women's movement may be the first in U.S. history to face the opposition of an organized antifeminist social movement. From the mid-1970s, a coalition of groups calling themselves profamily and prolife emerged. These groups, drawn from right-wing political organizations and religious organizations, oppose feminist gains in reproductive, family, and antidiscrimination policies. In addition, many gains have been set back by opposition to affirmative action programs and other equal rights policies. Political, legal, and media opposition to feminism continues to undermine women's equality (Faludi 1991).

Women's Struggles in the Twenty-First Century

Listen on MySocLab Audio: NPR: Women's Pay Disparity a Growing Campaign Issue

The women's movement is not over. Quite the contrary, the women's movement remains one of the most influential sources of social change, even though there is not a unified organization that represents feminism (Andersen 2011:354). Not only do mainstream feminist organizations persist, but also the struggles for women's rights continue. Today, many feminist activities occur at the grassroots level, where issues of race, class, and sexuality are important. In communities across the country women and men fight

> against the abuse of women, against corporate poisoning of their neighborhoods, against homophobia and racism, and for people-centered economic development, immigrants' rights, educational equity, and adequate wages. Many have been engaged in such struggles for most of their lives and continue despite the decline in the wider society's support for a progressive social agenda. (Naples 1998:1)

Regardless of whether they call themselves feminists, activists across the country and around the world are using their community-based organizing to fight for social justice. Instead of responding passively to the outside world, women are forging new agendas and strategies to benefit women.

■ CHAPTER REVIEW

1. U.S. society, like other societies, ranks and rewards women and men unequally.

2. Gender differences are not natural. They are social inventions. Although gender divisions make women unequal to men, different groups of men exhibit varying degrees of power, and different groups of women exhibit varying levels of inequality.

3. Men as well as women are gendered beings.

4. Gender works with the inequalities of race, class, and sexuality to produce different experiences for all women and men.

5. Many sociologists have viewed gender inequality as the consequences of learned behavior. More recently, sociologists have moved from studying gender as the individual traits of women and men to studying gender as social structure and social interaction.

6. Gender inequality is reinforced through language, interpersonal behavior, mass communication, religion, the law, and politics.

7. The segregation of women in a few gendered occupations contrasts with that of men, who are distributed throughout the occupational hierarchy, and women, even with the same amount of education and when doing the same work, earn less than men in all occupations.

8. Gender segregation is the basic source of women's inequality in the workforce. Work opportunities for women tend to concentrate in a secondary market that has few advancement opportunities, fewer job benefits, and lower pay.

9. The combined effects of gender and racial segregation in the labor force keep women of color at the bottom of the work hierarchy, where working conditions are harsh and earnings are low.

10. The global economy is strongly gendered. Around the world, women's labor is the key to global development strategies.

11. Gender inequality deprives society of the potential contributions of half its members, creates poverty among families headed by women, and limits the capacities of all women and men.

12. Feminist movements aimed at eliminating inequality have created significant changes at all levels of society. Despite a backlash against feminism, women and men across the country and around the world continue to work for women's rights.

■ KEY TERMS

Sex. Biological fact of femaleness and maleness.

Gender. Cultural and social definition of feminine and masculine.

Gendered. Differentiation of women's and men's behaviors, activities, and worth.

Feminist approach. View that supports equal relations between women and men.

Gender stratification. Differential ranking and rewarding of women's and men's roles.

Gendered institutions. All social institutions are organized by gender.

Male dominance. Beliefs, meanings, and placement that value men over women and that institutionalize male control of socially valued resources.

Patriarchy. Forms of social organization in which men are dominant over women.

Compulsory heterosexuality. The system of sexuality that imposes negative sanctions on those who are homosexual or bisexual.

Sexuality. A way of organizing the social world on the basis of sexual identity.

Capitalist patriarchy. Condition of capitalism in which male supremacy keeps women in subordinate roles at work and in the home.

Gender roles approach. Males and females differ because of socialization. The assumption is that males and females learn to be different.

Gender structure approach. Males and females differ because of factors external to them.

Androgyny. The integration of traditional feminine and masculine characteristics.

Gender segregation. Pattern whereby women and men are situated in different jobs throughout the labor force.

Glass ceiling. An invisible barrier that limits women's upward occupational mobility.

Sexual Orientation

((• Listen to Chapter 10 on **MySocLab**

The previous three chapters examined categories of people designated as minorities in society because of their impoverishment, race/ethnicity, or gender. The members of these social categories suffer from powerlessness, negative stereotypes, and discrimination. This chapter looks at another type of minority group. Unlike the other minorities, which are disadvantaged because of economic circumstances or obvious ascribed characteristics, the minority group examined in this chapter—gay men and lesbian women—is the object of discrimination because it is defined by the majority as deviant and therefore inferior. It is important to underscore a crucial point—*homosexuality is not inherently deviant, but it is defined and labeled as deviant*. In other words, the deviance ascribed to gays and lesbians is a social construction.

This chapter is divided into four sections. The first section examines the concept of heteronormativity and its implications. The next section presents what is known about the gay and lesbian community. The third section describes the various forms of past and current discrimination faced by gay men and lesbian women in the United States. The final section describes the coping strategies of gays and lesbians and their political activities aimed at changing the societal structures that are unfair to them.

10.1 Define deviant behaviors and understand the broader implications of the social construction of deviance.

Watch on **MySocLab Video:** Sexual Orientation

Explore on **MySocLab Activity:** Who Is Heterosexual? How Definitions Do Not Equal Identity

HETERONORMATIVITY

Heteronormativity is a term used to convey the belief that heterosexuality is the "normal" sexual orientation, and all other orientations are seen as deviant and thus marginalized. Heteronormativity implies that males and females fall into natural and complementary categories, and those sexual and marital relationships between men and women are the standards that all members of society should follow. The system of heteronormativity means that anyone who deviates from his or her expected sex, gender identity, gender role, or sexual orientation may be the subject of ridicule, harassment, and discrimination. The following discussion examines five important principles that help us better understand this concept of deviating from expected societal norms: (1) Deviance is socially constructed; (2) deviance is a relative, not an absolute, notion; (3) deviance is an integral part of all societies; (4) whoever holds the power determines who or what is deviant; and (5) the violators of important social norms are often punished and stigmatized.

(1) Because **deviance** is behavior that does not conform to social expectations, *it is socially constructed*. Societies create right and wrong by originating norms and saying that failure to follow the rules constitutes deviance. Whether an act is deviant depends on how other people react to it.

Even though sexuality has a biological base, it is also a social construction. Society impinges on this intensely private form of intimacy to shape our ideas about what is erotic, to define what is taboo, and to determine appropriate sexual partners and appropriate sexual behaviors. For example, during the 2004 Superbowl game halftime show, pop star Janet Jackson exposed her breast on national television. This act caused an outcry from the public, even though it is commonplace for women's breasts to be exposed in movies, on cable television, and in other forms of media. This reaction shows how behavior in one context is labeled as acceptable and in another context is labeled deviant. In the heteronormative system of contemporary U.S. society, **heterosexuality** (opposite-sex eroticism) is the expected—actually, demanded—sexual orientation. Thus, the term **compulsory heterosexuality** applies; that is, within U.S. society, the beliefs and practices of the majority enforce heterosexual behavior as normal while stigmatizing other forms of sexual expression. In fact, some people in the United States believe that **homosexuality** (sexual preference for someone of the same sex) or **bisexuality** (attraction to both sexes) is evidence of moral weakness or pathology. Thus, society has created homosexuality as deviance. For a closer look into the social construction of female and male sexuality, see "The Sexual Double Standard."

(2) Because deviance is not a property inherent in any particular kind of behavior, *deviance is a relative, not an absolute, notion.* Evidence for its relative nature is found in the

A Closer Look

THE SEXUAL DOUBLE STANDARD

In contemporary society, a prime example of the social construction of deviance and sexual behavior can be seen in the differential treatment of female same-sex sexuality versus male same-sex sexuality. Case in point: the well-publicized onstage kiss between pop icons Madonna and Britney Spears at the 2003 MTV Video Music Awards. It has received over 2,000,000 hits on Google and was voted the "best kiss of the decade" based on a poll by Selfridges. Now contrast that to the 2009 American Music Awards, where another pop star, Adam Lambert, kissed a male keyboard player. ABC received numerous complaints, and *Good Morning America* cancelled his subsequent appearance on their show. In an interview with CBS, Lambert refused to apologize and said that, as a gay man, he was being held to a different standard than female performers (for example, Janet Jackson groped one of her male dancers that same night, and no one complained). CBS then came under fire for replaying the footage of Lambert's performance and blurring out the infamous kiss, but then showing unedited the 2003 Madonna–Spears kiss. Why the double standard? Pepper Schwartz argues that lesbianism has been eroticized through heterosexual pornography.

As long as female performers in porno eventually show they are sexually available to men, their homosexual sex is seen as kinky rather than deviant. (Schwartz 2007:86)

Female same-sex sexuality is seen as erotic as long as the women engaging in it are defined as attractive, feminine, and still available to men. Schwartz argues that our culture tends to confuse heterosexuality with gender performance. Indeed, in interviews with gay youth in middle school, Benoit Denizet-Lewis found this to be clear. The students told her that openly gay youth that conformed to their expected gender role (either masculine or feminine) were often accepted and integrated fully into their school's social circles.

The sexual double standard illustrated by the Madonna–Spears kiss versus Adam Lambert's kiss clearly demonstrates how the same sexual behavior can be constructed in different ways. If Madonna and Britney Spears did not conform to societal standards of beauty and femininity, the societal reaction to their kiss would have undoubtedly been very different.

Madonna and Britney Spears at the 2003 MTV Video Music Awards.

Adam Lambert at the 2009 American Music Awards.

wide variation in definitions of deviance among societies and across history. For example, "On the streets of New York at the turn of the nineteenth century, men engaged in sexual acts with other men without any bearing on their identity as heterosexual, as long as they took what they thought of as the 'male part.' Women embraced their women friends, pledged their undying love, and slept with each other without necessarily interfering with their married lives" (Rupp 2007:55). In ancient Greece, homosexual relationships between men were expected. Men in ancient Greece and Rome were regarded as naturally bisexual, and one's sexual partner was not considered important. More importance was placed on how that sexual behavior was practiced. As Joan Roughgarden notes,

> *Ancient Greeks had a right way and wrong way of participating in male–male sexuality. In ancient Greece, male same-sex relationships were almost always between an older partner and a younger one. . . . The code for how a proper young man was to have male–male sex as the passive partner of an older man dictated that he never accept payment, that he refuse any unworthy active partner, that he avoid enjoyment, that he insist on an upright position, that he not meet the active partner's eye during orgasm, and that he avoid positions with penetration. The passive partner was understood to grant a favor to the active partner. (2004:367–368)*

🔍 **View on MySocLab Figure:** Sexual Orientation in the United States: Survey Data on Gender and Inequality

Historical and cross-cultural data support strongly that sexuality is a social construction, and that societal norms dictate appropriate and inappropriate sexual behavior in any given time period. In her essay on the social construction of heterosexuality, Pepper Schwartz argues,

> *Whatever the culture, its norms about masculinity and femininity are supposed to co-vary with heterosexual enactment, and gender itself is expected to be unambiguous and performed according to the cultural outlines of the moment. Even today, after the sexual and gender revolutions of the late 1960s and 70s, heterosexual dress codes, mannerisms, and body language are all strictly mandated. Although our culture has antiheroes who disdain these conventions . . . the majority culture creates cultural icons in its magazines, TV shows, movies, featuring models that tell us what exact gender displays portray heterosexual correctness. (2007:81)*

That deviance is relative rather than absolute can also be seen in the change in attitudes over time toward interracial sexual relationships. Prior to 1967, marriage and sexual relationships between people of different races (**miscegenation**) was defined as illegal through various state laws. In 1967 the Supreme Court ruled that anti-miscegenation laws were unconstitutional.

(3) *Deviance is an integral part of all societies.* According to Emile Durkheim, deviant behavior actually has positive consequences for society because it gives the nondeviants a sense of solidarity. By punishing the deviant, the group expresses its collective indignation and reaffirms its commitment to the rules. Indeed, it is the very process of defining deviance that gives the majority a firm sense of what those rules are in the first place. Rupp explains,

> *We know that, without the concept of homosexuality, there would be no heterosexuality. Without knowing which sexual desires and acts are deemed deviant, we would not know which ones passed muster. Knowing how identities are created, institutions established, communities built, and movements mobilized, we learn from the margins what the center looks like. (2007:56)*

Thus, when individuals in an organization condemn a gay or lesbian colleague, they are reaffirming that their sexuality—heterosexuality—is the only legitimate option. The negative sanctions applied to the deviant (gossip, avoidance, exclusion) serve to enforce conformity in the group by restraining other people from deviating and thus reaffirming compulsory heterosexuality.

The above photos show a 1959 rally to oppose racial "mixing" or integration and a 2005 rally to oppose same-sex marriage. They vividly demonstrate that societal norms dictate what is considered deviant behavior in any given period and that these social constructions are subject to change over time.

(4) *Whoever holds the power determines who or what is deviant.* Power is a crucial element in deciding who or what is deviant. As discussed throughout this chapter, certain social groups have relatively greater power and resources than others in getting their definitions of deviance to prevail. The major religious bodies in the United States, for example, have taken strong positions against homosexuality, and their opposition has influenced the laws and community norms.

(5) *The violators of important social norms are often* **stigmatized**. That is, deviants are not only believed to be different from the majority, but they are also set apart by being socially disgraced. The society—through the church, the medical community, and the law—stigmatizes gays as sick, sinful, and criminal. In the media, they are pejoratively labeled through stereotypes and language. From verbal harassment to physical violence to unequal civil rights, the consequences of deviating from the norm can be severe. This societal/community reaction to gays and lesbians has several consequences for them that are considered later in this chapter. The extremely negative reaction may keep many gays and lesbians invisible and fear of physical violence and discrimination may cause extreme personal distress. However, history has shown that power can be achieved in great numbers as gay and lesbian activists continue to mobilize and challenge the system of heteronormativity.

GAY AND LESBIAN COMMUNITY: AN OVERVIEW

Defining Homosexuality

10.2 Evaluate the problems of defining and conducting research on homosexuality.

👁 **Watch** on **MySocLab Video:** Michael Bailey: Being Gay in the U.S.

Homosexuality has become more visible in U.S. society as a result of mainstream media. This emergence of homosexuality into the mainstream of society has generated new questions about how homosexuality should be labeled and defined. The terms *sexual preference* and *sexual orientation* are both used to denote one's sexuality. The implications of each are important. **Sexual preference** implies a sense of choice regarding the sex of people to whom one is attracted, whereas **sexual orientation** implies a deterministic or biological view of sexual proclivities. Further complicating the issue is how precisely to define homosexuality. Should the definition be based on feelings, desires, actions, or self-identity? Some people may be attracted to persons of the same sex but they do not act on it or identify as homosexual. Others may have had same-sex sexual encounters, but do not identify as homosexual.

Alfred Kinsey's research in the late 1940s and early 1950s stunned society with his findings on sexuality. First, Kinsey argued that there should be a scale of sexuality, where individuals are rated from 100 percent homosexual to 100 percent heterosexual, with lots of combinations in between. He further astonished Americans by placing the percent of homosexuals at around 10 percent for men. In the 1990s, a study found that the incidence rate of homosexual *desire* was 7.7 percent for men and 7.5 percent for women, whereas the rate at which men *identify* themselves as gay was 2.8 percent, and the rate for which women *identify* themselves as lesbians was 1.4 percent (Laumann, Gagnon, and Michaels 1994).

In spite of these complexities, the system of heteronormativity assumes that heterosexuality is the "normal" sexual orientation, thus some researchers have attempted to explain any deviance from the norm by studying whether homosexuality has genetic or social origins. Homosexuality is fairly common in the animal world. It has been found that male sheep exhibit homosexuality at least as often as humans: Roughly 8 percent of rams turn out to have sex exclusively with other rams (Cloud 2007). At Oregon Health and Science University, researchers have been able to study the sheep's brains to examine the neurological basis of sexual attraction.

> The Oregon group's work has shown that gay rams have different brain structures from heterosexual ones, news that should cheer those who see homosexuality and heterosexuality as mere biological variations. (Cloud 2007:54)

Watch on MySocLab Video: Alternative Sexual Orientation

A small but growing scientific literature provides evidence of a biological basis for homosexuality in males (Associated Press 2005; Hamer and Rosbash 2010; Kristof 2003; Johnson 2003; Pillard and Bailey 1998; Thompson 1995). So far, however, the scientific evidence is inconclusive, and research on lesbians is rare. Most studies are based on very small, nonrandom samples. Some researchers are convinced that an area of the brain, the hypothalamus, is responsible. Others find that the size of the anterior commissure of the brain makes the difference, although these brain differences seem to be true for gay men but not for lesbians. According to a 2008 study, Swedish researchers found that gay men have brains that are strikingly similar to straight women in terms of symmetry, and lesbians have brains that are similar to straight men. The researchers analyzed the brains of ninety subjects using magnetic resonance imaging and found some interesting differences in the amygdala, the portion of the brain responsible for the complex interplay of thoughts and emotions (*Science Daily* 2008). In these types of studies, there is always a question of causation. In other words, were the brains different to begin with (at birth), or did parts of the brain change in response to environment?

Complicating the issue of biology versus society is research on twins. The chance that identical twins will both be gay ranges from about 25 percent to 50 percent, depending on the study (Kristof 2003; Roughgarden 2004). Recent findings also point to a possible "sibling factor," where men who have several older brothers—regardless of whether they were raised together—have an increased chance of being gay (Schmid 2006). Other researchers remain unconvinced, given the complexity of biology and environmental factors on individual behavior (Byne 1999). John D'Emilio, a historian of sexuality, expresses this ambiguity:

> There's a tremendous amount of evidence in history and cross-cultural studies to suggest that human sexual behavior and desire are enormously malleable, not just from culture to culture or from time period to time period, but in an individual's life. I'm not willing to say that there isn't a biological component, but there's too much else we haven't explored. (Quoted in Wheeler 1992:A9)

Whether sexual orientation has biological roots, social roots, or a combination of both is immaterial. As long as the system of heteronormativity defines other sexualities as deviant, prejudice, discrimination, and homophobia will continue.

The Numbers

Currently, there is no single nationwide survey they provides an accurate estimate of the numbers of gay men, lesbian women, and bisexuals. The Decennial Census does not include direct questions regarding sexual orientation; however, it does provide the number and percentage of "Unmarried Partner Households." According to the 2010 Census, same-sex unmarried partner households numbered 901,997 (0.8 percent).

A more accurate estimate of the size of the lesbian, gay, and bisexual community comes from the Williams Institute on Sexual Orientation and Gender Identity Law and Public Policy at the UCLA School of Law. Combining the results of population-based surveys, they estimate that there are more than 8 million adults in the United States that are lesbian, gay, or bisexual (see Figure 10.1) (Gates 2011). Key findings from their research indicate that:

- An estimated 3.5 percent of adults in the United States identify as lesbian, gay, or bisexual.
- Women are significantly more likely than men to identify as bisexual.
- Approximately 19 million Americans (8.2 percent) report that they have engaged in same-sex sexual behavior.
- Approximately 25.6 million Americans (11 percent) admit at least some same-sex sexual attraction.

Gates (2011) argues that understanding the numbers and size of the lesbian, gay, and bisexual population is an important step to inform public policy and research

FIGURE 10.1

Number and Percent of Adults Who Identify as Lesbian, Gay, or Bisexual in the United States

Source: Adapted from Gates, Gary J. 2011. "How Many People Are Lesbian, Gay, Bisexual, and Transgender?" The Williams Institute, UCLA School of Law. http://williamsinstitute.law.ucla.edu/wp-content/uploads/Gates-How-Many-People-LGBT-Apr-2011.pdf; page 6.

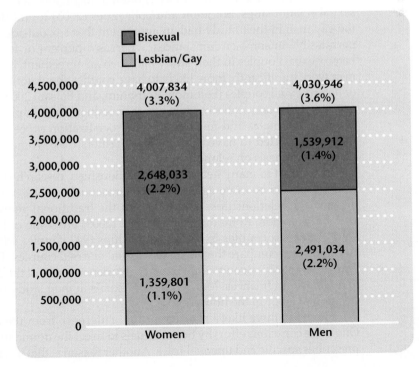

into health and economic disparity, discrimination, and marriage equality. In the 2000 census, numbers indicated that same-sex unmarried partners were present in 99.3 percent of all counties in the United States, which helped gay activists back up the claim that gays and lesbians are indeed "everywhere." The antigay right, on the other hand, argues for the lower numbers because it undercuts the gay movement for equality. Perhaps Congressman Henry Waxman gave the best response to the numbers issue: "One percent, 10 percent, discrimination is discrimination" (Cole and Gorman 1993:29).

Interpersonal Relationships and Domestic Arrangements among Gays and Lesbians

View on
MySocLab Figure:
Gay Marriage Timeline

With the ever-growing controversy surrounding the issue of same-sex marriage, some social scientists have turned to empirical investigations of gay couples. Their conclusions about sexual relationships point to a number of similarities and differences between homosexuals and heterosexuals and between gay men and lesbian women, some of which contradict the prevailing stereotypes.

Gays and lesbians are similar to heterosexuals in their desire for an intimate relationship with one special person. Because most homosexuals are denied marriage in most states, homosexual couples must turn to cohabitation relationships. Research has found that long-lived partnerships between gay men are not uncommon, but neither are they typical. Lesbians, on the other hand, tend to attach a high priority to domestic partnerships. Lawrence Kurdek has studied gay and lesbian couples over time and found that overall they are more similar than different; however, lesbians reported more trust and more equality in their relationships (Kurdek 2003). In another study, Kurdek found that lesbian couples reported higher levels of cohesion and higher levels of satisfaction than the heterosexual couples studied, whereas gay male couples reported lower levels of commitment compared to heterosexual couples (Kurdek 2001).

The issue of sexual exclusivity is often a major source of tension in male homosexual relationships. Solomon and colleagues (2005) found that over 40 percent of the gay men in their study had an agreement that sex outside their relationship was permissible in some circumstances, whereas 5 percent or fewer of the lesbian and heterosexual couples in their study had such an agreement. They also noted that gay men were significantly more likely to have conflict about nonmonogamy than lesbian or heterosexual couples (Solomon, Rothblum, and Balsam 2005:574). The tendency for gay men to be less sexually exclusive than lesbian women parallels the difference in heterosexual males and females and the socialization process whereby males learn they are expected to have more sexual partners than women, and women learn to place an emphasis on relationships.

In contrast to many heterosexual relationships, research shows that homosexual couples tend to be more egalitarian. Heterosexual couples, whether in cohabitation or marriage relationships, tend to accept the traditional gender roles for men and women. Solomon, Rothblum, and Balsam (2005) are some of the first researchers to study same-sex couples in legal relationships (947 couples who had civil unions in Vermont) and compare them to heterosexual married couples. Their findings indicate that gay and lesbian couples are more egalitarian in terms of the division of housework and household finances. Married heterosexuals in their study had a more traditional division of labor in the household.

There are three likely reasons for this difference from the heterosexual pattern. One is the conscious effort by homosexuals to reject the dominant marriage model that prescribes specific and unequal roles. Another reason is that in same-sex relationships, the partners have received the same gender-role socialization. Another source of equality in gay relationships is that there tends to be little income difference between the partners, a condition rare in heterosexual relationships in which most women have less earning potential than their male partners. Most gay and lesbian couples are dual-income units. And because both partners in a homosexual relationship are of the same sex, they are often subject to the same degree of sex discrimination in jobs and income. Whatever the reason, same-sex couples do not typically adopt "husband" and "wife" roles in their relationships but are more flexible in sharing housework (Peplau, Veniegas, and Campbell 2004).

Although there are many similarities between homosexual couples and heterosexual couples, homosexual couples face additional problems. Gay men and lesbian women are not encouraged to be open about their sexual orientation and their relationships, hence they may feel restricted in showing public affection toward their lovers. They may not be extended such commonplace courtesies as having a partner invited to an office party or to a retirement banquet. Sometimes, this lack of social support comes from family members. Solomon and colleagues (2005) found that same-sex couples were less likely than heterosexual couples to have contact with their family of origin.

In summary, lesbian and gay couples are similar to heterosexual couples in their quest for love and relationships. Research shows that they tend to be more egalitarian than heterosexual couples in their division of household work and finances and that gay male couples tend to be less monogamous than lesbian and heterosexual couples. This sometimes becomes a source of conflict for gay male couples. Another source of conflict for gay and lesbian couples resides in the lack of support received from the dominant society and, in many cases, from their own families.

PAST AND PRESENT DISCRIMINATION

10.3 Understand homophobia and its consequences.

Variance from the societal norm of heterosexuality is not a social problem; the societal response to it is. Society has defined what is appropriate sexual behavior and orientation. Consequently, people who differ from the approved orientation are objects of derision and contempt by members of society and are discriminated against by individuals and by the normal way that the institutions of society operate. This section examines that discrimination, both past and present.

Ideological Oppression

View on
MySocLab Figure:
Attitudes toward
Homosexual Relations,
1973–2010

Homophobia is fear and loathing of homosexuality and homosexuals. It shares many of the same roots with other prejudices. Like racism and anti-Semitism, homophobia includes "an intolerance toward otherness; a fear of lives, perspectives, and practices that one doesn't understand; and a visceral desire for a social hierarchy that puts some people on the rungs below you" (Angier 1993:4E). There is a long tradition of homophobia in Western society. Even though it is now politically incorrect to make racial, ethnic, and gay slurs, gay slurs are still heard in the movies, on television, and in schools. Homosexuals are often targets of ridicule, restricted from social interaction, and stigmatized. Public opinion on same-sex sexual behavior is sharply divided. The 2010 General Social Survey finds that:

- Forty-seven percent of Americans feel that sexual relations between two adults of the same sex is always or almost always wrong, while 41 percent feel that it is not wrong at all.
- Forty percent oppose same-sex marriage.

- Sixty-three percent of Americans age 70 and older feel that sexual relations between two adults of the same sex is always wrong, while 26 percent of those under age 30 said it was always wrong, showing a significant generation gap (Smith 2011).

For some people, the homosexual individual is an outcast. Gays are seen as an aberration, perhaps even a dangerous deviation, from so-called normal sexuality. When people believe that gays are immoral, they belittle their lifestyle, tell jokes about them, and even deny their rights to housing, jobs, and memberships in organizations; an example of this type of ideological oppression comes from the Boy Scouts of America, whose oath calls for members to be "morally straight." As a private organization, they maintain the right to exclude gays and lesbians (and atheists) from their ranks (Associated Press 2012).

An extreme consequence of homophobia is the possibility of verbal and physical assault, and cyber-bullying (see the "Speaking to Students" panel titled "Homophobia in Schools and Its Consequences"). In June 2004, the U.S. Senate voted to expand hate crime legislation to cover crimes that target people because of their sexual orientation, gender, or disability. According to the Uniform Crime Reports collected by the Federal Bureau of Investigation, in 2010 hate crimes involving sexual orientation ranked number three (19.3 percent of all hate crimes), just behind religion hate crimes (20.0 percent) and racial hate crimes (47.3 percent). These homophobic attitudes and behaviors cause many homosexuals to have personal problems with self-concept and other adjustment problems. The way that society views homosexuality is shaped significantly by our religious heritage and the views of the medical community.

- **Religion.**   The Judeo-Christian tradition considers homosexual behavior to be a sin. The Old Testament approves of sexual intercourse only within marriage and for the purpose of procreation. Homosexuality has therefore been expressly forbidden.

Speaking to Students

HOMOPHOBIA IN SCHOOLS AND ITS CONSEQUENCES

Adolescence is a difficult time of emotional, physical, and sexual changes. It is also a stage when peer approval is especially crucial for a positive sense of self. Today, many schools across the country have gay–straight alliance clubs, teens can watch mainstream media that include gays and lesbians in the programming, some novels and magazines are written for a gay and lesbian teen audience, and websites offer support and information for gay and lesbian teenagers. Despite such resources, the American Academy

of Pediatrics worries about gay and lesbian youths because they are subjected to abuse and isolation at this critical time in their lives. For the 2 million or so school-age children who are lesbian, gay, bisexual, or transgendered (LGBT), school can be an extremely difficult place. According to the 2009 National School Climate Survey (Gay, Lesbian and Straight Education Network 2010):

- Nine out of ten LGBT youth experienced harassment at school in the past year and

nearly two-thirds felt unsafe at school.
- 84.6 percent of LGBT youth report being verbally harassed.
- 40.1 percent of LGBT students reported being physically harassed, and 18.8 percent reported being physically assaulted because of their sexual orientation.
- 72.4 percent hear derogatory remarks such as "faggot" or "dyke" frequently or often at school.

These attacks on lesbian, gay, and bisexual students create a

The rejection of homosexual behavior that is found in the Old Testament is well known. In Genesis 19, two angels in disguise visit the city of Sodom and are offered hospitality and shelter by Lot. During the night, the men of Sodom demand that Lot hand over his guests for homosexual intercourse. Lot refuses, and the angels blind the men of Sodom. (Catholic.com 2004:1)

In all, roughly twenty Bible passages have been interpreted as involving homosexual behavior. Most fundamentalists and other Evangelical Christians believe that God hates homosexual behavior and that sexually active homosexuals will end up in Hell, not Heaven (Religious Tolerance.org 2009).

The New Testament continues the tradition of the Old Testament. The early Christians strived for human perfection unencumbered by the desires of the flesh—celibate religious leaders, sexual intercourse only within marriage, and condemnation of homosexuality. Speaking of homosexuality, the apostle Paul, for example, considered lustful behavior between men and between women as "vile passions . . . against nature" (Romans 1:26). Paul in Corinthians also wrote that homosexuals, along with fornicators, idolaters, adulterers, and thieves, would never inherit the kingdom of God.

Like all passages in the Bible, those pertaining to sexual behavior are hotly debated. Many scholars have contested the traditional interpretations of the Bible, whereas others feel the passages are unambiguously clear. Contemporary Christian churches and denominations are currently struggling between traditional views that are consistent with Christian history and a more modern approach of tolerance and acceptance.

For centuries, the Christian church ostracized homosexual people and gave its blessing to civil persecutions. The current expression of this position continues the heritage of moral condemnation toward gays. The Reverend Jerry Falwell, fundamentalist preacher and founder of the Moral Majority, for example, called the outbreak of AIDS among homosexuals a "form of judgment of God upon a society" (Crooks and Baur 1987:312).

hostile climate that can be unbearable for them. It can undermine their confidence and lead to feelings of isolation. It is no surprise that lesbian, gay, and bisexual teens are five times more likely to attempt suicide than their heterosexual peers (Pittman 2011).

At the very worst, teens can experience serious physical assault. In 1995, a 17-year-old student, Bill Clayton, committed suicide after being beaten and assaulted for being bisexual. In 1998, Matthew Shepherd, a gay student at the University of Wyoming, was beaten and killed because of his sexual orientation. In 2004, 18-year-old Scotty Joe Weaver was beaten, strangled, and stabbed. The authorities believe the killing was motivated by his sexual orientation. In 2008, Lawrence Fobes King, a 15-year-old student, was shot and killed by another 14-year-old male after asking him to be his valentine. Unfortunately, these are just a few of many examples of violence.

Sometimes, the intolerance, harassment, and homophobia come from the authority figures that teenagers are supposed to trust. For example, in 2002, the ACLU filed a lawsuit on behalf of an eighth-grader who was forced to sit in the principal's office during physical education class (for a week and a half) after the gym teacher heard that she was a lesbian (American Civil Liberties Union 2002). In 2003, the ACLU took action again, this time on behalf of a 14-year-old student. The ACLU claimed that school officials "outed" the gay student to his parents against his wishes, told him he must not discuss being gay while at school, forced him to read from the Bible, and disciplined him for being open about his sexual orientation (American Civil Liberties Union 2003).

To summarize, there are numerous support groups for gay and lesbian teens, growing numbers of gay–straight alliances in schools, more gay and lesbian characters on television, and attitude polls show growing support among youth for same-sex marriage. Despite these positive signs, on a day-to-day individual basis gay and lesbian youth continue to face pervasive harassment and threats of violence.

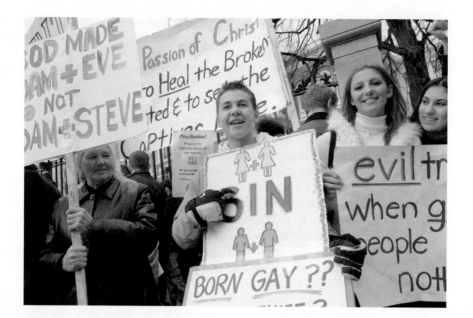

Religion fuels much of the protest against same-sex marriage.

The Reverend Pat Robertson, television evangelist, said in 1998 that the widespread practice of homosexuality will bring God's wrath: "[It] will bring about terrorist bombs, it'll bring earthquakes, tornadoes and possibly a meteor" (Wharton 1998:14A). In another extreme example of fundamentalist thinking on homosexuality, Pastor Peter J. Peters asserts, "The truth is, the Bible advocates discrimination against, intolerance of, and the death penalty for homosexuals" (Peters 1992:1).

The Roman Catholic Church has consistently reaffirmed its opposition to same-sex relationships, same-sex marriages, and same-sex adoptions. For example, in 1999, the Vatican ordered a Maryland-based priest and a nun to end their twenty-two-year ministry to lesbians and gays because they refused to condemn homosexuality as intrinsically evil (Associated Press 1999). More recently, Roman Catholic bishops drafted new guidelines that encourage parishes to reach out to gay Catholics who feel alienated by the Catholic Church, but at the same time, the guidelines reaffirm the Church's stance against homosexuality (Associated Press 2006).

The power of the church goes further than simply influencing beliefs, however. For example, in 1996 the Southern Baptist Convention voted to boycott Disney parks, movies, and products, for Disney's "promotion of homosexuality" because it provides the same healthcare benefits for the live-in mates of gay employees as it does for the spouses of straight workers and it allowed gay groups to organize an event at Disney World (Means 1996).

More recently, the American Family Association, a nonprofit Christian organization claiming the support of over 3 million people, called for boycotts of both Sears and Ford Motor Company for advertising during television programming that supports the "homosexual agenda" (Wildmon 2007).

Many congregations and denominations are more accepting of homosexuality. Some maintain that homosexuality must be condemned but, because of God's grace, homosexuals must *not* be condemned. Others are even more accepting, ranging from the acceptance of gay Christians as members to the ordination of gays as ministers. Although it is not a totally comprehensive list, Gaychurch.org has a listing of 6,826 "affirming" churches from all over the world. Such phrases as "affirming" signify that gay, lesbian, bisexual and transgendered people are accepted in the church.

Watch on **MySocLab Video:** ABC Nightline: One Town's Struggle with God, Gays, and Bigotry

The acceptance of gays and lesbians within religious denominations has reached a critical point in our history. The two most pressing and divisive issues concern (1) whether qualified gays and lesbians should be eligible to be priests, bishops, and ministers; and (2) whether the church should engage in rituals that recognize and bless same-sex unions. Conservative factions within these churches are threatening to break away if full acceptance of homosexuals becomes a reality. For example, the U.S. Episcopal Church confirmed an openly gay priest as bishop of New Hampshire in 2003, and as a result more than a dozen churches defected in protest (Moore 2006). In February 2010, the Episcopal Church ordained and consecrated a second openly gay bishop in the church's history (the Reverend Canon Mary Glasspool). Episcopal conservatives, upset with the move, have formed a rival church, the Anglican Church of North America.

The United Church of Christ is one of the first Christian denominations to approve a resolution endorsing same-sex marriage, and in 2009 the Evangelical Lutheran Church in America voted in favor of allowing practicing homosexuals in committed relationships to hold positions of authority within the sect. Strongly opposed to this decision were Lutheran members of CORE (Coalition for Renewal), representing over 400 conservative Lutheran congregations.

Perhaps the most telling example of this paradox regarding gays and lesbians is the December 2006 ruling by the Committee on Jewish Law and Standards. The leaders of the Conservative Jewish movement passed guidelines that opened the door for the ordination of gay rabbis and the recognition of gay marriage. However, in a separate vote, the group also upheld a 1992 statement that advises against gay ordinations and the recognition of same-sex marriages. The result is a mixed approach that will allow both liberals and the more orthodox in the movement to pursue whichever policies they prefer (Nichols 2006).

As the issue of same-sex marriage becomes more and more imminent, thorny theological questions surround the church's definition and treatment of homosexuals. Churches face an uncertain future and the possibility of alienating members as they vote on these important issues. There is an ideological divide between generations (with younger Americans being more in favor of same-sex marriage), between conservative and liberal factions within religious groups, and between individuals over the interpretations of scripture.

- **Medicine.**   The beliefs that people in the United States have about homosexuals have been shaped by religion, as we have seen, and also by the prevailing views of the medical community. Whereas religious ideology tends to view homosexuality as a sin, psychiatric theory, until 1973, considered homosexuality as an illness. As an illness, it was assumed to be curable, and many techniques were tried, including prefrontal lobotomies, crude forms of conditioning (such as drugs that induce a sensation of suffocation or emetics to induce vomiting), and even castration. These and more moderate strategies of psychoanalysis were singularly unsuccessful in treating this so-called malady.

    The American Psychiatric Association publishes the *Diagnostic and Statistical Manual*, which defines officially the conditions considered mental illnesses. In the first edition, homosexuality was labeled a mental illness. Some mental health professionals held the minority view that this label was wrong. Dr. Robert Spitzer, for example, said,

    With the exception of homosexuality, all other disorders were associated with impairment in general, occupational or social functioning, or inherently caused some distress. . . . The argument the gay activists were making was that any distress was a reaction to social pressure. (Mach 1987:44)

In 1973, after years of lobbying by gay activists and the efforts of other people, the American Psychiatric Association by a majority vote of its membership declassified homosexuality as a mental disorder; homosexual behavior was henceforth to be regarded simply as a manifestation of a preference, not as sick or bad. The Association recommends that treatment focus on the problems that may result from being part of a stigmatized group, problems such as guilt, anger, and low self-esteem.

> There is no published scientific evidence supporting the efficacy of "reparative therapy" as a treatment to change one's sexual orientation, nor is it included in the APA's Task Force Report, Treatments of Psychiatric Disorders. More importantly, altering sexual orientation is not an appropriate goal of psychiatric treatment. Some may seek conversion to heterosexuality because of the difficulties that they encounter as a member of a stigmatized group. Clinical experience indicates that those who have integrated their sexual orientation into a positive sense of self function at a healthier psychological level than those who have not. "Gay affirmative psychotherapy" may be helpful in the coming out process, fostering a positive psychological development and overcoming the effects of stigmatization. (American Psychiatric Association 2007)

In August 2009, the American Psychiatric Association's governing council formally adopted a resolution declaring that mental health professionals should not tell gay clients they can become straight through therapy or other treatments (Associated Press 2009).

Legal Oppression: The Law and the Courts

In fourteenth-century Europe, the common punishment for homosexuality was burning at the stake. The Puritans in the colonies continued the death penalty for this "crime." Around the time of the American Revolution, Thomas Jefferson and some liberal reformers of the day proposed changing Virginia law, replacing the death penalty for homosexuality with castration (Tivnan 1987).

The legal status of homosexuals has progressed considerably since the days of death and castration, but they are still not treated equally. According to the Human Rights Campaign, legally a person can be fired from his or her job in twenty-nine states just for being homosexual (2011). Furthermore, the marriage of homosexuals is recognized in just nine states and the District of Columbia. In addition to losing the symbolic importance of having a union legitimated by the state, same-sex couples and their families are denied access to more than 1,138 federal rights, protections, and responsibilities automatically granted to married heterosexual couples (Human Rights Campaign 2011).

This section begins by surveying the major historical developments in the law in three areas of great concern to the gay community: discrimination against gays by the military, family rights, and employment discrimination.

- **The Military.** Until recently, the U.S. armed forces discriminated against gays and lesbians. From 1982 to 1992, about 14,000 people were dishonorably discharged from the military as homosexuals. In 1993, newly elected President Clinton vowed to change the regulations so that homosexuals would not be discriminated against in the military. Many citizens, politicians, military leaders, and military personnel resisted this proposal. The result was a compromise—the "Don't Ask, Don't Tell, Don't Pursue" rule. This policy meant that the military was not to ask its personnel about their sexuality and was to prosecute only if gay and lesbian service members were blatant about their sexual orientation. In short, as long as homosexual service members "stayed in the closet," they were allowed to be in the military.

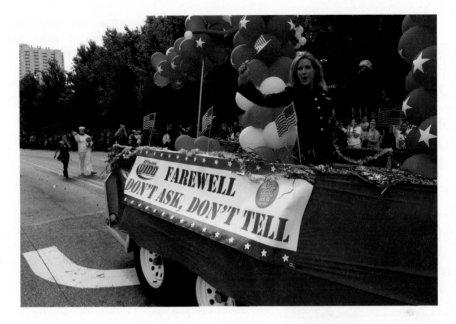

More than 12,000 military personnel were discharged for their sexual orientation under "Don't Ask, Don't Tell." The policy was officially repealed in 2011.

Since the "Don't Ask, Don't Tell" policy was adopted in 1994, more than 12,000 military personnel were discharged due to their sexual orientation. Analysts have noted that when America went to war after September 11, 2001, the numbers of discharges dropped dramatically, as more military personnel were needed. "As fighting in Afghanistan and Iraq continues, the Pentagon has discharged the fewest lesbian, gay, and bisexual service members since 1995. The Pentagon expelled 787 service members for being gay in FY2003, down 17% from FY2002, and 39% from FY2001. Gay discharge numbers have dropped every time America has entered a war, from Korea to Vietnam to the Persian Gulf to the present conflicts" (Servicemembers Legal Defense Network 2006:1).

In 1995, President Clinton ended fifty years of official federal discrimination against homosexuals by ordering that gays and lesbians were no longer considered security risks. This ruling meant that gays and lesbians in government would be granted access to classified government documents on the same basis as other federal employees. Although a small step forward, gays and lesbians in the military continued to face not only antigay harassment from their fellow military personnel and those in authority, but also the constant threat of being discharged.

In February 2000, Pentagon officials changed the name of the policy to reflect the problem of antigay harassment. In the wake of the murder of Private First Class Barry Winchell, the policy became "Don't Ask, Don't Tell, Don't Pursue, Don't Harass." A fellow service member murdered Winchell, believed to be gay, with a baseball bat in his barracks in 1999.

In September 2011, the law that banned openly gay Americans from serving in the U.S. military was officially repealed, ending almost eighteen years of discrimination. The repeal of Don't Ask, Don't Tell means that for the first time in United States history, service members are allowed to reveal their sexual orientation without fear of discharge.

- **Family Rights.** The United States has a history of regulating the sexual behavior of its citizens through laws regarding marriage. For example, African Americans were not allowed to legally marry until after the Civil War. Mixed-race couples were not allowed to legally marry until 1967. And until recently, same-sex marriages were forbidden in all states.

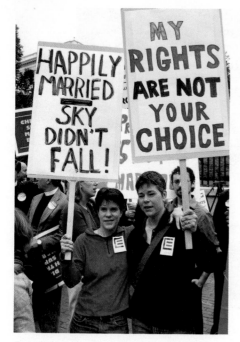

Same-sex marriage is legal in just nine states and the District of Columbia.

Because same-sex couples are not allowed to marry, they are denied of the Family and Medical Leave Act, which permits individuals to take leave from work to care for ill spouses; the right to inherit property from a partner in the absence of a will; and the right to family-related Social Security benefits, disability benefits, and military and veterans benefits (Human Rights Campaign 2011).

Bernard and Lieber set out to examine this issue from a monetary standpoint. They created a hypothetical gay couple, gave them two children and assumed that one partner would stay home for five years to care for the children. They gave their couple an income of $140,000 and considered the taxes in the three states that have the highest estimated gay population. They concluded that in the worst-case scenario, the couple's lifetime cost of being gay was $467,456. If the couple has good health insurance and lower taxes, the number is lower, and for wealthy couples with significant assets, the cost of being gay could spiral into the millions. All of these costs will disappear if the federal government legalizes same-sex marriage (Bernard, Siegel, and Lieber 2009:1).

As of February 2013, nine states and the District of Columbia have adopted same-sex marriage laws. These states join Belgium, Canada, the Netherlands, South Africa, Norway, Sweden, and Spain in allowing same-sex marriage. In a landmark case in 2003, the Supreme Court ruled that the Massachusetts Constitution allowed for same-sex marriages, and the state began to issue marriage licenses to same-sex couples in May 2004. Massachusetts was then followed by Connecticut, Iowa, Vermont, New Hampshire, the District of Columbia, New York, Washington, Maryland, and Maine. California granted same-sex marriage from June through November 2008, when voters passed a ban on same-sex marriage. The state Supreme Court later ruled that the estimated 18,000 gay couples who married between June and November would remain married with all the legal rights that that entails.

As an alternative to same-sex marriage, some states offer civil unions for same-sex couples. Civil unions fall something short of marriage, but the couples have the same rights and responsibilities as heterosexual couples in the matters of insurance, inheritance, child custody, and taxes. Like married couples, couples can apply for a divorce to dissolve their union. Unlike married couples, civil union couples are denied over 1,000 *federal* rights and are unable to transfer their civil union to another state should they wish to move.

Other states have passed laws granting some statewide benefits to unmarried couples without granting civil unions. These domestic partnerships range from granting broad benefits and responsibilities to same-sex partners (for example, in California and Nevada) to more limited benefits and protections known as reciprocal or designated beneficiaries (for example, in Colorado). While both civil unions and domestic partnerships expand the rights of same-sex couples, they fall short both legally and symbolically of marriage. The underlying assumption behind them takes us back to the system of heteronormativity, where same-sex relationships are viewed and treated as abnormal and inferior to heterosexual relationships.

In a resulting backlash to progressive changes, twenty-nine states have passed constitutional amendments that define marriage as the exclusive union of a man and a woman. These amendments mean that states refuse to recognize same-sex marriage licenses issued in other states and prohibit same-sex couples from receiving any marriage-based benefits.

Public opinion polls regarding same-sex marriage and civil unions demonstrate that this is a divisive issue that will be very important in political elections. In May 2012 President Barack Obama became the first United States president to publicly endorse same-sex marriage, setting off a firestorm of debate. Polls seem to indicate that there is a growing support for same-sex marriage (especially for those under age 30) signifying a shift in societal attitudes and the potential for social change in years to come (see Figures 10.2 and 10.3).

Barriers to marriage are just one form of legal oppression; parenthood is another battleground for lesbian and gay rights. The legality of homosexual parenthood varies from state to state, and the interpretation of the law often varies from judge to judge. For example, Florida, Mississippi, and Utah have laws that explicitly prohibit homosexual individuals and/or couples from adopting children, and Michigan has prohibited same-sex couples from adopting but does not prohibit single homosexual individuals from adopting. Other states may not explicitly prohibit same-sex adoption but may have requirements that only *married* couples may adopt, which thus prohibits same-sex couples from adopting. As of 2011, only sixteen states plus the District of Columbia allow same sex couples to jointly petition to adopt (Human Rights Campaign 2011). Despite restrictions, the proportion of same-sex couples who have adopted children has nearly doubled from 10 percent to 19 percent between 2000 and 2009 (Gates 2012).

Another situation is custody of children following a heterosexual marriage. In such a situation, judges routinely give custody to the heterosexual parent, assuming that this arrangement is better for the child. According to the American Civil Liberties

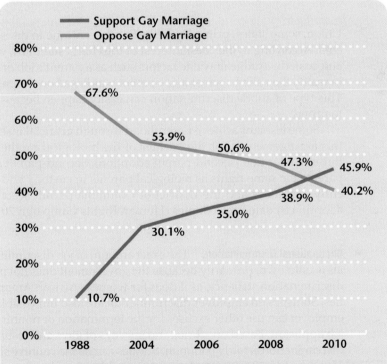

FIGURE 10.2

Support for Same-Sex Marriage: 1988–2010

Adapted from: Tom W. Smith. NORC/ University of Chicago, General Social Survey. 2011. "Public Attitudes Towards Homosexuality." http://news.uchicago .edu/sites/all/files/attachments/ Public%20Attitudes%20Toward%20 Homosexuality.pdf.

Support = Agreed or strongly agreed with the statement: Homosexual couples should have the right to marry one another.

Oppose = Disagree or strongly disagree with the statement: Homosexual couples should have the right to marry one another.

FIGURE 10.3

Support for Gay Marriage by Age Group, 2010

Adapted from: Tom W. Smith. NORC/University of Chicago, General Social Survey. 2011. "Public Attitudes Towards Homosexuality." http://news
.uchicago.edu/sites/all/files/attachments/Public%20Attitudes%20Toward%20Homosexuality.pdf.

Union, some states, primarily in the South, continue to discriminate against gay parents. According to the "best interest of the child" standard, when ruling on visitation and custody a judge may cite factors such as a parent's job or housing situation, when in reality the ruling against a gay parent was based on the parent's sexual orientation. This type of subtle discrimination can easily happen because it is almost impossible to prove.

Some lesbians achieve parenthood through artificial insemination. The trick with this arrangement is for the partner of the biological mother to achieve legal status through adoption (second-parent adoption). Second-parent adoption gives adoptive parents the same rights as biological parents in custody and visitation matters. Presently, ten states and the District of Columbia permit second-parent or stepparent adoption by same-sex couples (Human Rights Campaign 2011).

- **Occupational Discrimination.** The exact amount of job discrimination against homosexuals is unknown, primarily because the government does not provide gay employment discrimination statistics, as it does for women, African Americans, and other minorities. Statistics on employer discrimination are also impossible to calculate because an employer can use other excuses for the termination or nonhiring of a gay employee or job applicant. Based on stories and surveys of gays and lesbians, however, employer discrimination is fairly common. Studies across the country show that anywhere from 15 percent to 43 percent of gay men and lesbians have experienced discrimination and/or harassment in the workplace (Althauser and Greenberg 2011). For example, a 2004 survey in Topeka, Kansas, found that 16 percent of gay and lesbian respondents reported that they were denied employment because of their sexual orientation, 15 percent were fired because of their sexual orientation, and 35 percent had received harassing letters, e-mails, or faxes at work because of their sexual orientation (Colvin 2004). In another example, in 2005, a photographer named Laurel Scherer lost her photography contract with a ski resort in North Carolina after she and her partner were married in Massachusetts and ran their wedding announcement in their local newspaper (Gunther 2006). Many homosexuals fear that they will lose their jobs if their sexual orientation is revealed. Or, if not fired, they may experience other forms of discrimination, such as being passed over for deserved promotions, being given relatively low salary raises, and being harassed.

These fears are based on reality. Legally, a person can be fired from his or her job in twenty-nine states just for being homosexual (Human Rights Campaign 2011). Twenty-one states and the District of Columbia have passed laws prohibiting employment discrimination based on sexual orientation, but currently there is no *federal* law that protects lesbian, gay, bisexual, and transgender individuals from employment discrimination. The **Employment Non-Discrimination Act** (ENDA) is a bill introduced in the 112th Congress in 2011. If passed, it would provide basic federal protections against workplace discrimination on the basis of sexual orientation or gender identity (Human Rights Campaign 2011). ENDA would extend the current federal protections based on race, religion, sex, national origin, age, and disability.

A few employers are taking the lead in breaking down discrimination in the workplace. Corporate nondiscrimination clauses are being added to protect gay workers from harassment, and some companies are now offering domestic partner benefits. In fact, 87 percent of Fortune 500 companies have nondiscrimination policies on the basis of sexual orientation and more than half offer health benefits for domestic partners (Human Rights Campaign 2011). Coors Brewing Company, for example, offers all family benefits to gay and lesbian employees and their partners. Thus, gay employees of Coors and their partners receive medical and dental care, vision and hearing coverage, bereavement leave, and coverage for natural or adopted children or children of whom one partner has legal custody. Other large corporations that provide same-sex partner benefits include Microsoft, Walt Disney Company, Boeing, General Motors, Ford, DaimlerChrysler, Prudential, Motorola, General Mills, Honeywell, and Xerox. Some progressive corporations (e.g., Microsoft, AT&T, Xerox, Apple Computer, and Pacific Gas and Electric) provide diversity training to demystify homosexuality and to encourage gay and lesbian groups within the organizations. IBM is on the cutting edge as the number-one financial supporter of gay rights groups in the United States, and other corporations are following suit. "So it's clear where big business is going. What's interesting is to watch it pull the rest of the country along. It turns out that the most important factor shaping people's feelings about gay issues is not their age or even their religion—although those do matter—but whether they have relatives, friends, or coworkers who are gay" (Gunther 2006:5).

10.4 Explain the ideological and legal oppression of homosexuals.

FIGHTING THE SYSTEM: HUMAN AGENCY

The chapter to this point has documented the hostility, anger, and discrimination aimed at homosexuals in U.S. society. These reactions occur at the societal level through punitive religious ideology that condemns homosexuals' immorality and through court actions that discriminate. At the personal level, hostility occurs with looks, taunts, ostracism, and even violence. The objects of this assault—individual lesbian women, gay men, and bisexuals—may experience great personal stress as a result. Studies show that gay, lesbian, and bisexual youth attempt suicide at a rate five times higher than that of their heterosexual peers (Pittman 2011).

Gays use two basic strategies for living in a society hostile to their sexual orientation. One is to conceal their sexual orientation to avoid stigmatization, harassment, and discrimination. These closeted gays segregate their lives into gay and straight activities. When in the straight world, they conceal their sexual orientation from family, friends, co-workers, and other associates.

Gay activists, on the other hand, identify themselves openly as homosexuals. Rather than evade the efforts to stigmatize them, they challenge society in an effort to transform it. The gay men, lesbian women, and bisexuals who confront society are the reason that some positive changes can be seen in places like the military and in family rights, and are the focus of this section.

The negative sanctions from society, employers, friends, and family have kept lesbians and gay men for most periods of U.S. history from organizing to change a repressive situation. Political activist Emma Goldman in 1915 became the first person to speak publicly in favor of gay and lesbian rights. A few homosexual organizations were formed (the first, the Chicago Society for Human Rights in 1924, and the first modern gay rights organization, the Mattachine Society in 1950) for mutual support, but only a relatively few homosexuals were willing at the time to publicly declare their deviance from the norm of heterosexuality.

The 1960s provided a better climate for change when youths, African Americans, women, pacifists, and other groups questioned the norms and ideologies of the dominant society. This decade clearly was one of heightened awareness among the oppressed of their oppression and of the possibility that through collective efforts they could change what had seemed to be unchangeable.

The precipitating event for gay and lesbian unity occurred on June 28, 1969, when police raided the Stonewall Inn of New York's Greenwich Village. Instead of dispersing, as gays had always done in similar situations, the 200 patrons threw objects at the police and set fire to the bar. The riot lasted only 45 minutes, but it gave impetus to a number of collective efforts by gays to publicize police harassment of the gay community, job discrimination, and other indignities they faced. In effect, the Stonewall resistance came to symbolize the birth of the modern gay rights movement.

Following Stonewall, gay liberation groups emerged in many cities and on university campuses. Many neighborhoods in major cities became openly homosexual—most notably the Castro district in San Francisco, New Town in Chicago, and Greenwich Village in New York City. These communities included gay churches, associations of professionals, health clinics, and networks of gay-owned businesses to supply the gay community's needs. The proliferation of these organizations for lesbians and gays provided a supportive climate, allowing many of them to come out of the closet.

The increased numbers of public gays and lesbians have provided the political base for changing the various forms of oppression that homosexuals routinely experience. The Gay and Lesbian Alliance Against Defamation (GLAAD) promotes accurate and positive images of gays in television, films, and advertising; the Human Rights Campaign and Lambda Legal promote favorable legislation; the Gay Men's Health Crisis helps gay men deal with the reality of AIDS; and the National Gay and Lesbian Task Force furthers gay interests by attacking the minority-group status of homosexuals in a variety of political and ideological arenas.

Two countervailing forces in the 1980s affected the gay rights movement. The election of Ronald Reagan and his conservative agenda, along with the surge of Christian fundamentalism, inhibited the movement's momentum in the first part of the decade. The AIDS epidemic propelled the movement in the late 1980s. As it became clear that AIDS endangered the lives of gay males, the sense of a shared danger and the realization that they needed to push the government into action quickly inspired unity. More organizations formed, some directed specifically at the health needs of people with AIDS and others aimed at lobbying Congress and state governments for legislation important to gays.

On October 11, 1987, the largest gay rights demonstration occurred when approximately 250,000 lesbians, gay men, and their supporters marched in Washington, DC. They held a parade, had a huge marriage ceremony to protest the laws forbidding the marriage of gays, mourned their comrades who had died of AIDS, staged a mass civil disobedience action at the U.S. Supreme Court to protest the 1986 decision upholding state sodomy laws (840 people were arrested), and joined with other activist groups. The Reverend Jesse Jackson spoke at the rally:

> We are together today to say we insist on legal protection under the law of every American . . . for workers' rights, for civil rights, for the rights of religious freedom, the rights of individual privacy, for the rights of sexual preference. We come together for the rights of the American people. (Quoted in Freiberg 1987:15)

By 2012, forty-three years after Stonewall, many positive changes have occurred for the gay and lesbian community:

- At the time of Stonewall, forty-eight states had sodomy laws meant to outlaw homosexual sex. In 2003, those laws were overturned.
- In a groundbreaking decision, the Supreme Court in 1998 ruled unanimously that sexual harassment in the workplace applies to harassment between workers of the same sex. This ruling gives protections to all employees, male or female, homosexual or heterosexual, something unheard of in 1969.
- In 1982, more than 1,000 athletes from twelve countries competed in the Gay Games in San Francisco, an event beyond imagination in 1969; in 2010, Cologne hosted the games with over 10,000 participants.

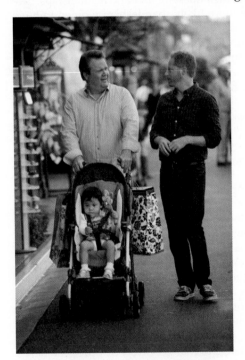

More television shows are featuring gay characters, such as ABC's sitcom Modern Family, *where gay couple Mitchell and Cameron adopt a baby.*

- In 1997, there were approximately 100 gay–straight alliances (GSAs)—clubs for gay and gay-friendly kids—on U.S. high school campuses. Today there are at least 3,500 GSAs.
- Prominent athletes have come out and announced to the world that they are gay—for example, former Olympic champion diver Greg Louganis, former NFL player Esera Tuaolo, former NBA player John Amaechi, and three-time MVP WNBA player Sheryl Swoops. Although the number of professional athletes who have come out is very small, these individuals are paving the way for a new generation of athletes.
- According to the Gay and Lesbian Victory Institute, there are over 1,000 openly LGBT appointed and elected officials across the United States (2012).
- Public opinion polls show a gradual acceptance of gays and lesbians, especially among the younger generation. The mainstream media is slowly incorporating more gays and lesbians into prime-time television shows, and MTV Network has a cable channel specifically for a lesbian, gay, bisexual, and transgender audience (LOGO). Perhaps the most prominent signs of progress are found in the movies *Brokeback Mountain* and *Milk*. *Brokeback Mountain* (a love story featuring two men) grossed more than $178 million worldwide and won four Golden Globe awards, including Best Motion Picture—Drama in 2005. *Milk* was based on the life story of Harvey Milk, the first openly gay man elected to public office. It was nominated for Best Motion Picture of the year and received Oscars for Best Actor (Sean Penn) and Best Screenplay (Dustin Lance Black) in 2008.

Homosexuals have also made some modest gains through court decisions, laws by progressive legislatures and city commissions, and acceptance of gays and lesbians by some religious leaders and a few congregations. But huge obstacles remain. The religious right refuses to yield on gay rights, making opposition to gay rights a defining issue. Gay issues such as the ordination of gay pastors and priests and the sanctification of same-sex unions continue to divide religious denominations and local churches.

This chapter began with the idea that whoever holds power in society has the power to define and label deviance. When examining sexual orientation, it is clear that powerful groups in society are currently in flux and disagreement over these definitions. On one hand, some progress has been made in certain areas of the law, the media, and the workplace, and President Obama has openly declared his support for same-sex marriage. On the other hand, major religious groups and politicians continue to disagree over these very issues, homophobia is still a problem in our schools, and the system of heteronormativity remains intact.

MySocLab ✔ Study and Review on MySocLab

▪ CHAPTER REVIEW

1. Unlike the status of most minorities, the minority status of gays, lesbians, and bisexuals is based on deviance from society's norms rather than on ascribed characteristics. This is due to the system of heteronormativity, where heterosexuality is viewed as the "normal" and expected sexual orientation, and all other orientations are viewed as deviant and inferior.

2. There are several important characteristics of social deviance: (a) It is socially created; (b) it is a relative, not an absolute, concept; (c) it is an integral part of all societies; (d) the powerful determine who or what is deviant; and (e) it creates an atmosphere in which deviants can be stigmatized for their behavior.

3. The response to same-sex sexual behavior varies by society and historical period. Although homosexuality is considered deviant behavior in contemporary U.S. society, it was not so considered in ancient Greece and Rome, nor was it deviant among some Native American tribes.

4. Defining homosexuality is not straightforward, as it may be defined based on feelings, desires, actions, or self-identity. Although there have been some studies pointing to biological origins of homosexuality, given the complex relationship between biology and environment there are no definitive conclusions. It is important to remember that (a) sexualities are shaped differently across time and location; and (b) the real issue is one of social justice, not origins.

5. Although the proportion of the population that is homosexual or bisexual is not known and is probably unknowable, the best estimate is that 3.5 percent of all adults self-identify as gay, lesbian, or bisexual.

In 2010, there were an estimated 902,997 same-sex unmarried partner households in the United States.

6. Lesbian and gay couples are similar to heterosexual couples in their quest for love and relationships. Gay men are more likely than lesbian women to have sex with someone other than their steady partners, a similarity shared with heterosexual males. Homosexual couples are much more likely than heterosexual couples to be egalitarian in sharing housework.

7. Variance from the societal norm of heterosexuality is not a social problem; the societal response to it is. Gays and lesbians confront ideological oppression stemming from traditional homophobic beliefs (especially religious). Gays and lesbians also confront legal oppression stemming from the law and court decisions.

8. In 2011, the "Don't Ask, Don't Tell" law that banned openly gay Americans from serving in the United States military was officially repealed, ending eighteen years of discrimination.

9. As of February 2013, nine states and the District of Columbia have adopted same-sex marriage laws. As a backlash to this progressive change, some states have adopted various forms of the Defense of Marriage Act, which defines marriage as the exclusive union of a man and woman. Public opinion polls show that support for same-sex marriage is growing, especially among those under age 30.

10. The challenge to change society's oppression based on sexual orientation began with the Stonewall Inn riot in 1969. Since then, gays and lesbians have organized communities, organized protests, and formed self-help and political lobbying organizations.

KEY TERMS

Heteronormativity. A system whereby heterosexuality is viewed as the "normal" sexual orientation, and all other orientations are seen as deviant and thus marginalized.

Deviance. Behavior that does not conform to social expectations.

Heterosexuality. Sexual orientation toward someone of the other sex.

Compulsory heterosexuality. Beliefs and practices that enforce heterosexual behavior as normal while stigmatizing other forms of sexual expression.

Homosexuality. Sexual orientation toward someone of the same sex.

Bisexuality. Sexual orientation toward or attraction to both sexes.

Miscegenation. Sexual relations or marriage between people of different races.

Stigma/stigmatized. Powerful negative social label that affects a person's social identity and self-concept.

Sexual preference. Person's choice regarding the sex of people to whom he or she is attracted.

Sexual orientation. Sexual attraction to the same or opposite sex is not a matter of choice but is determined by genetic or environmental factors.

Homophobia. Fear or loathing of homosexuality and homosexuals.

Employment Non-Discrimination Act. Modeled after Title VII of the Civil Rights Act of 1964, this federal bill (if passed) would provide basic protections against workplace discrimination on the basis of sexual orientation or gender identity.

Gay activists. Homosexuals who openly identify themselves as such and challenge society in an effort to eliminate the stigma and discrimination they face.

Disability and Ableism

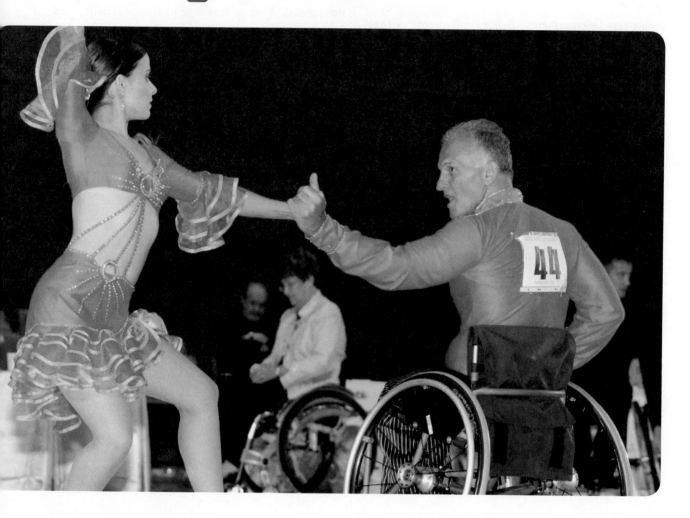

((• Listen to Chapter 11 on MySocLab

LEARNING OBJECTIVES

11.1 Understand the difference between the individual (medical) model of disability and the social model of disability.

11.2 Explain what constitutes a minority group.

11.3 Demonstrate how those with disabilities are vulnerable to abuse.

11.4 Describe the disability rights movement and the effects of the Americans with Disabilities Act of 1990.

This part of the book is devoted to various forms of inequality, examining categories of people experiencing discrimination, negative stereotypes, and powerlessness because of their being different from the dominant category in economic resources (the impoverished), racial classification (people of color), gender (females), and sexual orientation (gays and lesbians). This chapter turns our attention to another category of people defined as different and who constitute a minority group—those with physical, sensory, or cognitive impairments. This category is the largest minority group in the United States. People with disabilities, however, although sharing the characteristics of a minority group in most ways, differ in one significant way—it is a category in which most of us will eventually be included because of an accident, a virus, genetic heritage, or a degenerative disease.

The facts are these, according to the U.S. Census Bureau (2011b) and Centers for Disease Control and Prevention (n.d.):

- More than one in five U.S. residents (22.2 percent) has some form of impairment.
- Five percent of children 5 to 17 years old have disabilities.
- Twenty-seven percent of adults ages 18 to 64 have disabilities.
- Thirty-eight percent of adults age 65 and older have disabilities. This proportion increases rapidly with age as almost 75 percent of those 80 years and older have a disability. (See Table 11.1.)
- About 15 percent of people with a disability were born with it; 85 percent will experience a disabling condition in the course of their lives, usually from accidents, disease, environmental hazards, or criminal victimization (Russell 2000).

Social scientists, until recently, have largely ignored people with disabilities because their impairments were considered physical and psychic shortcomings, having little to do with the social. That assumption is false. The very definition of who is able and who is disabled is a social construction; the stereotypes and fears about people who are disabled are social constructions; and society creates financial, physical, and discriminatory barriers for people who are disabled.

TABLE 11.1
Prevalence of Disability among Adults, United States 2008

	Disability		No Disability	
	Number of People (in millions)*	Percentage of U.S. Population	Number of People (in millions)*	Percentage of U.S. Population
Total	50.6	22.2	117.2	77.8
Age				
18–44	15.3	13.5	96.2	86.5
45–64	20.8	27.4	55.1	72.6
65+	14.5	37.8	23.9	62.2
Sex				
Male	23.3	21.0	87.7	79.0
Female	27.3	23.4	89.5	76.6

*Slightly more than 1 in 4 of today's 20-year-olds will become disabled before reaching 67.

Source: Social Security Administration. 2011. "Social Security Basic Facts." Online: www.ssa.gov/pressoffice.htm.

Understand the difference between the individual (medical) model of disability and the social model of disability.

DEFINITIONS

The definition of disability influences how people relate to people whom they perceive to be disabled and how people who are disabled think of themselves. Because of the way disability is typically defined, people with disabilities may be feared, distrusted, pitied, overprotected, and patronized (Barton 1996:8).

Individual Model of Disability

The **individual model of disability** (also known as the *medical model of disability*) defines disability in terms of some physiological impairment due to genetic heritage, accident, or disease. The commonly held view is that since the focus of disability is on physical, behavioral, psychological, cognitive, and sensory tragedy, the problem is situated within the disabled individual (Gilson and Depoy 2000:208). The federal government, for example, defines *disability* as any physical or mental condition that substantially limits one or more major life activities and *disabled* as anyone who is regarded as having such an impairment. A person who is disabled might have difficulty performing activities such as personal care, walking, seeing, hearing, speaking, learning, or working (Taub and Fanflick 2000:13). The problem with focusing on the physical or mental impairment of people is that individuals are defined as deficient, inferior, and incomplete because they do not conform to what the majority in society define as "normal." Although some people with disabilities internalize these negative attitudes about themselves, others reject being defined as abnormal and thus dismiss the medical model as the dominant model of disability (Llewellyn and Hogan 2000).

Because the focus is on the individual, the goal of rehabilitation is for health practitioners to overcome, or at least minimize, the negative consequences of an individual's disability by addressing the person's special needs and personal difficulties. If possible, these health professionals would like to return disabled individuals to the "normal" condition of being able bodied. Although these goals seem appropriate, they make people with disabilities dependent on a vast army of allied professionals who dominate their lives (Barnes, Mercer, and Shakespeare 1999:25). Moreover, adaptation

The probability of disability increases with age with almost 75 percent of those 80 years and older having a disability.

to the environment—rather than changing the social arrangements that make life difficult for people with disabilities—is stressed during rehabilitation. The concentration on the biology of disability also defines people by only one dimension, ignoring their other qualities. To counteract this problem, we use the phrase "person with a disability" rather than "a disabled person," thereby reorienting our social construction so that it puts the human being first and the impairment second, rather than making the impairment the defining characteristic (Linton 1998:13).*

Finally, a note of caution. People with disabilities are a heterogeneous category. Although most have visible impairments, others have invisible disabilities such as chronic pain or dyslexia. Those who cannot hear face different societally induced problems than those who cannot see or those people who must use wheelchairs. Thus, as we discuss people with disabilities, we must remember that the people involved are complex, varying by type of disability and their other social locations (e.g., gender, race, social class, sexual orientation).

Social Model of Disability

The **social model of disability**, while acknowledging the biological conditions of disability, challenges the notion that disability is primarily a medical category. From this perspective, the real problem with physical and mental impairment is not physical but social: It is the way people with able bodies view people with disabilities and the institutionalization of these views that are the genuine handicaps (Duncan 2001; Oliver 1996). For adherents of the social model, the consequence of the power to define the identity of the disabled by professionals results in the disempowerment, marginalization, and dependency of people with disabilities (Barton 1996:9). The limited physical access, limited access to resources, and negative attitudes create barriers that interfere with the potential of people with disabilities to actualize their desired roles (Gilson and Depoy 2000). Furthermore, it is the way that people with disabilities are oppressed by societal views of normality. In effect, then, society disables people. Consider, for example, the argument by a man with a disability:

> [We] are disabled by buildings that are not designed to admit us, and this in turn leads to a whole range of further disablements, regarding our education, our chances for gaining employment, our social lives and so on. However, this argument is usually rejected, precisely because to accept it involves recognizing the extent to which we are not merely unfortunate, but are directly oppressed by a hostile social environment. (Brisenden 1986:176)

With the incredible medical, technological, and manufacturing advances available, many people made dysfunctional by infection, injury, or deleterious genes need not remain so if social arrangements are employed to address these deficits. Consequently, when the disability is not addressed, its persistence is a social rather than a biological phenomenon (Silvers 1998:16).

Congruent with this perspective, the Union of Physically Impaired against Segregation (UPIAS) in the United Kingdom promotes this definition of disability: "Disability is the disadvantage or restriction of activity caused by a contemporary social organization which takes no or little account of people who have physical impairments and

---

*The naming of people with disabilities is a complicated issue. On the one hand, many people with disabilities have wanted to keep disability as a characteristic of the individual as opposed to the defining characteristic. Yet beginning in the early 1990s, the term "disabled people" became popular among disability rights activists. Rather than keeping disability as a secondary characteristic, *disabled* became a marker of identity that they wanted to highlight as they protested for social change (Linton 1998:13).

thus excludes them from participation in the mainstream of social activities" (UPIAS 1976:3–4). The social model of disability redirects attention away from the individual and places the problem back on the collective responsibility of society (Llewellyn and Hogan 2000:159). The social model focuses on the experience of disability. It considers a wide range of social, economic, and political factors and conditions such as family circumstances, financial support, education, employment, housing, transportation, the built environment, disabling barriers and attitudes in society, and the impact of government policies and welfare support systems (Barnes, Mercer, and Shakespeare 1999:31).

Adherents of the social model see the goal of rehabilitation as being much different from the individual model. Rather than changing a person with a disability, a social model removes the social and environmental barriers to full participation (Gilson and Depoy 2000:208).

An academic offshoot of the social model is the area of "disability studies" (see Campbell 2009). This interdisciplinary concentration does not view disability as something inherently wrong but rather recasts disability as a difference that should be valued (Gray 2011:694).

Toward a More Complete Definition of Disability

The focus of the medical model is on **impairment** (the state of being mentally or physically challenged) and **disability**. The social model, in contrast, concentrates of the social impediments experienced by those with disabilities. The assumptions of both the medical and social models of disability are contradictory. Taken alone, each of these perspectives fosters a one-sided and therefore incomplete and faulty perception and interpretation of disability and people with disabilities (Shakespeare 2006). A synthesis that combines the best of each model will aid our understanding and allow for an acceptable definition.

The individual (medical) model is correct in that there is an **ontological truth** (a universal and undeniable reality) to the claim that disabilities result from some physiological or mental impairment. It follows, then, that disabled people do need medical support at specific points in their lives (Barton 1996:9). But this emphasis on locating problems and solutions within the disabled person is only half of the equation because it overlooks the role of society in defining and creating barriers for people with disabilities. The social model points to the very real (ontological) social barriers for most people with disabilities.

The definition of disability that we use combines the insights of the individual and social models: Disability, then, refers to a reduced ability to perform tasks one would normally do at a given stage of life that are exacerbated by the individual and institutional discrimination that people with disabilities encounter.

11.2 Explain what constitutes a minority group.

PEOPLE WITH DISABILITIES AS A MINORITY GROUP

Disability shares a number of characteristics common to the social constructions of race, sex and gender, and sexual orientation, thus making it a minority group as they are.* These characteristics are (1) being defined as different; (2) derogatory names; (3) their

*There are several ways to view people with disabilities. We use the minority groups model because of its (1) emphasis on social and economic discrimination; (2) consistency with our structural emphasis that explains systematic exclusion on the basis of gender, class, race, and sexual orientation; and (3) emphasis on social factors rather than biological and cultural ones (Block, Balcazar, and Keys 2001).

"differentness" as a master status; (4) categorization, stigma, and stereotypes; (5) exclusion and segregations; (6) the matrix of domination; and (7) discrimination.

Defined as Different

Minority groups are socially constructed categories. Which categories have minority status varies among societies and over time within a society. Society assigns some categories of people—in the United States, these categories are races other than Caucasian, certain ethnic groups, women, alternative sexual identities to the norm of heterosexuality, and people with disabilities—to minority status. The minority is composed of people with similar characteristics that are defined as significantly different from the dominant group. These characteristics are salient: They are visible, although not necessarily physical, and they make a difference. Whites dominate Blacks, Whites dominate Latinos, men dominate women, heterosexuals dominate homosexuals, and the able bodied dominate people with disabilities.

Derogatory Naming

Naming is not a neutral process; the names given to the members of minority groups by the majority have enormous symbolic significance that contributes to and perpetuates the dominance of the majority (Eitzen and Baca Zinn 1989; Hall 1985). These pejorative names belittle, trivialize, exclude, diminish, deprecate, and demean. In essence, pejorative names not only put the minority "down" but also separate and segregate. Just as "boy" can be blatantly offensive to minority men, so "girl" can have comparable patronizing and demeaning implications for women (Miller and Swift 1980:71). Gays and lesbians are called "queers" and "faggots," terms that clearly separate them from the heterosexual majority.

Consider the implications of names for people with disabilities, such as "invalid," "cripple," "freak," "gimp," "vegetable," "dumb," "deformed," "handicapped," and "retard." These labels imply not only impairment but also a lack of worth, marginality, and their dependence on the "able" (Barton 1996; Swain, French, and Cameron 2003:11–19).

Minority as a Master Status

Although people have many statuses simultaneously, typically, one status is dominant. This is known as a **master status**. The master status may be imposed by others, or it may be internalized by the individual, with exceptional significance for social identity. The master status of minority group members is the characteristic (or set of characteristics) that distinguish them from the majority. That is, African Americans or gays or homeless families are known and identified by others foremost by their race, sexual orientation, or impoverishment. Disability can be and often is a master status, as people frequently perceive those with disabilities first in terms of their disability and only second as individuals. That is, an impairment such as blindness or using a wheelchair is seen as the most salient part of a person's identity and therefore trumps all other statuses, such as occupation, educational attainment, and income level.

Categorization, Stigma, and Stereotypes

Not only are minority members singled out by their master status, but they also encounter the negative stereotypes and beliefs that accompany their defining characteristics. In other words, being a minority is not only a master status, but it is also a master status with a stigma. The stigma originates in the portrayals of people with disabilities in literature, movies, and television. Consider, for example, the people portrayed in the movies *The Hunchback of Notre Dame*, *The Phantom of the Opera*, *The King's Speech*, or *My Left Foot*. In this last example, Daniel Day-Lewis won an Academy Award for his portrayal of the Irish writer Christy Brown who overcame his cerebral palsy to write and paint with his foot. These portrayals of people with disabilities raise two issues. First, should a nondisabled actor be given such a part rather than a person with cerebral palsy? Second, is Hollywood sensitive to people with disabilities and not given to treating them in terms of stereotypes? In an enlightened version, the character with a disability would be depicted as a human with a disability and not as a victim of a disability (Rundle 2011).

A **stigma** is an attribute that is socially devalued and disgraced. The late sociologist Erving Goffman described stigma as a spoiled identity with negative consequences. Stigma implies being tainted with a shortcoming, or a failing, or a handicap. Because these individuals are defined as undesirable, they are subject to discrimination, including avoidance. Moreover, we tend to impute a wide range of undesirable attributes on the basis of the original stigma (Goffman 1963:3–5).

Some disabilities engender more stigma than others. In general, people with physical disabilities are less likely to be stigmatized than those with mental disabilities. Consider, for example, the difference between an older person with a broken hip compared to one with Alzheimer's disease.

Minority group members are stigmatized. The majority defines certain characteristics as different and abnormal and then discriminates against those in the category defined as inferior. Thus, some people are "in," whereas others are defined as "out," or they are either "us" or "them." In effect, the minority is defined as "other" because the members have characteristics that differ from the majority. The definition is simplified by making the distinctions binary. "'Race' becomes Black or White, 'gender' becomes male or female, 'sexual orientation' becomes gay or straight, and people are either disabled or normal" (Gordon and Rosenblum 2001:12). In each instance, the side defined as "other" is considered not only different but also deficient.

The disabled confront the dichotomous comparison with the able bodied, where they always come up short in one of two ways. Many internalize the inadequacy society regularly ascribes to them, thinking of themselves as incomplete or broken. Others reject the dichotomy dictated by society.

The dominant members of society perceive disability as a medical matter, associating disability with physiological, anatomical, or mental "defects." Viewed in this way, those with physical and mental impairments seem not only different but also lacking the "normal" interests and concerns that occupy others of their social class, race, gender, age, and gender orientation. In short, their "otherness" moves them to the margins of society as "inferiors."

The disabled, therefore, confront not only the challenges of living with their conditions but also the challenges of inequality characterized by ableism. The short definition of **ableism** is discrimination in favor of the able bodied (Tullock 1993). Implied in this definition is the notion that the abilities or characteristics of people with disabilities are inferior to able people (Linton 1998:9). As an example, research shows that those who murder children with disabilities are punished less severely by the criminal justice system than those who murder able children (Unnithan 1994).

Implicit in the ideology of ableism that permeates U.S. society is the belief that disability is an individual problem, susceptible to individual solutions. This frees the nondisabled to ignore or minimize social issues of accessibility, accommodation, and personhood (Duncan 2001).

View on
MySocLab Figure:
Needs of People with
Mental Disorders

Read on
MySocLab Document:
Hoops and Wheels

Exclusion and Segregation

Stigmatized race, sex/gender, and sexual orientation categories have traditionally been excluded from full participation in society by institutional barriers or custom. Historically, racial minorities have been excluded through Jim Crow segregation, Supreme Court rulings (e.g., *Plessy v. Ferguson*, which gave "separate but equal" facilities legal authority), and legislation that denied voting and other civil rights. Although recent laws have outlawed blatant discrimination by race, *de facto* segregation still exists in residential housing, in schools, and in private clubs. Women were once property of their husbands. Women today are underrepresented in the professions and in leadership positions in government, business, and religious organizations. Gays are not allowed as leaders in the Boy Scouts. Same-sex marriages are illegal in most states, and the right of gays and lesbians to adopt is difficult and in some states impossible because of legal barriers.

Historically, people with disabilities were often separated by segregated housing, sheltered workshops, and occasionally, in attics and basements to hide a family's shame. They have also been separated in nursing homes, asylums, and hospitals for "incurables." In the past, children with disabilities were separated from their "able" classmates in separate "special education" classrooms. However, the Individuals with Disabilities Education Act (IDEA), originally passed as the Education for All Handicapped Children Act in 1975, now requires that children be educated in the "least restrictive environment." This requirement generally has been interpreted to mean that children with disabilities should be "mainstreamed" in classrooms with typically developing children. Although inclusion is required by law, many children continue to be segregated in special education classes. Sometimes, of course, "special education" is reasonable, allowing educators to be more responsive to the "special" needs of children who cannot see, hear, think, or move as well as others. There are drawbacks, however, as those segregated as "different" are sometimes objects of abuse by other students. "Special education" teachers may be either more attentive to the conditions of their students than to their scholarship and/or they may have reduced expectations for these students, resulting in a negative self-fulfilling prophecy. The evidence is that children with disabilities who have been in segregated schooling are, in general, less well prepared than other children to exercise the skills and knowledge in the basic subjects of English, math, and science (Silvers 1998:24).

Despite the Americans with Disabilities Act, which requires the elimination of architectural barriers, many still remain, and thus people with disabilities are often separated from mainstream society by the lack of access to public transportation or by architectural barriers.

It does not matter if policy makers intend their policies to discriminate—what matters are the consequences of their actions. "Stairs, curbs, or small-print signs hung over doorways make admission nearly impossible. They may lack discriminatory intent, but they have the effect nonetheless" (Gordon and Rosenblum 2001:12).

Matrix of Domination

The hierarchies of stratification—class, race, gender, and sexual orientation—place socially constructed groups, and the individuals and families assigned to those groups, in different social locations (Baca Zinn, Eitzen, and Wells 2011). Placement in these hierarchies determines to what extent one will have or not have the rewards and resources of society. These are also systems of power and domination, as those from dominant race, class, gender, and sexuality groups play a part in and benefit from the oppression of subordinates.

Read on
MySocLab Document:
On Being Sane in Insane
Places

These stratification hierarchies are interrelated. People of color and women, for example, have fewer occupational choices than do White males. People of color and women typically earn less income for the work they do, resulting in advantage for White males. Thus, these systems of inequality intersect to form a **matrix of domination** in which each of us exists (Collins 1990). These intersections of oppression have important implications.

> First, people experience race, class, gender, and sexuality differently depending on their social location in these structures of inequality. For example, people of the same race will experience race differently depending on their location in the class structure as poor, working class, professional/managerial class, or unemployed and their location in the gender structure as male or female and in the sexuality system as heterosexual or homosexual.
>
> Second, class, race, and gender are components of both social structure and social interaction. As a result, individuals because of their social locations experience different forms of privilege and subordination. In short, these intersecting forms of inequality produce both oppression and opportunity.
>
> A third implication of the inequality matrix has to do with the relational nature of dominance and subordination. Power is embedded in each system of stratification, determining whether one is dominant or subordinate. The intersectional nature of hierarchies means that power differentials are linked in systematic ways, reinforcing power differentials across hierarchies. (Eitzen and Baca Zinn 2001:238–239; see also Baca Zinn and Dill 1996)

An important insight from this matrix of domination approach is that discrimination is more than additive. To be an African American lesbian with a disability, for example, is to be marginalized and experience discrimination in simultaneous and multiple ways. As one woman put it, "As a black disabled woman, I cannot compartmentalize or separate aspects of my identity in this way. The collective experience of my race, disability and gender are what shape and inform my life" (Hill 1994:7).

Thus, we cannot study classism, racism, sexism, homophobia, ableism, or any other oppression in isolation from each other (Block, Balcazar, and Keys 2001; Oliver 1996:37).

Discrimination

By definition, minority group members experience discrimination. They are the last to be hired and the first to be fired (e.g., the unemployment rate for African Americans is typically twice that for Whites). Racial minorities experience problems involving fairness in the criminal justice system, in obtaining loans, in housing, in schools, and in other institutions. So, too, do people with disabilities find discrimination throughout their lives. Some examples follow (from Russell 1998, 2000):

- Forty-seven percent of applicants genetically screened for insurance are denied health insurance because of "defects."
- Thirty-four percent of adults with disabilities live in households with an annual income of less than $15,000, compared to 12 percent of those without disabilities.
- Seventy percent of working-age disabled people are unemployed, and 79 percent report that they want a job. In addition, for those who are employed, many are underemployed in low-level, low-paying jobs.
- On average, workers with a disability make 85 percent (for men) and 70 percent (for women) of what their coworkers without disabilities earn. When people who are disabled are also Latino, African American, or Native American, there is an increased chance for unemployment and, for those who are employed, an even greater difference in wages than for their nondisabled co-workers (Kendall 2001).
- Under federal labor law, employers can pay people with disabilities less than the minimum wage, if they can show that the workers' disability makes them less

productive than able workers. This has led to exploitation, with some workers with disabilities receiving just 45 cents an hour (Ervin 2011).

The discrimination that people with disabilities experience is related to how they are perceived by the rest of society. If society is convinced that disabled people cannot have good lives, then there is no reason to invest in equal education, equal access, and equal opportunity for them (see the "Voices" panel "Your Fears, My Realities").

Voices

YOUR FEARS, MY REALITIES

Most of us are morally certain that we're not prejudiced against people with disabilities. Don't we root for Christopher Reeve and Jerry's Kids with our hearts and minds and checkbooks? (Many disabled people think we shouldn't, but that's another matter.)

Didn't we cheer for Jeannie Van-Velkinburgh when she was shot and paralyzed by Nathan Thill? Aren't we genuine admirers of Stephen Hawking and Muhammad Ali? How could we discriminate?

To understand disability discrimination, look close to home. Its most transparent feature is that it is caused by fear. We are the living proof that minds and bodies can go haywire and that it can happen to anyone at any time. Some people aren't ready for that news, so they react to us with overt anxiety or hostility.

But it's more subtle forms of discrimination that harm us the most. To cite one ubiquitous example, every family newspaper in the country runs occasional profiles of people with disabilities. They're usually found in the Living section, and they're usually fawning.

They marvel that we can keep our faith in the face of adversity, graduate from college, raise kids or maintain a generous attitude. If we appear to overcome our disabilities—something that's not really feasible for most of us—so much the better. Then we're brave, we're true, we inspire.

The trouble with these feel-good stories is that they become archetypal. By celebrating a single achiever as newsworthy and remarkable, they confirm society's low expectations for all other people with disabilities. Doesn't the exception prove the rule? And aren't we brave because we live lives that readers think they couldn't or wouldn't live themselves? Don't we inspire because we make them feel grateful that they're not like us?

The reading public loves our imagined triumphs of mind over matter, but not our real issues.

It loves us when we're docile, asexual, and childlike, but not when we vent our anger that the deck is stacked against us. It loved Van-Velkinburgh's courage at the crime scene and her readiness to move on with her life, but loved her less after a court appearance when she proved herself to be a real, mercurial person rather than patience on a monument. Real people are harder to deal with than idealized fictions.

After my injury in 1968, my business partner told me he would have killed himself under similar circumstances. Even my mother briefly toyed with the idea that I might be better off dead than disabled. "If I were paralyzed," people still tell me, "I couldn't handle it."

"Nonsense," I say, "you'd cope with it fine." But you seldom believe me. You think I'm still being brave, painting a happy face on the unspeakable. Disability discrimination is about your fears, not my realities.

Discrimination deepens when an entire nation takes this view of disability. If society is convinced that we can't have good lives, it's slow to invest in equal education, equal access, and equal opportunity. And even though most people know at heart that sooner or later they're likely to become disabled themselves, they're slow to act on readily achievable solutions because they're scared to death of disability's stigma. This is disability discrimination, and it's largely unconscious.

The result of this attitude—as successive Harris polls since the early 1980s have consistently shown—is that people with disabilities are the poorest minority in America. We have less money, less employment, less education, less transportation, less recreation, less of almost anything you can think of. We're the have-nots of this country.

It's not because people hate us. It's because they assume that our lives are so terrible that any effort to level the playing field is futile. And it's not because disability is so tough. It's because our cultural bias perpetuates the inequities.

Source: Barry Corbet. 2000. "Your Fears, My Realities." *Denver Post* (August 23):11B. Copyright © the Estate of Barry Corbet.

11.3 Demonstrate
how those with
disabilities are
vulnerable to abuse.

ISSUES OF GENDER, SEXUAL BEHAVIOR, AND FERTILITY

Although people with disabilities deal with a number of social barriers, our discussion here is limited to sexual relationships and related issues. We focus on sexuality because it demonstrates so clearly how social factors often negatively affect people with disabilities.

Gender Stereotyping

The foregoing section showed that people with disabilities are marginalized and stigmatized in U.S. society. This occurs, in part, because women and men with disabilities do not measure up to the cultural beliefs for each gender. For the physically disabled, their bodies are perceived as unattractive. The bodies of physically disabled men do not allow them to demonstrate the socially valuable characteristics of toughness, competitiveness, and ability (Messner 1992). **Hegemonic** (of the dominant belief system) masculinity privileges men who are strong, aggressive, independent, and self-reliant. But men who are physically disabled are perceived to have polar opposite traits; they are treated as weak, passive, pitiful, and dependent. Men with physical disabilities may cope with the fundamental incongruity by constructing their own sense of masculinity (Gerschick and Miller 2001). They may do all they can to meet society's definition of masculinity by becoming as athletic and competitive as possible (e.g., lifting weights, playing wheelchair basketball, participating in the paralympics). Others may redefine masculinity to fit their own unique characteristics (e.g., achieving a sense of independence by controlling those around them; redefining gender in terms of emotional relations rather than the emphasis on the physical). Still others may reject society's standards by either denying masculinity's importance in their life or by creating alternative masculine identities and subcultures that provide them with a supportive environment.

As difficult as dealing with disability is for men, it is as burdensome if not more so for women. Women with physical disabilities, similar to men, do not measure up to the cultural ideals of what it is to be a woman. Consequently, many think of themselves as asexual or unattractive. Many of these women feel undermined by a society that defines a woman's sexual attractiveness in terms of physical fitness and physical beauty, characteristics that are impossible for many of them to reach. Nancy Mairs writes about her physicality in this light:

> My shoulders droop and my pelvis thrusts forward as I try to balance myself upright, throwing my frame into a bony S. As a result of contractures, one shoulder is higher than the other and I carry one arm bent in front of me, the fingers curled into a claw. My left arm and leg have wasted into pipe stems, and I try always to keep them covered. When I think about how my body must look to others, especially to men, to whom I have been trained to display myself, I feel ludicrous, even loathsome. (1992:63)

Women with disabilities are disadvantaged over men with impairments when it comes to occupying traditional roles. Men with disabilities are more likely to be employed than women with disabilities, even filling socially powerful male roles, as did President Franklin D. Roosevelt (who used a wheelchair and crutches because of polio) or Representative James Langevin of Rhode Island, who in 2000 became the first quadriplegic elected to Congress, or former Senator Max Cleland of Georgia, who is missing both legs and an arm. Disabled women, on the other hand, are often even denied access to traditional female roles, as ableist and sexist stereotypes combine in much of the public, making it difficult even for the friends and relatives of disabled women to envision them as functional wives and mothers (Hanna and Rogovsky 1991).

In heterosexual relationships, men with disabilities are more likely to maintain their relationships, whereas women with disabilities are more likely to be abandoned (Shakespeare 1996:202).

Sexual Relationships

Increasingly, people with disabilities have positive and fulfilled sexual lives. Many form strong and happy relationships with other people with disabilities or with non-disabled partners. The growing disability rights movement (a topic discussed further later in this chapter), with its emphases on removing social barriers and social oppression, is important in this regard because it has helped provide people with disabilities a positive identity by working together to achieve common goals. The resulting activism has opened many possibilities as disabled people end their isolation, engage in political acts, and make friends with others in the movement. But sexual problems remain, not because of individual incapacity but because of prejudice, discrimination, and structural barriers (this section is taken primarily from Shakespeare 1996:192–209).

- **Assumptions about People with Disabilities: Asexual, Unlovely, and Undesirable.** Among the beliefs of nondisabled people about people with disabilities are a number that center on sexual difference:

  That we are asexual, or at best inadequate.

  That we cannot ovulate, menstruate, conceive or give birth; have orgasms, erections, [or] ejaculations; or impregnate.

  That if we are not married or in a long-term relationship, it is because no one wants us and not through our personal choice to remain single or live alone.

  That if we do not have a child, it must be the cause of abject sorrow to us and likewise never through choice.

  That any able-bodied person who marries us must have done so for one of the following suspicious motives and never through love: desire to hide his/her own inadequacies in the disabled partner's obvious ones; an altruistic and saintly desire to sacrifice their lives to our care; neurosis of some sort; or plain old-fashioned fortune-hunting.

  That if we have a partner who is also disabled, we chose each other for no other reason, and not for any other qualities we might possess. When we choose "our own kind" in this way, the able-bodied world feels relieved, until of course we wish to have children; then we're seen as irresponsible. (Morris 1991:20ff)

  Add to this list the assumptions discussed earlier that disabled people do not meet the societal standards for beauty and physical attractiveness. Also, "just as public displays of same-sex love are strongly discouraged, so two disabled people being intimate in public will experience social disapproval" (Shakespeare 1996:193).

- **Denial of Sex.** People with disabilities are often not welcome in nightclubs and other social venues where sex is on the agenda. They may not be admitted to a gay or straight facility because they are defined as "not sexy" and are believed to detract from the sexuality of the scene (i.e., their impairment was alienating to other patrons). Clubs designed for sexual interaction are often not designed for the disabled. They may be basements or other inaccessible buildings with steps, narrow hallways, flashing lights, and loud noise, which act as barriers for the disabled. Some lesbians with disabilities may find it difficult to meet with other lesbians because they often meet in inaccessible outdoor or sporting activities.

People who live in day centers, group homes, adult foster care homes, or other residential environments for people with disabilities may encounter policies and staff members who often deny their patients the right to form emotional or sexual relationships.

- **Difficulty in Finding Partners.**   People with disabilities often face barriers to access the environments where nondisabled people make contacts that lead to sexual encounters or romantic relationships. They may be blocked by inaccessible public transport, inadequate income, and inaccessible pubs and clubs, making it difficult to interact with potential partners. The workplace is a likely place for such encounters, but many disabled people lack access to paid employment. People with disabilities may also find churches, another common place for meeting potential partners, inaccessible because of physical or attitudinal barriers.

  Computer chat rooms or advertisements in lonely hearts newspaper columns provide an option to those with physical mobility difficulties. But these options are not usually accessible to people with visual impairments (the exception is software that "talks"). Moreover, the language used in these venues emphasizes one's physical attractiveness, thus disqualifying people with disabilities if they are honest about their impairments. This problem is minimized in the personal advertisements section of disability-related publications, where honesty is expected and the chances for rejection, so common in nondisabled settings, are reduced significantly.

  People who become disabled later in life often find that impairment interrupts their social networks and personal relationships, leaving them isolated. This is more likely for women with disabilities than for men with disabilities.

Physical and Sexual Abuse

The evidence is clear that people with disabilities, both children and adults, are more likely to be abused physically and sexually than those without disabilities (Mitchell and Buchele-Ash 2000). Because of the social context and the social opportunity, people with disabilities may experience quantitatively more abuse than the nondisabled (Shakespeare 1996:203).

> There are the ones who are chosen because they cannot speak of the horror. There are the ones who are chosen because they cannot run away, and there is nowhere to run. There are the ones who are chosen because their very lives depend on not fighting back. There are the ones who are chosen because there is no one for them to tell. There are the ones who are chosen because no one has even taught them the words. There are the ones who are chosen because society chooses to believe that, after all, they don't really have any sexuality, so it can't hurt them. (Cross 1994:165)

Those most vulnerable to physical and sexual abuse are deaf people who cannot speak and people with learning difficulties who may be lured into situations without understanding the consequences (for a chilling account of sexual assault of a girl with learning difficulties by athletes from her high school, see Lefkowitz 1998). The abuse may occur in institutional settings where staff members or other patients may take advantage of the vulnerable. In these settings, patients lack communication with the outside world, and the youngest or the most impaired are the most likely victims of those who have institutional power or personal power over them. Abuse can take other forms in institutions that are more like warehouses than welcoming environments. In such instances, the goal of profit surpasses patient care, resulting in savings through such activities as the overuse of drugs to control patients, inadequate health-care, thermostats set too low in the winter and too high in the summer, cheap food, and other forms of neglect (Press and Washburn 2000; K. Thomas 2001).

The Abortion Issue

The primary rationale for prenatal testing is to determine whether the fetus is "normal" or will result in a child with a disability. When the test affirms that possibility, the prospective parents have the choice and the legal right to terminate the pregnancy if they wish. For example, when a test reveals that a fetus has an extra twenty-first chromosome—the hallmark of Down syndrome—an estimated 90 percent of parents choose to terminate the pregnancy (Carmichael 2008). For a poignant argument against aborting a fetus with the extra chromosome, see the essay by columnist George F. Will about his son, Jon, who has Down syndrome (Will 2007:72).

This issue is a thorny one for those who favor a woman's right to choose (and we are among them) if we examine the ramifications of aborting "disabled" fetuses from the perspective of people with disabilities (these arguments are primarily from Hershey 2000).

Foremost, when a woman chooses to abort a fetus rather than to give birth to a disabled child, she accepts society's negative views about people with disabilities:

> She is making a statement about the desirability or the relative worth of such a child. Abortion based on disability results from, and in turn strengthens, certain beliefs: children with disabilities (and by implication adults with disabilities) are a burden to family and society; life with a disability is scarcely worth living; preventing the birth is an act of kindness; women who bear disabled children have failed. (Hershey 2000:558)

In short, the choice to abort a disabled fetus is a rejection of children and adults who have disabilities.

Second, most people with disabilities, despite the manifold medical and social difficulties associated with their conditions, affirm that their lives are meaningful and worthwhile. Laura Hershey, for example, has a rare neuromuscular condition. She must rely on a motorized wheelchair for mobility, a voice-activated computer for writing, and the assistance of Medicaid-funded attendants for daily needs such as dressing, bathing, eating, and going to the bathroom. She also has a house, a career, a partner, and a community of friends with and without disabilities. She says,

> My life of disability has not been easy or carefree. But in measuring the quality of my life, other factors—education, friends, and meaningful work, for example—have been decisive. If I were asked for an opinion on whether to bring a child into the world, knowing she would have the same limitations and opportunities I have had, I would not hesitate to say, "Yes." I know that many women do not have the resources my parents had. Many lack education, are poor, or are without the support of friends and family. The problems created by these circumstances are intensified with a child who is disabled. No woman should have a child she can't handle or doesn't want. Having said that, I must also say that all kinds of women raise healthy, self-respecting children with disabilities, without unduly compromising their own lives. (2000:559)

A similar defense for life is given by Harriet McBryde Johnson:

> Are we "worse off"? I don't think so. Not in any meaningful sense. There are too many variables. For those of us with congenital conditions, disability shapes all we are. Those disabled later in life adapt. We take constraints that no one would choose and build rich and satisfying lives within them. We enjoy pleasures other people enjoy, and pleasures peculiarly our own. We have something the world needs. (2003:53)

Third, in addition to traditional genetic testing, the Human Genome Project, which maps DNA, can predict hundreds, perhaps thousands, of disorders before birth and, in doing so, has the potential to eliminate hereditary diseases in a generation. It also presents a danger. Many in the disabled community fear that the widespread use of these genetic tools and abortion for the purpose of eliminating disability could inaugurate a new eugenics movement. Two examples from the twentieth century show how governments have viewed the lives of people with disabilities to have little value and indicated they should be extinguished (Silvers 1998):

- A 1939 German decree authorized physicians to put to death impaired persons who could not be cured. In the next two years, about 200,000 physically and mentally impaired children and adults were killed because they were judged to have "lives unworthy of life."
- As late as the 1930s, over half of the states in the United States had laws encouraging sterilization of people with disabilities, typically those with developmental disabilities, epilepsy, the blind, and the deaf.

Abortion, then, presents a major quandary for feminists who defend the right for women to choose, a right that can conflict with efforts to promote acceptance, equality, and respect for people with disabilities. Such is the dilemma of Laura Hershey, cited earlier, a prochoice feminist who is also disabled. She offers this solution to a highly complex issue:

> I wouldn't deny any woman the right to choose abortion. But I would issue a challenge to all women making a decision whether to give birth to a child who may have disabilities. The challenge is this: Consider all the relevant information, not just the medical facts. More important than a particular diagnosis are the conditions awaiting a child—community acceptance, access to buildings and transportation, civil rights protection, and opportunities for education and employment. Where these things are lacking or inadequate, consider joining the movement to change them. In many communities, adults with disabilities and parents of disabled children have developed powerful advocacy coalitions. I recognize that, having weighed all the factors, some will decide they cannot give birth to a child with disabilities. It pains me, but I acknowledge their right and their choice. (2000:563)

AGENCY

11.4 Describe the disability rights movement and the effects of the Americans with Disabilities Act of 1990.

People with disabilities have always had to acclimate to environments and social settings that were designed for the able bodied. As we have seen, they experience discrimination in housing, education, and work. Equal access is frequently denied because of transportation and architectural barriers in streets and buildings. Added to these structural barriers to equality are the stings of widespread stereotypes that demean them as inferior, unattractive, asexual, and pitiful. Their frustration with unequal access and discrimination has led many people with disabilities to become active in the disability rights movement. In joining with others, their feelings of isolation became feelings of a common bond and empowerment. This section focuses on their collective efforts and the results.

Disability Rights Movement

Explore on MySocLab Activity: Barriers to Full Participation: Limited Abilities

A **social movement** is a group that develops an organization and tactics to promote or resist social change. Its members share a belief system that defines common grievances and goals and group identity. The disability rights movement comprises a wide variety of individuals as well as local and national organizations with a common goal—equal rights for people who are disabled. It is a loose structure of organizations because many focus exclusively on people with particular disabilities (e.g., the National Federation of the Blind, the Disabled American Veterans, the National Association of the Deaf). But this network, although seemingly lacking unity, is united by the overarching objectives of empowerment and collective rights—human, civil, and legal—for people with disabilities.

Social movements capture the imagination of potential adherents when social conditions are right. Such was the case for people with disabilities when they observed the successes of other social protest movements such as civil rights in the 1950s and 1960s, the antiwar movement of the 1960s, and various oppressed groups such as women and gays/lesbians. People who once were resigned to living their lives in isolation came to believe that in joining with others they could make a difference as they saw protests and heard leaders argue that disability was not their fault but rather the failure of the political system to acknowledge their rights as human beings and to equality in society.

The disability rights movement began in the late 1960s with local organizing by Ed Roberts at the University of California at Berkeley and Judy Heumann in New York City, both of whom were postpolio quadriplegics. Roberts was instrumental in getting the Berkeley campus to provide students with disabilities peer counseling and support to gain access to university programs and housing (for a history of the fight for disabled rights, see Switzer 2003). By 1972, Roberts and others founded the Berkeley Center for Independent Living, in an apartment, which was the forerunner to the independent living movement, and its unofficial newspaper for the disability rights movement—the *Disability Rag* (now called *Ragged Edge*). Meanwhile, Judy Heumann filed a lawsuit when she was denied teaching certification because of her disability. Beginning with this action, others joined to form an organization called Disabled in Action (DIA), which had the goal to break down barriers to full societal participation of people with disabilities. In 1972, DIA, with 1,500 members, organized protests targeted at inaccessible public buildings, the Jerry Lewis telethon (which they believed perpetuated demeaning stereotypes of people with disabilities), and media organizations that either neglected or provided prejudicial coverage of disability issues. This group also blocked traffic in front of Richard Nixon's 1972 New York campaign headquarters to protest his veto of the Rehabilitation Act.

People with disabilities have organized successful protests to make their case to the public and policy makers.

Jack Ziegler/The New Yorker Collection/www.cartoonbank.com

View on
MySocLab Figure:
Children with Disabilities
Receiving SSI

Congruent with the politics of the times (e.g., the war on poverty, passage of the voting rights act), policy makers became more receptive to the civil rights of people with disabilities. Congress, for example, passed the Rehabilitation Act of 1973, which prohibited government agencies and contractors from discriminating against people with disabilities. In 1975, Congress passed the Education for All Handicapped Children Act (legislation that Judy Heumann had worked on as a legislative intern), which required a free and appropriate public education and related services to all children with disabilities. Also, the Developmental Disabilities Amendments of 1975 expanded services for people with such impairments as mental retardation and cerebral palsy and mandated a network of state protection agencies to monitor and protect their rights. In 1977, the Department of Health and Human Services (HHS) issued regulations that required all recipients of HHS funds to provide equal access (through ramps and elevators) to employment or services or lose their subsidies. Note well that HHS made these progressive changes only after sit-ins occurred in federal offices across the United States to protest the inaction by HHS on these issues.

Following the election of Ronald Reagan in 1980, the political climate changed for disability rights activists. The 1980s were characterized, in general, by weakened federal requirements, reduced budgets, deregulation, and judicial decisions that threatened previously established guarantees for the disabled. There were occasional victories such as success in organizing opposition to the Reagan administration's attempts to weaken several previously passed laws, including the Education for All Handicapped Children Act. They were defeated, however, when Reagan rescinded a Carter administration requirement that all new transit systems and newly acquired buses be wheelchair accessible. An organization within the disability rights movement, American Disabled for Accessible Public Transit (ADAPT), organized demonstrations in a number of cities to publicize the lack of access for many people with disabilities, but with only limited success during the chilly, politically conservative climate of the 1980s. Despite these setbacks, major progressive legislation was about to be enacted: the Americans with Disabilities Act of 1990.

Americans with Disabilities Act

When President George H. W. Bush signed the Americans with Disabilities Act of 1990 (ADA), it was called by some the most far-reaching civil rights legislation since the Civil Rights Act of 1964. The ADA was intended to eradicate discrimination against people with disabilities:

- The ADA prohibits discrimination in employment against qualified individuals. This means that people with disabilities can participate with equal opportunity in the application process, have an equal chance to perform essential functions, be provided with reasonable accommodations because of disability, and have equal benefits and privileges of employment. This law applies to all employers with fifteen or more employees.
- The ADA prohibits discrimination in programs run by public entities such as state and local governments, including public transportation.
- The ADA mandates that private businesses open to the public must make sure that all buildings, new and existing, are accessible to individuals with disabilities.
- The ADA requires telephone companies to make relay services available for hearing- and speech-impaired people.

Put more simply, because of this landmark legislation, accessibility is now commonplace: Parking lots reserve parking spaces for people with disabilities, bathrooms are equipped for wheelchair access, ramps and elevators provide access to public buildings, and elevators feature Braille floor numbers or audio assistance. These major changes represented in the provisions of the ADA did not occur because it was the right thing to do. The battle was won despite the opposition of the National Association of Manufacturers, the U.S. Chamber of Commerce, and the National Federation of Businesses. Despite the resistance of big business, the progressive legislation was passed because people with disabilities and their compatriots had organized rallies to publicize their grievances and used tactics of civil disobedience, such as disrupting public transportation and blocking access to city halls, to make their lack of civil rights more visible. Some policy makers were persuaded by the message and logic of the protesters, others by the potential political power of people, realizing that about one-fifth of Americans have disabilities. There were also the growing ranks of people with disabilities, including the aged, who, growing in numbers, are disproportionately affected by disabilities, and the increasing proportion of the population with HIV/AIDS. To the degree that people with disabilities act as a cohesive group, they have considerable political clout. Their growing sense of shared grievances and a common identity have made their voting as a bloc on certain issues more likely than ever. The result of this social movement has been legislation guaranteeing their civil rights and greater opportunities.

But there have been political setbacks to attempts to rectify inequities for people with disabilities:

- The media tend to treat the ADA as mainly a regulatory issue affecting private businesses rather than as a human rights issue facing society as a whole. Typically, the theme of their stories is the complaint that the ADA "goes too far" in forcing businesses to provide access and jobs (Jackson 2000).
- Among the provisions of the Fair Housing Act is the requirement that new multifamily housing with more units be accessible to people with disabilities. This regulation, according to Barry Corbet, an activist in the disability rights movement, is the most widely ignored law since Prohibition (Corbet 2000:9b).

- In addition to providing medical benefits to those 65 and over, Medicare also benefits the severely disabled. The beneficiaries who are disabled before age 65, however, must wait two years before becoming eligible. This means, for example, that people with amyotrophic lateral sclerosis (known as Lou Gehrig's disease), a neurological disorder that progressively deteriorates the spinal cord and the brain causing loss of muscle control and, typically, death in three years, must pay for their expensive care, drawing down their families' resources, requiring them in some cases to raid their children's college funds or sell their homes.

- In 1999, the U.S. Supreme Court narrowed the ADA, ruling that people with physical impairments that can be treated with medication or devices such as eye-glasses or hearing aids are not protected.

- In 2001, by a five to four majority, the U.S. Supreme Court held that state employees could not collect damages from their states for offenses under the federal ADA (Rosenbaum 2001).

- The Individuals with Disabilities Education Improvement Act mandated equal educational opportunities for disabled students. In 2005, the Supreme Court ruled that parents have the burden of proving that the school system does not provide a free, appropriate education for the special needs of their child. This ruling protects school districts from challenges, making equity more difficult to obtain.

- The 2010 update to the ADA required that Automatic Teller Machines (ATMs) be equipped with speech-enabled technology so that the 10 million or so visually impaired customers could use the machines without assistance. When the due date (March 15, 2012) for making these changes passed, more than half of ATMs had compliance issues (Sidel 2012). So, too, with hotels that resist the requirement that they must provide lifts to give people with disabilities access to pools and whirlpools (DeLollis 2012).

Despite legislative and judicial setbacks, the disabilities movement perseveres and continues to make a difference. In 2000, for example, a class-action suit, the first of its kind in the United States, was filed against Kaiser Permanente, a health maintenance organization (HMO), on behalf of all its California members with disabilities. The lawsuit argued that Kaiser discriminated against disabled patients by having inaccessible medical equipment (e.g., mammography machines that cannot be used by people in wheelchairs). The next year (2001), Kaiser agreed to a far-reaching settlement that included not only installing accessible medical equipment but also removing architectural barriers and instituting training programs, handbooks, and a complaint system to meet the needs of the disabled. In 2004, the Supreme Court ruled five to four in *Tennessee v. Lane* that courthouses must provide access to people with disabilities. This was a civil rights landmark case, according to Harriet McBryde Johnson, a lawyer in a power wheelchair:

> For many decades, long flights of stairs made statements about the grandeur and power of the law. They reflected prevailing assumptions about the abilities of the people who would be participating in public life. By design, they were humbling, even disempowering. Ramps, elevators and appropriate use of government spaces have the opposite effect. For people with disabilities, it is impossible to conceptualize equal protection of the law without them. (2004:12)

The Americans with Disabilities Act Amendments Act of 2008 became effective on January 1, 2009 (U.S. Equal Employment Opportunity Commission 2009). The act

Social Policy

A PROGRESSIVE STRATEGY FOR INCLUDING MORE DISABLED PERSONS IN THE WORKFORCE

There is an inherent tension between government mandates such as the Americans for Disabilities Act and the goal of business, which is to maximize profits. It costs businesses to supply ramps, elevators, voice-activated ATMs, and the like. So they resist the legislation, and once passed, typically "drag their feet" in achieving compliance.

Disability advocates argue that unemployment is one area where the various laws intended to bring people into the work force just have not worked. For example, in January 2012, the unemployment rate for people with disabilities was 50 percent higher than it was for their nondisabled peers

(much of the following is from Trottman 2012). Faced with this inequity, the Labor Department in the Obama administration proposed that businesses contracting with the federal government must have at least 7 percent of their labor force people with disabilities. The federal government has the leverage since roughly 200 businesses generate $700 billion in business with the government (including defense contractors, firms in healthcare, construction, and information-technology). The government said, in effect, if you want a government contract, then you must abide by this mandate or face the cancellation of your

contract or being barred from future contracts.

Should this plan become law, it would be a landmark rule compelling companies to meet a hiring quota. The companies involved argue that disabled workers are sometimes not hired because their impairments make them less than efficient workers. Disability advocates argue, on the other hand, that new technologies make it far easier for people with disabilities to complete work assignments.

What do you think? Should the government use its leverage to insist on an employment quota for people with disabilities? Does the goal of providing employment opportunities for those with physical and mental impairments trump the freedom of employers to hire the employees of their choosing?

met objections of the disability advocacy community that the original act was too narrowly defined. Specifically, the original was amended to emphasize that the definition of disability be construed in favor of broad coverage of individuals to the maximum extent permitted by the terms of the ADA. The effect of this change was to make it easier for an individual seeking protection under the ADA to establish that he or she has a disability within the meaning of the ADA.

To provide equal rights and opportunities for people with disabilities requires long-term solutions such as universal healthcare and a living wage. Some more readily achievable short-term goals, such as government actions to strengthen the ADA and other federal laws, will help the cause immeasurably. (See the "Social Policy" panel for a progressive strategy for improving the employment possibilities for people with disabilities.)

CONCLUSION

A fundamental progressive goal for society is social justice. The chapters in this inequality section show vividly that the United States is far from achieving that goal for racial/ethnic minorities, women, gays, and people with disabilities. In the words of Gail Schoettler, former lieutenant governor and treasurer of Colorado:

> The Civil Rights Movement made great strides. Yet as long as any person in America is denied a job or housing or simple courtesy because of her or his personal characteristics, whether they be disabilities or skin color or beliefs or sexuality, we have not affirmed the basic equal opportunity promised by our Constitution. (2000:2L)

■ CHAPTER REVIEW

1. About 20 percent of the U.S. population has some form of impairment. Approximately 15 percent of people with disabilities were born with the condition; 85 percent will experience a disabling condition in the course of their lives.

2. The individual approach (the medical model) defines disability in physiological terms, a physical or mental condition caused by the genes, accident, or disease. The goal is to return people with disabilities to "normal," and if this is not possible, to get them to adapt to their environment.

3. The social model, while acknowledging the biological basis of disability, focuses on the ways that social factors "disable" those with impairments. Some of these social factors are barriers to physical access, limited access to resources, and negative stereotypes.

4. People with disabilities constitute a minority group. Their marginality in society occurs because (a) they are defined as different; (b) the names given to them by society demean, diminish, trivialize, and deprecate; (c) the fact of disability establishes a master status by which people are categorized; (d) they are stigmatized; (e) they are excluded; (f) disability combines with other stratification hierarchies to form a matrix of oppression; and (g) they experience discrimination.

5. People with disabilities face a number of social barriers in the related areas of gender and sexuality. Women and men who are physically disabled are perceived as unattractive, asexual, and undesirable. Although both sexes are disadvantaged by the cultural expectations for what it takes to be feminine or masculine, women are more disadvantaged than men.

6. People with disabilities, both children and adults, are more likely to be abused physically and sexually than those without disabilities. Deaf people who cannot speak and people with learning disabilities are the most vulnerable to both types of abuse.

7. To counter their secondary status in society, many people with disabilities have taken an active part in the disability rights movement, a social movement with the goal of achieving empowerment and collective human, civil, and legal rights. Through the use of demonstrations and protest, this movement has succeeded, in part, to achieve favoring legislation that attempts to eliminate discrimination in housing, schooling, and the workplace, as well as the removal of architectural and other barriers to access to buildings and transportation. Most significant was the passage of the Americans with Disabilities Act of 1990, which, although flawed in its details and in its enforcement, advanced the cause of equality for people with disabilities.

■ KEY TERMS

Individual model of disability (also known as the medical model). Disability is defined in terms of some physiological impairment because of genetics, accident, or disease.

Social model of disability. The real problem with physical and mental impairment is not physical but social—the way people with able bodies view people with disabilities and the institutionalization of these views in limited physical access and other social barriers that interfere with the potential of people with disabilities.

Impairment. The state of being mentally or physically challenged.

Disability. Reduced ability to perform tasks one would normally do at a given stage of life that is exacerbated by the individual and institutional discrimination encountered.

Ontological truth. Universal and undeniable reality.

Master status. Status that has exceptional importance for social identity, overshadowing other statuses. Being defined as a member of a minority group is a master status.

Stigma. Attribute that is socially devalued and disgraced.

Ableism. Set of often contradictory stereotypes about people with disabilities that act as a barrier to keep them from achieving their full potential.

Matrix of domination. Intersections of the hierarchies of class, race, gender, sexuality, and disability in which each of us exists.

Hegemonic. Of the dominant belief system, which privileges the group in power.

Social movement. Group that develops an organization and tactics to promote or resist social change in society.

Crime and Justice

((• Listen to Chapter 12 on **MySocLab**

LEARNING OBJECTIVES

12.1 Explain the complicated nature of the definition of crime and how crime rates vary by sex, age, social class, and race.

12.2 Explain how the United States system of justice is biased against certain groups in society.

12.3 Discuss potential solutions to reduce crime in the U.S.

This chapter examines the nature of crime and how society reacts to criminal behavior in the processing of criminals. These topics are important because they help us understand the role of the powerful in regulating social behavior and the bias of the system against the powerless.

Explain the complicated nature of the definition of crime and how crime rates vary by sex, age, social class, and race.

CRIME IN SOCIETY

People are concerned with crime for obvious reasons. If left unchecked, crime destroys the stability necessary for the maintenance of an orderly society. In addition, public opinion polls routinely show that even when crime rates are low or declining, people harbor fears about being a potential victim of criminal activities (Saad 2010). Although legitimate, these concerns direct attention away from the deviance that results from the orderly working of society and from crimes that are much more costly than street crimes (which we tend to think are overwhelmingly the greatest criminal danger). These ironies will become apparent as we examine four aspects of crime: its definition, the incidence of crime, the kinds of people arrested, and the various types of criminal behavior.

What Is Crime?

Groups and individuals within society differ in their definition of crime. Some people equate crime with all antisocial behavior. Others argue that crimes are acts such as racism, sexism, and imperialism that violate basic human rights. Similarly, some people use moral rather than legal criteria to define what is or is not a crime. For example, Martin Luther King, Jr., and his followers believed that the laws enforcing racial segregation were morally wrong, so to violate them was not a crime but a virtue. Antiabortion activists believe that abortion is a crime regardless of what the formal law decrees.

Although there is no universally accepted definition of **crime**, the most common one—the breaking of a law—officially labels people and separates society into criminal and noncriminal categories. In other words, criminality is a social status that is determined by how an individual is perceived, evaluated, and treated by legal authorities. Generally, the law designates as criminal any behaviors that violate the strongly held norms of society. There is common agreement in the United States, for example, that the law should protect property from theft and vandalism. There is also universal agreement that society must protect its citizens from bodily harm (rape, assault, and murder). But, although there may be consensus in society on certain laws, the political nature of the lawmaking and enforcement process has important negative implications for the individuals caught up in them.

Consider, for example, how local and federal authorities treated antiwar protesters during the late 1960s and early 1970s. Their behavior was considered criminal because it threatened the power structure. What the powerful consider criminal depends, in fact, on what they perceive to be the intent of the individuals they observe. In the United States, society does not always forbid or condemn some acts of force that injure people or destroy property. Property damage during the celebration of sports victories, Halloween, or Mardi Gras is often overlooked or trivialized. Even 10,000 beer-drinking, noisy, and sometimes destructive college students on the beaches of Florida during spring break are allowed to go on such a binge because "kids will be kids." But if the same 10,000 college students were to destroy the same amount of property in a demonstration whose goal was to change the system, the acts would be defined as criminal and the police called to restore order by force if necessary. Thus, violence is condoned or condemned through political pressures and decisions. The basic criterion is whether the act supports or threatens existing social and political arrangements. If they are not supportive, then by definition the acts are to be condemned and punished.

A related implication of the political nature of crime is that the design of laws is influenced by a class bias. "The law and the legal order especially favor the very wealthy, but they favor enough of the rest of the population to appear to be equal. Yet the law clearly has never done a good job supporting the most marginalized sectors of the population: the poor in general, and African Americans, and other minorities" (Shelden 2001:15). This view pervades the criminal justice system, as discussed later in this chapter.

Because the definition of a crime depends on the current law, as society changes and as new interest groups become powerful, the laws and interpretations of the laws regarding criminal behavior may also change. Many behaviors once considered criminal no longer are, such as marrying someone of another race or selling liquor.

Finally, because crime is defined by the powerful in society, the organization and priorities of society are never regarded as harmful to human life (and therefore a moral crime). Yet the order of society itself can be very destructive to some categories of people, as Carmichael and Hamilton showed in their classic 1967 book, *Black Power*. They noted that when White terrorists bombed a Black church in Birmingham, Alabama, and killed five children, the act was deplored by most elements of U.S. society. But when hundreds of Black babies die each year in Birmingham because of the effects of racism, no one in the power structure gets upset and calls this violence. Although high infant mortality and rates of preventable disease, which are perpetuated through discrimination, take many more lives than civil disorder or street crimes, the term *violence* is not applied to these crimes (Carmichael and Hamilton 1967:4). Forty years later, the infant mortality rate was *still* twice as high for Blacks as for Whites (*Washington Post* 2007), but this is not labeled a moral crime by the dominant society.

Crime Rates

The innately political nature of crime is clearly evident when one examines the official crime rates, which emphasize certain types of crimes (those of the powerless) while minimizing or ignoring others. These discrepancies have profound implications because they mean, in effect, that some categories of people are disproportionately labeled criminals.

There are two basic sources of national crime statistics in the United States. The first is the *Uniform Crime Reports* (UCR), published yearly by the FBI (Federal Bureau of Investigation 2012). The *UCR* statistics are based on the arrest figures and reports supplied by 17,000 law enforcement agencies. This means that there is the potential to underreport the actual extent of crime because they list only crimes reported to the police.

Official crime rates from the *UCR* are also misleading because they imply that the amount of crime varies a good deal from year to year or from region to region. These changes may occur, but the official statistics make real variations difficult to determine. In some cases, the actual incidence of crime may not change, but the accuracy of reports may be in question. For example, in a recent survey of retired police officers in New York City, the officers said that the intense pressure to produce annual reductions in crime led some supervisors and precinct commanders to manipulate crime statistics (Rashbaum 2010). Other police departments in Atlanta, Dallas, New Orleans, Washington, and Baltimore have also been accused of tampering with crime data.

Another problem with these statistics is that they focus on traditional crimes and omit white-collar crimes, corporate crime, organized crime, and political crimes. The FBI statistics (called index crimes) emphasize violent crimes (murder, forcible rape, robbery, and aggravated assault) and property crimes (burglary, larceny, motor vehicle theft, and arson). This focus has the effect of directing public attention almost exclusively to crimes involving violence and property, in which the poor and minorities are thought to be the major perpetrators, and away from the crimes of the affluent.

The second major source of crime statistics comes from the National Crime Victimization Survey (NCVS), conducted annually by the Bureau of Justice Statistics (BJS) department. Instead of gathering crime data from police departments, these crime statistics come from a nationally representative survey of households. The benefit of using these statistics to gauge the amount of crime in society is that they include crimes regardless of whether they were reported to the police. According to the NCVS, only 51 percent of all violent victimizations and 39 percent of all property crimes were reported to the police in 2010 (Truman 2011).

- **Violent Crimes and Property Crimes.** According to NCVS data, from 2009 to 2010 violent and property crime rates declined 13 percent and 6 percent respectively. Overall, U.S. residents experienced 3.8 million violent crimes and 14.8 million property crimes (Truman 2011). This represents a 40.5 percent decrease in violent crime rates and a 28 percent decrease in property crimes since 2001 (see Table 12.1).

- **Murder and Nonnegligent Manslaughter.** According to the *Uniform Crime Report* data (Federal Bureau of Investigation 2012), 14,748 people were murdered nationwide in 2010. Looking closely at the 2010 statistics, two things are apparent: (1) The majority of murder victims and murder offenders are male (77.4 percent of victims; 90.3 percent

TABLE 12.1
Number of Victimizations and Percent Change, by Type of Crime, 2001 and 2010

Type of Crime	2001	2010	Percent Change 2001–2010
ALL CRIMES	24,215,700	18,725,710	−22.7%
VIOLENT CRIME*	5,743,820	3,817,380	−33.5%
Rape/Sexual Assault	248,250	188,380	−24.1%
Robbery	630,690	480,750	−23.8%
Assault	4,864,890	3,148,250	−35.3%
PROPERTY CRIME	18,283,510	14,769,990	−19.2%
Household Burglary	3,139,700	2,923,430	−6.9%
Motor Vehicle Theft	1,008,730	606,990	−39.8%
Theft	14,135,090	11,239,560	−20.5%

*Excludes homicide because NCVS is based on interviews with victims and therefore cannot measure murder.

Source: Truman, Jennifer L. 2011. *Criminal Victimization, 2010.* National Crime Victimization Survey. Bureau of Justice Statistics, U.S. Department of Justice. (September 2011).

of offenders), and (2) given their numbers in the general population, Blacks are over-represented among both victims and offenders. According to the 2010 Census, Blacks are 12.6 percent of the population, yet they make up 50.4 percent of murder victims and 53.1 percent of offenders. We will explore further the issues of sex, race, and crime in the next section.

Looking more generally at crime rates over time, crime rates for all types of crimes appeared to rise in the 1990s with a trend toward decreasing rates since 2000. At the same time:

- Expenditures increased 420 percent for police departments, 660 percent for the Department of Corrections, and 503 percent for the Judicial Branch from 1982 to 2006 (Bureau of Justice Statistics [BJS] 2010).
- The prison population increased from 319,598 in 1980 to 2,266,800 in 2010. Currently there are 7.1 million people (1 in 33 adults) in jail, prison, on parole, or on probation (Bureau of Justice Statistics 2012).

Let's examine what kinds of people are arrested and labeled as criminals in U.S. society.

Demographic Characteristics of People Arrested for Crimes

Read on MySocLab Document: Race and Class in the American Criminal Justice System

The data from official sources clearly indicate that people from certain social categories are more likely than others to be arrested for criminal activities. We examine these categories of sex, age, social class, and race.

Forty-eight states allow the shackling of female inmates while they are giving birth.

- **Sex.** Overall, men are more likely to be both the offender and the victim in a crime. Although this has remained fairly consistent over the years, women's crime rate is increasing. In terms of arrests, in 2010 men accounted for 74.5 percent of individuals arrested, but this represents a 6.8 percent decrease in their crime rate from 2001, whereas women's crime rate increased 10.5 percent over that same period. *Uniform Crime Report* data show some interesting arrest trends by sex from 2001 to 2010. In the twenty-nine different crimes reported, women's rate increased in thirteen categories while men's rate increased in five. Women experienced the largest increase in arrests (over a 30 percent increase) for larceny-theft, vagrancy, and driving under the influence. Overall, the number of males arrested for property crimes in 2010 declined 7.2 percent from 2001, while the number of females arrested for property crimes rose 27.1 percent in the same period.

  In spite of these increases, the incarceration rate for women was 67 per 100,000 in 2010, compared to the rate of 938 per 100,000 men. In other words, the national imprisonment rate for males was about fourteen times the imprisonment rate for females in 2010.

- **Age.** According to the Bureau of Justice Statistics (2012), incarceration rates peak for males and females between the ages of 25 and 34 and drop off sharply for males after age 49 and for females after age 44. This "maturation leads to less crime" phenomenon occurs across White, Black, and Hispanic populations.

- **Social Class.**   The bulk of the people processed by the criminal justice system for committing street crimes are the undereducated, the poor, the unemployed, or those working at low-level, alienating jobs. There are several explanations for this relationship. First, the kinds of crimes listed by the FBI are those of the lower classes (white-collar and corporate crimes, for example, are omitted). Second, the police and others in the criminal justice system assume that lower-class people are more likely to be criminals. Thus, they place more personnel in lower-class neighborhoods, which ensures that they will find more criminal activity. Third, economic deprivation may induce people to turn to crime to ease their situations. The evidence is clear that direct interpersonal types of crime (robbery, larceny, assault) are committed disproportionately by those in poverty. In addition, the National Crime Victimization Survey indicates that lower income households are more likely than higher income households to experience property crime (Truman 2011). In fact, households in the lowest income category were victims of burglary at a rate that was more than two times higher than the rate for households earning $75,000 or more.

  Social class is also significant for crimes in the upper strata of the stratification system. Those in lofty occupational and political roles commit white-collar crimes. Embezzlement, computer crimes, fraud, bribery, manipulation of the stock market, land swindles, and the like involve people at the other end of the social hierarchy from those most likely to engage in street crimes. The irony is that although white-collar, political, and corporate crimes do much more harm to society than do the crimes by the poor, crimes by the poor are seen as the crime problem.

View on
MySocLab Figure:
Call-Back Rates by Race-
Ethnicity and Criminal
Record

- **Race.**   People labeled as criminals in the United States are disproportionately people of color—African Americans, Hispanics, and Native Americans. The rates of sentenced prisoners in the United States show that Black males have a disproportionately high rate of incarceration. In 2010, Black males were incarcerated at a rate of 3,074 per 100,000, compared to 459 White males per 100,000 (see Figure 12.1). The rate for Black males age 30–34 was 7,299 incarcerated per 100,000, which means that approximately

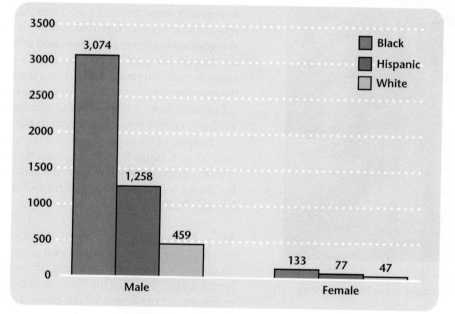

FIGURE 12.1

Estimated Rate of Sentenced
Prisoners under State and
Federal Jurisdiction by Sex
and Race, 2010

Note: Rates per 100,000 in each
population group. For example,
3,074 Black males incarcerated per
100,000 Black males.

Source: Guerino, Paul, Paige
M. Harrison, and William J. Sabol.
2011. "Prisoners in 2010." Bureau of
Justice Statistics, U.S. Department
of Justice. Online: http://bjs.gov/
content/pub/pdf/p10.pdf.

7.3 percent of the Black male population age 30–34 was incarcerated in 2010 (Guerino, Harrison, & Sabol 2011).

View on MySocLab Figure: Inequality and Crime

Although racial minorities have more contact with the criminal justice system than Whites do, this statistic does not mean that race causes crime. Racial minorities commit many crimes on the street because the social conditions of unemployment, poverty, and racism fall more heavily on them. Especially in urban centers, more and more African Americans are jobless and are living in poverty and in conditions conducive to high rates of violence and crime. Moreover, we should remember that the official statistics reflect arrest rates and are not necessarily a true indication of actual rates. The bias of the system against the poor, and especially poor minorities, makes the likelihood of their arrest and conviction greater than for well-to-do Whites, as shown in the section on the criminal justice system.

Categories of Crime

The *Uniform Crime Reports* of the FBI focus on traditional types of crime, which tend to be concentrated among the young and the poor. The focus on traditional crime ignores other types that may actually be more costly to society in terms of lives and property—organized, white-collar, corporate, and political crime. Another type of crime—moral order crime—is significant in enforcement costs but not necessarily in human costs.

View on MySocLab Figure: Property Crime Rates

- **Traditional Street Crimes.** These are the crimes emphasized by the police, the government, and the media. They are the FBI's index crimes of burglary, larceny, auto theft, robbery, rape, assault, and murder. These are serious crimes against property or **violence** against people that many people consider to be the whole of crime. People accused of these crimes are ones who typically clog the courts and prisons. The perpetrators of these types of crimes are disproportionately people on the economic margins of society—the poor, the uneducated, the unemployed, the homeless, and racial minorities.

  In evaluating this type of crime, we need to consider two types of offenders. One type is a habitual offender, who, for whatever reason, continues his or her criminal patterns. For all seven major traditional crime categories, the majority of those arrested are repeaters. Obviously, the career criminal must be converted to a new way of life, to a legitimate career that offers all the gratifications received through criminality, if rehabilitation is to be successful.

  The other type is a one-time-only criminal (the accidental or incidental criminal). Progressives maintain that such people should not be punished harshly, for that would be counterproductive. For example, locking up a one-time offender might have the unintended consequence of hindering a person's employment prospects and perhaps creating a career criminal.

  Conservatives, on the other hand, argue for swift and severe punishment to deter the person from a life of crime and to reinforce the notion in the rest of society that crime does not pay. The criminal justice system in the United States has mainly approached criminality from this conservative perspective.

  This growth in punitiveness was accompanied by a shift in thinking about the basic purpose of criminal justice. In the 1970s, the sociologist David Garland argues, the corrections system was commonly seen as a way to prepare offenders to rejoin society. Since then, the focus has shifted from rehabilitation to punishment and stayed there. Felons are no longer persons to be supported, but risks to be dealt with. And the way to deal with the risks is to keep them locked up. (Loury 2007:2)

Since the 2007 to 2009 economic recession, we are starting to see a change in this philosophy. Because it costs states a large amount to put offenders in prison, cash-strapped states are increasingly turning to alternative sentencing methods and streamlined probation and parole for low-level offenders. It costs approximately $79 a day to keep an inmate in prison but $3.50 a day to monitor the same person on probation or parole (Richburg 2009). Texas, known for its hard sentencing laws and conservative judges, implemented new rules in 2007, including shortened probation (from ten years to five), increasing the rate of offenders receiving parole, and more drug and DWI (driving while intoxicated) courts. They have consequently seen a significant decrease in their prison population (Richburg 2009). As states see their budgets dwindling, many are considering these cheaper alternatives to prison. In 2010, the combined U.S. prison population decreased 0.3 percent, the first decline since 1972 (Guerino, Harrison, and Sabol 2011).

- **Crimes against the Moral Order.** To enforce the morality of the majority, legislation defines certain acts as criminal if they are deemed offensive. Violations of these laws are **moral order crimes**. Examples of this type of crime are gambling, recreational drug use, and prostitution. Sometimes these acts that violate the moral order are called **victimless crimes** because, even though they may offend the majority, they do not harm other people. The argument for such laws is that the state has a right to preserve the morals of its citizens in the interest of promoting social stability and consensus.

  Should an individual have the right to choose among alternative forms of behavior without fear of social sanction if that behavior does not harm other people? The answer to this question is not as unqualified as it may seem; many so-called victimless crimes in fact hurt other people, at least indirectly. The family members of an alcoholic, drug addict, or compulsive gambler are affected both materially and emotionally by his or her habit. Overindulgence in alcohol or a drug increases the probability of automobile accidents. Prostitution is a victimless crime, except that some people are unwillingly forced to become prostitutes.

  A fundamental problem with legislating morality, aside from putting limitations on individual freedoms, is that it labels people as "criminals" on the basis of the tastes of those in power. Thus, **secondary deviance** (deviant behavior that is a consequence of the self-fulfilling prophecy of a negative label) may result not because someone harmed another but because his or her act was presumed by powerful others to be harmful to them.

  The detection, arrest, and prosecution of victimless criminals is an enormous and expensive task. More than half the arrests and roughly 80 percent of the police work in the United States are related to the regulation of private morals (alcohol abuse, pornography, juvenile runaways, drug use, prostitution, and gambling). In 2010, 51 percent of federal inmates were serving time for drug offenses (Guerino, Harrison, and Sabol 2011). If these private acts were legalized, then the police, the courts, and the prisons would be free for other, more important duties. Formerly illicit activities could become legitimate businesses providing tax revenues to local and state governments. Most important, organized crime, which now acquires most of its income from providing illegal goods and services, would no longer be able to hide its investments and profits. Thus, laws against victimless crimes are indirectly responsible for maintaining organized crime.

  Moral order crimes also contribute to the corruption of the police and courts. Although many police officers are unwilling to accept bribes from murderers and thieves, they may accept them from the perpetrators of victimless crimes, using the justification that they believe these crimes are harmless and impossible to control anyway. This rationale opens the way for people involved in organized crime to buy protection for their illicit activities.

- **Organized Crime.** **Organized crime** is a business syndicate that seeks profit by supplying illegal goods and services such as drugs, prostitution, pornography, gambling, loan sharking, sale of stolen goods, money laundering, and even disposal of hazardous wastes. In short, people can and do organize to provide what others want, even if it is illegal. In fact, the illegality of what people want ensures that someone will supply the goods or service because the profits are so high.

    Several characteristics of organized crime serve to perpetuate it. First, organized crime supplies illegal goods and services that are in great demand. So, one reason for the continued existence of organized crime is that it fills a need of supply and demand. If moral order crimes were decriminalized, organized crime would be left with products and services that could be easily and cheaply supplied by legitimate sources, and its profits and existence might be eliminated.

    A second characteristic of organized crime is that it depends on the corruption of police and government officials for survival and continued profitability. Bribery, campaign contributions, delivery of votes, and other favors are used to influence police personnel, government attorneys, judges, media personnel, city council members, and legislators.

    Another characteristic of organized crime is its use of violence to enforce conformity with the organization. There are strict rules for conduct and means of enforcing those rules. Individuals who cheat or fail to meet their obligations are disciplined severely. Violence is also used to eliminate competition. When rival organizations vie for the monopoly of a geographic territory or the distribution of a particular service or product, the struggle is often extremely violent.

Movies like The Godfather *contribute to stereotypes regarding Italians and organized crime.*

Finally, organized crime is structured to ensure efficiency. This organization is not composed just of members of a criminal society. There are criminals, of course, but many of these people are linked with legitimate members of society as well. Together, the criminal and legitimate elements combine to form networks within cities, regions, and even nations.

In 2008, after a fifteen-year hiatus, the Organized Crime Council (which makes reports to Congress) met and turned its attention to the transnational nature of organized crime. These crime networks that we know as organized crime are often controlled by a racial or ethnic group. The stereotype, thanks to movies like *The Godfather*, is that Italians dominate them. However, the Organized Crime Council reports that the top organized crime threat in the United States is from Eurasian/Russian crime syndicates (Finklea 2010).

- **White-Collar Crime.** The public, influenced by the media and the FBI reports, focuses its fears on traditional street crimes such as assault and robbery. Even though these are legitimate concerns, crime of the street variety (typically by the young, poor minority person) is much less significant in cost and social disruption than are **white-collar crimes**—those committed by middle-class and upper-middle-class people in their business and social activities (such as theft of company goods; embezzlement; bankruptcy fraud; swindles; tax evasion; forgery; theft of property by computer; passing bad checks; illicit copying of computer software, movies, and music; and fraudulent use of credit cards, automatic teller machines, and telephones). Some examples of the magnitude of white-collar crimes follow:

  - Telephone marketing swindlers cheat U.S. consumers out of an estimated $40 billion annually.
  - Time theft by employees (e.g., faked illness, excessive breaks, and long lunches) costs U.S. businesses as much as $200 billion annually.
  - Surveys by the Internal Revenue Service consistently find that three of ten people cheat on their income taxes. The IRS estimated that Americans underpaid their taxes by $400 billion in 2006 (*Time* 2006). This does not include the monies received from the selling of goods and services for cash and tips that go unreported to the government (that if reported would generate an estimated $345 billion in taxes annually).
  - Otherwise law-abiding citizens routinely copy or purchase pirated computer software, videos, and music. Many also engage in cable TV theft. Others photocopy copyrighted materials, even though these activities are against the law.
  - A poll of workers found that they had seen 37 percent of their co-workers take office supplies or shoplift, 25 percent steal product or cash, and 18 percent claim falsely that they had worked extra hours (*Business Week* 2002).
  - According to Bureau of Justice Statistics, in 2010, 7.0 percent of American households (8.6 million) had at least one member who was a victim of identity theft (2012).
  - Executives at major corporations such as Enron, Global Crossing, and WorldCom, knowing that their companies were soon to lose much of their value, sold stock for personal gain worth about $5 billion from 1999 to 2005.
  - In what has been called the largest securities fraud in history, Wall Street financier Bernard Madoff used what is called a **Ponzi scheme** to con investors out of approximately $65 billion. He was sentenced to 150 years in prison in 2009.

Although we know that white-collar crimes are expensive and extensive, we do not know by how much. The statistics just noted understate the actual amount because

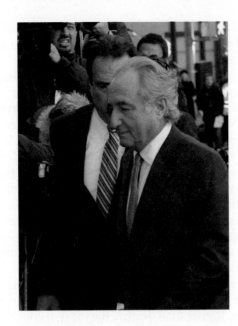

Wall Street financier Bernard Madoff conned investors out of approximately $65 billion.

many of them are so difficult to detect. Moreover, the victims are often embarrassed at their naivete in having been bilked. Whatever the numbers, the losses are huge. Suffice it to say that the criminal activities of the relatively well-to-do are widespread and expensive. What is remarkable, however, is how lenient U.S. society is to such wrongdoers when they are caught. Moreover, for the relatively few who are sentenced to prison (compared to street criminals), they serve relatively light sentences.

- **Corporate Crime.** Business enterprises can also be guilty of crimes, which are known as **corporate crimes**. The list of illegal acts committed in the name of corporate good includes fraudulent advertising, unfair labor practices, noncompliance with government regulations regarding employee safety and pollution controls, price-fixing agreements, stock manipulation, copyright infringement, theft of industrial secrets, marketing of adulterated or mislabeled food or drugs, bribery, swindles, selling faulty merchandise, and overstating earnings to increase the value of company stock. The magnitude of such crimes far surpasses the human and economic costs from other types of crime. Some examples follow:

  - The National Highway and Traffic Safety Administration has recorded 203 deaths and more than 700 injuries, amid thousands of complaints, involving rollover-prone Ford Explorers that crashed following sudden tread separation on factory-installed Firestone tires. Internal corporate memos at the two corporations reveal that Ford and Firestone "willfully and knowingly kept unsafe products on the market" (Milchen and Power 2001:9).
  - In 2000, the world's largest auction houses, Sotheby's and Christie's, agreed to pay $512 million to settle claims that they cheated buyers and sellers in a price-fixing scheme dating back to 1992.
  - Bayer sold a blood-clotting medicine for hemophiliacs, a medicine that carried a high risk of transmitting AIDS, in Asia and Latin America while selling a new, safer product in the West (Bogdanich and Koli 2003).
  - In 2004, Schering-Plough settled with the government for $345 million because it charged private insurers much lower prices on Claritin than it charged the government programs of Medicare and Medicaid (Schmit 2004).

- In recent years Exxon, International Paper, United Technologies, Weyerhaeuser, Pillsbury, Ashland Oil, Texaco, Nabisco, and Ralston-Purina have been convicted of environmental crimes.

- Cosco did not tell the Consumer Product Safety Commission of the more than 200 children who had been injured by its tandem stroller and did not recall the stroller until more than a year after it began receiving what turned out to be 3,000 complaints. "This is a pervasive problem in a wide range of products used by children. . . . Product manufacturers frequently conduct internal investigations but remain publicly silent as complaints about alleged defects pile up. In the past three years, 75 percent of the most dangerous problems that led to recalls were never voluntarily reported to the government" (O'Donnell 2000:1B).

- Archer Daniels Midland (ADM) pled guilty and was fined $100 million (the company had revenues of $13.6 billion) for its role in conspiracies to fix prices and eliminate competition and allocate sales in the lysine and citric acid markets worldwide. In return for its guilty plea, ADM was granted immunity against charges of price fixing on other products.

- ConAgra executives knowingly resold eighty tons of meat in 2000 that South Korea customs agents had quarantined because they said it contained a potentially lethal bacteria. Rather than destroy the meat or cook it to kill the pathogens, the meat was sold to other countries with lower standards than South Korea's (Migoya 2002).

- Costain Coal pled guilty to twenty-nine counts and no contest to three counts of misconduct at a Kentucky mine shaft site where an explosion killed ten workers. These counts included violations of the Mine Safety Act's mandatory health and safety standards and false statements on records filed by the company.

- Halliburton has been found guilty repeatedly of overcharging the government for fuel, services (food and housing of troops), and construction during and following the first and second Iraqi wars. Moreover, contrary to federal laws prohibiting companies from doing business with countries supporting terror—Iraq, Iran, and Libya—Halliburton circumvented these restrictions by setting up subsidiaries in foreign countries (Herbert 2003a).

- Several newspapers—the *Dallas Morning News*, *Newsday*, and the *Chicago Sun-Times*—admitted that they had overstated weekday circulation (the greater these figures, the more the newspapers can charge for advertising) (McCarthy 2004).

These examples make three points. First, the goal of profit is so central to capitalistic enterprises that many corporate decisions are made without consideration for the consequences to their customers and employees. But not only are entrepreneurs indifferent to people, society is also essentially indifferent to certain offenders. The punishments meted out to individual white-collar criminals, and especially to corporate officials, are incommensurate with their misdeeds. Moreover, criminal corporations are treated much more gently than criminal individuals. For instance, states commonly have "three strikes and you're out" laws (i.e., if found guilty of three felonies, you go to prison for life), but these do not apply to corporations. Second, the companies that are criminally prosecuted represent only a fraction of corporate wrongdoing. And third, the costs of corporate crimes far outweigh the costs of street crimes.

> The General Accounting Office, the investigative arm of Congress, estimates that health care fraud alone costs up to $100 billion each year. Another estimate suggests that the annual cost of antitrust or trade violations is at least $250 billion. By comparison, the FBI estimated that in 2002, the nation's total loss from robbery, burglary, larceny-theft, motor

vehicle theft and arson was almost $18 billion. That's less than a third of the estimated $60 billion Enron alone cost investors, pensioners, and employees. (Drutman 2003:2)

- **Political Crime.** Typically, **political crimes** are seen as any illegal acts intended to influence the political system. The operant word in this definition is *illegal*. Is it illegal to disobey unjust laws such as laws supporting racial segregation? Is it illegal to oppose tyranny? If the answer to these questions is yes, then Martin Luther King, Jr., and George Washington must be considered political criminals. The definition given here assumes that the political system is always right and that any attempt to change it is wrong. Although antithetical to the heritage of the early American colonists and the Declaration of Independence, such thinking is typical of how those in power interpret any attempt to change the existing political system.

  Another way to conceive of political crime is to concentrate on the deviance of the people in power. One example of this type of political crime is the imprisonment or harassment by the powerful of those who act against established authority. Such acts include the jailing of Martin Luther King, Jr., the FBI's infiltration of dissident groups, the Internal Revenue Service's intimidation of people on President Nixon's "enemies list," and the punishment of people involved in providing housing, transportation, and jobs to refugees escaping political repression in Guatemala and El Salvador (the Sanctuary Movement).

  Government itself can be engaged in illicit activities. Some examples are the involvement in covert actions to overthrow legitimate governments, such as the Reagan administration's policy to aid the Contra effort in Nicaragua; the U.S. attack on Panama to capture its leader, Manuel Noriega; the suppression of popular revolts in countries favorable to the United States; the use of secrecy, lying, and deceit; the use of people as unwilling and unknowing guinea pigs in medical experiments; and war crimes. For example:

  - The government revealed in 1995 that the Department of Energy conducted 435 human radiation experiments involving 16,000 people during the Cold War. Included among these experiments was one in which eighteen people were injected with plutonium without their knowledge or consent (Eisler 2000).
  - From 1932 to 1972, the U.S. Public Health Service followed 400 African American men with syphilis without treating them. The purpose of the research was to determine the natural course of syphilis. In 1947, when penicillin was found to be an effective treatment for syphilis, it too was withheld from the men and their families (Washington 2006).

  We have seen that there are a number of different types of crimes and criminals. However, the laws and their enforcement apparatus selectively focus on traditional street crimes. The social reaction to these crimes is the subject of the remainder of this chapter.

12.2 Explain how the United States system of justice is biased against certain groups in society.

UNJUST SYSTEM OF JUSTICE

Justice refers to the use of authority to uphold what is lawful in a completely impartial and fair manner. Even though fairness is the goal of the U.S. system of justice, it is far from realized. The law itself, the administration of the law by the police and judges, and the prisons all express bias against certain categories of people. To document this assertion, we examine the criminal justice system from multiple directions: laws, police, the judicial process, and the U.S. correctional system.

Laws

Of all the requirements for a just system, the most fundamental is a body of nondiscriminatory laws. Many criminal laws are the result of public consensus on what kinds of behaviors should be punished (such as murder, rape, and theft). The laws devised to make these acts illegal and to specify the extent of punishment for violators are nondiscriminatory because they do not single out a particular social category as the target. Although these laws in themselves are not discriminatory, the remainder of this chapter demonstrates that the administration of them often is.

Other laws, however, do discriminate because they result from the exertions of special interests to translate their objectives into public policy. In contrast, some segments of society (such as the poor, minorities, and youth) rarely have access to the lawmaking process and therefore often find the laws unfairly aimed at them. Vagrancy, for example, is really a crime that only the poor can commit.

One example of this interest group approach to the law is the pre–Civil War and Jim Crow legislation in the South. The majority created laws to keep the races separate and unequal. Here are a few specific examples of the historical bias of the law against Blacks:

- The law played a critical role in defining and sanctioning slavery. For instance, the law made slavery hereditary and a lifetime condition.
- The slave codes denied Blacks the rights to bring lawsuits or to testify against a White person.
- The slave codes denied Blacks the rights to marriage.
- Jim Crow laws codified the customs and uses of segregation.
- After Reconstruction, the grandfather clause, the literacy test, and the poll tax were legal devices designed to keep Blacks from voting.
- In the nineteenth century, the law allowed only White men to sit on juries.

Explore on MySocLab Activity: Stereotypes of Crime and Justice

Not only is the formation of the law political, so, too, is its administration. At every stage in the processing of criminals, authorities make choices based on personal bias, pressures from the powerful, and the constraints of the status quo. Examples of the political character of law administration include attempts by the powerful to coerce other people to their view of morality, resulting in laws against pornography, drug use, and gambling; pressure exerted by the powerful on the authorities to crack down on certain kinds of violators, especially individuals and groups who are disruptive (protesters); pressure exerted to keep certain crimes from public view (embezzlement, stock fraud, the Iran-Contra scandal); pressure to protect the party in power, elected officials, and even the police department; and any effort to protect and preserve the status quo.

Police

Formal law enforcement policy begins with the police. They decide whether a law has been broken. They interpret and judge what behavior is "disorderly," how much noise constitutes a "public nuisance," when a quarrel becomes a "criminal assault," when protest becomes illegitimate, and what constitutes "public drunkenness." Their authority to interpret these questions suggests that the police have great decisional latitude. Unlike other agencies in the criminal justice process, the police in their work often deal with their clients in isolation.

Given the great discretionary powers of the individual police, one must determine whether police officers as a group tend to hold particular biases that affect their perceptions and actions. Several characteristics of the job and the types of people attracted to it suggest that certain biases may prevail among this occupational category.

The job itself causes police personnel to develop a distinctive way of perceiving the world. Foremost is that they are given the authority to enforce the law. They have power, even the ultimate power of legitimate force, at their disposal to uphold the law. As authorities sworn to uphold the law, police support the status quo. Naturally, then, they find people who defile the flag or otherwise protest against the system abhorrent.

Second, the danger inherent in their occupation promotes a particular worldview among the police. The element of danger tends to make them suspicious of behavior that is nonconforming or otherwise unusual. In the interests of self-defense, they tend to assume the worst of people they believe to be dangerous (minorities, protesters, drug users).

The police also tend to be socially isolated. Because they have actual power over other citizens, police personnel are the objects of hostility for many, but especially for minority group members. This hostility is manifested in abusive language and other forms of harassment. The result, of course, is that the police, even those relatively free of prejudice toward minorities, tend to become hostile toward members of certain social categories over time. The harassment directed toward the police also increases the threat of danger to them. The result is a self-fulfilling prophecy: The police, harassed by victimized categories in society, in turn harass their tormentors, which leads to charges of police brutality and the justification to be hostile toward them.

This characterization presupposes that the police are relatively free of prejudice, at least at the beginning of their career. This assumption, however, is not always true. The evidence is clear that suspects who are poor, minority, and male are more likely to be formally arrested than suspects who are white, affluent, and female. **Racial profiling** (the practice of targeting citizens for police encounters on the basis of race) is common. DWB (driving while Black or Brown), or more recently, DWM (driving while Muslim) or FWM (flying while Muslim) is not a crime, but because of racial profiling by the police, there is the assumption of criminal behavior. For example, over 80 percent of the automobile searches by the New Jersey state police on the New Jersey Turnpike during the 1990s were conducted on vehicles driven by African Americans and Latinos (Kocieniewski and Hanley 2000). A report of Missouri police found that they stop Black motorists at a rate 30 percent higher than White drivers and search them 70 percent more often (Associated Press 2001). This targeting of racial minorities by the police is based on the assumption that racial minorities are more likely than Whites to commit crime (Lichtenberg 2006).

A 2008 report by the American Civil Liberties Union in Arizona found that black and Latino drivers were two and a half times more likely than white drivers to be searched, and Native American drivers were three and a quarter times more likely than whites to be searched, despite the fact that they were *less* likely than Whites to be found with contraband (ACLU 2009). The ACLU concludes,

The disproportionate rates at which minorities are stopped and searched, in addition to the often high concentrations of law enforcement in minority communities, continue to have a tremendous impact on the over-representation of minorities (and especially members of African American, Latino, and Native American communities) in the American criminal justice system. (2009:12–13)

Read on MySocLab Document: Explaining and Eliminating Racial Profiling

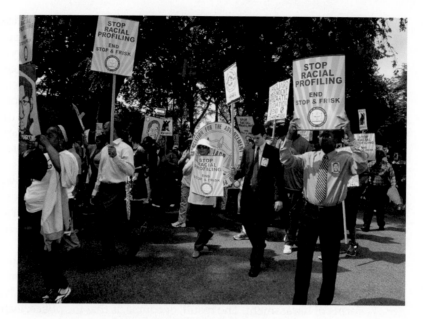

Protestors march in New York City against racial profiling and the New York Police Department's "Stop and Frisk" policy.

The police engage in racial profiling also in ways other than in traffic encounters. For example, the police are much more likely to engage in a crackdown on the use of crack than on the use of drugs on a middle-class college campus, even though the level of drug use may be higher on campus. The result is that a greater proportion of African Americans are arrested for drug charges than middle-class Whites, thereby reinforcing the stereotypes and the rationale for further use of racial profiling (see Chapter 13).

Judicial Process

Watch on MySocLab Video: ABC 20/20: Justice and Privilege

How fair is the process by which lawbreakers are prosecuted, tried, convicted, and sentenced? Given that the courts deal only with those whom the police arrest, clearly the process begins with a bias. The question is, Do the courts increase the degree of unfairness or not? A related question involves the operation of the principle that individuals brought before the courts are presumed to be innocent: How great is the gap between principle and practice?

To answer these questions, let us examine the formal procedures of the justice system for the commission of a serious crime. The police arrest the probable offender and bring him or her before a magistrate. The magistrate examines the evidence and decides whether to allow the alleged offender to be free on bail. The case is then turned over to a prosecuting attorney, who formally charges the defendant. This charge is subject to review by a judge at a preliminary hearing or by a grand jury. If the defendant pleads not guilty, then he or she comes to trial, where the facts of the case are argued by the prosecuting and defense attorneys before a judge and jury. If the jury finds the defendant guilty, he or she is sentenced by the judge to a term in prison or to a term of probation.

- **Magistrate and the Setting of Bail.** The primary functions of the magistrate are to inform defendants of their right to counsel, to assign them counsel if so requested, to set a date for a preliminary hearing, and to set bail. In the last procedure, the magistrate exercises considerable discretion.

Bail is the posting of money by the accused to guarantee that he or she will be present at the time of trial. The Constitution provides the right to bail in noncapital cases. Bail allows accused people to stay out of jail, thereby retaining their family, community, and work responsibilities; most important, it allows them a chance to investigate and prepare their cases.

Several practices in setting bail, however, undermine the principle of treating all people fairly. The primary problem is that the amount of bail to be posted is left to the discretion of the magistrate, who may set high bail to "teach the accused a lesson" or to "protect the community." Magistrates have often taken such an approach when the defendants have been political protesters and minority group members. This practice violates the Eighth Amendment, which specifically forbids the setting of excessive bail; moreover, the concept of preventive detention contradicts the presumption of innocence that is supposed to be at the heart of the judicial process.

The setting of bail is also unfair because magistrates tend to determine the amount of bail by the type of crime alleged instead of by the accused's ability to pay. Moreover, the accused or their families typically obtain bail money from professional bondspersons, who receive 5 to 10 percent of the total as their fee. If the bail were set at $10,000 for everyone accused of a felony and the accused had to pay a bondsperson a fee of $1,000, clearly the accused who were poor would suffer the greatest hardship.

The obvious result of the system of setting bail is that the poor remain in jail and the wealthy are released, either because the latter have their own money or bail or because bail bondspersons consider them less risky. This result highlights another problem: the power of bail bondspersons to decide whom they will bond and whom they will not. Of course, the poor are considered more risky. Moreover, bondspersons may refuse to grant bail as a "favor" to the police.

Thus, the biggest problem with the bail-setting practice as it now operates is that it tends to imprison the poor. Time spent in jail before trial varies by locality and by the backlog of pending cases. In some jurisdictions, defendants who cannot make bail spend as long as eighteen months in jail awaiting trial. Clearly, this situation violates the principle that the accused person is presumed innocent until proven guilty, for it provides punishment before conviction. And the difference between those who languish in jail before their trial and those who are free is money.

- **Plea Bargaining.** Fewer than 10 percent of the people charged with crimes ever go to trial. The thousands of cases that bypass the trial process do so because either the charges are dropped or the people accused plead guilty to the original or lesser charges. The latter event is called **plea bargaining** because the defendants bargain away their right to a trial in return for their guilty plea and a more lenient punishment than if they were found guilty of the original charge. Plea bargaining has become the rule, not the exception, in the disposition of criminal cases in the United States.

  There are many pressures on defendants, lawyers, prosecutors, and judges to encourage plea bargaining. Foremost is the overwhelming caseload facing police, prosecutors, and judges. Without guilty pleas to speed defendants through the system, the criminal justice process could not function because of impossibly crowded courts. One obvious solution is for judges to encourage guilty pleas by implementing the agreements negotiated by prosecutors and defense counsel. Similarly, prosecutors encourage plea bargaining because of their large caseloads. In addition, prosecutors must have a high conviction rate, and plea bargaining achieves this goal at relatively little expense.

Defendants are pressured in several ways to plea bargain. People who are assigned as defense counsel typically encourage their clients to "cop a plea." One reason they encourage plea bargaining is that assigned counsel receive little compensation, and they would rather return quickly to their more lucrative private practice. Counsel may also feel that plea bargaining is in the best interests of the client because it will reduce time spent in jail awaiting trial. District attorneys often force plea bargaining on defendants by charging them with more serious crimes (carrying heavier penalties). Compelling defendants to plea bargain has the effect of reducing caseloads. A defendant who refuses to bargain faces the possibility of serving a longer sentence and for a more serious offense. Public defenders also encourage plea bargaining to reduce the burden of their large caseloads on their small investigative staffs. They would rather concentrate their efforts on capital crimes.

There are special pressures on defendants who are poor or of moderate means to plead guilty. They will be unable to bear the expense of a lengthy trial. Moreover, those unable to make bail must await trial in jail. These factors deter poor defendants from insisting on their rights. Although overcrowding in the courts may make it a necessity, plea bargaining subverts the basic foundations of the system of criminal justice. Contrary to the Bill of Rights, the practice operates on an implicit assumption of guilt. It fails to distinguish between the innocent and the guilty, thus penalizing the innocent and rewarding the guilty. Moreover, because it reduces sentences, plea bargaining erodes the elements of deterrence on which criminal sanctions are based. The procedure especially discriminates against the poor. The poor defendant, already in jail, is pressured by court-appointed counsel to bargain from a position of weakness. In a plea-bargaining situation, the need for competent and conscientious counsel outweighs all other factors. Yet it is inevitable that a lawyer receiving a handsome fee for his or her services will be more interested in a client's welfare than will an overburdened and undercompensated court-appointed one.

- **Adversary System.** An intrinsic feature of the U.S. criminal justice system is the concept of adversary roles. In the **adversary system**, the state and the accused engage in a public battle to argue and provide evidence before an impartial judge or jury. For this principle to work, the adversaries must be relatively equal in ability, incentive, and resources. But this is not usually the case. The state has enormous resources (police, crime labs, detectives) with which to build its case. The accused, if wealthy, can match the resources and expertise of the state. In the famous O. J. Simpson case, for example, the defendant spent between $5 million and $6 million for a team of lawyers, jury selection experts, DNA authorities, and other specialists. In what would have been a speedy trial and probably an open-and-shut case of guilt for a poor defendant, the Simpson team was able to contest every piece of evidence by the prosecution, present counter-theories, and raise a reasonable doubt among the jurors:

    *The Simpson case has demonstrated perhaps more starkly than ever before that in the American justice system, as in so much else in this country, **money changes everything**—and huge amounts of money change things almost beyond recognition. (Gleick 1995:41; emphasis added)*

    But the Simpson case was an anomaly. Of all felony defendants in the United States, 80 to 90 percent are too poor to hire their own lawyer and are represented by court-appointed attorneys. These poor defendants are especially disadvantaged by the adversary system. Obviously, they cannot pay for detective work, hire expert witnesses, and do the other things necessary to build their case.

- **Trial by Jury.** Fundamental to a fair system of criminal justice is the right to a trial by a jury consisting of a representative body of citizens. In practice, however, certain categories of people are underrepresented on juries: minorities, people not registered to vote, students, and low-prestige occupational groups. The result is that the poor, especially the poor from minority groups, are typically not judged by a jury of their peers (see the "A Closer Look" panel "Jena Six").

  The failure of juries to reflect communities is significant because the people least represented are those most likely to challenge community norms. This situation puts a special burden on defendants accused of political crimes (such as antiwar and civil rights protest).

  In selecting a jury, the attorneys for the state and the accused attempt to choose jurors who are likely to favor their particular side. The selection process tends to be unfair, however. The state, with enormous investigatory and financial resources at its disposal, may use the police and the FBI to investigate minute details about each prospective juror. Unless the accused is very wealthy, the defense usually decides on the bases of intuition and superficial information.

A Closer Look

JENA SIX

In high schools across the country teachers and administrators must deal with school fights on a regular basis. Most of the time, the students are punished or suspended, and the public never hears about them. This was not the case, however, for the infamous "Jena Six." In December 2006, racial tensions were mounting at Jena High School in central Louisiana. One particular day, a Black student sat under a tree that was known to students as the "White tree" where only White students could sit. The next day, three nooses were hanging from the tree.

The principal expelled the White students responsible, but the school board and superintendent overruled him, reducing the punishment to in-school suspensions. As tensions mounted, there was a fight in which a White student suffered a concussion and multiple bruises. Six Black students were arrested and faced felony charges of attempted murder with potential fines of more than

$90,000 and potential sentences of up to twenty years. They became known as the "Jena Six."

A judge reduced the charges against five of the six boys and only one of the Jena six went to trial. Mychal Bell (16 years old) was initially tried as an adult for aggravated assault and conspiracy.

He was tried before a white judge and an all-white jury. He had only a court-appointed counsel who called no witnesses. The prosecutor argued that the gym shoes on his feet constituted a "deadly weapon." He was convicted, jailed with prohibitive bond and faced 20 years in prison. (Jackson 2007:1)

The severity of the charges caught the attention of civil rights groups across the country, and protests mounted. An online civil rights group raised more than $275,000 for legal defense for the Jena Six,

and in September 2007 more than 40,000 demonstrators went to Jena to protest unequal justice for the students. In December 2007, Mychal Bell pleaded guilty to second-degree battery and was sentenced to eighteen months in jail.

In 2009, the case was resolved when the other five students pleaded no contest to simple battery and agreed to fines and seven days of probation. The civil rights group (ColorofChange.org) that raised the money for their defense said in a press statement:

Today's plea deal shows that the original charges in the case were unfair and vastly overblown. The story of the Jena six was an extreme example of what can happen when a justice system biased against black boys operates unchecked. But it's also an example of what can happen when hundreds of thousands of people across the country stand up to challenge unequal justice. (quoted in Facing South 2009:1)

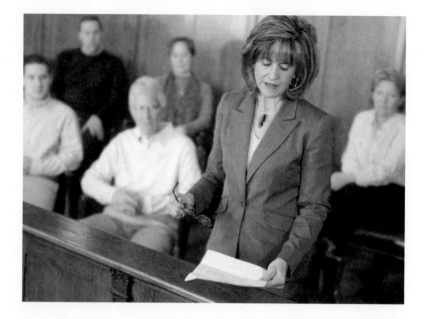

Individuals from poor minority groups are typically not judged by a jury of their own peers.

Trial outcomes are also affected to some extent by whether the case is heard by a jury or a trial judge. The research suggests that juries tend to be more lenient than judges. This points to another inequity of the judicial system: Because jury trials increase the probability of acquittal for defendants, they should be equally available to all people.

- **Judicial Sentencing.** Until the 1970s, judges were given considerable latitude in determining the exact punishment for convicted criminals. The discretion of the judges was almost without limits, and sometimes the results were very inconsistent from judge to judge and even by a particular judge. This discretionary sentencing permitted individualized justice. In other words, the judge could take into account the peculiar factors of the case in the sentencing decision. Although this ideal is a worthy one, the procedure resulted in a kind of courtroom roulette, depending on the law in the jurisdiction, the ideology of the judge, media attention, and other factors. Most telling among these other factors were the social class and racial characteristics of the defendants, with a strong tendency for middle- and upper-class Whites to receive lighter sentences than lower-class Whites and racial and ethnic minorities.

Beginning in the 1970s, there was a movement to curb the discretionary power of judges with the passage of mandatory and determinate sentencing laws. **Mandatory sentencing** forced judges to incarcerate violent and habitual criminals. **Determinate sentencing** means that for a given offense, the judge must impose a sentence (sometimes a fixed sentence and sometimes a range, depending on the state), within the guidelines of the law, depending on the crime and the offender's past record. Typically, a sentencing commission would be appointed in a state to determine these penalties.

The leading example of mandatory sentencing is the "three strikes and you're out" law passed by the federal government (1994) and many state legislatures. The essence of this law is that someone found guilty of three serious crimes would be locked up for life with no hope for parole (serious is defined differently by the various states, with some accepting only violent crimes in this category, whereas others may include low-level property crimes and drug offenses). This provision is popular because it is punitive on so-called habitual criminals and thus will lower the crime rate. There are several problems with this get-tough policy, however. First, despite having the highest imprisonment rates of all industrialized countries, the United States still has the highest crime rates, so clearly "three strikes" is not working. Second, this mandatory provision increases the demand on limited prison space. Third, the prisons are increasingly populated by lower-level offenders (small-time thieves, repeat property criminals, and drug offenders). The percentage of inmates in federal prisons convicted of violent crimes, for example, has decreased while the proportion there for drug offenses has increased to almost half of all federal prisoners (see Figure 12.2).

As mentioned previously, the rising prison population coupled with tough economic times has caused some states to ease their mandatory sentencing regulations and seek cheaper alternatives to imprisonment. In 2003, Delaware and Washington, for example, reduced prison terms for nonviolent drug offenders, thus saving millions and reducing prison overcrowding (we further examine the issue of U.S. prisons in the following section).

Critics of the system argue that in spite of mandatory and determinate sentencing laws, the judicial sentencing process continues to be biased. This becomes obvious

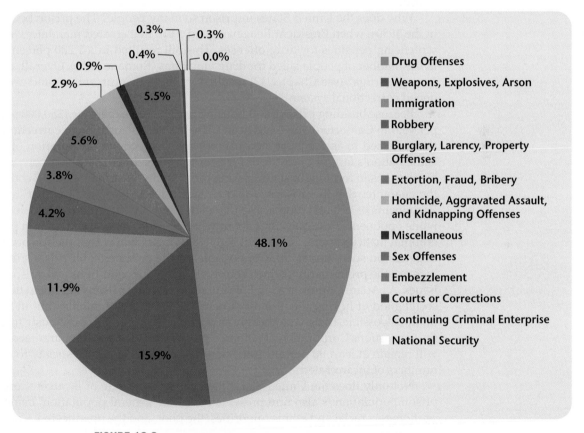

FIGURE 12.2

Types of Offenders in Federal Prison, 2012

Source: Federal Bureau of Prisons, U.S. Department of Justice. Prisoner Population as of June 23, 2012. Online: http:www.bop.gov.

when looking at who actually receives the death penalty—**capital punishment**. As of April 2012, thirty-five states and the federal prison system held 3,170 prisoners under sentence of death. Of these inmates, 98 percent are male, and *50 percent have less than a high school education*. Racial minorities are also disproportionately found on death row (e.g., Blacks are 12.6 percent of the population, but they made up 42 percent of those awaiting execution in 2012).

In sum, the bias that disadvantages minorities and the poor throughout the system of justice continues as parole board members, corrections officers, and others make judgments that often reflect stereotyped notions. The facts make the case that at every stage of the judicial process the poor and racial minorities are at a distinct disadvantage. From the decision to arrest or let go with a warning, to the setting of bail, to trial and sentencing, disparities persist.

U.S. Correctional System

In 2010, the total number of people in the U.S. correctional population (incarcerated, on supervised probation or parole) was 7.1 million. This translates to 1 in every 33 adults (Glaze 2011). In terms of incarceration, over 1.9 million were incarcerated in 2010 (1 in every 104 adults in the United States), by far the highest rate in the world.

Why does the United States imprison so many people? The prison boom started in the 1980s, when President Reagan signed a bill that created mandatory minimum sentencing penalties for drug offenses. This bill resulted in a 1,200 percent increase in the number of people jailed for drug violations (Romano 2011). Overall, America's "war on drugs" (see Chapter 13) resulted in massive incarceration and an overburdened correctional system.

Because building prisons and housing prisoners is expensive ($50,000 per inmate per year in California), there has been a rise in the privatization of correctional facilities (referred to as the **prison-industrial complex**). Corrections Corporation of America is the nation's largest operator of for-profit prisons. In 2011 the company offered to buy prisons in forty-eight states, asking for a twenty-year management contract plus the guarantee that the prisons would remain at least 90 percent full (Kirkham 2011). Proponents of privatization argue that states can benefit from the infusion of cash, while opponents raise questions about whether profit motive should be a part of our criminal justice system. Some civil rights advocates worry that the for-profit model depends on spending as little as possible on the prisoners and prisons in order to increase the profit margin, which could result in poor conditions and prisoner safety issues. As Adam Gopnik argues, "the interest of private prisons lies not in the obvious social good of having the minimum necessary number of inmates but in having as many as possible, housed as cheaply as possible" (2012:74). As previously mentioned, the Corrections Corporation of America will buy prisons only if guaranteed that they will remain at least 90 percent full. Shouldn't it be our goal as a society to *reduce* the numbers of incarcerated?

Not only does the United States have a very high rate of incarceration, but the prison population is also unrepresentative of the general population, being disproportionately racial and ethnic minorities, the poor, and the uneducated. Consider the following:

- More than half of all black men without a high school diploma go to prison at some time in their lives (Gopnik 2012).

- In 2010, Black males had an imprisonment rate that was seven times higher than white males (3,074 per 100,000 Black male residents compared to 459 per 100,000 White males).
- According to the Innocence Project, nearly 70 percent of the 242 people that have been exonerated by DNA testing are racial minorities (that is, they were convicted of crimes and later DNA testing found them to be innocent) (2012).
- African American youth make up 30 percent of those arrested while they only represent 17 percent of the overall youth population. Furthermore, African American youth are nine times more likely than white youth to receive an adult prison sentence (Shelton 2009).

That the members of the disadvantaged in society (the poor and the minorities) are disproportionately represented in the prison population reinforces negative stereotypes already prevalent among the majority of the population. The large number of African Americans and the poor in prison is taken as proof that those groups have criminal tendencies. Moreover, the high **recidivism rate** (the return to crime by ex-prisoners; 50 to 60 percent of inmates in U.S. prisons or jails are not there for the first time) is viewed as further proof of the criminality of the poor, the uneducated, and minority groups. But, as we have seen, the criminal justice system is not just. Economic resources make a crucial difference at every stage in the process, while institutional discrimination has also kept minorities disproportionately underrepresented among police, lawyers, judges, and juries.

With an overcrowded prison system and a high recidivism rate, it is clear that the correctional system is not working as it stands. As criminologist Jeffrey Reiman states, "Prison produces more criminals than it cures" (2007:32). See the "Social Policy" panel "Halden, the World's Most Humane Prison" for an alternative approach to incarceration.

Social Policy

HALDEN, THE WORLD'S MOST HUMANE PRISON

In 2010, Halden prison opened in southeastern Norway. Halden is not your typical prison; there are no bars, and prisoners have private cells with large windows for sunlight and private bathrooms. The prisoners enjoy flat screen televisions in their rooms and mini-refrigerators. Ten to twelve cells share a common living room and kitchen, where they cook for each other and socialize. The facility also includes a gym, a training room, a chapel, a library, a sound studio, and a school. There is a free-standing two-bedroom house to host families during overnight visits, and the grounds include jogging trails and a rock-climbing wall. The architects designed the prison to avoid an institutional feel, and the entire prison was built under the principle that repressive prisons do not work. Instead, at Halden they believe that treating prisoners humanely will boost their chances of reintegrating into society (Adams 2010).

Halden brings up the fundamental question: What are prisons for? Are they for punishment or rehabilitation? Obviously, in Norway they believe that prisons are for rehabilitation. Because many of the prisoners come from dysfunctional homes, at Halden they promote a sense of family. The guards do not wear guns, and routinely eat and socialize with the inmates (Adams 2010).

This approach is a far cry from the U.S. approach to incarceration, and it appears to be working. Officials in Norway claim that within two years of their release, 20 percent of Norway's prisoners end up back in jail (a much lower recidivism rate than the United States rate of 50–60 percent) (Adams 2010).

STOPPING THE CRADLE TO PRISON PIPELINE

As this chapter has shown, the United States has the highest incarceration rate in the industrialized world. We spend billions of dollars each year to imprison more of our citizens than any other country, and our system of justice does not treat all groups of people equally. The president of the Children's Defense Fund, Marion Wright Edelman, wrote,

> Nationally, one in three Black boys and one in six Latino boys born in 2001 are at risk of going to prison during their lifetimes. Although boys are more than five times as likely to be incarcerated as girls, the number of girls in the juvenile justice system is significant and growing. This shamefully high incarceration rate of Black youths is endangering our children at younger and younger ages and poses a huge threat to our nation's future. America's cradle to prison pipeline is putting thousands of young people on a trajectory that leads to marginalized lives, imprisonment, and often premature death. (2009:1)

 Watch on **MySocLab Video:** ABC Primetime: Juvenile Corrections

The Children's Defense Fund has started a "Cradle to Prison Pipeline Crusade," aimed at preventing children from entering the pipeline and helping the children already trapped there. A number of states are working on plans to break the pipeline. The Children's Defense Fund points to Missouri as a model for the rest of the country.

> The state of Missouri used a rehabilitative and therapeutic approach to overhaul its juvenile justice system that has been hailed as a national model for juvenile justice reform. The philosophy behind Missouri's program is to treat youths as potentially productive members of society instead of lost causes in a prison cage. The results are clear. Missouri's juvenile recidivism rate has only eight percent of those incarcerated coming back into juvenile custody and eight percent going into Missouri's prisons. It is one of the best success stories in the country. (Edelman 2009:1)

Read on **MySocLab Document:** Violent Girls or Relabeled Status Offenders? An Alternative Interpretation of the Data

The pipeline to prison is connected to many of the topics in this book, especially racial inequality, poverty, and education. High school dropouts are almost three times as likely to be incarcerated as high school graduates, and, as we have seen, half the prison population awaiting execution does not have a high school diploma. Thus, the Children's Defense Fund points to early childhood intervention programs (such as Head Start) and education reform as key components in stopping the pipeline for at-risk youth. The challenge for states is to make the commitment and invest in *prevention*, rather than continue to spend a disproportionate amount of funds and resources on corrections and punishment.

MySocLab ✓ Study and Review on MySocLab

■ CHAPTER REVIEW

1. Criminality is a social status determined by how an individual is perceived, evaluated, and treated by legal authorities. What is a crime depends on the law, which is created by the powerful. Crime, then, is innately political.

2. There are two basic sources of crime statistics in the U.S. The FBI's *Uniform Crime Reports* is based on reports gathered from law enforcement agencies across the country. These statistics focus on street crimes against people and property. They

omit white-collar crimes, corporate crimes, political crime, and organized crime.

3. The second major source of crime statistics is the National Crime Victimization Survey. These statistics come from surveys of households, thus they also include crimes *not* reported to the police.

4. The rates of violent crimes (including homicide) and property crimes are lower now than in 2001. At the same time, expenditures for police departments and courts have increased over time, and there are over 7 million people in jail, prison, on parole, or on probation.

5. According to the official crime statistics, (a) more males than females commit crimes, (b) young adults ages 25–34 have the highest street crime rates, and (c) the poor, undereducated, unemployed, and racial minorities are more likely to be arrested and labeled as criminals.

6. Victimless crimes are private acts designated as criminal by powerful interest groups that are able to legislate morality. Making these acts criminal creates several problems: (a) They are costly to enforce, and, if legal, they would bring in significant tax revenues; (b) they make organized crime profitable; and (c) they contribute to the corruption of the police and courts. Moreover, so-called victimless crimes are rarely victimless—they do harm people.

7. Organized crime is a business syndicate that supplies illegal goods and services. Organized crime thrives because of (a) the high demand for illegal goods and services, (b) corruption among the police and government officials, (c) violence and intimidation, and (d) its well-organized operation at all levels—locally, regionally, nationally, and internationally.

8. Losses resulting from individual white-collar crime amount to many times the monetary loss from street crimes. Yet official agencies do not devote as much attention to white-collar crimes, and the few criminals that are apprehended often receive relatively light sentences.

9. Corporate crimes are the most dangerous and expensive to society because they involve unsafe working conditions, pollution of the environment, unsafe products, and fraud.

10. Political crimes are of two types: (a) acts that threaten the power structure and (b) illegal acts by those in power.

11. The system of justice is fundamentally unjust. The laws favor the powerful. The Crime Index channels police activities toward certain criminal acts (street crimes) and away from others (white collar). The poor are disadvantaged at every stage of the judicial process because lawyers, bail, and an adequate defense are costly. Thus, for similar offenses, the powerless are more likely than the powerful to be found guilty, to be sentenced far more harshly, to wait longer for parole, and if sentenced, to die—actually to be executed.

12. The U.S. incarcerates more people than any other country, a boom that began in the 1980s with the "war on drugs." Corporations have taken advantage of cash-strapped states and have bought or manage correctional facilities as a for-profit enterprise.

13. The "cradle to prison pipeline" is the idea that some children in American society are at great risk to end up in the American correctional system. Solutions to the crime problem must veer away from the current ideology of punishment to focus on prevention and breaking this pipeline.

■ KEY TERMS

Crime. An act that breaks the law.

Violence. An act of force perceived by the powerful as threatening to the status quo.

Moral order crimes. Acts that violate laws that enforce the morality of the majority.

Victimless crimes. Acts that violate moral order crimes; they may offend the majority, but they do not harm other people.

Secondary deviance. Deviant behavior that is a consequence of the self-fulfilling prophecy of a negative label.

Organized crime. A business operation that seeks profit by supplying illegal goods and services.

White-collar crimes. Illicit acts committed by middle-class and upper-middle-class people in their business and social activities.

Ponzi scheme. An investment fraud that involves the payment of purported returns to existing investors from funds contributed by new investors (rather than from any legitimate investment activity).

Corporate crimes. Illegal acts by business enterprises.

Political crimes. Illegal acts intended to influence the political system. Also, the abuse of authority by those in power. Finally, actions by governments that are illegal or immoral.

Racial profiling. The practice of targeting citizens for police encounters on the basis of race.

Bail. Posting of money by the accused to guarantee that he or she will be present at the trial.

Plea bargaining. Arrangement between the prosecution and the accused whereby the latter pleads guilty in return for a reduced charge.

Adversary system. The U.S. system of justice, whereby the state and the accused engage in a public battle to argue and provide evidence before an impartial judge or jury.

Mandatory sentencing. By law, judges must incarcerate certain types of criminals.

Determinate sentencing. For a given offense, a judge must impose a sentence that is within the guidelines of the law.

Capital punishment. Killing of a criminal by the state.

Prison-industrial complex. The privatization of correctional facilities.

Recidivism rate. Percentage of offenders who, after their treatment or punishment has ended, are arrested and convicted of new offenses.

Drugs

((• Listen to Chapter 13 on **MySocLab**

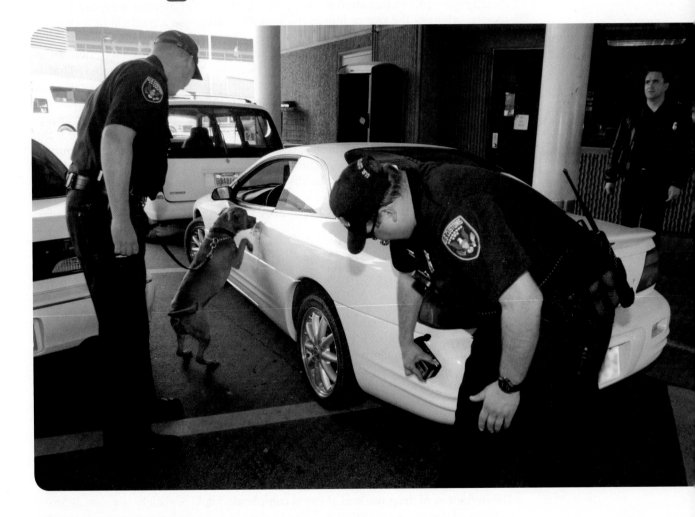

LEARNING OBJECTIVES

13.1 Explain the politics behind the definition of drugs and the current United States drug laws.

13.2 Discuss the most commonly abused illegal and legal drugs and how drug use varies by class, race, and gender.

13.3 Give examples which demonstrate how the U.S. "war on drugs" is racist.

13.4 Discuss alternatives to the current war on drugs.

Throughout history, people have sought to alter their consciousness through the use of both legal and illegal substances. A **drug** is any substance that affects the structure or function of the body when ingested. This broad definition includes such substances as aspirin, caffeine, nicotine, heroin, and alcohol. Every society accepts some drugs as appropriate and regards others as unacceptable. Some drugs are considered dangerous, and others are harmless. But the definitions vary from society to society, and within U.S. society they are inconsistent and often ambiguous.

Many people in the United States are concerned about the drug problem. But what is meant by "the drug problem"? Is drug use equated with abuse? Why are alcohol and tobacco legal drugs when they are addictive, physically harmful, and socially disruptive? Put another way, why is the use of alcohol accepted by U.S. society, whereas the use of marijuana is not? Is drug use a medical or a criminal problem?

Three points should be made at the outset of this discussion. First, definitions concerning drugs and drug-related behaviors are socially constructed. That is, definitions about drugs are not based on some universal standard but rather on meanings that people in groups have imputed to certain substances and behaviors. Second, as is true with all social problems, members of different societies or groups (e.g., religious and political) within a society often differ in their beliefs about this phenomenon. Third, the definition of drugs by the most powerful interest groups in a society will become part of the law and be enforced on others. Thus, the labeling of some drugs as licit and others as illicit involves politics. Therefore, in examining such topics as the history of drug laws, the extent of drug use and abuse, types of drugs, and the consequences of official drug policies, this chapter continually refers to the **politics of drugs**.

13.1 Explain the politics behind the definition of drugs and the current United States drug laws.

THE POLITICS OF DRUGS

Drugs are a social problem in U.S. society. Yet not all drugs are considered problems, nor are all people who take drugs. Some drugs are legal, and others are not. Some drugs caused problems once but are now considered safe; some that were not considered problems now are. Some drug use is labeled "abuse," whereas other use is not. Ironically, the drugs most objected to and most strictly controlled are not those most dangerous to users and society. Marijuana and heroin, though illegal, are less dangerous than are barbiturates, alcohol, and nicotine, which can be legally obtained and used indiscriminately. To explain such irrationality, we must understand how drugs and their use came to be considered safe or illicit.

Historical Legality of Drugs

The definition of drug use and abuse is complicated in U.S. society because different patterns of use are acceptable for different people. Some religious groups forbid the use of any drugs, even for medicinal purposes. Others accept medicines but reject all forms of drugs, including caffeine, for recreational use. At the other extreme are groups that may use drugs in their religious rituals to expand the mind. Time also changes interpretation. Early in the twentieth century, for example, it was socially acceptable for men to smoke tobacco, but not for women to do so. Then around 1950 or so, it became socially acceptable for women to smoke tobacco, and smoking was regularly seen in movies and on television. Now, increasingly, smokers of both sexes find their smoking unacceptable in public places.

A bottle of opium from the nineteenth century, when it was legal.

Not only is there variance from group to group within society and from time to time, but there has also been virtually no consistency concerning the legality of drugs historically. The history of the acceptance or rejection of opiates (such as opium, morphine, and heroin) in the United States affords a useful example because it parallels what happened to public attitudes toward other drugs.

Opiates were legal in the nineteenth-century United States and were widely used as painkillers in the Civil War, with many soldiers becoming addicted. Morphine was legally manufactured from imported opium, and opium poppies were legally grown in the United States. Opium was widely dispensed in countless pharmaceutical preparations.

The only nineteenth-century context in which opiates were declared illegal was one created by anti-Chinese sentiment. The Chinese, who were imported to the West Coast to provide cheap labor to build the railroads, brought opium with them. At first, their opium dens were tolerated. But as the cheap Chinese labor began to threaten the White labor market, there was agitation to punish the Chinese for their "evil" ways. San Francisco and several other West Coast cities passed ordinances around 1875 prohibiting opium dens. These laws were, as some analysts have noted, aimed at the Chinese, not the drug.

The early 1900s were characterized as a period of reform. A number of individuals and groups wanted to legislate morals; the Eighteenth Amendment, which prohibited the sale and use of alcohol, was passed in 1919 as a result of pressure from these reform forces. These groups rallied against **psychoactive drugs** because they believed them to be sinful. They fought against "demon rum" and "demon weed," as well as other moral evils such as gambling and prostitution. They believed that they were doing God's will and that, if successful, they would provide a better way of life for everyone. Therefore, they lobbied vigorously to achieve appropriate legislation and enforcement of the laws to rid the country of these immoral influences.

As a result of these reform efforts, Congress passed the Harrison Narcotics Act of 1914. This act was basically a tax law requiring people who dispensed opium products to pay a fee and keep records. The law was relatively mild. It did not prohibit the use of opium in patent medicines or even control its use. It did, however, establish a Narcotics Division in the Treasury Department (which eventually became the Bureau of Narcotics). This department assumed the task (which was not specified in the formal law) of eliminating drug addiction. Treasury agents harassed users, physicians, and pharmacists. The bureau launched a propaganda campaign to convince the public that there was a link between drug use and crime. Finally, the bureau took a number of carefully selected cases to court to broaden its powers. In all these endeavors, the bureau was successful. The net result was that a medical problem became a legal problem.

This point cannot be overemphasized: Prior to the Harrison Act, drug addicts were thought (by the public and government officials) to be sick and in need of individual help. They were believed to be enslaved and in need of being salvaged through the humanitarian efforts of others. But with various government actions (laws, court decisions, and propaganda) and the efforts of reformers, this image of addicts changed from a "medical" to a "criminal" problem. Once defined as a criminal problem, the solution became incarceration.

Factors Influencing Drug Laws and Enforcement

Read on
MySocLab Document:
Association Is Not
Causation: Alcohol
and Other Drugs
Do Not Cause Violence

The previous section shows how differently a drug can be viewed over time. Clearly, current policies regarding opium (most common in the form of heroin) are repressive, but alcohol and tobacco continue to be socially acceptable drugs. These differences, especially because the laws do not reflect the drugs' relative dangers to users, demonstrate that official drug policies are arbitrary and problematic. What, then, are the factors that affect the focus of our drug laws? We examine two factors: cultural reasons and interest groups.

- **Cultural Reasons.** Drug laws and policies tend to reflect how people typically perceive drug use. Certain drugs have negative stereotypes, and others do not. Government may have orchestrated these stereotypes or they may be the result of faulty research, propaganda of reformers, negative portrayals in the media, religious ideology, and so on. In the 1940s, for example, most people in the United States shared the assumption that marijuana smokers were "dope fiends." They believed that marijuana users were criminals, immoral, violent, and out of control (an idea encouraged in anti-drug propaganda films like *Reefer Madness* in 1936). Until about 1965, public consensus supported the strict enforcement of marijuana laws. Marijuana was believed to be a dangerous drug associated with other forms of deviance, such as sexual promiscuity and crime. Even college students were virtually unanimous in their condemnation of marijuana smokers as deviants of the worst sort. But the social upheavals of the 1960s included experimentation with drugs and the questioning of society's mores. Rapid changes in attitudes and behavior occurred, especially among the young and college educated. Most significantly, the use of marijuana skyrocketed. In 1965, 18,815 people were arrested for violations of state and local marijuana laws, and these numbers continue to increase each year. By 2010, over half of all arrests for drug abuse violations were for marijuana (either possession or selling), totaling 853,839 arrests in one year (Drugwarfacts.org 2012).

  Public opinion polls reveal that Americans are divided over the legalization of marijuana. A 2011 Gallup poll found that 50 percent of Americans were in favor of legalizing marijuana, and 46 percent were opposed (Newport 2011). Those opposed believe that marijuana is physically addictive and that its use leads to the use of hard drugs (in other words, they believe it is a **"gateway drug"**). Research has shown both notions to be false. Marijuana is not physically addictive; it does not cause people to use heroin or other harder drugs. Despite the facts, however, the public generally accepts the negative stereotypes and thus fears the drug and supports strict enforcement.

  Some drug use has been interpreted as a symbolic rejection of mainstream values, and in this situation those supporting the status quo condemn the drug. Drugs such as alcohol and nicotine do not have this connotation. Because marijuana use was closely associated with the youth protest of the 1960s, many construed it as a symbol of an alternative lifestyle, a rejection of the traditional values of hard work, success through competition, initiative, and materialism and as support for socialism, unpatriotic behavior, sexual promiscuity, and rejection of authority. As long as this view prevailed, punitive measures against marijuana users seemed justified to many if not most citizens.

- **Interest Groups.** The approaches for controlling drug use have more to do with the power and social class structure of society than with the inherent characteristics of the substance being controlled. Just as the early anti-opium laws were aimed at Chinese workers, not at opium itself, so the reform movements aimed at prohibition of alcohol represented retaliation by the old middle class—rural, Protestant, native born—against the largely Catholic urban workers and immigrants who threatened their privileged status. Jenkins examines the relationship between power and drug laws and finds,

> Historical examples are not hard to find. Joseph Gusfield's book Symbolic Crusade explained the temperance movement in nineteenth-century America in terms of underlying conflicts between old-established elite groups, who were mainly Anglo-Saxon and Protestant, and newer Catholic populations, who were German and Irish. As Catholics viewed alcohol consumption more tolerantly than did Protestants, temperance laws became a symbolic means of reasserting WASP power and values. Other writers have suggested ethnic agendas for the campaigns to prohibit opium in the 1880s (as part of an anti-Chinese movement) and marijuana in the 1930s (which stigmatized a drug associated with African Americans and Mexicans). Repeatedly, African Americans have been the primary targets of such movements, whether the drug in question was cocaine in the progressive era, heroin in mid-century, or crack in the 1980s. During the drug war launched by Presidents Reagan and Bush, for example, the crack cocaine favored by black users attracted savage penalties in the form of severe mandatory sentences for dealing and possession, while lesser sanctions were inflicted upon the mainly white users of cocaine in its powdered form. (1999:13)

A final example of the relationship between social class and drug policy can be found in the current drive to liberalize marijuana laws. When marijuana was used primarily by the lower working class (such as Mexican Americans), the law against its use was extremely punitive. In the 1960s, this changed when middle-class, White, affluent college youth became the primary users. However much parents may have disagreed with their children's use of marijuana, they did not want them treated as criminals and stigmatized as drug users. The ludicrousness of the gap between the punishments for marijuana use and for alcohol use became readily apparent to the educated. As a result, White, affluent, and powerful people in most communities and states mounted a push to liberalize the laws.

Mosher and Akins (2007) argued that by demonizing certain drugs and not others, the government, the criminal justice system, and the media all serve their own interests. For example, a significant part of U.S. agriculture and consumer industry is engaged (with government support) in the production and marketing of nicotine and alcohol products. Even though it is well known that tobacco is harmful to users, the government will not ban its use because of the probable outcry from farmers, the states where tobacco is a major crop, and the tobacco manufacturers, wholesalers, retailers, transporters, and advertisers. Marijuana, on the other hand, is merchandised and sold illegally, so there is no legitimate economic interest pushing for its legalization.

Similarly, the pharmaceutical industry works diligently to dissuade Congress from further restricting amphetamines and other pills. In 1970, pushed by President Nixon, Congress passed the Comprehensive Drug Abuse Prevention and Control Act. Some forces tried to include amphetamines in the dangerous-drug category in that bill, but without success. The law declared marijuana possession a serious crime but did not do the same for amphetamines, despite irrefutable evidence that they are more dangerous to the user.

The illegal status of some drugs enables illicit economic interests to flourish. Underworld suppliers of drugs oppose changes in the law because legalization would seriously reduce their profits. They therefore promote restrictive legislation. The result is often a strange alliance between underworld economic interests and religious/moral interests seeking the same end—prohibition of the drug—but for opposite reasons. Thus, a member of Congress could safely satisfy religious zealots and organized crime alike by voting for stricter drug laws.

The law enforcement profession is another interest group that may use its influence to affect drug policy. If drugs and drug users are considered threats, then budgets to seize them will be increased. More arrests will be made, proving the necessity of enforcement and, not incidentally, the need for higher pay and more officers. Perhaps the best example of this syndrome is provided by the activity of the Narcotics Bureau, created by the Harrison Act of 1914. As mentioned earlier, the bureau was instrumental in changing the definition of opiate use from a "medical" activity to a "criminal" one. The bureau used a number of tactics to "prove" that its existence was necessary: It won court cases favorable to its antidrug stance; it vigorously used the media to propagate the "dope fiend" mythology; and it used statistics to incite the public or to prove its own effectiveness.

In effect, the Narcotics Bureau created a **moral panic**. Moral panics occur when a social problem is defined as a threat to societal values and interests. Moral panics often involve the exaggeration of social phenomena and can result in changes in social policy. Some examples include the media's portrayal of crack cocaine and "crack babies" in the 1980s; the "dope fiend" mythology promoted by the United States government in the early 1900s and again in the 1960s; and more recently, the media portrayal of methamphetamine, "meth babies," and methamphetamine-related crime.

Although *all* drugs are associated with certain harms to individuals and to society, the current drug laws are illogical. They reflect successful political lobbying by a variety of powerful interest groups, with the less powerful suffering the consequences. Despite the drug laws and shifting definitions of certain drugs, an examination of the extent of drug use in U.S. society demonstrates the prevalence of this social problem among all social groups.

DRUG USE IN U.S. SOCIETY

13.2 Discuss the most commonly abused illegal and legal drugs and how drug use varies by class, race, and gender.

Drugs are used worldwide for pleasure and medicinal purposes. The average U.S. family has about thirty different drugs in its medicine cabinet and numerous alcoholic beverages in its liquor cabinet. Approximately 90 percent of the people in the United States are daily caffeine users, and roughly 45 million Americans currently smoke cigarettes. One of the most comprehensive studies on drug use is the annual National Household Survey on Drug Use and Health conducted by SAMHSA (Substance Abuse and Mental Health Services Administration 2012a). According to the most recent reports for 2010, 51.8 percent of the population over age 12 (~131.3 million people) reported being a current user of alcohol, 27.4 percent (69.6 million people) used tobacco in the past month, and 8.9 percent (22.6 million people) used an illicit drug in the past month (see Figure 13.1). A 2011 University of Michigan survey (Monitoring the Future) found that 40 percent of twelfth-graders had used some illicit drug and 63.5 percent had used alcohol in the last year (Johnston et al. 2012). In 2010, there were over 1.6 million state and local arrests for drug abuse violations (Federal Bureau of Investigation 2012). In short, psychoactive drugs, both legal and illegal, are important to a significant portion of Americans.

Commonly Abused Illegal Drugs

- **Marijuana.** Very much like alcohol, marijuana is a social drug. Marijuana comes from the hemp plant *Cannabis sativa*, a plant cultivated for at least 5,000 years and found throughout the world. It is the world's fourth most widely used psychoactive drug

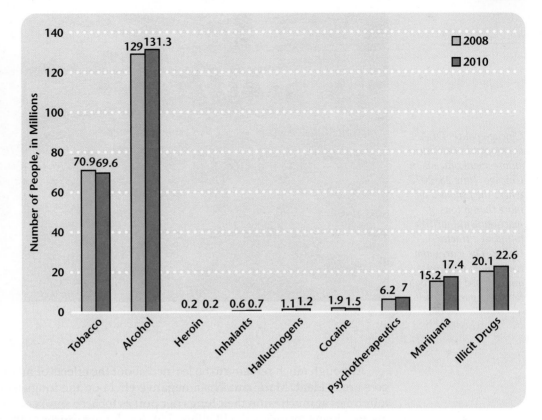

FIGURE 13.1

Past Month Drug Use among Persons Age 12 and Older: 2008 & 2010

Note: "Illicit Drugs" category includes marijuana.

Sources: SAMHSA, Substance Abuse and Mental Health Services Administration. 2009. "Results from the 2008 National Survey on Drug Use and Health: National Findings." Office of Applied Studies. NSDUH Series H-36, HHS Publication NO. (SMA) 09-4434. Rockville, MD. Substance Abuse and Mental Health Services Administration (SAMHSA). 2012. "Results from the 2010 National Survey on Drug Use and Health: Summary of National Findings." Office of Applied Studies. NSDUH Series H-41, HHS Publication NO. (SMA) 11-4658. Rockville, MD.

(following caffeine, nicotine, and alcohol) and, by far, the most widely used illicit drug in the United States. In 2010, approximately 17.4 million Americans used marijuana at least once in the month prior to being surveyed, and an estimated 4.6 million Americans use marijuana on a daily or almost daily basis (SAMHSA 2012a). Although it is often thought that marijuana is a relatively harmless drug, in 2010, marijuana was a factor in 461,028 hospital emergency room visits in the United States (SAMHSA 2012b).

The main active chemical in marijuana is tetrahydrocannabinol (THC), which stimulates the brain cells to release the chemical dopamine. Dopamine produces a relaxing effect, increases the intensity of sense impressions, and provides a "high" akin to one produced by alcohol.

 Read on MySocLab Document: Becoming a Marijuana User

Marijuana is a widely misunderstood drug. Under the Controlled Substances Act, the Drug Enforcement Administration classifies marijuana as a **Schedule 1 drug**. That is, it has high potential for abuse and no currently accepted medical use in treatment in the United States. Many consider marijuana addictive, asserting that it creates psychological dependence. Some researchers have argued that it causes lower levels of sex hormones to be produced in males and breaks up chromosomes, causing genetic problems for future generations.

Chicago police, DEA agents, and other law enforcement officials in Chicago, June 28, 2012, where they showed off more than 8 tons of marijuana authorities found in a tractor-trailer. The marijuana was grown in Mexico and shipped to Chicago for street gangs to sell.

View on
MySocLab Figure:
Marijuana: Trends
in Annual Use,
Risk, Disapproval,
and Availability,
Grades 8, 10, and 12

Although much remains to be learned about the effects of marijuana, some dangers are evident. Marijuana has a negative effect on the lungs (smokers get about four times as much tar in their lungs per puff as tobacco smokers). As a result, smoking marijuana increases the likelihood of developing cancer of the neck or head, as well as increasing the risk of chronic cough, bronchitis, and emphysema. Its use also increases dangers for people with damaged hearts. According to the National Institute on Drug Abuse, heavy marijuana use is also associated with depression, anxiety, job-related problems and higher job turnover, lower high school graduation rates, and lower grades (2012). A final danger is arrest and a criminal record, the consequence of its use being officially defined as criminal. On the positive side, we know that marijuana is not physiologically addictive; there is no evidence of a lethal dose; and it has been found to have positive effects for certain medical problems, such as migraine headaches, muscle spasms associated with epilepsy and multiple sclerosis, glaucoma, and asthma. Of special note is the successful use of marijuana to reduce or eliminate the nausea that accompanies chemotherapy treatments for cancer. It can also stimulate appetite in the chronically ill. Currently, eighteen states and Washington, DC, have laws that remove the state-level criminal penalties for growing or possessing medical marijuana (the possession limits vary in each state), something that the U.S. Drug Enforcement Administration is openly against (DEA 2012). It is the current position of the U.S. Drug Enforcement Administration that smoking marijuana is harmful, and there are safer medicinal drug alternatives that have been approved by the Federal Drug Administration. In the states that have removed state-level criminal penalties, individuals who use marijuana for medical purposes are not exempt from federal laws because marijuana is still classified as a Schedule 1 drug.

There is growing evidence that marijuana use is on the rise, as the daily use rate for twelfth-graders is at its highest rate since 1981. Roughly one in fifteen high school seniors is a daily marijuana user (Johnston et al. 2012). Furthermore, among teenagers

Speaking to Students

GENERATIONAL FORGETTING

Monitoring the Future (MTF) is a long-term study of American adolescents, college students, and adults conducted by the University of Michigan. Conducted annually since 1975, MTF demonstrates drug use and drug attitude trends over time and reveals interesting patterns (see Johnston et al. 2012). The authors of MTF find that determinants of use are at least partly affected by perceived benefits and perceived risks associated with each drug. For example, the perceived risk associated with marijuana use has been falling for the past five years, and daily use among teenagers is on the rise. In another example, the rise in abuse of prescription drugs may be related to the fact that many of the drugs are advertised on television and prescribed by doctors, so the perceived risk associated with taking them is lessened. When a new drug emerges (like bath salts), or an old drug makes a comeback, there is a lag time when the risks associated with that drug are unknown. "Generational Forgetting is when drugs make a comeback in popularity because knowledge among youth of the drug's adverse consequences faded as generational replacement took place" (Johnston et al. 2012:7). According to MTF, LSD and methamphetamine were widely used in the 1960s and then made a comeback in the 1990s due to generational forgetting. Similar patterns can be seen for heroin, cocaine, PCP, and crack cocaine. Today, LSD, inhalants, and ecstasy are all showing signs of a comeback and generational forgetting, that is, the perceived risk associated with these drugs has declined. It would appear, then, that educating the public on the risks associated with each different drug type is an important component to reducing drug use in the population.

the perceived risk for using marijuana has been falling in the last five years, perhaps the result of the debate over medical marijuana (Johnston et al. 2012). For a closer look at drug use patterns over time, see the "Speaking to Students" panel "Generational Forgetting."

- **Hallucinogens.** Also called psychedelics, hallucinogens produce sensory experiences that represent a different reality to the user. The person may react to trivial everyday objects as if they had great meaning. Emotions may be greatly intensified. Among the perceptual phenomena experienced by some is the feeling that one is looking at oneself from the outside. Hallucinogens occur naturally in the peyote cactus, some mushrooms, and certain fungi and other plants. Bad experiences with psychedelics include panic associated with loss of control, the common hallucination that spiders are crawling over the body, paranoia and delusions, and occasionally suicide. The psychedelic drug phencyclidine (PCP) is perhaps the most dangerous. This drug, which is relatively easy to manufacture, can cause psychotic reactions (hallucinations, combative or self-destructive impulses), loss of bowel and bladder control, slurred speech, and inability to walk. Taken in large quantities, it can induce seizures, coma, and death. There is no evidence that physical dependence develops for any of the hallucinogenic drugs. For some people, though, psychological dependence occurs. In 2010, 1.2 million people reported using a hallucinogen in the previous month (SAMHSA 2012a).

The drug ecstasy is a synthetic drug with stimulant and hallucinogenic effects. Users say that ecstasy produces a high for up to six hours with feelings of euphoria, empathy, and heightened senses. Ecstasy is one of several popular drugs known as "club drugs," used by youth at all-night dance parties, dance clubs, and bars. In 2010, 4.7 percent of Americans reported using ecstasy in the past year (SAMHSA 2012a). According to research by the University of Michigan, ecstasy use declined among eighth, tenth, and twelfth graders since its peak in 2001, but rates increased for twelfth graders between 2010 and 2011 (Johnston et al. 2012). Regular use can produce blurred vision, confusion, sleeplessness, depression, muscle cramping, fever, chills, hallucinations, and anxiety. Used in combination with alcohol, the effects can be dangerous. The most serious effect of ecstasy is that the drug interferes with the body's ability to regulate temperature. The sharp increase in body temperature can result in severe dehydration, or, on the opposite extreme, an individual will drink too much water and can suffer from water poisoning of their bloodstream.

- **GHB (Gamma Hydroxybutyrate).** GHB is a central nervous system depressant that, similar to the drug Rohypnol or "roofie," can produce amnesia (an idea made popular in the movie *The Hangover*). It is a colorless, odorless liquid that is mixed with alcoholic drinks or fruit juices. It relaxes or sedates the body, slowing breathing and the heart rate. Users feel euphoric, then sleepy. Overdose results in nausea, vomiting, drowsiness, and headache and can escalate to loss of consciousness, seizures, and a comatose state. GHB has two qualities that make it a favorite date-rape drug: (1) It knocks out users and their short-term memory, and (2) it clears quickly from the body, so laboratory tests might not detect it.

Watch on
MySocLab Video:
Opium Addiction

- **Narcotics (Opiates).** Narcotics are powerful depressants that have a pronounced effect on the respiratory and central nervous systems. Medically, they are used very effectively to relieve pain, treat diarrhea (paregoric), and stop coughing (codeine). These drugs, which include opium and its derivatives (morphine and heroin), also produce a feeling of euphoria.

  Opiates are highly addictive and highly dangerous. Prolonged users experience severe withdrawal symptoms. Because the drug is not regulated, it can include harmful impurities and be of varying potency. As a result, between 3,000 and 4,000 users die annually of heroin overdoses. The sharing of needles is a major cause of hepatitis and, in recent years, HIV infection (the precursor of AIDS). Efforts to supply clean needles to the addict population are resisted by government officials because that would appear to condone, even promote, an illegal activity. Another danger associated with heroin is the high cost of purchasing the illegal drug (maintaining a heroin addiction can cost hundreds of dollars per day). The users must spend much of their time finding ways to supply their habit, which may include theft or prostitution. The possession of heroin is a criminal offense, leading to incarceration. Taken together, then, the criminal activities an addict turns to plus the complications of poor-quality drugs and infection lead to a relatively high rate of deaths.

  The annual prevalence of heroin use has remained fairly constant among teenagers, hovering around 0.8 percent for twelfth graders in 2011 (Johnston et al. 2012). More disturbing are trends for other opiate-based painkillers such as Vicodin and OxyContin. The potential for addiction to painkillers and other prescription drugs was made public when Rush Limbaugh, a well-known conservative radio host, admitted to being addicted to prescription painkillers in 2003, as well as the drug-related deaths of popular stars Anna Nicole Smith, Brittany Murphy, and Michael Jackson. The authors of the Monitoring the Future study note that "these prescription-type drugs have become more important in the nation's larger drug abuse problem, reflecting their gradual increase in popularity over an extended period of time while the use of a number of illegal drugs (e.g., LSD, ecstasy, and heroin) has receded considerably" (Johnston et al. 2007:14). According to the Centers for Disease Control and Prevention (2012), prescription drugs have now surpassed heroin and cocaine as the leading cause of fatal overdoses.

- **Cocaine.** Cocaine is a strong central nervous system stimulant. It stimulates an area in the brain that regulates the sensation of pleasure, intensifying sexual highs and producing euphoria, alertness, and feelings of confidence. An estimated 15 percent of people who try cocaine become addicted. Two studies conducted in 2004 used rats to demonstrate this addictive nature of cocaine. In a French study, rats were given cocaine for three months, and then the scientists cut the rats' drug supply. They found that a certain percentage of the rats were very persistent in trying to get their cocaine, even if it meant getting shocked electrically. In the British study, they also found that rats were willing to experience shocks on their feet to get their fix of cocaine, but only those rats that had been taking cocaine for a long time. The rats that had been taking cocaine for only a short time gave up after their first electric shock (reported in *Medical News Today* 2004).

  In 2010, there were 1 million current cocaine users (SAMHSA 2012a). Repeated use of cocaine can produce paranoia, hallucinations, sleeplessness, tremors, weight loss, and depression. Snorting cocaine (the typical procedure) draws the cocaine powder through the nasal passages, leading to permanent damage to the mucous membranes and serious breathing difficulties. Moreover, snorting allows the cocaine to be absorbed rapidly into the bloodstream and subsequently the brain. If the user desires a more potent dosage, cocaine can be injected in solution directly into the veins or chemically converted and smoked in the process called *freebasing*. Another variation is to mix cocaine with heroin, which combines a powerful stimulant with a potent depressant.

  Crack is a smokable form of cocaine, created by mixing cocaine, baking soda, and water and heating them. This potent drug provides an almost instant rush, reaching the brain within eight seconds, with peak effects within a few minutes. Because crack's effects are more short-lived and more intense than powder cocaine, there is a greater urge toward repeated use. Crack, compared with powder cocaine, is cheaper and provides a quicker high.

- **Methamphetamine.** Also known as speed, crystal, crank, chalk, glass, or ice, methamphetamine is part of a subclass of amphetamines. It is a powerful addictive stimulant that affects the central nervous system. It can be injected, smoked, snorted, and ingested orally or anally. Methamphetamine use decreases appetite, heightens energy levels, enables people to be physically active for long periods, and provides a sense of euphoria similar to that of cocaine (Covey 2007).

  Methamphetamine use is associated with a number of negative effects, both short- and long-term. Short-term effects include higher pulse rate, higher blood pressure, increased body temperature, convulsions, irritability, and nervousness. During the coming-down period, the user may become agitated and potentially violent (Covey 2007). Long-term effects include severe psychological and physical dependence, violent behavior and paranoia, chronic fatigue, depression, open sores and infections on the skin from picking and scratching at imaginary bugs, tooth decay and dental deterioration, and severe weight loss. Methamphetamine acts as a corrosive on the gums and teeth and softens the teeth so that they literally melt away.

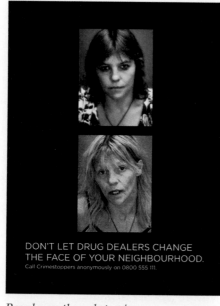

DON'T LET DRUG DEALERS CHANGE
THE FACE OF YOUR NEIGHBOURHOOD.
Call Crimestoppers anonymously on 0800 555 111.

Regular methamphetamine use can cause dramatic physiological damage both inside and outside the body, as shown in these photos of the changed facial appearance of this young woman.

Methamphetamine use and addiction has become a frequent topic in the mass media. Much as it did during the "crack epidemic" of the 1980s and 1990s, the media is again using the word *epidemic* to describe the problem. The government has turned its attention to methamphetamine as well. Congress passed the Comprehensive Methamphetamine Control Act of 1996, the Methamphetamine Anti-Proliferation Act of 2000, and the Combat Methamphetamine Epidemic Act (CMEA) of 2005. The first of these acts doubled the maximum penalties for possession of the drug and possession of equipment used to manufacture the drug from four to ten years. All three acts also focus on limiting the sale of ingredients that can be used to manufacture methamphetamine. The CMEA of 2005 regulates the retail over-the-counter sales of ephedrine, pseudoephedrine, and phenylpropanolamine, which are common ingredients in cough, cold, and allergy products. Those drugs are now placed out of customer reach, customers must show identification and sign a log book, and customers are limited to no more than 9 grams of ephedrine per month.

Studies on the amount of methamphetamine use are mixed. Many substance abuse authorities believe that use and distribution are on the rise, thus resulting in an "epidemic" (for a review of these studies, see Covey 2007). On the other hand, the U.S. DEA claims that the number of meth labs has decreased as a result of the Combat Methamphetamine Epidemic Act, and prominent research studies show a decline in use. In 1999, 4.7 percent of high school seniors had used methamphetamine in the past year compared to 1.4 percent in 2011 (Johnston et al. 2012). Similarly, the National Survey on Drug Use and Health shows that numbers of past-month users have declined from 731,000 in 2006 to 353,000 in 2011 (SAMHSA 2012a). Despite these declining numbers, the spread of methamphetamine use has been "likened to an epidemic moving from the West and Southwest to the rest of the country" (Covey 2007:23).

Legal but Dangerous Drugs

At the beginning of this chapter, we pointed out that the definitions concerning drugs and drug-related behaviors are socially constructed; that is, these definitions shift and change over time. Nothing illustrates this more poignantly than looking at the legality of certain drugs and the age at which the consumption of such drugs becomes *defined* as legal. For example, in 1992, Congress directed all states to establish 18 as the minimum age to purchase and smoke cigarettes. In Alaska, the minimum age is 19. That a person can simply step over a state line and his or her behavior will be defined as illegal or not demonstrates this social construction.

- **Nicotine.** Nicotine is the active ingredient of tobacco. Cigarette smoking remains the leading preventable cause of death in the United States—accounting for one of every five deaths (443,000 people) each year (Centers for Disease Control and Prevention 2012). This figure includes approximately 49,400 deaths per year from secondhand smoke exposure. Nicotine is a stimulant that raises blood pressure, increases the heart rate, dulls the appetite, and provides the user with a sense of alertness. As a stimulant, nicotine is responsible for a relatively high probability of heart disease and strokes among cigarette smokers. In addition to the nicotine, smokers inhale various coal tars, nitrogen dioxide, formaldehyde, and other ingredients that increase the chances of contracting lung cancer, throat cancer, emphysema, and bronchitis. Former Surgeon General Richard Carmona has reported that smoking causes no fewer than twenty-six diseases, including cancers of the stomach, uterus, cervix, pancreas, and kidneys (*Arizona Daily Star* 2004). Moreover, inhaling secondary tobacco smoke contributes to respiratory infections in babies, triggers new cases of asthma in previously unaffected children, and exacerbates symptoms in asthmatic children. Because of all the health problems associated with smoking, the CDC estimates that the cost of smoking to the nation for the years 2000 to 2004 was approximately $193 billion in medical costs and lost worker productivity (Centers for Disease Control and Prevention 2012).

Current estimates indicate that approximately 45.3 million adult Americans smoke cigarettes. Looking at patterns of smoking behavior, several points are clear (Centers for Disease Control and Prevention 2012): (1) More adult men smoke than women (21.5 percent versus 17.3 percent); (2) smoking and education are inversely related (that is, as education level goes up, the incidence of smoking goes down; see Figure 13.2); and (3) cigarette smoking is more common among adults living below poverty level than among those not in poverty (28.9 percent versus 18.3). Thus, the poor and uneducated are more likely to smoke.

Although the tobacco industry is enormous, it is faced with declining sales due to public smoking bans, increased tobacco taxes, and public antismoking campaigns. The tobacco companies have responded in three ways. First, the tobacco companies have invested heavily in the federal, state, and local campaigns of politicians in the hope of favorable legislation (regarding such issues as public smoking, selling through vending machines, reining in the Federal Drug Administration, and the extent of liability in impending lawsuits). The tobacco industry gave $1.5 million in contributions to federal candidates in the 2009 to 2010 election cycle (The Campaign for Tobacco-Free Kids 2012).

The second strategy of the tobacco companies is to increase their advertising in the United States and attempt to hook new users. According to the CDC (2012),

FIGURE 13.2

Past Month Cigarette Smoking among Adults Age 18 and Over, by Education: 2010

Source: Substance Abuse and Mental Health Services Administration (SAMHSA). 2012. "Results from the 2010 National Survey on Drug Use and Health: Summary of National Findings." Office of Applied Studies. NSDUH Series H-41, HHS Publication NO. (SMA) 11-4658. Rockville, MD.

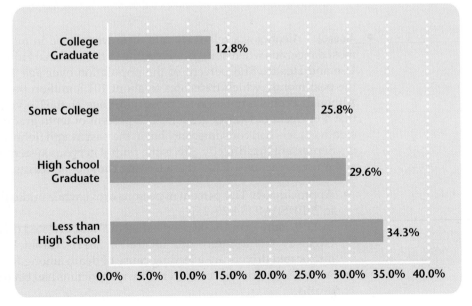

in 2006 (latest data available), tobacco companies spent $12.4 billion on advertisements and promotions. This amounts to $34 million per day, or annually $42 for every person in the United States and more than $275 for each adult U.S. smoker. This advertising is aimed primarily at minorities, women, and youth. Consider the following:

- Studies have found a high density of tobacco billboards in racial and ethnic minority communities. A study by the University of Pittsburgh School of Medicine found that there are 2.6 times as many ads per person in predominantly Black neighborhoods as there are in predominantly White neighborhoods (Toland 2007).
- Tobacco companies have marketed specifically to Hispanics and American Indians, including the promotion of cigarette brands like Rio, Dorado, and American Spirit (Centers for Disease Control and Prevention 2012).
- In 2007, R.J. Reynolds unveiled a new product called "Camel No. 9," a cigarette with a decorative pink band, a tiny pink camel, and an ebony box with hot-pink and teal accents. With the slogan "light and luscious," it is clearly a product targeting women and young girls (Quindlen 2007).
- Smoking is featured in many video games targeting youth. For example, the game "The Chronicles of Riddick: Escape from Butcher Bay" has players win packs of cigarettes, and the game makes fun of the warning labels on the packs (Perry 2010).
- In 2007, a report by the Harvard School of Public Health showed that cigarette companies increased the amount of nicotine in their cigarettes by an average of 11 percent from 1998 to 2005 (reported in Siegel 2007). Although tobacco companies deny claims of a deliberate increase in nicotine, antismoking groups argue that this was a calculated move to hook new smokers on their product.

A third strategy of the tobacco companies is to increase advertising and sales overseas to compensate for declining domestic sales. According to Kluger (2009),

> This year tobacco companies will produce more than 5 trillion cigarettes—or about 830 for every person on the planet. In China, 350 million people are currently hooked on tobacco, which means the country has more smokers than the U.S. has people. (50)

- **Alcohol.** Alcohol is a relatively safe drug when used in moderation but one of the most dangerous when abused. According to the National Household Survey on Drug Use and Health, 51.8 percent of the population over age 12 consumed alcohol in the past month, which translates to about 131.3 million people (SAMHSA 2012a). Although alcohol is not legal for those under age 21, the University of Michigan found that 40 percent of twelfth graders, 27.2 percent of tenth graders, and 12.7 percent of eighth graders had consumed alcohol in the past month (Johnston et al. 2012). Alcohol is a depressant that directly affects the central nervous system, slowing brain activity and muscle reactions. Thus, it is a leading cause of accidents:

- Approximately 11.4 percent of persons drove while under the influence of alcohol in 2010 (SAMHSA 2012a).
- In 2010, more than 10,000 people died in alcohol-related driving crashes (National Highway Traffic Safety Administration 2012). Automobile accidents involving intoxicated drivers are a leading cause of death among teenagers.
- Approximately seven out of ten drowning victims had been drinking prior to their deaths.

Alcohol consumption is related to other problems as well:

- Underage drinking costs Americans $62 billion per year in injuries, deaths, and lost work time (reported in Portillo 2006).
- There are intangible and immeasurable expenses due to disrupted families, spouse and child abuse, desertion, and countless emotional problems that arise from drinking. Most significant, two-thirds of victims who suffered violence from an intimate (a current or former spouse, boyfriend, or girlfriend) reported that alcohol had been a factor (Bureau of Justice Statistics 2007).
- Among youth (high school and college), excessive drinking is related to risky sexual behavior, vandalism, racist acts, homophobic violence, and sexual assault.
- One of the strongest risk factors for attempted suicide in both adults and youth is alcohol use.

Watch on
MySocLab Video:
Housing Alcoholics

Continued use of large quantities of alcohol can result in indigestion, ulcers, degeneration of the brain, and cirrhosis of the liver; over 20,000 Americans die of cirrhosis of the liver each year. Malnutrition is often associated with prolonged use of alcohol; a pint of whiskey provides about half of a person's daily calorie requirements but without the necessary nutrients. Heavy consumption also reduces the production of white blood cells, so alcoholics have a low resistance to bacteria. Alcoholics, in addition, run the danger of permanent destruction of brain cells, resulting in memory loss and sometimes psychotic behavior. Chronic use also results in physiological addiction. Withdrawal can be very dangerous, with the individual experiencing convulsions and delirium. The conclusion is inescapable, then, that alcohol is a dangerous legal drug for individuals and societies.

Drug Use Patterns by Class, Race, and Gender

Drug use and abuse is most often discussed as an individual's choice, an individual's behavior, and an individual's problem. However, examining drug use from a sociological standpoint reveals interesting patterns by class, race, and gender. These patterns demonstrate that a person's place in the social structure can increase or decrease the odds that he or she will use drugs and alcohol. Drug use is not uniform throughout society. For example, men of all ages and races are more likely than women to use illicit drugs. Even marital status matters—married women are less likely to use tobacco, engage in binge alcohol use, or use an illicit drug compared to divorced, separated, never married, or cohabitating women. In terms of social class, intravenous drug users continue to be found predominantly among the inner-city poor. This practice places them at great risk of exposure to the AIDS virus from the sharing of needles.

The disproportionate use of drugs by the poor is not limited to illicit drugs. As indicated previously in Figure 13.2, cigarette smoking is inversely related to education level. The lower the education level, the greater the incidence of cigarette smoking. The CDC estimates that nearly 28.9 percent of people living below the poverty line smoke. Statistics also reveal interesting differences by race/ethnicity and smoking. Native Americans have the highest rates of smoking (35.8 percent), and Asians have the lowest rates of smoking (12.5 percent; SAMHSA 2012a).

Alcohol use also varies greatly by race, social class, and age. Whites are more likely to report current use (defined as consuming any alcohol in the past month) than any other racial group (56.7 percent compared to 42.8 percent for Blacks and 38.4 percent for Asians) (SAMHSA 2012a). Youth in general are more likely to report binge and heavy use, with the highest prevalence among 21- to 25-year-olds. College students often are heavy binge drinkers during their college years. In fact, research

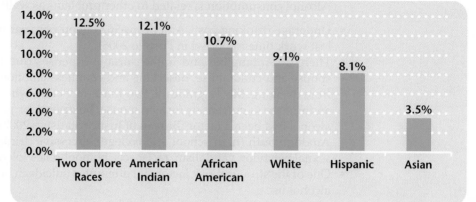

FIGURE 13.3

Past Month Illicit Drug Use among Persons Age 12 and Older, by Race/Ethnicity: 2010

Source: Substance Abuse and Mental Health Services Administration (SAMHSA). 2012. "Results from the 2010 National Survey on Drug Use and Health: Summary of National Findings." Office of Applied Studies. NSDUH Series H-41, HHS Publication NO. (SMA) 11-4658. Rockville, MD.

indicates that around 63.3 percent of college students drink alcohol, and 42.2 percent binge drink (defined as five or more drinks in a row; SAMHSA 2012a). Gender, too, is relevant, as Black women are much more likely than White women to be abstainers. Recall that the incidence of smoking decreases with higher levels of education. The opposite is true for drinking. The rates of current alcohol use increase with increasing levels of education.

Although Whites report a higher incidence of current alcohol use, illicit drug use reveals a different pattern. Individuals of two or more races report the highest rates of illicit drug use, followed by Native Americans (see Figure 13.3). Illicit drug use is also higher in large metro areas than in nonmetro areas (SAMHSA 2012a).

Recently, tobacco and alcohol companies have come under fire for targeting minority neighborhoods. They sponsor sports tournaments and music festivals in predominantly Black neighborhoods and purchase considerable advertising in Black publications. In 2004, cigarette companies came out with a new line of flavored cigarettes that antismoking activists claim specifically targets minority teens. The packaging features graffiti artists and other hip-hop imagery that appeals to minority youth (Associated Press 2004a).

In looking at the statistics, it is clear that drug use cuts across all class, racial, and gender lines. It is how the drugs (and the persons using those drugs) are defined that determines drug treatment and handling by the authorities. For example, in 2010 an estimated 5.1 million persons used pain relievers nonmedically, and they are often middle- and upper-class Whites (2.2 million used tranquilizers, 1.1 million used stimulants, and 374,000 used sedatives; SAMHSA 2012a). Unlike the poor—who tend to use illicit drugs and therefore are hassled by the authorities and treated in prisons and public hospitals—the more affluent tend to use legal and prescription drugs and are treated by private physicians. Thus, their addiction is typically protected and hidden from public awareness.

Explore on MySocLab Activity:
The Downward Spiral: Drug Use and Socioeconomic Status

Why Use Drugs?

It is clear that *all* drugs have the potential for harm, even those drugs that seem completely risk free. Aspirin, for example, may seem like a drug with few side effects, but taken in large doses, it can result in ulcers and stomach bleeding. A person needs only listen closely to commercials advertising drugs to see their potential for harm. By law, drug companies must state the possible side effects, and often they are numerous—from bowel problems to sexual dysfunction. So why do we subject ourselves to potential harm?

Listen on
MySocLab Audio:
NPR: Texas Considers
"Conscience Clause"
for Pharmacists

- **Medical Pressures.** In recent times, chemists have created numerous synthetic substances that have positive health consequences. Vaccines have been developed to fight diseases such as polio, mumps, smallpox, diphtheria, and measles. Many of these contagious diseases have been eliminated by the wonders of science. Similarly, antibiotics were created as cures for a number of infectious diseases. The public quickly accepted these drugs as beneficial. As a result, Americans are a highly drugged society, and total prescription drug expenditures in 2010 reached $307.4 billion (Berkrot 2011). In fact, U.S. residents spend far more on prescription drugs than do people in other developed countries, and rising costs have even driven some to smuggle prescriptions from other countries.

- **Cultural Pressures.** The United States has become a "quick-fix" society, with individuals seeking instant results and striving to meet cultural ideals about perfection. In seeking mental perfection, physical perfection, and improved physical performance, Americans have increasingly turned to artificial substances and enhancements to meet those ideals. In the early 1950s, chemists made a breakthrough in drugs that treated mental disorders such as depression, insomnia, aggression, hyperactivity, and tension. These drugs (tranquilizers, barbiturates, and stimulants) have since been widely prescribed by doctors for these problems. **Psychopharmacology**, the science of drugs that affect the mind, is on the verge of developing pills that will enrich memory, heighten concentration, enhance intelligence, and eliminate shyness or bad moods.

  Recently, there has been much controversy over the use of so-called behavior drugs for children. The CDC estimates that in 2010 ADHD (attention deficit/hyperactivity disorder) diagnoses in children rose to 5.2 million (Centers for Disease Control and Prevention 2012). From 2001 to 2004, there was a 49 percent rise in the use of ADHD drugs by children under the age of 5 and an astonishing 369 percent increase in spending on such drugs. In fact, this spending exceeded the spending for antibiotics and asthma medication for children (Johnson 2004). The symptoms for ADHD are inattentiveness, fidgeting, not listening, being easily distracted, making careless mistakes, and excessive talking. Stimulants such as Ritalin, Adderall, Concerta, and Dexedrine are prescribed to have the paradoxical effect of calming and focusing children who are chronically inattentive and hyperactive. These drugs stimulate the central nervous system, with many of the same pharmacological effects of cocaine. They affect the brain by enhancing the chemical dopamine, the neurotransmitter that plays a major role in cognition, attention, and inhibition. Their side effects are nervousness, insomnia, and loss of appetite. Although these stimulants for children are often successful, their widespread use raises some important questions:

  - The United States consumes 80 percent of the world's methylphenidate (the generic name for Ritalin). Are American youth more hyperactive than youth in other countries?
  - Is hyperactivity the inevitable by-product of a society-wide addiction to speed—to cellular phones, faxes, email, overnight mail, ever-faster computers? How are children affected by the high-stimulus activities that saturate their lives—video games, interactive television, hundreds of cable channels, and fast-action movies with vivid violence?
  - According to the CDC (2011), 13.2 percent of boys have received a diagnosis of ADHD compared to 5.6 percent of girls. Is the preponderance of boys diagnosed

as hyperactive because adults find that boys are more difficult to control than girls?

- What is the role of the pharmaceutical companies in the rapid growth of medications for ADHD? This is a billion-dollar sector of the pharmaceutical market.
- What is the role of managed-care companies and insurers in promoting the medication of children for ADHD? These organizations are concerned with costs (see Chapter 17), and it is much cheaper to prescribe pills, thus avoiding referring children to more expensive mental health specialists.
- Ritalin and other stimulants prescribed for ADHD work on the brain much like cocaine does. Children using this drug are "wired" every day, raising concern over its long-term effects. This is not the only way that children are wired. Companies promote energy drinks (high in caffeine) targeting youth by using names like Rockstar, Monster, Red Bull, and Venom. Are we creating an entire generation (called by some the "Rx generation") with a "sweet tooth for cocaine"?

View on MySocLab Figure: Age 12 and Older Reporting Nonmedical Use of Prescription-Type Psychotherapeutic Drugs, by Type of Drug

The widespread use of these stimulants leads to their abuse by adolescents and adults seeking pharmacological highs. Taken in larger amounts than prescribed and crushed and snorted, these drugs produce euphoria, greater energy and productivity, increased sexual appetite, and an overall feeling of being a lot smarter. As a result, the DEA says that drugs to treat ADHD rank among today's most stolen prescriptions and most abused drugs (Drug Enforcement Administration 2012). The Monitoring the Future study found that in 2011, 2.6 percent of high school seniors, 2.6 percent of tenth graders, and 1.3 percent of eighth graders had abused Ritalin in the previous year (Johnston et al. 2012).

Not only has U.S. society become increasingly concerned with mental perfection, but also the cultural ideals of physical perfection are overwhelming. Drugs can offer a way to meet these ideals. Consider the following:

- The largest area of growth in nonsurgical cosmetic procedures is in Botox injections (2,619,739 procedures in 2011). The injected toxin blocks the nerve impulses, temporarily paralyzing the muscles that cause wrinkles (American Society for Aesthetic Plastic Surgery 2012).
- In 2003, the FDA approved Humatrope, a brand of human growth hormone, for healthy children with short stature (defined as height more than 2 standard deviations below the mean for their age and sex).
- Ephedra, found in products to aid weight loss, enhance sports performance, and increase energy, was banned in 2004 after it was linked to deaths and reports of serious health problems.

Mental perfection and physical perfection pave the way for other performance pressures as well. The pressure to succeed in competitive situations may also encourage some people to take drugs. Individuals who want to be especially alert or calm to do well may take a drug to accomplish their goal. Sports present an excellent example of drug use to enhance performance. Athletes use two types of drugs: **restorative drugs** (to heal a traumatized part of the body) and **additive drugs** (to improve performance). Amphetamines, human growth hormones, hormones such as androstenedione (the favorite of home-run king Mark McGwire) and Creatine, and anabolic steroids are the additive drugs commonly used by athletes. Amphetamines increase alertness, respiration rate, blood pressure, muscle tension, heart rate, and blood sugar. The user is literally "psyched up" by amphetamines. Moreover, these drugs have the capacity to abolish a sense of fatigue. Growth hormones increase body size and strength. Anabolic steroids are male hormones that aid in adding weight and muscle. If an athlete wants to be a world-class weightlifter, shot putter, or discus thrower, the pressures are great

The reputation of professional baseball has been tarnished with accusations of steroid abuse.

to use anabolic steroids: They make the user stronger, and many competitors use such drugs to get the edge on the competition. Football players, even in high school, may use drugs to gain weight and strength to be a "star." In 2011, approximately 1.2 percent of high school seniors reported using androstenedione or anabolic steroids in the previous year (Johnston et al. 2012). At the 2012 London Olympics, the World-Anti Doping Agency banned over 100 athletes from competing in the games due to doping suspensions. Also in 2012, the U.S. Anti-Doping Agency stripped Lance Armstrong of his seven Tour de France titles and banned him from cycling for life due to the use of banned performance enhancing drugs. Clearly, the use of performance enhancing drugs by professional athletes is an ongoing problem.

Performance pressures have also extended into the bedroom, with drugs like Viagra, Cialis, and Levitra available to aid with sexual performance. Viagra, approved by the FDA in 1998, is a $2 billion-per-year seller for Pfizer, Inc.

The pressures to use drugs are unrelenting. They come from doctors, coaches, parents, teachers, peers, and advertising. People may learn to drink in families where social drinking is an integral part of meals, celebrations, and everyday relaxation. In situations such as cocktail parties, guests are expected to drink alcoholic beverages as part of the social ritual. Peer groups are also important for the entry of the individual into the world of illicit drug use. The person learns from others how to use the drug and how to interpret the drug's effects positively. Similarly, the pressures to meet society's ideals of mental and physical perfection and performance can be overwhelming, with drugs offering a "quick-fix" solution.

📖 **Read** on
MySocLab Document:
Millions for Viagra, Pennies for Diseases of the Poor

U.S. OFFICIAL POLICY: A WAR ON DRUGS

13.3 Give examples which demonstrate how the U.S. "war on drugs" is racist.

In 1971, President Richard Nixon called drug abuse "public enemy number one," and thus began the U.S. "war on drugs." The U.S. drug war is fought on two fronts: stopping the flow of drugs into the United States and using the criminal justice system to punish those who sell and use illegal drugs within the United States. The federal government spent over $15 billion in 2010 on the War on Drugs (a rate of about $500 per second) (Drugsense.org 2012). In fact, the drug war has cost taxpayers more than $1 trillion since 1971 (Associated Press 2010b).

Stopping the supply of drugs into the country (**interdiction**) involves the use of customs agents at the borders inspecting the baggage of passengers and cargo from planes, trucks, and ships. It involves working with other countries (especially Colombia, Peru, Ecuador, Bolivia, and Mexico) to destroy the places where drugs are grown, manufactured, and processed and to destroy the transportation networks to the United States (by sea and air, and by land through Mexico). These efforts involve the State Department, the Treasury Department, the Coast Guard, various branches of the military, and the Central Intelligence Agency (CIA). These agencies train local soldiers and supply them with equipment (helicopters, radar, and surveillance aircraft) and supplies (herbicides, guns, and munitions). This means, of course, that the United States is involved in destroying the crops (e.g., opium poppy and coca) of local farmers. It means the involvement of the United States (through the CIA) in local politics, siding with pro-U.S. factions against anti-U.S. factions, or involvement in civil wars, where rebels finance their operations with drugs in the fight against the established governments. It encourages violence, threats, and bribery as drug cartels use any means to keep their lucrative businesses flourishing (see the "Social Problems in Global Perspective" panel on the drug war in Mexico).

The policy of interdiction clearly is a failure. Drugs are found by the U.S. Customs, sometimes in large amounts. But massive amounts of drugs cross U.S. borders and enter an intricate distribution system within this country. Despite all our

Social Problems in Global Perspective

Mexico's Drug War

There is a war going on in Mexico. In 2006, Mexican President Felipe Calderón declared war on the country's drug cartels. Putting 45,000 army troops on the streets, he pledged to arrest the cartel leaders, confiscate their drugs, and seize the large amounts of cash that they need to operate. Since then, an estimated 35,000 to 40,000 people have died in drug-related violence. The drug cartels have conducted kidnappings, executions, and assaults. In early 2009, the police chief in Ciudad Juarez resigned after drug traffickers began to make good on their promise to kill police officers in the city until the chief stepped down (Navarrette 2009). The gangs have dumped severed heads in front of town halls and have essentially terrorized the Mexican people to put pressure on the government to back down. In 2011, thirty-five bound, tortured bodies were dumped onto a main thoroughfare during rush hour in the city of Veracruz (Associated Press 2011). On a positive note, since Calderón declared war in 2006, the five main drug cartels have been reduced to two (the Sinaloa and Zeta cartels) that are fighting for control over the country's drug market and trafficking routes (Associated Press 2011).

The United States has a large stake in Mexico's war, as it is estimated that 90 percent of all the cocaine flowing into the United States comes from Mexico, and 90 percent of the guns seized in drug-related violence in Mexico come from the United States (Navarrette 2009). In addition, the Mexican drug cartels have established a presence in approximately 230 U.S. cities. The United States has stepped in and provided $1.5 billion in funds (part of the $1.8 billion Merída Initiative) to help combat the war on drugs in Mexico and Central America. In addition, they have added officers and announced new security measures at the border. But according to some experts, the American demand for illegal drugs plays the most important role in fueling Mexico's drug war. "No matter how much law enforcement or financial help the U.S. government provides Mexico, the basics of supply and demand prevent it from doing much good" (Crary 2009:1).

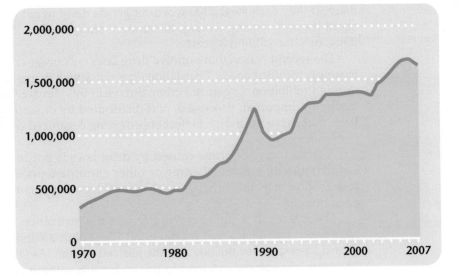

FIGURE 13.4

Adult Drug Arrests,
1970–2007

Source: This chart can be found on the Bureau of Justice Web site, Key Facts at a Glance, on the following page: http://bjs.ojp.usdoj.gov/content/glance/drug.cfm.

efforts, we have not stopped the supply; we have only dented it and made the drugs that enter the United States more expensive. The drug policy of interdiction also fails because it has led to strained relations with drug-producing nations in South America. By fighting our battles on their soil, the United States is often viewed as the villain.

The second front in the war on drugs occurs within the United States. Beginning in the 1970s, the courts became more punitive toward people selling or possessing illegal drugs. In New York State, for example, a law was passed in 1973 requiring a minimum sentence of fifteen years to life for a first-time offender caught selling as little as 2 ounces or possessing 4 ounces of cocaine or heroin. The police, too, became more active in ferreting out buyers and sellers through the use of undercover agents, wiretaps, and sting operations. As a result, the number of adults arrested for drug offenses grew from about 500,000 in 1980 to approximately 1.7 million in 2007 (Bureau of Justice Statistics 2010; see Figure 13.4). In fact, the United States imprisons a larger fraction of its population for drug offenses than European nations do for all crimes. This has led to tremendous overcrowding of both the courts and the prisons, resulting in a huge and costly growth in the number and size of prisons. (In California it costs approximately $47,000 per year to incarcerate one prisoner.)

Consequences of Official Drug Policies

The drug laws in the United States are irrational, and they do not achieve their intended goals of deterring crime by severely punishing the seller and user. There are three reasons this approach does not work to deter crime. First, by making drugs illegal and therefore dangerous to produce, transport, and sell, society pushes the cost to many times what it would be if they were legally available. Thus, heroin users, for example, are often forced into crime to sustain a high-cost habit. Crimes committed to produce money for drugs are typically nonviolent (prostitution, shoplifting, selling drugs, and burglary), but their cost is enormous. Suppose, for example, that there are 100,000 addicts in New York City with habits each costing $50 daily. If they each steal $300 worth of goods daily to get the $50 (a 6-to-1 ratio is about the way fencing works), the amount stolen in the city would be $30 million daily, or $10.68 billion a year!

The second reason that punitive drug laws encourage crime is that someone has to supply the illicit goods. Legislation does not dry up demand, as was vividly shown during Prohibition. Organized crime thrives in this climate. Illegal drugs are, for the most part, imported, processed, and distributed by organized crime groups. Drug laws, then, have the indirect effect of providing organized crime with its most lucrative source of income.

A third source of crime caused by drug laws is police corruption. Black market activities by organized crime or other entrepreneurs are difficult without the cooperation of police officials or drug enforcement agents, so their assistance is often bought.

The end result of police corruption and the realization that drug laws are arbitrary (such as the fact that marijuana is illegal but alcohol is legal) causes widespread disrespect for the law and the judicial system. As Garrison Keillor has said, "A marijuana grower can land in prison for life without parole while a murderer might be in for eight years. No rational person can defend this . . ." (2005:26). A final source of irreverence toward the law is the overzealousness of narcotics agents. In their efforts to capture drug law violators, agents have sometimes violated the constitutional rights of individuals (wiretapping, search and seizure without a warrant, entrapment, use of informants who are themselves addicts, and so on). All these abuses have contributed to an attitude of insolence on the part of many people toward agents of the law.

Criminal laws create crime and criminals. If there were no law regulating a behavior, then there would be no criminal. So it is with drug laws. Prior to 1914, heroin users were not criminals, nor were marijuana users before 1937. The drug laws, then, have created large numbers of criminals. By labeling and treating people as criminals, the justice system creates further crime (secondary deviance). In other words, efforts at social control actually cause the persistence of the deviant behaviors they are designed to eliminate. Several interrelated processes are at work here. First, as noted earlier, the drug user is forced to rely on illegal and very expensive sources. This reliance typically forces the user into crime or interaction with the criminal fringes of society. Second, when processed by the criminal justice system, the individual is stigmatized, which makes reintegration into normal society very difficult. All these factors encourage those pejoratively labeled by society to join together in a deviant drug subculture.

Official drug policies have been predicated on the assumption that punitive laws and rigorous enforcement were necessary to eradicate the menace of certain drugs. The policies, however, have had just the opposite effect. They have harmed the drug users in a variety of unnecessary ways; they have cost society untold billions of dollars in enforcement costs and have clogged courts and prisons; they have resulted in additional indirect and direct crime; and they have kept organized crime very profitable.

Is the Drug War Racist?

The official policy of the federal government is to punish the sellers and users of illicit drugs. The problem is that the laws and the punishment for their violation are unfair to African Americans and other racial minorities. Four facts buttress this allegation. First, recall that the data on past month illicit drug use by race reveals

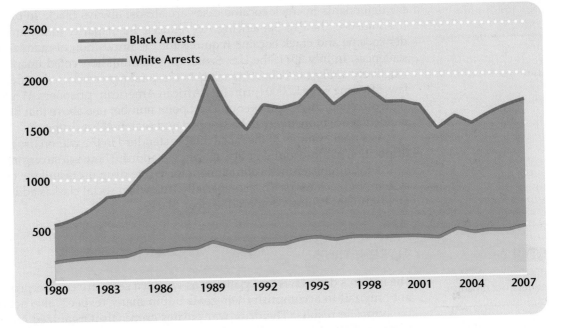

FIGURE 13.5

U.S. Rates of Adult Drug Arrests by Race, 1980–2007

Source: "Decades of Disparity: Drug Arrests and Race in the United States," March 2009. Human Rights Watch (Figure 1, page 6).

a rate of 10.7 percent for African Americans and 9.1 percent for Whites. According to the 2010 Decennial Census, there are 223,736,465 Whites and 38,929,319 African Americans in the United States. Given their numbers in the general population, this means that overall there are more Whites using illicit drugs than Blacks, yet the data show consistently that *African Americans are more likely to be imprisoned for drug offenses.* In every year from 1980 to 2007, Blacks were arrested nationwide on drug charges at rates relative to the population that were 2.8 to 5.5 times higher than White arrest rates (see Figure 13.5). In some states, Blacks were arrested at rates up to 11.3 times greater than the rate for Whites (Human Rights Watch 2009).

Second, federal drug enforcement has waged its war against drugs almost exclusively in minority neighborhoods. The issue is one of targeting—studies show that Blacks are more likely to be stopped while driving and searched. As Glasser notes,

> In Florida blacks were seventy-five times more likely than whites to be stopped and searched for drugs while driving. And it turned out that these racially targeted stops were the explicit result of a Drug Enforcement Administration program begun in 1986, called Operation Pipeline, that "trained" 27,000 state troopers in forty-eight states to spot cars that might contain drugs. Most of the cars spotted were driven by blacks. And this happened even though three-quarters of monthly drug users are white! (2006:25)

Third, historically the laws have differed in the severity of punishment if violated. Although powder cocaine and crack cocaine are the same drugs, prior to the Fair Sentencing Act of 2010, federal law treated them quite differently. Under previous law, crack offenses led to sentences 100 times more severe than powder cocaine sentences (Diamond and Millhiser 2011). This unfair 100-to-1 ratio was racist because the defendants in crack cocaine cases are almost always Black. In order to remedy this injustice, the Fair Sentencing Act reduces the disparity in the amounts of powder cocaine and crack cocaine required for the imposition of mandatory minimum sentences. In July 2011, the U.S. Sentencing Commission voted unanimously to retroactively apply the Fair Sentencing Act to prisoners convicted under the previous law, affecting over 12,000 (primarily African American) prisoners. While a step in the right direction, this not does counteract point number one above that Blacks and other minorities are more likely to be stopped and searched for drugs.

As a final example of the racial double standard in the war on drugs, consider the disposition of those found guilty of drug violations. There is a strong tendency for the courts to administer medical treatment for White drug users and the criminal justice system for Black users. This is especially true when social class is added to the racial mix—affluent Whites compared to poor Blacks.

ALTERNATIVES

13.4 Discuss alternatives to the current war on drugs.

The nation's drug laws and policies, as we have seen, are counterproductive. They not only fail to accomplish their goals but in many respects also actually achieve the opposite results. The drug war creates criminals. Organized crime flourishes because of official drug policies. The criminalization of drugs encourages corruption within the criminal justice system, and it reduces the freedoms guaranteed by the Constitution. As conducted, the war on drugs is unfair to racial minorities through racial profiling. It overburdens the courts and prisons, and most significant, it does not work.

The United States has alternatives concerning drug policy: (1) Continue to wage the war on drugs by enacting and enforcing criminal laws, (2) legalize drugs and regulate them through licensing and taxation, (3) take a public health approach, with an emphasis on decriminalization, and (4) address the social causes of drug use. We have already considered the first option—the criminalization of drug use—so we concentrate here on the other alternatives.

Regulation of Trade or Use through Licensing and Taxation

Legalizing a drug but regulating its use, as is now the case with alcohol, tobacco, and prescription drugs has some obvious benefits:

- It ensures the products' conformity to standards of purity and safety.
- It dries up the need for vast criminal networks that distribute drugs.
- It provides the government with revenues.
- Prison space and police activities would be reserved for the truly dangerous.

Opponents argue that government regulation would actually condone the use of drugs. This apparent approval, together with the easy availability and relatively low prices, would promote experimentation and use of the drug, perhaps increasing the number of users. While the majority of public opinion polls show that the public is not in favor of the legalization of all drugs, polls do indicate that attitudes are shifting regarding the legalization of marijuana (see Figure 13.6), especially for those under the age of 30.

Under the government regulation option, the biggest population to deal with would be the heroin addicts. These users are a special problem to themselves and society. Their habits are the most expensive, so of all drug users, they are most likely

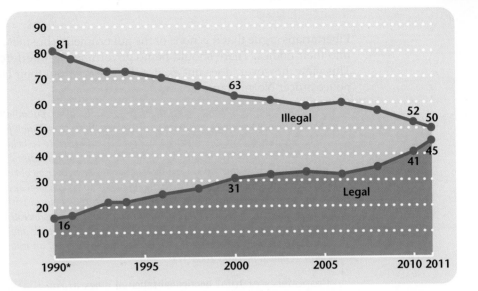

FIGURE 13.6

Should Marijuana Use Be Legal?

*1990–2008 data from the General Social Survey.

Source: Pew Research Center. Feb. 22–Mar. 1, 2011. QA63 Found in: http://people-press.org/files/2011/03/711.pdf, page 17.

to turn to crime. Their habit also requires almost full-time diligence in securing the drug; and being "strung out," they do not function normally in society. How, then, should the government deal with them? Hard-liners argue that they should be classified as criminals and incarcerated. Other people suggest that addicts could remain in society and be relatively productive if drugs were supplied to them cheaply, under government regulation and medical supervision.

This can be accomplished through **heroin maintenance**, which treats addicts as medical problems rather than criminal problems. Methadone or buprenorphine are medications that can be taken orally for the treatment of narcotic withdrawal and dependence. Taken once per day, methadone suppresses withdrawal symptoms for 24 to 36 hours. The drug does not make the user drowsy, it does not impair cognitive functions, and it does not interfere with driving a car or operating machinery. Although it is also addictive, the net effect is that a methadone user can continue to be a productive member of society without having to steal for his or her habit.

A number of the nation's heroin addicts are on **methadone maintenance**. Most states control and closely monitor the distribution of the drug. A benefit to this close monitoring is that there is no sharing of needles, a common problem among heroin users. Thus, it helps to control the spread of HIV infection.

In addition, methadone costs about $13 per day, a cheaper alternative to incarceration where the average cost in state prison is approximately $67 per day. Through the methadone maintenance program, addicts are not labeled as criminals. They are considered to have a medical, not a moral, problem. Equally important is that addicts remain participating members of the community.

Critics of methadone maintenance argue that such programs encourage wider use of hard drugs. They also assert that these plans will not be acceptable to most citizens, who will continue to label addicts as criminals and sinful. Liberals, although likely to approve of either plan over the current criminal model, foresee a danger in government control over an addict population dependent on it for drugs. Also, such programs attack the problem at the individual level (blaming the victim) and ignore the social and cultural sources of drug use.

Noninterference

Libertarians argue that it is none of the government's business what drugs people put into their bodies. There should be no governmental interference in this private act. This view, however, does not excuse drug users from their behavior. Former Seattle police officer Norm Stampler says,

> If I choose to inject, inhale, sniff, snort, or for that matter, put a bullet in my brain, that's a choice I should have as an adult. Where the line is drawn for society is if I choose to be irresponsible in committing those acts. Then I need to be held accountable for my behavior. For instance, if I furnish a kid with drugs, or if I abuse a spouse, then I need to be held accountable for my criminal actions. The hypocrisy of keeping the prohibition on these substances going, yet making no moves to ban alcohol as a choice for adults, is staggering. We know there are far greater problems associated with alcohol abuse. Just as with alcohol, though, I think it should be viewed as a basic civil liberty for people to be able to use whatever drugs they want, and second, to treat the abuse of drugs as a medical problem, which is what it is. It is a public health issue, not an issue for the law to deal with. (Quoted in Talvi 2005:27)

Proponents of total **decriminalization of drugs** argue that all societies throughout known history have had psychoactive drugs. Legislation and strict enforcement will not curb the tendency among many people to want to alter their consciousness artificially. Such acts should be neither penalized nor encouraged because it is none of the government's business what individuals do to themselves. The United States could follow the example of other countries such as Brazil, Uruguay, Portugal, and Mexico, who have all changed their laws to eliminate jail time for people carrying small amounts of drugs for personal use (see the "Social Policy" panel titled "Portugal's Drug Policy").

Critics suggest that decriminalization will encourage the spread of drug use. Drug use will spread because drugs will be readily available and because commercial interests will see potential profits in these formerly illicit drugs and will produce them and promote their use. Finally, and perhaps most significant, some argue that drug use is not an isolated act that affects only the user. In short, although many people believe that drug use is a "victimless vice," there is always a victim.

What, then, is the answer to drug use? Probably some combination of these alternatives makes the most sense. Clearly, the arguments about the solution will continue to incite passion. There will be those who are concerned with the use of certain drugs and who feel that society must control such deviance. They insist on imposing their morals on others. At the other extreme are those who are more concerned with how the laws and their rigorous enforcement cause social problems. As the various segments of society continue the debate, legislation will be proposed and eventually passed. The astute observer should note the role of interest groups in what is decided and also who benefits and who loses by the decision reached.

Address the Social Causes of Drug Use

When one looks at drug use across the United States, it is clear that drugs are correlated with poverty, education, gender, social location, and race/ethnicity. The United States has spent billions of dollars tackling the supply side of drugs through regulating its borders and other social control efforts, yet an effective drug policy must also focus on reducing the demand for drugs. Addressing social problems such as poverty, violence, and racial-ethnic inequality is a necessary first step in lowering drug use rates in America.

PORTUGAL'S DRUG POLICY

In the late 1990s, Portugal had incredibly high rates of drug abuse, crime, and the highest rate of drug-related AIDS deaths in the European Union (Specter 2011). Faced with a problem that was not going away, Portuguese leaders decided on a bold and controversial move and in 2001 they passed a law that made Portugal the first country to fully decriminalize personal drug use. To be clear, drugs are *not* legal in Portugal, but an individual caught with small amounts of drugs for personal use is not jailed. Instead, the individual meets with a panel from the Commission for the Dissuasion of Drug Addiction, usually consisting of a lawyer or judge, a doctor, and a social worker. The panel then recommends a small fine or treatment, or nothing is done at all. Users are most often sent to counseling or treatment programs, thus drug users are viewed

as having medical or psychological problems rather than as criminals. In fact, the Portuguese government moved responsibility for drug control issues from the Justice Department to the Ministry of Health (Specter 2011). Proponents of the law argue that since 2001:

- The number of people seeking treatment has grown.
- Rates of drug-related deaths and infectious diseases have fallen.
- Drug-related court cases have dropped 66 percent (Associated Press 2010c).
- Drug-related new HIV cases have dropped 75 percent (Associated Press 2010c).
- Decriminalization did not bring a surge in use: The number of regular users has held steady.
- Street drug overdoses have dropped.

- Decriminalization has allowed the Portuguese justice system to focus its energies on more significant criminals and more dangerous crimes.

The Portuguese model is typically called "harm reduction," which means that rather than trying to eliminate drug abuse, the goal is to minimize the negative consequences of drug use. As part of the program, outreach health workers drive the streets and provide addicts with clean needles and health screens. Opponents of the law argue that harm reduction is not effective; all it does is create more docile drug addicts with no incentive to actually quit their addiction. Regardless, it is hard to ignore the positive consequences of harm reduction when comparing the model to the United States' $1 trillion "War on Drugs" where punitive drug laws have overburdened the prison system and 8.9 percent (22.6 million) of Americans used an illicit drug in the past month (SAMHSA 2012a).

MySocLab ✓ Study and Review on MySocLab

■ CHAPTER REVIEW

1. Whether drugs in U.S. society are defined as legal or illegal is based not on their potential for harm to the users or society but on politics—the exercise of power by interest groups and the majority to legislate their views on others.

2. The acceptability of certain drugs such as marijuana or heroin has varied historically. Opiates, once legal in the United States, became illegal for two reasons: (a) Members of the White working class on the West Coast felt threatened by cheap Chinese labor and sought coercive measures against those

Chinese, and (b) religious groups interpreting opiate use as a moral evil mounted successful pressure. The result was the Harrison Narcotics Act of 1914, which established a Narcotics Division of the Treasury Department whose goal was to eliminate drug addiction. Behavior once considered a medical problem became a criminal problem, and the solution became incarceration.

3. Laws defining which drugs are legal and which are not reflect negative stereotypes held by the general public and efforts for control by interest groups

(such as religious groups, the pharmaceutical industry, and organized crime) and law enforcement professionals. The result is that current drug laws are illogical. They are not related to the danger of the drugs but reflect the political interests of the powerful.

4. Most people in the United States take some drug on a regular basis. Those drugs considered legal are caffeine, alcohol, nicotine, tranquilizers, amphetamines, and barbiturates. Illegal drugs used by millions in U.S. society are marijuana, cocaine, methamphetamine, inhalants, psychedelics, and heroin.

5. The prevailing culture, group norms, and social pressures strongly affect the patterns of drug use and their behavioral effects. Drug use varies by age, education level, race, gender, and social class. Men of all ages are more likely than women to use illegal drugs.

6. The pressure to use drugs may come from doctors, coaches, pharmaceutical firms, tobacco and alcohol companies, and one's friends and associates. Drugs are used increasingly to meet cultural standards of mental and physical perfection.

7. The U.S. war on drugs has cost taxpayers more than $1 trillion since 1971. It entails stopping drugs from coming into the country and punishing those who use and sell drugs. In large part, this war has not succeeded.

8. Drug laws promote crime in at least three ways: (a) Users often engage in criminal activity because the drugs, being illegal, are so expensive; (b) punitive drug laws encourage organized crime by making importation, processing, and distribution of illegal drugs extremely lucrative; and (c) people selling illicit drugs often corrupt the police.

9. The drug war appears to be racist because of four patterns in the criminal justice system: (a) Blacks and Latinos are overrepresented in the prison population for drug offenses given their numbers in the population and their drug usage statistics; (b) drug enforcement occurs almost exclusively in minority neighborhoods; (c) prior to the Fair Sentencing Act of 2010, although crack cocaine and powder cocaine are basically the same, the government punished the (primarily Black) users and sellers of crack much more severely; and (d) the courts tend to administer medical treatment for White drug users and the criminal justice system for Black users.

10. Government can adopt alternative policies toward drug use: (a) prohibition of trade and use through enforcement of criminal penalties (the current policy); (b) regulation through licensing and taxation; (c) noninterference (ignoring drugs because what people do to themselves is not the government's business); and (d) addressing the underlying social causes of drug use to reduce the demand for drugs.

■ KEY TERMS

Drug. A chemical that alters the perceptions and/or moods of people who take it.

Politics of drugs. The labeling of some drugs as licit and others as illicit depends on the definition of drugs by the most powerful interest groups, which are able to get their definitions incorporated into the law.

Psychoactive drug. Chemical that alters the perceptions and/or moods of people who take it.

Gateway drug. The belief that the use of a drug will lead to the use of other hard drugs like heroin and cocaine.

Moral panic. Moral panics occur when a social problem is defined as a threat to societal values and interests. Moral panics typically involve the exaggeration of a social problem; the public response to it is also exaggerated.

Schedule 1 drug. Classified by the Drug Enforcement Administration as a drug that has high potential for abuse and no currently accepted medical use.

Psychopharmacology. Science of drugs that affect the mind.

Restorative drugs. Chemicals that heal a traumatized part of the body.

Additive drugs. Chemicals that improve performance.

Interdiction. Public policy of stopping the flow of drugs into the United States by guarding the borders and by curtailing the creation, processing, and distributing of drugs in other countries.

Heroin maintenance. British approach to heroin addiction that treats addicts as sick rather than as criminal; thus, addicts are placed under the jurisdiction of physicians who administer drugs to their patients.

Methadone maintenance. Used for heroin maintenance, this treatment provides a heroin substitute (methadone) to addicts under medical supervision.

Decriminalization of drugs. Legalization of drugs.

The Economy and Work

(((Listen to Chapter 14 on **MySocLab**

This chapter is divided into three parts. The first part describes the two polar types of economic systems: capitalism and socialism and the social problems associated with each. The second examines the great economic trends of our time: the transformation of the economy, globalization, and the Great Recession. Each of these major trends is the source of many social problems. The final section is devoted to the problems of work.

CAPITALISM AND SOCIALISM

Industrialized societies organize their economic activities according to one of two fundamental forms: capitalism or socialism. Although no society has a purely capitalist or socialist economy, the ideal types provide opposite extremes on a scale that helps us measure the U.S. economy more accurately.

Capitalism

Four conditions must be present for pure **capitalism** to exist—private ownership of property, personal profit, competition, and a government policy of laissez-faire. These necessary conditions constitute the underlying principles of a pure capitalist system. The first is private ownership of property. Individuals are encouraged to own not only private possessions but, most important, also the capital necessary to produce and distribute goods and services. In a purely capitalist society, there would be no public ownership of any potentially profitable activity.

The pursuit of maximum profit, the second essential principle, implies that individuals are free to maximize their personal gains. Most important, the proponents of capitalism (see the panel on Adam Smith) argue that profit seeking by individuals has positive consequences for society. Thus, seeking individual gain through personal profit is considered morally acceptable and socially desirable.

Competition, the third ingredient, is the mechanism for determining what is produced and at what price. The market forces of supply and demand ensure that capitalists produce the goods and services wanted by the public, that the goods and services are high in quality, and that they are sold at the lowest possible price. Moreover, competition is the mechanism that keeps individual profit seeking in check. Potential abuses such as fraud, faulty products, and exorbitant prices are negated by the existence of competitors who soon take business away from those who violate good business judgment. So, too, economic inefficiency is minimized as market forces cause the inept to fail and the efficient to succeed.

These three principles—private property, personal profit, and competition—require a fourth condition if true capitalism is to work: a government policy of laissez-faire, allowing the marketplace to operate unhindered. Capitalists argue that any government intervention in the marketplace distorts the economy by negatively affecting incentives and freedom of individual choice. If left unhindered by government, the profit motive, private ownership, and competition will achieve the greatest good for the greatest number in the form of individual self-fulfillment and the general material progress of society.

Critics argue that capitalism promotes inequality and a host of social problems because the object is profit, not enhancing the human condition. Put another way: Capitalism is about profit, not social justice.

The economy of the United States is not purely capitalistic. Taxes are levied on the population to raise monies for the common good, such as the federal interstate

Adam Smith

Adam Smith (1723–1790), a Scottish economist, is the godfather of laissez-faire capitalism. His *Inquiry into the Nature and Causes of the Wealth of Nations*, written in 1775, presented a logical vision of how society was bound inextricably by the private decisions of entrepreneurs and consumers alike.

Of the many issues that Smith addressed, one is paramount for our concerns: How does society hang together when everyone is pursuing his or her own self-interest? For Smith the answer is in the laws of the marketplace: The needs of society and its citizens are met by each person producing what will bring a profit. But if all entrepreneurs are profit hungry, what will prevent them from taking unfair advantage of their consumers? The answer, simply, is competition. The existence of competition will keep prices fair and product quality high.

The market also regulates the incomes of those who produce the goods. If wages are too high in one kind of work, other workers will rush to that type of job, bringing down the exorbitant wages. Similarly, if wages are too low, then workers will change to better-paying jobs. The marketplace also reduces the possibility of surpluses because entrepreneurs, foreseeing the problem, will move to more profitable arenas where the demand and profits are high. Thus, the laws of the marketplace provide an "invisible hand" that regulates the economy without government intervention. The government is not needed to fix prices, to set minimum wages, or to protect against consumer fraud. All that is needed is a free and competitive marketplace. The question, of course, is whether the nature of the marketplace in a world of huge multinational corporations, multimillion-member labor unions, and conglomerates is the same as it was in the eighteenth century.

highway system, the air traffic control system and the subsidizing of airports, flood control projects, the defense establishment, the postal system, and disaster relief. In many ways, the government interferes with the market by monitoring the safety of food and drugs, prohibiting the sale of certain products, regulating the environment, insisting on health and safety regulations in workplaces, issuing licenses, protecting the civil rights of women and minorities, taxing income, subsidizing certain business activities, overseeing the banking and insurance industries, and raising or lowering interest rates.

Moreover, although U.S. social programs are less generous than those found in the social welfare states, there is nonetheless minimal help for victims of natural disasters, preschool training for children of the poor, low-interest student loans, Medicare, and Medicaid.

Socialism

Socialism is an economic system in which the means of production are owned by the people for their collective benefit. The five principles of socialism are democratism, egalitarianism, community, public ownership of the means of production, and planning for common purposes. True socialism must be democratic. Representatives of a socialist state must be answerable and responsive to the wishes of the public they serve. Nations that claim to be socialist but are totalitarian violate this fundamental aspect of socialism. The key to differentiating between authentic and spurious socialism is to determine who is making the decisions and whose interests are being served.

Thus, it is a fallacy to equate true socialism with the politicoeconomic systems found in Cuba or the People's Republic of China. These societies are socialistic in some respects; that is, their material benefits are more evenly distributed than those in the United States. But their economies and governments are controlled by a single political party in an inflexible and authoritarian manner. Although these countries claim to have democratic elections, in fact the citizens have no electoral choice but to rubber-stamp the candidates of the ruling party. The people are denied civil liberties and freedoms that should be the hallmark of a socialist society. In a pure socialist society, democratic relations must operate throughout the social structure: in government, at work, at school, and in the community.

The second principle of socialism is egalitarianism: equality of opportunity for the self-fulfillment of all, equality rather than hierarchy in decision making, and equality in sharing the benefits of society. For some socialists, the goal is absolute equality. For most, though, equality means a limit to inequality, with some acceptable disparities in living standards. This more realistic goal of socialism requires a fundamental commitment to achieving a rough parity by evening out gross inequities in income, property, and opportunities. The key is a leveling of advantages so that all citizens receive the necessities (food, clothing, medical care, living wages, sick pay, retirement benefits, and shelter).

The third feature of socialism is community, which is the "idea that social relations should be characterized by cooperation and a sense of collective belonging rather than by conflict and competition" (Miller 1991:406). This sense of the collective is evidenced by a relatively high taxation rate to provide for the common good—such as universal healthcare, paid maternity leave, subsidized childcare, universal preschool programs, and a generous retirement program (see the "Social Policy" panel, which provides the example of the Swedish Welfare State).

The fourth characteristic of socialism is the public ownership of the means of production. The people own the basic industries, financial institutions, utilities, transportation, and communications companies. The goal is serving the public, not making profit.

The fifth principle of socialism is planning. The society must direct social activities to meet common goals. This means that socialists oppose the heart of capitalism, which is to let individuals acting in their own interests in the marketplace determine overall outcomes. For socialists, these uncoordinated activities invite chaos, and although they possibly help some people in the society, they do damage to others. Thus, a purely socialist government requires societal planning to provide, at the least possible individual and collective cost, the best conditions to meet the material needs of its citizens. Planning also aims to achieve societal goals such as protecting the environment, combating pollution, saving natural resources, and developing new technologies. Public policy is decided through the rational assessment of the needs of society and how the economy might best be organized to achieve them. In this situation, the economy must be regulated by the government, which acts as the agent of the people. The government sets prices and wages; important industries are run at a loss if necessary. Dislocations such as surpluses or shortages or unemployment are minimized by central planning. The goal is to run the economy for the good of the society.

Critics of democratic socialism argue that "the nanny state" minimizes individual freedom and choice. Government monopoly is inefficient because of a centralized bureaucracy making "one-size-fits-all" decisions. Taxes are high to pay for the social programs, robbing individuals of their earned income. And, the argument goes, the "cradle-to-grave" social programs for individuals and families reduce their motivation

Social Policy

THE SWEDISH WELFARE STATE

Sweden, although a capitalist economy for the most part, is socialist in its generous welfare provisions that level the extremes in wealth and poverty. The Swedish system is based on the principle that the government is responsible to provide basic services for the entire population. In broad outline, the present welfare system includes the following provisions:

- *A national health insurance program.* Patients choose their own physicians, and health services are subsidized for all residents of Sweden.
- *A family support program for parents and children.* Prenatal care, delivery, and postnatal care are free. All children under the age of 20 receive free medical and dental care. Working parents may take a leave from work to care for their infant for a total for both parents of 480 days

(divided as they choose) while being compensated at 80 percent of their wages. Either parent may take time off for the care of a sick child (60 days a year per child), with compensation for lost earnings. All children ages 4 and 5 are provided three hours of free preschooling a day.

- *Care of the elderly.* Everyone who has lived in Sweden for at least three years is entitled to at least a minimum pension. Full pension is for those who have lived in Sweden for forty years. The elderly receive a housing subsidy. Institutionalized care is provided when needed, but the preference is for the elderly to receive nursing care in their homes, which is subsidized, whenever possible.
- *Subsidized housing.* The government provides nonprofit municipal housing, establishes rent ceilings, subsidizes financing,

and provides housing allowances. These provisions allow lower-income families to afford decent housing.

To provide these many and expensive services of the welfare state, Swedish taxes are relatively high. Direct taxes include an income tax on employment, income from capital, business income, a national property tax on real estate, and an inheritance tax. Directly, there are a state sales tax and consumption taxes to curb the use of energy (oil and gas, electrical power, and motor vehicles), tobacco, gaming, and alcohol. As a result, the total tax revenue for Sweden as a percentage of gross domestic product in 2009 was 49.7 percent (compared to 28.2 percent for the United States, 40.6 percent in Germany, 39.0 percent in the United Kingdom, and 33.4 percent for Canada).

Source: Updated version from D. Stanley Eitzen. 2010. "The Swedish Welfare State." In D. Stanley Eitzen (ed.), *Solutions to Social Problems: Lessons from Other Societies*, 5th ed. (Boston: Allyn & Bacon).

to succeed, an attitude that, when held by many, limits creativity, economic productivity, and growth.

14.2 Describe the transformation of the U.S. economy from industrialized to an information/service economy.

MEGA ECONOMIC TRENDS

The structure of contemporary society shapes families and individuals within them. Three interrelated trends of great magnitude especially affect our jobs, incomes, and our futures—globalization, the structural transformation of the economy, and the Great Recession (this section is taken largely from Baca Zinn, Eitzen, and Wells 2014: Chapter 4).

Globalization

Among other changes, the new technologies have, most significantly, magnified the connections among all peoples across the globe (the following is dependent in part on Eitzen, Baca Zinn, and Smith 2013, Chapter 8; and Eitzen and Baca Zinn 2012).

The Internet makes worldwide communications instantaneous. Money moves across political boundaries with a few keystrokes. Low wages in one country affect wages elsewhere. A drought in one part of the world drives up prices for commodities everywhere, and overproduction of a product in one region brings down the prices of that product elsewhere. A collapse in the stock market of one nation has ramifications for financial markets around the world. Movies, television, and advertising from one society affect the tastes, interests, and styles in other places. Polluted air from China, for example, rides the jet stream and in five days reaches the west coast of the United States and Canada. Deforestation in the developing nations has a major effect on climate change everywhere. Global warming, caused by the burning of fossil fuels, changes climates, generates megastorms, and increases the spread of tropical diseases around the world. A disease such as HIV/AIDS left Africa some fifty years ago and now infects 34 million people worldwide and 1.2 million in North America. H1N1 became a **pandemic** (worldwide health danger) within a few months. There has been a dramatic increase in migration flows, especially from poorer to richer nations. With sophisticated weapons systems, no nation is immune from assault from other nations or terrorist acts by revolutionary groups.

Each of these is an example of **globalization** (the processes by which everyone on Earth becomes increasingly interconnected economically, politically, culturally, and environmentally). Connections among peoples outside their tribes or political units are not new, but the linkages now are increasing geometrically, with few, if any, groups unaffected. We concentrate here on economic globalization.

Although trade between and among nations is not new, global trade entered a new phase after World War II. What have evolved are a global trade network, the integration of peoples and nations, and a global economy, with a common ideol-

ogy: capitalism. Former colonies have established local industries and sell their raw materials, products, and labor on the global market. The United States emerged as the strongest economic and military power in the world, with U.S. corporations vitally interested in expanding their operations to other societies for profit. The shift to a global economy has been accelerated by the tearing down of tariff barriers. The North American Free Trade Agreement (NAFTA) and the General Agreement on Tariffs and Trade (GATT), both passed in 1994, are two examples of agreements that increased the flow of goods (and jobs) across national boundaries. In 2005 President Bush signed the Central American Free Trade Agreement (CAFTA), which institutes a Western Hemisphere–wide version of NAFTA.

The globalization of the economy is not a neutral process. Decisions are based on what will maximize profits, thus serving the owners of capital and not necessarily workers or the communities where U.S. operations are located. In this regard, private businesses, in their search for profit, make crucial investment decisions that change the dynamics in families and communities. Most significant are the corporate decisions regarding the movement of corporate money from one investment to another (called **capital flight**). This shift of capital takes several forms: investment in plants located in other nations, plant relocation within the United States, and mergers. Although these investment decisions may be positive for corporations, they also take

Container ships enter U.S. ports with goods produced elsewhere to be sold here. The merchandise is relatively cheap, but there is a high cost in fewer jobs for U.S. workers.

away investment (disinvestment) from others (workers and their families, communities, and suppliers).

The Transformation of the Economy: From Manufacturing to Services

The Industrial Revolution, which began in Great Britain in the 1780s, was a major turning point in human history. With the application of steam power and, later, oil and electricity as energy sources for industry, mining, manufacturing, and transportation, fundamental changes came to the economy, the relationship of people and work, family organization, and a transition from rural to urban life. In effect, societies are transformed with each surge in invention and technological growth (Drucker 1993).

The U.S. economy was once dominated by agriculture, but in the twentieth century, while agricultural productivity increased, the number employed in an agrarian economy declined precipitously. Manufacturing replaced agriculture as the dominant economic activity, indicating a **structural transformation of the economy**. Now we are undergoing another transformational shift—from an economy dominated by manufacturing to one characterized by service occupations and the collection, storage, and dissemination of information. Reflecting this shift, from 2000 to 2010, some 54,621 U.S. factories shut down and the number of employees in manufacturing fell from 17 million to 11.5 million (Bureau of Labor Statistics, reported in Lind 2011). Accompanying this decline, as workers left manufacturing for other jobs, their new jobs tended to pay less, had less job security, and provided fewer benefits such as health insurance and pensions.

While manufacturing declined in the United States, transnational corporations shifted their manufacturing to low-wage economies. Manufacturers moved offshore because profits are greater and because giant retailers (e.g., Walmart) have compelled manufacturers to move offshore in search of lower prices for consumers and higher profits for themselves (Meyerson 2010:A16–A17). This migration of jobs takes two forms, both related to capital flight: offshoring and outsourcing (Friedman 2005). **Offshoring** is when a company moves its production to another country, producing the same products in the same way, but with cheaper labor, lower taxes, and lower benefits to workers. Apple, for example, employs 700,000 workers in China making its iPhones, iPads, and the like (Isaacson 2011:546). **Outsourcing** refers to taking some specific task that a company was doing in-house—such as research, call centers, accounting, or transcribing—and transferring it to an overseas company to save money and reintegrating that work back into the overall operation.

This move to low-wage economies has three negative effects on U.S. workers. First, many have lost their jobs. Second, the wages of those production workers who have not lost their jobs remain relatively low because if they seek higher wages, their employers threaten to move the jobs elsewhere. And, third, workers' unions have been weakened because they, too, have lost clout. When workers had strong unions, the wages and benefits were enough for a middle-class lifestyle.

This phenomenon of outsourcing has three roots. First, there is the worldwide communications revolution spawned by the Internet. Second, there is a supply of qualified workers in English-speaking countries, most notably India but also the Philippines, Barbados, Jamaica, Singapore, and Ireland. And, third, these workers are willing to work for one-fifth or less the salary of comparable U.S. workers. The kinds of jobs affected by outsourcing are software engineers, accountants, architects, engineers, art designers, x-ray technicians, and airplane maintenance. In this latter instance, airlines such as Jet-Blue and U.S. Airways tune up their planes in El Salvador, where mechanics make $4,500 to $15,000 a year, compared to the average in the

United States of $52,000 annually (*Business Week* 2008). Also negatively affected are lower-level white-collar jobs such as customer service representatives, telemarketers, record transcribers, and those who make airline and hotel reservations.

The Changing Nature of Jobs

Explore on MySocLab Activity: Stanford and the Silicon Valley

Every new era poses new problems of adjustment, but this one differs from the agricultural and industrial eras. The earlier transformations were gradual enough for adaptation to take place over several decades, but conditions are significantly different now. The rate of change now is phenomenal and unprecedented.

Joseph Schumpeter (1950) described a process inherent to capitalism that he called "creative destruction." By this he meant that as the economic structure of capitalism mutates, some sectors will lose out while others gain. For example, in 1917, the largest U.S. corporation, with three times the assets of its nearest competitor, was U.S. Steel, which employed 268,000 workers. Today U.S. Steel is worth about one-fifth what it was in 1917 and employs only one-tenth of the workers that it once did. Replacing U.S. Steel at the apex of the nation's corporate elite are companies such as Apple, Intel, and Merck. Today the largest employer in the United States is Walmart. These facts illustrate how manufacturing, the backbone of the U.S. economy in the twentieth century, is no longer dominant. It has been replaced by the service sector and knowledge-based companies. Whereas in the past people mostly worked at producing goods, now they tend to do work in offices, banking, insurance, retailing, healthcare, education, custodial work, restaurant work, security, and transportation.

Businesses are profitable and more productive than ever, but they do so with fewer workers. Among the reasons for this are that Americans work more hours than any other Western nation (an average of 1,804 hours a year, compared to 1,434 for German workers) (Begala 2011). More important, machines are replacing humans in the work place (automation). Robots replace humans doing routine work such as picking fruit, welding, assembling, painting, and scanning products for defects. Now robots can see, feel, move, and work together. As a result, factory production is up by one-third, but factory employment has dropped by about one-third (Davidson 2012).

Automation affects white-collar workers as well as blue-collar workers (Lyons 2011). Software replaces law clerks in the search for previous court opinions. Self-service in the checkout lines at supermarkets and other stores replaces workers. The Internet, for example, allows people to make their own travel arrangements, reducing or eliminating the need for travel agents, or to buy and sell stocks, making stockbrokers unnecessary. Also, software is available that helps people do their tax returns without the need of a tax specialist. Within firms, computer programs take care of payrolls, inventory control, and delivery schedules, reducing the need for accountants. Primarily because of voice mail, laser printers, and word processors, hundreds of thousands of secretarial and clerical jobs have been eliminated.

As the economy shifted away from manufacturing to services and information/knowledge some sectors of the economy fade in importance or will even die out completely. These sectors are known as **sunset industries** (e.g., steel, tires, shoes, toys, film cameras, and textiles). Literally millions of blue-collar jobs, most of which were unionized with good pay and benefits, were lost and not replaced.

The employer/employee relationship is also being reshaped. The Internet is revolutionizing how business is transacted. More than 30 million American workers work in temporary, contracted, self-employed, leased, part-time, and other "nonstandard" arrangements (**contingent work**). These workers under contingent employment (i.e.,

"He's working from home today."

John Klossner/The New Yorker Collection/cartoonbank.com

employees who work part time, in temporary jobs, or as independent contractors) typically lack an explicit contract for ongoing employment and thus receive sporadic wages. They earn less than their counterparts who do the same work, and they have fewer benefits such as health insurance, family leave, and retirement, thus costing their employers up to 30 percent less than regular employees (Davidson 2009).

One version of contingent employment is **homeshoring** or **homesourcing** in which independent contractors work from their homes. These workers make a wage but pay for their healthcare and retirement. They also furnish their own equipment (telephone, computer). The independent contractor benefits by flexible hours and saving on childcare, transportation, and clothing.

Another type of contingent employment is that of temporary workers ("temps"). This trend represents a dramatic change in work. Businesses argue that they need this arrangement for flexibility in a rapidly changing competitive economy. These growing numbers of temporary workers are not tied to an employer, which makes them free to choose from available work options. There is a downside to this trend, however: About 60 percent of these nonstandard jobs are low quality, paying less than regular full-time jobs held by similar workers. Temps earn on average 40 percent less per hour than full-time workers. In short, this trend has meant the proliferation of marginal jobs, with employers now shifting the burden of fringe benefits to individual workers and their families.

A generation or so ago, workers tended to work for one or two employers during their working years. Employers were loyal to their workers ("If you do your job, you'll have a job") and workers were loyal to their employers. But the nature of work has changed dramatically. Now many workers are not allied with an employer, working, as we have seen, as contingent workers. Millions of workers are dismissed as their employers modernize the plants or move them elsewhere. Still other workers find their skills not keeping up with technological changes. Others leave jobs for other jobs. Sociologist Richard Sennett has calculated that young workers today with at least two years of college can expect to change jobs at least eleven times before retirement (reported in Schwartz 2004).

But while jobs have shrunk by the millions in the last two decades, many millions more have been created in **sunrise industries** (those industries characterized by increased output and employment). Such jobs are involved in the production of high-tech products (computers, software, medical instruments, bioengineering, robotics). Also, lower-end service jobs such as sales clerks, restaurant workers, janitors, and security guards are relatively plentiful (and have the advantage of being immune to outsourcing). The important point for workers is that these new industries pay less and have fewer benefits than the old ones (a point that we will return to later in this chapter).

The Great Recession (2007–2010 and Beyond)

Listen on MySocLab Audio: NPR: Experts Fear Financial Crisis Will Hurt World's Poor

The transformation and the economy and the effects of globalization have created considerable economic havoc in the past few decades. Adding to the dislocations brought about by these epochal changes is the Great Recession, which began in 2007 and, while technically over in 2009, the economic problems associated with it continue.

- **Prelude to the Economic Crisis.** As the economy shifted away from manufacturing to services and information/knowledge, some sectors (sunset industries) of the economy faded in importance or even died. Tens of millions of jobs, mostly unionized jobs with good pay and benefits, were lost permanently, creating displaced workers. Moreover, weak unions plus the competition from low-wage economies led many U.S. corporations to reduce or eliminate their benefits (health insurance, retirement) to workers. Wages were also negatively affected.

  Thus, the transformation of the economy, at least in the short run, marginalized millions, increased unemployment, drove social mobility downward, and made many millions insecure about their jobs, healthcare, and retirement. To cope with these problems, employees worked more hours a week, putting in 350 more hours a year than the average European, more women worked in the labor force (70 percent, almost double the percentage in 1970), and families went deeper into debt with credit cards, car loans, college loans, and home equity loans. Families were also buying homes because home values had risen for half a century, most steeply from 1997 to 2006. This price appreciation tempted many to speculate, "flipping" recently purchased houses for a quick profit. Others took advantage of easy credit to refinance by taking out second mortgages to remodel their homes or to purchase "big ticket" items such as automobiles and boats.

  Mortgage market lenders encouraged this housing "bubble." About 20 percent of home loans in 2005 were "subprime"—that is, loans sold to people with questionable credit records. These loans went disproportionately to African Americans and Latinos, many buying homes for the first time. They were offered no-money-down loans, with what appeared to be low interest rates. The "low" rates were for the first two years but then the loans increased substantially when the "variable rate" clause (found in the fine print of the loan contract) was enforced. In 2011 Bank of America agreed to a record $335 million settlement with the Justice Department, agreeing that its financial mortgage unit from 2004 to 2008 had discriminated against more than 200,000 African American and Latino borrowers by charging higher fees and interest rates than charged to Whites and steering them into subprime mortgages.

  Add to this mix the reckless and irresponsible deal making on Wall Street, which involved an intricate, intertwined system of loan brokers, mortgage lenders, Wall Street trusts, hedge funds, offshore tax havens, and other predators (Hightower 2007; see also Moyers and Winship 2009). For example, subprime loans were bundled and sold to third parties. These "derivatives" were financial contracts between a buyer and a seller that derive value from an underlying asset, such as a mortgage or a stock. This allowed banks and insurance firms to leverage their assets by as much as forty times the value of the underlying asset. There were five agencies at the federal level that could have regulated these reckless practices but did not because they assumed the financial players would police themselves (Hightower 2007).

View on MySocLab Figure: Percentage of each group who say they did the following because of the recession . . .

The Ensuing Economic Crisis.   These forces converged in 2007, creating a "perfect storm" of economic devastation. It began when subprime borrowers began defaulting on their mortgages. That sent housing prices tumbling, unleashing a domino effect on mortgage-backed securities (Gandel and Lim 2008). Banks and brokerages that had borrowed money to increase their leverage had to raise capital quickly. Some, like Merrill Lynch and Bear Stearns, were forced to sell their assets to other banks at bargain rates (Bear Sterns was sold to JPMorgan for $236 million, down from its value of $20 billion a year earlier). Others, like Lehman Brothers, failed. The stock market dropped precipitously. Credit dried up. Business slowed, causing companies to lay off workers by the hundreds of thousands. What happened in the United States affected markets elsewhere, causing a worldwide recession and a further slowing of business activity here and abroad. The result was the worst economic downturn in the United States since the Great Depression of the 1930s. Let's consider the contours of the crisis, beginning with unemployment.

Unemployment.   Since the 1970s, retaining a job has become more precarious (Kalleberg 2009). This trend accelerated in the recent recession as some 8.8 million American workers lost their jobs from late 2007 to January 2012. The official government's unemployment rate jumped from 4.6 percent in mid-2007 to 10 percent through January 1, 2010. The rate receded to 8.5 percent in early 2012 (13.1 million people), but these official data underreport the actual number of unemployed by omitting the 8.6 million who work part-time but want to work full-time and the 2.5 million who are out of work but do not actively seek work. We will return to this topic later in this chapter. The official unemployment data do tell us how long people have been out of work. During the Great Recession the share of the unemployed out of work for more than half a year went from 17.5 percent in 2007 to a staggering 45.5 percent in March 2011 (Shierholz 2012).

Housing Woes.   The value of homes grew rapidly in the new millennium, reaching a peak in 2006. By this time many homeowners were on the financial edge

Leo Cullum/Conde Nast Publications/www.cartoonbank.com/The New Yorker Collection

as they purchased overvalued houses, assuming their value would increase even more. But the housing bubble burst, causing values to decline precipitously, losing $4 trillion in value from 2005 to the end of 2008 and another $2 trillion in the next three years (Allegretto 2011). The newly unemployed found they could not meet their monthly payments. Those who purchased subprime mortgages were especially vulnerable. By 2009 some 1.5 million homes owned mostly by African Americans were lost through subprime foreclosures. Banks repossessed 1 million homes in 2010. During the Great Recession, the value of the average home plummeted by more than 30 percent. This meant that more than one-fourth of home owners (11 million) were "under water" (i.e., they owed more on their mortgages than their homes were worth). Many either walked away from their now unaffordable mortgages, or after missing payments, their mortgages were foreclosed by lenders. This created a downward spiral, decreasing home values further. Adding to the loss of home value was the accompanying drop in the building of new homes with the construction industry losing 2 million jobs from 2005 to 2010. This, of course, made the Great Recession even worse.

The Great Recession's negative impact on housing began to recede in 2012. In 2011 some 1.89 million homes were issued notices of foreclosure. The next year the number of homes repossessed was down 17 percent (Veiga 2013).

Renters are not immune from the nation's housing crisis. This occurs in several ways (Armour 2008). First, when owners of apartments are foreclosed on, their renters are evicted, even though they have been paying their rents. According to the National Low Income Housing Coalition, renters make up an estimated 40 percent of families facing eviction because of foreclosure (Fireside 2009). Those who were evicted usually lost their security deposits and any prepaid rent. Second, homeowners forced into foreclosure become tenants, which drives up rents. Third, the cost of renting in many areas of the country was high, as demand exceeds the supply. By 2010 some 53 percent of renters were paying 30 percent or more of their household income on

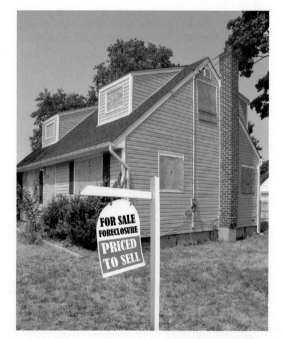

Some areas of the U.S. experienced serious declines in housing values during the Great Recession, resulting in distress sales, foreclosures, and owners walking away from their mortgages.

housing (30 percent is the government threshold to determine if housing is unafford-able). Approximately one in four renters pays more than half their income on rent (Schmit and Hansen 2011).

The housing problem is especially acute for low-income families, for whom there is a critical shortage of affordable housing. The dwindling supply of affordable hous-ing for the poor represents a long-term trend (the following is from Timmer, Eitzen, & Talley 1994:18–24). Since the 1970s, rents have increased and the stock of low-income housing has shrunk. Well over a million single-room occupancy (SRO) hotels have been demolished. SROs and other low-cost rental housing have disappeared because of several related trends. The first is **gentrification** (the process of converting low-income housing to condominiums or upscale apartments for the middle and upper-middle classes). Second, urban developers and real estate interests have bought up properties for speculation. Third, federally financed urban renewal projects demolished blighted properties in poor and working-class neighborhoods but failed to replace the housing because of lack of funding.

These long-term trends have depleted the supply of affordable homes for the poor. Then the Great Recession hit, adding to the housing crisis. The few available housing units became even more scarce (and more expensive) because of those middle-class families who were evicted from their homes (or walked away from their "under water" mortgages) and moved down to the relatively cheap housing once exclusively used by the poor.

Financial Decline.   During the height of the Great Recession, the stock market value lost over $7 trillion, individuals lost over $1 trillion in their retirement sav-ings, and 2.4 million workers lost health insurance that there were getting through their jobs. In short, surveys revealed that more than 24 million Americans shifted in 2008 from lives that were "thriving" to ones that were "struggling" (Page 2009). Minorities were especially hard hit by the Great Recession, with the gap between them and Whites increasing. According to the Pew Hispanic Center (Kochhar, Fry, and Taylor 2011):

- Median household wealth among Latinos dropped by 66 percent from 2005 to 2009 compared to 53 percent for African Americans, and 16 percent for Whites.
- In 2009 the median wealth of White households was eighteen times that of Latino households and twenty times that for Black households.
- About a third of Latino and Black households had zero or negative net worth in 2009, compared to 15 percent of White households.

Watch on
MySocLab Slideshow:
Debt Addiction

Personal Bankruptcies.   The current economic crisis with rising unemployment, plummeting home values, staggering stock market losses, and increased indebted-ness added to these usual reasons for bankruptcy (medical catastrophe, financial missteps, and divorce). From March 2008 to March 2009, about 1.2 million debtors filed for bankruptcy, an increased of 46 percent from the year earlier (Baker 2009). In 2009, the number of personal bankruptcies increased another 32 percent. For 2010, there were 1.55 million bankruptcy filings, compared to 1.44 million the previous year (Ladika 2012).

A major source of bankruptcy is the inability to pay for catastrophic healthcare needs. Employers have increasingly cut back on their contribution to health insur-ance, either dropping coverage altogether, or by decreasing their obligation to provide health insurance, including introducing high-deductible health insurance. Of course, those who lose jobs also lose their health insurance. Because the cost of healthcare is so expensive (e.g., a heart by-pass costs $200,000; a premature baby close to $1 million), the uninsured are just a catastrophic illness or accident away from economic ruin. The Public Broadcasting System reported that 700,000 go bankrupt each year because of medical bills (Public Broadcasting System 2009).

Watch on MySocLab Video: ABC 20/20: The Ultimate Rags to Riches Story

Downward Social Mobility. The "American dream," in effect, a middle-class dream, is that one's family will own a home, own at least one late-model car, and be able to provide adequate healthcare and a college education for the children. Through the 1950s and 1960s, this dream was realized by increasingly more Americans as average real wages (i.e., wages adjusted for inflation) increased and the economy created new jobs and opportunities. The result was that many Americans after World War II were able to move up into a growing and vibrant middle class. This trend peaked in 1973, and since then families have tended to either stagnate or decline in their level of affluence. The transformation of the economy, fueled by globalization, had the effect of shrinking the middle class as the gap between the "haves" and the "have-nots" increased. This trend downward accelerated with the Great Recession, which began in 2007, with unemployment rates climbing dramatically, personal debt rising, and the housing bubble bursting. All this while the costs for healthcare, college, consumer goods, and transportation continued to rise. Clearly, the American middle class—the middle 40 percent of households in income—was in distress as many of these families plunged in income and resources, thus moving down in social class. Some declared bankruptcy. Some were forced from their homes and had to relocate. Some families became poor, hungry, and even homeless.

Poverty. The official poverty rate increased 27 percent between the onset of the Great Recession and 2010, a period of time when the total population of the United States grew by less than 3.3 percent (Seefeldt et al. 2012). This was an increase of 9.6 million people in the "poverty" category from 2007 to 2010. Concomitant with this increase in the number of poor people have been the policy decisions at the federal and state levels to reduce the "safety net" that aids the poor. In effect, the poorest among us suffered the harshest effects of the economic decline. Already on the economic margins, they have been pushed down even further.

Hunger. The Great Recession caused a dramatic increase in hunger in the United States. In 2007, 13 million were considered "food insecure," the government term meaning that they had difficulty getting enough food due to lack of resources. By 2009 the number had increased by 4.4 million to 17.4 million. Three other indicators of added numbers needing food aid:

- By April 2011, 45 million Americans received food stamps, the highest in the program's history. This was an increase of 14 million from just three years earlier.
- Some 32 million low-income children received free or reduced-cost school lunches through the federal National School Lunch Program.
- Privately funded food banks and soup kitchens reported record numbers of people needing their services.

The New Homeless. The extent of homelessness is difficult to know because those without a permanent home may be doubling up with relatives, sleeping in vehicles, and the like, not just in shelters. Thus the official numbers of the homeless understate the actual count. Given that caveat, the official number of homeless prior to the Great Recession was about 1 in 400 Americans (750,000) without a home on any given night, and about 1.6 million experienced homelessness at some point in a given year. During the Great Recession millions more were at greater risk of becoming homeless. As we have seen, 9.6 million families were spending more than half of their income on housing. Foreclosures brought evictions, even for renters when their apartment buildings were foreclosed. The newly unemployed could not make their mortgage payments or their rents. Costly medical bills put some in bankruptcy. As a result, the number of homeless increased by 38 percent from 2007 to 2010 (National Center on Family Homelessness 2011). This rise in the homeless population constitutes, for the most part, the **new homeless**. Unlike the traditional homeless, composed mostly of the long-time poor and the near poor, the new homeless include middle-class families who never expected to find themselves without shelter—victims of the Great Recession.

14.3 Understand how the structure of work is a major source of social problems.

WORK AND SOCIAL PROBLEMS

Work is central to the human experience. People everywhere engage in physical and mental activities that enhance the physical and social survival of themselves and others. Societies are organized to allocate work to produce the goods and services needed by the society and its members for sustenance, clothing, shelter, security, and even luxury. Work provides individuals and their families with their social identity, economic resources, and social location. Work dominates their time and is a primary source of life's meaning because it constitutes their contributions to other people.

The world of work also has a dark side, however. The structure of work is a major source of social problems. Work is alienating for many people. The organization of work sometimes exploits, does harm to workers, and often dehumanizes them. The distribution of work and how it is rewarded are major sources of inequality in society. This section focuses on these social problems generated by the social organization of work.

Control of Workers

With the advent of the Industrial Revolution, more and more families left agrarian life, moved to cities, and worked in factories. Work in these factories was sometimes difficult, sometimes dangerous, often tedious, and usually boring. There was always the threat of lowered productivity and worker unrest under these adverse conditions. The factory owners and their managers used several tactics to counteract these potential problems and especially to maintain high productivity—scientific management, hierarchical control, technical control, and extortion.

Scientific management (also called Taylorization, after its founder, Frederick Taylor) came to the fore in U.S. industry around 1900. The emphasis was on breaking down work into very specialized tasks, the standardization of tools and procedures, and the speeding up of repetitive work. These efforts to increase worker efficiency and therefore to increase profits meant that workers developed a very limited range of skills. Instead of a wide knowledge of building cars or furniture, their knowledge was severely curtailed. This specialization had the effect of making the workers highly susceptible to automation and to being easily replaced by cheaper workers. But this scientific management approach also had a contradictory effect. In its attempt to increase efficiency by having workers do ever more compartmentalized tasks, it increased the repetition, boredom, and meaninglessness of work—hence, the strong tendency for workers to become alienated and restless.

Closely related to scientific management is the use of bureaucracy to control workers. Work settings, whether in factories, universities, offices, or corporations, are organized into bureaucratized hierarchies. In this hierarchy of authority (chain of command), each position in the chain gives orders to those below, taking responsibility for their actions and following orders from above. The hierarchical arrangement controls workers by holding out the possibility of advancement, with more prestigious job titles, higher wages, and greater benefits as one moves up the ladder. Those who hope to be upwardly mobile in the organization must become obedient rule followers who do not question authority.

Workers are also controlled by management's use of technology to monitor and supervise them. Some businesses use lie detectors to assess worker loyalty. Psychological tests and drug tests (80 percent of major companies require employees to undergo urine tests for drugs) are used to screen applicants for work. E-mail and use of the Internet are monitored. Telephone taps have been used to determine whether workers use company time for personal use. Closed-circuit television, two-way mirrors, and other devices have been used by management to determine whether workers are using their time most productively. The most common contemporary technology for worker control is the computer. The computer can count keystrokes, time phone calls, monitor frequency of errors, assess overall employee performance, and even issue warnings when the employee falls short of the ideal.

A final management tool to control workers is extortion. If workers become too militant in their demands for higher wages, safe working conditions, or benefits, management can threaten them with reprisals. In the past, owners threatened to hire cheaper labor (new immigrants, for example) or to use force to end a strike. Today, the most common and successful management tool is the threat to move the plant to a nonunion state or even outside the United States if the union does not reduce its demands or to replace the workers with robots or other forms of automation.

Alienation

Alienation is the separation of human beings from each other, from themselves, and from the products they create. In capitalism, according to Karl Marx, worker alienation occurs because the workers do not have any control over their labor, because they are manipulated by managers, because they tend to work in large, impersonal settings, and because they work at specialized tasks. Under these circumstances, workers use only a fraction of their talents and have no pride in their own creativity and in the final product. Thus, we see that worker alienation is linked with unfulfilled personal satisfaction.

In the absence of satisfaction and personal fulfillment, work becomes meaningless. When this meaninglessness is coupled with management's efforts to control workers, the repetitious nature of the work, and the requirement of punching a time clock, many workers feel a profound resentment. This resentment may lead workers to join together in a union or other collective group to improve their working conditions. For many workers, though, the alienation remains at a personal level and is manifested by higher worker dissatisfaction, absenteeism, disruption in the workplace, and alcohol or other drug abuse on the job.

Alienation is not limited to manual workers. The work of white-collar workers such as sales clerks, secretaries, file clerks, bank tellers, and data entry clerks is mostly routine, repetitive, boring, and unchallenging. These workers, like assembly line workers, follow orders, do limited tasks, and have little sense of accomplishment.

Dangerous Working Conditions

In a capitalist economy, workers represent a cost to profit-seeking corporations. The lower management can keep labor costs down, the greater its profits. Historically, low labor costs meant that workers received low wages, had inferior or nonexistent fringe benefits such as healthcare and pensions, and worked in unhealthy conditions. Mines and factories were often extremely unsafe. The labor movement early in the 1900s gathered momentum because of the abuse experienced by workers.

After a long and sometimes violent struggle, the unions were successful in raising wages for workers, adding fringe benefits, and making the conditions of work safer. But the owners were slow to change, and worker safety was, and continues to be, one of the most difficult areas. Many owners of mills, mines, and factories continue to consider the safety of their workers a low-priority item, presumably because of the high cost.

About thirty years ago, the federal government instituted the Occupational Safety and Health Administration (OSHA) to make the workplace safer. However, OSHA's resources are inadequate to meet the challenge of ensuring safe working conditions for workers. In 2009, for example, there was only one OSHA inspector for every 66,258 workers (Wedekind 2009:7).

Worker safety is a serious concern. In an average year between 5,000 and 6,000 workers are killed on the job by explosions, electrocutions, fires, cave-ins, and the like. Another 50,000 to 60,000 die annually from cancers, black lung, and other occupational diseases due to long-term exposure to chemicals, asbestos, pesticides, and solvents (Hightower 2010).

Minorities, especially Latinos, have the highest work-related death rates. According to the Bureau of Labor Statistics, the fatality rate for Latino workers was 3.7 per 100,000 full-time workers in 2009, 12 percent higher than the rate for the entire work force (reported in Greenhouse 2010). The reason for the higher Latino rate is the influx of Latino immigrants who take the dangerous and hard-to-fill jobs in construction, meatpacking plants, and as farm laborers. Undocumented workers often are exploited because if they complain, they will be deported. They usually do not join unions, which help protect workers, and they do not protest when conditions are dangerous. See the "A Closer Look" panel on the dangers in meatpacking factories, where recent immigrants are overrepresented.

Significant occupational dangers continue to plague workers, especially those in certain jobs, such as loggers, fishers, structural iron and steel workers, refuse collectors, roofers, electrical power line installers and repairers, miners, and farmers. In addition to falls, fires and explosions, cave-ins, violent weather, and equipment malfunctions, there are also dangers from invisible contaminants such as nuclear radiation, chemical compounds, coal tars, dust, and asbestos fibers in the air. These dangers from invisible contaminants are increasing because the production of synthetic chemicals has increased so dramatically.

This discussion raises some critical questions: Should profits supersede human life? Are owners guilty of murder if their decisions to minimize plant safety result in

A Closer Look

THE MOST DANGEROUS JOB IN THE UNITED STATES

In 1906, Upton Sinclair published *The Jungle*, an exposé of the meat-packing industry in the United States. In addition to the widespread contamination of meat, Sinclair noted the mistreatment of meat-packing workers, mostly Eastern European immigrants, employed at dangerous, dirty, low-wage jobs. In time, the industry was unionized, and by the 1950s, meatpacking workers had one of the highest paid manufacturing jobs. But by the 1970s, the industry had changed. Big companies bought out smaller ones. The plants moved from urban areas such as Chicago and Kansas City, where unions were strong, to rural areas such as Arkansas, North Carolina, Texas, Colorado, Kansas, Nebraska, and Iowa, where unions were weak. Employees are mostly

recent immigrants from Mexico, some unable to speak English, and some in the United States as undocumented workers. Thus, they are vulnerable and unlikely to challenge authority (Schlosser 2001).

Just as Sinclair noted a century ago, the workers in the slaughterhouse once again had one of the lowest paid manufacturing jobs and one of the most dangerous (Schlosser 2006). A report of conditions in Nebraska's meatpacking plants revealed that the production line speed was brutally high with more over 400 cattle slaughtered and processed every hour (more than six animals per minute) at large packing plants. This high rate of speed leads to worker injuries. Workers using knives in these production lines can make 20,000

cutting motions a day, making them especially susceptible to repetitive motion injuries (carpal tunnel syndrome) (Midwest Coalition for Human Rights 2011). Other typical injuries are falling on slippery floors, being mangled by meat processing machines, being cut, and asphyxiation from fumes (Human Rights Watch report, cited in Greenhouse 2005). Moreover, the meatpacking companies violated human and labor rights by suppressing their employees' efforts to organize a union. In this regard, the U.S. Court of Appeals in 2006 upheld a ruling by the National Labor Relations Board that the Smithfield Packing Company, between 1992 and 1998, had violated a number of labor laws and created an atmosphere of intimidation and coercion to prevent workers from joining the United Food and Commercial Workers (UFCW) union (Schlosser 2006).

industrial deaths? (See the "A Closer Look" panel on a preventable mining disaster.) Who is a greater threat, the thug in the streets or the executives in the suites? Criminologist Jeffrey Reiman answers these questions, arguing that:

> Is a person who kills another in a bar brawl a greater threat to society than a business executive who refuses to cut into his profits to make his plant a safe place to work? By any measure of death and suffering, the latter is by far a greater danger than the former. Because he wishes his workers no harm, because he is only indirectly responsible for death and disability while pursuing legitimate economic goals, his acts are not called "crimes." Once we free our imagination from the blinders of the one-on-one model of crime, can there be any doubt that the criminal justice system does not protect us from the gravest threats to life and limb? It seeks to protect us when danger comes from a young lower-class male in the inner city. When a threat comes from an upper-class business executive in an office, the criminal justice system looks the other way. This is in the face of growing evidence that for every two American citizens murdered by thugs, more than three American workers are killed by the recklessness of their bosses and the indifference of their government. (2007:87)

Sweatshops

A **sweatshop** is a substandard work environment where workers are paid less than the minimum wage and are not paid overtime premiums and where other labor laws are violated. Although sweatshops occur in various types of manufacturing, domestically they occur most frequently in the garment industry. The U.S. Department of Labor estimates that more than half of the nation's 22,000 garment factories are sweatshops, mostly in New York, California, Texas, Florida, and Georgia, but also offshore in U.S. territories like American Samoa, Guam, and Saipan where the garments are labeled "Made in the USA" (cited in Lendman 2010). The workers in these places make clothes for such brands as Levi Strauss, Esprit, Casual Corner, the Limited, and the Gap and for such merchandisers as J.C. Penney, Sears, and Walmart. The workers, mostly Latina and Asian immigrant women, are paid much less than the minimum wage, receive no benefits, and work in crowded, unsafe, and stifling conditions.

At the extreme, modern-day slavery exists in the United States. Although the exact number is unknown, the Central Intelligence Agency has estimated that as many as 50,000 people are trafficked into or transited through the United States annually as sex slaves, domestic servants, garment slaves, and agricultural laborers (cited in Copblock.org 2011).

U.S. corporations also sell products produced by workers, many of whom are children, working in sweatshop conditions in other countries. Foxconn, for example, employs 1.2 million workers in China who assemble 40 percent of the electronics equipment sold worldwide, much of it in the United States to companies such as Microsoft, Hewlett-Packard, Dell, Amazon, and Apple. It is the largest supplier of Apple's hugely popular iPads and iPhones. Workers at Foxconn and other plants are typically young women who work up to 14-hour shifts six or seven days a week. The

A Closer Look

THE UPPER BIG BRANCH MINE DISASTER: PREVENTABLE?

In the month prior to the worst mining disaster in four decades, the U.S. Mine Safety and Health Administration (MSHA) cited Massey Energy for fifty-three safety violations in its Upper Big Branch Mine in West Virginia. On April 5, 2010, an explosion in that mine killed twenty-nine miners. After this disaster, the MSHA investigated and issued 369 citations and orders on the owner, Massey Energy, including twenty-one "flagrant violations" of safety and health standards. The report concluded that the explosion that caused this tragedy was entirely preventable. It was the result of an ingrained culture of greed and recklessness that put profits before workers' safety. Among the charges by the MSHA

(reported in Jameson 2011; Mauriello 2011; and Daly 2011):

- Mine managers were given advanced notice by Massey as to when federal and safety inspectors were to visit the mine.
- The company kept two sets of safety books, one that included known dangers and another version for miners and inspectors that minimized the dangers.
- The explosion was caused when methane was ignited from outdated equipment; inoperable sprinklers combined with already unsafe working conditions.
- Ventilation levels were dangerously low due to the company's failure to comply with its ventilation plan.

- Management showed an intentional pattern of covering up safety hazards.
- When inspectors identified safety hazards, Massey often failed to take corrective action.
- There was an atmosphere of intimidation that kept workers from bringing safety concerns to inspectors.

Massey was acquired by Alpha Natural Resources in June 2011 for $7.1 billion, thereby assuming Massey's legal liabilities for the disaster. Alpha agreed to a $209.5 million settlement. Of that, $46.5 million went to families of the victims, $128 million to fund mine safety upgrades and research and training, and $35 million in penalties for federal mine safety violations. The settlement, approved by the Justice Department, allowed Alpha to escape pleading guilty to any criminal charges.

work environment is characterized by military-type discipline (Arthur 2012). Workers are exploited in sweatshops throughout the low-wage countries (e.g., China, India, Bangladesh, Vietnam, Cambodia, Indonesia, Nicaragua, and Haiti) making shoes, apparel, athletic equipment, toys, and tools for American consumers.

Unions and Their Decline

Historically, labor unions have been extremely important in changing management–labor relations. Joining together, workers challenged owners to increase wages, add benefits, provide worker security, and promote safety in the workplace. Through the use of strikes, work slowdowns, public relations, and political lobbying, working conditions improved, and union members, for the most part, prospered. In wages and benefits, union workers earn more than nonunion workers. Consider the following differences between union workers and unorganized workers:

- The median yearly earnings of workers in 2010 were $47,684 for union workers, compared with $37,284 for employees not represented by unions (Bureau of Labor Statistics, reported in Bauerlein and Jeffery 2011:21).
- Union members are more likely to have employer-provided health insurance, pensions, and paid sick leave than non-union workers (vanden Heuvel 2010).
- Women union members earn 33 percent more than women nonunion workers.
- African American union members earn 35 percent more than African American nonunion workers.
- Latino union members earn 51 percent more than Latino nonunion workers (A. Levin 2004).
- There are fewer fatalities and injuries in underground coal mines that are unionized than at nonunion mines (Morantz 2011).

Despite all of the benefits, unions have lost their power since about 1980, as membership declined from a high of about 35 percent of wage and salary workers in the mid-1950s, and 20 percent in the early 1980s, to 11.9 percent in 2010. With such small and dwindling numbers, labor unions are in danger of becoming irrelevant. The reasons for the decline in union membership (and clout) are several. First, there was a direct assault against unions by Republican presidents Reagan, George H. W. Bush, and George W. Bush. Each of these administrations was unsympathetic with strikes and sometimes used federal leverage to weaken them. Similarly, their appointees to the post of Secretary of Labor and the National Labor Relations Board (NLRB) were probusiness rather than prolabor.

Second, public opinion has turned against unions because some of them are undemocratic, scandal ridden, and too zealous in their demands. Public opinion has also turned against organized labor because of a probusiness, procapitalist bias by Republicans, especially since the Reagan administration. Third, businesses do all they can to block unions. Typically, companies are required to have a union vote if 30 percent of workers sign a petition. When such an election does occur, companies have won more than half the time, versus 28 percent in the early 1950s. The anti-union vote by workers is the result usually of an all-out assault by the company, including information arguing that unionization may lead to downsizing or even closing plants, "worker appreciation" days with free barbecues or pizza, the selective firing of workers who are union activists (an illegal activity, but it happens in about one-fourth of the union drives, according to a commission study established by President Clinton), and other forms of intimidation. Walmart, for example, has been formally cited numerous times for using illegal tactics to deny its workers the right to join a union. The 2010 Supreme Court decision to allow corporations to spend unlimited amounts for or against a political candidate has disastrous consequences for unions because business is so anti-union. Corporations will support anti-union candidates while working to defeat pro-union candidates. After a few election cycles, very few pro-union legislators at the state and federal levels will remain in office.

A major reason for the decline of union strength is the transformation of the economy. Manufacturing jobs, which are in decline, have historically been pro-union, whereas service jobs, which are increasing, have been typically nonunionized. Similarly, the advent of computers, modems, and fax machines has increased the number of people who work at home as temporary and part-time workers. These workers are the least likely to join unions.

And, finally, some corporations have moved their operations to nonunion states. Automobile manufacturers, for example, have bypassed the industrial (and heavily unionized) North and have opened assembly plants in the South, where there is an anti-union climate. Nissan became the first foreign car maker in the South (in Tennessee and later in Mississippi), followed by Toyota (Kentucky, Texas, and Alabama), Honda, Mercedes-Benz, Hyundai (Alabama), and BMW (South Carolina). Now the aircraft industry is involved in a similar migration with Boeing building an assembly line in South Carolina for its 787 Dreamliner jet.

These forces have given the strong advantage to management. This trend has several negative consequences. First, faced with the threat of plants closing or moving to nonunion localities or to low-wage nations, unions have chosen, typically, to give back many of the gains they made during the 1960s and 1970s. Thus, workers have lost real wages and benefits. A second consequence of union decline is that the workplace may be less safe: Some of the most injury-prone industries, like cattle, pig, chicken, turkey, and catfish processing and textiles, have clustered in right-to-work (i.e., nonunion) states across the South.

A major consequence of union decline is the further dwindling of the middle class. Union jobs in manufacturing brought many relatively unskilled workers into the middle class. This trend is reversed now with robots replacing assembly line workers and with the relatively few remaining manufacturing jobs migrating to the South or overseas.

With union strength dwindling, incomes have stagnated or declined. This has consequences for the economy as workers will not be able to purchase enough goods and services to encourage economic growth and societywide prosperity. In short, demand for products will fall, resulting in employers laying off workers or reducing their wages and benefits further.

Those nations with strong unionized labor (e.g., Canada, Germany, and Sweden) have a social democratic conception of society, which means universal healthcare, progressive income taxes, and more equitable government programs.

Discrimination in the Workplace: Perpetuation of Inequality

View on MySocLab Figure: Women in the Labor Force: A Global View

Women and minorities have long been the objects of discrimination in U.S. industry. Currently (and we have progressed mightily), approximately 50,000 charges of discrimination by organizations are filed annually with the Equal Employment Opportunity Commission. The charges now and in the past have centered on hiring policies, seniority rights, restricted job placement, limited opportunities for advancement, and lower pay for equal work. A number of court suits (and those settled out of court) illustrate that discriminatory policies have been common among such major corporations as AT&T, General Motors, and Northwest Airlines and in such industries as banking and steel.

Two mechanisms operating in the U.S. economy perpetuate inequalities in the job market by social class, race, and gender—the segmented labor market and male dominance.

- **Segmented Labor Market.** The capitalist economy is divided into two separate sectors that have different characteristics, different roles, and different rewards for laborers within each. This organization of the economy is called the segmented labor market, or the dual labor market. The primary sector is composed of large, bureaucratic organizations with relatively stable production and sales. Jobs within this sector require developed skills, are relatively well paid, occur in good working conditions, and are stable. Within this sector there are two types of jobs. The first type, those in the upper tier, are high-status professional and managerial jobs. The pay is very good for the highly educated people in these jobs. They have a high degree of personal autonomy, and the jobs offer variety, creativity, and initiative. Upward mobility is likely for those who are successful. The second type, the lower-tier jobs within the primary sector, are held by working-class people. The jobs are either white-collar clerical or blue-collar skilled and semiskilled. The jobs are repetitive, and mobility is limited. The jobs are relatively secure because of unionization, although they are much more vulnerable than those in the upper tier. When times are difficult, these workers tend to be laid off rather than terminated.

  The secondary economic sector is composed of marginal firms in which product demand is unstable. Jobs within this sector are characterized by poor working conditions, low wages, few opportunities for advancement, and little job security. Little education or skill is required to perform these tasks. Workers beginning in the secondary sector tend to get locked in because they lack the skills required in the primary sector, and they usually have unstable work histories. A common interpretation of this problem is that secondary-sector workers are in these dead-end jobs because of their pathology—poor work history, lack of skills, and lack of motivation. Such an explanation, however, blames the victim. Poor work histories tend to be the result of unemployment caused by the production of marginal products and the lack of job security. Similarly, these workers have few, if any, incentives to learn new skills or to stay for long periods with an employer because of the structural barriers to upward mobility. And unlike workers in the primary sector, workers in the secondary sector are more likely to experience harsh and capricious work discipline from supervisors, primarily because there are no unions.

  The significance of this dual labor market is threefold. First, placement in one of these segments corresponds with social class, which tends to be perpetuated from generation to generation. Second, employment in the secondary sector is often so inadequately paid that many full-time workers live in poverty, as noted in Chapter 7. And third, the existence of a dual labor market reinforces racial, ethnic, and gender divisions in the labor force. White males, although found in both segments, are overrepresented in the upper tier of the primary sector. White females and White ethnics tend to be clerks in the lower tier of the primary sector. Males and females of color are found disproportionately in the secondary sector. These findings explain why unemployment rates for African Americans and Latinos are consistently much higher than the rate for Whites (usually at least double). They explain the persistent wage differences found by race and gender. That is why there is a vast overrepresentation of people of color and women living in poverty. These facts are especially relevant as the workforce is increasingly composed of racial and ethnic minorities, most notably Latinos.

- **Male Dominance at Work.**   Closely tied to segmented labor markets is the dominance of men in work-related roles. This dominance is reflected in two ways—males tend to make the rules and enforce them, and males receive unequal (i.e., greater) rewards.

Current gender inequality results from a long history of patriarchal social relations in which men have consciously kept women in subordinate roles at work and in the home. Men as workers consistently have acted in their own interests to retain power and to keep women either out of their occupations or in subordinate and poorly paid work roles. Historically, through their unions, males insisted that the higher-status and better-paying jobs be exclusively male. They lobbied legislatures to pass legislation supportive of male exclusiveness in occupations and in opposition to such equalization measures as minimum wages for women. Also, the male unions prevented women from gaining the skills that would lead them to equal-paying jobs. The National Typographical Union in 1854, for example, insisted not only that women be refused jobs as compositors but also that they not be taught the skills necessary to be a compositor (Hartmann 1976).

Throughout U.S. history, business owners have used gender inequality in the workplace to their advantage. Women were hired because they would work for less money than men, which made men all the more fearful of women in the workplace. Capitalists even used the threat of hiring lower-paid women to take the place of higher-paid men to keep the wages of both sexes down and to lessen labor militancy.

In contemporary U.S. society, men and women, with some exceptions, are accorded different, and unequal, positions in religious, government, school, work, and family activities. Looking only at work, women and men do different work both in the family and in the labor force. This division of labor between the sexes preserves the differential power, privilege, and prestige of men (see Chapter 9). Men are over-represented in administrative and supervisory roles. Women are found disproportionately in jobs where they follow orders. Women are found, as just noted, more often than men in the secondary job market, where jobs are menial, poorly paid, and with little or no benefits. Take the pay differential, for example. Women's pay lags behind men's in virtually every sector of the economy. In 2010, full-time female workers made 77 cents for every dollar earned by their male counterparts.

Job Insecurity

A generation ago, workers had realistic hope of lifetime employment with the same employer. That is no longer the case. Corporate America has been downsizing for over thirty years, replacing workers with automation or with workers outside the United States. Mergers have brought more downsizing. When SBC merged with AT&T in 2005, for example, 13,000 jobs were eliminated. Those who kept their jobs found that their wages had stagnated and that their employers often had reduced their benefits. Downsized workers, if they find work, typically work for lower wages than previously.

The Bureau of Labor Statistics supplies the official unemployment statistics. The official unemployment rate in the United States since 2000 has ranged from a low of 3.9 percent in October 2000 to a high of 10.2 percent in late 2009. The official unemployment rate is misleading, however, because it understates, dramatically, the actual magnitude of unemployment. The unemployment rate does not include those discouraged persons who have stopped looking for jobs within the past four weeks. If these **discouraged workers** were added to the official unemployment rate of 10 percent, it would add 2.3 million people. The official rate also does not include those part-time workers who would prefer to work full time, adding another 9.2 million. If both of these categories are included, the actual rate of unemployment/underemployment would be 17.2 percent (Rugaber 2009). The official government data, by undercounting joblessness, diminishes the perceived severity of unemployment and therefore reduce the zeal to do anything about the problem.

Unemployment is commonly believed to be functional (i.e., have positive consequences) for society by reducing inflationary pressures. It is also kept relatively high by capitalists because high unemployment deflates wages and therefore increases profits. When there are unemployed people willing to work, workers will not make inordinate demands for higher wages for fear that they will be replaced by cheaper labor. Thus, even unionized labor becomes relatively docile when unemployment is high.

Unemployment affects some groups more than others. This **reserve army of the unemployed** (unemployed people who want to work) is disproportionately composed of people of color (Latinos, African Americans, Native Americans), teenagers, and residents in declining cities. Typically, the official unemployment rate for African Americans is at least twice as high as the rate for Whites. In 2011, for example, the African American unemployment rate averaged 15.8 percent, twice the White average of 7.9 percent. These proportions by race tend to be relatively constant, whether the overall unemployment rate is high or low, whether the economy is in a boom or a slump (see Figure 14.1). Thus, the labor market assigns people of color disproportionately not only to the low-paying jobs but also to jobs that are the most unstable, precisely the situation of the secondary sector in the segmented labor market.

An important consequence of the reserve army of the unemployed being composed primarily of racial minorities is that it inflames racial antipathies against them by people who hold unstable jobs. These job holders perceive their enemy as the people below them (commonly, recent immigrants), who will work for lower wages, rather than as the capitalists who oppose full employment and adequate wages for all people.

There are clear demographic reasons for the shortage of jobs now and for the near future. In the past thirty years or so, an unusually large number of women entered the labor force, motivated by the necessity of supplementing family income and the need for self-fulfillment in nontraditional roles. About seven in ten married women with children work outside the home. The other demographic force behind unemployment pressures was the very large numbers of young people entering the job market during the 1970s. The baby-boom generation—those 10 million more babies born between 1946 and 1956 than in the previous ten years—reached the job-seeking stage in the 1970s. These baby boomers increased the pressure for jobs and depressed the wages of people with jobs. The immense burden they put on jobs, wages, and promotions will affect jobs not only for those preceding them but also most notably for those following

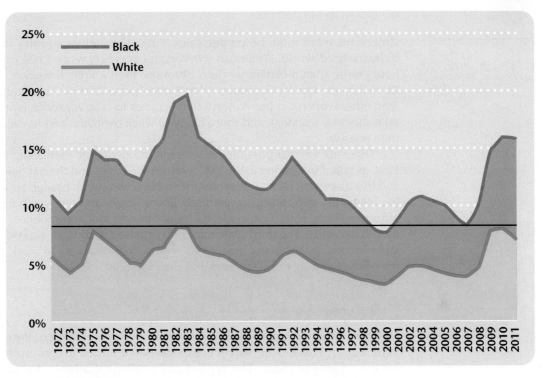

FIGURE 14.1

Black and White Annual Unemployment Rates, 1972 to 2011

Source: Algernon Austin. 2012. "For African Americans, 50 Years of High Unemployment." Economic Policy Institute (February 22).

them. In the 1970s, an astonishing 21 million new jobs were created. But because of the unprecedented number of women and young people entering the job market, the labor force grew by more than 24 million, leaving a shortfall of 3 million jobs.

But as important as these demographic trends are in explaining the unemployment problem, they are relatively minor when compared with the effects of the structural transformation and globalization that are occurring in the U.S. economy.

Benefits Insecurity

With relatively weak unions, high unemployment, and competition from low-wage economies, U.S. corporations have been reducing their benefits to workers. Some corporations have even declared bankruptcy to renege on benefits promised to their workers (e.g., United Airlines, Delta Airlines, Northwest Airlines, and Delphi Corporation, the largest U.S. auto parts maker). Others (e.g., General Motors, Chrysler, Caterpillar, Harley-Davidson, and Kohler) have negotiated with unions to set up a two-tiered system. The first tier maintains benefits to those already hired. New hires, on the other hand, will not only receive lower wages than those in the first tier but a greatly reduced benefits package as well. Another strategy by employers is to shift retirement plans from defined benefit (a guaranteed retirement benefit based on years of service) to one based on the investments of employees (e.g., 401k). This relieves employers from future obligations. In effect, then, corporations, which used to provide for the risks of old age and ill health of their workers, shifted those risks off the corporate ledger and onto the worker (Hacker 2006).

Increased Workload

Americans work more hours per week than in any other country in the advanced industrialized world. American workers, on average, work 1,804 hours a year, 135 hours more than a British worker, 240 more than a French worker, and 370 hours more than the typical German worker (Greenhouse 2009:6). Americans are less likely than other workers in the Western democracies to take vacations (and more likely to take shorter vacations), and more likely to work overtime and to even work at more than one job.

There are several possible reasons for U.S. workers' increasing their workload. First, as noted in Chapter 2, the gap between the haves and the have-nots is widening, and this disparity creates incentives for employees to work harder. Second, the widening inequality gap results in relatively lower wages and net worth for the less-than-affluent, which, with the increased cost of housing and automobiles, makes working more a necessity. The third reason for the increased workload, and one articulated by labor unions, is that many businesses require their workers to work more to reduce the costs of adding more workers and their benefits.

Worker Compensation

Median household income fell 9.8 percent from the beginning of the Great Recession to June 2011. This loss in worker compensation is added to continuing loss of wages for forty years or more. The typical male college graduate, for example, earned about 12 percent less in 2009 than his counterpart did in 1969. For the median man with a high school degree, his earnings fell by 47 percent during those forty years (Rampell 2012).

Moreover, in this time of stagnant or declining wages, the cost for healthcare and college tuition have skyrocketed.

Ironically, wages declined during this prolonged period while worker productivity (i.e., output per hour worked) actually rose. This lag is a consequence, as shown throughout this chapter, of technology (computers, robots), efficiency of production, workers fearing that they will be laid off if they do not produce, and fewer workers working more. See Figure 14.2, which shows increases in manufacturing output and profits, while jobs decreased.

Several factors depress the wages of workers. First, union membership has declined. Second, competition from low-wage countries depresses wages in the United States. For example, Delphi Corporation in 2005, unable to compete with low-wage economies, slashed its wages for production workers from $27 an hour to $10 (decreasing a full-time worker's annual income from about $56,000 to $20,800). Third, many corporations, if not moving overseas, have moved their operations to the largely nonunion South, the less-unionized West, and to rural areas where wages are lower. Fourth, corporate management has systematically replaced workers with machines as well as contingent workers—independent contractors, temporary workers, part-time workers, and home-based workers. The salient features of contingent workers are that they are disproportionately women, their wages are relatively low, and they are typically without traditional benefits. Finally, low wages result from a minimum wage (raised to $7.25 in 2009) that is not a living wage (which should be at least $10 an hour).

The higher one looks at the wage distribution, the wider the gap in compensation. As noted in Chapter 2, the gap between those at the top (corporate executives) and the workers who produce the products or services is huge. At the bottom, about 30 million

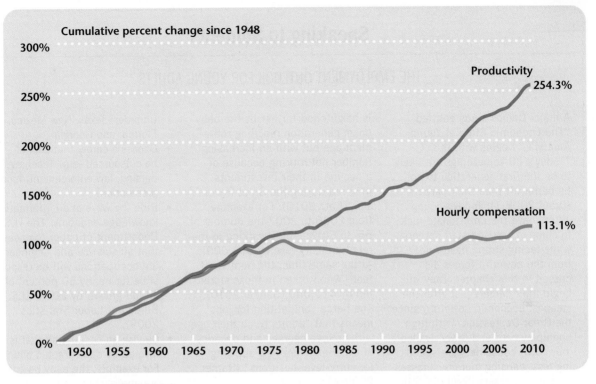

FIGURE 14.2

Growth of Real Hourly Compensation for Production/Nonsupervisory Workers and Productivity 1948, 2011

Source: Lawrence Mishel. 2012. "The Wedges between Productivity and Median Compensation Growth." Economic Policy Institute (April 26).

workers earn less than $10 an hour, typically without health insurance and other benefits. They are disproportionately African American, Latino, and female.

Consequently, many Americans are not making it financially. In 2010, some 46.2 million were living below the poverty line, and 49.9 million Americans were without health insurance. Racial and ethnic minorities were disproportionately disadvantaged. Black households had only 60 percent of the median income of Whites, and Latinos had but 70 percent of the median income of Whites in 2010. Full-time, year-round women workers made only 77 cents for every dollar earned by full-time men workers. Thus, the U.S. economy does not work for everyone. The roots of the problems found in the U.S. economy are found in the changes associated with globalization and its structural transformation.

The Problem: Workers or Jobs?

The argument is advanced often in the business community that there is a jobs/skills mismatch. That is, if graduating students were better prepared, the jobs would be there for them. But this conventional argument misses the point. The problem is not a lack of education but a lack of good jobs. Jobs have moved away to low-wage economies or non-union locales in the South and West. Jobs have been replaced by robots, scanners, and the like. The largest number of jobs that are available, for the most part, pay minimum wage or slightly above with few if any benefits (Katz-Fishman 1990:23).

Speaking to Students

THE EMPLOYMENT OUTLOOK FOR YOUNG ADULTS

A major Demos study entitled "The Economic State of Young America," begins with this: "Today's 20-somethings are likely to be the first generation to not be better off than their parents" (Draut 2008:1). Today's young adults have the unfortunate luck to come of age and start careers while facing strong headwinds from the powerful forces discussed in this chapter. They will begin their careers just after the steepest economic downturn since the Great Depression. With high unemployment and fewer available jobs, U.S. consumers are spending less, causing more businesses to release workers (Raum 2009). The shift from a manufacturing economy to one based on services will cause employers to continue lowering wages and benefits for their workers. Jobs are being created and destroyed in this dynamic economy, fueled by the economic transformation, with more jobs destroyed than created, resulting in a disconnect between the demand for labor and the supply (Benson 2009). Because they are new to the job market, young adults will be the last to be hired and the first to be fired. Unions no longer have the power to ameliorate the vicissitudes of work. Future job growth will be concentrated in the lower-wage sector of the economy. The jobs squeeze is heightened further by the baby boom generation reaching retirement age but with an increasing number not retiring because of a decline in their investments incurred during the Great Recession (Kotz 2010). For example, from 2000 to 2007 the number of 55- to 64-year-olds working in the retail industry rose by 553,000. At the same time, the number of teens who worked in those stores fell by 419,000 (Gandel 2010). The fierce competition for jobs means that "adults twice their age with college degrees and decades of experience are now applying for entry-level positions" (Ratner 2009:21).

In short, the American economy is not providing enough jobs, "and nowhere near enough good jobs, to maintain the standard of living that most Americans have come to expect" (Herbert 2009: para 4).

How does one cope with this insecure work world? Some young people will succeed, but most will find the job world harsh. The forces that converge to make finding good jobs troublesome will not be going away soon. Here are a few ideas to ponder as you face a difficult economic environment.

• Jobs are migrating away from the industrial heartland to the South and Southwest. The states with the highest job growth are (in order) Texas, New Mexico, Florida, and Georgia.

• Choose a career that cannot be outsourced (e.g., teaching, nursing, law enforcement, food preparation).

• Ride the wave of an information/knowledge economy. The U.S. Department of Labor foresees that all science and engineering occupations will be responsible for nearly 60 percent of all job growth by 2018 (U.S. Bureau of Labor Statistics 2009).

• Choose an occupation that is favored by demographic change. For example, the baby boomers are approaching old age. Moreover, the old are living longer. This increases the need for doctors, nurses, pharmacists, nursing aides, home health aides, recreational therapists, and for people to plan and construct retirement homes and gerontology clinics.

• Choose an occupation that will solve social problems endorsed by the public. For example, the world faces a dangerous overheating of the environment. Green jobs, such as producing solar panels or wind turbines, weatherizing homes, and engineering clean energy projects will add an estimated 2.5 million jobs in the United States by 2018 (Walsh 2009).

In summary, the problems associated with work in U.S. society are structural in origin. The source is not in unmotivated or unwilling or undereducated workers. To understand the work setting in our society, we must understand globalization and the nature of capitalism, where profit—not the human consequences—guides managerial decisions. And in looking at unemployment, we must recognize that the economy fails to produce enough jobs with living wages and adequate benefits for the workers to maintain a middle-class lifestyle. Finally, in examining this labor market, we must understand that the economy is undergoing a profound transformation. The next few generations will be caught in the nexus between one stage and another, and many will suffer because of the dislocations. (See the "Speaking to Students" panel.) So, too, will a society that refuses to plan, but, rather, lets the marketplace dictate the choices of economic firms.

MySocLab

✓ **Study** and **Review** on **MySocLab**

■ CHAPTER REVIEW

1. There are two fundamental ways in which society can organize its economic activities: capitalism and socialism.

2. Capitalism in its pure form involves (a) private ownership of property, (b) the pursuit of personal profit, (c) competition, and (d) a government policy of allowing the marketplace to function unhindered.

3. Socialism in its pure form involves (a) democracy throughout the social structure; (b) equality of opportunity, equality rather than hierarchy in decision making, and equality in sharing the benefits of society; (c) public ownership of the means of production; (d) community; and (e) planning for common purposes.

4. The economy of the United States is in the midst of a major structural transformation. This fundamental shift is the consequence of several powerful converging forces: (a) technological change, (b) the globalization of the economy, (c) capital flight, and (d) the shift from an industrial economy to a service/information economy.

5. These forces combine to create considerable discontinuity and disequilibrium in society. The trend toward robotics and other forms of super-automation reduces the jobs for the unskilled and semiskilled. This high-tech society, however, creates a need for workers skilled in communication, reasoning, mathematics, and computer programming. The proportion of workers traditionally found in these jobs (White males) is declining, while the proportion of new workers is increasingly non-White. Because non-Whites are disadvantaged economically and educationally, there is a skills mismatch. This skills gap offers the disadvantaged the potential of upward mobility if they, governments, schools, and businesses, meet the challenge.

If not, the gap between the advantaged and the disadvantaged will continue to widen.

6. Deindustrialization and the shift to a service economy have reduced the number of jobs providing a middle-class standard of living and have expanded the number of lower standard-of-living jobs. The result is a bifurcation of the labor force into the haves and the have-nots.

7. Societies are organized to allocate work to produce the goods and services required for survival. The way work is organized generates important social problems.

8. Owners and managers of firms and factories control workers in several ways: (a) through scientific management, (b) through bureaucracy, (c) by monitoring worker behavior, and (d) through extortion.

9. Blue-collar and white-collar workers in bureaucracies and factories are susceptible to alienation, which is the separation of human beings from each other, from themselves, and from the products they create. Specialized work in impersonal settings leads to dissatisfaction and meaninglessness.

10. A primary goal of business firms in a capitalist society is to reduce costs and thus increase profits. One way to reduce costs is not to provide adequately for worker safety.

11. Labor unions have declined in numbers and power. This decline has resulted in lower real wages and benefits, less-safe work conditions, and a declining middle class.

12. Another work-related problem is discrimination, in which women and minorities have long received unfair treatment in jobs, pay, and opportunities for advancement. Two features of the U.S. economy promote these inequities: (a) the segmented labor market and (b) capitalist patriarchy.

13. The official government data on unemployment hide the actual amount by undercounting the unemployed in two ways: (a) people not actively seeking work (discouraged workers) are not counted; and (b) people who work at part-time jobs are counted as fully employed.

14. Unemployment has positive consequences for some people. Having a certain portion unemployed tends to keep inflation in check, according to some economists. Also, unemployment benefits capitalists by keeping wages down.

■ KEY TERMS

Capitalism. The economic system based on private ownership of property, guided by the seeking of maximum profits.

Socialism. The economic system in which the means of production are owned by the people for their collective benefit.

Pandemic Worldwide health danger.

Globalization. The processes by which the earth's peoples are increasingly interconnected economically, politically, culturally, and environmentally.

Capital flight. Investment choices that involve the movement of corporate monies from one investment to another (investment overseas, plant relocation, and mergers).

Structural transformation of the economy. Fundamental change in the economy resulting from several powerful contemporary forces: technological breakthroughs in microelectronics, the globalization of the economy, capital flight, and the shift from a manufacturing economy to one based on information and services.

Offshoring. When a company moves its production to another country, producing the same products but with cheaper labor, lower taxes, and lower benefits to workers.

Outsourcing. The process of transferring a specific task (such as accounting or transcribing) to a foreign firm to save money and reintegrating that work back into the overall operation.

Sunset industries. Industries declining in output and employment.

Contingent work. Employment arrangement whereby employees work as temporaries or independent contractors, freeing employers from paying fringe benefits.

Homeshoring (homesourcing). The process of employing home-based independent contractors.

Sunrise industries. Industries characterized by increased output and employment.

Gentrification. The process of converting low-income housing to condominiums or upscale apartments.

New homeless. Middle-class families who never expected to be poor but became so because of the Great Recession.

Scientific management. Efforts to increase worker efficiency by breaking down work into very specialized tasks, the standardization of tools and procedures, and the speeding up of repetitive work.

Alienation. Separation of human beings from each other, from themselves, and from the products they create.

Sweatshop. Substandard working environment where labor laws are violated.

Discouraged workers. People who have not actively sought work for four weeks. These people are not counted as unemployed by the Bureau of Labor Statistics.

Reserve army of the unemployed. Unemployed people who want to work. Their presence tends to depress the wages of workers and keeps those workers from making demands on employers for fear of being replaced.

LEARNING OBJECTIVES

15.1 Explain the myths versus realities of family life in the United States.

15.2 Explain how societal economic transformations affect family life.

15.3 Describe the effects of social class on families in the United States.

15.4 Explain the difficulties of managing work and family with little support from the system.

15.5 Understand the divorce rate and the consequences of divorce.

15.6 Examine the causes and consequences of violence in families.

amily changes occurring in the last few decades have led some social analysts to conclude that the family is in serious trouble, that we have lost our **family values**, and that the "breakdown of the family" causes social problems. The **family** is an easy target for those who blame social problems on bad people doing bad things. They assume that when the family fails, the rest of society fails. This view of the world is flawed in two fundamental respects. First, it reverses the relationship between family and society by treating families as the building blocks of society rather than as *a product of social conditions*. Second, it ignores the structural reasons for family breakdown and the profound changes occurring throughout the world. Even in very different societies, families and households are undergoing similar shifts as a result of global economic changes.

Some social problems have their locus in family settings. Although many of these problems are rooted in conditions outside the family, they become family problems that affect growing numbers of children and adults. This chapter examines the family as a social institution and the social problems that have their locus in family life. The chapter is divided into five parts. The first section shows the gap between common images of the family and family life as it is actually experienced in this society. The remaining four sections examine representative family-based social problems: the economic disadvantages for some families and current changes in the larger economy that are producing new problems for families, problems in balancing work and family without social supports, divorce, and domestic violence. The theme of this chapter is that family life and family problems are connected with other social institutions.

THE MYTHICAL FAMILY IN THE UNITED STATES

15.1 Explain the myths versus realities of family life in the United States.

There are many myths about families. These beliefs are bound up with nostalgia and cultural values concerning what is typical and true about families. The following myths, based on folk wisdom and common beliefs, are rarely challenged except by social scientists and family scholars.

1. *The myth of a stable and harmonious family of the past.* Most people think that families of the past were better than families of the present. They are believed to have been more stable, better adjusted, and happier. However, family historians have found that there is no golden age of the family. Many children were raised by single parents or stepparents, just as now. Divorce rates were lower because of strong religious prohibitions and community norms against divorce, but this does not mean that love was stronger in the past. Many "empty" marriages continued without love and happiness to bind them.

   Read on MySocLab Document: How History and Sociology Can Help Today's Families

   Historian Stephanie Coontz has reexamined our assumptions about family history. Her book *The Way We Never Were* (1992) exploded the myth that the family has recently "gone bad." In her more recent book, *Marriage: A History* (Coontz 2005), she shows how marriage changed from an economic and political institution to a voluntary love relationship. This change, not the loss of family values, is what makes marriage more fragile today. Family life of the past was quite different from the stereotype. Desertion by spouses, the presence of illegitimate children, and other conditions that are considered modern problems existed in the past. Part of the family nostalgia holds that there were three generations living under one roof or in close proximity. This image of the three-generational family is also false. Few examples of this "classical family of western nostalgia" (Goode 1983:43) have been found by family historians.

2. *The myth of separate worlds.* This is the positive image of the family as a place of love and trust, where individuals escape from the outside world. It makes a distinction between "public" and "private" realms with the family as a "haven in a heartless world." Here, social relations are thought to be different from those in the world at large. Of course, love, intimacy, and trust are the glue for many families, but this glorification of private life tends to mask the dark side of some families, where emotional and physical aggression are commonplace and where competition between spouses and among children sometimes destroys relationships. This myth ignores the harsh effects of economic conditions such as globalization and the Great Recession (e.g., poverty or near poverty, unemployment and underemployment, **downward mobility** or the threat of downward mobility). It ignores the social inequalities (racism, sexism, ageism, homophobia) that prevent many people from experiencing the good things in life. And the idealized family view masks the inevitable problems that arise in intimate settings (tensions, anger, and even violence in some instances).

3. *The myth of the monolithic family form.* We all know what a family is *supposed* to look like. It should resemble the Ozzie and Harriet form. We get this image from our ministers and priests, from our politicians, from children's literature, and from television. This image is of a White, middle-class, heterosexual father as breadwinner, mother as homemaker, and children at home, living in a one-family house. This model, however, represents a small proportion of U.S. households. Less than 10 percent of households consist of married couples with children in which only the husband works. Today, it makes more sense to talk about "types of families" (Mabry, Giarrusso, & Bengston 2004:93). Contemporary family types represent a multitude of family forms, including single-parent households, stepparent families, extended multigenerational households, gay and straight cohabiting couples, child-free couples, transnational families, lone householders with ties to various families, and many other kinds of families.

4. *The myth of a unified family experience.* We assume that all family members experience family life in the same way. This image hides the diversity within families. The family is a gendered institution. Women and men experience marriage differently. There are gender differences in decision making, in household division of labor, and in forms of intimacy and sexuality. Similarly, divorce affects them differently. Remarriage patterns differ by gender, as well. Girls and boys experience their childhoods differently, as there are different expectations, different rules, and different punishments according to gender.

5. *The myth of family decline as the cause of social problems.* Partly because of the myths about the past, and partly because the family has changed so much in the past few decades, many conclude that the breakdown of the family is responsible for today's social ills. Fatherless families and women working outside the home are said to be the reasons for poverty, violence, drug addiction, and crime. Divorced or unwed mothers, in this view, are damaging children, destroying families, and tearing apart the fabric of society.

15.2 Explain how societal economic transformations affect family life.

U.S. FAMILIES IN HISTORICAL PERSPECTIVE: THE FAMILY IN CAPITALISM

Family forms in the United States are closely related to economic development. Industrialization moved the center of production from the domestic family unit to the workplace. Families became private domestic retreats set off from the rest of society.

Watch on MySocLab Slideshow: Families

View on MySocLab Figure: Family Structure: U.S. Families with Children Under Age 18 Headed by Mothers, Fathers, and Both Parents

Men went off to earn a wage in factories and offices, while women remained in the home to nurture their children. From the rise of the industrial economy until World War II, capitalism operated within a simple framework. Employers assumed that most families included one main breadwinner—a male—and one adult working at home directing domestic work—a female; in short, jobs with wives. As a result, many men received the income intended to support a family.

The private family with a breadwinner father and a homemaker mother was an important historical development, but economic conditions precluded this pattern for many families. With industrialization, wave after wave of immigrants filled the industrial labor force. Through their labor, entire families became a part of society. Immigrant families did not separate themselves into private units. Instead, they used extended family ties to adjust in the new society. Family members helped their newly arrived kin and other members of their ethnic groups.

Many immigrants came to the United States in family groupings, or they sent for families once they were established in cities. Kin helped locate jobs and housing, and they provided other forms of support. Contrary to the typical portrayal of immigrants, their transplanted kinship and ethnic bonds did not disintegrate but rather were rebuilt in the new society (Early 1983; Vecoli 1964).

The developing capitalist economy did not provide equal opportunities for all. Racial-ethnic people did not have the opportunity to become part of the industrial labor force. Instead, they labored in nonindustrial sectors of the economy, which often required family arrangements that were different from those in the dominant society. The breadwinner–homemaker pattern never applied to immigrants and racial minorities because they were denied the opportunities to earn a family wage. So, many married women took jobs to make ends meet. Some women took in boarders or did piecework; some worked as maids in middle-class and upper-class homes; and some became wage workers in sweatshops, department stores, and offices. For these families, the support of the community and extended family members was crucial (Albelda 1992:7).

Families have always varied with the social conditions surrounding them. From the original settlement of the American colonies through the mid-twentieth century,

The "breadwinner–homemaker" pattern does not apply to people who lack the opportunities to earn a family wage.

families of European descent often received economic and social supports to establish and maintain families. Following World War II, the GI Bill, the National Defense Education Act, the expansion of the Federal Housing Authority and Veterans Administration loan subsidy programs, and government funding of new highways provided the means through which middle-class Whites were able to achieve the stable suburban family lives that became the ideal against which other families were judged (Coontz 1992). These kinds of supports have rarely been available for people of color and, until quite recently, were actively denied them through various forms of housing and job discrimination. Family history makes it clear that social forces have always created many different family types.

What we think of as "the family" is an ideal. It implies a private retreat set apart from society. This image masks the real relationship between families and the larger society. A better way of understanding how families are related to social institutions is to distinguish between families and households. *Family* refers to a set of social relationships, whereas **household** refers to residence or living arrangements (Jarrett and Burton 1999; Rapp 1982). To put it another way, a household is a residence group that carries out domestic functions, whereas a family is a kinship group (Holstein and Gubrium 1999:31). A good example of the importance of distinguishing between family and household is the restructuring of family obligations and household composition after divorce (Ferree 1991:107).

15.3 Describe the effects of social class on families in the United States.

STRATIFICATION AND FAMILY LIFE: UNEQUAL LIFE CHANCES

In previous chapters, we examined growing inequalities in the distribution of social opportunities. These stratification hierarchies—class, race, and gender—are changing and reshuffling families and individuals. In this section, we examine the effects of social class on families in the United States. Of course, the social patterning of inequality occurs along many other dimensions, including age, family characteristics, and place of residence (see Table 15.1).

Families are embedded in a class hierarchy that is "pulling apart" to shrink the middle class while more families join the growing ranks of the rich or the poor (Usdansky 1992). This movement creates great differences in family living and no longer guarantees that children's placement in the class system will follow that of their parents. Still, a family's location in the class system is the single most important determinant of family life.

Social and economic forces produce different family configurations. In a stratified society, family structures differ because households vary systematically in their ability to acquire, accumulate, and transmit wealth, wages, or welfare (Rapp 1982). Households in different parts of the class structure have different ways of acquiring the necessities of life. Inheritance, salaries, wages, welfare, or various involvements with the hidden economy, the illegal economy, or the irregular economy provide different connections with society's opportunity structures. The social networks or relationships outside the family—at work, school, church, and voluntary associations—are the social forces that shape class and racial differences in family life.

The middle-class family form is idealized in our society. This form, a self-reliant unit composed of a breadwinning father, a homemaker mother, and their children, has long been most characteristic of middle-class and upper-middle-class families. Middle-class families of the twenty-first century are quite different from television's stereotyped family of the 1950s. Today, many families can sustain their class status only through the economic contributions of employed wives. Such families must

TABLE 15.1

People and Families in Poverty by Selected Characteristics, 2010

Characteristics	Below Poverty Percent	Characteristics	Below Poverty Percent
People		Nativity	
Total	15.1	Native	14.4
Family Status		Foreign born	19.9
In families	13.2	Naturalized citizen	11.3
Householder	11.7	Not a citizen	26.7
Related children under 18	21.5	Region	
In unrelated subfamilies	45.5	Northeast	12.8
Reference person	42.6	Midwest	13.9
Children under 18	49.8	South	16.9
Unrelated individual	22.9	West	15.3
Male	21.7	Residence	
Female	24.1	Inside metropolitan areas	14.9
Race		Inside central cities	19.7
White	13	Outside central cities	11.8
Black	27.4	Type of Family	
Asian	12.1	Married-couple	6.2
Hispanic origin	26.6	Female householder (no husband present)	31.6
Age			
Under 18	22	Male householder (no wife present)	15.8
18–64 years	13.7		
65 years and older	9		

Source: DeNavas-Walt, Carmen, Bernadette D. Proctor, and Jessica C. Smith, U.S. Census Bureau, Current Population Reports, P60-239, *Income, Poverty, and Health Insurance Coverage in the United States: 2010*, U.S. Government Printing Office, Washington, DC, 2011, pp. 15–16.

find ways to provide care for their children. How families in different class locations provide childcare in the twenty-first century is the subject of a recent study by sociologist Karen Hansen. Her research challenges the myth that middle-class families are self-sufficient and disconnected from kin. Even if they are middle class, families with two breadwinners must build social networks to help them care for children. In today's world, they have increased their reliance on kin. Hansen concluded that structural changes have given rise to middle-class families that are "not-so-nuclear" (Hansen 2005).

Although middle-class families *appear* to be self-sufficient, they are supported by conditions in the larger society. When exceptional economic resources are called for, nonfamilial institutions usually are available in the form of better medical coverage, expense accounts, and credit at banks (Rapp 1982:181).

These connections with other institutions are what distinguish middle-class family life from family life in other social classes. The strongest links are with the occupations of middle-class family members, especially those of the husband–father. Occupational roles greatly affect family roles and the quality of family life (Schneider and Smith 1973). Occupations are part of the larger opportunity structure of society. Occupations that are highly valued and carry high income rewards are unevenly distributed. The amount of the paycheck determines how well a given household can acquire needed resources.

In the working class, material resources depend on wages acquired in exchange for labor. When such hourly wages are insufficient or unstable, individuals in households must pool their resources with other people in the larger family network. The pooling of resources may involve exchanging babysitting, sharing meals, or lending money. Pooling is a way of coping with the tenuous nature of connections between household and opportunity structures of society. It requires that the boundaries of "the family" be expanded. This is one reason that the idealized nuclear family is impossible for many people to sustain. At the lower levels of the class hierarchy, people lack the material resources to form autonomous households.

The fluid boundaries of these families do not make them unstable. Instead, this family flexibility is a way of sustaining the limited resources that result from their place in the class system. Minority single-parent families, which are criticized as being disorganized, are often embedded in a network of sharing and support. Variation in family organization is often a way of adapting to society.

Middle-class families with husbands and wives in careers have both economic resources and built-in ties with supportive institutions such as banks, credit unions, medical facilities, and voluntary associations. These ties are connected with some occupations and middle-class neighborhoods. They are structurally determined. Such institutional linkages strengthen the autonomy of middle-class families. But the middle class is shrinking, and many middle-class families are without middle-class incomes because of changes in the larger economy. Changes in family structure have also contributed to the lowering of family income. High divorce rates, for example, create many more family units with lower incomes.

Turning to the upper class, we find that family boundaries are more open than are those of the middle class, even though class boundaries are quite closed. Among the wealthy, "the family" includes not only the nuclear family but also the extended family. The elite have multiple households (Rapp 1982:182). Their day-to-day life exists within the larger context of a network of relatives (Dyer 1979:209).

Wealthy families are nationally connected by a web of institutions they control. In this social class, families throughout the country are linked by private schools, exclusive colleges, exclusive clubs, and fashionable vacation resorts. In this way, the elite remains intact and the marriage market is restricted to a small (but national) market (Blumberg and Paul 1975:69). Marriage legally clarifies the lines of inheritance in a way that is less important to those without property (Hansen 2005:69). Family life of the elite is privileged in every sense, as Stein, Richman, and Hannon (1977:22) reported: "Wealthy families can afford an elaborate support structure to take care of the details of everyday life. Persons can be hired to cook and prepare meals and do laundry and to care for the children." The vast economic holdings of these families allow them to have a high degree of control over the rewards and resources of society. They enjoy freedoms and choices not available to other families in society. These families maintain privileged access to **life chances** and lifestyles.

Kinship ties, obligations, and interests are more extended in classes at the two extremes than they are in the middle (McKinley 1964:22). In the upper extreme and toward the lower end of the class structure, kinship networks serve different functions. At both extremes, they are institutions of resource management. The kin-based family form of the elite serves to preserve inherited wealth. It is intricately tied to other national institutions that control the wealth of society. The kin-based family form of the working and lower classes is a primary institution through which individuals participate in social life as they pool and exchange their limited resources to ensure survival. It is influenced by society's institutions, but it remains separate from them.

15.4 Explain the difficulties of managing work and family with little support from the system.

Explore on **MySocLab Activity:** Family Diversity: Who Takes Care of Whom?

CHANGING FAMILIES IN A CHANGING WORLD

Economic Transformation and Family Life

Large-scale economic trends are reshaping U.S. families and households. (The following is adapted from Baca Zinn, Eitzen, and Wells 2011:92–132.) In Chapter 14, we discussed the powerful forces that are transforming the U.S. economy: (1) globalization, (2) technological change, (3) capital flight, and (4) the shift from an industrial economy to a service economy. These forces combine to affect families both directly and indirectly. They have reduced the number of jobs providing a middle-class standard of living and have expanded the number of lower-standard-of-living jobs. This results in increased job insecurity and fewer benefits such as health insurance, family leave, and retirement. (See Figure 15.1 on children, poverty and health insurance.) These changes create a shrinking middle class, and downward social mobility for many.

The Great Recession (also detailed in Chapter 14) has magnified these difficulties and created considerable discontinuity for family life. For example, wages for the employed have stagnated, and their benefits have been reduced or eliminated. Unemployment has risen sharply. Investments in stocks and home buying have declined precipitously, causing high rates of foreclosures and bankruptcies. The economic decline has increased the numbers of individuals and families who are "food insecure" and homeless. Tough economic conditions have caused couples to delay marriage and if married to delay childbearing. Financial woes are a major source of financial discord. The bond for some couples may be strengthened as the partners work together to find solutions. Many others find their bonds weakened or severed by difficult economic times. See the "A Closer Look" panel "Layoffs Can Stress Family Ties."

The economic transformation and the Great Recession have had dire consequences for many in the middle class. Katherine Newman describes the experience of the downwardly mobile middle class:

> They once "had it made" in American society, filling slots from affluent blue collar jobs to professional and managerial occupations. They have job skills, education, and decades of steady work experience. Many are, or were, home owners. Their marriages were (at least initially) intact. As a group they savored the American dream. They found a place higher up the ladder in this society and then, inexplicably, found their grip loosening and their status sliding. Some downwardly mobile middle-class families end up in poverty, but many do not. Usually they come to rest at a standard of living above the poverty level but far below the affluence they enjoyed in the past. They must, therefore, contend not only with financial hardship but with the psychological, social, and practical consequences of "falling from grace," of "losing their proper place" in the world. (1988:8)

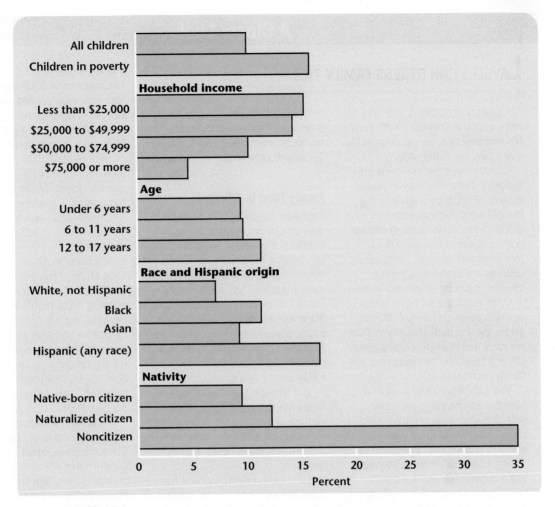

FIGURE 15.1

Uninsured Children by Poverty Status, Household Income, Age, Race and Hispanic Origin, and Nativity: 2010

Source: Carmen DeNavas-Walt, Bernadette D. Proctor, and Jessica C. Smith. 2011. U.S. Census Bureau, Current Population Reports, P60, *Income, Poverty and Health Insurance Coverage in the United States: 2010.* U.S. Government Printing Office, Washington, DC, p. 24.

Thus, individual self-esteem and family honor are bruised. Moreover, this ordeal impairs the chances of the children, as children and later as adults, to enjoy economic security and a comfortable lifestyle.

Downward mobility also occurs within the stable working class, whose link with resource-granting opportunity structures has always been tenuous. Many downwardly mobile families find successful coping strategies to deal with their adverse situations. Some families develop a tighter bond to meet their common problems. Others find support from families in similar situations or from their kin networks. But for many families, downward mobility adds tensions that make family life especially difficult. Family members experience stress, marital tension, and depression. Newman suggests that these conditions are normal given the persistent tensions generated by downward mobility. Many families experience some degree of these pathologies and yet somehow endure. But some families disintegrate under these pressures, with

A Closer Look

LAYOFFS CAN STRESS FAMILY TIES

The gloomy economy is affecting more than the unemployment lines. It's also having a dramatic impact on many families nationwide.

Unemployed professionals are suddenly becoming stay-at-home parents. Pink slips are triggering marital woes. College students have dropped out, taken jobs, or moved home because their parents can't foot their tuition bills. Some young couples are postponing having children because of job problems.

After earning a six-figure salary and almost all his family's income, Ed Simon was laid off in March from his sales and marketing management job at a consumer products firm. His family is still reeling.

His wife, Lori, used to work a half day so she could be home with the kids. Now she's working more, and Simon is Mr. Mom to Ari, 13, and Daniel, 7. Instead of taking business trips and managing a department, he spends his day clipping coupons and attending parent-teacher conferences.

"It's provided a whole lot of conflict. Now I'm telling my wife she has to spend more time with the kids," says Simon, 43, of Princeton, NJ. "It's a complete role reversal, and it's very tough. My wife comes home, and I'm at the kitchen sink saying, 'You have no idea how hard this is.' "

Mounting research suggests there's a strong connection between economic swings and family stability. These are some of the major trends:

Family Time Is Affected

Research indicates that a failing economy forces many working parents to put in longer hours on the job, leaving them with less time for their children. That's because layoffs have intensified job pressures by leaving fewer employees to shoulder the workload. As a result of longer hours, seven of ten Americans feel they don't have a healthy balance between work and life, according to a May survey by Expedia.com.

But while the work day may be longer for those with jobs, a growing number of parents are experiencing the opposite extreme—they've been laid off, and that means staying home.

Long-term unemployment has been spreading fastest in families with young children, according to a study by the Children's Defense Fund in Washington, DC.

The proportion of families with an unemployed parent jumped by nearly a percentage point to 6.6 percent from 2000 to 2001 because of the economic slump that began early in 2001, according to the Department of Labor. In an

average week in 2001, 4.8 million families had at least one member who was unemployed—a rise of 665,000 families from 2000.

They're fathers like Rich Miller, 48, who found himself out of work in May 2002, when the New York office of his advertising agency closed. Miller started his own media placement company, Smarter Media, and tends bar on the weekends to help make ends meet.

It's been tough on his marriage. Says Miller, "The financial issues add an additional strain and magnify other problems. It's changed our life."

But he can also work from home, which means more time with his 8-year-old son, Joshua. "He does appreciate the time we have together," says Miller of Hamilton Square, NJ.

Parental involvement can be shaped by economic trends. A U.S. Census Bureau report found that fathers had more time to spend with their preschool-age children during the recession in 1990 and 1991. But as the economy picked up and job opportunities became more abundant, dads were less likely to provide care.

Working Parents Feel Stressed

While the quantity of family time in some cases increases, the quality often suffers. Unemployment

serious problems of physical brutality, incapacitating alcoholism, desertion, and even suicide (Newman 1988:134–140).

Although families throughout the social structure are changing as a result of macroeconomic forces, the changes are most profound among the working class. Blue-collar workers have been hardest hit by the economic transformation. Their jobs have been eliminated by the millions because of the new technologies and competition from other lower-wage (much lower) economies. They have been disproportionately fired or periodically laid off. Sometimes their places of work have shut down entirely and leaves jobless people worrying about money and finding work, while those in the labor force wrestle with job insecurities.

That tension spills into the home. Working women with young children are most likely to say they have little time to relax, according to a 2002 *USA Today*/CNN/Gallup poll.

"People are working under double anxiety," says Niels Nielson, author of *Princeton Management Consultants Guide to Your New Job*. He founded an unemployment support group, JobSeekers, and started a human resources and general management firm, Princeton Management Consultants. "They're working longer hours and dealing with the prospect of being laid off. The family feels the strain. It's a double whammy."

Relationships Have More Pressures

Job relocations, unemployment, and financial concerns are testing many marriages. More than 70 percent of unemployed workers say family stress has increased since they lost their jobs, according to a poll by the National Employment Law Project.

Financial worries also take a toll. Calls about financial matters to counselors at ComPsych, a Chicago-based employee assistance provider, were up 58 percent in 2002. The majority of calls were for

problems such as debt and bankruptcy instead of the typical calls they get for subjects such as money management advice.

Jim Holmes, 42, and his wife, Susan Smith, 40, were both unemployed for about two months last year. Shortly after they relocated from Los Angeles to Seattle for his wife's job, she was laid off, and he was still looking for work.

Today, Holmes is a planner with the city, and his wife is teaching and doing research at the University of Washington. While the stretch without an income gave them extra time with their children, Max, 11, and Sabrina, 6, it also was a time of worry.

"We had a good time together," says Holmes, of Issaquah, WA. "But it was stressful at the same time. . . . You'd worry about how it affects [the children's] lives."

While tensions may mount, research suggests a difficult economy actually tends to depress divorce rates. The reason: Couples have fewer financial resources, making it more cost-efficient to stay together. The divorce rate (which is shaped by numerous factors, including the economy) dipped from 4 percent in 2000 to 3.9 percent in 2002, according to the National Center for Health Statistics.

"It usually takes another job for a spouse to leave," says Carl Steidtmann, chief global economist at Deloitte Research in New

York. "Divorce is an expensive proposition for a lot of people, and in a down economy you wait for a better time."

Many Are New to Unemployment

Many of the families affected by the economy are college-educated professionals with years of career experience. About 35 percent of workers unemployed for six months or longer in 2002 were over 45 years old, according to an analysis by the Economic Policy Institute (EPI) in Washington. About 18 percent of the long-term unemployed had college degrees, and 20 percent were executive, professional, and managerial workers.

"These are people who aren't accustomed to being unemployed," says economist Jeffrey Wenger. "What kind of coping strategies do they come up with? Because you've had such a stable environment for a long time, it's possible to have family friction."

There are other spillover effects of a downturn. One-third of unemployed workers have had to interrupt their own or a family member's education, according to a recent National Employment Law Project study of laid-off workers. And one in four has moved in with a family member or into other housing. . . .

Source: Armour, Stephanie. 2003. "Layoffs Can Stress Family Ties." *USA Today* (June 27):B1–B2.

moved to other societies. Their unions have lost strength (in numbers and clout). And their wages have declined.

Because family life is intertwined with social forces, we should not be surprised that economic transformations are producing changes that make family life difficult for many. In 1950, some 60 percent of U.S. households fit the intact nuclear households form—a household composed of a male breadwinner, his full-time wife, and their dependent children. Although this family form was dominant in society, its prevalence varied by social class. The pattern clearly prevailed in working-class households,

Watch on MySocLab Video: Judith Stacey: How a Family Is Defined

for example, but was much less likely among the poor, where women have always had to work outside the home to supplement family income.

This model for the family, which sociologist Judith Stacey (1990, 1991) calls the **modern family**, was disrupted by the destabilizing effects of globalization on jobs in the United States and by the challenges women face in maintaining traditional ways. Stacey found that working-class families, especially the women in them, created innovative ways to cope with economic uncertainty and domestic upheavals. In effect, these women were and are the pioneers of emergent family forms. Stacey calls these new family forms **postmodern families** because they do not fit the criteria for a modern family. Now there are divorce-extended families that include ex-spouses and their lovers, children, and friends. Households now expand and contract as adult children leave and then return home only to leave again. The vast majority of these postmodern families have dual earners. Many now involve husbands in greater childcare and domestic work than in earlier times. Kin networks have expanded to meet economic pressures. Parents now deal with their children's cohabitation, single and unwed parenthood, and divorce. The result is that fewer than 10 percent of households now conform to the modern family form. According to Stacey,

> No longer is there a single culturally dominant family pattern, like the modern one, to which the majority of Americans conform and most of the rest aspire. Instead, Americans today have crafted a multiplicity of family and household arrangements that we inhabit uneasily and reconstitute frequently in response to changing personal and occupational circumstances. (1991:19)

These postmodern family forms are new to working-class and middle-class families as they adjust to globalization and deindustrialization, *but they are not new to the poor*. The economic deprivation faced by the poor has always forced them to adapt in similar ways: single-parent families, relying on kin networks, sharing household costs, and multiple wage earners among family members.

As families struggle, they often change. Economic difficulties produced by the Great Recession have moved family life even further in the direction of postmodern family forms. For example, housing woes and unemployment have pushed relatives to "double up" and share living quarters. Sometimes these arrangements are multigenerational, with adults sharing their home with their children, grandchildren, and one or two elderly parents. The 2010 census found that 5.1 million households were multigenerational, with three or more generations (Tavernise 2010). Grandparents provide a safety net for their children's children when their children cannot provide for them. But these grandparents typically are struggling during the Great Recession with the loss of retirement savings because of the stock market crash and the resulting loss of 401(k)s and IRAs. The added load of dependent grandchildren coupled with much less retirement income has severely eroded their "golden years." Another family form emerging from the economic crisis is the married couple that lives in the same house even though the individuals no longer want to live together. They continue to live together because it is too costly to maintain two homes. So they build walls, real and imaginary, to create separate spaces for each in the same larger space—still married, still living together, but living apart emotionally.

Many households are composed of two generations as adult children, faced with low-paying jobs and high college and/or credit-card debts move in with their parents. Twenty-nine percent of young adults between the ages of 15 and 34 have moved back in temporarily with their parents (Mintz 2012). See the "Speaking to Students" panel "Moving Back Home."

15.4

Speaking to Students

MOVING BACK HOME

The extended economic downturn that began in 2007 will affect families for years to come. The Great Recession has produced an increase of young, primarily middle-class, adults returning to their parents' homes after being away to college or having otherwise lived independently.

Among people aged 18–24, almost two-thirds of men (60 percent) live with their parents. Half of women in this group do (U.S. Census Bureau 2011a). "These 'boomeranged' adults are a generation facing an historic

transformation in the route to a successful job and family life" (Mintz 2012). In the 1950s and 1960s, the pattern was to finish school and then leave the family of origin. Leaving the childhood home was an important and inevitable rite of passage for young adults. Owning a house and starting a nuclear family was their dream. "Failure to launch" was a social disgrace.

Today's economic conditions have changed patterns of how and when people form families. Moving back home for financial reasons often comes before living

independently or marrying. This sequence is no longer a stigma.

Is this trend a good thing or a bad thing? Will young people unused to struggle return to the immature dependence of childhood with free food and laundry service? Or will moving back in with mom and dad provide a gradual transition to successful adulthood in today's economy? Some family experts say that pulling together in a household to survive may make young adults more responsible—like the frugal and self-reliant Depression Era generation. What do you think?

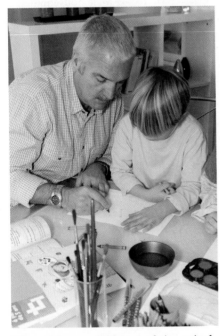

More and more children are being raised by grandparents.

The Great Recession has disproportionately laid off men. Of every five jobs lost, men have lost four of them during this economic crisis (Reed 2009). In Chapter 9, we saw that growing proportions of women are entering the workforce in downturn-resistant sectors like education and healthcare. This has significant ramifications for family dynamics as women become primary breadwinners "while also retaining their household responsibilities. Meanwhile, husbands must reconstruct their definition of contributing to the family enterprise, often swapping a paycheck for a broom" (della Cava 2009:D2).

Today's Diverse Family Forms

Families are constantly changing through their connections with other social institutions, especially the economy. Among the most prominent changes are those in family form and composition. To understand current trends in family life, we must return to the distinction between households and families discussed earlier in this chapter. (The following is based on Ahlburg and De Vita 1992; Bianchi and Casper 2000:8; and Lichter and Qian 2004.) The U.S. Bureau of the Census defines a *household* as all persons living in a housing unit. A *household* may consist of one person who lives alone or of several people who share a dwelling. A *family*, on the other hand, includes household members who are related by blood, marriage, or adoption and who reside together. All families comprise households, but not all households are families under the Census Bureau's definition. Family households include families in which a family member is the householder—the person who owns or rents the residence. These households can also include nonfamily members such as a boarder or friend. A **nonfamily household** includes the householders who live alone or share a residence with individuals unrelated to the householder, such as college friends sharing an apartment.

Some nonfamily households substitute for families and serve many of the same functions. Same-sex couples are one example (Lichter and Qian 2004:2). The growth of the nonfamily household (that is, persons who live alone or with unrelated individuals) is one of the most dramatic changes to occur during the past four decades, as shown in Figure 15.2.

In 1970, 81 percent of households were family households; by 2010, just 66 percent were family households. At the same time, nonfamily households, which consist primarily of people who live alone or who share a residence with roommates or with a partner, have been on the rise. The fastest growth has been among persons living alone. They may consist of elderly individuals who live alone, college-age youths who

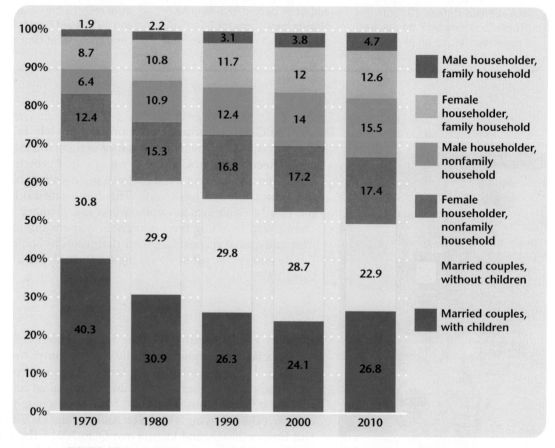

FIGURE 15.2

Households by Type: 1970–2010 (percent distribution)

Source: Fields, Jason C. 2004. "America's Families and Living Arrangements: 2003." Current Population Reports, P20-553. Washington, DC: Bureau of the Census, p. 4. U.S. Census Bureau, 2010. *Families and Living Arrangements: Historical Times Series.* Table HH-1: Households by Type: 1940 to Present.

share an apartment, cohabiting couples, individuals who delay or forgo marriage, or those who are "between marriages" (Ahlburg and De Vita 1992:5; Rawlings 1995:22).

Another dramatic shift in household composition has been the decline in the percentage of households with children. Two-parent households with children dropped from 40 to 23 percent of all households between 1970 and 2010 (Fields 2004; U.S. Census Bureau 2010). This downward trend reflects the postponement of marriage and children and the shift toward smaller families. However, household composition varies considerably among different segments of the population. Minorities are more likely than Whites to live in households that include children. In 2010, 40 percent of African American households and 54 percent of Latino households had at least one child under age 18, compared with 31 percent of White households (U.S. Census Bureau 2010) This difference arises primarily because minority populations tend to have a younger age structure than the White population (that is, a greater share of minorities are in the prime childbearing ages), and minorities tend to have higher fertility rates than Whites (De Vita 1996:34). In the next decade, the overall composition of households is projected to continue to shift, with a decreasing proportion of family households and continued growth of nonfamily households.

Macrolevel changes produce a wide range of family structures, including one-parent families, cohabiting couples (both gay and straight) with children, dual-worker families, and many varieties of extended families such as divorce-extended families and multigenerational families. Still, married couples with children continue to be a prominent family pattern. Parents and children now live in increasingly diverse settings, including intact biological families, stepfamilies and blended families, and single-parent families. Structural changes have made families more diverse and altered family experiences.

Read on
MySocLab Document:
Stepfamilies in the United
States: A Reconsideration

Balancing Work and Family with Few Social Supports

Regardless of their form, families now face new challenges. One of the greatest changes in the past few decades has been the increased participation of women in the labor force. Since 1960, the rise of women's participation in the labor force has been dramatic (see Chapter 9). In 2010, 70 percent of married women with dependent children (birth through age 17) were in the workforce. The rise in **dual-worker families**, or in married-couple families in which both spouses are in the labor force, has both positive and negative consequences for family life. Because mothers work, families have been able to keep their incomes from falling, but this does not mean that the economy is working for families. According to the Families and Work Institute, two-thirds of parents say that they do not have enough time with their children and two-thirds of married workers say that they don't have enough time with their spouse. Nearly half of all employees with families report conflicts between their job and their family life, more so than a generation ago (Boushey 2007:A2).

Very few jobs make it easy to balance work and family needs. (The following is based on Baca Zinn, Eitzen, and Wells 2011:210–212.) Workplaces have been slow to respond the needs of their employees who are or will soon be parents. The traditional organization of work—an inflexible eight-hour workday—makes it difficult for parents to cope with family problems or the conflicting schedules of family members. Unlike some other countries, the United States has only recently become aware of the complex struggle that most workers face in trying to combine paid work and family work. Only in the past decade or so have political, business, and professional leaders had very much to say about work and family. In the 1990s, the federal government made modest efforts to help families cope with childcare through tax credits, programs for subsidizing the childcare costs of low-income parents, and the **Family and Medical Leave Act of 1993 (FMLA)**.

The FMLA requires employers of fifty or more people to provide twelve weeks of unpaid leave to any worker who has a medical emergency or needs to care for an adopted or newborn child or a seriously ill child, spouse, or parent. FMLA does not cover part-time workers. A total of 41 million workers in the United States—nearly half of the private workers—are ineligible for family leave under this law. The FMLA of 1993 remained unchanged until 2009, when several points of clarification were added to the original legislation. The 2009 bill also expands military family leave entitlements, permitting eligible employees to take up to twenty-six weeks of leave to care for a service member with a series injury or illness (U.S. Department of Labor 2009). See the "Social Policy" panel comparing U.S. government support for working families with other nations around the globe.

More than two-thirds of all children under the age of 5 are in a childcare arrangement on a regular basis by someone other than a parent. Many of these children are young because 75 percent of women go back to work by a child's ninth month. The

Social Policy

How Europe Supports Working Parents and Their Children

Many rich countries do a far better job than the United States does of supporting workers who are balancing the competing demands of employment and parenthood. Several European countries, especially in northern and western Europe, provide extensive work/family reconciliation policies—including paid family leave, public early-childhood education and care, and working-time measures that raise the quality and availability of reduced-hour work. The European Union puts a common floor under several of these national standards.

Parents in much of Europe have access to multiple forms of paid family leave, for both mothers and fathers. Equally important, these programs provide wage replacement, usually financed by social insurance, in order to spread the costs between women and men, across generations, and among enterprises. Social-insurance financing also minimizes employers' resistance to hiring young workers, especially women, who they anticipate will be leave-takers.

The Nordic countries—including Denmark, Finland, Norway, and Sweden—provide especially generous family leave rights and benefits. Most new parents have the right to take approximately one year of leave, and they receive about two-thirds or more of their pay. Family leave policies in the Nordic countries also offer parents substantial flexibility. Denmark and Sweden allow parents to take their allotted leaves in increments until their children are 8 years old. Norway and Sweden allow parents to combine prorated leaves with part-time employment, and Finland and Norway permit parents to use portions of their leave benefits to purchase private childcare instead. Recent reforms add incentives for fathers to take leaves, to encourage more gender-egalitarian usage.

Across Europe, publicly supported childcare serves a large proportion of infants and toddlers while their parents are working for pay. In Denmark, for example, three-quarters of 1- and 2-year-olds are now served in publicly financed childcare settings; half of the children in this age range are in public care in Sweden and more than a third in Norway. In many European countries—including Belgium, France, and Italy—nearly all children from age 3 to the start of primary school are enrolled in full-day preschools. Throughout Europe, public policy measures assure that early childhood education and care are affordable. Parents typically pay income-scaled fees for infant and toddler care, while educationally oriented preschools (for children age 3 and older) are usually free for all families.

Parents are further aided by a package of working-time measures, some of which are required by the European Union. European children may attend daycare centers or nursery schools, go to the home of a provider, or be cared for by a relative, neighbor, or babysitter (Zaslow and Tout 2002).

The United States has no comprehensive childcare system. This lack of a system differentiates us from the other industrialized nations. Currently, the federal government is involved modestly in providing for childcare through two programs. First, it permits the deduction of childcare payments on income tax returns. This amounts to about a $4 billion tax credit, which is considerable. The problem, however, is that by being tied to taxes, it benefits the most affluent families and has negligible effects on the poor because they do not earn enough to take advantage of it. Second, the welfare legislation of 1996 included approximately $4 billion in new childcare funds over six years. "But the new law forces so many parents into the work force that this increase falls far short of what is needed to meet the new demand for child care generated by the law, much less to ensure that vulnerable children receive good care" (Children's Defense Fund 1997:38).

The government's less-than-adequate childcare programs are fundamentally flawed in at least two respects. Foremost, they are underfunded. The amounts the federal government promised simply do not meet childcare needs. The other problem

countries set their standard weekly work hours individually and, across western and northern Europe today, full-time work is generally defined as between 35 and 39 weekly hours. All EU-member countries are required to grant workers a minimum of four weeks of paid time off each year. Furthermore, EU law requires that all member countries ensure part-time workers prorated pay and benefits comparable to what full-time workers receive, in order to make shorter-hour work more economically feasible. In addition, since 2000, several countries—including Germany, the Netherlands, and the United Kingdom—have granted workers new rights to request work-schedule changes; employers may refuse, but their refusals are subject to public review.

These work/family measures are provided alongside universal health insurance, which adds crucial economic support for families, and gives workers flexibility when seeking employment that best meets their families' needs.

All told, the comprehensive work/family policy packages operating in several European countries offer parents considerable latitude in allocating their time between paid work and care, and indemnify them against substantial fluctuations in disposable income.

Generous work/family policies are good for parents, children, and worker productivity, and especially benefit lower-income workers who tend to have less bargaining power and cannot afford to pay for help privately. Public systems equalize access and affordability, across family types and throughout the income spectrum, leading to outcomes that are more equitable than what market-based systems produce.

Moreover, expansive work/family policies are compatible with good economic outcomes. Consider GDP-per-hour-worked, a powerful indicator of productivity. The six top-ranked countries in the world are European countries with comprehensive work/family policies, including France, the Netherlands, Belgium, and Norway.

Furthermore, the World Economic Forum's Competitiveness Index includes, among the top five countries globally, Denmark, Sweden, and Finland—three countries with extensive work/family policies.

In recent decades, many European countries have restructured their social policies to trim costs and improve economic outcomes. However, programs that support workers with family responsibilities—including paid leave, childcare, and rights to high-quality reduced-hour work—were singled out for protection and growth rather than cutbacks, both by the EU and in many individual countries. Clearly, high-income industrialized countries can perform productively and competitively while granting workers rights and benefits that recognize the realities of family life.

Source: Reprinted with permission from Janet Gornick, "Atlantic Passages," *The American Prospect*, Volume 18, Number 3: March 01, 2007. The American Prospect, 2000 L Street NW, Suite 717, Washington DC 20036. All rights reserved.

Availability of quality daycare is often the biggest problem facing working parents.

is that they rely on the states to implement the programs and to match the federal grants if they are to receive monies. The states, through their governors, legislatures, and social service bureaucracies, vary greatly in their enthusiasm for childcare, their licensing and monitoring of childcare programs, and the standards they set to ensure quality in childcare. If history is a guide, then it is likely that many states will not commit the greater resources needed to receive the federal funds.

Single Parents and Their Children

Today, one-fourth of all U.S. children live with just one parent, up from 12 percent in 1970. The disproportionate number of single-parent families headed by a woman is a consequence, first, of the relatively high divorce rate and the very strong tendency for divorced and separated women to have custody of the children. Second, there is the relatively high rate of never-married mothers (in 1960, 5 percent of U.S. babies were born to unmarried mothers; in 2010, 40 percent were). To counter the common myths, the facts indicate that more than three-fourths of out-of-wedlock births are to women age 20 and older. Moreover, although the *unwed birthrate* for African Americans and Latinos is higher than for Whites, there are *more unwed births* among Whites than among African Americans and Latinos.

The important question to answer concerning this trend is, What are the effects on children of living in mother-only families? Research has shown consistently that children from single-parent homes are more likely than children from intact families to have behavioral problems. McLanahan and Booth's (1991) review of the research on children from mother-only families, compared to children from two-parent families, shows the following:

Watch on
MySocLab Video: ABC
Nightline: Single Mothers

- They have poorer academic achievement. This relationship is even more negative for boys than for girls.
- They are more likely to have higher absentee rates at school.
- They are more likely to drop out of school.

- They are more likely to marry early and to have children early, both in and out of marriage.
- If they marry, they are more likely to divorce.
- They are more likely to commit delinquent acts and to engage in drug and alcohol use.

Because 76 percent of one-parent families are headed by women, the common explanation for the disproportionate pathologies found among the children of single parents has been that the absence of a male adult is detrimental to their development. The presence of both mothers and fathers contributes to the healthy development of the child (Marsiglio et al. 2001). Also, the absence of a spouse makes coping with parenting more difficult. Coping is difficult for any single parent—female or male—because of three common sources of strain: (1) responsibility overload, in which single parents make all the decisions and provide for all their family's needs; (2) task overload, in which the demands of work, housekeeping, and parenting can be overwhelming for one person; and (3) emotional overload, in which single parents must always be on call to provide the necessary emotional support. Clearly, when two people share these parental strains, it is more likely that the needs of the children will be met.

Although the factors just described help to explain the behavioral differences between children from one-parent and two-parent homes, they sidestep the major reason—a fundamental difference in economic resources. As Andrew Cherlin has argued, "It seems likely that the most detrimental aspect of the absence of fathers from one-parent families headed by women is not the lack of a male presence *but a lack of a male income*" (Cherlin 1981:81; emphasis added). There is a strong likelihood that women raising children alone will be financially troubled. In 2010, for example, 31 percent of children living in single-parent families headed by a woman were poor, compared with 6 percent of children in married-couple families (DeNavas-Walt et al. 2011).

The reasons for a disproportionate number of mother-headed families that are poor are obvious. First, many single mothers are young and never married. They may have little education, so if they work, they have poorly paid jobs. Second, many divorced or separated women have not been employed for years and find it difficult to re-enter the job market. Third, and more crucial, jobs for women, centered as they are in the bottom tier of the segmented job market, are poorly paid (women, we must underscore again, presently earn about 81 cents for every dollar earned by men; see Chapter 9). Fourth, half the men who owe child support do not pay all they owe, and a quarter of them do not pay anything; women who do receive child support find that the amount covers less than half the actual cost of raising a child.

The economic plight of single-parent families is much worse for families of color. Women of color who head households have the same economic problems as White women who are in the same situation, plus the added burdens of institutional racism. In addition, they are less likely to be receiving child support (their husbands, unlike White husbands, are much more likely to be poor and unemployed), and they are more likely to have been high-school dropouts, further reducing their potential for earning a decent income. The financial difficulties of women heads of households are sometimes alleviated in part by support from a kinship network. Relatives may provide childcare, material goods, money, and emotional support. The kin network is an especially important source of emergency help for African Americans and Latinos. But for many, kin may not be near or helpful.

In summary, the behavioral social costs attributed to the children of single mothers are, in large part, the result of living in poverty. Lack of income has negative effects on intellectual development and physical health (Guo and Harris 2000). Living in poverty translates into huge negatives for single mothers and their children—differences in healthcare, diet, housing, neighborhood safety, and quality of schools, as well as economic disadvantages, leading to a greater probability of experiencing low self-esteem, hopelessness, and despair.

Societal Response to Disadvantaged Children

As a nation, the United States has taken deliberate actions to reduce poverty among the elderly while simultaneously allowing childhood poverty to increase. (The following is adapted from Baca Zinn, Eitzen, and Wells 2011:477–480.) In 1970, the proportion of elderly in poverty was double the national average, yet by 2010, the poverty rate among the elderly was below the national average (9 percent compared to the national rate of 15 percent). The poverty rate for children under age 18 in 1970 was more than one-third lower than that for the elderly. By 2010, this situation had changed, with 22 percent of children under age 18 living in poverty (DeNavas-Walt et al. 2011; see Figure 15.3).

During the last twenty years, federal benefits to the elderly have risen from one-sixth of the federal budget to 30 percent (to about $300 billion annually). This increase occurred because federal policymakers created programs such as Medicare and Medicaid and because Social Security benefits were indexed to offset inflation. Conversely, however, these same decision makers did not provide adequately for needy families with children. The government actually reduced the programs targeted to benefit children (e.g., the children's share of Medicaid, Aid to Families with

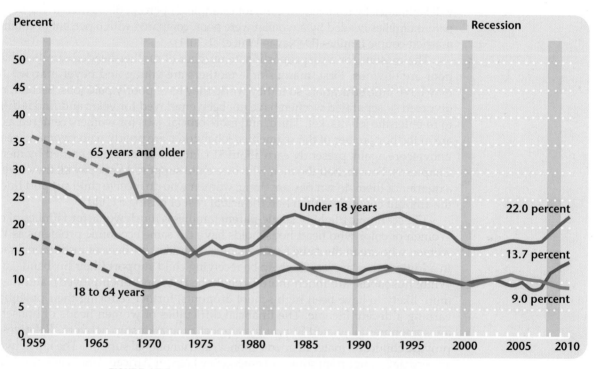

FIGURE 15.3

Poverty Rates by Age: 1959 to 2010

Source: Carmen DeNavas-Walt, Bernadette D. Proctor, and Jessica C. Smith. 2011. U.S. Census Bureau, Current Population Reports, P60, *Income, Poverty and Health Insurance Coverage in the United States: 2010.* U.S. Government Printing Office, Washington, DC, p. 17.

Dependent Children [AFDC], Head Start, food stamps, child nutrition, and federal aid to education).

Childhood poverty is especially acute for racial minorities. The bias against children in federal programs is heightened for minority children. The late senator Daniel Patrick Moynihan pointed out that there are two ways the federal government provides benefits to children in single-parent families. The first is Aid to Families with Dependent Children. The majority of the children receiving this type of aid are Black or Hispanic. Since 1970, the government has decreased the real benefits by 13 percent. The other form of assistance is Survivors Insurance (SI), which is part of Social Security. The majority of children receiving SI benefits are White, and these benefits have increased by 53 percent since 1970 (adjusted for inflation). Moynihan, writing eight years before the 1996 welfare legislation, said,

> To those who say we don't care about children in our country, may I note that the average provision for children under SI has been rising five times as fast as average family income since 1970. We do care about some children—majority children. It is minority children— not only but mostly—who are left behind. (1988:5)

Another telling illustration is that although Congress in 1996 eliminated AFDC and severely cut food stamps and school nutrition programs for the poor, it did not cut cash and food programs for poor senior citizens.

The decisions to disproportionately help the elderly reflect the electoral power that the elderly have compared to the young. The elderly are organized, with several national organizations dedicated to political action that will benefit their interests. The American Association of Retired Persons (AARP), for example, is the nation's largest special-interest organization, with more than 40 million members. With the elderly making up 16 percent of the voting public (and much more in states such as Florida and Arizona, which have high concentrations of elderly people), politicians tend to pay attention to their special needs.

Children, on the other hand, have no electoral power and few advocates (an exception is the Children's Defense Fund). Their parents, especially those who are poor, are not organized. So, in a time of fiscal austerity, the needs of children—prenatal care for poor women, nutritional and healthcare, daycare, and better schools—are underfunded. The irony is that the political right wing, which claims to be profamily, limits its political agenda to antiabortion legislation and court cases and ignores or fights governmental assistance to needy children and their struggling parents.

The argument is not that the elderly and the young should compete for scarce resources and that one or the other should win. Rather, both age groups are dependents and are in need. The test of a civilization is the condition of its dependents. So far, the United States has opted to care moderately well for one and not at all for the other.

DIVORCE

15.5 Understand the divorce rate and the consequences of divorce.

Most people in the United States marry, but not all marriages last forever; some eventually are dissolved. Some marriages become intolerable because they are filled with tension and violence (as shown in the next section of this chapter). Some marriages fail because the love the wife and husband once shared diminishes for various reasons. Still other marriages break up because of the relentless strains brought about by poverty.

Divorce—the formal dissolution of marriage—is a relatively common experience in the United States. Politicians, clergy members, editorial writers, and others have shown great concern over the current high rates of marital dissolution in the United States. Although estimates vary, most scholars agree that between 40 and 50 percent of all first marriages end in divorce (Visher, Visher, and Pasley 2003). Various government documents from the Census Bureau ("Marital Status and Living Arrangements"), the Centers for Disease Control and Prevention, and the National Center for Health Statistics reveal the following patterns for first marriages (summarized in Coontz 2007):

- One in five marriages ends in divorce or separation within five years.
- Couples who separate do so, on average, after seven years and divorce after eight years.
- One in three marriages dissolves within ten years.
- Divorce patterns for African Americans differ from those of Latinos and Whites. Latinos have divorce rates that are about the same as those of Whites, but African Americans are more likely to experience economic hardships that lead to marital disruption and divorce rates that are twice as high as Whites.

Listen on MySocLab Audio: NPR: Military Combats High Divorce Rate

Some of the many reasons for the increased divorce rate include increased independence (social and financial) of women, economic restructuring that eliminates many jobs for men and makes women's employment necessary, women's inequality, greater tolerance of divorce by religious groups, and reform of divorce laws, especially the adoption of no-fault divorce in many states (i.e., one spouse no longer has to prove that the other was at fault to obtain a divorce). An important reason is the striking change in public attitudes toward divorce. Divorce is a difficult step and one that commands sympathy for the partners and children. But it is no longer considered a moral violation. Instead, divorce is generally accepted today as a possible solution for marital difficulties.

Consequences of Divorce

Divorce is an intensely personal event, and this intensity makes the breakup a painful experience, even when both parties want the marriage to end. In this section, we review the personal side of divorce—the consequences for ex-wives and ex-husbands and for their children. (This section is adapted from Baca Zinn, Eitzen, and Wells 2011:385–389.)

- **"His" and "Her" Divorce.** Both partners in a divorce are victims. Each is affected, in the typical case, by feelings of loneliness, anger, remorse, guilt, low self-esteem, depression, and failure. Although ex-spouses tend to share these negative feelings, the divorce experience differs for husbands and wives in significant ways because of the structure of society and gender inequality.

- **"His" Divorce.** Ex-husbands have some major advantages and a few disadvantages over their ex-wives. Men have the advantage of being better off financially than their former wives. Typically, they were the major income producers for their families, and after the separation their incomes stay disproportionately with them.

  Another benefit that men have over women after divorce is greater freedom. If there are children, they usually live with the mother (about 85 percent), so most men are free from the constraints not only of marriage but also of childcare. Thus, they are freer than ex-wives to date, travel, go to school, take up a hobby, or work at a second job. Especially significant is sexual freedom because males tend to have more money and leisure time.

The experience of ex-husbands on some counts, however, is more negative than that of ex-wives. Many divorced men, especially those from traditional marriages, experience initial difficulty in maintaining a household routine. They are more likely to eat erratically, sleep less, and have difficulty with shopping, cooking, laundry, and cleaning. And because ex-wives usually have legal custody of the children, ex-husbands are able to see their children only relatively rarely and at prescribed times. Thus, they may experience great loneliness because they have lost both wife and children.

The image of liberated ex-husbands as swinging bachelors does not fit many men. Some find dating difficult. They find that women in general have changed or that they themselves have changed. Many men withdraw from relationships because of their fear of rejection. They may also be wary over concerns about AIDS or other sexually transmitted diseases.

- **"Her" Divorce.**   Contrary to common belief, about two-thirds of divorces are initiated by women (Sweeney 2002). The only exception is that older wives in long-term unions are less likely than their husbands to file for divorce (Hacker 2003:27). This is an interesting anomaly because women benefit less from divorce than men. To be sure, many ex-wives are relieved to have ended an onerous relationship, and some are even freed from a physically abusive one. Some are now liberated from a situation that stifled their educational and career goals. Of course, divorce also frees spouses to seek new and perhaps more fulfilling relationships.

  For women, the negatives of divorce clearly outweigh the positives. Women oriented toward traditional gender roles tend to feel helpless and experience a loss of identity associated with their husbands' statuses. Divorced mothers who retain sole custody of their children often feel overwhelmed by the demands of full-time parenting and economic survival. The emotional and schedule overloads that usually accompany solo parenting leave little time for personal pursuits. The result is that divorced women often experience personal and social isolation, especially the feeling of being locked into a child's world. White women cope less well with divorce than do African American women. Presumably, this is because Black women have better social supports (extended family networks, friendship and church support networks) than do White women (Fine, Ganong, and Demo 2005).

  Both ex-husbands and ex-wives tend to lose old friends. For the first two months or so after the divorce, married friends are supportive and spend time with each of the former mates. But these contacts soon decline because, as individuals, divorced people no longer fit into couple-oriented activities. This disassociation from marital friends is especially acute for women because their child-raising responsibilities tend to isolate them from adult interactions.

  On the positive side, women tend to have stronger family and friendship networks than men. These networks provide support, explaining, in part, why women fare better emotionally than men after divorce (Faust and McKibben 1999). Moreover, because most women receive custody of their children after divorce, they are more connected to their children than noncustodial fathers.

  The biggest problem facing almost all divorced women is a dramatic decline in economic resources. Paul Amato, after examining the relevant research, concludes that "overall, mothers' postseparation standard of living [is] only about one half that of fathers" (Amato 2001:1277). As Lenore Weitzman argued, for most women and children,

> [Divorce] means precipitous downward mobility—both economically and socially. The reduction in income brings residential moves and inferior housing, drastically

diminished or nonexistent funds for recreation and leisure and intense pressures due to inadequate time and money. Financial hardships in turn cause social dislocation and a loss of familiar networks for emotional support and social services, and intensify the psychological stress for women and children alike. On a societal level, divorce increases female and child poverty and creates an ever-widening gap between the economic well-being of divorced men on the one hand, and their children and former wives on the other. (1985:323)

Divorce has drastic social and economic effects on women and their children. It is a major social problem created by institutions that perpetuate gender discrimination and by divorced fathers who do not contribute to the support of their children (Arendell 1990).

Children of Divorce

Watch on **MySocLab Video:** Divorce and Adolescence

Approximately 65 percent of divorcing couples have minor children, meaning that about 1 million children are involved in new divorces annually. This means that about two-fifths of children—one in three White children and two in three African American children—by age 16 will experience the permanent disruption of their parents' marriage. Most of them will remain with their mothers and live in a fatherless home for at least five years. Most significant, many children of divorce effectively *lose* their fathers (Amato and Booth 1996). "Ten years after a divorce, fathers will be entirely absent from the lives of almost two-thirds of these children" (Weissbourd 1994:68). Some are twice cursed by the broken relationships of their parents. About one-third of White children and one-half of Black children whose mothers remarry will experience a second divorce before the children reach adulthood.

The crucial question is, What are the consequences of divorce for children? There is clearly the possibility of emotional scars from the period of family conflict and uncertainty prior to the breakup. Children will be affected by the permanency of divorce and the enforced separation from one of the parents. Most commonly, this is separation from their father.

There are the possible negative effects of being raised by a single parent who is overburdened by the demands of children, job, economics, and household maintenance. And there are the negative consequences that may result from the sharp decline in resources available to the family when the parents separate. The data are consistent: Female-headed single-parent families, compared to two-parent families and to male-headed single-parent families, have much lower incomes. This severe decline in family resources for female-headed single-parent families produces a number of challenges for children's adjustment, often including moving to a different home and school, eliminating or greatly reducing the probability of a college education, and other alterations in lifestyles. As a result of all of these possible outcomes of divorce, children may experience behavioral problems, decline in school performance, and other manifestations of maladjustment.

Summaries of the research on the consequences of divorce on children (Amato 2001; Amato, Booth, Johnson, and Rogers 2007; Fine, Ganong, and Demo 2005; Wallerstein 2003) reveal that children with divorced parents score lower than children with continuously married parents on measures of academic success, conduct, psychological adjustment, self-concept, and social competence. Although the differences between children from divorced and two-parent families are small, they are consistent. Research also finds that children are better off on a variety of outcomes if parents in high-conflict marriages divorced than if they remained married. But because only some divorces are preceded by a high level of conflict, "divorce probably helps fewer children than it hurts" (Amato 2001:1278).

We must note that the long-term effects of divorce are difficult to measure. Does divorce actually cause the problems displayed by divorced children? Could it be that these troubled children are being raised by troubled parents who eventually divorce (Cherlin 1999)? Heatherington points out that many of the adjustment problems of children are the result of inept parenting and destructive family relations that were present *before* divorce and not the consequences of divorce (Heatherington 2002:63). We simply cannot know, for example, how the children from a particular family would have fared if the parents had stayed together in a tension-filled household. Reviews of the studies on the effects of divorce on children find that "the 'large majority' of children of divorce . . . do not experience severe or long-term problems: most do not drop out of school, get arrested, abuse drugs, or suffer long-term emotional distress" (Coontz 2007:100; Amato and Cheadle 2005).

15.6 Examine the causes and consequences of violence in families.

VIOLENCE IN U.S. FAMILIES

The family has two faces. It can be a haven from an uncaring, impersonal world, a place where love and security prevail. The family members love each other, care for each other, and are accepting of each other. But there is also a dark side of the family. The family is a common context for violence in society. "People are more likely to be killed, physically assaulted, sexually victimized, hit, beat up, slapped, or spanked in their own homes by other family members than anywhere else in our society" (Gelles 1995:450). The intensity that characterizes intimate relationships can give way to conflict. Some families resolve the inevitable tensions that arise in the course of daily living, but in other families conflict gives way to violence.

Violence and the Social Organization of the Family

((•)) **Listen on MySocLab Audio:** NPR: Ohio Marriage Law Hampers Efforts Against Domestic Abuse

Although the family is based on love among its members, the way it is organized encourages conflict. First, the family, like all other social organizations, is a power system; that is, power is unequally distributed between parents and children and between spouses, with the male typically dominant. As we saw in Chapter 9, male dominance has been perpetuated by the legal system and religious teaching. Threats to male dominance are often resisted through violence. Parents have authority over their children. They feel they have the right to punish children to shape them in ways the parents consider important.

Unlike most organizations, in which activities and interests are relatively narrow, the family encompasses almost everything. Thus, there are more "events" over which a dispute can develop. Closely related to this phenomenon is the vast amount of time in each day that family members spend interacting. This lengthy interaction increases the probability of disagreements, irritations, violations of privacy, and the like, which increase the risk of violence. Family privacy is another characteristic that enhances the likelihood of violence. The rule in our society that the home is private has two negative consequences. First, it insulates the family members from the protection that society could provide if a family member becomes too abusive. Second, the rule of privacy often prevents the victims of abuse from seeking outside help.

Intimate Partner Violence

Violence between husbands and wives, cohabiting partners, and dating couples in the form of beating, slapping, kicking, and rape is relatively common in U.S. society as well as in countries around the world. That such violence occurs between persons who supposedly joined together because of their mutual love is puzzling indeed. (This section is adapted from Baca Zinn, Eitzen, and Wells 2011:343–353.)

Intimate partner violence is difficult to define. Researchers cannot agree on a common definition. As a result, the estimations of this phenomenon vary. The estimates of the incidence of intimate partner violence provided here use the definition in the National Violence Against Women (NVAW) Survey. This survey, undertaken by the National Institute of Justice and the Centers for Disease Control and Prevention (CDC), is the most recent national study of intimate partner violence. The NVAW Survey defines **intimate partner violence** to include rape, physical assaults, and stalking perpetrated by current and former spouses, cohabiting partners, and dating partners (Tjaden and Thoennes 2000:5).

- **Incidence of Intimate Partner Abuse.**   Conclusions about the incidence of violence among intimate partners vary according to who is included within the category of intimate partners and what actions are defined as abusive. Some studies continue to focus only on married couples, while others exclude dating couples. Some include same-sex partners, and others do not. Some researchers define domestic violence to include emotional abuse in addition to physical harm. This variation makes it difficult to obtain data on the extent of intimate partner abuse. Nonetheless, research consistently shows that it is a pervasive problem in the United States and a serious public health concern. The findings of the NVAW Survey allow for the following estimated of the scope of the problem:

  - Over 33 million Americans have been victims of intimate partner violence at some point in their lifetime.
  - Every year, around 1.3 million women and more than 800,000 men are physically assaulted by an intimate partner; many of these individuals are victimized repeatedly.
  - In comparing the experience of abused women and abused men, we find that abused women are assaulted more frequently and are more likely to be injured than are men.
  - Injuries inflicted by intimate partners are frequently severe enough to require medical care; approximately 550,000 female victims and 125,000 male victims require medical treatment every year (Tjaden and Thoennes 2000).

  Both women and men are victims of intimate partner violence; nonetheless, ample evidence—including the most recent study from the Centers for Disease Control and Prevention—documents that most victims of domestic violence are women. This report, titled the *National Intimate Partner and Sexual Violence Survey (NISVS)*, found that one in four women has been the victim of severe physical violence by an intimate partner while one in seven men experiences severe physical violence by an intimate partner. In addition, female victims experienced multiple forms of violence while male victims most often experienced physical violence (Centers for Disease Control and Prevention 2012).

- **Class, Race, and Intimate Violence.**   Although the statistics on intimate violence are somewhat unreliable, we do have a more precise understanding about the conditions under which this phenomenon occurs. Foremost, the connection to social class is clear. Although battered women are found in all social strata, they tend to be found primarily in families threatened by economic hardships. This relationship is generally viewed as the outcome of the stresses of poverty or the lack of resources. Managing family life in a context that may include, for example, crowded and substandard housing, unstable work, unreliable transportation, and neighborhood crime is difficult. In such situations, domestic violence against women would be viewed as the outcome of the "pileup of stressors" associated with inadequate resources (Fox et al. 2002:749).

Men's unemployment puts their partners at increased risk for abuse (Tjaden and Thoennes 2000). Unemployment increases economic strains as bills accumulate and debt rises. In addition, unemployment can be devastating for men who believe it is their responsibility to be the primary provider (Gelles and Cornell 1990:75).

Poverty also limits women's range of responses to abuse (Coker 2005:370). Sufficient material resources are key to escaping an abusive situation; inadequate material resources is the primary reason women do not separate from abusive partners.

An individual's vulnerability to abuse is shaped not only by her gender and class but also by her race (Sokoloff and Dupont 2005:02). The NVAW Survey (Tjaden and Thoennes 2000) found that 25 percent of White women reported having been victimized by an intimate partner. For African Americans, the figure was 29 percent; for Hispanics, it was 23 percent; for Native Americans, it was 31 percent; and for Asian Americans, it was 15 percent. These data show that except for Asian Americans, people of color are more susceptible to domestic violence than Whites. There may be some basis for this generalization. Chapter 8 revealed that minority individuals experience disadvantages related to being a member of a minority group, such as a relatively high probability of joblessness, low wages for doing society's "dirty work," substandard housing, inferior schools, high-crime neighborhoods, and police harassment. Minorities have high rates of poverty and must contend with the stresses that accompany poverty.

We must view the apparent overrepresentation of people of color among the abusers and abused with caution. When demographic and socioeconomic factors are controlled, minorities are no more likely to be violent. In other words, racial differences in domestic abuse have less to do with racial patterns than they do with social class (Johnson and Ferraro 2000).

Child Abuse and Neglect

Gelles and Straus have concluded that "with the exception of the police and the military, the family is perhaps the most violent social group and the home the most violent social setting in our society" (Gelles and Straus 1979a:15). "Adult family members who abuse each other also tend to abuse their children" (Mignon, Larson, and Holmes 2002:15). "A small child has more chance of being killed or severely injured by its parents than by anyone else. For children, the home is often the most dangerous place to be" (Collins and Coltrane 1995:476–477). Child abuse is even more prevalent than intimate partner violence. Every week, child protective services (CPS) agencies receive nearly 60,000 referrals alleging child abuse or neglect: CPS agencies investigated the family environments of 3.5 million children in 2007 (U.S. Department of Health and Human Services 2009). This problem is reviewed here, focusing on the definition, incidence, causes, and consequences of child abuse. (The following discussion is adapted from Baca Zinn, Eitzen, and Wells 2011:356–362.)

- **Definition.** What is child abuse? The extreme cases of torture, scalding, beatings, and imprisonment are easy to place in this category. But there are problems in determining whether many other actions are abusive. For example, one definition of child abuse is violence "carried out with the intention of, or perceived as having the intention of, physically hurting the child" (Gelles and Straus 1979b:336). This definition includes everything from spanking to murder. The problem is that spanking is used by nine in ten parents and is considered legitimate and acceptable behavior. At what point does appropriate punishment become excessive? This is an important question for counselors, social workers, health practitioners, and the courts to address because the consequences for children and parents are enormous. To have a definition that is too lax imperils the health and safety of children, and to have one that is too stringent jeopardizes parents who might incorrectly receive the label of "child abuser," have their children taken from them, and even be imprisoned.

  The Child Abuse Protection and Treatment Act provides minimum federal guidelines that states must use in defining child maltreatment. These guidelines provide four categories of child maltreatment: neglect, physical abuse, sexual abuse, and emotional abuse. Most states include terminology that defines physical abuse as "physical injury due to punching, beating, kicking, biting, burning, or otherwise harming a child" (U.S. Department of Health and Human Services 2008). This type of abuse involves a range of behaviors, including the inadequate feeding of a child or lack of provision of sanitary living conditions. These forms of neglect may be just as damaging to children, physically and mentally, as physical aggression. This type of problem is complicated, too, because the neglect may or may not be willful on the part of parents.

  We have chosen an all-inclusive definition of **child abuse:** "the distinctive acts of violence and nonviolence and acts of omission and commission that place children at risk" (Gelles 1976:136). This is consistent with the government's definition in the Child Abuse Prevention and Treatment Act of 1996: "[Child abuse is, at a minimum, any act or failure to act] resulting in imminent risk of serious harm, death, serious physical or emotional harm, sexual abuse, or exploitation" (cited in Mignon, Larson, and Holmes 2002:19). We should not be misled, in using this broad definition, into thinking that all forms of child abuse and neglect are essentially alike, caused by the same sources, and subject to a uniform treatment (Gelles 1976). We generalize about this problem, but the reader is warned that child abuse is, like all social problems, very complex.

- **Incidence.** The precise extent of child abuse and neglect is impossible to know, for two reasons. First, studies of the phenomena have not used uniform definitions; and second, the issue is extremely sensitive to the people involved. To be the perpetrator or victim of child abuse is generally something for which people are stigmatized. Acts of violence and neglect are hidden from society because they occur in private. When asked by a survey researcher if they have ever physically abused their children, abusing parents will most likely deny such an act. Thus, many statistics are taken from police, teachers, social workers, and medical personnel who must assume that the children were victims of abuse. Obviously, such subjective observations are subject to error. As one illustration of the problem of subjectivity, we can note that the parents and children of the middle and upper classes are commonly viewed quite differently by authorities than are those from the lower classes. Trained personnel are more likely to assess a poor child with a black eye as a victim of child abuse than a child from a rich family. Also, of course, many cases of abuse and neglect are never seen by authorities. Official statistics, then, always underreport the actual incidence.

Although there are problems with defining and determining the exact incidence of child abuse, the government provides annual statistics. In 2008, the Department of Health and Human Services (DHHS) reported 772,000 substantiated cases of child abuse and neglect, including the deaths of 1,740 children. The rate of child abuse and neglect in 2008 was 10.3 cases per 1,000 children. This represents a decline from a rate of 12.5 in 2001 (U.S. Department of Health and Human Services 2010).

- **Contexts.**   The reasons for the abuse and neglect of children by parents are complex and varied, involving personal, social, and cultural factors. The most commonly assumed cause for abusive behavior toward children is that the perpetrators are mentally ill. This assumption, however, is a myth that hinders the understanding of child abuse (Gelles 1976:138). In the view of experts, only about 10 percent of maltreating parents have severe personality disorders or psychoses. This is not to say that personal factors are unimportant. Obviously, abusive parents let their aggressive feelings go too far. There are several possible reasons that they do. One important reason is that abused children have a higher probability of becoming abusive parents than do nonabused children. In short, violence tends to beget violence. Some caution is advised concerning this relationship, however. The evidence is that about 30 percent of physically abused children grow up to be abusive adults. Although this is much higher than the overall societal rate of between 2 and 3 percent, we must not ignore the fact that seven in ten abused children *do not* become abusive adults (Gelles 1993:15).

  A relatively common trait of abusing parents is chronic substance abuse. This activity reduces the normal restraints inhibiting aggression in the individual. Parents' alcoholism has long been associated with child abuse. Recent years have seen an increase in reports of child abuse in households in which parents used methamphetamines (Children's Defense Fund 2005). Substance abuse is also associated with a number of other factors that produce strain and disruption in stable family patterns: greater unemployment, poor health, low self-esteem, isolation, and preoccupation with self.

  Finally, a caution from Gelles and Straus: "When our explanations focus on 'kinds of people'—mentally disturbed, poor alcoholics, drug abusers, etc.—we blind ourselves to the structural properties of the family as a social institution that makes it our most violent institution with the exception of the military in time of war" (Gelles and Straus 1988:51).

  The Children's Defense Fund states the relationship between social class and child abuse starkly: "Poverty is the single best predictor of child abuse and neglect. Children who live in families with annual incomes of less than $15,000 are 22 times more likely to be abused or neglected than those with annual incomes of $30,000 or more" (2005:113).

  In fact, rising and falling rates of child maltreatment are closely tied to changes in the poverty rate. Most poor children are not abused or neglected. In 2010, nearly 16 million children were poor, but fewer than 1 million U.S. children (representing all social classes) were confirmed as abused or neglected (U.S. Department of Health and Human Services 2011).

  Unemployment is another condition associated with child abuse. It may lead to poverty, low self-esteem (because of being a failure in a success-oriented society), and depression. The unemployed are also homebound, increasing their interaction with children.

- **Consequences.**   Many consequences of child abuse are obvious. More than 1,700 children die annually from abuse. Emergency rooms, clinics, and therapists treat hundreds of thousands more. Less obvious are the long-term consequences of child abuse and neglect. Hundreds of studies have provided evidence on the health outcomes, cognitive behavior, and social behavior outcomes. The following is drawn from the summary of this body of literature provided by Chalk, Gibbons, and Scarupa (2002):

Health Outcomes

- Various types of brain injuries are associated with childhood maltreatment, particularly when physical abuse and neglect occur in the first three years of life.
- Abuse and neglect may be associated with physical defects, growth and mental retardation, and speech problems.
- Maltreated children tend to have heightened levels of depression and low self-esteem.

Cognitive and Educational Outcomes

- Some studies find associations between abuse and neglect and language deficits, reduced cognitive functioning, and attention deficit disorders.
- Both neglected and physically abused children tend to do poorly in school, as evidenced by low grades, low standardized test scores, and frequent retention in the same grade.

Social and Behavioral Outcomes

- Antisocial behavior and physical aggression are two of the most consistent outcomes, along with fear and anger, of physical child abuse.
- Maltreatment can have a negative impact on children's emotional stability and self-regulation, problem-solving skills, and the ability to cope with or adapt to new or stressful situations.
- Maltreated children are at risk of getting into trouble with the law and running away from home.
- Several studies have suggested a link between childhood victimization and substance abuse in later life.

Violence in the family presents the ultimate paradox—the physical abuse of loved ones in the most intimate of social relationships. The bonds between wife and husband, parent and child, and adult child and parent are based on love, yet for many people these bonds represent a trap in which they are victims of unspeakable abuses.

Although it is impossible to know the extent of battering that takes place in families, the problem these forms of violence represents is not trivial. The threat of violence in intimate relationships exists for all couples and for all parents and children. Violence in the family, however, is not only a problem at the microlevel of family units. It also represents an indictment of the macrolevel—society, its institutions, and the cultural norms that support violence.

All forms of intimate violence occur within a social context. This social context of intimate violence includes a patriarchal ideology that condones and maintains the power of men over women. The social context includes a media barrage with the consistent message that violence solves social problems. The social contexts include an economy in which poverty, unemployment, and corporate downsizing jeopardize millions of families. The social context includes institutional sexism, institutional racism, and institutional heterosexuality, which make life more difficult for certain categories of people, especially limiting the possibilities for women, people of color, and lesbians and gays. In short, these social forces create the conditions that foster abuse in intimate relationships.

Although the existence of family violence is strongly affected by social forces, individuals acting singly, or with others, can and do shape, resist, and challenge the forces affecting their lives. Concerned citizens—abused women, feminists, and others—have worked through organizations to change the societal forces that encourage abuse. They have also worked to change laws and procedures to protect the victims of abuse.

MySocLab ✓ Study and Review on MySocLab

■ CHAPTER REVIEW

1. The family is one of the most idealized of all of society's institutions. There are disparities between the common images of the family and real patterns of family life. New sociological research has given us a better understanding of the U.S. family in past and present.

2. Families are closely connected with conditions in the larger society. Their location in class and race hierarchies gives them different resources for family life and creates variation in family form.

3. Changes in the U.S. economy have created discontinuity in family life. Globalization and other transformations have reduced the number of jobs. As the need for skilled labor has diminished, many blue-collar families have experienced unemployment or underemployment. Jobs providing a middle-class standard of living have also disappeared and produced downward mobility for families across the country. These difficulties have been magnified by the Great Recession, which has produced high rates of unemployment and changed the shapes of families in many ways.

4. A major demographic trend since World War II has been the sharp rise in mothers with young children who work outside the home. Few jobs make it easy to balance work and family. Thus, a critical need has emerged in society for accessible and acceptable childcare. In general, U.S. society has been unresponsive to this need.

5. More than one-fourth of all households with children are single-parent families, and most are headed by women. Single-parent families have a number of unique problems, the most prominent being a lack of economic resources.

6. Twenty-two percent of all children in the United States live in poverty.

7. The economic situation of children has worsened relative to the elderly.

8. The divorce rate in U.S. society is the highest in the world. The reasons for this high rate are the increased social and financial independence of women, increased affluence, greater tolerance of divorce by religious groups, no-fault divorce laws, and a more lenient public attitude toward divorce.

9. There are several important consequences of divorce: (a) Males and females experience divorce differently, with males having more advantages than females; (b) the economic resources (life chances) for children are reduced; and (c) the trauma for children is heightened for young children, for boys, for large families, and for children whose mother goes to work for the first time after divorce.

10. Researchers on family violence have concluded that the family is among the most violent social groups and that the home is among the most violent settings in U.S. society. The way that families are organized in the United States—the unequal distribution of power, patterns of male dominance, the intensity of interaction, and privacy—encourages conflict.

11. Although family violence occurs across the socioeconomic spectrum, both intimate partner violence and child abuse are correlated with socioeconomic hardship.

Family values. Conservative phrase supporting the two-parent family. The implication is that all other family arrangements are the source of social problems.

Family. Social arrangements whereby people related by ancestry, marriage, or cohabitation live together, form an economic unit, and often raise children.

Downward mobility. Movement to a lower social class.

Household. Residential unit in which members share resources. These units vary in membership and composition. A household is not always a family (parents and children), and a family is not always a household (because it may be separate geographically).

Life chances. Opportunities throughout one's life cycle to live and to experience the good things in society.

Modern family. Nuclear family that emerged in response to the requirements of an urban, industrial society. It consisted of an intact nuclear household unit with a male breadwinner, full-time homemaker wife, and their dependent children.

Postmodern families. Multiple family forms and household arrangements that have emerged as a result of a number of social factors, such as women in the labor force, divorce, remarriage, and cohabitation arrangements.

Nonfamily household. Persons who live alone or with unrelated individuals.

Dual-worker family. Family in which both spouses are in the labor force.

Family and Medical Leave Act of 1993. Federal law providing workers in establishments with more than fifty workers the right to unpaid job-protected leave for meeting family health needs.

Divorce. The formal dissolution of a marriage.

Intimate partner violence. Use of force, including rape, physical assaults, and stalking, perpetrated by current and former spouses, cohabiting partners, and dating partners.

Child abuse. Distinctive acts of violence and nonviolence and acts of omission and commission that place children at risk.

Education

((• Listen to Chapter 16 on **MySocLab**

LEARNING OBJECTIVES

16.1 Understand the consequences of having schools under local control.

16.2 Assess the ways that schools perpetuate class and race inequality.

16.3 Discuss possible solutions to address the inequities in our education system.

This chapter examines one of society's basic institutions—education. The organization of education in society is both a source of and a potential solution to some of our most vexing social problems. The chapter is divided into three main sections. The first describes the characteristics of U.S. education. The second section describes the current role of education in perpetuating inequality in society. The concluding section describes alternatives to eliminate the race and class biases in education.

16.1 Understand the consequences of having schools under local control.

CHARACTERISTICS OF EDUCATION IN THE UNITED STATES

Education as a Conserving Force

The formal system of education in U.S. society (and in all societies) is conservative because the avowed function of the schools is to teach newcomers the attitudes, values, roles, specialties, information, skills, and training necessary for the maintenance of society. In other words, the special task of the schools is to preserve the culture, not to transform it. Thus, the schools indoctrinate their pupils in the culturally prescribed ways. Children are taught to be patriotic. They learn the myths of the superiority of their nation's heritage; they learn who the heroes are and who the villains are. As Terry Everton notes,

> Compulsory schooling defines good citizens as those who play by the rules, stay in line, and do as they're told. Learning is defined by how well we memorize and regurgitate what someone else has deemed we need to know. Creativity is permitted within the parameters of the guidance of licensed professionals whose duty it is to make sure we don't get too wacky with our ideas or stray very far from the boundaries of normalcy. (2004:55)

There is always an explicit or implicit assumption in U.S. schools that the American way is the only really right way. When this assumption is violated on the primary and secondary school level by the rare teacher who asks students to consider the viability of world government or who proposes a class on the teachings of Karl Marx

Children are taught to be patriotic as part of their cultural indoctrination.

or about world religions, then strong enough pressures usually occur from within the school (administrators, school board) or from without (parents, the Christian right) to quell the disturbance. As a consequence, creativity and a questioning attitude are often curtailed in school.

Mass Education

Watch on MySocLab Video: Current Issues in U.S. Education

People in the United States have a basic faith in education. This faith is based on the assumption that a democratic society requires an educated citizenry so that individuals can participate in the decisions of public policy. For this reason they not only provide education for all citizens but also compel children to remain in school at least until the eighth grade or until age 16 (although the law varies somewhat from state to state).

Who can quarrel with the belief that all children should be compelled to attend school because it should be for their own good? After all, the greater the educational attainment, the greater the likelihood of larger economic rewards and upward social mobility. However, to compel a child to attend school for six hours a day, five days a week, forty weeks a year, for at least ten years, is quite a demand. The result is that many students are in school for the wrong reason. The motivation is compulsion, not interest in acquiring skills or curiosity about their world. This involuntary feature of U.S. schools is unfortunate because so many school problems are related to the lack of student interest. It is no surprise that despite two decades of intense educational reform, approximately 24.5 percent of public high school students will not graduate with their senior class (Aud et al. 2012).

On the positive side, as a result of the goal of and commitment to mass education, an increasing proportion of people have received a formal education. In 2010, 85.6 percent of Americans over the age of 25 were high school graduates, and another 28.2 percent had a bachelor's degree or higher (U.S. Census Bureau 2010).

Preoccupation with Order and Control

Most administrators and teachers share a fundamental assumption that school is a collective experience requiring subordination of individual needs to those of the school. U.S. schools are characterized, then, by constraints on individual freedom. The school day is regimented by the dictates of the clock. Activities begin and cease on a timetable, not in accordance with the degree of interest shown or whether students have mastered the subject. Another indicator of order is the preoccupation with discipline (i.e., absence of unwarranted noise and movement and concern with the following of orders).

In their quest for order, some schools also demand conformity in clothing and hairstyles. Dress codes are constraints on the freedom to dress as one pleases. School athletic teams also restrict freedom, and the school authorities condone these restrictions. Conformity is also demanded in what to read and how to give the answers the teacher wants.

The many rules and regulations found in schools meet a number of expressed and implicit goals, but many of those goals may be outdated. In the past, the school year was developed around the farm calendar and the emphasis on order and conformity intended to prepare children for jobs in factories. We have now shifted from the industrial age to the information age as many factories have moved overseas. Is the regimented factory-based school system the best educational approach in this new information age?

Roz Chast/The New Yorker Collection/www.cartoonbank.com

A Fragmented Education System

Certain trends indicate that the educational system in the United States is moving toward greater fragmentation rather than less. Today, more parents are opting to send their children to private schools (about 10 percent or 5.9 million students) or to school them at home (about 2.9 percent or 1.5 million students in 2007) (National Center for Education Statistics 2012).

Taxpayer-funded charter schools are also growing rapidly. These schools are based on a hybrid "free-market" system in which educators, students, and parents choose a curriculum and educational philosophy free from the dictates of school boards and educational bureaucracies but are financed publicly. In 2010, 5,000 public schools were charter schools with more than 1.6 million students (Aud et al. 2012).

Vouchers are another plan that splinters the educational system. This plan gives parents a stipulated amount of money per child that can be used to finance that child's education in any school, public or private. This plan sets up an educational "free market" in which schools have to compete for students. This competition will, theoretically, improve schools because they must provide what parents want for their children, whether that be better discipline, emphasis on learning the fundamentals, religious instruction, focus on the arts, vocational training, or college preparation.

Seventy percent of Black charter students attend schools where at least 90 percent of students are minorities.

Each of these educational reforms that are underway has strengths and weaknesses. Most important, they represent a trend that is rapidly dividing and subdividing the educational system. For many, this is viewed as a strength, representing the core American values of individualism and competition. Others see this trend as fragmenting further an already disaggregated educational system. Moreover, they see private schools, charter schools, and voucher systems as working against inclusiveness through segregation. For example, 70 percent of Black charter students attend schools where at least 90 percent of students are minorities (Blume 2010). This segregation serves to increase the gap between racial-ethnic groups and social classes in U.S. society.

Local Control of Education

View on **MySocLab Figure:** A Typical School District's Educational Bureaucracy

Although the state and federal governments finance and control education in part, the bulk of the money and control for education comes from local communities. There is a general fear of centralization of education under federal control. Local school boards (and the communities themselves) jealously guard their autonomy. Because, as is commonly argued, local people know best the special needs of their children, local boards control allocation of monies, curricular content, and the rules for running the schools, as well as the hiring and firing of personnel.

There are several problems with this emphasis on local control. First, tax money from the local area traditionally finances the schools. Whether the tax base is strong or weak has a pronounced effect on the quality of education received (a point we return to later in this chapter).

Second, local taxes are almost the only outlet for a taxpayers' revolt. Dissatisfaction with high taxes (federal, state, and local) on income, property, and purchases is often expressed at the local level in defeated school bonds and school tax levies. A current population trend—families with school-age children declining while the number of elderly Americans is rising—increases the ever-greater likelihood of the defeat of school bonds.

Third, because the democratic ideal requires that schools be locally controlled, the ruling body (school board) should represent all segments of that community. Typically, however, the composition of school boards has overrepresented the business and professional sectors and overwhelmingly underrepresented blue-collar workers, the poor, and various minority groups. The result is a governing body that is typically conservative in outlook and unresponsive to the wishes of people unlike themselves.

Fourth, local control of education may mean that the religious views of the majority (or, at least, the majority of the school board) may intrude in public education. An explicit goal of the Christian Coalition, a conservative religious organization founded by Pat Robertson, is to win control of local school boards. Its agenda opposes globalism, restricts sex education to abstinence from sexual intercourse, promotes school prayer and the teaching of biblical creationism in science classes, and censors books that denigrate Christian values (favorite targets are, for example, *Catcher in the Rye* by J. D. Salinger and John Steinbeck's *The Grapes of Wrath*).

The following are some examples of attempts by states and cities to install religious values in schools:

- In 2002, the Cobb County Board of Education in Georgia voted to insert a sticker in school biology textbooks that reads: "This textbook contains material on evolution. Evolution is a theory, not a fact, regarding the origin of living things. The material should be approached with an open mind, studied carefully, and critically considered" (Slevin 2005). Eleven parents filed suit against the school board, challenging the constitutionality of the textbook warning sticker. On December 19, 2006, a settlement was announced in which the school board agreed not to restore the warning sticker or take any actions that would prevent or hinder the teaching of evolution (National Center for Science Education 2006).
- In 2005, the Kansas State Board of Education adopted standards of teaching science whereby evolution was to be represented as scientifically controversial. In February 2007, the board overturned that decision, ruling that evolution should be treated in a scientifically appropriate and responsible way (National Center for Science Education 2007).
- Although the U.S. Supreme Court outlawed the posting of the Ten Commandments in public schools, numerous local school boards believe they can survive legal challenges if the commandments are posted in a display with other historical documents, such as the Magna Carta and the Declaration of Independence (D. Johnson 2000).
- In 2002, the Texas Board of Education objected to a sixth-grade social studies book that read, "Glaciers formed the Great Lakes millions of years ago," because this statement was counter to the creation timeline of religious conservatives. The book was changed to read, "Glaciers formed the Great Lakes in the distant past" (Russell 2003).
- In March 2010, the Texas Board of Education voted to approve a social studies curriculum that portrays conservative ideas in a more positive light, emphasizes the role of Christianity in the nation's founding, and stresses the superiority of American capitalism (McKinley 2010). Furthermore, the board adopted a resolution that seeks to curtail references to Islam in Texas textbooks, "as social conservative board members warned of what they describe as a creeping Middle Eastern influence in the nation's publishing industry" (Castro 2010:1).

As illustrated by these and a number of other lawsuits in recent years, the separation of church and state remains a volatile subject in the United States.

A Lack of Curriculum Standardization

The local control of education results in another much-debated characteristic of U.S. education—the lack of curriculum standardization across more than 100,000 K–12 schools and fifty states. Compared to most high-performing countries, the United States is unique in its lack of a common national curriculum, although there are signs that this may change in the future.

In a push for a common national curriculum, the National Governors Association Center for Best Practices has joined with others to form the Common Core State Standards Initiative, an initiative to develop international benchmarks for all states so that all students are prepared to be competitive in a globalized market. The federal government was not involved in the development of the standards; this is purely a state-driven initiative. Parents, teachers, school administrators, and experts across the country have developed the set of common standards, and as of March 2013 forty-five states and the District of Columbia have voluntarily adopted them.

While there has been a national push for education based on common standards, there has been a simultaneous push to preserve local control of education. This idea is embodied in the 2001 **No Child Left Behind Act**. Signed by George W. Bush in 2002, the goal of the NCLB legislation was to close the gaps that plague education in the United States and make schools accountable for success or failure. For example, according to National Assessment of Educational Progress data, only 35 percent of the nation's eighth graders are proficient or better in mathematics and just 34 percent are proficient or better in reading (Aud et al. 2012). Compared with other industrialized nations, which have prescribed national curricula or highly specified national

The No Child Left Behind Act was signed by President Bush in 2002.

standards, U.S. students rank near the bottom in achievement. To improve performance, NCLB legislation required states to develop academic standards in reading, math, and science. States, districts, and schools would then be responsible to ensure that all children achieve these state standards by 2013–2014. Adequate yearly progress is measured by a single, statewide assessment system given annually to all students from third to eighth grade. On the basis of these tests, schools are given a grade of "passing" or "failing." In the 2009 to 2010 school year, 38 percent of schools were labeled as "failing to make adequate yearly progress" (Education News 2011). This percentage varies by state, with a low of 5 percent of schools in Texas failing to make progress, to a high of 91 percent of schools in the District of Columbia. In 2007, more than 1,000 of California's 9,500 schools were branded as "chronic failures," and state officials predict that all 6,063 public schools serving poor students will be declared in need of restructuring by 2014 (Schemo 2007).

Although this legislation has been heralded as the most ambitious federal overhaul of public schools since the 1960s, there are a number of problems. First and foremost, instead of one system, we have fifty. Each state was permitted to set its own proficiency benchmarks, with some setting a high and others setting a low standard. Because the federal government rewards those who meet the standards, the ones with high standards are punished, while the ones with low standards are unfairly rewarded. In their 2007 report "The Proficiency Illusion" (Cronin et al. 2007), researchers from the Thomas B. Fordham Institute examine No Child Left Behind in detail. In their comprehensive review, they found:

- State tests vary greatly in their difficulty, with Colorado, Wisconsin, and Michigan having the lowest proficiency standards in reading and math.
- Improvements in the passing rates on state tests can largely be explained by declines in the difficulty on those tests, rather than true growth in student learning.
- The tests in eighth grade are consistently and dramatically more difficult than those in earlier grades. Many states set the bar much lower in elementary school, giving false impressions to parents and teachers that students are doing well.

Critics of No Child Left Behind argue that there is no attempt to address the funding inequities among rich and poor districts within a state that help perpetuate the achievement gaps, the chronic underfunding of poorer schools, or child poverty itself (Metcalf 2002). To rectify this, in March 2010 President Obama announced that an allocation of $900 million in grants would be awarded to help turn around the nation's lowest performing schools. Unfortunately, the 2007 to 2009 economic recession has left states in fiscal crisis, and budget cuts to education are rampant, resulting in teacher layoffs and the reduction in school programs and supplies. It remains to be seen what effect this will have on state standards and educational outcomes.

In sum, the lack of a common national curriculum has several negative consequences. First, there is a wide variation in the preparation of students, as states have the ability to raise or lower their standards. Second, because families move on the average of once every five years (and the rate is probably higher for families with school-age children), there are large numbers of children each year who find the requirements of their new schools different, sometimes very different, from their previous schools. Finally, not only are many American students graduating without the skills necessary to compete in an information economy, but they also appear to be ill poised to compete in a *global* economy.

"Sifting" and "Sorting" Function of Schools

Schools play a considerable part in choosing the youth who come to occupy the higher-status positions in society. School performance also sorts out those who will occupy the lower rungs in the occupational-prestige ladder. Education is, therefore, a selection process. The sorting is done with respect to two different criteria: a child's ability and his or her social class background. Although the goal of education is to select on ability alone, ascribed social status (the prestige and socioeconomic status of one's family, race, and religion) has a pronounced effect on the degree of success in the educational system. The school is analogous to a conveyor belt, with people of all social classes getting on at the same time but leaving the belt in accordance with social class—the lower the class, the shorter the ride.

16.2 Assess the ways that schools perpetuate class and race inequality.

EDUCATION AND INEQUALITY

Education is presumed by many people to be the great equalizer in U.S. society—the process by which the disadvantaged get their chance to be upwardly mobile. The data in Figure 16.1 show, for example, that the higher the educational attainment, the higher the income. But these data do not in any way demonstrate equality of opportunity through education. They show clearly that Blacks and Hispanics with the same educational attainment as Whites receive lower economic rewards at every educational level. These differences reflect discrimination in society, not just in schools. This section examines the ways that the schools help to perpetuate class and race inequities.

The evidence that educational performance is linked to socioeconomic background is clear and irrefutable (we include race/ethnicity along with economic status since they are highly correlated).

- African American, Latino, and Native American students lag behind their White peers in graduation rates and most other measures of student performance. The National Assessment of Educational Progress (NAEP) defines the **status dropout rate**

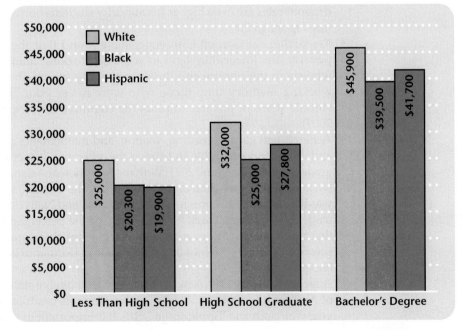

FIGURE 16.1

Median Annual Earnings of Full-Time Salary Workers Ages 25–34 by Educational Attainment and Race/Ethnicity, 2010

Source: Table adapted from Aud, Susan, William Hussar, Frank Johnson, Grace Kena, Erin Roth, Eileen Manning, Xiaolei Wang, and Jijun Zhang. 2012. "The Condition of Education 2012." (NCES 2012-045). U.S. Department of Education, National Center for Education Statistics. Washington, D.C. (Page 289). http://nces.ed.gov.

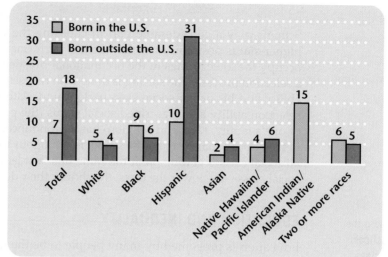

FIGURE 16.2

Status Dropout Rates (percentages) of 16- through 24-Year-Olds in the Noninstitutionalized Group Quarters and Household Population, by Nativity and Race/Ethnicity: American Community Survey (ACS) 2010

Noninstitutionalized group quarters include college and university housing, military quarters, facilities for workers and religious groups, and temporary shelters for the homeless. Among those counted in noninstitutionalized group quarters in the American Community Survey (ACS), only the residents of military barracks are not included in the civilian noninstitutionalized population in the Current Population Survey.

Source: U.S. Department of Commerce, Census Bureau, American Community Survey (ACS), 2010. Chart adapted from Aud, Susan, William Hussar, Frank Johnson, Grace Kena, Erin Roth, Eileen Manning, Xiaolei Wang, and Jijun Zhang. 2012. "The Condition of Education 2012." (NCES 2012-045). U.S. Department of Education, National Center for Education Statistics. Washington, D.C. (Page 83). http://nces.ed.gov.

as the percentage of 16- to 24-year-olds that are not enrolled in school and have not earned a high school diploma or equivalency. In 2010, the status dropout rate for Asian/Pacific Islanders was 4 percent; for Whites it was 5 percent; for Blacks it was 8 percent; and for Hispanics it was 15 percent (Aud et al. 2012). The status dropout rates are even higher for minority students born outside the United States (see Figure 16.2).

- Researchers at Cornell University have found that the longer children live in poverty, the lower they tend to score on working-memory tests. In fact, those who spent their entire childhood in poverty scored about 20 percent lower on working memory than those who were never poor. They conclude that the chronic stress of poverty impairs the cognitive development of children (Stein 2009).

- Achievement gaps in reading, writing, and mathematics persist between minority and White students. Table 16.1 shows the difference in average math scores of eighth graders in 1990, 2009, and 2011. With the exception of Asian/Pacific Islander students (who scored higher than all other groups), the average score for White students was higher than the scores for Black, Hispanic, and Native American/Alaska Native students in all three years. Note also that as the percentage of students in a school that are eligible for free or reduced lunch goes up, the average math scores go down, providing further evidence that educational performance is linked to socioeconomic background.

- A recent study by UCLA indicates that, in the twelve states studied, less than half of American Indian and Alaska Native students graduate from high school each year (Faircloth and Tippeconnie 2010). It is important to note that graduation rates

TABLE 16.1
Average Math Scores for 8th Graders in 1990, 2009, and 2011 by Race/Ethnicity, Sex, and Percent of Students in School Eligible for Free/Reduced-Price Lunch

	1990	2009	2011
SEX			
Male	263	284	284
Female	262	282	283
RACE/ETHNICITY			
White	270	293	293
Black	237	261	262
Hispanic	246	266	270
Asian/Pacific Islander	275	301	303
American Indian/Alaska Native	++	266	265
PERCENTAGE OF STUDENTS IN SCHOOL ELIGIBLE FOR FREE OR REDUCED-PRICE LUNCH			
0–25 Percent	—	298	300
26–50 Percent	—	284	287
51–75 Percent	—	274	276
76–100 Percent	—	260	264

—Not available
++Reporting standards not met (too few cases)

Source: Table adapted from Aud, Susan, William Hussar, Frank Johnson, Grace Kena, Erin Roth, Eileen Manning, Xiaolei Wang, and Jijun Zhang. 2012. "The Condition of Education 2012." (NCES 2012-045). U.S. Department of Education, National Center for Education Statistics. Washington, DC (page 207). http://nces.ed.gov.

Read on MySocLab Document: The Hispanic Dropout Mystery: A Staggering 30 Percent Leave School, Far More than Blacks or Whites. Why?

Read on MySocLab Document: Racial Stratification and Education in the United States: Why Inequality Persists

in all racial-ethnic groups also vary greatly by gender. For a closer look at gender and education, see the "A Closer Look" panel "Leaving Boys Behind?"

• The high dropout rate for Hispanics and African Americans translates into a lifetime of poor outcomes. According to Thornburgh, "Dropping out of high school today is to your societal health what smoking is to your physical health, an indicator of a host of poor outcomes to follow, from low lifetime earnings to high incarceration rates to a high likelihood that your children will drop out of high school and start the cycle anew" (2006a:32).

These social class and racial gaps in academic achievement are found in almost every school and district in the United States. On the surface, these patterns reinforce the social Darwinist assumptions that the affluent are successful because they are intelligent, and, conversely, the poor and minorities are at society's bottom because they do not have the requisite abilities to be successful. Similarly, dysfunctional families, unmotivated students, and the culture of poverty are believed by some to explain the academic achievement gap. We argue, to the contrary, that structural factors explain why the poor and minorities are disadvantaged in our supposedly meritocratic educational system. In effect, the educational system is stacked in favor of middle- and upper-class children. Many interrelated factors explain why the education system tends to reinforce the socioeconomic and racial differences in the United States. We examine a few of these in the following sections.

A Closer Look

LEAVING BOYS BEHIND?

In the 1990s, researchers and popular writers started writing about the "girl crisis" in America. According to books like *Reviving Ophelia: Saving the Selves of Adolescent Girls* (Pipher 1994) and *Failing at Fairness: How Our Schools Cheat Girls* (Sadker and Sadker 1994), girls were believed to be suffering when they hit adolescence. In 1992, the American Association of University Women (AAUW) published "How Schools Shortchange Girls," a study conducted by the Wellesley College Center for Research on Women. The report claimed that girls across the country were victims of a pervasive bias in schools. Teachers paid more attention to male students, gave them more time and feedback on their work, and did not encourage girls, especially in the areas of math and science. As a result, millions of dollars in grants were awarded to study the plight of girls in education (Sommers 2000).

More recently, writers have been focusing on a different crisis in education, that of boys, not girls. Christina Hoff Sommers writes,

The research commonly cited to support the claims of male privilege and sinfulness is riddled with errors. Almost none of it has been published in peer-reviewed journals. Some of the data are mysteriously missing. Yet the false picture remains and is dutifully passed along in schools of education, in "gender equity" workshops, and increasingly to children themselves. . . . A review of the facts shows boys, not girls, on the weak side of an educational gender gap. (2000:14)

According to Garibaldi, boys are increasingly disengaged in the "feminized" classroom (2006). Through movies, television, and rap music, pop culture teaches young boys it is not "cool" to like or do well in school and that to be masculine is

to be disengaged and anti-authority (Wenzl 2007). Those who propose that it is boys who are in crisis offer the following arguments:

- Boys are less likely to graduate from high school (65 percent versus 72 percent of girls; Greene and Winters 2006).
- Boys are, on average, a year and a half behind girls in reading and writing (Sommers 2000).
- Each year women receive more bachelor's and master's degrees than men (Mead 2006).
- Boys are more likely to be held back a grade, drop out, and be suspended from school (Sommers 2000).
- Girls continue to score higher on the Scholastic Aptitude test in the area of writing. On the newly revamped SAT in 2006, girls scored an average of eleven points higher in writing (College Board 2006).

So what is the truth concerning the gender gap in education? In a 2006 report by the Education Sector, Mead argued that "the real

Financing Public Education

Approximately 49.5 million U.S. children attend public schools (5.5 million attend private schools and about 1.5 million are homeschooled). These schools receive funds from three governmental sources—about 9 percent from the federal government; about 47 percent from the state, depending on the allocation within each state; and 44 percent from local taxes in each district within the state (Villano 2009). The result of this distribution is that schools are funded unequally in the United States, with public schools being more successful in educating children in middle-class communities but often failing children in poor neighborhoods.

Equal opportunity in education (at least as measured by equal finances) has not been accomplished nationwide because wealthier states are able to pay much more per pupil than are poorer states. The top-spending states, for example, invest more than double the amount per pupil than those states spending the least. Because the federal government provides only about 9 percent of the money for public schools, equalization from state to state is impossible as long as education is funded primarily by state and local governments because both entities vary in wealth and commitment to public education.

View on MySocLab Figure: The Unequal Funding of Education story is not bad news about boys doing worse; it's good news about girls doing better" (2006:1). In the report, using data from the National Assessment of Education Progress, Mead argued that American boys are scoring higher and achieving more than they have in the past, but girls have improved their performance on some measures even faster, which makes it appear as though boys are doing "worse." The data seem to indicate that younger boys are doing quite well, but older boys are starting to slip when they reach twelfth grade. Mead argued that twelfth-grade girls are sliding as well. She argued, "The fact that achievement for older students is stagnant or declining for both boys and girls, to about the same degree, points to another important element of the boy crisis. The problem is most likely not that high schools need to be fixed to meet the needs of boys but rather that they need to be fixed to meet the needs of *all* students, male and female" (2006:4).

In the battle over who is in crisis and more disadvantaged, two very important ideas seem to get left out.

First of all, regardless of the statistics that more boys are dropping out of school and are less likely to go to college, women still, on average, earn less than men at every level of education. Furthermore, women continue to attain a small percentage of high-level jobs in corporations, politics, and other occupations, and they continue to be responsible for the majority of domestic work. In her criticism of the "boy crisis" literature, Douglas writes,

In 1999, one year before Sommers' book came out, the top five jobs for women did not include attorney, surgeon, or CEO. They were, in order, secretaries, retail and personal sales workers (including cashiers), managers and administrators, elementary school teachers and registered nurses. In 2007, when presumably some of the privileged, pampered girls whose advantages over boys Sommers had kvetched about had entered the workforce, the top five jobs for women were, still secretaries in first place, followed by

registered nurses, elementary and middle school teachers, cashiers, and retail salespersons.

Farther down the line? Maids, child care workers, office clerks and hairdressers. Not a CEO or hedge fund manager in sight. And, in the end, no president or vice president in 2008. But what about all those career-driven girls going to college and leaving the guys in the dust? A year out of college, they earn 80 percent of what men make. And 10 years out? A staggering 69 percent. (2010:1–2)

Second, for every statistic that indicates a gender gap, there is an even larger gap by social class and race. Mead argues that "the gaps between students of different races and classes are much larger than those for students of different genders—anywhere from two to five times as big, depending on the grade. . . . Overall, poor, Black, and Hispanic boys would benefit far more from closing racial and economic achievement gaps than they would from closing gender gaps" (2006:5).

View on MySocLab Figure: Starting Salaries of U.S. College Graduates, BA or BS Degree: Public School Teachers Compared with Private Industry

The disparities in per-pupil expenditures within a given state are also great, largely because of the tradition of funding public schools through local property taxes. This procedure is discriminatory because rich school districts can spend more money than poor ones on each student—and at a lower taxing rate. Thus, suburban students are more advantaged than are students from the inner city; districts with business enterprises are favored over agricultural districts; and districts with natural resources are better able to provide for their children than are districts with few resources. In some states, the disparity in spending for each pupil may be as much as three times more in affluent districts than in poor areas. Following are some examples:

- In Illinois, in 2007–2008 the New Trier Township High School District spent $21,137 per student, while the Farmington Central Community Unit School District spent only $6,728 per student, reflecting the large disparity in their local tax bases (New America Foundation 2009).
- According to the U.S. Census Bureau, in the 2008–2009 school year Camden, New Jersey, schools spent $23,356 per student, while the Tom's River Regional School District spent $12,005 per student (2011a).

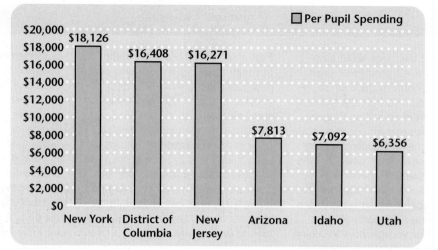

FIGURE 16.3

States with the Highest and Lowest Spending per Student, 2009

Source: U.S. Census Bureau, Public Education Finances: 2009.

Watch on
MySocLab Video:
Inequities in Education

Explore on
MySocLab Activity:
High School Dropouts and Educational Funding

- In Scarsdale Union Free School District, New York (the wealthiest school district in the country), the median household income is $238,000, and per pupil spending is $26,742 per year. In Barbourville Independent School District, Kentucky (the poorest school district in the country), the median household income is $16,607, and per pupil spending is $8,178 per year (Sauter et al. 2012).

Nationwide, data from the U.S. Census Bureau show that in 2009, per-pupil spending ranged from a high of $18,126 in New York to a low of $6,356 in Utah (see Figure 16.3). This gap is even greater when one considers the monies raised in each district from fundraisers, soda machine contracts, and foundation contributions.

There have been a number of court challenges to unequal funding within states, and systems in several states have been judged unconstitutional. Various schemes have been proposed to meet the objections of the courts, but inequities remain even in the more progressive states. Progressive plans to address financial inequities are fought by the affluent districts and their constituents because, they argue, their taxes should be spent on their children, not the children of others.

Overall, research shows that poor students and the schools serving them have fewer computers and other supplies; have teachers who are underpaid and have less teaching experience; are more likely to attend schools in need of repairs, renovations, and modernization (Filardo et al. 2006); and have higher pupil–teacher ratios. See the "Speaking to Students" panel "In-School Marketing" for a look at what some schools are doing to generate more funds.

In sum, the financing of public education is upside down. The schools and students who need the most help receive the least, whereas those with advantages are advantaged all the more. In a study of school construction spending across the nation between 1995 and 2004, Filardo and colleagues found that out of the billions of dollars spent on school facilities, the least-affluent school districts (also those with predominantly minority student enrollment) made the lowest investment per student, and the most affluent districts made the highest investment (2006). Further, the money spent on schools serving low-income students was more likely used to fund basic repairs, but schools in more affluent districts were more likely to add science labs, technology, or other new programs. As stated by President Barack Obama, "For low-income students, the schools are made less decrepit; for wealthier students, they are made more enriching. . . . For all students to achieve, all must be provided adequate resources: effective teachers, inspiring school leaders, and enriching classroom environments" (2006:1).

Speaking to Students

IN-SCHOOL MARKETING

We live in an advertising age. Through television, radio, billboards, movies, and the Internet, Americans are bombarded with advertisements. Research shows that the average American is exposed to 61 minutes of on-screen ads and promotions per day (Stelter 2009), and the average American living in a big city sees up to 5,000 advertisements per day (Story 2007).

In an effort to make up for declining school revenues, many school districts allow companies to market their products within the school environment in exchange for cash or computers and other supplies. Teenagers provide a target audience for marketers who want to catch consumers early and create brand loyalty. Smart companies understand that teenagers have enormous spending power, and they are ready and willing to capitalize on this through in-school marketing. In elementary, middle, and high schools, direct advertising can be found on:

- Book covers and educational posters in hallways.
- Sponsored educational materials. Teaching materials that

are provided by companies can be very popular with teachers. The problem with advertising on teaching materials is that the companies producing such materials are not focused on education as the ultimate goal, but rather on selling their product (Carney 2007).

- Channel One (a division of Alloy Media and Marketing) broadcasts daily to nearly 6 million teens in approximately 8,000 schools.
- School buses: Some school districts have sold advertising space on the side of their buses, and others broadcast radio programs with advertisements.
- Vending machines: Schools can have exclusive product sponsorships and can even receive bonuses if certain sales quotas are met (Carney 2007).
- Athletics fields, scoreboards, and gymnasium walls.
- Fundraising items such as cookie dough, magazines, and other branded products.

Critics of this arrangement argue that advertising within

an educational institution is exploitative.

Children, legally required to be in school, provide advertisers with a captive audience that is more likely to believe the advertising messages because they are displayed in a school/learning environment (Carney 2007:2).

In this way, marketing to students is dangerous because it seems as though the school endorses the product. A superintendent in Manassas Park says, "To me, it kind of cheapens the education mission, and it takes a captive audience and shoves advertising down their throats" (quoted in Birnbaum 2009:1).

Others argue that in tight economic times schools are forced to do whatever it takes to bring in resources. Furthermore, in a culture saturated with advertising, students will be exposed to ads whether they are presented within the school environment or presented outside of school. Because this is the case, schools might as well benefit from the practice of marketing to students.

So the question for students, parents, and educators is, should education be "commercial-free"?

Family Economic Resources

The average SAT (Scholastic Aptitude Test) scores for youth from families whose annual income was $200,000 or more was 381 points higher than for youth from families whose income is $20,000 or less (1702 versus 1321). By race, Whites scored about 300 points higher than African Americans on average (Marklein 2009). How are we to explain these differences on the SATs by income and race? One factor highly correlated with income is parents' education level. For SAT takers in the class of 2004, scores were approximately fifty points higher than the national average for those whose parents had a graduate degree and thirty-nine points lower than the national average if their parents had only a high school diploma (Carnahan and Coletti 2006).

Many benefits come from economic privilege. Poor parents (disproportionately people of color), most without health insurance, are unable to afford prenatal care, which increases the risk of babies being born at low birth weight, a condition that may lead to learning disabilities. As these poor children age, they are less likely to receive adequate nutrition, decent medical care, and a safe and secure environment. These deficiencies increase the probability of their being less alert, less curious, and less able to interact effectively with their environment than are healthy children.

Poor children are more likely than the children of the affluent to attend schools with poor resources, which, as we have seen, means that they are less likely to receive an enriched educational experience. In their analysis of a nationally representative sample of kindergarten children, Lee and Burkam argue,

> Low-SES [socioeconomic status] children begin school in kindergarten in systematically lower-quality elementary schools than their more advantaged counterparts. However school quality is defined—in terms of higher student achievement, more school resources, more qualified teachers, more positive teacher attitudes, better neighborhood or school conditions, private vs. public schools—the least advantaged U.S. children begin their formal schooling in consistently lower-quality schools. This reinforces the inequalities that develop even before children reach school age. (2002:3)

Similarly, most poor young people live in communities that have few opportunities to apply academic skills and build new ones because such opportunities are either not available or not accessible (libraries, planetariums, summer camps, zoos, nature preserves, museums). The lack of community resources is especially destructive during the summer months, the time when children doing least well in school (a group that is disproportionately poor) slide backward the furthest.

Children from poor families cannot afford private early development programs, which prepare children for school. They can be in Head Start, but these government programs have funding for only about 60 percent of those eligible.

The level of affluence also affects how long children will stay in school because schools, even public schools, are costly. There are school fees (many school districts, for example, charge fees for participation in music, athletics, and drama), supplies, meals, transportation, and other costs of education. These financial demands pressure youngsters from poorer families to drop out of school prematurely to go to work. The children from the middle and upper classes, not constrained by financial difficulties, tend to stay in school longer, which means better jobs and pay in the long run.

The affluent also give their children educational advantages such as home computers; travel experiences abroad and throughout the United States; visits to zoos, libraries, and various cultural activities; and summer camps to hone their skills and enrich their experiences in such activities as sports, music, writing, and computers. Another advantage available to the affluent is the hiring of tutors to help children having difficulty in school or to transform good students into outstanding ones.

The well-to-do often send their children to private schools (about 10 percent of U.S. children attend these schools). Parents offer several rationales for sending their children to private schools. Some do so for religious reasons. Another reason is that private schools, unlike public schools, are selective in whom they accept. Thus, parents can ensure that their children will interact with children similar to theirs in race (some private schools were expressly created so that White children could avoid attending integrated public schools) and social class. Similarly, private schools are much more likely than public schools to get rid of troublesome students (e.g., behavioral problems and low achievers), thereby providing an educational environment more conducive to learning and achievement. A final reason for attending private schools is that the most elite of them provide a demanding education and entry to the most elite universities, which, in turn, lead to placement in top positions in the professional and corporate occupational worlds.

The preceding arguments show that a family's economic resources are correlated to their child's educational success. From test scores to dropout rates, some students are more advantaged than others.

Higher Education and Stratification

As noted earlier, obtaining a college degree is an important avenue to later success. Because the payoff in jobs and pay is directly related to the prestige of the college or university attended, colleges play an important role in maintaining the stratified structure of society. From those who receive no college education to those who attend private, elite universities, each tier in the hierarchy results in different life chances.

On the lowest tier of the hierarchy are those who cannot afford to attend college. Although economic success is possible without a college degree, for most individuals, no college education translates into a lifetime of lower earnings and low-mobility jobs. Throughout the 1980s and 1990s, the cost of college rose at a rate more than twice the inflation rate. In 2010–2011, on average, the total annual expenses to attend a four-year private school (tuition, fees, room and board) were $39,800 compared to $20,100 for a four-year public school for in-state students (Aud et al. 2012). The cost of room, board, fees, and tuition at the nation's most exclusive schools is over $50,000 for a single school year. The high costs, coupled with declining scholarship monies, prohibit college attendance not only for the able poor but also increasingly for children of the working and lower middle classes. A comparison of students

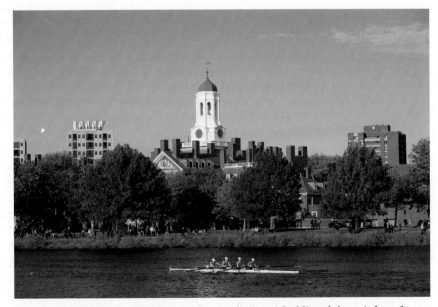

America's elite schools, like Harvard, have a distinguished list of alumni, from former presidents to U.S. ambassadors.

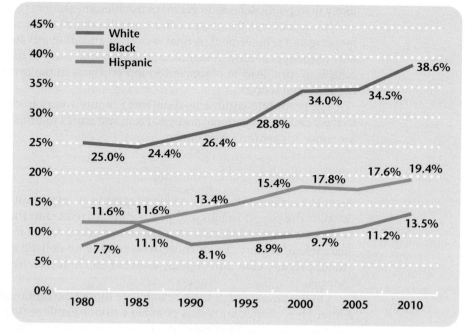

FIGURE 16.4

Percentage of 25- to 29-Year-Olds with a Bachelor's Degree or Higher, by Year and Race/Ethnicity

Source: Chart adapted from Aud, Susan, William Hussar, Frank Johnson, Grace Kena, Erin Roth, Eileen Manning, Xiaolei Wang, and Jijun Zhang. 2012. "The Condition of Education 2012." (NCES 2012-045). U.S. Department of Education, National Center for Education Statistics. Washington, D.C. (Page 286). http://nces.ed.gov.

from different income groups shows that 14 percent of those from the lowest income group will enroll in college, compared to 64 percent of those from the highest income group (Symonds 2006).

Because racial minorities are much more likely than Whites to be poor or near poor, they are underrepresented in colleges and among college graduates. The percentages of all racial groups who have completed a bachelor's degree or higher have increased since 1980, but the gaps between Whites and Blacks and Whites and Hispanics remains (see Figure 16.4). The disproportionately low number of college degrees earned by minorities is reflected in the relatively low number of students who attend and complete graduate school. This, of course, results in a low proportion of minorities in the various professions in the near future. Of special significance is the low minority representation among full-time faculty in higher education now and projected for the future.

For students who do attend college, money stratifies. The poorest, even those who are talented, are most likely to attend community colleges, which are the least expensive (today 6 million of the nation's college students attend community colleges).

Students with greater resources are likely to attend public universities. State schools are subsidized by their legislators according to their level of prestige. Similar to the funding of public education from kindergarten through high school, the funding of public higher education benefits the already advantaged and neglects the already neglected. And, as we have already noted, the costs of public universities are high and continue to rise.

Finally, on the highest tier of the hierarchy are the students with the greatest financial backing who are the most likely to attend elite and prestigious private institutions. The most prestigious schools have the most resources, which means they can hire the most prestigious professors, maintain the most complete libraries and research facilities, and equip state-of-the-art classrooms. Despite falling endowments due to the economic recession, in 2011 Harvard had an endowment valued at $31.7 billion, Yale had an endowment worth $19.3 billion, and Stanford had an endowment worth $16.5 billion (National Association of College and University Business Officers [NACUBO] 2012).

Although talent is an important variable, it is money—not ability—that places college students in this stratified system. For example, admission committees at elite universities give students from upper-class families favorable ratings if they are children of alumni or children of big contributors to the university's fundraising campaigns (this is a reverse form of affirmative action, benefiting the children of the affluent, the most notable example being George W. Bush's acceptance into Yale). Reporter Daniel Golden argued that these children of celebrities, politicians, and wealthy executives, called "development cases," are often admitted to elite colleges with SAT scores sometimes 300 or 400 points lower than those of some rejected applicants (Golden 2006).

Opponents of affirmative action argue that affirmative action policies undermine the meritocratic nature of colleges by rewarding and advancing students not on the basis of ability or talent, but rather on their race or minority status. In reality, the meritocratic system is undermined by the admittance and advancement of students who are well-connected or have relatives who are alumni, politicians, or donors to the institution. According to a five-year study of 146 top colleges, white students with below average qualifications were twice as prevalent as black and Hispanic students who were admitted under affirmative action policies (Schmidt 2007). While some of these white students may be recruited as athletes, most are so-called "development cases," admitted to keep their relatives happy with the institution.

A degree from a prestigious school opens doors of opportunity rarely available to graduates of the less-prestigious schools, yet entry goes disproportionately to the already advantaged.

Segregation

Schools in the United States tend to be segregated by social class and race, both by neighborhood and, within schools, by ability grouping. Schools are based in neighborhoods that tend to be relatively homogeneous by socioeconomic status. Racial and economic segregation is especially prevalent at the elementary school level, carrying over to a lesser degree in the secondary schools. Colleges and universities, as we have seen, are peopled by a middle- and upper-class clientele. Thus, at every level, children tend to attend a school with children like themselves in socioeconomic status and race. According to a study of Southern California schools by the University of California, Los Angeles, the typical Latino student in the Los Angeles Unified School District goes to a school where just 6 percent of the students are White (Orfield, Siegel-Hawley, and Kucsera 2011). This same study found that the typical Black student in San Diego attends a school where just 6 percent of the students are White. According to Fuentes (2007), Latinos living in New York attend schools that are 80 percent non-White. In short, the progress toward desegregation peaked in the late 1980s and has retreated because of racially segregated neighborhoods and school districts across the country challenging integration policies.

At the college level, some universities have also addressed the issue of segregation through the use of race-conscious admissions. At the University of Michigan, for example, the admissions committee uses a point scale whereby students need 100 points to be accepted to the university. Prior to 2003, underrepresented ethnic minorities received an automatic twenty-point bonus toward admission. A 2003 Supreme Court decision (*Gratz v. Bollinger*) found this system to be unconstitutional and too close to a quota system. At the same time, however, another Supreme Court decision (*Grutter v. Bollinger*) upheld that race could still be considered in the admission process, but minorities could not be awarded a fixed quantity of extra points. This decision has come under fire from the public. In 2006, Michigan residents voted overwhelmingly in favor of barring the state from granting preferences based on skin color or gender in public contracting, employment, and education (Brown 2006). However, in 2011 a federal appeals court ruled that Michigan cannot ban the use of affirmative action in college admissions, saying it violates the U.S. Constitution. The controversy continues with never-ending court battles and public debate.

In summary, the statistics are difficult to ignore, and they paint a picture of a segregated educational system where students attend schools largely populated by their own race and socioeconomic group. Speaking about school segregation, Gary Orfield writes: "Isolation by poverty, language, and ethnicity threatens the future opportunities and mobility of students and communities excluded from competitive schools, and increasingly threatens the future of a society where young people are not learning to live and work effectively across the deep lines of race and class in our region" (Orfield, Siegel-Hawley, and Kucsera 2011:4).

Tracking and Teachers' Expectations

In 1954, the Supreme Court declared segregated schools unconstitutional. As we have seen, many schools remain at least partially segregated by social class and race because schools draw students from residential areas that are more or less homogeneous by class and race. Segregation is reinforced further by the tracking system within the schools. **Tracking** (also known as ability grouping) sorts students into different groups or classes according to their perceived intellectual ability and performance. The decision is based on grades and teachers' judgments but primarily through standardized tests. The result is that children from poor families and from ethnic minorities are overrepresented in the slow track, whereas children from advantaged backgrounds are disproportionately in the middle and upper tracks. The rationale for tracking is that it provides a better fit between the needs and capabilities of the student and the demands and opportunities of the curriculum. Slower students do not retard the progress of brighter ones, but teachers can adapt their teaching more efficiently to the level of the class if the students are relatively homogeneous in ability. The special problems of the different ability groups, from gifted to challenged, can be dealt with more easily when groups of students share the same or similar problems. The arguments are persuasive.

Although these benefits may be real, tracking is open to serious criticisms. First, students in lower tracks are given low-level work that increases the gap between them and students in the higher tracks, thereby reinforcing the U.S. stratification system. Kozol (2005) found evidence of tracking in his discussions with poor high schools students. For example, he found that minority students were funneled into vocational classes geared toward low-level employment (like sewing classes) rather than classes with academic substance that would prepare them for college. Thus, the tracking system is closely linked to the stratification system—that is, students from low-income families are disproportionately placed in the lowest track, resulting in a reinforcement of the social class structure.

Second, students in the upper track develop feelings of superiority, while those in the lower track tend to define themselves as inferior. As early as the second grade, students know where they stand on the smart-to-dumb continuum, and this knowledge profoundly affects their self-esteem. These psychological wounds can have devastating effects.

Third, the low-track students are tracked to fail. The negative labels, low teacher expectations, poor education resources (e.g., the highest track is much more likely to have access to computers and to have the most talented teachers), and reluctance of teachers to teach these classes (there is a subtle labeling among teachers regarding who gets to teach what level) all lead to a high probability of failure among students assigned to the lowest track. Given all these negatives, it is not surprising that students who are discipline problems or who eventually drop out come disproportionately from the low track.

The tracking system is powerful in its negative effects. There are four principal reasons this system stunts the success of students who are negatively labeled: stigma, self-fulfilling prophesies, beliefs about future payoffs to education, and the creation of negative student subcultures.

- **Stigma.** Assignment to a lower track carries a strong **stigma** (a label of social disgrace). Such students are labeled as intellectual inferiors. Their self-esteem wanes as they see how other people perceive them and behave toward them. Thus, individuals assigned to a track other than college prep perceive themselves as second class, unworthy, stupid, and in the way. Clearly, assignment to a low track is destructive to a student's self-concept.

- **Self-Fulfilling Prophecy.** A self-fulfilling prophecy (see Chapter 7) is an event that occurs because it is predicted, and people alter their behavior to conform to the prediction. This effect is closely related to stigma. If placed in the college-prep track, students are likely to receive better instruction, have access to better facilities, and be pushed more nearly to their capacity than are students assigned to other tracks. The reason is clear: Teachers and administrators expect great things from the one group and lesser things from the other. Moreover, these expectations are fulfilled. Students in the higher track do better, and those in the lower track do not. These behaviors justify the greater expenditures of time, faculties, and experimental curricula for those in the higher track.

  An example comes from a classic controversial study by Rosenthal and Jacobson (1968). Although this study has been criticized for a number of methodological shortcomings, the findings are consistent with theories of interpersonal influence and with the labeling view of deviant behavior. In the spring of 1964, all students in an elementary school in San Francisco were given an IQ test. The following fall, the teachers were given the names of children identified by the test as potential academic spurters, and five of these children were assigned to each classroom. The spurters were chosen by means of a table of random numbers. The only difference between the experimental group (those labeled as spurters) and the control group (the rest of the class) was in the imaginations of the teachers. At the end of the year, all the children were again tested, and the children from whom the teachers expected greater intellectual gains showed such gains (in IQ scores and grades). Moreover, they were rated by their teachers as being more curious, interesting, happy, and more likely to succeed than were the children in the control group.

  The implications of this example are clear. Teachers' expectations have a profound effect on students' performance. When students are overrated, they tend to overproduce; when they are underrated, they underachieve. The tracking system is a labeling process that affects the expectations of teachers (and fellow students and parents). The limits of these expectations are crucial in the educational process. Yet the self-fulfilling prophecy can work in a positive direction if teachers have an unshakable conviction that their students can learn. Concomitant with this belief, teachers should hold themselves, not the students, accountable if the latter should fail. Used in this manner, the self-fulfilling prophecy can work to the benefit of all students.

- **Future Payoff.** School is perceived as relevant for students going to college. Grades are a means of qualifying for college. For the non-college-bound student, however, school and grades are much less important for entry into a job. At most, students need a high school diploma, and grades really do not matter as long as one does not flunk out. Thus, non-college-bound students often develop negative attitudes toward school, grades, and teachers. This is reflected in the statistic that students from the lowest income quarter are more than six times as likely to drop out of high school as students from the highest income quarter (U.S. Department of Education, National Center for Educational Statistics 2006).

  As we have seen, being on the lower track has negative consequences. Lower-track students are more rebellious, both in school and out, and do not participate as much in school activities. Finally, what is being taught is often not relevant to their world. Thus, we are led to conclude that many of these students tend to feel that they are not only second-class citizens but perhaps also even outcasts. What other interpretation is plausible in a system that disadvantages them, shuns them, and makes demands of them that are irrelevant?

- **Student Subculture.** The reasons given previously suggest that a natural reaction of people in the lower track would be to band together in a **student subculture** that is antagonistic toward school. This subculture would quite naturally develop its own system of rewards because those of the school are inaccessible.

  These factors (stigma, negative self-fulfilling prophecy, low future payoff, and a contrary student subculture) show how the tracking system is at least partly responsible for the fact that students in the lower tracks tend to be low achievers, unmotivated, uninvolved in school activities, and more prone to break school rules and drop out of school. To segregate students either by ability or by future plans is detrimental to the students labeled as inferior. It is an elitist system that for the most part takes the children of the elite and educates them to take the elite positions in society. Conversely, children of the non-elite are trained to recapitulate the experiences of their parents.

  The conclusion is inescapable: Inequality in the educational system causes many people to fail in U.S. schools. This phenomenon is the fault of the schools, not of the children who fail. To focus on these victims is to divert attention from the real problem—the inadequacies of the school system.

16.3 Discuss possible solutions to address the inequities in our education system.

POSSIBILITIES FOR PROMOTING EQUALITY OF OPPORTUNITY

A fundamental tenet of U.S. society is that each individual, regardless of sex, race, ethnicity, religion, sexuality, age, and social class, has the opportunity to be equal on her or his own merits. In other words, the system must not impede individuals from reaching their potential and from gaining the unequal rewards of an unequal society. The data presented in this chapter show that U.S. schools tend to block the chances of minority and poor children in their quest to be successful in society. This section outlines several programs that schools and society could adopt to promote equality of opportunity for all children.

We must realize at the start that if the situation for poor and minority children is difficult now, it will worsen significantly if changes are not made. This assertion is based on three societal trends. The first, documented throughout this book, is that the gap between the affluent and the poor is widening. Also, as the demographic mix of the nation continues to change, increasing numbers of children of color from relatively poor families will attend schools. Today about 22 percent of schoolchildren have a foreign-born parent (mostly Latino and Asian), a proportion that will likely increase. The poor and children of immigrants are disproportionately found in inner cities in increasingly segregated neighborhoods. With the poor and people of color clustered in cities, these local governments, faced with a declining tax base, will be less and less able to provide the services required of their citizens, including education. Similarly, certain regions—the Pacific Coast, the Southwest, and Florida—are especially affected by immigration, placing an extraordinary financial burden on those states and localities.

The second trend that will negatively affect the educational opportunities of minorities unless changes are made is that the number of minority students is increasing and will in the next decades make Whites the numerical minority (as they are today in many school districts). Moreover, racial and ethnic minorities are concentrated in poor states (the South and Southwest), in poor geographical regions (Appalachia, the Ozarks, along the Rio Grande, and in the Mississippi delta), and in poor sections of cities. This is significant because racial/ethnic minorities have higher rates of poverty, more unemployment, and lower educational attainment than do the more fortunate majority. In effect, under current policies, children of minorities are disadvantaged economically and are at greater risk of educational failure. So, wherever these children are overrepresented, there will be disproportionately less local money to meet their educational needs (because of the lower tax base). Ironically, the poor require more money than the affluent to catch up, such as enriched preschool, after-school programs, summer reading programs, and small classes, yet the richest school districts spend more per student.

In addition to the rise in the proportion of racial minority students, several demographic trends makes reform difficult. One demographic trend negatively affecting education is the aging of society (see Chapter 5). As a greater proportion of the population no longer has children in school, there will be a greater reluctance on their part to vote for tax increases directed at education. Another population trend is for increased enrollments from the baby boom echo—that is, the children of children of the disproportionately large baby boom generation are in school or soon will be, swelling the numbers significantly. This means that more classrooms and teachers are needed at a time when many states are making cuts to education due to the economic recession.

All the previously mentioned demographic changes point to a society that is at risk for increasing the gap between rich and poor students. The next sections discuss several programs that schools and society could adopt to promote equality of opportunity for all children.

Provide Universal Preschool Programs

View on MySocLab Figure: Childcare Arrangements of Preschoolers with Employed Mothers by Race/Ethnicity

The most important variable affecting school performance is not race but socioeconomic status. Regardless of race, children from poor families tend to do less well in school than do children from families who are better off. Long-term studies are beginning to show that the United States needs to invest in preschool-age children from disadvantaged families to counter some of these poor outcomes. In fact, the

Studies have shown that investing in preschool-age children results in positive life outcomes.

earlier the investment, the better. For example, in a forty-year study of 123 low-income children, intensive preschool attention resulted in higher academic achievement, higher earnings, and lower rates of criminal activity compared to a control group (reported in Farrell 2006). Although the program was expensive ($10,600 investment per pupil), researchers estimated that the benefit-to-cost ratio comes to $17 for every $1 invested.

Offer Free Education

Beginning with preschool, there must be a commitment to a free education for all students. Presumably, public education at the elementary and secondary levels is free, but this assumption is a fallacy, as discussed earlier. Although circumstances vary by district, typically children must pay for their supplies, textbooks, laboratory fees, locker rental, admission to plays and athletic events, meals, and participation in extracurricular activities. Some districts waive these costs for poor families, but waivers do not occur uniformly across school districts, and the procedures for granting these waivers are often degrading (i.e., done in such a way that other people know who receives the handouts). These costs are regressive because they take a larger proportion of the poor family's budget, thereby increasing the pressure to withdraw the child from school, where he or she drains the family resources.

By making education absolutely free to all children, communities could reduce dropout rates among the poor. A program of greater scope would also provide a living allowance for each child from a poor family who stayed in school beyond the eighth grade. This program would be analogous to the GI Bill, which provided similar benefits to soldiers returning after World War II. Special care must be given to provide these benefits, as did the GI Bill, without making their acceptance degrading.

An important way to produce equal opportunity is to provide a free college education to all students who qualify. This means the elimination of tuition and fees and an allowance for books for everyone, plus grants and loans for students in need to pay for living expenses while attending college. Students could then "give back" through community service or working on campus. An example comes from the College of the Ozarks, where students pay no tuition and work at least fifteen hours a week on campus (students are graded on their work performance in addition to their academics).

Set National Education Standards

The government should provide national education standards, a national curriculum, and national tests. As noted before, the No Child Left Behind Act was a step in this direction, but it allows each of the fifty states to set its own standards. There are more than 16,000 school districts and 100,000 schools in the United States. We must require that each school district and school, rather than acting on its own, meet specific standards for school achievement agreed to by a national consensus among educational leaders. The minimum result of this requirement would be that students, whether growing up in Nebraska or New York, would learn the same basic materials at about the same time. It would also mean that as students move with their families from one locality to another, they would not be at a disadvantage because of the esoteric schooling they had received. The fact that forty-five states and the District of Columbia have voluntarily adopted the standards promoted by the Common Core State Standards Initiative is an important step in this direction.

Reduce Funding Disparities across States and Districts

Another reform at the federal level would be to spend the federal monies unequally to equalize differences among the states. In effect, the federal government must take the money it receives in taxes and, like the fictional character Robin Hood, take disproportionately from the wealthy states and redistribute it to the poor states. Otherwise, the gap between the rich and poor states will be maintained.

Nationwide, the traditional property tax system of raising money for education locally is under assault. The supreme courts in various states are ruling in case after case that the states are failing the children in the poorer districts. States should be encouraged to distribute their funds to eliminate or minimize disparities between rich and poor districts. This could be done by the federal government's withholding funds from states with discrepancies between their poor and rich districts that exceed federal guidelines. In such cases, the federal government could channel its monies directly to the poorer districts within the offending states.

Reduce Class and School Size

Schools can be restructured to better meet the needs of students. A beginning would be to reduce class size. A Tennessee study (Project Star) found that students in smaller classes tended to achieve higher grades, had better high school graduation rates, and were more likely to attend college, and the gap between Black–White academic achievement narrowed by 38 percent (Herbert 2001). Not only small classes but smaller schools are also beneficial, generating higher graduation rates, more participation, less alienation, and less violence. Results from the National Longitudinal Study of Adolescent Health, a federally funded survey of 72,000 junior high and high school students, found that when the number of students in a school exceeded 1,200, students became more isolated from one another. Isolation contributes to the greater likelihood of engaging in risky behavior such as drug use, violence, and early sexual activity (reported in Fletcher 2002).

Attract and Retain Excellent Teachers

Watch on MySocLab Video: Attracting and Retaining Good Teachers

Schools need to attract and retain excellent teachers. This means higher salaries, mentoring of new teachers, and paying teachers a bonus for teaching in difficult school situations. This is especially challenging when states are inclined to make large cuts to education as they attempt to balance their budgets.

Extend the School Day and Year

The United States devotes the shortest amount of time to teaching its children of any advanced nation. The six-hour day and the nine-month calendar instituted to accommodate farm life have not changed since the nineteenth century. Pushing for an extended school year, President Obama said,

> We can no longer afford an academic calendar designed when America was a nation of farmers who needed their children at home plowing the land at the end of the day. That calendar may have once made sense, but today, it puts us at a competitive disadvantage. Our children spend over a month less in school than children in South Korea. That is no way to prepare them for a 21st century economy. (Quoted in Thomma 2009:1)

Hold Educators Accountable

Virtually every state has instituted statewide examinations in the past decade, linking the results to such things as grade promotion, high school graduation, and teacher and principal salaries. The cornerstone of the No Child Left Behind legislation is to have nationwide testing, mandating annual tests in grades 3 through 8, plus one in high school, with penalties for those schools that fail. There are difficulties with this assessment of schools, as noted earlier. Do you punish schools from economically disadvantaged districts with children who are more proficient in a language other than English? When a school fails, do you punish, or do you invest in more resources (tutoring, after-school programs, summer school, smaller class size, modern-schools wired for the future)?

As witnessed in cases in Virginia and Georgia, the pressure on teachers and administrators that their schools score well may lead to cheating or to manipulating their rankings by assisting students during test-taking, exempting special education students and slow learners from taking the tests, or through the subtle encouragement of slow learners to drop out of school.

These criticisms are valid and important, but they do not invalidate the need for standards and evaluation. The key is to heavily invest in poor children, beginning in preschool, and to enrich their school with meaningful experiences and talented, caring teachers. With such a commitment, over time all children can be held to the same standards and their schools held accountable.

Reform the Educational Philosophy of Schools

The reforms listed earlier do not question the structure and philosophy of the educational system. The present system is predicated on the needs of an industrial society in which citizens must follow orders, do assigned tasks in the appropriate order and time span, and not challenge the status quo. According to Everton, "This is why school sucks. Rather than do what it pretends to—educate, foster curiosity, expand our intellects, and promote diversity—compulsory schooling segregates people on the basis of how well they're willing to do what they're told. . . . Compulsory schooling is at its best when diluting intellects in preparation for lifetimes of subservience to corporate masters" (2004:55).

But these behaviors will not be appropriate for life in the twenty-first century. The future will likely require people who can cope with rapid turnover—changes in occupations, human relationships, and community ties. Moreover, the citizens of the future must be able to cope with myriad choices. Does an educational system built on order, a rigid time schedule, and the lecture method adequately prepare youngsters for life as it is and will be? The proponents of these and other alternatives are critical of U.S. education. They conclude that schools are failing not only children from the ghettos of large cities but also suburban and small-town youngsters. Wallis and Steptoe write,

> For the past five years, the national conversation on education has focused on reading scores, math tests and closing the "achievement gap" between social classes. This is not a story about that conversation. This is a story about the big public conversation the nation is not having about education, the one that will ultimately determine not merely whether some fraction of our children get "left behind" but also whether an entire generation of kids will fail to make the grade in the global economy because they can't think their way through abstract problems, work in teams, distinguish good information from bad or speak a language other than English. (2006:52)

Today's economy demands that schools rethink their educational philosophy and focus more on twenty-first-century skills. Those skills include (1) knowing more about the world as global citizens, (2) thinking outside the box, (3) becoming smarter about new sources of information, and (4) developing good people skills (Wallis and Steptoe 2006).

The demands of the twenty-first century require students to work cooperatively, to be knowledgeable about technology, and to think outside the box.

Chapter 16 • Education   427

Restructure Society

The approaches to equality described previously focus on changing either individual students or the schools. But if equality of opportunity is truly the goal, education cannot accomplish it alone. Closing the achievement gap between advantaged and disadvantaged students cannot be accomplished without a society-wide assault on racism and poverty. Poverty can be eliminated only through fundamental revisions in the economic and familial institutions. This is not to say that reform of the schools should be ignored. Efforts to improve our schools should parallel attempts to restructure the other institutions of society.

MySocLab ✓ Study and Review on MySocLab

■ CHAPTER REVIEW

1. The system of education in the United States is characterized by (a) conservatism—the preservation of culture, roles, values, and training necessary for the maintenance of society; (b) a belief in compulsory mass education; (c) a preoccupation with order and control; (d) fragmentation; (e) local control; (f) a lack of curriculum standardization across the country; and (g) reinforcement of the stratification system through the sifting and sorting of students.

2. The belief that our society is a meritocracy, with the most intelligent and talented at the top, is a myth. Education, instead of being the great equalizer, reinforces social inequality.

3. Educational outcomes are strongly linked to social class, race, and ethnicity.

4. The schools are structured to aid in the perpetuation of social and economic differences in several ways: (a) by being financed principally through property taxes so that rich school districts spend more per student; (b) by offering an educational experience that is correlated to a family's economic resources; (c) by increasing the cost of attending college; (d) by segregating students by race and social class; and (e) by tracking according to presumed level of ability.

5. The tracking system is closely correlated with social class; students from low-income families are disproportionately placed in the lowest track. Tracking thwarts the equality of educational opportunity for the poor by generating four effects: (a) a stigma, which lowers self-esteem; (b) the self-fulfilling prophecy; (c) a perception of school as having no future payoff; and (d) a negative student subculture.

6. Demographic changes such as the increasing number of minority students and students with a foreign-born parent are widening the gap between poor and rich students.

7. The government needs to invest in preschool programs to improve the life chances of disadvantaged youth.

8. Beginning with preschool and continuing through college, there must be a societal commitment to free education.

9. The federal government could promote equality of opportunity by providing national educational standards, a national curriculum, and national tests.

10. The federal government must level the playing field by distributing money unequally to the states according to need and encouraging states to minimize economic disparities among their school districts.

11. Promoting equality of opportunity and excellence in the public schools requires (a) reducing class and school size; (b) attracting and retaining excellent teachers; (c) extending the school year; (d) holding educators responsible for their students' outcomes; and (e) changing the philosophy of schools to meet the needs of the twenty-first century and global economy.

12. The restructuring of schools will not meet the goal of equality of educational opportunity, radical critics argue, unless the society is also restructured. This change requires a society-wide assault on racism and poverty and a redistribution of wealth to reduce the inequalities that result from economic advantage.

No Child Left Behind Act. Federal legislation requiring states to develop academic standards in reading, math, and science. All children must reach these standards by 2013–2014.

Status dropout rate. The percentage of 16- to 24-year-olds that are not enrolled in school and have not earned a high school diploma or equivalency.

Tracking. Ability grouping in schools.

Stigma. Powerful negative social label that affects a person's social identity and self-concept.

Student subculture. Members of the disadvantaged band together in a group with values and behaviors antagonistic toward school.

The Healthcare System

((Listen to Chapter 17 on **MySocLab**

LEARNING OBJECTIVES

17.1 Understand the extent of the healthcare crisis in the United States.

17.2 Explain how the healthcare system has shifted from physician-centered care to managed care, and the consequences of this shift.

17.3 Explain how access to healthcare varies by social class, race, and gender.

17.4 Compare and contrast the Bismarck, the Beveridge, and the National Health Insurance models of healthcare.

17.5 Discuss some alternatives to improve the healthcare delivery system in the United States.

This chapter is devoted to analyzing the system of healthcare in the United States. How does the current system work? Who benefits and who does not from the current system? Is reform needed? What reforms, if any, emerged from the Obama and Democratic Party initiatives? To answer these questions the chapter is divided into six parts: (1) a description of the contours of the health crises, (2) the social organization of the healthcare system, (3) the unequal access to healthcare, (4) models of national healthcare: lessons from other developed nations, (5) the politics of healthcare reform, and (6) the Affordable Health Care Act of 2010.

17.1 Understand the extent of the healthcare crisis in the United States.

CRISES IN HEALTHCARE: COST, COVERAGE, AND CONSEQUENCES

Rising Healthcare Costs

In 2010 Americans spent $2.6 trillion on healthcare. The United States has experienced a steep growth rate in medical expenses. In 2010 healthcare costs were 17.8 percent of its GDP on healthcare, up from 5 percent in 1960 and 13.6 percent in 2000. This is much more, both in amount spent per capita and percentage of gross domestic product, than any other advanced modern nation, spending around 50 percent more per person than the next highest spending countries, Switzerland and Norway. Compared to the U.S., where healthcare spending accounts for over 17 percent of GDP, Switzerland spends 11.4 percent and Norway 9.6 percent.

There are several reasons healthcare in the United States is so expensive compared to other countries. Most significant, profit drives the U.S. system: private hospitals, insurance companies, and medical equipment manufacturers seek greater returns on their investments. A report by Health and Human Services stated that in 2010 the largest insurance companies—WellPoint, United Health, Cigna, Aetna, and Humana—combined for over $15 billion in profits, a 22 percent increase from 2009. Most significant, profits for the ten largest insurance companies increased 250 percent over the last decade (Alazraki 2011).

Second, the system is inefficient. Especially costly is the paperwork involved in insurance claims from hundreds of different insurance firms. Physicians and hospitals have to hire additional personnel to deal with the layers of paperwork. According to research published in the *New England Journal of Medicine*, 31 percent of the money spent on healthcare goes for paperwork and administration (reported in Bennett 2010).

Third, many physicians practice **defensive medicine**—tests and procedures doctors perform primarily to protect themselves from lawsuits. The practice of defensive medicine means, in effect, that much of the healthcare that is delivered—as much as one-third, according to a Dartmouth study—is unnecessary (cited in Saporito 2005).

Fourth, lawsuits alleging malpractice on the part of physicians, pharmaceutical companies, and hospitals account for about 4 percent of total healthcare costs (Weitz 2004:235).

Fifth, science keeps inventing costly new tests, new drugs, and new treatments. Because health insurers pay doctors and clinical facilities most of what they charge, there are financial incentives to use the new and expensive technologies. Related to this, many physicians, to increase their incomes, install expensive equipment in their offices (ultrasound, magnetic resonance imaging, etc.). Research shows that self-referring doctors order tests for their machines far more frequently than doctors who refer patients to radiologists and other specialists (D. Levin 2004).

Another source of the high cost of healthcare in the United States is the shortage of primary-care physicians and the overuse of specialists. The income of general practitioners (primary-care physicians) is less than half, on average, of what specialists make. Thus, the financial incentive is for medical students to choose the specialty route. The services of specialists are costly, and they are more prone than primary-care physicians to rely on expensive technical procedures for their livelihood. Because there is a shortage of general practitioners, fewer patients go to them on a regular basis, which means they are less likely to receive preventive care. One estimate is that if everyone went to a general practitioner regularly, healthcare costs would go down by $67 billion a year (Carmichael 2010).

A final reason for the costly healthcare system is the wide use of prescription drugs, the greatest part of the healthcare bill of Americans. The cost in 2010 was $307.4 billion for prescription drugs. Drug costs are an especially heavy burden on the elderly, who take an average of four prescription drugs per person.

The U.S. pharmaceutical industry is comprised of profit-seeking companies that conduct research, manufacture, advertise, and sell their products. The United States is the only developed nation that allows direct-to-consumer marketing of pharmaceuticals. Significantly, the pharmaceutical companies spend more on advertising than on research and development. As a result of these factors the profit margin for pharmaceutical firms averages 17 percent, much more than found in other industries. Drug prices in the United States compared to the cost in other industrialized countries are 35 percent to 55 percent higher. Prices in Canada, for example, are one-half to one-fourth the prices in the United States (Wright 2009). As long as drug companies hold the patent to a drug, the prices rise from year to year. In 2008 the price for brand-name drugs rose 8.7 percent, more than double the inflation rate (Werner 2009). When the patent expires, the price drops immediately as generic copies are sold. When several drug manufacturers produce a similar generic, the price drops further due to the competition (Barry 2008).

To summarize, the U.S. healthcare system is comprised of various commercial enterprises seeking profits. Consider the emphasis on profit by the health insurance firms. The money paid by the insurance industry to physicians, hospitals, and pharmacies for treating insured patients is referred to as "medical loss."

> *That is, when health insurance actually pays for somebody's healthcare, the industry considers it a loss. . . . Insurance executives, securities analysts, and the business media carefully watch each company's medical loss ratio to make sure that the actual medical payments don't eat too deeply into administrative costs and profits. According to their filings with the Securities and Exchange Commission, most for-profit insurance companies maintain a medical loss ratio of about 80 percent,* which is to say that 20 cents of every dollar people pay in premiums for health insurance doesn't buy any healthcare *(emphasis added). (Reid 2009:37)*

Does the High Cost of Healthcare Translate into Good Health Consequences?

With the United States spending 50 percent more per capita on healthcare than any other country, it seems reasonable to expect that Americans would be the healthiest people on Earth, yet Americans do not fare as well as those in Western Europe, Scandinavia, Canada, and Japan. Consider the following rankings (taken from Reid 2009:30–34, 241–244):

- The World Health Organization rated the national healthcare systems of 191 countries in terms of "fairness" and the United States ranked fifty-fourth.
- The Commonwealth Fund concluded that the United States is the worst of the developed countries on "avoidable mortality." That is, deaths before age 75 from conditions that are at least partially modifiable with effective medical care. Some of these conditions are asthma, diabetes, and kidney transplants.

- The United States ranks forty-seventh in average life expectancy.
- According to the Commonwealth Fund, the United States tied for last among twenty-three nations in healthy life expectancy at age 60. This predicts not only how long a 60-year-old will live but also how that person can expect to live before the onset of predictable ailments of the elderly.
- The United States ranks last among twenty-three wealthy countries in keeping newborns alive. The **infant mortality rate** (babies who die within one year of birth) for the United States is more than twice as high as the rate in the top-ranked countries (Sweden and Japan).

Christopher Murray, a physician and health economist at Harvard, summarized the meaning of these last three rankings: "Basically you die earlier and spend more time disabled if you're an American rather than a member of most other advanced societies" (quoted in Reid 2009:244). See the "A Closer Look" panel for the unequal health consequences for children in the United States.

A Closer Look

CHILD HEALTH

Without a healthy start in life, a child can fall behind developmentally and have trouble catching up, physically, emotionally, socially, and academically. Unmet health and mental health needs greatly increase the likelihood of a child entering the cradle-to-prison pipeline. The lack of access to healthcare often is a result of the lack of health coverage. While Medicaid and the Children's Health Insurance Program (CHIP) provide health coverage to more than 36 million children each year, still more than 8 million children—one in ten—remain uninsured. Two-thirds of these uninsured children are eligible for coverage in Medicaid or CHIP but are not enrolled largely due to state-imposed barriers that differ across states. Children of color are disproportionately uninsured and as a result suffer more from preventable and treatable health conditions from birth through adulthood.

- One in five Native American children, one in six Hispanic children, and one in eight Black children are uninsured compared to one in fourteen White children.
- Black and Hispanic children, poor children, and uninsured children are more likely than White, higher income, and insured children to be in poor health. Black and Hispanic children are almost three times as likely to be in poor or only fair health as White children and are more likely to have an unmet medical need due to cost than White children.
- The United States has the second-highest infant mortality rate among thirty-two industrialized nations, and its low birthweight rate is tied for twenty-second among those same thirty-two nations. Infants born to Black mothers are almost twice as likely to be born at low birthweight as infants born to White mothers and more than twice as likely to die before

their first birthday. The rate of babies born at low birthweight has increased by 22 percent since 1984. After four decades of decline, infant mortality rates increased in 2002 and again in 2005 and 2007.
- Overall, children from different races and ethnicities have very similar immunization rates. However, income matters: Poor Black children are less likely to be fully immunized than higher-income Black children.
- Medicaid and the Children's Health Insurance Program (CHIP) work for children. The challenge is getting all children who are eligible enrolled. Currently, these programs insure one in three children in the United States who would otherwise likely go uninsured. Although still too high, the number of uninsured children in America is the lowest it has been in twenty years.

Source: Children's Defense Fund. 2011. *The State of America's Children 2011.* Washington, DC: Children's Defense Fund, p. E2.

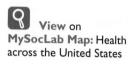

17.2 Explain how the healthcare system has shifted from physician-centered care to managed care, and the consequences of this shift.

View on **MySocLab Map:** Health across the United States

THE HEALTHCARE SYSTEM IN THE UNITED STATES PRIOR TO THE 2010 REFORM

The healthcare system in the United States has four unique characteristics. First, there are separate health systems for different categories of people. Second, the system relies heavily on for-profit private insurance to pay the bills and for-profit hospitals to care for the sick. And, third, the system is dominated by privately owned managed care.

Different Plans for Different Categories

Each of the advanced nations has one health program for its people. The United States, in sharp contrast, maintains separate systems for different categories of people (this section depends on Reid 2009:16–21).

- **The Plan for Workers.** For most working people under age 65, health insurance is linked to employment. That is, the worker and the employer share the premiums for a health insurance policy (in 2011 the cost for a family plan for a family of four amounted to a premium of $4,129 for the worker and $10,944 for the employer). But there are problems with this employer-based insurance coverage. Foremost, employers are not required to provide health insurance for their employees. Indeed, the proportion of employers including a healthcare package declined from 80 percent of all companies in 1991 to 60 percent in 2011. If not dropping health insurance coverage, employers may require employees to pay a larger proportion of the premiums or pay higher deductibles for coverage. Employers have also reduced their health costs by employing more part-time workers and independent contractors because they do not receive any benefits. Finally, basing insurance on employment means that when someone becomes unemployed or leaves an employer to work for another, he or she loses the coverage previously held.

- **The Plan for Native Americans, Military Personnel, and Veterans.** For certain categories healthcare is provided and financed by the federal government. Native Americans receive free care in government clinics. Those in the active military are cared for as needed. The Department of Veterans Affairs owns and operates clinics and hospitals for military veterans. Health practitioners in these settings are government employees. The cost of healthcare for these selected categories is free for those who qualify.

- **The Plan for Those 65 and Over.** The government has a near universal health plan for the elderly—**Medicare**. This system covers about 45 million elderly and people with disabilities of any age. Workers pay a payroll tax for Medicare, and when they become eligible most of their health expenses are paid for by the government.

View on **MySocLab Map:** Percent Uninsured

- **The Plan for the Uninsured.** The uninsured have access to medical care if they can pay the bills out-of-pocket at the time of treatment. The other alternative is to go to the emergency room in a public hospital. Public hospitals are required to attend to the medical needs of the indigent.

Private Insurance

The healthcare system for most Americans depends on the health insurance industry. Health insurance is a necessity. However, 49.9 million people—16.3 percent of the population—were uninsured in 2010, which means that they were essentially left outside the healthcare system (see Table 17.1 for the characteristics of the uninsured).

TABLE 17.1
The Medically Uninsured, 2008

Characteristics	Percent Who Are Uninsured
Total	46.3 million (15.4%)
Age	
Under 18	9.9
18–24	28.6
25–34	26.5
35–44	19.4
45–64	14.4
65 and older	1.7
Race/Ethnicity	
Whites	10.8
Asian Americans	17.6
African Americans	19.1
Latinos	30.7
Nativity	
Native	12.9
Foreign born	33.5
Household Income	
$75,000 or more	8.2
Less than $25,000	24.5
Work experience	
Worked full time	17.2
Worked part time	25.4
Did not work	26.0

Source: Carmen DeNavas, Bernadette D. Proctor, and Jessica C. Smith. 2009. "Income Poverty and Health Insurance Coverage in the U.S.: 2008." *Current Population Reports*, P60-236 (September), p. 21.

Because the health insurance firms are for-profit entities, they use various techniques to enhance their profits. Raising rates is the most common one. In 2009, for example, when WellPoint's profit was $2.9 billion, its branch in California raised premiums by as much as 39 percent (Lingeman 2010). Other profit-enhancing tactics are (Reid 2009:38–40, 230):

- They hire armies of adjusters and investigators to examine claims looking for reasons to deny payment.
- They apply "rescission," which is the legal term for "We're canceling your coverage." This occurs, typically, when an insured person, because of injury or disease, requires long-term expensive care. The justification for cancellation may be that the individual's problem is the result of being overweight, having a risky lifestyle, or not following doctor's orders.
- They do not insure people with a "preexisting condition." In other words, they refuse to insure the very people who need their services the most.

Despite these considerable shortcomings, health insurance is crucial. Individuals cannot go it alone; they need health insurance either from the government or private insurance companies. Without health insurance, bad things happen. Some examples: A Harvard study found that uninsured patients with traumatic injuries were almost twice as likely to die in the hospital as similarly injured patients with health insurance (Gawande et al. 2009). Lack of health insurance kills 45,000 adults a year, according to a study by the *American Journal of Public Health*. "More Americans die of lack of health insurance than terrorism, homicide, drunk driving, and HIV combined" (Sklar 2009:15). And, according to a Harvard University study, more than 62 percent of all personal bankruptcies are the result of overwhelming medical expenses (cited in Keller 2011).

Many Americans have inadequate insurance coverage. These underinsured are often left with medical bills they cannot afford to pay, spending more than 10 percent of their income yearly on healthcare costs and risking bankruptcy if they have a major illness. The problems of the underinsured stem from required deductibles and copayments; long waiting periods before insurance covers preexisting conditions; caps on insurance reimbursement per treatment, per year, or per lifetime; and lack of insurance for certain costs, such as nursing home care and prescriptions (Weitz 2004:243).

Significantly, the uninsured and underinsured are less likely than the insured to receive preventive care. They are more likely to avoid the high costs of doctors, medical tests, and hospitals, putting them at a much higher risk for chronic disease, disability, and premature death.

For-Profit Hospitals

Traditionally, hospitals in the United States have been nonprofit organizations run by churches, universities, and municipalities. Since the mid-1960s, however, private profit-oriented hospitals and hospital chains have emerged, and they have grown rapidly through mergers and acquisitions. These transactions, plus the explosive growth of outpatient centers, have resulted in a reduction of available hospital beds and the number of hospitals.

Also, after a merger or acquisition, the new company can purge its rolls of costly customers or, at a minimum, force them to pay steep premium hikes. This corporate strategy, which is detrimental to many patients, is, however, in compliance with the insurance laws in most states.

In addition to downsizing in the hospital industry, there has been a simultaneous process of concentration of ownership. For example, Columbia/HCA Healthcare Corporation, the world's largest for-profit hospital chain, owned, at the end of 2006, some 173 hospitals, 107 outpatient diagnostic and surgery centers, and hundreds of nursing homes, home care units, blood centers, and psychiatric facilities. Columbia's strategy has been to purchase nonprofit hospitals, creating quasi-monopolies. They then slash basic services and increase the price of services to boost profits. Richard E. Rainwater, a cofounder of Columbia, calls this strategy for hospital empire building "the Wal-Mart approach to healthcare" (Weiss 1997:68).

A number of strategies are employed by the for-profit hospitals to optimize profits. They avoid low-income areas by locating in states and neighborhoods with well-insured populations. Often they build hospitals without emergency departments, neonatal intensive units, or burn units because such facilities often lose money. For-profit hospitals have a special interest in minimizing their care for emergency patients because emergency facilities attract Medicaid and charity cases, and federal law requires that hospitals must care for all emergencies, even if the patients have no insurance. Thus, hospitals without emergency departments or with inadequate emergency facilities can avoid having to provide treatment for little or no reimbursement (Weiss 1997:72).

Private hospitals treat people who can afford their services, often leaving aside those who cannot. This practice is called **patient dumping**. These practices help the hospital's bottom line, but they do not help the poor who need specialized care. Also, patient dumping decreases the quality of care at public hospitals because it increases overcrowding and increases the demand on the limited resources of public hospitals. The practice of patient dumping also indirectly increases the profits of private hospitals by increasing the desire of many of the affluent to choose them over public hospitals.

Another strategy to increase profits is to purchase all the nonprofit hospitals in an area, creating a monopoly—and with a monopoly comes higher prices for services. Still other organizations purchase hospitals that are nonunion, which allows them to keep salaries and wages relatively low. They can also skimp on the quality of supplies, the level of cleanliness, and the level of staffing. Thus, as hospitals have become increasingly owned by private, profit-seeking interests, the cost of medical care has increased.

To summarize, proponents of for-profit hospitals argue that they are more efficient than nonprofits. Critics counter that they charge more, provide less charitable care, and have lower personnel costs because of lower patient-staff ratios (Budrys 2012:40).

Managed Care Networks

 Watch on MySocLab Video: Managed Care

Doctors used to practice alone or in a small group of doctors, treating patients, setting fees, and billing patients. Now 93 percent of medical school graduates will become employees of large clinics, managed care companies, or hospital systems (the following depends on Glasser 2009). We focus here on the surge to managed care systems that began in the 1970s. This shift to physicians as employees has important implications for the doctor–patient relationship. The relationship has become depersonalized. In the past the focus was on knowing one's patients and, in a small practice, knowing one another's patients. Patients in managed care, in contrast, often do not see the same physician. The human relationship between doctor and patient has evaporated.

> The care you get—and how long you get it—is only the care your health plan will reimburse your doctor for. . . . Personal knowledge and concern have evaporated in the world of employee–physicians, replaced by cookie-cutter best-practice guidelines and rules on prescribing drugs, acceptable lengths of hospital stays and the number of clinic patients a doctor must see per hour.
>
> And why not? Everyone in medicine knows that these are no longer the physician's patients. They belong to the insurance companies, the health plans, the hospitals. With that understanding comes personal indifference and professional exhaustion. (Glasser 2009:24)

The implication is that managed care has taken management of patients' health away from physicians and put it in the hands of ancillary personnel in corporate headquarters. Thus, physicians in managed care networks no longer have the freedom to practice what they believe is the best medicine for their patients.

Read on MySocLab Document: Healing in a Hurry: Hospitals in the Managed-Care Age

Managed care networks, as in other profit-oriented medical entities, seek to enhance the bottom line by maximizing the number of healthy and insured patients while restrict the number who are sick. In other words, the sickest patient is a cost center to be avoided. This is accomplished by **medlining** (the practice in healthcare of avoiding the sick, similar to the practice of redlining, the practice in lending and insurance of avoiding deteriorating neighborhoods or racial minority neighborhoods). One medlining strategy is to not have physicians who treat severe conditions (e.g., cardiologists) in the network. Similarly, when building clinics or recruiting doctors, the managed care network can limit exposure to the chronically sick by seeking those in affluent locales, where the incidence of AIDS and tuberculosis, for example, is low.

17.3 Explain how access to healthcare varies by social class, race, and gender.

UNEQUAL ACCESS TO HEALTHCARE

In examining the structure of a society and any of its institutions, the analyst of social problems asks, Who benefits and who suffers from the way it is organized? When healthcare delivery is the focus, the answer to this question is clear: Glaring inequities result in some categories of people being less healthy than others. Our examination of this structural inequity focuses on the three fundamental structures of inequality—class, race, and gender—which are key determinants of health (i.e., the distribution of health and disease) and healthcare delivery (i.e., the distribution of treatment). These structures of inequality make a difference, not surprisingly, with the already advantaged being advantaged even more and the already disadvantaged being disadvantaged further.

Social Class

Economic disadvantage is closely associated with health disadvantages. Put another way, how people live and die depends in large measure on the social class to which they belong (Navarro 1991:2). The poor are more likely than the affluent to suffer from certain forms of cancer (cancers of the lung, cervix, and esophagus), hypertension, low birth weight, hearing loss, diabetes, and infectious diseases (especially influenza and tuberculosis). For example, one study found that 13.9 percent with family incomes under $20,000 were diagnosed with diabetes, whereas 6.5 percent those with incomes over $80,000 had diabetes (Painter 2008). Using education as an indicator of social class, men with less than twelve years of education are more than twice as likely to die of heart disease and more than three times as likely to die as a result of injury, compared to those with thirteen or more years of education (Reuss 2001).

The physical health of poor people is more likely to be impaired than is the health of the more well-to-do because of differences in diet, sanitation, shelter, exposure to environmental hazards (e.g., air pollution, lead, untreated water), unsafe work conditions, medical treatment, and lifestyle. Regarding lifestyle, for instance, the lower a person's social class, the more likely he or she uses tobacco. Child health, as another example, varies by family income. Table 17.2 compares the health outcomes for poor and nonpoor children.

An obvious health advantage of the affluent is access to health-promoting and health-protecting resources and, when needed, access to medical services, typically paid for, at least in part, with health insurance. The lower the prestige and the lower the wages in the job, the less likely the pay will include a health benefits package provided by an employer.

The uninsured, of course, cannot afford the costs for physicians, dentists, and hospitals, so they often do without. Poor pregnant women, for example, often do not receive prenatal and postnatal healthcare. The consequences are a relatively high maternal death rate (typically from hemorrhage and infection) and a relatively high

Explore on MySocLab Activity: Social Context and Healthcare

View on MySocLab Figure: Income and Illness: People So Sick That They ...

TABLE 17.2
Poverty Matters

Health Outcomes	Low-Income Children's Higher Risk
Death in infancy	1.6 times as likely
Premature birth (under 37 weeks)	1.8 times as likely
Low birth weight	1.9 times as likely
No regular source of health care	2.7 times as likely
Inadequate prenatal care	2.8 times as likely
Family had too little food sometime in the last 4 months	8.0 times as likely

Source: Reprinted by permission from Children's Defense Fund, *The State of America's Children 2004*. Washington, DC: Children's Defense Fund.

infant mortality rate. Ironically, when the uninsured go to a doctor, they pay more for services than the more well-to-do insured patients. The reason is that health insurance companies insist on discounts. The result is that a doctor may charge $25 for a routine exam insured by a group insurance plan but charge $175 for the same exam for a person without insurance. For the role of inequality in the health of all citizens, see the "Social Problems in Global Perspective" panel.

Medicaid is the government health program for the very poor. It is funded jointly by the federal government and each state. Each state administers its version of Medicaid with few federal guidelines. Thus, Medicaid varies among states in quality, eligibility of patients, coverage, and the adequacy of fees for the services of physicians and hospitals. The consequence of this policy makes obtaining Medicaid services a function of the state in which one lives, rather than level of poverty or need. Also, when states

Social Problems in Global Perspective

THE MORE EQUAL THE SOCIETY, THE HEALTHIER THE CITIZENS

British health researchers Richard Wilkinson and Kate Pickett (2010), citing reams of research findings, make a provocative argument that among rich industrialized societies, the most equal societies are healthier than the more unequal ones. Put another way, the wealthiest and most unequal societies score lower than the more equal societies on every measure of health, happiness, and well-being (Conniff 2010).

It's not just that the poor are better off in the more equal societies (such as the Scandinavian countries, Netherlands, Japan), but

people in all income levels in these societies are. Conversely, rich people and poor people are less healthy in the more unequal countries. In the United States, for example, the culture based on competitiveness and individualism assaults the affluent, causing higher rates than in the more equal countries of hypertension, diabetes, heart disease, mental disorders such as depression, anxiety, and alcohol addiction.

Wilkinson and Pickett say:

The [health and social] problems in rich countries are not caused by

the society not being rich enough (or even by being too rich) but by the scale of material differences between people within each society being too big. What matters is where we stand in relation to others in our own society. (2010:25)

The evidence shows that reducing inequality is the best way of improving the quality of the social environment, and so the real quality of life, for all of us. . . . National standards of health . . . are substantially determined by the amount of inequality in a society. If you want to know why one country does better or worse than another, the first thing to look at is the extent of inequality. (29–30)

The infant mortality rate in the United States is more than twice as high as the rate in the countries with the lowest rate.

are short of funds, Medicaid is a likely target for budget cuts, as happened during the Great Recession. Because Medicaid is a partnership between the state and federal governments, state cuts bring a matching loss of federal money as well.

Millions of poor people in the United States are treated under Medicaid, but there are serious problems with this program. Many physicians refuse to treat Medicaid patients (because the government does not reimburse them enough for their services), resulting in delayed medical attention, and then typically in hospital emergency departments, where such patients cannot be turned away. This overburdens hospitals and postpones treatment, as patients often must wait many hours before being seen by a physician. Often the examination is superficial and the treatment careless because the attending physicians are overwhelmed by the numbers of patients.

Even when the poor do go to physicians, hospitals, and clinics, they are more likely than the more affluent to receive inferior services. The poor are more likely to receive care in inadequate (in number of staff and quality of equipment) health-care facilities. Without medical insurance, they are relegated to crowded emergency departments staffed by overworked nurses and physicians. Poor communities have fewer hospitals, and the quality of those hospitals is lower than in more affluent communities. Research shows, for example, that the best-performing hospitals are concentrated in higher-income counties. Consequently, heart patients in wealthier communities have a better chance of getting recommended treatments at their local hospitals than do patients in lower-income areas. The common belief is that the poor are accountable for their health deficiencies. The poor, from this perspective, have cultural norms that differ from the majority. Their lifestyle is less likely than the lifestyle of the more affluent to include proper exercise for a healthy heart. Their diets are more likely to contain relatively high amounts of fat. They are more likely to smoke cigarettes and to abuse drugs. The children of the poor, for instance, are more likely than the children of the affluent to be born addicted to crack and to be victims of fetal alcohol syndrome.

The essence of this argument is that the problems of ill health that beset the poor disproportionately are a consequence of their different lifestyle. This line of reasoning blames the poor for their failure to follow healthier lifestyles.

This approach, however, ignores the fundamental realities of social class. Williams (1990), in his comprehensive review of the social science literature on socioeconomic status and health, argued that privilege in the social stratification system translates both directly and indirectly into better health in several major ways. First, the privileged live in home, neighborhood, and work environments that are less stressful. The economically disadvantaged, on the other hand, are more subject to the stresses (and resulting ill health) from high rates of street crime, financial insecurity, marital instability, death of loved ones, exposure to unhealthy work conditions where they are exposed to hazardous risks and toxic substances, and exposure to pollution and toxic wastes in their neighborhoods. Poor workers are more likely than the nonpoor to be in jobs with low job security. The poor have more stress and hypertension (high blood pressure) because of living in crowded conditions and worrying about having enough resources for food, utilities, and rent. The poor also may not have adequate heat, ventilation, and sanitation, which means that they are more susceptible to infectious and parasitic diseases.

Second, the privileged have more knowledge of positive health habits (adequate sleep, refraining from smoking, drinking moderately, good nutrition, maintaining normal weight, physical exercise, and monitoring cholesterol and blood pressure levels) and the resources to implement them.

Third, the children of privilege have healthier environments in the crucial first five years of life. Many adults from disadvantaged backgrounds suffer throughout their lives because of an unhealthy environment (especially exposure to lead) in their formative years.

Fourth, the privileged have better access to and make better use of the healthcare system (the primary subject of this chapter). Early intervention at the onset of a disease and medical management of a chronic illness affect both the survival rates and the quality of life. The fewer the economic resources, the less likely a person will receive preventive care and early treatment. This is because medicine in U.S. society is a market commodity and thus is dispensed unequally to the people who can afford it.

As strong as the case is for providing equal access to medical care to all people, it is not the most fruitful approach to correcting the differences in health by socioeconomic class. The answer, most fundamentally, is to reduce the inequalities of class (and race and gender) that perpetuate poor health among the disadvantaged.

Race/Ethnicity

To examine health outcomes by race implies that there are biological differences among the races. Since race is a socially constructed concept rather than biologically based, the differences in health outcomes by race are, almost entirely, a consequence of disproportionate poverty and discriminatory treatment.

Non-White people in the United States are disproportionately poor (e.g., about one in four Latinos and African Americans are below the poverty line). This fact combined with racial discrimination leads to unfavorable patterns of health and healthcare delivery for them. Let's examine some of these health differences by race.

- **Life Expectancy.** Perhaps the best illustration of the difference that race makes on health is in life expectancy. The life expectancy for African American males in 2008 was 5.4 years less than for White males, and for Black females it is 3.7 years less than for White females. The discrepancy is even wider for Native Americans, who have the poorest health of any racial category in the United States, with a life expectancy ten years below that of the nation as a whole.

- **Infant Mortality.** The rate of infant mortality in the United States reveals striking differences by race. According to the Centers for Disease Control and Prevention (MacDorman and Mathews 2011), the Black infant mortality rate in 2009 (13.3 per 1,000 live births) was almost twice the White rate (6.7 per 1,000). Native Americans had a relatively high rate (9.2). Among Latinos, the rate for Puerto Ricans (7.7) was more than 50 percent higher than for infants of Cuban origin (5.2), a difference explained in large part by social class differences. The same relationship is found among Asians, with rates for Filipinos almost double that for infants of Chinese origin.

- **Maternal Mortality.** Statistics reveal that the death rate of African American women due to complications during birth is more than triple the rate for White mothers. The main reason for this racial disparity is that Black women are less likely to receive prenatal care.

- **Prenatal Care.** There is a substantial racial disparity in early prenatal care, with about nine of ten White mothers receiving it, compared to about three of four Latino and African American mothers.

- **Low Birth Weight.** Low birth weight is closely related to two factors: mothers not receiving adequate prenatal care and prospective mothers smoking during pregnancy. African Americans are twice as likely to be born with a low birth weight than are White children. This differential by race has remained about the same since 1960.

- **Heart Disease.** Heart disease in all its forms is the nation's leading cause of death. The evidence is that Black men are twice as likely as White men to die from heart disease before the age of 65. Overall, the national death rate from heart disease for African American men is 841 per 100,000 compared to 666 White men. A study of a national sample of 237,000 Medicare patients from 1999 through 2005 found that Black patients are less likely to receive implantable heart devices than White patients (reported in Rubin 2007).

- **Cancer.** The death rate from cancer is about three and one-half times greater for Black males than for White males. The rate for Black women is also higher than it is for White women. The problem, generally, is that African Americans (and Latinos) are more likely to be diagnosed with cancer in its later stages, making survival less likely. This, of course, is not because of race per se but because of the greater likelihood that African Americans and Latinos are poor and uninsured.

  The cancer rate is higher for African Americans than Whites for all cancers except stomach cancer and breast cancer. The latter anomaly may be explained by the apparent fact that the younger a mother is at the birth of her first child, the lower the breast cancer risk, and Black women tend to have children at younger ages. Once cancer is detected in both Blacks and Whites, Whites have a much higher survival rate. Latinos have the lowest incidence of breast cancer, but their chances of survival are not as good as Whites. Overall, Asian American women are much less likely than White or Black women to develop breast cancer, and their five-year survival rate is the best. However, for cervical cancer, the rate for Vietnamese Americans is higher than for Whites. The apparent reason for this higher rate for Vietnamese Americans is their very low early screening rates; because most of them are recent immigrants, they may be unfamiliar with the concept of preventive care or they are too poor to visit a doctor. Related to this last point, the 1996 welfare reform passed by Congress barred recent immigrants from receiving federally funded Medicaid until they had been in the country for five years (Scher 2001), and, as stated, many Vietnamese Americans are recent immigrants.

- **Dementia.**   According to the Alzheimer's Association, African Americans are almost twice as likely as Whites to have Alzheimer's and other forms of dementia, and Latinos are about one and a half times more likely to be affected (cited in Marcus 2010). The various forms of dementia are associated with high rates of diabetes and heart disease, both of which are disproportionately high among Blacks and Latinos.

- **Vision Problems.**   More than 9 million people in the United States have visual impairment, caused usually by glaucoma, diabetes, and retinal diseases. African American adults are nearly twice as likely as Whites to be legally blind or vision impaired. Latinos are more likely than Whites to be blind, primarily because of complications from diabetes, a disease they are three times more likely than Whites to have.

- **Communicable Diseases.**   The diseases especially found among the poor (e.g., influenza, pneumonia, and tuberculosis) are disproportionately found among non-Whites because they are disproportionately poor. Tuberculosis occurs fourteen times more frequently among African Americans than Whites, and it is four times more likely to occur among Hispanics than Whites. Native Americans are four times more likely to die from tuberculosis and dysentery than are non–Native Americans.

  Cultural or lifestyle differences offer some explanations. This blaming-the-victim approach argues that racial minorities do not take proper care of themselves. Their diets tend to be high in fat, sugar, and salt. They are more likely to smoke (a fact not lost on the tobacco companies, as they target their products and advertising to African Americans and Latinos). They are less likely than members of the majority to exercise. Thus, Blacks, for example, have a high incidence of obesity, hypertension, and heart disease.

  But even though lifestyle differences among the races account for some variations in health, other factors are more important. Economic factors explain much of the variation. Minority racial and ethnic groups are disproportionately poor. This means that many of them must live in rat-infested neighborhoods, where they are exposed to diseases carried by these vermin. Their neighborhoods also have high concentrations of lead (in the paint and plumbing), which exposes their children to many health dangers, including brain damage. Living in poverty also means living in inadequate shelter, where exposure to the cold leads to complications such as bronchitis and pneumonia. Living in overcrowded situations leads to the spread of communicable diseases. A low income means reliance on a diet of cheap, fattening, nonnutritious food.

  Living in poverty also results in the disruption of social networks and in heightened fears and anxieties caused by arson, drug abuse, and violent crime. Regarding this last point, Blacks are nearly six times more likely than Whites to be murdered, are almost twice as likely to be robbed, and are raped at a rate nearly double that of Whites.

  The poor also are less likely to receive adequate medical attention. Many, as noted earlier, do not have medical insurance, and being poor, they cannot afford medical care on a regular, preventive basis. The absence of insurance coverage is related to race, with Latinos and African Americans much less likely to have medical insurance than Whites. As stated earlier, recent immigrants are denied Medicaid until they have been in this country for five years. Thus, they delay going to the physician, dentist, or hospital until the health problem is too serious to ignore. This may mean that the problem is too advanced for a cure.

  But even when African Americans and Latinos seek medical attention, they often are given less attention than Whites. For example, according to a study of 7,000 patients, Black men were 25 to 30 percent less likely to get standard tests to detect a heart attack than were White men (Fischman 2007).

The poor in general, and African Americans and other racial minorities in particular, are much more likely than Whites to rely on emergency and hospital outpatient departments than on a family physician. The two most important reasons for this are that they cannot afford a family physician and, even if they can afford one, physicians are in short supply where the poor live. Most of the uninsured live in areas that have inadequate medical care, including a shortage of primary-care physicians.

There are four negative outcomes from this for racial minorities. First, they do not meet regularly with a physician who is familiar with their health history. Second, the number of hospitals in the poor sections of cities and where rural poverty is prevalent is declining. Third, federal cutbacks since the 1980s have resulted in decreased medical attention for the poor. And fourth, even when health services are accessible, racial minorities may face racial discrimination in attempting to obtain care.

Thus, a major reason for the high death rate of African Americans from cancer is because they often do not have access to quality healthcare. But the link may be stronger than that—when African Americans (and other racial minorities) have access to good medical care, they do not receive the same treatment as do Whites, a consequence of economics, and possibly of discrimination. Racial minorities (and women), for example, wait longer than White men for liver transplants and are less likely to undergo bypass surgery or angioplasty, resulting in their reduced heart disease survival.

Poverty and its associated problems are exacerbated by the social inequalities associated with race. To be African American, Latino, or Native American means, for many people, to be considered inferior, even to be despised. Thus, hierarchy and its attendant discrimination create tensions and stresses. African Americans have higher blood pressure than do Whites. Is the reason genetic or social in origin? African Americans, especially those with low income, have higher hypertension (high blood pressure) rates than the more well-to-do. This is partially the result of a poor diet. But it also is reasonable to assume that the stress associated with hypertension results from blocked social mobility, anger over perceived and real injustices, fear of crime, and being treated as a social inferior.

Gender

Read on MySocLab Document: Health Care Reform—A Woman's Issue

The health of women and the healthcare they receive reflect primarily their status in society and only secondarily their physiological differences from men. Women do have significant health advantages over men; for example, their life expectancy exceeds that of males by about seven years. These advantages begin in the womb, where female fetuses have a 10 percent higher survival rate than do male fetuses. These advantages continue after birth and throughout the life cycle, as male death rates exceed female death rates at all ages. Women are less likely than men to die from the leading causes of death, including heart disease, cancer, accidents, suicide, and homicide (the only exceptions are death from diabetes and Alzheimer's).

There are both biological and social reasons for some of the health advantages that women have over men. During early childhood, girls have biological benefits over boys, as exhibited by their greater resistance to infectious and chronic diseases. As adults, women in the past were more protected than were men, at least until menopause, especially from heart disease and hypertension, because of the hormone estrogen.

More important, though, than the biological differences between the sexes are the significant social differences that also account for gender differences in health. The adolescent and young adult male gender role includes being assertive and daring. This accounts for the greater likelihood of males being in automobile accidents (five out of seven victims of traffic accidents are men), driving while drunk, and using more alcohol (men are three times as likely to be alcoholics), illegal drugs, and cigarettes (recently, however, the number of women who smoke is increasing, so the difference between men and women is converging). Males also are more likely than females to work at risky jobs (including military combat).

The female gender role is more conducive to good health in several ways. Women are expected to be more knowledgeable about health matters and thus to be more aware of changes in their bodies than are men. Women are also more likely to see a physician or be admitted into a hospital than are men (traditional men tend to see this behavior in males as a sign of weakness).

Women on average are less likely than men to have medical insurance. This is because they are more likely than men to work at part-time jobs or doing contingent work, thus not qualifying for employer-supplied health insurance. Also, insurance coverage for women stops under their husbands' policies when they are widowed or divorced. These disadvantages are strongest for women between ages 45 and 64 (before they qualify for Medicare) and especially for African American and Latina women in this age category (about 35 percent of women compared with two-thirds of men). As a result, millions of women are too poor to buy health insurance but earn too much to get public aid.

Whether one has health insurance is literally a matter of life and death. Using the example of breast cancer, researchers have found that uninsured women are less likely to receive cancer-screening services than are women with private insurance, less likely to have their breast cancer adequately evaluated, less likely to get regular mammograms, and less likely to have their breast cancer aggressively treated (Jackson 2006).

Women face two major health risks. One is childbearing, which can be unhealthy, even deadly, for mothers. The other health risk is a consequence of traditional gender roles. Because women in U.S. society are evaluated by their physical appearance, they are much more likely than men to suffer from anorexia nervosa and bulimia (conditions that result when individuals take extraordinary measures to lose weight). Women are also much more likely than men to risk surgery for cosmetic reasons (tummy tucks, liposuction, breast implants or reduction, and facelifts), which may have negative health effects.

The advantage women have over men in mortality rates is overshadowed by the advantages men receive from the medical profession. First, the medical schools and the medical profession are dominated by males. Women in medicine are vastly over-represented in the nurturant, supportive, underpaid, and relatively powerless roles of nurse and aide, or if they are physicians, they are most likely to be in general practice or specialize in pediatrics.

Second, until 1990, when the government confirmed that women had been intentionally left out of federally funded medical research, much medical research has excluded women as subjects. For example, the major study on whether taking daily doses of aspirin can reduce the risk of a heart attack used 22,071 subjects—all men. In most cases, a drug proved effective in men is also effective for women. But the differences in hormone proportions and the menstrual cycle can be important. In the aspirin study, it would have been useful to determine whether taking aspirin prevents heart attacks in premenopausal women, in only postmenopausal women, or not in any women. Another study used 12,866 male subjects to explore the links between heart disease and high cholesterol, lack of exercise, and smoking. By excluding women from the study, the medical profession has no clear scientific proof whether the linkages among these variables found for men also occur for women.

The National Women's Health Resource Center has noted that other major health studies have overlooked women. As in the aspirin and heart disease studies, research using only male subjects has studied diet, exercise, and cholesterol; Type A behavior and heart disease; binge drinking; and alcohol and blood pressure.

Third, research appears to put women's health priorities second to men's. For example, the National Institutes of Health has spent much less of its research budget on women's healthcare issues than on men's issues. Perhaps this explains why medical research has yet to come up with an acceptable, safe, and effective male contraceptive. This deficiency has meant that women have had to bear the responsibilities and health risks of contraception. This oversight in medical research is gradually being rectified. Recent research has uncovered genes linked to hereditary breast cancer, made advances in the prevention of osteoporosis, and created drugs to fight ovarian cancer.

Fourth, female patients interacting with male physicians encounter a number of sexist practices. These include paternalistic attitudes; insensitivity toward the special problems of women surrounding the menstrual cycle, childbirth (see the "Voices" panel), and menopause; siding with husbands who were leery of vasectomies and performing, rather, tubal ligations on wives, even though the cost and medical risk were much greater; and requiring more specific tests for men than for women during diagnostic examinations. Another example of male physicians' insensitivity to women often occurs during an unwanted pregnancy. Many male physicians often consider women's interests secondary to fetal survival.

Fifth, women are discriminated against in the treatment they receive or do not receive. For example, a study found that women with cardiac complaints were about 50 percent more likely than men to experience delays by emergency medical services (Boyles 2009). Moreover, women are less likely than men to receive implantable heart devices (Rubin 2007).

HIV/AIDS: The Intersection of Class, Race, and Gender

Since the killer HIV/AIDS (acquired immunodeficiency syndrome) epidemic began in 1981, the worldwide death toll is 30 million people. According to the World Health Organization, over 34 million were infected in 2010 worldwide, including 3.4 million children. In 2010, some 2.7 million were newly infected with HIV. The global epidemic appears to have peaked in 1996, and the disease seems to be stable in most regions, except for sub-Saharan Africa where 5 percent of the adult population is infected (Avert 2011).

The first known cases of AIDS were reported in the United States in 1981. Since then, an estimated 1.7 million people have been infected with HIV with more than 615,000 deaths. Approximately 1.2 million people are currently infected with HIV, with about 50,000 added each year, with 17,000 deaths annually (Healy and Maugh 2011). Having HIV is no longer a death sentence, however, because new drugs are available that are effective in preventing HIV from becoming AIDS. The problem is that these new drugs go only to those who can afford them, and to a fortunate few who are poor but live in states with generous assistance, resulting in the benefits

Voices

DOES THE DOCTOR'S GENDER MATTER?

[A] female OB or a female nurse can sympathize a little more with what you are going through than a male. . . . [Male attendants] could possibly watch their wives go through it, but they don't know what it's like exactly.

—Tricia, White mother of two

I wanted to be sure to be heard, and I know with medicine, being a child of a physician, I just [know] at times that women's concerns can be seen as over-reactive, exaggerating, unfounded concerns.

—Tonya, African American mother of one

You know, when I said to her, "Gee, this really hurts over here," she could relate to it. With a guy, it was kind of like, "It's all just in your mind." She really could relate to everything. And her personality was wonderful, and she had a great bedside manner. She listened to your questions.

—Jill, White mother of two

These women's comments exemplify many others' feelings about women as doctors.* A 1996 study of women's childbirth experiences in a mid-Atlantic state found that the gender of the doctor did affect many women's reproductive experiences. Eight (or 42 percent) of nineteen interviewees specifically chose female doctors. Some explained that they had had prior bad experiences with male OB-GYNs or intimates and thus had switched to female doctors at some point. Other women specifically wanted a doctor who should be "more caring," hinting that feelings and emotions during pregnancy and childbirth were important. Others explained that they wanted to be on more "equal footing" with their attendant.

Vicki, a mother of two from England, recounted her experience with a male OB-GYN:

Yeah, he basically gave me no information. When I asked him about birth courses, you know, . . . he told me to go to the birthing course at the hospital. And [the class]

*All names of women have been changed to ensure confidentiality.

was mostly on drugs, it was very strange. And he patted me on the head and said, "I'll handle it, don't you worry about a thing." And I didn't like that, and I didn't want any part of it [the second time].

The authoritative medical knowledge that this doctor held supposedly gave him the right to withhold certain types of information from Vicki, leaving her with little knowledge of what would happen during birth. He assumed that Vicki would be comfortable simply allowing him to "handle it." The desire to be heard and informed is also evident in this next woman's response:

Just from the different experiences I've had, [female doctors will] sit down and listen to you more, they'll understand your concerns, or they'll answer questions you might not have thought of that they've known. . . . Just in general, they seem more, not more caring or sympathetic, just open to other ideas, instead of being a leader person. (Heidi, White mother of three)

The fact that female doctors often have had their own birthing experiences was an additional reason to choose them, for experience was equated with greater competency, knowledge, and understanding of the birth process. Thus, female doctors brought comfort for many women on many levels. Stephanie, a White mother of two, stated: "You have a lot going on, you know, they're prodding and poking you and I just felt—because I'm a modest person—I just knew that I would be more comfortable with a female [doctor]." Rachel, a White mother of one, stated that she "would be more comfortable [asking a] myriad of questions with a woman. I felt that I could get a little bit more of an insight especially because [my doctor] had had children as well." And Natasha, another White mother of one, suggested that she was not comfortable "talking about this kind of stuff to begin with, so I have a hard time talking about this stuff even with a woman. I probably would have been red in the face the whole time talking to a man."

In contrast to the situations explained here, women who received prenatal care from male doctors did not necessarily "choose" the gender of their doctor. Of those who had male doctors, only three out of eleven (approximately 25 percent) stated that the gender of their doctor mattered to them. Thus, we can assume that the rest of the women interviewed simply followed a pre-established model for birth (perhaps going to doctors whom relatives or friends recommended), which included birth in a hospital setting with a male doctor in charge. If gender did matter to a woman, then she was more likely to seek out a female doctor.

Source: Heather E. Dillaway. 2000. Michigan State University, Department of Sociology. This essay was written expressly for *Social Problems*.

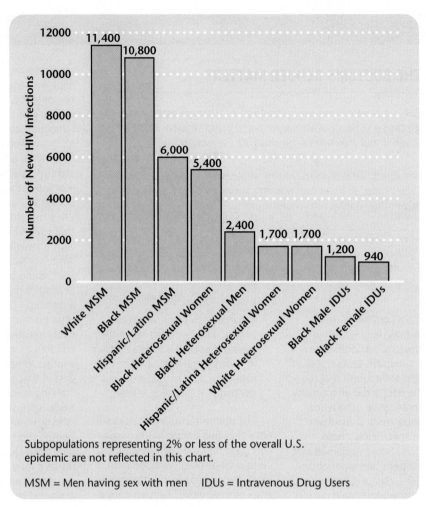

Subpopulations representing 2% or less of the overall U.S. epidemic are not reflected in this chart.

MSM = Men having sex with men   IDUs = Intravenous Drug Users

FIGURE 17.1

Race/Ethnicity of Persons (Including Children) with HIV/AIDS Diagnosed During 2007

Source: Centers for Disease Control. "HIV in the United States: Factsheets." http://www.cdc.gov/hiv/resources/factsheets/us.htm.

Watch on MySocLab Video: ABC Primetime: AIDS in Black America

disproportionately going to those with class and racial privilege. Especially hard hit are minority men and women (see Figure 17.1). Consider the following facts for the United States (Centers for Disease Control and Prevention 2012):

- Although African Americans make up about 13 percent of the population, they account for about half (46 percent) of all people in the United States who live with HIV.
- HIV/AIDS is the leading cause of death for Blacks 25 to 44 years of age (the fifth leading cause of death for Whites and the fourth leading cause for Latinos).
- The number of people with HIV per 100,000 population in 2010 was 15.3 for Whites, 44.7 for Latinos, and 116.0 for African Americans.
- Two-thirds of new infections among women occur in Black women. In 2007, the rate of new AIDS cases for Black women was twenty-two times that of White women and five times greater than the infection rate for Latinas. The rate of AIDS for Black men was almost eight times the rate for White men.

Those most susceptible to HIV/AIDS are men who have sex with other men (71 percent) and intravenous drug users who share needles. For women, 75 percent received the virus from heterosexual contact and 23 percent from drug injections. Young Black gay men are the most vulnerable. According to the CDC,

> *The AIDS virus continues to spread widely among African Americans, who represent just 14% of Americans ages 13–29 but account for half of new infections in that group. . . . Young black gay and bisexual men account for 55% of infections among African Americans in that age group. . . . (Cited in Sternberg 2010:7D)*

MODELS FOR NATIONAL HEALTHCARE: LESSONS FROM OTHER SOCIETIES

The United States, as we have stated, spends much more for healthcare, both in total dollars and as a percentage of its gross national product, than any other nation. Yet, all major indicators of national health show that other nations are getting more for their health dollars than does the United States. Almost 50 million Americans do not have health insurance, and millions more are underinsured. The system is fragmented, inefficient, and wasteful. Most important, the for-profit system that prevails in the United States lacks a social mission; it is more responsive to Wall Street than to Main Street. Economist Robert Kuttner says this:

> *The only way to cut through this mess is, of course, to have universal health insurance. All insurance is a kind of cross-subsidy. The young, who on average need little care, subsidize the old. The well subsidize the sick.*
>
> *With a universal system, there is no private insurance industry spending billions of dollars trying to target the well and avoid the sick, because everyone is in the same system. There is no worry about "portability" when you change jobs, because everyone is in the same system. And there are no problems choosing your preferred doctor or hospital, because everyone is in the same system. (1998:27)*

Given this gloomy health climate, are there reforms that would improve the healthcare system in the United States? Other advanced societies have found ways that fit their history, politics, economy, and national values. The general patterns fit into three basic arrangements (the following depends on Reid 2009:17–20).

The Bismarck Model

Named after Otto von Bismarck, who invented the welfare state in Germany in the nineteenth century, this system is found today in Germany, Japan, France, Belgium, and Switzerland. Like the U.S. system, it uses private health insurance plans, usually financed by both employers and employees. Unlike the United States, though, Bismarck-type plans cover everyone, and the insurance companies do not make a profit. There is tight government regulation of medical services and fees to contain cost.

The Beveridge Model

This system, named after a British reformer, is found in Great Britain, Italy, Spain, Cuba, and most of Scandinavia. Healthcare is provided and financed by the government. There are no medical bills since medical treatment is a public service, like the public library (Reid 2009:18). Most hospitals and clinics are owned by the government, and many doctors are government employees. There are private doctors who are reimbursed by the government for their services. There are low costs because the government controls what physicians can do and what they can charge. Ironically,

> *The two purest examples of the Beveridge Model—or "socialized medicine"—are both found in the Western Hemisphere: Cuba and the U.S. Department of Veterans Affairs. In both*

of those systems, all the healthcare professionals work for the government in government-owned facilities, and patients receive no bills. (Reid 2009:18)

The National Health Insurance Model

View on **MySocLab Figure:** Spending on Healthcare, Selected Countries

This system, found in Canada, Taiwan, and South Korea, includes elements of both Bismarck and Beveridge models. Healthcare providers are private, but the payer is a government-run insurance program. This is known as a **single-payer plan**. The government insurance plan (either a federal or a provincial plan) collects monthly premiums from every citizen and pays the medical bills.

> *Since there's no need for marketing, no expensive underwriting offices to deny claims, and no profit, these universal insurance programs tend to be cheaper and much simpler administratively than American-style private insurance. As a single-payer covering everybody, the national insurance plan tends to have considerable market power to negotiate for lower prices [for lower pharmaceutical costs, for example]. (Reid 2009:18–19)*

Most advocates of universal health insurance argue that the United States should adopt a single-payer plan similar to the Canadian plan. This plan would serve all citizens at lower cost; Canada spends 10 percent of its gross domestic product (GDP) on healthcare, compared to 17.8 percent in the United States. Canadians spent $3,678 per person in 2009 on healthcare, compared to $6,714 for each American, yet Canada has better health outcomes (see Figure 17.2). It would be more efficient not only in serving everyone but also in reducing bureaucracy and paperwork; health administration costs in the United States are double the costs in Canada. David Himmelstein

FIGURE 17.2

Health Outcomes: United States vs. Canada

Source: Reprinted from "Healthcare for All," the Fall 2006 *YES!* Magazine, PO Box 10818, Bainbridge Island, WA 98110.

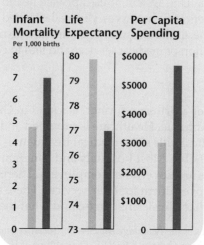

Side-by-Side: No Comparison

Canada   U.S.

Canada and the U.S. used to be twins on public-health measurements. Here's how it looks after 35 years of Canadian universal health care:

Infant Mortality Per 1,000 births   Life Expectancy   Per Capita Spending

Social Policy

A CANADIAN DOCTOR DIAGNOSES U.S. HEALTHCARE

Michael M. Rachlis

Universal health insurance is on the American policy agenda for the fifth time since World War II. In the 1960s, the United States chose public coverage for only the elderly and the very poor, while Canada opted for a universal program for hospitals and physicians' services. As a policy analyst, I know there are lessons to be learned from studying the effect of different approaches in similar jurisdictions. But, as a Canadian with lots of American friends and relatives, I am saddened that Americans seem incapable of learning them.

Our countries are joined at the hip. We peacefully share a continent, a British heritage of representative government, and now ownership of GM. And, until fifty years ago, we had similar health systems, healthcare costs, and vital statistics.

The United States' and Canada's different health insurance decisions make up the world's largest health policy experiment. And the results?

On coverage, all Canadians have insurance for hospital and physician services. There are no deductibles or co-pays. Most provinces also provide coverage for programs for home care, long-term care, pharmaceuticals, and durable medical equipment, although there are co-pays.

On the United States side, 46 million people have no insurance, millions are underinsured, and healthcare bills bankrupt more than 1 million Americans every year.

Lesson No. 1: A single-payer system would eliminate most U.S. coverage problems.

On costs, Canada spends 10 percent of its economy on healthcare; the United States spends 16 percent. The extra 6 percent of GDP amounts to more than $800 billion per year. The spending gap between the two nations is almost entirely because of higher overhead. Canadians don't need thousands of actuaries to set premiums or thousands of lawyers to deny care. Even the U.S. Medicare program has 80 to 90 percent lower administrative costs than private Medicare Advantage policies. And providers and suppliers can't charge as much when they have to deal with a single payer.

Lessons No. 2 and 3: Single-payer systems reduce duplicative administrative costs and can negotiate lower prices.

Because most of the difference in spending is for non-patient care, Canadians actually get more of most services. We see the doctor more often and take more drugs. We even have more lung transplant surgery. We do get less heart surgery, but not so much less that we are any more likely to die of heart attacks. And we now live nearly three years longer, and our infant mortality is 20 percent lower.

Lesson No. 4: Single-payer plans can deliver the goods because their funding goes to services, not overhead.

The Canadian system does have its problems, and these also provide important lessons. Notwithstanding a few well-publicized and misleading cases, Canadians needing urgent care get immediate treatment. But we do wait too long for much elective care, including appointments with family doctors and specialists and selected surgical procedures. We also do a poor job managing chronic disease.

However, according to the New York-based Commonwealth Fund, both the American and the Canadian systems fare badly in these areas. In fact, an April U.S. Government Accountability Office report noted that U.S. emergency room wait times have increased, and patients who should be seen immediately are now waiting an average of 28 minutes. The GAO has also raised concerns about two- to four-month waiting times for mammograms.

On closer examination, most of these problems have little to do with public insurance or even overall resources. Despite the delays, the GAO said there is enough mammogram capacity.

These problems are largely caused by our shared politico-cultural barriers to quality of care. In nineteenth-century North America, doctors waged a campaign against quacks and snake oil salesmen and attained a legislative monopoly on medical practice. In return, they promised to set and enforce standards of practice. By and large, it didn't happen. And perverse incentives like fee-for-service make things even worse.

Using techniques like those championed by the Boston-based Institute for Healthcare Improvement, providers can eliminate most delays. In Hamilton, Ontario, seventeen psychiatrists have linked up with 100 family doctors and eighty social workers to offer some of the world's best access to mental health services. And in Toronto, simple process improvements mean you can now get your hip assessed in one week and get a new one, if you need it, within a month.

(continued)

Lesson No. 5: Canadian health-care delivery problems have nothing to do with our single-payer system and can be fixed by re-engineering for quality.

U.S. health policy would be miles ahead if policymakers could learn these lessons. But they seem less interested in Canada's or any other nation's experience than ever. Why?

American democracy runs on money. Pharmaceutical and insurance companies have the fuel.

Analysts see hundreds of billions of premiums wasted on overhead that could fund care for the uninsured. But industry executives and shareholders see bonuses and dividends.

Compounding the confusion is traditional American ignorance of what happens north of the border, which makes it easy to mislead people. Boilerplate anti-government rhetoric does the same. The U.S. media, legislators, and even presidents have claimed that our "socialized" system doesn't let us choose our own doctors. In fact, Canadians have free choice of physicians. It's Americans these days who are restricted to "in-plan" doctors.

Unfortunately, many Americans won't get to hear the straight goods because vested interests are promoting a caricature of the Canadian experience.

Source: Michael M. Rachlis. 2009. "A Canadian Doctor Diagnoses U.S. Health-care." *Los Angeles Times* (August 3), online: http://www.latimes.com/news/opinion/la-oe-nachlis3-2009aug03,0,538126.story.

and Steffie Woolhandler, cofounders of Physicians for a National Healthcare Program, argued that if the United States cut its medical bureaucratic costs to Canadian levels, it would save nearly $400 billion annually (cited in Hastings Center 2009: para 5). (See the "Social Policy" panel for an analysis of the Canadian and U.S. healthcare systems, written by a Canadian physician.)

17.5 Discuss some alternatives to improve the healthcare delivery system in the United States.

REFORMING THE HEALTHCARE SYSTEM OF THE UNITED STATES

The United States is the only developed nation without some form of universal healthcare. There have been attempts to reform the U.S. healthcare system going back to 1912, but they have all failed. Teddy Roosevelt campaigned for a national healthcare plan in 1912, but he was defeated by Woodrow Wilson. In 1915 Congress debated a bill providing for universal medical coverage, but when the United States declared war with Germany in 1917, the issue died. In 1935 President Franklin D. Roosevelt passed the Social Security Act. This legislation originally included healthcare reform but it was dropped because it was considered too divisive. In 1943 Congress considered a bill to establish a national medical care and hospitalization fund, but it failed to pass. In 1949 President Harry Truman called for the creation of a national health insurance plan, but the American Medical Association denounced it as "socialized medicine" and when war broke out with North Korea, it was abandoned. In 1965 President Lyndon Johnson sought to enact universal healthcare. He dropped the universal aspect of it but was able to establish Medicare and Medicaid. In 1974 President Richard Nixon proposed a version of national healthcare similar to the Obama proposal of 2009, but the Watergate scandal intervened and it did not survive. (At the same time, Canada adopted its single-payer plan.) In 1976 President Carter pushed for a mandatory health plan, but an economic recession derailed it. In 1986 President Reagan signed COBRA, a requirement that employers allow former workers to stay on the company health plan after leaving a job for eighteen months. President Bill Clinton in 1993 presented a national healthcare plan to Congress, which required businesses to cover their workers and mandated everyone to have health insurance, but it failed to pass. Then in 2009 President Obama, faced with a dysfunctional system, made the overhaul of the healthcare system his primary goal.

The Politics of Health Reform

During 2009 and 2010 the members of Congress engaged in heated debate over health reform. The sides coalesced into two contentious factions—Democrats generally favoring change and Republicans blocking reform measures with unanimous opposition. Undergirding the arguments was a basic philosophical issue: Is the organization of healthcare a concern of government (the Democratic position), or should it be left to the marketplace (the Republican position)? At a practical level, roughly $2.6 trillion, the amount spent on healthcare annually, was at stake. The division of that money was at the center of the debate. Insurance and pharmaceutical companies feared losing their profits. Doctors, hospitals, and managed care networks were concerned about their futures. Individuals and families worried about how changing the system would affect their pocketbooks as well as the quality of healthcare they would receive. In short, there were interest groups with a huge stake in the status quo. The result was a bitter struggle, with a variety of tactics employed by the forces for and against changing the healthcare system. We focus here on the efforts opposing reform.

• **Influencing the Public.**   Interest groups on all sides of the healthcare debate spent more than $210 million on television advocacy advertising in 2009 (Seelye 2010). An orchestrated campaign was also waged by conservative commentators such as Rush Limbaugh and media outlets such as Fox News to persuade the public that Obama and the Democrats were leading the country down a wrong and dangerous path, with an ever-greater government intrusion into the lives of individual Americans. Among their arguments were that the government overreach was tantamount to losing freedom, that it would subsidize abortion, that it would lead to "death panels" composed of Washington bureaucrats, and that it would be too costly.

The efforts by those opposed to healthcare reform were successful in turning public opinion against reform and in turning some people such as Tea Partiers into rabid opponents. The signs at their rallies showed Obama as Hitler, displayed communist symbols such as the hammer and sickle, and stated: "Obamacare: Socialized Medicine," "Obama Lies and Granny Dies," "No Socialism—No Death Panels!" "Obama Care: Goodbye to Old People!" and "Congress Ain't My Doctor."

© Mike Keefe, The Denver Post and InToon.com.

- **Influencing Congress.** In 2009 there were 3,098 health-sector lobbyists in Washington—nearly six for each member of Congress. Their efforts were intended to either block reform legislation or to shape the resulting legislation to maintain their advantage (Sklar 2009). The nonpartisan Center for Responsive Politics found that the federal lobbying by health and health insurance industries amounted to $648 million in 2009, the most money ever by a business sector for federal lobbying (cited in Seelye 2010). One interested industry, the pharmaceutical and health products industry, spent $266.8 million on lobbying in 2009, an all-time record for a single industry (Jackson 2010).

  Another tactic to influence the final composition of healthcare legislation was funneling money to key legislators. Nearly 60 percent of the healthcare industry's campaign contributions to members of Congress went to lawmakers sitting on five powerful committees where the health reform legislation was crafted. The hope behind these contributions was that the influential legislators would form the legislation to their advantage. Max Baucus, for example, chair of the Senate Finance Committee, was the leading recipient of Senate campaign contributions from the hospitals, insurers, and other medical interest groups, receiving $1.5 million in 2007 and 2008 (Eggen 2009).

- **Legislative Blockage by the Minority.** The Republicans, as the minority party in both houses of Congress, agreed on a strategy of total opposition to health reform. For example, when the Senate voted on a crucial healthcare bill on Christmas Eve 2009, not a single Republican voted in favor. In the 435-seat House, only one Republican broke ranks. There were two roots to this negativism. For some, opposition was based on principle, that it was wrongheaded to go with a government plan rather than let the marketplace determine healthcare. For others, their extreme partisanship was political—to deny Obama a major victory (Klein 2010:21).

  Also, the Republicans in the Senate used the rules of that body such as the filibuster to block health reform legislation (see Chapter 2). The rules require sixty votes to stop a filibuster by the minority party, and the Republicans used this to block change (*Nation* 2009:3).

Lisa Benson/Cartoonist Group

The Obama Plan

Watch on
MySocLab Video:
Obama Healthcare Plan

Because the Democrats controlled both houses of Congress, different bills reforming healthcare passed in the House and in the Senate. The final bill that emerged from a conference committee did not provide universal health insurance through a single payer plan, which dismayed progressives. It did increase the role of government in the healthcare system, which upset conservatives. The Affordable Health Care Act (also known as "Obamacare") was passed in 2010, with some provisions to take effect immediately and others delayed until 2014.

What emerged in the struggle for passage was legislation with these changes to the status quo.

- There was a mandate that everyone take out health insurance, just as drivers are legally required to have car insurance or pay a fine. The government would subsidize people with low incomes, covering their premiums through expanded Medicaid coverage or tax credits. The rationale for the mandate was twofold: to protect people from the consequences of going unprotected and to prevent society from having to pay for the health costs of the uninsured (Coy 2012).
- Individuals could keep their existing insurance plans if they choose.
- Exchanges were created on which small businesses and people who buy their own coverage directly from insurers could choose from an array of private plans that would compete for their business.
- A Medicare oversight board was created with authority over reimbursement rates.
- There was security for those who were laid off or changed employers, or switched to employers that do not offer insurance as they were now guaranteed coverage.
- Individuals could not be denied coverage for a preexisting medical condition or because their medical bills were too expensive.
- Insurance companies were blocked from putting lifetime caps on coverage.
- Young adults were covered by their parents' policy until age 26.
- Approximately 31 million previously uninsured became insured.

- **What the Plan Is Not.** The Affordable Health Care Act was not socialism. If it were, the government would provide the health insurance, own the hospitals, and hire health professionals as employees. The government was to regulate and subsidize health insurance, but it was not a takeover of the American healthcare system. Although considered in the legislative process, a public option was not included in the final bill. This would have allowed the government to compete with private insurance, thus providing more competition, lower rates, and more government intrusion in the marketplace. In short, the plan kept healthcare as a mostly private system.

The plan did not hurt the commercial health insurers. Although constrained by no longer being able to turn away costly patients, health insurers benefitted by an increased number of insured people because everyone was required to have insurance, and they did not have to compete with government insurance.

The Supreme Court and the Affordable Health Care Act

Attorneys-General from twenty-six states (each a Republican from a Republican-dominated state) filed challenges to the Affordable Health Care Act with the Supreme Court—most particularly to the constitutionality of its centerpiece—the individual mandate that everyone buy some kind of health insurance or face penalties. In late June 2012, two years after passage, the Supreme Court ruled by a 5–4 vote to uphold

In 2012 the Supreme Court ruled by a 5–4 vote to uphold the constitutionality of the individual mandate and most of the provisions of the Affordable Health Care Act.

the constitutionality of the individual mandate and most of the provisions of the Affordable Health Care Act.

- **The Big Picture.** The Court's decision moved the United States closer to the other advanced industrial societies that guarantee health insurance to their citizens. Not perfectly, since approximately 20 million will still be left uninsured. But clearly the Act, validated by the Supreme Court, was a move in that direction.

  The Affordable Health Care Act affirmed the high value that Americans have for equality of opportunity as it did do much to help the disadvantaged (children, young adults, women, the very poor, those suffering from chronic medical conditions, and those uninsured by their employers). Most particularly, 30 million people without health insurance will be covered by 2016.

- **The Ingredients of the Affordable Health Care Act.** Prior to the Supreme Court decision, the Affordable Health Care Act was in limbo. It was not clear whether the Act was constitutional, as constitutional law professors differed in their interpretations and judges on various lower courts gave decisions on both sides of the issues. With the decision by the Court, however, the Act was now the law of the land.

  Some parts of the Act, already in effect, remained so: (1) Young adults could stay on their parents' health insurance up to age 26 (affecting 3.1 million young adults); (2) insurers could not deny coverage to children with preexisting health problems; (3) insurers could no longer limit how much policies would pay out to each person annually and over a lifetime (affecting 105 million); and (4) seniors and people with disabilities could save money through improved Medicare prescription benefits (affecting 5.3 million).

  According to the Act, beginning in 2014: (1) Almost everyone would be required to have insurance or pay a fine. This sounds ominous, but it affects only 7 percent of the population, and most of them will be eligible for subsidies to help purchase their coverage (Urban Institute study, reported in Pugh 2012); (2) businesses employing more than fifty employees would face fines if they did not offer coverage for their employees; (3) newly created insurance markets would make it easier for individuals and small businesses to purchase affordable coverage; (4) insurance companies were now limited to spending no more than 15 cents out of every dollar on non-medical costs (overhead);

(5) insurers would be prohibited from denying adults and children coverage or from charging them more if they had preexisting health problems; (6) health insurance was expanded to include psychiatric disorders; and (7) the Medicaid system would be expanded to include all people within 133 percent of the poverty line.

This last point was addressed by the Supreme Court when it ruled that the federal government could not deny funds to the states for their existing Medicaid programs if they rejected the expansion of Medicaid called for under the Affordable Health Care Act. In effect, the states could not be compelled to expand Medicaid, that is, they were free to choose to not cover all of their low income residents through their Medicaid programs (Starr 2012). Some states, whose leadership was hostile to this healthcare legislation, will likely refuse to comply when the law goes into effect. Rick Perry, the Texas governor, for example, refused to enlarge the Texas Medicaid program, arguing that it would make "Texas a mere appendage of the federal government when it comes to healthcare." By opting out, Texas chose to not cover the 6.2 million poor people, including 1.2 million children, who lacked health insurance (Fernandez 2012). In doing so, the states also refused the influx of federal money to cover the newly eligible Medicaid beneficiaries for the first three years, and 90 percent thereafter. If a few states opt out of the Medicaid expansion, there will be gap from state to state in coverage. The poor in the South and much of the Midwest will be denied the benefits of other states.

The Future of the Affordable Health Care Act

The Affordable Health Care Act was not perfect. It angered progressives who felt that it did not go far enough to provide universal healthcare. Moreover, it left most private healthcare in the hands of a for-profit insurance industry, with huge administrative costs and paperwork. Conservatives were hostile to the healthcare reform because it gave too much power to the federal government. Moreover, it was questioned by Speaker of the House John Boehner, who asked: Why change a system that is the greatest healthcare system in the world? And, it caused anxiety among the public, who were unsure of such a major change—an overhaul of one-sixth of the economy— and how the change would affect their lives and their taxes.

Republican politicians vowed to repeal the Affordable Health Care Act, but the 2012 reelection of Obama and a Democratic majority in the Senate legitimized the reforms. However, some provisions need to be improved. Costs need to be contained. The remaining uninsured need to be included in health reform. Most significant, in the words of economist Robert H. Frank: "[The Supreme Court decision] will at last enable our distinctly dysfunctional healthcare system to evolve into something better" (quoted in Huffington 2012, para 4).

MySocLab ✓ **Study** and **Review** on **MySocLab**

■ CHAPTER REVIEW

1. The U.S. healthcare system is the most expensive among advanced nations. The reasons: (a) profit drives the system, (b) inefficiency, (c) defensive medicine to ward off expensive lawsuits, (d) overuse of specialists, (e) the wide use of prescription drugs, and (e) investor-owned enterprises.

2. The high cost of healthcare does not translate into better health outcomes compared with other advanced nations.

3. The U.S. healthcare system has unique characteristics: (a) different plans for different categories of people, (b) private insurance, (c) for-profit hospitals, and (d) managed care networks.

4. Economic disadvantage is closely related to health disadvantages. The poor are much more likely than the affluent to die in infancy, to suffer from certain diseases, and as adults to die sooner. They are less likely to receive medical attention because of being uninsured (46 million) or underinsured (50 million), and when they do receive medical care, to receive inferior service.

5. The most commonly held explanation for the strong relationship between social class and health is that the poor are responsible for their disproportionate ill health because of ignorance or neglect. This approach blames the victim because it ignores the primary role that privilege plays in good health and the lack of privilege in poor health. The fundamental solution for reducing socioeconomic differences in health is to reduce the inequalities in society that perpetuate poor health among the disadvantaged.

6. Race is also related to health, with non-Whites disadvantaged by a combination of economic disadvantage and racial discrimination.

7. Health and ill health are also related to gender differences. Women have health advantages over men because of their physical differences and differing gender expectations. Women are placed at risk, however, by childbearing, the greater likelihood of unnecessary surgery such as hysterectomies and tubal ligations, the relative lack of medical research using women as subjects, and the still-common sexist practices by physicians, who are predominantly male.

8. AIDS, once a death sentence, can now be controlled for the most part by combinations of very expensive drugs. Those with HIV (the precursor to AIDS) who are most likely to die from AIDS are the poor in the developing nations and the poor in the United States who live in states that do not subsidize the expensive treatments. Although the number of new cases of AIDS has dropped appreciably among Whites in the United States, it has remained high among young Black gay men, Black users of intravenous drugs, and Black heterosexual women.

9. There are three major systems of universal healthcare employed by other advanced societies: the Bismarck model, the Beveridge model, and the national health insurance model (single-payer plan). The United States does not have a universal healthcare plan.

10. In 2010, after heated debate, Congress passed the Affordable Health Care Act. Included in the reform bill that passed were these provisions: (a) mandates for everyone to have medical insurance, (b) an oversight board, (c) guarantees that insurance companies cannot deny coverage, and (d) coverage of young adults through their parents' policy until age 26. The Supreme Court in 2012 upheld the Act.

11. Obamacare is not socialism. It is not a government takeover of the healthcare system. The plan keeps healthcare in a mostly private system.

■ KEY TERMS

Defensive medicine. The practice of requiring extra diagnostic tests and medical procedures to protect the physician from liability.

Infant mortality rate. Number of deaths before age 1 per 1,000 live births.

Medicare. Government program that provides partial coverage of medical costs primarily for people age 65 and older.

Patient dumping. Practice by physicians and private hospitals of treating only patients who can afford their services.

Medlining. Practice of managed care organizations of limiting the number of patients with health problems while maximizing the number of healthy patients.

Medicaid. Government health program for the poor.

Single-payer plan. Tax-supported health program in which the government is the sole insurer.

National Security in the Twenty-First Century

 Listen to Chapter 18 on **MySocLab**

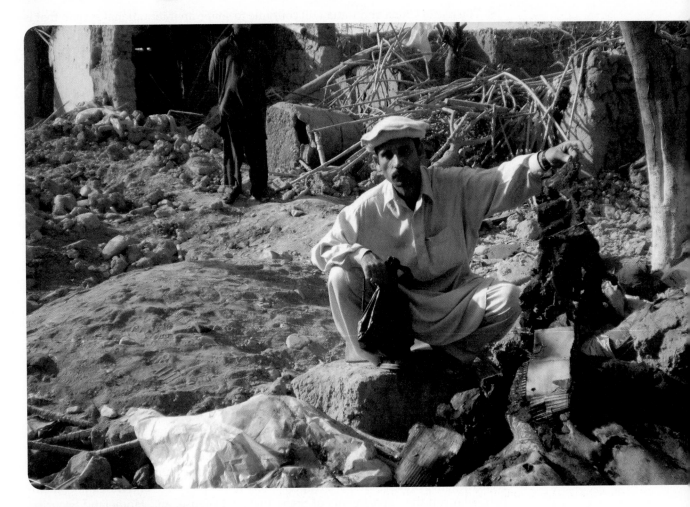

LEARNING OBJECTIVES

18.1 Describe the defense budget of the U.S. military and the size, strength, and cost of the U.S. military.

18.2 Understand the global threat of nuclear weapons to the United States.

18.3 Understand threats of domestic and international terrorism.

18.4 Understand the consequences of the United States' invasion of Afghanistan and Iraq.

18.5 Discuss the changes in warfare in the twenty-first century.

The mission of the Department of Defense is to protect the American people and advance the nation's interests (U.S. Department of Defense 2010). Every four years the Pentagon reviews the mission of the military in the light of changes in international and domestic environments. The 2010 Quadrennial Review provides the current state of U.S. **national security:** "The United States faces a complex and uncertain security landscape in which the pace of change continues to accelerate" (p. iii). Among the challenges for defending the nation's interests are (U.S. Department of Defense 2010:iii–iv):

- The rise of China and India will continue to shape an international system that is no longer easily defined.
- Globalization has transformed the process of technological innovation while lowering the entry barriers for a wider range of actors to acquire advanced technologies.
- Nonstate actors (i.e., terrorist groups) will continue to gain influence.
- The proliferation of weapons of mass destruction (WMDs) continues to undermine global security. The instability or collapse of a WMD-armed state is among the most troubling concerns.
- Several powerful trends such as demographic pressures, increasingly limited resources (e.g., arable land, water, oil), the effects of climate change, the emergence of new strains of disease, and rapid urbanization may exacerbate future conflicts.

Reflecting the new realities, the Defense Department states,

The U.S. military must prepare for a combination of humanitarian missions, untraditional threats such as cyberattacks, environmental disasters, terrorist groups seeking weapons of mass destruction and as many as two major conflicts. (The Quadrennial Defense Review, reported in Youssef 2010:1A)

The sections of this chapter describe (1) the magnitude of the military establishment, (2) the threat of nuclear weapons, (3) the threat of domestic terrorism, (4) the threat of international terrorism, and (5) conducting war in the twenty-first century.

THE U.S. MILITARY ESTABLISHMENT

18.1 Describe the defense budget of the U.S. military and the size, strength, and cost of the U.S. military.

Nation-states organize to defend their national security by protecting borders, guarding their national interests, and shielding their citizens and businesses abroad with armies, military bases, intelligence networks, embassies, and consulates. National security in the United States is a responsibility of the president and the cabinet members who run the departments of State, Justice, Defense, and Homeland Security. National defense does not necessarily mean involvement in a war, but it often has. As of 2010, for example, the United States had been at war for forty-seven of its 230 years, or for 20 percent of its history (Bumiller 2010).

The Size of the U.S. Military

Read on
MySocLab Document:
Military Partisanship

The size of the U.S. military establishment is enormous. Here are the facts:

- In September 2011 there were 1,468,364 active military personnel. This is an all-volunteer military (see the "Speaking to Students" panel). Conscription can be enacted by request of the president and approval of Congress.

Speaking to Students

RECRUITING AN ALL-VOLUNTEER MILITARY

The Pentagon in 2009 had a $5 billion recruiting budget. In that year the U.S. military met its annual recruiting goals for the first time in thirty-five years. This shift occurred because of three factors. The first was unplanned. That is, the economic downturn (the Great Recession) and rising joblessness led more youths to enlist (Tyson 2009). Pentagon research shows that a 10 percent increase in the national unemployment rate generally translates into a 4 to 6 percent improvement in recruiting (reported in *The Progressive* 2009).

A second reason for the rise in volunteer recruits in 2009 was that recruits were enticed by an average signing bonus of $14,000 compared to $12,000 in 2008.

Third, military recruiters were armed with information on each potential recruit, giving them an edge in gaining rapport and softening them up to the decision to join up.

In the past few years, the military has mounted a virtual invasion into the lives of young Americans. Using data mining, stealth websites, career tests, and sophisticated marketing software, the Pentagon is harvesting and analyzing information on everything from high school students' GPAs and SAT scores to which video games they play. Before an Army recruiter even picks up the phone to call a prospect, the soldier may know more about the kid's habits than do his own parents. . . .

To put all of its data to use, the military has enlisted the help of Nielsen Claritas, a research and marketing firm whose clients include BMW, AOL, and Starbucks. Last year, it rolled out a "custom segmentation" program that allows a recruiter armed with address, age, race, and gender of a potential "lead" to call up a wealth of information about young people in the immediate area, including recreation and consumption patterns. The program even suggests pitches that might work while cold-calling teenagers. "It's just a foot in the door for a recruiter to start a relevant conversation with a young person," says Donna Dorminey of the U.S. Army Center for Accessions Research. (Goodman 2009:21–22)

- In 2009 there were 848,000 members of the guard and reserve (more than the standing army of France). These are people who can be "called up" by the Defense Department to fight in war.
- There were 678,025 civilians on the military payroll in 2009. Most of them do clerical work, report writing, and technical jobs.
- The military operates 865 military bases and other facilities in 135 nations located on every continent. The cost to maintain these bases exceeds $100 billion a year.
- The headquarters of the Department of Defense is the Pentagon in Washington, DC. It is one of the world's largest office buildings, with 17.5 miles of corridors.
- The military has a worldwide satellite network providing constant intelligence, surveillance, and communication.
- The United States has the world's largest navy, larger than the next thirteen navies combined (Pena 2010). Included in the fleet are fifty-seven nuclear-powered attack and cruise-missile submarines, more than the rest of the world combined (Ramirez 2010).
- The carbon footprint of the military is huge (e.g., the military uses 4.6 billion gallons of fuel annually).
- The government outsources some military operations to private firms. There are more of these nonmilitary personnel (53 percent) in Iraq and Afghanistan

than military personnel. For example, there were more than 218,000 private U.S. contractors in Iraq and Afghanistan in 2009 (Schwartz 2009).

- In 2010 there were 21.8 million military veterans with 9 million of them 65 and older, and 3.4 million with a service-connected disability. In 2011 the budget for Veterans Affairs was $122 billion.
- There are 1,271 government agencies and 1,931 outside contractors devoted to counterterrorism (*USA Today* 2010).

The Cost of Maintaining U.S. Military Superiority

Military might has been the typical security strategy of nations. Since World War II, the United States, for example, has spent more than $20 trillion (adjusted for inflation) on military defense. The **defense budget**, which represents the government's spending plan for the military for fiscal 2012 (which began on October 1, 2011) was $741 billion. The military budget included an operating budget of $549 billion, plus funding for the Iraq and Afghanistan wars at $192 billion, including an extra $33 billion for expanding the war in Afghanistan. Not included in the military budget are the indirect costs of war: veterans benefits, including healthcare and disability costs, federal debt payments due to military expenditures, covert intelligence operations, federal research on military and space programs, cleaning up toxic waste from the development and production of nuclear weapons, and homeland security. Taken together, actual military spending for fiscal 2012 was $1.2 trillion (Hellman 2011).

The United States with a formal military budget of $741 billion ($2.2 billion a day) outspends all other nations on national security. The Stockholm International Peace Research Institute estimated that the world's military expenditures in 2011 totaled $1.74 trillion (SIPRI 2012). The United States accounted for 41 percent of that amount. Military spending by the United States and its NATO allies account for about 70 percent of world military spending. If other allies and friends of the United States such as South Korea are included, then the total share of global military outlay hits 80 percent (Bandow 2010: para 12). Put another way, the United States spends more on defense than the next fourteen countries combined. It outspends its nearest rival in military expenditures, China, by five times, and Russia, the world's third military power, by ten times (Wittner 2012), and twenty-nine times the combined spending of the six "rogue" states (Cuba, Iran, Libya, North Korea, Sudan, and Syria; Greenwald 2010a).

There are at least four reasons why U.S. defense spending is so high and continues to grow. First, there is the ongoing fear of nuclear weapons. Russia, which has a huge nuclear arsenal, although much less a threat than before 1990, remains a potential threat to U.S. security. Rogue states such as North Korea and Iran pose a significant threat as they join the nuclear club.

Second, the world, even without the Soviet threat, is an unsafe place, where terrorism and aggression occur and must be confronted and contained. Several nations, including regimes with expansionist agendas and hated enemies, have nuclear weapons or soon will have them. They also have chemical and biological weapons. Several nations are suspected of supporting terror and working to develop **weapons of mass destruction** (nuclear, biological, or chemical weapons capable of large-scale deaths and destruction). Iran, in particular, is a special worry in the tense Middle East, especially for Israel.

Third, defense expenditures bring profits to corporations, create jobs, and generate growth in the economy. For example, many corporations benefited from the wars in Afghanistan and Iraq as Defense Department contracts more than doubled from

2000 to 2009. The four largest contractors in 2009 were Lockheed Martin ($30.9 billion), Boeing ($20.0 billion), Northrup Grumman ($17.5 billion), and Raytheon ($5.9 billion) (*Forbes* 2011). (See the "A Closer Look" panel on Lockheed Martin.) With huge contracts available, these corporations spend millions on lobbying ($131 million in 2011). Corporate military contractors are eager for more contracts, for the following reasons (Parenti 2008:80):

- There are few risks. Unlike manufacturers who must worry about selling the goods they produce, defense corporations have a guaranteed contract.
- Almost all contracts are awarded without competitive bidding and at whatever price the corporation sets. If the cost exceeds the bid (cost overruns), then the government picks up the tab.

A Closer Look

LOCKHEED MARTIN

- Government contracts 2009: $30.9 billion
- Total lobbying and campaign contributions in 2009: $12 billion

Lockheed Martin was formed in 1995 with the merger of two of the world's premier technology companies—Lockheed Corporation and Martin Marietta Corporation. The company employs about 140,000 people worldwide.

It has 1,000 facilities in 500 cities, forty-six states, and in seventy-five nations and territories. Lockheed Martin is the world's number one military contractor, as well as the world's largest arms exporter. It dominates the fighter aircraft sector and is heavily involved in transport aircraft, missiles, and space systems.

In addition to lobbying and campaign contributions, Lockheed Martin has links with the government and the Pentagon that make it easier to obtain government contracts. For example, its board of directors includes a number of former high-ranking government officials: the former head of the U.S. Strategic Command, former vice president of the Joint Chiefs of Staff, former deputy Secretary of Homeland Security, former Secretary of Commerce, and a former Secretary of Defense (Derysh 2009). One of the above, former Secretary of Defense Pete Aldridge, in the month before he left the Pentagon to join Lockheed's board, approved a $3 billion contract to build twenty Lockheed planes. Furthermore, while on Lockheed's Board of Directors, Aldridge was appointed by President George W. Bush to chair the president's commission on space exploration—a possible conflict of interest (SourceWatch 2008).

Lockheed has also been able to exercise its influence in a larger way—in support of the invasion of Iraq. The company's former vice president, Bruce Jackson, chaired the Coalition for the Liberation of Iraq, a bipartisan group formed to promote Bush's plan for war in Iraq. Jackson was also involved in corralling the support for the war from Eastern European countries, going so far as helping to write their letter of endorsement for military intervention. Not surprisingly, Lockheed also has business relations with these countries.

In the last few years, the SEC has investigated Lockheed for insider trading and falsifying its accounts. Lockheed Martin leads all defense contractors with a number one ranking on the "contractor misconduct" database maintained by the Project on Government Oversight (Hartung 2011). These instances include age, race, and sex discrimination, contract fraud, unfair business practices, contractor kickbacks, federal election law violation, environmental violations, improper charges, nuclear safety violations, pricing irregularities, and overcharges. In 2010, the Secretary of Defense, Robert Gates, fined the military officer overseeing the Pentagon's new F-35 stealth-fighter-jet program for cost overruns and technical failures and punished Lockheed Martin by withholding $615 million in fees. Despite the ongoing cases of misconduct (a serious example of corporate recidivism), Lockheed Martin continues to be the number one supplier of military goods to the government.

- The Pentagon directly subsidizes defense contractors with free research and development, public lands, buildings, and renovations.
- Defense spending does not compete with the consumer market. Moreover, the market is virtually limitless, as there are always more advanced weapons systems to develop and obsolete weaponry to replace.

Members of Congress are eager to support an expansive military machine for two reasons. First, only a rare politician would campaign to reduce the military for fear of being labeled unpatriotic and thereby risk defeat in the next election. Second, politicians gain support from their constituents if they bring military money to their corporations, communities, and state. The corporations supplying military supplies exploit this by distributing their operations across many states and many districts within those states.

Lawmakers even team up with defense contractors to fight for certain targeted programs even when the Pentagon says that it does not need the weaponry in question. For example, every year from 2006 through 2009, the Pentagon argued that it had enough C-17 cargo planes (produced by Boeing for about $250 million apiece). But every year, Congress overruled the military and authorized more funds for these planes ($2.5 billion in the 2010 budget) (Elgin and Epstein 2009:47).

In 2009, California led the way with defense contract expenditures in that state totaling $27.9 billion, followed by Virginia ($23.4 billion) and Texas ($21.1 billion) (StateMaster n.d.). Even a small state such as Kansas has three major bases, has 40,000 members in the military, and receives a military boost to the economy of $7.7 billion (Milburn 2009). In sum, business, labor, the states, Congress, and academia combine to present a unified voice supporting massive and increasing military expenditures. Opposing this behemoth are only faint voices from individuals and groups seeking to reduce the huge costs of the military-industrial complex.

Finally, the disproportionate amount that the United States appropriates for war is based on the assumption that by having the world's costliest military force and being so far ahead of other nations in military strength and technology, no one would dare challenge us militarily. Although other nations may have more people (China and India), they do not have the United States' sophisticated weaponry, weapons

"Oh, that's good, sir, that's very good—'What if they gave a war and nobody profited.'"

Charles Barsotti/The New Yorker Collection/www.cartoonbank.com

delivery systems, and nuclear stockpile. The United States chooses to retain this superiority because its leaders believe there is "peace through strength."

This strategy succeeded for the most part during the Cold War years, as the United States and the Soviet Union engaged in an expensive arms race to strike first if necessary and to scare the other side into not attacking first. The attacks on the World Trade Center and the Pentagon showed that this rationale does not hold for the terrorism that we confront in the twenty-first century.

THE THREAT OF NUCLEAR WEAPONS

18.2 Understand the global threat of nuclear weapons to the United States.

Nuclear weapons involve the most destructive technology on Earth. During the **Cold War** (the intense tension and arms race between the United States and the Soviet Union that lasted from the end of World War II until 1990), the two superpowers had most of the nuclear weapons. The United States spent almost 8 trillion in 2012 dollars on nuclear weapons in the last half of the twentieth century. That nuclear budget was more than that half-century's federal combined spending on Medicare, education, disaster relief, social services, non-nuclear research, environmental protection, highway maintenance, and prisons (Maddow 2012:219). The United States and Russia in 2009 possessed 96 percent of the world's nuclear warheads, each aimed at the other.

Other nuclear power holders were France, Britain, China, Israel, Pakistan, India, and North Korea (*Guardian* 2009). The year 1998 was a turning point, as the world entered a new nuclear era when India tested five bombs, followed two weeks later by its rival neighbor, Pakistan.

Thus, in this globalized world, we face a threatening situation in which as many as forty countries have the capacity to develop nuclear weapons in a very short time span. Two nations, thought of as "rogue nations" by the United States and its allies, are North Korea, which has tested a bomb several times since 2006, and Iran, which is believed to be close to developing nuclear weapons.

> What we have now is not a tight club of nuclear powers with interlocking interests and an appreciation for the brutal doctrine of "mutually assured destruction" but an unpredictable host of potential Bomb throwers: a Stalinist Bomb out of unstable North Korea; a Shiite Bomb out of Iran; a Sunni Bomb out of Pakistan; and, down the road, possibly out of Egypt and Saudi Arabia as well; and, of course, an al-Qaeda Bomb out of nowhere. (Powell 2006:32)

The newcomers to the nuclear club, unlike the charter members, are not governed by elaborate rules and sophisticated technology designed to prevent accidents and firing in haste. Instead, they are dealing with the savagery of ethnic strife, intense religious differences, and insecure nations. Moreover, there is the danger of nuclear weapons or weapons-grade materials falling into the hands of terrorists—"the one enemy we know would probably not hesitate to use them" (Keller 2003:51).

Nuclear technology is expected to accelerate as nations turn to atomic power for their domestic energy requirements. This technology gives them the ability to make reactor fuel, or with the same equipment and a little more effort, bomb fuel. Thus, the tension and the threat will continue to accelerate.

THE TERRORISM THREAT

18.3 Understand threats of domestic and international terrorism.

Terrorism is a major national security threat, as the United States experienced with the ramming of hijacked planes into the World Trade Center and the Pentagon on September 11, 2001. **Terrorism** is any act intended to cause death or serious injury to civilians or noncombatants to intimidate a population and weaken their will or draw attention to the perpetrator's cause. Thus, terrorist acts are political acts. In the case of the September 11 terrorist attack, al-Qaeda, Osama bin Laden's organization, sought to show the vulnerability of the United States and to rally other extremist Islamists in a war against—in their words—"the Great Satan." So, too, was the bombing of the federal building in Oklahoma City by ex-soldier Timothy McVeigh, who had grievances with the U.S. government. Also, when Joseph Stack flew an airplane into a building housing Internal Revenue Service offices in Austin, Texas, to advance his political grievances, it was an act of terrorism (Greenwald 2010b). Similarly, the killing of abortion doctors and the bombing of abortion clinics are terrorist acts, making political statements and intimidating their opponents.

Terrorism is "not an enemy; it is a methodology of using violence to gain political objectives" (Greider 2004:11). It is a tactic used historically by groups against governments and organizations viewed as unjust and oppressive. Terrorists believe that they are legitimate combatants, fighting for a just cause, by whatever means possible. The warfare is asymmetric—that is, terrorism is the method of less well-armed and less powerful opponents. Because, typically, they do not have sophisticated weapons, terrorists use what is cheap and available. Instead of guided missiles, they use suicide bombers—"the poor man's air force" (Davis 2006). Because they do not have weapons of mass destruction, they use "weapons of mass disruption" such as arson, infecting computers with viruses (cyberterrorism), and disrupting mass transit. They instill fear through kidnapping, raping, and torturing victims and even showing the beheading of these victims on television. Note that terrorism as a method of asymmetric warfare is not exclusively a Muslim or al-Qaeda method but also a method used, for example, by the American revolutionaries, the Irish Republican Army, the Viet Cong, and antidictatorial forces in Latin America.

Terrorism is a social construction (Turk 2004). That is, what is defined as terrorism and who is labeled a terrorist are matters of interpretation of events and their presumed causes. Consider the different meanings for these words: terrorist/freedom fighter or suicide bomber/martyr.

"*The terrorist barriers seem to be working.*"
Frank Cotham/The New Yorker Collection/www.cartoonbank.com

> *The powerful conflict parties, especially governments, generally succeed in labeling their more threatening (i.e., violent) opponents as terrorists, whereas attempts by opponents to label officially sanctioned violence as "state terrorism" have little chance of success unless supported by powerful third parties (e.g., the United Nations). (Turk 2004:272)*

While terrorism is typically seen as having international implications, it can be domestic in origin as well. We begin the discussion with the internal terrorist threat: attacks by Americans on Americans.

Domestic Terrorism

Typically, we think of terrorism as deadly acts committed by foreigners, usually Islamic fundamentalists from the Middle East. Thus, when a bomb destroyed the federal building in Oklahoma City in 1995, killing 168, the immediate suspects were Muslim extremists. But Timothy McVeigh and Terry Nichols, two U.S. military veterans, were convicted of that crime. (McVeigh received the death penalty for detonating the bomb and was executed in 2001; Nichols was sentenced to life imprisonment for his involvement in planning the attack.) As extreme as the Oklahoma City bombing was, the act of an American detonating a bomb to harm other Americans is not unusual because there are about 2,000 illegal bombings annually within the United States.

Foreigners acting alone or as agents of their organization or government killing Americans is relatively easy to understand, but Americans killing Americans is more difficult to comprehend. The history of the United States, however, is full of examples of various dissident groups that have used violence against their neighbors to achieve their aims (Hewitt 2003). Colonists, farmers, settlers, Native Americans, immigrants, slaves, slaveholders, laborers, strike breakers, anarchists, vigilantes, the Ku Klux Klan and other White supremacist organizations, antiwar protesters, radical environmentalists, and prolife extremists have acted outside the law to accomplish their ends.* Just in recent years antiabortion terrorists have bombed abortion clinics and murdered abortion doctors. One of those doctors, George Tiller, was wounded in 1993, his clinic was bombed and vandalized, and then in 2009 he was killed by an antiabortion zealot. Also, various extremists have bombed African American churches, Jewish synagogues, and Islamic mosques throughout the United States, U.S. Bureau of Land Management and Forest Service offices, and the 1996 Olympic Games in Atlanta. In addition to bombings, there have been acts of arson, beatings, killings, and letters/packages with bombs or anthrax addressed to political targets.

Extreme actions by the government have persuaded some individuals to become part of extremist groups. The government's actions in conducting the Vietnam War and its reactions to protesters (e.g., the killing of Kent State students by the National Guard) led some groups such as the "Weathermen" to use violence to further their cause. Two events in the 1990s energized the Patriot movement. In 1992 the Bureau of Alcohol, Tobacco, and Firearms (ATF) attacked Randy Weaver, a White supremacist in Idaho, for gun violations. In the process Weaver's wife and son were killed by ATF snipers. The second event was the 1993 assault by ATF on David Koresh

---

*It is important to note that the law can be a friend or an enemy. The agents of government (e.g., police, FBI, military, National Guard, and the courts) defend the law even with force, but what if a group considers the law immoral, as do prolife supporters or Martin Luther King, Jr., who led protests against the Jim Crow laws in the South? Is it appropriate for them to use unlawful acts to overturn what they consider a bad law?

and the Branch Davidians near Waco, Texas. This siege, again over guns violations, ended with the deaths of eighty-six men, women, and children. Those in the Patriot movement interpreted these acts as government run amok, using its power to take away the liberties that individuals are granted by the Constitution. Thus, the membership in this movement, "far from thinking itself outside the law, believes it is the critical force making for a restoration of the Constitution" (Wills 1995:52). See the "Voices" panel for a letter from Timothy McVeigh, airing his grievances with the U.S. government.

The Patriot movement faded somewhat in the late 1990s, although pockets remained. But ten years later the momentum was revived. In 2011 the number of hate groups rose to 1,018, up from 602 in 2000 (*SPLC Report* 2012). The U.S. Department of Homeland Security issued a report warning that current political and economic conditions resembled those of the early 1990s, when there was an upsurge in right-wing extremism that culminated in the Oklahoma City bombing (Blow 2009; Krugman 2009).

There was a resurgence of populist anger, coinciding with the Great Recession, that emerged in 2009. Leading the charge was the Tea Party movement (there is some dispute over the name's origin: Was it taken from the 1773 tax revolt, or is it an acronym for "taxed enough already"?). This movement is a platform for conservative populist discontent. It embodies a brand of politics historically associated with libertarians, populists, and those on the fringe: militia groups, hate groups, and anti-immigration advocates. Tea Party activists, although divided on a number of issues, agree that "government is too big. Spending is out of control. Individual freedom is at risk. And President Barack Obama's policies are making it all worse" (Associated Press 2010a: para 1). The catalyst was the election of Barack Hussein Obama, the first African American president. This raised two fears for some in the

Voices

A LETTER FROM TIMOTHY MCVEIGH

Three years before he ignited a bomb that destroyed the federal building in Oklahoma City, killing 168 people, Timothy McVeigh wrote a letter to his hometown newspaper, the Lockport (N.Y.) *Union-Sun & Journal*, listing his concerns about the government.

Crime is out of control. Criminals have no fear of punishment. Prisons are overcrowded so they know they will not be imprisoned long. . . .

Taxes are a joke. Regardless of what a political candidate "promises," they will increase taxes. More taxes are always the answer to government mismanagement. . . .

The "American Dream" of the middle class has all but disappeared, substituted with people struggling just to buy next week's groceries. Heaven forbid the car breaks down! . . .

Politicians are out of control. Their yearly salaries are more than an average person will see in a lifetime. They have been entrusted with the power to regulate their own salaries, and have grossly violated that trust to live in their own luxury. . . .

Who is to blame for the mess? At a point when the world has seen communism falter as an imperfect system to manage people, democracy seems to be headed down the same road. No one is seeing the "big" picture. . . .

What is it going to take to open up the eyes of our elected officials? AMERICA IS IN SERIOUS DECLINE.

We have no proverbial tea to dump; should we instead sink a ship full of Japanese imports? Is a Civil War imminent? Do we have to shed blood to reform the current system? I hope it doesn't come to that. But it might.

movement: that he was African American and that he was a Muslim. There is more than a hint of racism here. "For some white Americans of a certain age and background, the sight of a black man in the Oval Office, even one who went to Harvard Law School and conducts himself in the manner of an aloof WASP aristocrat, is an affront" (Cassidy 2010: para 2). Also, there is an anti-Islam strain among some in the movement. Summarizing this line of thought, Southern Poverty Law Center's Mark Potok, said:

> For many extremists, President Obama is a lighting rod, a symbol of all that's wrong with the country. He's the "Kenyan" president, the "secret Muslim" who is causing our country's decline. (SPLC Report 2012:1)

Fanning these flames, one segment of the movement—the birthers—questioned the legitimacy of Obama to be president because, they argued, his birth certificate was bogus and his father was an African. These fears were fomented by conservative talk show hosts on radio and cable television, who "have gone out of their way to provide a platform for conspiracy theories and apocalyptic rhetoric" (Krugman 2009: para 5). Most significant, under Obama and the Democrats, broad federal programs were initiated, such as national healthcare; bailouts of Wall Street banks (actually begun by President Bush), General Motors, and Chrysler; the $787 billion stimulus (TARP); and an immense and rapidly growing national debt. These were interpreted as moving the nation toward a totalitarian socialist state, with subsequent loss of freedoms, again fueled by talk show rhetoric from the political Right. Obama, by the way, receives on average of thirty death threats a day (a 400 percent increase from the number received by President George W. Bush; Harnden 2009).

Obama's government programs were not only perceived as centralizing authority (an orchestrated "power grab") but also that they benefit the wealthy and educated elites but not average people (see the "A Closer Look" panel airing the grievances of the Texas Suicide Flyer). And many of these average people were suffering in the bad economy. They were worried about their jobs, their retirement incomes, and their mortgages and paying for their children's education. Some were concerned that Whites were losing their numerical majority to non-Whites. For them, immigration, especially illegal immigration, has to be stopped. As Bill O'Reilly of Fox News complained to Senator John McCain about the number of undocumented Latino immigrants:

> Do you understand what the New York Times wants, and the far-left want? They want to break down the white, Christian, male power structure, of which you're a part and so am I. They hate America, and they hate it because it's run primarily by white, Christian men. They want to bring in millions of foreign nationals to basically break down the structure that we have. (Quoted in Benjamin 2009: para 5)

The Tea Party movement is difficult to define because there is no single Tea Party. "This is an amorphous, factionalized uprising with no clear leadership and no central structure" (Barstow 2010: para 15). Comprised within the movement are a number of local groups, often focusing on different issues. Some followers are gun rights activists, some rally against taxes, some want state sovereignty, some are White Supremacists, whereas others are concerned about the federal government's interference in their freedoms. Connecting the disparate issues that preoccupy many Tea Party supporters is the strong feeling of impending governmental tyranny. This theme permeates the Far Right's commentary, the Tea Party websites, Facebook pages, Twitter feeds, and YouTube videos (Barstow 2010). Although many of these are relatively benign, some are not. In fact, the Simon Wiesenthal Center (Jewish human rights

A Closer Look

THE TEXAS SUICIDE FLYER'S MANIFESTO

Reminiscent of the 9/11 attack, on February 18, 2010, Joseph Stack flew his single-engine plane into an Austin, Texas, office building that housed the Internal Revenue Service, killing two and injuring thirteen. He left behind a manifesto listing his grievances against Big Government and Big Business. Specifically, he railed against (Benjamin 2010):

- A crippled economy dominated by political and corporate potentates.
- A campaign and election system rotted by special interests and money.
- Government bailouts of corporate and banking interests, paid for with taxes from the "little guy."
- Excessively complicated tax laws that baffle small business owners and individuals.

Stack's manifesto calls for a citizen's movement to change this foul system, and to change it through violence:

I know I'm hardly the first one to decide I have had all I can stand.

It has always been a myth that people have stopped dying for their freedom in this country, and it isn't limited to the blacks, and poor immigrants. I know there have been countless before me and there are sure to be as many after. But I also know that by not adding my body to the count, I insure nothing will change. I choose to not keep looking over my shoulder at "big brother" while he strips my carcass. I choose not to ignore what is going on all round me. I choose not to pretend that business as usual won't continue. I have just had enough.

I can only hope that the numbers quickly get too big to be whitewashed and ignored that the American zombies wake up and revolt; it will take nothing less. I would only hope that by striking a nerve that stimulates the inevitable double standard, knee-jerk government reaction that results in more stupid draconian restrictions people wake up and begin to see the pompous political thugs and their mindless minions for what they are. Sadly, though I spent my entire life trying to believe it wasn't so, *but violence not only is the answer, it is the only answer.* (emphasis added; Stack 2010: para. 32–33)

Rich Benjamin argues that Stack's complaints echo the issues raised by the Tea Party movement and should be taken seriously because they resonate with the protestations of so many.

Deplorable though he might be, Stack is not quite a "random bad apple." His act might be uncommon, but his jumbled populism is not. His crime is in no way excusable, but it spotlights a larger problem that both political and corporate elites like to caricature or dismiss: visceral populist anger. Stack may have suffered from mental illness, but he is also an acute symptom of this nation's neglected wounds. (2010: para. 16)

organization) noted that there was a 25 percent rise from 2008 to 2009 in the number of "problematic" social networking groups on the Internet. The report found that there are over 10,000 networking groups, portals, blogs, chat rooms, and videos on the Internet that promote racial violence, anti-Semitism, homophobia, hate music, and terrorism (cited in Parsons 2009).

This movement represents a passionate rebellion that has the potential to change the political landscape. It is important to note that most Tea Partiers are non-violent, yet the movement has a violent edge, fueled by frustration, anxiety, fear, and anger. Research shows that in difficult economic times, extremist groups emerge and flourish—groups such as Skinheads, neo-Nazis, militias, White Supremacists, and "Sovereign citizens," who believe that they do not have to pay taxes or obey most other laws, such as having a driver's license. (When Scott Roeder, the convicted killer of abortionist Dr. George Tiller, was arrested, sheriff deputies stopped his car because it had no license plate. Instead there was a tag declaring him a "sovereign" and immune from state law.) During hard times, membership in these extremist groups increases, and the number of hate crimes (against gays, Muslims, recent immigrants, and people of color) rises dramatically.

At Tea Party rallies there are occasional placards that incite violence. There are pictures of Obama, redrawn as Hitler, the use of Nazi symbols such as swastikas, and signs reading "Death to Obama" and "Death to Michelle and her two stupid kids."

To reiterate: Most Tea Partiers are not violent, but they are angry, upset, and they feel threatened. The movement represents a genuine backlash against current trends (Berlet 2010). And for some this backlash includes the seeds for violence by some individuals and groups.

International Terrorism

The context for international terrorist activity in today's world varies. The terrorists may be seeking separation from the dominant group by establishing an independent state, which is the goal of the Basques in Spain, the Chechnyans in Russia, and Northern Ireland, which seeks independence from Great Britain. They may be rival religious groups such as the Protestants and Catholics in Northern Ireland or Sunnis and Shiites, warring Muslim sects in the Middle East. Ethnic/religious groups in the former Yugoslavia—Serbs (Eastern Orthodox), Croatians (Catholics), and Bosnians (Muslims)—have fought each other with brutal tactics for centuries. Palestinian terrorists attack the Israeli government that keeps them in secondary status. Israeli extremists attack the Israeli government (e.g., the assassination of a moderate leader) when they believe that it will compromise with the Palestinians, as do Palestinian extremists who fear their leaders are not being militant enough with Israel. Various African countries have warring tribes seeking control through ethnic cleansing, and governments such as in Sudan use ethnic militias to terrorize through killings, rapes, and destruction of villages and farms to quell rebellious groups.

Globalization has quickened the pace, scale, and fear of terrorism. As nations become all the more connected, they are increasingly vulnerable to terrorist attacks. The United States, in particular, is relatively unprotected from terrorist attacks because it is a mobile, open society with porous borders that are difficult to police. Every day, over a million people enter the country legally (and many others illegally), as do almost 3,000 aircraft and over 16,000 containers on 600 ships. Satellite communications give the world an instant look at the consequences of terrorist acts. This capability heightens the motivation of terrorists, who seek to dramatize their grievances to a wide audience. Modern societies provide a huge array of possible targets for terrorists. The United States, for example, has 60,000 chemical plants and 103 nuclear plants that could be sabotaged. So, too, could hydroelectric dams, power grids, oil refineries, oil and natural gas pipelines, water treatment plants, and factories. Transportation systems (planes, trains, cargo ships) can be easily disrupted with explosions or computer glitches.

Clearly, humankind lives in an increasingly dangerous world—the context in which nations must seek national security. This section broadly outlines the challenges to the United States by the new terrorism; the U.S. response to terrorism, using the wars in Afghanistan and Iraq as the case study; and the consequences of this response for these nations, the United States, and the world.

By Mike Smith. *Las Vegas Sun.* United Features Syndicate.

Mike Smith EDT/King Features Syndicate.

Understand the consequences of the United States' invasion of Afghanistan and Iraq.

U.S. NATIONAL SECURITY AND THE WAR ON TERROR

The U.S. attacks on Afghanistan and Iraq were the result of a number of historical events that converged to bring about the response of war.

Prelude to the War on Terror

Horrible and incomprehensible as the 9/11 attacks were, terrorism by Islamic radicals against the United States and its citizens was not born on that day. A chronology of terrorist acts directed at the United States by Islamic groups before 9/11 includes the following:

- In 1983, Shiite Muslim suicide bombers destroyed U.S. Marine and French para-trooper barracks in Lebanon, killing 299, including 241 Americans.
- In 1988, terrorists linked to Libya bombed a Pan Am 747 headed for the United States over Lockerbie, Scotland, killing 270 passengers and residents of the town.
- In 1993, a truck bomb was detonated in the garage of the World Trade Center, killing six and injuring more than 1,000.
- In 1995, the Army training headquarters in Riyadh, Saudi Arabia, was bombed, killing five Americans and wounding thirty-one.
- In 1996, nineteen U.S. soldiers were killed and 372 Americans injured by an attack on military housing in Dhahran, Saudi Arabia.
- In 1998, car bombs, organized by al-Qaeda, exploded outside U.S. embassies in Tanzania and Kenya, killing 224 people, including twelve Americans.
- In 2000, the USS Cole was attacked in a Yemen harbor by al-Qaeda suicide bombers in a small boat, killing seventeen sailors and injuring thirty-nine.
- On September 10, 2001, the National Security Agency intercepted messages that said, "The match is about to begin" and "Tomorrow is zero hour." These messages were not translated until September 12 (Dickinson and Stein 2006).

The Precipitating Event

On the morning of September 11, 2001, four commercial planes left East Coast airports loaded with passengers and fuel for cross-country flights. These flights were taken over by hijackers who piloted the planes to new destinations, and the course of history was changed. The first plane left Boston for Los Angeles but headed instead for New York City, where it rammed into the World Trade Center's north tower, setting its upper floors ablaze. Fifteen minutes later, a second plane, scheduled for a Boston to Los Angeles flight, steered into the south tower of the World Trade Center. Within the next hour, both towers, each 110 stories high, melted from the intense heat and collapsed. A third plane departed from Washington, DC, for Los Angeles, but turned around and plunged into the Pentagon. The fourth plane left Newark for San Francisco, changed direction, but, possibly because of heroic passengers attacking the hijackers, failed in its mission, presumably to dive into the White House or Capitol Hill, crashing instead in rural Pennsylvania. Thus, within about two hours, these four planes, commandeered by terrorists in synchronized suicide missions, had attacked two symbols of the United States—the World Trade Center, the hub of U.S. capitalism, and the Pentagon, the headquarters of the world's greatest military—killing nearly 3,000 people, about the same number of Americans who died at Pearl Harbor. "Not since the Civil War have we seen as much bloodshed on our soil. Never in our history did so many innocents perish on a single day" (Gergen 2001:60).

A Rush to War

Explore on MySocLab Activity: The War on Terror and Those Who Fight It

Responding to the acts of terrorism against the United States that took place on September 11, 2001, President Bush, just nine days later, declared the war on terror. The president could have declared the 9/11 event a criminal act, limiting the response

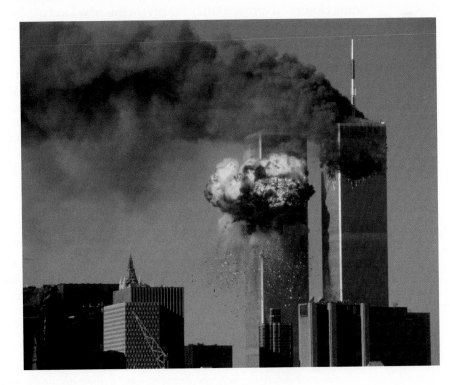

The events of September 11, 2001, changed the course of history.

to capturing the criminals and bringing them to justice. The decision, however, was to declare a war. Moves against al-Qaeda—the terrorist group that carried out the 9/11 attacks—would begin the war, he said, but the war would not end "until every terrorist group of global reach has been found, stopped, and defeated." The president advised Americans to expect "a lengthy campaign, unlike any other we have ever seen." He explained,

> We will starve terrorists of funding, turn them one against another, drive them from place to place, until there is no refuge or no rest. And we will pursue nations that provide aid or safe haven to terrorism. Every nation, in every region, now has a decision to make. Either you are with us, or you are with the terrorists. From this day forward, any nation that continues to harbor or support terrorism will be regarded by the United States as a hostile regime. (Bush 2001a:3)

- **A War Like No Other.** This "war on terror" was to be a war like no other. In the twentieth century, wars were fought by nations over land, resources, and ideology. But the terrorists of 9/11 did not represent a nation, and they were not intent on occupying territories. Terrorists do not have battleships and airfields to be targeted. Instead of an organized army, they are loosely organized through small groups with embedded "cells" to carry out terrorist activities. Containment, the strategy of the Cold War, was no longer possible when there are, as the U.S. State Department noted, thirty-seven foreign terrorist organizations with bases in at least twenty-five nations and the Palestinian territories. These terrorists located around the globe do not wear uniforms but rather live in their host countries as students or workers, just as other residents. If the leaders are identified and killed, others will take their place. Combat includes the use of conventional force as well as car bombs and suicide bombers (the "guided missiles" of the poor). In this new warfare, the combatants will not know victory. "There's no land to seize, no government to topple, no surrender that will bring closure" (Parrish 2001:2). Finally, in this new kind of warfare, great advantages in military technology, as demonstrated by the successful attacks on the World Trade Center and Pentagon, do not make a nation safe.

- **The War in Afghanistan.** With broad international support, Operation Enduring Freedom launched the war on October 7, 2001, as President Bush had promised, against the Taliban of Afghanistan, which supported al-Qaeda. The immediate war offensive moved rapidly so that control of all the major cities of Afghanistan had been wrested from Taliban control within two months of the beginning of combat. A year after starting the operation, the U.S. government claimed that "al-Qaeda went on the run . . . losing their power, their safe havens and much of their leadership. . . . They are fragmented and their leaders are missing, captured, killed or on the run" (The White House 2002a:1).

  This optimistic view proved to be wrong in the long run. At the beginning of 2012, more than ten years after the war began, the United States was still at war with terrorists in Afghanistan.

- **The Bush Doctrine.** Believing in the rightness of their cause and the evil of the terrorists, the Bush administration developed guidelines for U.S. military actions in the war on terror and the longer-range plan for national security in the twenty-first century. This policy, known as the **Bush Doctrine**, has its roots in a particular vision about America's role in the world.

  > The great struggles of the twentieth century between liberty and totalitarianism ended with a decisive victory for the forces of freedom—and a single sustainable model for national

success: freedom, democracy, and free enterprise. . . . These values of freedom are right and true for every person, in every society—and the duty of protecting these values against their enemies is the common calling of freedom-loving people across the globe and across the ages. . . . Today, the United States enjoys a position of unparalleled military strength and great economic and political influence. We seek . . . to create a balance of power that favors human freedom: conditions in which all nations and all societies can choose for themselves the rewards and challenges of political and economic liberty. (The White House 2002b:i)

From this vision flow the strategic principles that guide U.S. military actions in the war on terror.

The Line in the Sand.   Addressing the nation on the day of 9/11, President Bush said, "We will make no distinction between the terrorists who committed these acts and those who harbor them" (Bush 2001b:1). He clarified later that the United States was drawing a line in the sand, and that all world nations had a "decision to make." "Either you are with us, or you are with the terrorists," the president proclaimed (Bush 2001a:3). Later, that binary principle of "us versus them" led the president to his now famous designation of Iraq, Iran, and North Korea as an "axis of evil" and his denunciation of our allies such as France and Germany when they chose not to join in the Iraq war.

Unbounded U.S. Military Superiority.   A second principle of the Bush Doctrine calls for building a military "beyond challenge" and for "experimentation with new approaches to warfare" to give the United States the "capability to defeat any attempt by any enemy" and "dissuade potential adversaries . . . with hopes of surpassing, or equaling, the power of the United States" (The White House 2002b:29–30). In a separate classified policy statement, the Bush Doctrine policy makers even declared that the United States reserves the right to respond to danger with overwhelming force—including potentially nuclear weapons—if necessary (*Washington Times* 2003).

Unilateral Preventive War and Regime Change.   The Bush administration asserted the right of the United States to carry out preventive wars unilaterally to remove governments (regime change) that it deems to be engaged in long-range plans to develop weapons of mass destruction (WMDs) and to support terrorism. This pillar of the Bush Doctrine, an astonishing departure from U.S. practice and tradition, was first conveyed by the president in a graduation speech to West Point cadets. "We must take the battle to the enemy, disrupt his plans, and confront the worst threats before they emerge. If we wait for threats to fully materialize, we will have waited too long" (quoted in Ricks 2006:38). "We cannot let our enemies strike first. The overlap between states that sponsor terror and those that pursue WMD compels us to action. . . . To forestall or prevent such hostile acts by our adversaries, the United States will, if necessary act preemptively" (quoted in Ricks 2006:62).

   The Bush Doctrine includes the assertion that the United States can engage in a **preventive war** as well as a **preemptive war**. The late historian Arthur Schlesinger notes the differences in these two principles.

The distinction between "pre-emptive" and "preventive" is well worth preserving. It is the distinction between legality and illegality. "Pre-emptive" war refers to a direct, immediate, specific threat that must be crushed at once; in the words of the Department of Defense manual, "an attack initiated on the basis of incontrovertible evidence that an enemy attack is imminent." "Preventive" war refers to potential, future, therefore speculative threats. (Quoted in Singh 2006:18–19)

Using this distinction, Robert Singh said, "The Iraq war was as clear an instance of preventive war—illegal under the U.N. Charter—as possible" (Singh 2006:19).

The Bush Doctrine does not require imminent threat for the United States to swing into full offensive military force; it requires only distant threat as determined by U.S. leaders. This is the "One Percent Solution," as enunciated by Vice President Cheney (hence, also known as the "Cheney Doctrine"): "If there was even a one percent chance of terrorists getting a weapon of mass destruction . . . the United States must now act as if it were a certainty" (quoted in Suskind 2006:62). In March 2003, Operation Iraqi Freedom became the first proof of U.S. commitment to this principle for national security in the war on terror.

The Spread of Democracy. The assumption is that the national interests of the United States are best pursued by spreading democratic forms of governance. As President Bush said in his 2004 speech at West Point,

> Some who call themselves "realists" question whether the spread of democracy in the
> Middle East should be any concern of ours. But the realists in this case have lost contact
> with a fundamental reality. America has always been less secure when freedom is in retreat.
> America is always more secure when freedom is on the march. (Quoted in Singh 2006:20)

The War in Iraq

With early positive results in Afghanistan, the Bush administration's attention turned to Iraq. The Bush administration justified a preventive war against Iraq because its leader, Saddam Hussein, was guilty of mass murder against his own people, but also because, it was alleged, he was amassing weapons of mass destruction (nuclear, chemical, and biological), and there was a strong connection between Saddam Hussein and al-Qaeda's terrorism. A debate rages as to whether these last two charges are factual, as claimed by the Bush administration or was the Bush administration convinced too easily by evidence that showed them what they wanted to see? Or was the president acting reasonably on information that appeared solid at the time? (*USA Today* 2007:13A). Historians will eventually provide a definitive answer to this crucial debate that during the war and postwar years was so highly politicized.

Operation Iraqi Freedom began in March 2003 without a clear United Nations mandate. As in the war in Afghanistan, the initial offensive moved swiftly. Some 340,000 U.S. military personnel were deployed in the Persian Gulf region, along with more than 47,000 British troops and smaller numbers from a few other nations, to carry out the initial invasion of Iraq. After just twenty-five days, the United States and coalition forces were in some degree of control of all major Iraqi cities. President Bush declared an end to major combat operations on May 1, 2003, yet the war continued until the last troops were withdrawn in December 2012. No weapons of mass destruction were found, and the rationale for the war shifted to bring democracy to Iraq, which would serve as a model for democracy for other nations in the Middle East to adopt.

After almost nine years of war, the Pentagon declared an official end to its mission in Iraq in late 2011. There was no clear sense of what had been won or lost in this war (Shanker, Schmidt, and Worth 2011). The conflict claimed 4,486 American lives and 32,226 more Americans wounded in action. The aftermath of the war proved complicated and very costly for the United States. Iraqi institutions were not equipped to restore civil order, rebuild the infrastructure, and provide basic services because they were challenged by a persistent Iraqi resistance movement and sectarian violence.

Although most of the U.S. troops were withdrawn from Iraq, the U.S. continued its influence both directly and indirectly. There is a huge U.S. embassy in Baghdad. How involved is the United States, through this embassy, in the internal affairs of Iraq? Moreover, the Iraqis have bought more than $15 billion of U.S. military hardware, including fighter planes, tanks, armored personnel carriers, and surveillance drones. The Iraqis insist these are for defensive purposes. But how will these purchases of weapons be interpreted by its neighbors in Iran, Syria, Turkey, and Israel? Will they increase or lessen tensions in the Middle East? And how will the supplying of these weapons by the United States be interpreted?

The Afghanistan War

Listen on MySocLab Audio: NPR: The Long War in Afghanistan

As the Iraq War wound down, President Obama increased U.S. military presence briefly in Afghanistan. The goal, however, was to gradually withdraw most of the troops by the end of 2014, coinciding with the NATO decision to remove all troops from Afghanistan in 2014. From that point on, primary combat responsibilities belong to the Afghan army. The United States will keep about 20,000 military personnel in Afghanistan for another ten years, at an annual cost of $4 billion. Regardless of U.S. involvement, Afghanistan will likely continue is perpetual civil war between the Pashtun tribes in the south and ethnic factions in the north (Klein 2012). So, as *USA Today* editorialized, "A clear-cut victory [in Afghanistan] is no more attainable than it was in Vietnam, Korea or Iraq" (2012:8A).

The Costs of the Iraq and Afghanistan Wars

View on MySocLab Figure: Deaths of Americans in Eleven U.S. Wars

- **Loss of Human Life.** At mid-2012, the Pentagon's official death toll from both wars was 6,460 U.S. service members. In addition to the deaths of U.S. military personnel, there were the deaths of 1,344 other coalition soldiers (CNN 2012). Other deaths were Iraqi and Afghani soldiers/police, U.S. defense contractors, humanitarian workers, journalists, insurgents, and civilians. The number of civilian deaths in Iraq is unknown, with estimates varying from 100,000 to 920,000 deaths. If the high estimate is accurate, the total is 303 times as many people killed in Afghanistan and Iraq than in the terrorist attacks of September 11, 2001 (Unknown News 2010).

- **The Injured.** Estimates of the injured vary. Some limit the number injured to U.S. troops. Thus, the Pentagon official count of injured in Afghanistan and Iraq is 38,000. This gives a false impression in two ways. First, if all casualties were included (U.S. and coalition troops, Afghan and Iraqi troops and civilians, contractors, and journalists, the total would be as high as 1.74 million (Unknown News 2010). Second, just counting U.S. troops, at the beginning of 2012 some 320,000 U.S. veterans had brain injuries (Griffis 2012). Moreover, the Department of Veterans Affairs estimates that 170,000 veterans suffer hearing damage and 200,000 veterans have mental problems (reported in Sandels 2010). The number of troops with brain and spinal injuries is high because of better protective equipment and improvements in medical trauma care; more injured troops are surviving these wars than in previous wars. Although this is good news, the downside is that because of the terrible force of explosions the combat soldiers experience, more are surviving with brain injuries.

In addition, the trauma of war haunts many soldiers when they return home. More than 17 percent of returning soldiers suffer from post traumatic stress disorder (PTSD), with symptoms of flashbacks, nightmares, feelings of detachment, irritability,

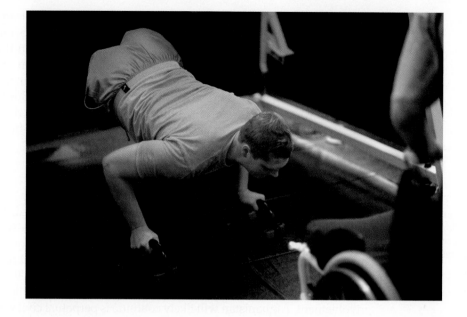

More than 80,000 troops were injured or wounded in the Iraq War.

trouble concentrating, and sleeplessness. Those who have been deployed more than once have a 50 percent increase in acute combat stress over those who have been deployed only once (Thompson 2007). Indicative of the higher stress levels felt by wartime troops, in 2012, a Veterans Administration investigation found that in 2010 there were an average of thirty-three suicide attempts by veterans a day, with eighteen being successful (Somander and Gilani 2011). Put another way, 20 percent of all deaths in the military are by suicide, compared to 7 percent of all deaths among civilian men ages 17 to 60 (Thompson and Gibbs 2012).

Often overlooked in the injuries of war are the consequences of long separations and psychological trauma on the intimate lives of soldiers and their spouses, resulting in a rising divorce rate. Their divorce rate for fiscal 2011 was 3.7 divorces per 100 marriages, up from 2.6 in 2001, when the conflict began. The incidence of spouse abuse within military couples has also increased as the war progressed, especially with male veterans with PTSD, who are two to three times more likely than veterans without PTSD to engage in intimate partner violence (Somander and Gilani 2011).

The trauma of war is not limited to soldiers but affects civilians who are also in harm's way. They fear air raids, attacks by unseen drones, and other forms of violence. A study of Iraqi children by the Iraqi Ministry of Health, for example, found that around 70 percent of primary school students suffered symptoms of trauma-related stress such as bed-wetting, stuttering, voluntary muteness, and increased aggressive behavior (Palmer 2007).

- **The Displaced.** According to Brown University's analysis, the wars displaced 7.815 million people (3.315 million Afghan civilians, 3.5 million Iraqi civilians, and 1.0 million Pakistani civilians) (reported in Moyers 2012).

- **Monetary Costs.** Before the invasion of Iraq, the Bush administration estimated that combat operations there would cost about $50 billion. According to Brown University's Watson Institute for International Studies, nearly ten years after the wars began, the

United States had spent between $2.3 trillion and $2.7 trillion on these conflicts (Brown University 2011). These costs will continue after the wars cease, as the war debt is repaid and the care and treatment of many U.S. military veterans continues indefinitely for brain and spinal injuries.

A major cost of the wars was that it drained resources from social programs that could have lessened their severity as societal social problems. *New York Times* columnist Bob Herbert interviewed Nobel laureate economist Joseph Stiglitz, asking how the massive funds for the military might have been better spent. Stiglitz replied,

> *About $560 billion, which is a little more than half of [the Stiglitz] study's conservative estimate of the cost of the war, would have been enough to "fix" Social Security for the next 75 years. If one were thinking in terms of promoting democracy in the Middle East, the money being spent on the war would have been enough to finance a mega-mega-mega-Marshall Plan, which would have been so much more effective than the invasion of Iraq. (Quoted in Herbert 2006: para. 12)*

The "Social Policy" panel "Shifting Some Military Spending to Alternative Programs" provides some further suggestions for funneling military spending into social spending.

Social Policy

SHIFTING SOME MILITARY SPENDING TO ALTERNATIVE PROGRAMS

The United States spends as much on military spending as the next fourteen nations combined. By itself, the United States accounts for 41 percent of all global military spending. Moreover, America's allies account for another 21 percent of the world's military spending. In effect, the United States and its friends and allies account for more than two-thirds of the military spending worldwide (Lindorff 2010). When is enough enough? Are we overspending on defense at the expense of other crucial societal concerns? Because we spend so much on the military, is it reasonable to assume that the United States could reduce its spending on defense without jeopardizing national security?

President Eisenhower said: "Every gun that is made, every warship launched, every rocket fired signifies, in the final sense, a theft from those who hunger and are not fed, those who are cold and are not clothed." Similarly, Martin Luther King, Jr. pointed out: "When a nation becomes obsessed with the guns of war, social programs must inevitably suffer" (quoted in Solomon 2010). Could policymakers reduce the military budget by one-fourth or so (or even more) and put that money to work on mass transit, low-cost housing, job training, green jobs, subsidized education, infrastructure projects, and the like? If so, we could produce more jobs than when we create military projects.

It is commonly argued that military spending is more productive than most industries in creating jobs. Actually, research shows that for each $1 billion spent, over 17,000 jobs would be created in clean energy, or about 20,000 in health care, and over 29,000 in education, compared to that same $1 billion spent in the military, resulting in 11,600 jobs (Garrett-Peltier 2010).

If we take the formal military budget of about $700 billion (not the actual one of $1.2 trillion, which includes veterans' benefits, homeland security, and the like), a reduction of 25 percent (about $175 billion), could be achieved immediately by withdrawing from Iraq and Afghanistan, cutting weapons systems that the Pentagon has deemed unnecessary, and closing half of the 800 U.S. military bases abroad (Mazzetta and Clark 2010). That $175 billion could be used to reduce the national debt or provide health coverage for 40 million people, or build/renovate 20,000 schools (Mazzetta and Clark 2010).

These wars were funded primarily with borrowed money. As a result, at least $1.5 trillion has been added to the nation's national debt. By 2011 about $185 billion in interest had been paid on war spending, and another $1 trillion will accrue in interest alone through 2020. This adds significantly to the national debt of $16 trillion (in 2012). This huge amount is used by some legislators to justify massive cuts in social programs.

The Legacy of the Wars

The United States chose to respond to the 9/11 terrorist attacks by invading Afghanistan and later Iraq. This response has had enormous consequences for the United States, for the people of Afghanistan and Iraq, for the Middle East, and for international relations. Recognizing that the U.S. involvement in the Middle East continues and the end results are unknown, this section outlines the consequences of the wars and speculates on the long-term legacy of U.S. actions.

The Bush Doctrine was the first attempt at a grand strategy since the end of the Cold War. But did it work? Did it eliminate the threat from terrorist networks and rogue states? Did it spread democracy to the Middle East? Did it unify these fractured nations?

Supporters of the wars argued that Saddam Hussein had been captured, tried, and executed and bin Laden assassinated. But while the deaths of these terrorist leaders were symbolically significant, they did not destroy al-Qaeda and prevent future acts of terrorism. Terrorism now emanates from places like Iran, Yemen, Pakistan, and Somalia.

The long-term consequences of the U.S. military interventions in Afghanistan and Iraq appear to be serious and far reaching. We do not know the full extent of the ramifications, but we have some clues. We begin with the successful scenario, followed by a number of negative possibilities.

- **The Effort Is Successful.** Vice President Cheney gave this optimistic prediction of our wars to stifle terrorism:

  > Ten years from now, we'll look back on this period of time and see that liberating 50 million people in Afghanistan and Iraq really did represent a major, fundamental shift, obviously, in U.S. policy in terms of how we dealt with the emerging terrorist threat—and that we'll have fundamentally changed circumstances in that part of the world. (Quoted in Nye 2006: para. 2)

  Cheney was correct on two counts. First, the U.S. effort freed Iraq from the tyranny of Saddam Hussein in Iraq and the leadership of bin Laden in the al-Qaeda organization. But are the Iraqis and Afghans better off? Will democracy get a foothold in these countries and spread across the Middle East as apologists for the war believe? Ten years after the war in Iraq began, the answers to these questions are negative. Long term, these are questions for historians to answer. And, second, Cheney asserted that the Middle East will be fundamentally changed by U.S. efforts. He was correct, but will the U.S. war on terror bring about beneficial changes for that region? Or will they be overwhelmingly detrimental?

- **Iraqis and Afghans Turn against the United States.** The United States did liberate Iraq from the oppressive Saddam Hussein regime and Osama bin Laden is dead, but in the process, the wars destroyed much of Iraq's and Afghanistan's infrastructure (e.g., roads, bridges, buildings, private homes, and the means for providing essential services such as electricity and water). The United States was held responsible for this destruction, which was compounded by the slow rebuilding of the infrastructure because of terrorist acts, bureaucratic mismanagement, scandal, profiteering, and insufficient funds.

As the *New York Times* editorialized, "The United States' failure to restore utilities and rebuild schools and hospitals has turned once sympathetic Iraqis against the American presence in their country" (*New York Times* 2006: para. 2).

Read on **MySocLab Document:** Blowback: U.S. Actions Abroad Have Repeatedly Led to Unintended, Indefensible Consequences

The war on terrorism has not been won. Actually, U.S. involvement in the Middle East has caused resentment among local populations. In effect, U.S. violence and occupation increased the threat of terrorism (McGovern 2012). Or, as the late historian Howard Zinn asked: "Is our war in Afghanistan ending terrorism, or provoking it" (Zinn 2008)? It provokes terrorism as a consequence of the U.S. meddling in the affairs of other sovereign nations but also because of the collateral damage (the deaths and injuries to civilians) from indiscriminate shelling or drone attacks. Muslims have been outraged by videos showing Marines urinating on Taliban bodies, the burning of the Koran, and soldiers holding up body parts of their enemies as trophies. These acts enhanced the threat of terrorism rather than diminishing it.

- **The Civil War in Iraq Is Polarizing the Sunni–Shiite Schism Worldwide.** The United States was ineffective in bringing the Sunnis and Shiites together in Iraq. Even as the United States withdrew, militias from both sides continuously attacked each other's neighborhoods and holy places. Both sides in this civil war used car bombs, suicide bombers, roadside bombs, and guerrilla-style ambushes.

  Ethnic and regional political divisions in Iraq have been exacerbated by the war, and these resulting sectarian schisms are increasing tensions in the Muslim world. The continuing war by these religious factions is viewed by Arabs on regional television across the region, inflaming sectarian passions and resulting in similar clashes between Sunnis and Shiites in Egypt, Pakistan, Saudi Arabia, and elsewhere. Even in Muslim neighborhoods in the United States, these tensions are felt as, for example, when Shiite shopkeepers were victims of arson, presumably perpetrated by Sunnis, in Dearborn, Michigan.

  Of the world's 1.3 billion Muslims, 85 percent are Sunni. Shiites are a majority in five countries, most notably Iran and Iraq. These Shiite nations form a crescent from Iran to Lebanon. The Sunnis fear the growing power influence of Iran and the new Shiite government in Iraq brought to power by the war. Ironically, the United States finds itself favoring the Shiite government in Iraq but favors Sunni leaders everywhere else, which angers both sides (Feldman 2007).

  Shiite leaders sense that the United States incites sectarianism as a way of blunting Iran's influence:

  > The growing Sunni–Shiite divide is roiling an Arab world as unsettled as at any time in a generation. Fought in speeches, newspaper columns, rumors swirling through cafes and the Internet, and occasional bursts of strife, the conflict is predominantly shaped by politics: a disintegrating Iraq, an ascendant Iran, a sense of Arab powerlessness and a persistent suspicion of American intentions. (Shadid 2007:6)

- **Loss of U.S. Image and Credibility in the Arab World.** A goal of the Iraq and Afghanistan wars was to install a pro-U.S. democracy there with the intention that this model would eventually spread democracy and freedom throughout the Arab world. The war and the occupation, however, turned more and more people in that region against the United States. Polls by Zogby International and the Pew Research Center in 2010 and 2011 found that many in the Arab world had an unfavorable rating of the United States. Moreover, these already low ratings declined even more in the first years of the Obama administration compared with the ratings at the end of the Bush administration. For example, favorable ratings of the United States fell at least 9 percent in Morocco, Egypt, Saudi Arabia, and the United Arab Emirates from 2008 to 2010. In Egypt the favorable rating fell from 30 percent to 5 percent (Al Jazeera 2011; Ukman 2011).

Among the reasons Muslims have less regard for the United States since the Iraq and Afghanistan wars were the perceived indirect attack on Muslims, and the widespread assumption that the United States involvement was to take advantage of the oil supply in Iraq, the secret prisons, and the torture of Muslims (per the images of prisoners at Abu Ghraib and Guantanamo Bay, Cuba), expanding the war in Afghanistan, the assassination of Osama bin Laden, and the continued U.S. support of Israel.

Watch on
MySocLab Video:
Survey of U.S. Troops

Inhumane Treatment of Suspected Terrorists Aids the Cause of the Terrorists. The Geneva Conventions are international agreements on humane treatment of combatants and civilians by opposing governments and military forces during times of war. The first of these treaties dates back to 1864, and since then, the agreements evolved so that nearly every nation (188 of them) was a signatory to the Geneva Conventions at the beginning of the war on terror. Although the Bush administration never suggested that the United States withdraw from these core provisions of international law, there has been a pattern of circumventing them. The pattern began after the 2001 military campaign in Afghanistan, which netted thousands of captive Taliban supporters and suspected al-Qaeda operatives, many of whom were imprisoned and subjected to sometimes barbaric treatment in "defiance of American and international law" (Conason 2007:12). This practice continued during the Obama administration, as suspects were kidnapped and taken to prisons around the world for months and years at a time. Under American law, these acts were illegal.

Listen on
MySocLab Audio:
NPR: Interrogation and
National Security

In 2006, Congress passed the Military Commissions Act. When President Bush signed this act, he announced: "In memory of the victims of September 11, it is my honor to sign [this Act] into law" (quoted in Sussman 2007:7). This act (Herman 2006):

- Significantly broadens the definition of "enemy combatant" and makes it a matter of presidential discretion. An "enemy combatant" is defined as a person who is designated by the commander-in-chief as someone who has engaged in hostilities against the United States.
- Removes habeas corpus rights of noncitizens. **Habeas corpus**, a human right considered fundamental to the western world since the Magna Carta (CE 1215), prevents the police from arresting and holding someone without cause. In other words, enemy combatants are denied the right to challenge their detentions in civil courts.
- Permits aggressive interrogations in secret prisons. The act does not list acceptable and unacceptable "methods of interrogation." The legislation keeps methods open-ended and subject to the president's interpretation of the Geneva Conventions.
- Suspension of normal rules of evidence and due process. The act, unlike the procedures in U.S. courts, permits the use of hearsay and coerced evidence and evidence obtained in warrantless searches, and it fails to allow prisoners on trial ensured access to the evidence against them.

The Military Commissions Act may eventually be declared unconstitutional by the Supreme Court because it violates the Bill of Rights. But in the meantime, the

U.S. reaction to terrorism was a "five-year transformation from beacon of freedom to autocratic torture state" (Rall 2006:19).

- **The Erosion of Civil Liberties at Home.** Faced with the threat of terrorism, the president sought, and Congress passed, the USA PATRIOT (Uniting and Strengthening America by Providing Appropriate Tools Required to Intercept and Obstruct Terrorism) Act of 2001. This act was hailed by supporters as a crucial piece of legislation giving the nation's law enforcement and intelligence-gathering personnel the "tools they need" to catch terrorists and stop another 9/11. The provisions of the USA PATRIOT Act:

  - Expanded the ability of law enforcement personnel to conduct secret searches and conduct phone and Internet surveillance and to access a wide range of personal financial, medical, mental health, and student records. Government monitoring of communication between federal detainees and their lawyers is allowed. Judicial oversight of these investigation activities is reduced by the act.
  - Expanded the legal definition of terrorism beyond previous laws in a manner that subjects ordinary political and religious organizations to surveillance, wiretapping, and criminal action without any evidence of wrongdoing.
  - Allowed FBI agents to investigate any American citizen without probable cause of crime if they say it is for "intelligence purposes." As a result, some American citizens, mostly of Arab and South Asian origin, have been held in secret federal custody for weeks or months, many without any charges filed against them and without access to lawyers.
  - Allowed noncitizens to be jailed based on suspicion, even without evidence. Suspects can be detained indefinitely without judicial review, and hundreds have been detained. Immigration hearings for post-9/11 noncitizen detainees are conducted in secret.

Some argue that ordinary law-abiding folks have nothing to fear from laws like the USA PATRIOT Act unless they are involved in some kind of clandestine activity. But this reaction misses the point according to critics. The USA PATRIOT Act is only one of hundreds of laws and legal regulations rewritten by the Bush administration to create barriers to the possibility of terrorists penetrating U.S. borders. More than any other legal change, it points out the uncanny contradiction of the war on terror policies. Under the Bush Doctrine, the United States has conducted aggressive military campaigns to liberate Afghans and Iraqis and bring democracy to "the greater Middle East." Yet, the actions of the government have restricted civil liberties that are the foundation of the U.S. Constitution and democracy. How can we expand democracy in the wider world when we do not practice it in fortress America?

Senator Russ Feingold from Wisconsin was the only senator to vote against the PATRIOT Act. His rationale delivered to his colleagues was,

> There is no doubt that if we lived in a police state, it would be easier to catch terrorists. If we lived in a country where the police were allowed to search your home at any time for any reason; if we lived in a country where the government was entitled to open your mail, eavesdrop on your phone conversations, or intercept your e-mail communications; if we lived in a country where people could be held in jail indefinitely based on what they write or think, or based on mere suspicion that they were up to no good, the government would probably discover and arrest more terrorists, or would-be terrorists, just as it would find more lawbreakers generally. But that would not be a country in which we would want to live, and it would not be a country for which we could, in good conscience, ask our young people to fight and die. In short, that country would not be America. (2001:2)

Watch on MySocLab Video: NYC Terrorist Plot

To conduct the war on terror, domestic surveillance programs have been conducted by the FBI, the Defense Department, Homeland Security, and the National Security Agency (all of which are justified as inherent in the "wartime" powers of the president). Here are some examples of domestic spying:

- Surveillance by the FBI and local police of domestic activist organizations (e.g., American Friends Service Committee, Greenpeace, and United for Peace and Justice; Dunn 2006).
- The departments of Justice, State, and Homeland Security buy commercial databases that track Americans' finances, phone numbers, and biographical information (Woellert and Kopecke 2006).
- Using a "national security letter," the FBI can demand that an Internet provider, bank, or phone company turn over records of who you call and e-mail; where you work, fly, and vacation; and the like. No judge has to approve the demand. Moreover, the individual under surveillance is unaware of what is happening because it is classified (*USA Today* 2005).
- The Department of Homeland Security recruited utility and telephone workers, cable TV installers, postal workers, delivery drivers, and others who regularly enter private homes to become federal informants, informing of suspicious persons, activities, and items that they observed (Conason 2007:194).
- To qualify for federal homeland security grants, states must assemble lists of "potential threat elements"—individuals or groups suspected of possible terrorist activity (Kaplan 2006).
- The Justice Department funded a private contractor, Matrix (Multistate Anti-Terrorism Information Exchange), which used "data mining" technology to search public records and matched them with police files to identify some 120,000 "suspects" with "high terrorist factor" scores.

Proponents argue that the dangers are serious, and these and other security measures are needed to make the nation secure by making it easier to identify, prevent, and punish terrorists.

Critics, on the other hand, argue that these measures go too far in expanding the government's abilities to intrude on citizens' lives, thereby weakening individual rights. Citizens have guarantees from the Constitution that protect them from government surveillance, reading the mail, and listening to phone conversations of its citizens—in short, Americans have the right to privacy and freedom from unreasonable search and seizure. Moreover, there is a high probability that the invasion of privacy will not be randomly distributed but more likely will be directed to noncitizens, Muslims, and people who look "Middle Eastern."

There is a fine line between what is needed for security and protecting the freedoms that characterize the United States. If we stray too far toward restricted freedoms, we end up, ironically, terrorizing ourselves. Another irony is that President Bush declared on the night of the assault on the World Trade Center and Pentagon that "America is the brightest beacon for freedom in the world and no one will keep that light from shining," yet the domestic antiterrorism actions taken by the government "darken that very beacon of freedom by making a new attack on our own people's already endangered civil liberties" (Hightower 2001:1).

18.5 Discuss the changes in warfare in the twenty-first century.

TWENTY-FIRST CENTURY WARFARE

The conduct of war has changed since the Korean and Vietnam conflicts in the 1950s and 1960s. Wars used to require collective national sacrifice with a draft, rationing, and higher taxes. All of that has changed with the wars in Afghanistan and Iraq.

A volunteer military replaced the draft. Because the military offers educational opportunities and financial inducements, youth from poor and working-class families are overrepresented in the military. These volunteers tend to come from economically struggling, mostly rural areas, with few job opportunities. For example, the death rate for rural soldiers is 24 per million adults, a rate 60 percent higher than the death rate for soldiers from cities and suburbs (15 deaths per million; Engelhardt 2007). In terms of social class, 75 percent of those killed came from U.S. towns where the per capita income was below the national average (*Newsweek* 2007). As a result, most Americans do not have family members in the fight. Thus, they are emotionally insulated from the war.

The number of military personnel is kept at a minimum in two ways. One method is to extend the combat tours of the military personnel and to give them multiple combat tours. This overworking of soldiers takes its toll in mental fatigue increasing the likelihood of post-traumatic stress syndrome (PTSD). One manifestation of the stress is the relatively high rate of suicide. In the past ten years, for example, the U.S. army lost more soldiers to suicide than to enemy fire in Afghanistan (Maddow 2012:204).

The second tactic used to limit the size of the military has been to privatize many military functions. In other words, the Pentagon hires private contractors to do work once done by soldiers, in effect outsourcing such activities as cooking, maintenance work, building and remodeling structures, furnishing transportation, providing security (just a bit ironic), data processing, and gathering intelligence. The privatizing of the military benefits the Pentagon by allowing the expansion of war activities, shifting parts of the Pentagon budget to other government agencies, but keeping many activities away from public view. In short, this allows the military to go beyond the limits set by Congress without political consequences. Moreover, the number of deaths and injured among private contractors are not included in the toll of wars, thus hiding the actual cost of lives from civilian notice. But they die, nevertheless, for U.S. goals. In 2011, for example, more contractors working for American companies died than did U.S. soldiers in Afghanistan (Nordland 2012).

The contractors provide security, but they also conduct clandestine raids against suspected insurgents. Thus, they are private forces deployed in a war zone free from public scrutiny and shielded from accountability, oversight, and legal constraints (Scahill 2007:13; see also, Scahill 2009).

Typically, during wartime the government reevaluates tax and spending policies to add revenue and to shift resources from less vital pursuits to pay the additional costs of conducting and winning the war. Not so in the twenty-first century, as the president and Congress, for the first time in modern history, went into a major war by reducing the tax burden on the wealthy. The costs were shifted to later generations as the national debt rose and its immense size ($16 trillion in 2012), was used to justify reducing social programs. In effect, then, the cost of the wars was not shared equally among the citizens of the United States. Directly and indirectly the less advantaged bear the brunt of wars, while the impact of these conflicts does not impact the rest of U.S. society.

The public has also been shielded from the loss of American lives in the wars of the twenty-first century. From 2003 to 2008, for example, the Bush administration banned news photographers from the ceremonies when flag-draped caskets were removed from planes at U.S. air bases. Moreover, the president and vice president did not attend military funerals, and the Pentagon effectively banned images of wounded troops when it required news agencies to get signed consent forms from soldiers photographed after they were wounded (Maddow 2012). So, instead of shared grief and national honor for the loss of American lives, the grief is privatized to the families of the fallen. Among Rachel Maddow's recommendations, after reviewing the various aspects of wars as they are now fought, is that "going to war, being at war, should be painful for the entire country, from the start" (Maddow 2012:249; see also Ricks 2012). But that is not how wars are conducted in the twenty-first century. Americans have been systematically made oblivious to the grisly human price of war (Shane 2012). This makes it too easy for leaders to lead us toward war.

Wars are also distant to many combatants as conventional warfare has been replaced in part by a "shadow power," composed of private corporations, mercenaries, drone strikes, electronic surveillance, and stealth engagements by special forces.

Drone strikes are especially relevant to twenty-first century warfare. These are unmanned aerial vehicles used for surveillance and bombing strategic targets. The United States has deployed 7,000 drones in six countries. The CIA and the U.S. military operate the drones but a far distance from the strikes (as far away as Langley, Virginia). Not only does this remove combatants from the enemy, drone operations are classified and thus cannot be openly debated in Congress, thus removing the program from public view and responsibility (Cole 2012).

Drones are used to assassinate those responsible for terrorist attacks. This has meant strikes in sovereign nations without their permission (acts that Americans would not tolerate if they were directed at the United States). The United States, for example, conducted over 300 drone strikes in Pakistan from 2004 to 2012, over the strong objections of the Pakistani government. These stealth attacks have assassinated suspected terrorist leaders but their collateral damage has also killed innocents, leading to intense hatred of the United States and increasing support of the terrorists (*The Nation* 2012). In particular, drone strikes lead many Pakistanis and Yemenis, driven by hatred and revenge, to join militant groups opposed to the United States (Mothana 2012).

Drones and other new technologies have freed the executive branch from seeking approval of Congress. President Obama and his administration unilaterally order the killing of foreigners located far from the battlefield without the oversight of the other

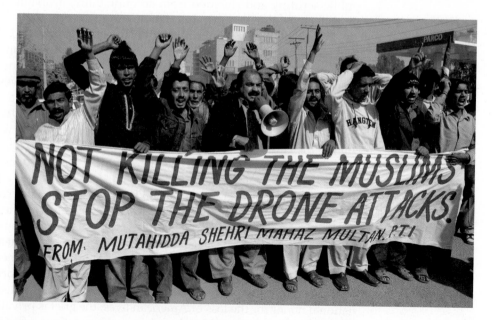

Stealth attacks by drones have assassinated suspected terrorist leaders, but their collateral damage has also killed innocents, leading to increased support for terrorists in their war against the United States.

branches of government (*New York Times* 2012). This trend of presidents bypassing Congress on matters of war began with Kennedy and Johnson in the Vietnam War and later with Reagan, and continuing to the present, with an ever greater convergence of power in the executive branch (Maddow 2012).

Two final points regarding national security threats in the twenty-first century: First, throughout most of U.S. history, the threat to national security was organized violence by nation-states. This threat, while still plausible, has diminished. Now ethnic tribes and clans, drug cartels, ethnic nationalists, and religious fundamentalism are the threats. But these potential enemies will not be defeated by conventional means. As former Senator Gary Hart observed, our strategic weapons, large Army divisions, and navy warships will have little impact on the new enemies (Hart 2011:76).

What does this mean for national security in the twenty-first century? Does the United States continue to require intercontinental ballistic missiles, nuclear submarines, aircraft carriers, stealth fighters, and the like for its national defense? They were needed in the age of conventional warfare, but are they needed in the new realities of terrorism? The cost of fighting these twenty-first century threats is considerably less than fighting conventional wars. These costs could be reduced by hundreds of billions without jeopardizing the nation's security (Reich 2012). If history is a guide, however, the costs of wars will continue to expand as the military-industrial-complex uses lobbying, campaign contributions, and spreading its production networks across manufacturing sits in many Congressional districts.

Second, not only is warfare itself changing, so, too, are the treats to security from global problems such as resource depletion (especially water but also energy and metals), climate degradation, the maldistribution of food, significant migrations from the southern hemisphere to the northern hemisphere, and global pandemics.

In sum, if we do not solve national security problems, then the other social problems discussed in this text are immaterial. These global social problems, although seemingly far away and removed from everyday life, hold the ultimate consequences to our individual and collective security.

MySocLab ✓ Study and Review on MySocLab

■ CHAPTER REVIEW

1. Military might, to be second to none in power, is the principle guiding national security in the United States. The U.S. military is the largest and most expensive in the world. Military spending is high because (a) of the fear of nuclear weapons held by others; (b) there are nations with expansionist agendas; (c) defense spending benefits business, labor, the states, the members of Congress, and academia; and (d) outspending others is said to give the United States "peace through strength."

2. Nuclear weapons are the most destructive weapons on earth. The United States and Russia possess 96

percent of the world's nuclear warheads. As many as forty countries have the capacity to develop nuclear weapons.

3. Terrorism is a strategy of using violence to gain political advantage. It is a social construction. That is, what is defined as terrorism and who is labeled a terrorist are matters of interpretation.

4. Domestic terrorism (Americans killing Americans) has occurred throughout U.S. history. The current threats come from individuals and groups focusing on particular issues such as abortion or gun control or a more generalized fear of government overreach and government mistakes, as well as feeling

powerless against not only by big government but also big banks and big Wall Street. The Tea Party movement embodies these fears and is a source of unrest. Most movement followers are not violent, but the seeds of violence are.

5. The war on international terror is like no other war because terrorists do not represent a nation but are loosely organized and are willing to use tactics such as suicide bombers.

6. The Bush Doctrine that emerged to guide national security in response to the September 11, 2001, attacks included the following principles: (a) the right of the United States to engage unilaterally in preventive wars and to change governments it deems to be dangerous, (b) the spread of democracy, (c) the building of a military beyond challenge, and (d) dividing nations into those who are with us and those who are against us.

7. The war on terror has been very costly in human life, injury, and treasure. The costs to the United States in conducting this war are not evenly distributed. The soldiers come disproportionately from minorities, the working and lower classes, and rural areas.

8. The possible long-term negative consequences of these wars include (a) the loss of Iraqi and Afghani support, (b) the polarizing of the Sunni–Shiite schism worldwide, (c) the loss of U.S. image and credibility in the Arab world, (d) unintended support for the cause of the terrorists through U.S. actions against suspected terrorists, and (e) the loss of civil liberties in the United States.

9. The cost of wars in casualties and treasure are now minimized for the public by outsourcing military functions to private contractors, not counting casualties by contractors in the official statistics, distributing the costs of the military to a number of departments, and by limiting debates on military matters in Congress.

10. The conduct of wars in the twenty-first century differs from earlier times. The combatants are volunteers, many combatants have been replaced by mercenaries, attacks are often carried out by unmanned drones or by special forces.

■ KEY TERMS

National security. The ways nations organize to protect borders, guard their national interests, and shield their citizens and businesses abroad with armies, military bases, intelligence networks, embassies, and consulates.

Defense budget. The government's spending plan for maintaining and upgrading the military defenses of the United States.

Weapons of mass destruction (WMDs). Nuclear, biological, and chemical weapons capable of large-scale death and destruction.

Cold War. The tension and arms race between the United States and the Soviet Union from World War II until 1990.

Terrorism. Any act intended to cause death or serious injury to civilians or noncombatants to intimidate a population and weaken their will or draw attention to the perpetrator's cause.

Bush Doctrine. The policy guiding U.S. military actions in the "war on terror" and the long-range plan for national security in the twenty-first century.

Preventive war. A war in response to a presumed future threat.

Preemptive war. A war in response to a direct, immediate, and specific threat.

Habeas corpus. A basic human right in the Western world that prevents the police (or government) from arresting and holding someone without cause.

Progressive Plan to Solve Social Problems

 Listen to Chapter 19 on **MySocLab**

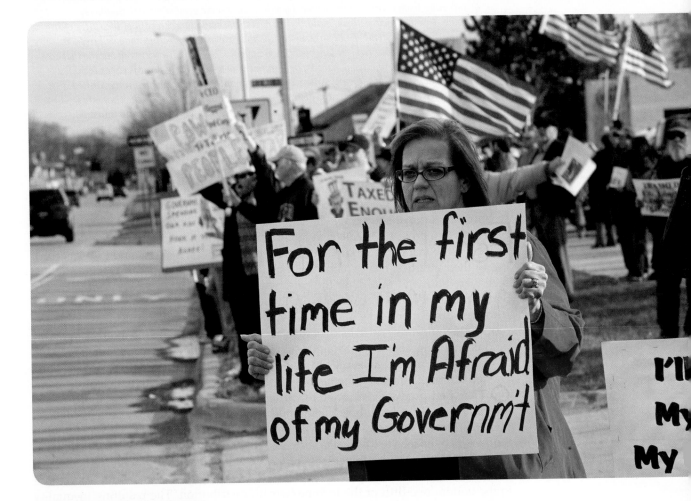

LEARNING OBJECTIVES

19.1 Describe the sociological imagination and how it can be used to seek solutions to social problems.

19.2 Understand the principles that should guide public policy in reducing or eliminating social problems.

19.3 Explain how the United States could finance a progressive agenda.

19.4 Assess the obstacles to instituting a progressive social agenda.

Social problems are social. That is, they are human arrangements, created and sustained by people. The politicoeconomic system of a society, from which social problems emanate, does not simply evolve from random events and aimless choices. The powerful in societies craft policies to accomplish certain ends within the context of historical events, budgetary constraints, and the like. Addressing the issue of inequality, Claude S. Fischer and his colleagues say,

> *The answer to the question of why societies vary in their structure of rewards is . . . political. . . . By loosening markets or regulating them, by providing services to all citizens or rationing them according to income, by subsidizing some groups more than others, societies, through their politics, build their ladders [the height and breadth of the rungs of the stratification system]. To be sure, historical and external constraints deny full freedom of action, but a substantial freedom of action remains. . . . In a democracy, this means that the inequality that Americans have is, in significant measure, the historical result of policy choices Americans—or, at least, Americans' representatives—have made. In the United States, the result is a society that is distinctly unequal. Our ladder is, by the standards of affluent democracies and even by the standards of recent American history, unusually extended and narrow—and becoming more so. (1996:8)*

In other words, America's level of inequality, which is greater than found in any of the Western democracies, is by design (Fischer et al. 1996:125).

Social policy is about design, about setting goals and determining the means to achieve them. Do we want to regulate and protect more, as the well-developed welfare states do, or should we do less? Should we create and invest in policies and programs that protect citizens from poverty, unemployment, and medical inattention, or should the market economy sort people into winners, players, and losers according to their abilities, efforts, and the luck or misfortune of the families into which they were born and raised? In the past two decades, decision makers in the United States have opted to reduce drastically the welfare system (e.g., elimination of Aid to Families with Dependent Children [AFDC]) while the taxes on the affluent have been reduced significantly and subsidies such as the tax exemption on the interest and taxes paid on housing have been retained. Congress and state legislatures have reduced or completely rejected subsidies to low-income families for childcare, medical care, and job training. Similarly, the boards of corporations, faced with major profit gains and increased productivity, have rewarded their executives with ever more generous salaries and stock options. Meanwhile, these same corporations have downsized their workforces, reduced entry-level wages, hired more temporary and contingent workers, moved jobs to low-wage societies, and reduced health and other benefits to employees. Thus, the combined acts of federal and state governments and corporations have increased the gap between the top one-fifth ("the fortunate fifth") and those in the bottom one-fifth of the income/wealth distribution. The resulting inequality gap is a major source of social problems.

The important sociological point is that if societies are designed, and some of the arrangements result in social problems, they can be changed to reduce or eliminate those problems. In other words, the design can be changed.

Such change is not easy, though. Social arrangements can be tradition bound and often imbued with religious approval, which impedes efforts at change. The status quo is defined as natural, and those who challenge it are seen as "impractical, ridiculous, crazy, dangerous and/or immoral. By definition, the conventional wisdom of the day is widely accepted, continually reiterated and regarded not as ideology but as reality itself" (Willis 1998:19). But change is possible. In the words of the late progressive Senator Paul Wellstone,

It's the power that won the eight-hour day, women's right to choose, civil rights laws, and the end of the Vietnam War. Grassroots movements brought about these and most great changes that have advanced the people of this country. People organized, protested, educated one another, kept up the pressure, and held their ideals high. [In doing so] the collected voices of concerned and committed Americans spoke clearly and loudly enough to be heard over those who resisted change. (1998:1)

 19.1 Describe the sociological imagination and how it can be used to seek solutions to social problems.

SOCIOLOGY, SOCIAL PROBLEMS, AND SOCIAL CHANGE

This textbook is a sociological introduction to the understanding of social problems, their sources, and their consequences. Let us look more closely at the discipline of sociology and make explicit what has been implicit throughout this book.

The Sociological Imagination and Social Problems

Among the components of the sociological imagination (see Chapter 1) is that it involves moving away from thinking in terms of the individual and her or his problem and focusing rather on the social, economic, and historical circumstances that produce the problem for many. In other words, when seeking solutions to social problems, we focus on changing the social structure rather than on changing problem people.

As an example, changing attitudes to reduce or eliminate racism, although important, does not solve the underlying problem of institutional racism in U.S. society. Changing the structure of society to ensure equality of opportunity for jobs, income, education, housing, and healthcare is the solution.

Sociological Paradox: Structure and Agency

Throughout the discussions in this book, we have emphasized the power of social context and the social forces that so strongly affect human behavior (the following is from Eitzen, Baca Zinn, and Smith 2010:521–522). As sociologist Peter Berger says,

Society not only controls our movements, but shapes our identity, our thoughts and our emotions. The structures of society become the structures of our own consciousness. Society does not stop at the surface of our skins. Society penetrates us as much as it envelops us. (1963:121)

This **deterministic view** is too strong, however. Although society constrains what we do, it does not determine what we do (Giddens 1991:863). Although society and its structures are powerful, the members of society are not totally controlled. We are not passive members. We can take control of the conditions of our own lives. Human beings cope with, adapt to, and change social structures to meet their needs. Individuals, acting alone or with others, can shape, resist, challenge, and sometimes change the social organizations and social institutions that impinge on them. These actions constitute **human agency**.

The paradox of sociology—the power of society over its members versus the power of social actors to change society—has several important meanings and implications. Foremost, society is not a rigid, static entity composed of robots. People in interaction are the architects of society in an ongoing project. That is, society is created, sustained, and changed by people.

Second, the social forms that people create often take on a sacred quality—the sanctity of tradition—that constrains behavior in socially prescribed ways. The sociological insight is, to restate the previous point, that what many consider sacred and unchangeable is a social construction and can therefore be reconstructed.

A third implication is that because social structures are created and sustained by people, they are imperfect. There are both positive and negative consequences of the way people have organized. Many are content with the status quo because they benefit from it. Others accept it even though they are disadvantaged by it. But some also seek change to improve the social structure or, perhaps, to transform it into something completely different. They are the agents of change.

In sum, the essence of agency is that individuals, through collective action, are capable of changing the structure of society and even the course of history. But although agency is important, we should not forget the power of the structures that subordinate people, making change difficult or, at times, impossible.

A Sociological Dilemma: Recognition and Rejection

Sociologists wish to be taken seriously by those in power. We are experts on social life. We have answers, not all by any means, but many, nonetheless, based on empirical research (see any issue of the sociological journals *Contexts* and *American Sociological Review*). But society's governmental and corporate leaders rarely seek sociological expertise in tackling social problems. Repeatedly, for example, sociologists have pointed out to political deaf ears that it "costs less to educate people than to leave them untrained. It costs less to provide prenatal care than to care for underweight babies. It costs less to house people than to build prisons to warehouse them" (Jackson 1998:20). It costs less and is more effective to deal with children before they get into trouble than to ignore them and put them in the criminal justice system after they have become disheartened, alienated, and angry because they have no hope of conventional success. But this understanding goes unheeded as budgets for Head Start–type programs dry up and budgets for prisons escalate.

Sociologists Barbara Risman and Donald Tomaskovic-Devey conveyed this dilemma of having helpful knowledge but being marginal in our effectiveness as public intellectuals:

> One of the wonderful things about being sociologists is knowing that collectively we have something powerful to contribute to the understanding of most, probably all, problems faced by society. One of the most frustrating things about being sociologists is how rarely we see sociological knowledge guiding the social choices and strategies of others. This happens at all levels, from the construction of global warming policy, to campaign finance reform, to affirmative action in our own universities, to couples struggling to create egalitarian relationships. (1998:vii)

Why is this the case? Why are sociologists rejected by those in power? Several related reasons combine to make sociologists marginal (the following is from Risman and Tomaskovic-Devey 1998; and Eitzen and Baca Zinn 1998:8–9). Foremost, the sociological perspective is subversive. That is, sociology undermines everything because it questions all social arrangements, whether religious, political, economic, or familial. Such an approach is threatening to those in power. As Risman and Tomaskovic-Devey say, "Our insights, regardless of how intellectually and empirically powerful they might be, are not always welcomed by the privileged" (1998:vii). But it is not just the powerful elites who are threatened; it is those who are powerful because they are in the majority by virtue of their social class position, their race/ethnicity, their gender, or their sexual orientation. Sociology unmasks the institutional classism, racism, sexism, and homophobia that is present in the "normal" and "accepted" ways that social structures work to discriminate against the powerless and keep them "in their place."

Watch on MySocLab Video: Culture and Human Freedom

The message of sociologists is rejected by many because it challenges the core of society's dominant ideology. The economy of the United States is capitalism. This system has its strengths, but it also leads to many social problems, as has been amply shown throughout this book.

Related to capitalism is the emphasis in U.S. society on individualism. Unlike Canada, the Scandinavian countries, and the nations of Western Europe, the United States focuses more on individual achievement and competition, letting the losers fend mostly for themselves. In essence, we say for the most part, you are on your own; get an education; get a job; take care of yourself and your family; and you are not obligated to take care of others. Thus, government programs to help the economically disadvantaged are minimal. The governments of the other Western democracies have a different philosophy. They are much more inclined to provide for the common good (e.g., generous welfare programs to lift people out of poverty; universal health insurance; more public resources for parks, orchestras, and mass transit). Sociologists are quick to point out the difference between the United States and its peers, noting that although the United States is the wealthiest country, compared with other modern industrialized nations it has the highest proportion of people living in poverty, the highest proportion of children growing up in poverty, and the most unequal income and wealth distributions. Thus, the individualism that pervades U.S. society has a severe downside, leading to serious social problems. But because the individualist ideology is a core belief of most Americans, any criticism of it is viewed with alarm, as being unpatriotic. Thus, when sociologists examine and report what they see as the consequences of public policy, which has as its foundation the emphasis on individualism, they are moved to the margins of public discourse about social problems.

We assume that many of the readers of this book have found the sociological examination of social problems uncomfortable. Perhaps you have found it subversive because it questions underlying assumptions about U.S. society. Even though this critical approach may be uncomfortable to many people, it is necessary to understand human social arrangements and find solutions to social problems. Thus, we ask that you think sociologically: (1) to view social arrangements critically and (2) to view social problems as emanating from social structure, not bad people. In essence, we ask that you overcome the societal bias against sociology by adopting the sociological imagination as you consider what society should do about its social problems.

19.2 Understand the principles that should guide public policy in reducing or eliminating social problems.

PROGRESSIVE PRINCIPLES TO GUIDE PUBLIC POLICY

This book has focused on the structural basis for social problems. These problems are formidable, but not insolvable. We can do something about them. This effort to change problematic social arrangements is the essence of human agency.

What, then, do we do to solve social problems? The first step must be to determine the facts. We must challenge the myths that often guide public opinion and policy makers. Providing the facts and demythologizing social life have been major goals of this book.

The second step is to establish, as a society, the principles that will guide public policy to accomplish the common good. This, we realize, is politically impossible at the moment for at least three related reasons. Foremost, underlying many of the problems in the United States is the power of money over the decision-making process, a problem that was magnified by the 2010 Supreme Court ruling giving corporations and other organizations the right to give unlimited amounts of money to affect the political process. The problem, of course, is that the powerful use money to retain and expand their power, and the relatively powerless (e.g., single mothers, the homeless, renters, children, the working poor, recent immigrants, and contingent workers) are left with no effective political voice. This is not democracy; it is a **plutocracy** (a government where the wealthy class rules).

Until campaign finance is straightened out, no significant change is possible (Lessig 2010; Moyers and Winship 2010). As it is, politics is guided by the "golden rule": Those who have the gold will make the rules. Donald Kaul, writing about the Supreme Court decision, provides this dire assessment:

> The decision, Citizens United vs. Federal Election Commission, *ended limits on the money corporations and unions can spend on influencing elections, thus writing a finish to the experiment in democracy we've been conducting for 220 years.*
>
> *We'll still have elections and rallies and arguments and tea parties. So what? It's all a show, the political equivalent of professional wrestling. (2010:23)*

If money rules, we do not have a democracy. The public must demand campaign finance reform and accept nothing less.

The second stumbling block to change is that politicians (at both state and federal levels) are "incapable of tackling long-term social and economic challenges, whether the solutions come from the left or the right" (Harwood 2010: para. 5). The reason: One rarely gets elected to public office by asking citizens to sacrifice by paying higher taxes to pay for problems with long-term positive consequences for society. Consider infrastructure: The American Society of Civil Engineers prepares a "report card" on the state of the infrastructure—roads, bridges, dams, levees, ports, water systems, sewage systems, the electric grid, etc. The most recent grade was "D," and the cost of bringing all systems up to adequacy was estimated at $2.2 trillion over five years (cited in Fallows 2010). Is there a politician who would run on a platform to remedy this serious (and very costly) problem now and with higher taxes? Added to this is the political component: Many (e.g., about 20 percent of adult Americans identified with the Tea Party movement in 2010) view government as the problem, not the solution. Hence, for them, the government has no role in solving national problems. What, then, is the solution to the crumbling infrastructure? But not only the physical infrastructure but the social infrastructure as well needs fixing. Do we not need public investment in healthcare, education, childcare, and nutrition programs? Or are these problems to be left to local decisions or the marketplace? The problem is not only weak legislators who vote on the safe side to get reelected. "The fault lies everywhere. The president, the Congress, the news media and the public are to blame. Shared sacrifice is not part of anyone's program" (Herbert 2010: para. 12). Significant in their culpability are the people who favor candidates who, for example, pledge to never vote for higher taxes. This unwillingness of lawmakers to sacrifice for the public good is the dark side of democracy.

The third obstruction to solving social problems is gridlock among decision makers at the state and federal levels (Beinart 2010). We concentrate here on Congress. To begin, as noted in Chapter 2, the filibuster in the Senate has made it virtually impossible to enact important legislation. This has worsened as Congress has become more divided in the last twenty years or so. In the late 1960s, for example, senators filibustered less than 10 percent of major legislation, but in 2009 Senate Republicans filibustered 80 percent of important legislation. Behind this is the polarization of Congress. Winners in primary elections, where only members of a party can vote, tend to side with their party's base, which has unyielding beliefs about civil rights, abortion rights, climate change, immigration, spending on the military, the role of the

Politicians seem unable to raise taxes to improve the crumbling infrastructure because they fear that they will be defeated by those favoring small government and reduced taxes.

federal government, and the regulation of the free market system. The result is fewer moderates becoming candidates in the general election and less compromise with the opposition when elected. This is exacerbated by the practice of **gerrymandering**, the carving up of districts by the party in power to maintain their favorable balance of power. The politicians favored in this arrangement have no incentive to compromise. Compromise and bipartisanship are rare qualities in today's politicians and political bodies. These are further complicated by the dysfunctional political structure of Congress.

Assuming that the bias of money in politics, the short-term outlook of politicians, and the gridlock in our political bodies can be overcome—dubious assumptions at best—let us propose some principles that we believe ought to guide public policy to reduce or eliminate major social problems that plague U.S. society. We realize, of course, that this is a controversial exercise, but we ask you to ponder these proposals and improve on them.

1. *A call for policies and behaviors that enhance our moral obligation to our neighbors (broadly defined) and their children, to those unlike us as well as those similar to us, and to future generations.* This principle runs counter to our societal celebration of individualism. But, we argue, the emphasis on individualism over community leads to exacerbated inequality; the tolerance of inferior housing, schools, and services for "others"; and public policies that are punitive to the economically disadvantaged. Moreover, exaggerated individualism is the antithesis of cooperation and solidarity—the requirements of community.

What happens when the gap between the rich and the poor widens? This phenomenon of income inequality has implications for democracy, crime, and civil unrest. The inequality gap "erodes social solidarity" (Gitlin 1995:225).

The welfare states of Canada, Western Europe, and Scandinavia have comprehensive social supports for their peoples. They provide universal healthcare insurance systems. They have a much more ample minimum wage than does the United States. They provide generous pensions and nursing home care for the elderly. They have paid maternity (and in some cases paternity) leave. Education is free through college. These benefits are costly, with income, inheritance, and sales taxes considerably higher than in the United States. The tradeoff is that poverty is rare, and the population feels relatively safe from crime and from the insecurities over income, illness, and old age. Most important, there is a large middle class with a much stronger feeling of community and social solidarity than is found in the United States. And, the people are better off. As Robert Borosage stated:

> On every social indicator—health, longevity, education, social cohesion, crime, generosity—more equitable societies fare better than richer, less equitable ones like our own. (2010:12; see also Wilkinson and Pickett 2010)

In sharp contrast, the United States has the highest poverty rate by far among the industrialized countries, a withering bond among those of different social classes, a growing racial divide, and an alarming move toward a two-tiered society. Should we move further toward an extreme bipolar society, the following is likely to occur:

> If you had a million dollars, where would you want to live, Switzerland or the Philippines? Think about all the extra costs, monetary and otherwise, if you chose a vastly unequal country like the Philippines. Maybe you'd pay less in taxes, but you'd wind up shuttling between little fenced-in enclaves. You'd have private security guards. You'd socialize only in private clubs. You'd visit only private parks and beaches. Your kids would go to private schools. They'd study in private libraries. (James Fallows, quoted in Carville 1996:87)

The United States is not the Philippines, but we are already seeing a dramatic rise in private schooling and homeschooling and in the number of walled and gated affluent neighborhood enclaves on the one hand and ever greater segregation of the poor and especially poor racial minorities in deteriorating neighborhoods and inferior schools on the other. Personal safety is more and more problematic as violent crime rates increase among the young and disaffected.

Finally, democracy is on the wane as more and more people opt out of the electoral process, presumably because, among other things, they are alienated and their

Kirk Anderson/Artizans Entertainment Inc.

choice among politicians is limited to those whose interests favor the wealthy, not the economically disadvantaged.

There is a flaw in the individualistic credo. We cannot go it alone entirely—our fate depends on others. Thus, it is in our individual interest to have a collective interest. As sociologist Alan Wolfe, discussing the Scandinavian countries, has put it,

> The strength of the welfare state—indeed, the accomplishment that makes the welfare state the great success story of modern liberal democracy—is the recognition that the living conditions of people who are strangers to us are nonetheless our business. (1989:133)

2. Acceptance of the first principle leads to the second: *A call for government programs that provide for people who cannot provide for themselves.* This is a call to bring all members of society up to a minimum standard of dignity. At a minimum, this includes universal health insurance, jobs, a living wage that places workers above the poverty line, and guaranteed and adequate pensions.

This position is opposite the direction of current policy makers in Congress and the state legislatures, whose stance is to reduce rather than expand the already constricted U.S. welfare safety net. The ideological consensus among the Republicans, the Blue Dog (conservative) Democrats, and various pressure groups has two related propositions. First, government subsidies exacerbate social problems rather than solve them. Second, individuals who fail are to blame for their failure. Ironically, these propositions are assumed by the powerful to hold for individuals but not for corporations.

📖 **Read on MySocLab Document:** The End of Welfare as We Know It: An Overview of the PRWORA

Since the 1930s, the United States has had a social safety net of AFDC, food stamps, Head Start, subsidized housing, and the like to help those in need. Conservatives see this safety net as the problem because they believe that it destroys incentives to work and encourages poor single mothers to have children. They argue, then, that welfare is the problem and that social problems will get worse if we are more generous to the poor. By this logic, if we spend less on welfare, we save money, government is reduced, and the lot of the poor improves. Thus, since about 1970, the federal government has gradually reduced or eliminated welfare programs. Has this dismantling of a relatively meager welfare program helped the poor? Has it made society safer?

From the progressive position, the poor have fared badly "because of an erosion of their labor market opportunities, not because of an erosion of their work ethic" (Danziger and Gottschalk 1995:4).

3. Acceptance of these principles leads to a third: *A special commitment to children, all children, and to implement this commitment with viable, universal programs.* In sociologist Jay Belsky's words,

> The time has come for this nation to regard child care as an infrastructure issue and make the same kind of investment in it that we talk about making in our bridges and roads and that we initially made in these vital transportation systems. We need to recognize that, in the same way that the massive capital investment in transportation and communication systems resulted in huge capital gains that we continue even to this day to realize, investment in child care can bring with it comparable long-term benefits. To gain insight into the costs, specifically foregone opportunity costs of not endeavoring to improve child care and increase options for families, imagine for a moment an America with the automobile but without paved roads. (1990:11)

Such a commitment to children involves providing prenatal and postnatal medical care, childhood immunization, protection from exposure to toxic chemicals, adequate nutrition, the elimination of child poverty, access to preschool and after-school programs, safe neighborhoods, and equitably financed schools.

Jonathan Kozol, the longtime children's advocate, speaking on behalf of these children, said this:

> "Conservatives," [Kozol] said, "now demand that poor children prove their worthiness before aid can be considered while liberals wring their hands and capitulate to the ethos of our time." In New York's South Bronx, as many as 25 percent of children are born HIV-positive while the nation's richest neighborhoods in Manhattan, a 12-minute bus ride away, look on and do nothing. Across the country, the story is the same everywhere.
>
> [Kozol] noted that the nation balks at spending $6,000 a year to educate poor children while it unhesitatingly spends $60,000 a year to incarcerate them when their hopelessness leads to crime. "What honorable Judeo-Christian society would pay 10 times as much to punish a child as to educate him? The neglect of America's children," argued Kozol, "is nothing less than collective sin." (Quoted in Judson 1997:2A)

Kozol's term "collective sin" is important for our consideration because the neglect of children is not just a matter of the neglect of individual parents, as it sometimes is, but much more important, it is a matter of society's neglect. As a society, the United States could eliminate poverty, provide universal healthcare, and ensure that all children receive preschool training. But as a society, we continue to look the other way (see the "Looking Toward the Future" panel, which insightfully describes an imaginary society that collectively provides for all children).

4. *A call to redistribute societal resources to lift those urban and rural areas that are economically disadvantaged.* Some areas of the nation are especially at risk. There are many pockets of rural poverty, such as Appalachia, the Mississippi Delta, and the Rio Grande Valley in Texas, where jobs are few and poorly paid and poverty rates are many times higher than the national average. These areas need federal assistance for schools, job training, and infrastructure. They need government subsidies through tax rebates to encourage businesses to locate there and hire local workers (the subsidies to be received when company performance conditions—jobs, pay, benefits to workers—are met).

There are extraordinary numbers of recent immigrants in California, Texas, and Florida who are poor and have special needs such as job training. Those people need jobs, shelter, food, and services such as education and healthcare. Those states especially affected by immigration need help from the federal government to supply assistance to the immigrants. At present, immigration is a federal policy, but the states are left with the financial responsibility (as mentioned in Chapter 5). This overburden results in either the immigrants not receiving the necessary assistance or the states stretching their welfare budgets too thin for the immigrant and nonimmigrant poor. Clearly, these states need federal assistance to meet the special needs of recent immigrants.

The other important area of neglect is the declining central cities. As noted in Chapter 6, the central cities have been abandoned by the middle classes, who have moved to the suburbs, and by corporations that have moved their businesses (and jobs) to the suburbs, to other parts of the country, or out of the country. The tax base in the cities has eroded, leaving declining transit systems, parks, and services, most notably schools. This erosion contributes to cutbacks in services and more flight to the suburbs. The high unemployment and continued job flight leads to despair, hopelessness, drug and alcohol abuse, and crime, further justifying the decisions of businesses and families to leave.

Looking Toward the Future

THE CHILDSWAP SOCIETY: A FABLE

Sandra Feldman, president of the American Federation of Teachers, wrote of a pretend society in which a national child lottery was held every four years:

Every child's name was put in—there were no exceptions—and children were randomly redistributed to new parents, who raised them for the next four years. Babies were not part of this lottery. Parents got to keep their newborn children until the next lottery, but then they became part of the national childswap. The cycle was broken every third swap, and kids were sent back to their original parents until the next lottery. So by the time you were considered an adult, at age 26, the most time you could have spent with your birth parents was ten years. The other sixteen were simply a matter of chance.

Maybe one of your new parents would be the head of a gigantic multinational company and the most powerful person in the country or the president of a famous university. Or you might find yourself the child of a family living in a public housing project or migrant labor camp. . . . People in the childswap society took the lottery for granted. They didn't try to hide their children or send them away to other countries;

childswapping was simply a part of their culture. And one thing the lottery did was to make the whole society very conscientious about how things were arranged for kids. After all, you never knew where your own child would end up after the next lottery, so in a very real sense, everyone's child was—or could be—yours. As a result, children growing up under this system got everything they needed to thrive, both physically and intellectually, and the society itself was harmonious.

What if someone wrote a story about what American society in the [early twenty-first] century takes for granted in the arrangements for its children? We might not want to admit it, but don't we take for granted that some kids are going to have much better lives than others? Of course. We take for granted that some will get the best medical treatment, and others will be able to get little or none. We take for granted that some kids will go to beautiful, well-cared-for schools with top-notch curriculums, excellent libraries, and computers for every child, and others will go to schools where there are not enough desks and textbooks to go around—wretched places where even the toilets don't work.

We take for granted that teachers in wealthy suburban schools will be better paid and better trained than those in inner-city or rural schools. We take for granted, in so many ways, that the children whom the lottery of birth has made the most needy will get the least. "After all," we say to ourselves, "it's up to each family to look after its own. If some parents can't give their children what they need to thrive, that's their problem."

Obviously, I'm not suggesting that the United States adopt a childswap system. The idea makes me cringe, and, anyway, it's just a fable. But I like to imagine what would happen if we did. We'd start with political figures and their children and grandchildren, with governors and mayors and other leaders. What do you suppose would happen when they saw that their children would have the same chance as the sons and daughters of poor people—no more and no less? What would happen to our schools and healthcare system—and our shameful national indifference to children who are not ours? I bet we'd quickly find a way to set things straight and make sure all children had an equal chance to thrive.

Source: From Sandra Feldman, "The Child-Swap Society." Reprinted by permission of the American Federation of Teachers, AFL-CIO. www.aft.org/presscenter/speechescolumns/wws/1998/0198.htm.

🔍 **View on MySocLab Figure:** Urban Growth and Urban Flight

Policies of the federal government are partly responsible for urban decay:

We have spent trillions building non-metro roads, but nowhere near that on metro ones or mass transit. Federal annual funding for mass transit has never been more than a fifth of highway funding, and state ratios are even more unbalanced. The overwhelming share of federal and state economic development funding also goes to non-metro sites—more highways, sprawl—supporting infrastructure, exurban tax credits and low-interest loans

for new development. Similarly, the deliberate siting of military bases and other govern-
ment facilities outside cities or more developed regions remains a deliberate national policy.
(Rogers 1998:14)

The federal government can reverse these anti-urban policies, thus helping to revitalize the cities. To date, there is no political will to do so. These politicians choose to ignore the human and economic costs of this neglect.

5. *Although some social policies should be made and administered at the local level, others must be largely financed, organized, and administered by the federal government.* This principle is based on the assumption that some issues are national in scope and require uniform standards (e.g., nutrition guidelines, immunization timetables, preschool, elementary through high school goals, the certification of teachers, and healthcare guarantees). Other policies, such as reducing poverty, require the massive infusion of money and compensatory programs, coupled with centralized planning.

While dismantling the welfare system, the strategy has been to cut funds and move the programs from the federal level to the states (called **devolution**). This devolution trend has the effect of making benefits very uneven, as some states are relatively generous while others are much less so. The distinguished historian, the late Arthur Schlesinger, Jr., has said this about the role of the federal government vis-à-vis the state governments:

> *It is a delusion to say that, because state government is closer to the people, it is more responsive to their needs and concerns. Historically it is national government that has served as the protector of the powerless. It is national government that affirmed the Bill of Rights against local vigilantism and preserved natural resources against local greed. The national government has civilized industry, secured the rights of labor organizations, improved income for the farmer, and provided a decent living for the old. Above all, the national government has vindicated racial justice against local bigotry. Had the states' rights creed prevailed, the U.S. would still have slavery. And historically the national government has been more honest and efficient than state and local governments. . . . As for bureaucracy, duplication, and waste, will there be more or less if a single federal agency is to be replaced by fifty separate state agencies? (Quoted in Shanker 1995:E7)*

19.3 Explain how the United States could finance a progressive agenda.

IS A PROGRESSIVE SOCIAL POLICY POSSIBLE?

Three questions remain: (1) Why should we adopt a progressive social agenda? (2) How do we pay for these programs? (3) Is there any hope for enacting progressive solutions to social problems?

Should a Progressive Plan Be Adopted by U.S. Society?

Why should the United States adopt a progressive plan to deal with its social problems? Foremost, these are serious problems, and market solutions will not alleviate them. Reliance on the bottom line (profits) means, for example, that companies will move their operations wherever labor is cheapest. It means lobbying to remove government oversight of their operations. Market-based strategies result in winners and losers and, moreover, it means opposition to social programs to help these "losers." We are convinced that public policy based on abandoning the powerless exacerbates social problems.

A second reason to favor progressive solutions has to do with domestic security. We ignore the problexms of poverty, wealth inequality, and a rationed healthcare system at our own peril. If we continue on the present path of ignoring these problems or reducing or eliminating programs to deal with them, we will be less secure, and we will have more problem people who require greater control—and at an ever greater social and economic cost.

The final argument for a progressive attack on social problems is an ethical one. We need, in our view, to have a moral obligation to others. We need to restore a moral commitment to the safety net. We should take the moral high ground, as Jonathan Kozol has argued: "There is something ethically embarrassing about resting a national agenda on the basis of sheer greed. It's more important in the long run, more true to the American character at its best, to lodge the argument in terms of simple justice" (quoted in Nore 1991:36).

Or consider this moral warning from an unlikely source, the very conservative British Chancellor of the Exchequer Kenneth Clarke, who explained his resistance to calls for a minimalist state: "This is a modern state. It is not the fifties . . . not southeast Asia. I believe in North American free-market economics, but I do not wish to see [here in Great Britain] the dereliction and decay of American cities and the absolute poverty of the American poor" (*The Nation* 1996:5).

Financing the Progressive Agenda

There are several sources of additional funds. The first is to reduce defense spending. We are the world's mightiest nation by far, and although there no longer is a Soviet threat, there is the threat of terrorism. The United States maintains a global network of bases, many of which are not needed. Similarly, there are expensive forms of military equipment are no longer required. The U.S. defense budget is enormous—$740 billion for fiscal year 2011—a sum that exceeds the amount spent by all of our allies combined. If the United States reduced annual military spending by $200 billion, it would still outspend everyone else—by a lot.

A second source of funds would be to reduce or eliminate corporate welfare and subsidies to the wealthy. At the moment, corporations receive much more than $100 billion in direct subsidies and tax breaks. The wealthiest Americans pay lower tax rates and have more tax loopholes than found in any other modern nation. Annually, we have about $400 billion in "tax expenditures" (i.e., money that is legally allowed to escape taxation). The economically advantaged receive most of these tax advantages.

A third source of funds is to increase the taxes on the wealthy, the opposite position of the Bush administration and the Republican-controlled Congress. Congress, with the urging of President Bush, provided tax cuts in 2001, 2002, and 2003, totaling $1.7 trillion over ten years. Imagine if the government took that money ($170 billion a year) to help pay for various aspects of the physical infrastructure (repairing or replacing aging bridges and water systems, providing better transportation systems, replacing crumbling school buildings), and social infrastructure (e.g., universal healthcare, adequate pensions, a living wage, free education through college, and subsidized daycare).

Finally, we should increase tax revenues. Totaling federal, state, and local taxes equals 30 percent of the gross domestic product. This is the lowest rate of any industrialized nation. In comparison, the English pay 36 percent, Germans and Canadians pay 37 percent, the French pay 44 percent, and at the high end the Swedes pay 56 percent. In addition, we should enact a truly progressive income tax.

Is There Any Hope of Instituting a Social Agenda Based on Progressive Principles?

The final issue—and, of course, the crucial issue—is: Is there any hope of mounting a successful progressive program? At first, the negative side seems overwhelming. We have already mentioned several formidable obstacles: (1) the widely held belief in individualism as the core of American ideology, (2) the current anger by the Tea Partiers and others at the federal government that appears more beholden to Wall Street than to Main Street; this level of anger and angst is the highest in two decades, and (3) the two major parties and political candidates are financed by Big Money, and Big Money favors the status quo. Big Money opposes public investment in healthcare, education, and various social supports.

There are at least three other barriers to progressive change. The first is the massive multitrillion-dollar debt ($15.9 trillion in July 2012), which is viewed by politicians of both parties as a giant weight on government that makes it difficult to fund existing programs, let alone institute new ones. The momentum is to cut programs. Adding to this impetus toward reduced government is the overall low tax rates, which limit revenues to the federal government.

Another major obstacle is the present weakness of the union movement in the United States. Each of the generous welfare states of Canada, Scandinavia, and Western Europe has a heavily unionized workforce. Unions use their collective power to work for pensions, universal healthcare, worker safety, a strong minimum wage, and other benefits to workers and their families. This condition is not present in the United States.

The final barrier to progressive change is that those who will benefit most from progressive social policies (the poor, the working poor, racial minorities, inhabitants of the inner cities, and the rural poor) are the least likely to vote, and they do not have the money to fund lobbyists and politicians sympathetic to their needs. So their speech (which the Supreme Court has defined as spending money to support political causes) is limited, whereas the speech of the advantaged is not. The disaffected do not vote because neither political party speaks to their needs. Is it because there is little difference between Republicans and Democrats, both of whom direct their attention to the White, affluent voters?

The Tea Party movement, which is opposed to progressive reforms, steps into this vacuum to speak to the needs of the politically alienated. There is a question, though, as to whether the Tea Party movement is a passing fad, reflecting a transient political mood, or one with a lasting impact (Schmitt 2010).

Given these obstacles to progressive change, is there a possibility that the progressives might eventually prevail? We are in the midst of societal upheaval. The Great Recession has ravaged the middle class. Employment is difficult to obtain and keep. Wages are stagnant, yet the big banks and corporations, bailed out by the government when they were on the brink of disaster, are reaping large benefits. This leads to two possible scenarios. One is that the Tea Party movement gains momentum and is successful in reducing government significantly by lowering taxes and by reducing government programs. This dooms progressive social policies at least in the near term. But there is an alternative scenario.

Looking at lessons from history (Dionne 1996; Weisberg 1996), more than 100 years ago, the Progressive movement began as a reaction to unchecked capitalism, the robber barons, economic exploitation, and political corruption. Out of the Progressive era came an activist government that addressed problems of the workplace by instituting workplace safety regulations, prohibiting child labor, mandating the eight-hour workday, and providing disability compensation. The government broke up business monopolies, established a national parks system, and gave women the vote.

During the depths of the Great Depression, President Roosevelt and Congress passed sweeping social programs including Social Security, unemployment insurance, AFDC, and massive public building projects that provided jobs, wages, and physical infrastructure (bridges, dams, roads, parks, schools, gymnasiums, libraries, rural electrification, and water conservation).

Following World War II and lasting for about three decades, society became more inclusive with the racial integration of the armed forces, sports, and workplaces. Despite significant opposition, civil rights protections, including the right of all citizens to vote, were mandated by the law. After World War II, Congress opened up college education to all social classes by passing the GI Bill, which made a college education a reality for millions of returning veterans of all class and racial backgrounds.

In short, there are times in U.S. history when progressive steps were taken. Former secretary of labor Robert Reich summarized,

> Nations are not passive victims of economic forces. Citizens can, if they so choose, assert their mutual obligations to extend beyond their economic usefulness to one another and act accordingly. Throughout our history the United States has periodically asserted the public's interest when market outcomes threatened social peace—curbing the power of great trusts, establishing pure food and drug laws, implementing a progressive federal income tax, imposing a forty-hour workweek, barring child labor, creating a system of social security, expanding public schooling and access to higher education, extending health care to the elderly and so forth. We effected part of this explicitly through laws, regulations, and court rulings, and partly through social norms and expectations about how we wanted our people to live and work productively together. In short, this nation developed and refined a strong social compact that gave force to the simple proposition that prosperity could include almost everyone. The puzzle is why we seem to have stopped. (1998:12)

The choices are there for legislators and the public. Small government or big government. A society of individuals on their own or a society working for the common good. In our view, if we take the individualistic view, then there will be a further unraveling of social solidarity, and our society will be less secure. And, a hopeful note that may lead to a search for new answers—perhaps a new progressive era, just as it did 110 years ago.

Two necessary conditions for progressive social policies to prevail are a strong union movement and a class-based labor party or Social Democratic party. Although the labor movement has been moribund for two decades or so in the United States, there is, under the right conditions, the resurgence of labor with a shift toward more organizing and more ambitious and aggressive approaches against hostile employers and unfriendly laws. Should that occur, then there is hope not only for a labor renaissance but also for an organized push for progressive social policies.

A new progressive era will work only if a class-based party emerges. In particular, progressive leaders need to articulate a vision, a sense of direction, that builds a sense of community. Our future, we must recognize, depends on the welfare of all in the community in which we live and the society of which we are a part, not just on our own accumulated wealth.

The alternative vision that we have proposed may seem very radical. We do not think so. Most of the suggestions are found in one form or another in each of the Western social democracies except the United States. Can we learn from them? Should we learn from them? Can we afford massive policy changes? Can we afford not to make them?

HUMAN AGENCY: SOCIAL CHANGE FROM THE BOTTOM UP

Sociologists know that social problems emanate from social structure. That is why the progressive agenda, which aims at changing social structure, makes sense. The progressive agenda that we propose is aimed at societal changes, at macrosolutions. But what can we do as individuals in families, at work, in our churches, and in our communities, to bring about changes to solve social problems? What can we do to make a difference—to be agents of social change?

We begin with the premise, already stated, that individuals can make a difference through collective action. Individuals need to join with others who share their goals to have any hope of success. Sociologists Kenneth Kammeyer, George Ritzer, and Norman Yetman show the importance of collective actions for individuals to be effective agents of change:

> As individuals, we are limited in our ability to make the societal changes we would like. There are massive social forces that make change difficult; these forces include the government, large and powerful organizations, and the prevailing values, norms, and attitudes. As individuals protesting to officials, we have minimal power. As individuals standing against the tide of public opinion, we have little hope of exerting influence. As individuals confronting a corporate structure, we are doomed to frustration and failure. But if we combine with others who share our convictions, organize ourselves, and map out a course of actions, we may be able to bring about numerous and significant changes in the social order. Through participation in a social movement, we can break through the social constraints that overwhelm us as individuals. (1997:632–633)

Individuals Protesting and Organizing for Change

Throughout U.S. history, individuals have organized to change elements of society that they deemed unethical, unjust, racist, sexist, or oppressive. Harlan Cleveland puts it this way:

> The tidal waves of social change of our lifetimes—environmental sensitivity, civil rights for all races, the enhanced status of women, recognition of the rights of consumers and small investors—were not generated by the established leaders in government, business, labor, religion, or higher education. They boiled up from people (and new leaders) who had not previously been heard from. (1992:16)

Let's examine briefly two representative movements.

- **Racial Minorities.**   Although collective efforts by African Americans for freedom and justice have occurred throughout their history in the United States, a major shift to bring justice to Blacks occurred in 1955. Before then, racial segregation in the South was as entrenched as was apartheid in South Africa. But in 1955 an African American woman, Rosa Parks, was jailed in Montgomery, Alabama, for not giving her seat on a bus to a White man, as was the custom fortified by the law. As a result of this courageous act, the Black community in Montgomery mobilized to bring down the segregated public busing system (Eitzen and Stewart 2007:1–3). A leader emerged, a young local minister, Martin Luther King, Jr., who inspired Blacks to use nonviolent resistance to overthrow their oppressors and their unfair laws and practices. The Blacks boycotted the transportation system for 381 days, walking to work or using a carpooling network. The city eventually abolished segregation in public transportation—a clear case of agency, as the powerless successfully changed an unfair system through their collective power.

Under the leadership of Martin Luther King, Jr., African Americans and other civil rights supporters mobilized to desegregate public facilities in the South.

Under the leadership of Reverend King, African Americans and White sympathizers mobilized to desegregate other public facilities in the South. There were sit-ins in restaurants, waiting rooms, and churches, and wade-ins at public beaches. Economic boycotts were organized. Court cases were initiated. Brave students became the first African Americans to attend formerly segregated schools. And there were protest marches to publicize grievances. These efforts were violently resisted by Whites. King and others were jailed. Demonstrators were abused verbally and physically. There were lynchings, bombings, drive-by shootings, and other forms of intimidation to keep Blacks "in their place," especially to keep them from registering to vote. The Blacks persisted, however. Their cause was to change the laws and the political establishment that kept them second class. In the words of the late historian Howard Zinn:

> So black people in the South decided they had to do something by themselves. They boycotted and sat in and picketed and demonstrated, and were beaten and jailed, and some were killed, but their cries for freedom were soon heard all over the nation and around the world, and the President and Congress finally did what they had previously failed to do—enforce the 14th and 15th Amendments to the Constitution. Many people had said: The South will never change. But it did change. It changed because ordinary people organized and took risks and challenged the system and would not give up. That's when democracy came alive. (2005: para. 7)

King's movement was bent on tearing down the segregationist norms and practices and substituting new ones. To a limited but nonetheless significant extent, the movement succeeded. Schools were desegregated with the help of federal troops. The 1964 Civil Rights Bill banned discrimination in public facilities, education, employment, and any organization receiving government funds. The 1965 Voting Rights Act prohibited the use of literacy and similar tests to screen voting applicants and allowed federal examiners to monitor elections.

But although civil rights battles have been won, the war for racial equality is still being fought in legislatures, in the courts, in school districts, in the workplace, and in neighborhoods. These are the facts from 2010 of the ongoing structural legacy of racism (DeNavas-Walt, Proctor, and Smith 2011; Rivera et al. 2009):

- Black households earned $32,068 a year, compared to $54,620 for White households.
- The Black poverty rate was 27.4 percent, compared to 13 percent for Whites.
- Among young Black males aged 16–19, the unemployment rate was 38.4 percent, while their White counterparts were at 23 percent.
- The median Black household had only 12 cents for every dollar of wealth the median White household had (Austin 2012).
- Life expectancy for Black men was six years shorter than for White men.

So the war for racial equality is far from over. Individuals and groups need to continue to take agency seriously, working to change institutional racism in all its forms.

- **Workers.** Early in the nineteenth century, U.S. workers were nonunionized. As a result, work conditions were often unsafe, work was poorly paid, and child labor was commonplace. Eventually, despite the aggressive opposition of business owners, workers formed unions. With unionization, workers were no longer alone in their bargaining with management. Collectively, workers had power to demand and receive higher wages and benefits and safer working conditions or they would strike or boycott the products of the company. Their unions were engaged politically, lobbying for social legislation and working for the election of candidates sympathetic to the cause of workers. Unquestionably, unions have improved the conditions for U.S. workers.

  By the 1990s, unions had lost much of their power. Union membership has declined significantly. The result has been a worsening of conditions for workers—declining wages and benefits, increasing job insecurity, and the tendency of management to hire temporary workers. In this climate, the Teamsters in 1997 conducted a strike against United Parcel Service (UPS, a company that at the time employed 340,000 workers worldwide and delivered 80 percent of all packages shipped by ground in the United States; the following is from Brecher 1998). Although better working conditions and wages were part of the Teamsters' demands, the major point of contention was that UPS hired too many part-time workers who were paid much less than full-time workers. The Teamsters wanted UPS to make many of the part-timers into full-time positions. Because this issue was an important one for labor, the AFL-CIO supported the Teamsters with loans of $10 million a week and promoted solidarity rallies in a number of cities. Faced with this opposition and the loss of $30 million a day in profits because of the strike, UPS accepted a settlement that created 10,000 new full-time jobs, promoted a minimum of 10,000 part-timers to full-time status, and granted full-timers a raise of 15 percent over five years and part-timers a raise of 37 percent, to reduce the wage differential. "It's a big win not only for the union but for labor," said Robert Ridley, a 44-year-old UPS driver in Austin, Texas. "This was labor against corporate America" (Brecher 1998:27). And labor, composed of individual working women and men with power gained collectively, won.

  In sum, society's structural arrangements are not inevitable. Individuals converging across lines of race, ethnicity, gender, and sexual orientation can work at the grassroots level organizing opposition, educating the public, demonstrating to promote a cause, electing allied candidates, using the courts, or employing other tactics to transform society. Human beings are the agents of change if they choose to be. The choice is ours.

Frances Fox Piven, the eminent social scientist, in writing about the need for social change to solve our current social problems, said,

> No one has ever successfully predicted the movements when ordinary people find their footing, discover new capacities for solidarity and power and new visions of the possible. Still, the development of American democracy depended on the perennial emergence of popular revolt in the past, and it does once again. (1996:67)

MySocLab ✓ **Study** and **Review** on **MySocLab**

■ CHAPTER REVIEW

1. The politicoeconomic system of a society, from which social problems emanate, is the result of historical events and conscious choices by political elites.

2. Social policy is about the way society should be designed—setting goals and determining the means to achieve them. If societies are designed, and some of the arrangements result in social problems, they can be changed to reduce or eliminate those problems.

3. The sociological paradox involves two opposing forces affecting human behavior. On the one hand, social forces constrain what we do. But although societies and their structures are powerful, people are not totally controlled. They shape, resist, challenge, and sometimes change the social organizations and social institutions that impinge on them. These actions constitute human agency.

4. Sociologists, as the experts on social life, have answers to many social problems based on empirical research, but society's governmental and corporate leaders rarely seek their advice. Sociologists tend to be rejected by those in power because their perspective is subversive, and they challenge the core of society's dominant ideology.

5. We propose five progressive principles to guide public policy: (a) policies and behaviors that enhance our moral obligation to others; (b) government provision of benefits to people who cannot provide for themselves; (c) a special commitment to all children to ensure health, safety, preparation for school, and equal funding for schools; (d) a redistribution of jobs and resources to economically troubled rural and urban locations; and (e) addressing many problems with federal money, standards, and administration.

6. A progressive agenda is needed because (a) it would reverse the current trend toward greater inequality; (b) it would make society more secure; and (c) it would promote social justice.

7. A progressive agenda, although expensive, could be financed by reducing the military budget, eliminating corporate welfare and subsidies to the wealthy, using the budget surplus for social programs, and increasing tax revenues.

8. Despite many obstacles, there are several possibilities for progressive change. The conservatives who control government could go too far with their market-based strategies, thereby alienating many who would resist. Historically, there have been progressive periods (the progressive era of the 1890s, the Great Depression, the thirty years following World War II) when social programs were instituted, corporate power thwarted, and inclusive policies implemented.

9. Social change can occur from the bottom up—from individuals acting collectively with a plan and mobilizing for action. Throughout U.S. history, individuals sharing a vision have organized to change elements of society. Case studies of successful changes were presented using racial minorities and workers.

■ KEY TERMS

Deterministic view. Belief that some variable controls social life.

Human agency. Individuals acting alone or with others shape, resist, challenge, and sometimes change the social organizations and the social institutions that impinge on them.

Plutocracy. Government in which the wealthy class rules.

Gerrymandering. The practice by the political party in power to carve up voting districts in a manner that keeps them in power.

Devolution. Process of shifting federal programs to the states.

BIBLIOGRAPHY

All highlighted entries are new to the thirteenth edition.

Abbott, Greg. 2009. "Colonias Prevention." (October 8). Online: http://www.oag.state.tx.us/consumer/border/colonias.shtml.

Acker, Joan. 1990. "Hierarchies, Jobs, Bodies: A Theory of Gendered Organizations." *Gender and Society* 4:139–158.

Acker, Joan. 1992. "Gendered Institutions: From Sex Roles to Gendered Institutions." *Contemporary Sociology* 21 (September):565–568.

Acosta, R. Vivian, and Linda Jean Carpenter. 2012. *Women in Intercollegiate Sport, the Thirty-Five Year Update: 1977–2012.* Unpublished manuscript.

Adams, William Lee. 2010. "Postcard: Halden." *Time* (May 10):14.

Adamson, Rebecca. 2009. "Foreword to Dedrick Muhammad," *Challenges to Native American Advancement.* New York: Institute for Policy Studies.

Adamuti-Trache, Maria, and Lesley Andres. 2008. "Embarking on and Persisting in Scientific Fields of Study: Cultural Capital, Gender, and Curriculum along the Science Pipeline." *International Journal of Science Education* 30(12):1557–1584.

Adler, Ben. 2011. "Wheels of Progress." *The Nation* (October 17):22–24.

Ahlburg, Dennis A., and Carol J. De Vita. 1992. "New Realities of the American Family." *Population Bulletin* 47 (August): entire issue.

Alazraki, Melly. 2011. "Health Insurers Post Healthy Profits but Remain Cautious in 2011." *AOL. Original.* (February 4). Online: http://www.dailyfinance.com/2011/02/04/health-insurers-post-healthy-quarterly-profits-cautious-2011-outlook.

Albelda, Randy. 1992. "Whose Values, Which Families?" *Dollars & Sense,* No. 182 (December):6–9.

Albelda, Randy. 2012. "Different Anti-Poverty Programs: Same Single-Mother Poverty." *Dollars and Sense* (January/February):11–17.

Albelda, Randy, and Chris Tilly. 1997. *Glass Ceilings and Bottomless Pits: Women's Work, Women's Poverty.* Boston: South End Press.

Al Jazeera. 2011. "U.S. Standing Plunges Across Arab World." (July 14). Online: http://www.aljazerra.com/indepth/features/2011/07/20117141044137.

Allegretto, Sylvia. 2011. "The State of Working America's Wealth 2011." *Economic Policy Institute* (March 24). Online: http://www.epi.org/publication/the_state_of_working_americas_wealth_2011.

Allen, Walter R., and Angie Y. Chung. 2000. "Your Blues Ain't Like My Blues: Race, Ethnicity and Social Inequality in America." *Contemporary Sociology* 29 (November): 796–805.

Alter, Jonathan. 2007. "The Other America: An Enduring Shame." In D. Stanley Eitzen and Janis E. Johnston (Eds.), *Inequality: Social Class and Its Consequences.* Boulder, CO: Paradigm Publishers, pp. 35–42.

Alter, Jonathan. 2010. "High–Court Hypocrisy." *Newsweek* (February):15.

Althauser, Seth, and Sarah Greenberg. 2011. "The Employment Non-Discrimination Act: What You Need to Know." *Center for American Progress.* Online: http://www.americanprogress.org/issues/2011/07/endafaq.html.

Amato, Paul R. 2001. "The Consequences of Divorce for Adults and Children." In Robert M. Milardo (Ed.), *Understanding Families into the New Millennium: A Decade in Review.* Minneapolis: National Council on Family Relations, pp. 1269–1287.

Amato, Paul R., and Alan Booth. 1996. "A Prospective Study of Divorce and Parent–Child Relationships." *Journal of Marriage and the Family* 58 (May):356–365.

Amato, Paul R., Alan Booth, David R. Johnson, and Stacy J. Rogers. 2007. *Alone Together: How Marriage in America Is Changing.* Cambridge, MA: Harvard University Press.

Amato, Paul R., and Jacob Cheadle. 2005. "The Long Reach of Divorce: Tracking Marital Dissolution and Child Well-Being across Three Generations." *Journal of Marriage and Family* 67:191–206.

American Association of University Women (AAUW). 1992. "How Schools Shortchange Girls." Executive Summary. AAUW Report. Washington, DC: American Association of University Women Educational Foundation.

American Association of University Women (AAUW). 1999. *Gender Gaps: Where Schools Still Fail Our Children.* New York: Marlowe & Company.

American Civil Liberties Union (ACLU). 2002. "ACLU Sues on Behalf of CA 8th Grader Barred from Gym Class Because of Sexual Orientation." (December 17). Online: http://www.aclu.org/lgbt/youth/12027prs20021217.html.

American Civil Liberties Union (ACLU). 2003. "ACLU Warns Arkansas School to Stop Persecuting Gay Student." (March 13). Online: http://www.aclu.org/lgbt/youth/12051prs20030313.html.

American Civil Liberties Union (ACLU). 2007. "Rights of Lesbian and Gay Parents after Heterosexual Divorce." Online: http://www.aclu.org/getequal/par/divorce.html.

American Civil Liberties Union (ACLU). 2009. "The Persistence of Racial and Ethnic Profiling in the United States: A Follow-Up Report to the U.N. Committee on the Elimination of Racial Discrimination." Online: http://www.aclu.org/files/pdfs/humanrights/cerd_finalreport.pdf#page=13.

American Psychiatric Association. 2007. Gay, Lesbian, and Bisexual Issues. Online: http://healthyminds.org/glbissues.cfm.

American Society for Aesthetic Plastic Surgery. 2012. Online: http://www.surgery.org.

American Sociological Association. 2003. *The Importance of Collecting Data and Doing Scientific Research on Race.* Washington, DC: American Sociological Association.

Amott, Teresa. 1993. *Caught in the Crisis: Women and the U.S. Economy Today.* New York: Monthly Review Press.

Andersen, Margaret L. 2011. *Thinking About Women: Sociological Perspectives on Sex and Gender.* Boston: Pearson Education, Inc.

Andersen, Margaret L., and Howard F. Taylor. 2000. *Sociology: Understanding a Diverse Society.* Belmont, CA: Wadsworth.

Angier, Natalie. 1993. "Bias against Gay People: Hatred of a Special Kind." *New York Times* (December 26):4E.

Angier, Natalie. 2000. "Scientists: DNA Shows Humans Are All One Race." *Denver Post* (August 22):2A, 5A.

Arendell, Terry. 1990. "Divorce: A Woman's Issue." In Christopher Carlson (Ed.), *Perspectives on the Family: History, Class, and Feminism.* Belmont, CA: Wadsworth, pp. 460–478.

Arizona Daily Star. 2004. "Carmona Cites Smoking as a Culprit in 26 Diseases." (May 28).

Armour, Stephanie. 2008. "Renters Can't Escape Housing Crisis." *USA Today* (April 2):1B–2B.

Armour, Stephanie. 2009. "2008 Foreclosure Filings Set Record." *USA Today* (January 15). Online: http://www.usatoday.com/money/economy/housing/2009-01-14-foreclosure-record-filings_N.htm.

Arthur, Charles. 2012. "Foxconn Lifts Wages for Under 20% as Apple Lets ABC News into Plant." *Guardian* (February 20). Online: http://www.guardian.co.uk/technology/2012/feb/20/foxconn-apple-china-wages.

Associated Press. 1999. "Priest, Nun Told to End Ministry to Gays." (July 14).

Associated Press. 2001. "Report: Blacks Searched More Often." (June 1).

Associated Press. 2004a. "Ads for Flavored Smokes Decried as Minority-Targeted." (August 19).

Associated Press. 2004b. "Data: Renting Tough on Minimum Wage." (December 21).

Associated Press. 2005. "Study: Gays' Response to Sex Chemical Differs." (May 10).

Associated Press. 2006. "Catholic Bishops' Document Calls for Reaching Out to Gays." (October 29).

Associated Press. 2009. "Therapy to Turn Gays Straight Is Repudiated." (August 6).

Associated Press. 2010a. "'Tea Party' Movement Faces Uncertain Future." (February 5).

Associated Press. 2010b. "AP Impact: After 40 Years, $1 Trillion, US War on Drugs Has Failed to Meet Any of Its Goals." (May 13).

Associated Press. 2010c. "Portugal's Drug Policy Pays Off; US Eyes Lessons." (December 26).

Associated Press. 2011. "Just Two Gangs Now Battle to Control Drugs in Mexico." (October 2).

Associated Press. 2012. "Boy Scouts Oust Gay Den Mother, Angering Parents." (April 27).

Astore, William. 2012. "America Has Become the World's Arms Dealer—But at What Cost to Ourselves and the World?" *Alternet* (January 24). Online: http://www.alternet.org/153878.

Aud, Susan, William Hussar, Frank Johnson, Grace Kena, Erin Roth, Eileen Manning, Xiaolei Wang, and Jijun Zhang. 2012. "The Condition of Education 2012." (NCES 2012-045). U.S. Department of Education, National Center for Education Statistics. Washington, D.C. Online: http://nced.ed.gov.

Austin, Algernon. 2010. "Budget Cuts and Our Children's Future." *American Prospect* 21 (November):A18–A19.

Austin, Algernon. 2012. "Wealth Losses by Race and Ethnicity." Economic Policy Institute (June 20). Online: http://www.epi.org/blog/wealth-losses-race-ethnicity.

Avert. 2011. "Worldwide HIV and AIDS Statistics." Online: http://www.avert.org/worldstats.htm.

Babones, Salvatore. 2012. "U.S. Income Distribution: Just How Unequal?" Inequality.org (February 14). Online: http://inequality.org/unequal-americas-income-distribution-just-how-unequal.

Baca Zinn, Maxine, and Bonnie Thornton Dill. 1996. "Theorizing Difference from Multicultural Feminism." *Feminist Studies* 22 (Summer):1–11.

Baca Zinn, Maxine, D. Stanley Eitzen, and Barbara Wells. 2011. *Diversity in Families*, 9th ed. Boston: Allyn and Bacon.

Baca Zinn, Maxine, D. Stanley Eitzen, and Barbara Wells. 2014, forthcoming. *Diversity in Families*, 10th ed. Boston: Pearson.

Baca Zinn, Maxine, Pierrette Hondagneu-Sotelo, and Michael A. Messner. 2010. *Gender Through the Prism of Difference*, 4th ed. New York: Oxford University Press.

Bailey, Jon M. 2009. "The Top 10 Rural Issues for Health Care Reform." Center for Rural Affairs (March).

Bajaj, Vikas. 2011. "Microlenders, Honored with Nobel, Are Struggling." *New York Times* (January 5). Online: http://www.nytimes.com/2011/01/06/business/global/06micro.html.

Bakalian, Anny, and Mehdi Bozorgmehr. 2011. "Middle Eastern and Muslim American Studies Since 9/11." *Sociological Forum* 26(3):714–727.

Baker, Mike. 2009. "Bankruptcies Surge in Spite of Law." Associated Press (April 19).

Bales, Kevin. 1999. *Disposable People: New Slavery in the Global Economy.* Berkeley: University of California Press.

Bales, Kevin. 2000. *New Slavery: A Reference Book.* Santa Barbara, CA: ABC-CLIO.

Balswick, Jack, with James Lincoln Collier. 1976. "Why Husbands Can't Say 'I Love You.'" In Deborah S. David and Robert Brannon (Eds.), *The Forty-Nine Percent Majority.* Reading, MA: Addison-Wesley, pp. 58–59.

Balswick, Jack, and Charles Peck. 1971. "The Inexpressive Male: A Tragedy of American Society." *Family Coordinator* 20:363–368.

Bamshad, Michael J., and Steve E. Olson. 2003. "Does Race Exist?" *Scientific American* (December):78–85.

Bandow, Doug. 2010. "Military Spending—for What?" *The Japan Times* (January 19). Online: http://search.japanTimess.co.jp/cgi-bin/en201000119db.html.

Banfield, Edward C. 1977. *The Unheavenly City Revisited.* Boston: Little, Brown.

Barlow, Maude. 2008. "Where Has All the Water Gone?" *The American Prospect* (June).

Barnes, Colin, Geof Mercer, and Tom Shakespeare. 1999. *Exploring Disability: A Sociological Introduction.* Malden, MA: Blackwell.

Barnett, Rosalind, and Caryl Rivers. 2004. *Same Difference.* New York: Basic Books.

Barry, Patricia. 2008. "Generic Drug Prices Go Down Sharply." AARP Bulletin (May 15). Online: http://www.bulletin.aarp.org/yourhealth9Medications)articles/aarp_report_generic_drugs.

Barsamian, David. 1997. "Howard Zinn." *The Progressive* 61 (July):37–40.

Barstow, David. 2010 "Tea Party Movement Lights Fuse for Rebellion on Right." *New York Times* (February 16). Online: http://www.nytimes.com/2010/02/16/politics/16teaparty.html?

Bartlett, D. L., and J. B. Steele. 2000. "How the Little Guy Gets Crunched." *Time* (February 7):40–43.

Barton, Len. 1996. "Sociology and Disability: Some Emerging Issues." In Len Barton (Ed.), *Disability and Society: Emerging Issues and Insights.* London: Longman, pp. 3–17.

Basow, Susan. 1996. "Gender Stereotypes and Roles." In Karen E. Rosenblum and Toni-Michelle Travis (Eds.), *The Meaning of Difference.* New York: McGraw-Hill, pp. 81–96.

Bauerlein, Monike, and Clara Jeffery. 2010. "Too Many? Too Much?" *Mother Jones* (May/June):4.

Bauerlein, Monike, and Clara Jeffery. 2011. "The Speedup." *Mother Jones* (July/August):18–25.

Bean, Frank D., Jennifer Lee, Jeanne Batalova, and Mark Leach. 2004. *Immigration and Fading Color Lines in America.* New York: Russell Sage Foundation and Population Reference Bureau.

Becerra, Jorge, Peter Damisch, Bruce Holley, Monish Kumar, Matthias Naumann, Tjun Tang, and Anna Zakrzewski. 2012. "The Battle to Regain Strength." The Boston Consulting Group (May). Online: http://www.begperspectives.com/images/bgg_the_battle_to_regain_strength_may_2012_tem80.

Beck, Joan. 1995. "Preschool Can Help Close the Poverty Gap." *Denver Post* (January 19):7B.

Becker, Howard S. 1967. "Whose Side Are We On?" *Social Problems* 14 (Winter):239–247.

Begala, Paul. 2011. "Who Are You Calling Lazy?" *Newsweek* (December 5):8.

Begley, Sharon. 2011. "Are You Ready for More?" *Newsweek* (January 6):40–46.

Beinart, Peter. 2010. "Why Washington's Tied Up in Knots." *Time* (March 1):20–24.

Beinin, Joel. 2010. "Knowing the 'Other': Arabs, Islam, and the West." In Hazel Rose Marcus and Paula M.L. Moya (eds.), *Doing Race: 21 Essays for the 21st Century.* New York: W. W. Norton & Company, Inc., pp 199–215.

Belsie, Lourent. 2009. "Why Do Firms Lobby?" *Christian Science Monitor* (April 10). Online: www.law.KU-edu/media/inthenews/2009/2009/April/10/lobbying.shtml.

Belsky, Jay. 1990. "Infant Day Care, Child Development, and Family Policy." *Society* (July/August):10–12.

Bender, William, and Margaret Smith. 1997. "Population, Food, and Nutrition." *Population Bulletin* 51 (February): entire issue.

Benedetto, Richard. 2001. "President Asks Mayors to Back Faith-Based Plan." *USA Today* (June 26):11A.

Bengston, V. L., C. Rosenthal, and L. Burton. 1990. "Families and Aging: Diversity and Heterogeneity." In R. H. Binstock and L. K. George (Eds.), *Handbook of Aging and Social Sciences*, 3rd ed. San Diego, CA: Academic Press, pp. 263–287.

Benjamin, Rich. 2009. "Pockets of White America Are in the Throes of an Existential Crisis." *AlterNet* (December 19). Online: http://www.AlterNet.orgg/module/printversion/144672.

Benjamin, Rich. 2010. "Texas Suicide Flyer Had Real Populist Grievances." *AlterNet* (February 20). Online: http://www.AlterNet.org/rights/145745.

Bennett, Amanda. 2010. "Lessons of a $618,616 Death." *Business Week* (March 15):32–40.

Benokraitis, Nijole, and Joe R. Feagin. 1995. *Modern Sexism*, 2nd ed. Upper Saddle River, NJ: Prentice Hall.

Benson, Clea. 2009. "Uncreative Destruction." *Congressional Quarterly* (October 26):2444–2450.

Berger, Peter. 1963. *Invitation to Sociology: A Humanistic Perspective*. Garden City, NY: Doubleday Anchor Books.

Bergman, Jake, and Julia Reynolds. 2002. "The Guns of Opa-Locka: How U.S. Dealers Arm the World." *Nation* (December 2):19–22.

Berkrot, Bill. 2011. "U.S. Drug Spending Slows; Hits \$307 Billion in 2010: Report." *Reuters* (April 19). Online: http://www.reuters.com/article/2011/04/19/us-drug-spending-idUSTRE7314G920110419.

Berlet, Chip. 2010. "Taking Tea Partiers Seriously." *The Progressive* 74 (February): 24–27.

Berman, Ari. 2012. "How a Filthy Rich 196 People Will Buy Our Election!" *Alternet* (February 16). Online: http://www.alternet.org/154172.

Bernard, Tara Siegel, and Ron Lieber. 2009. "The High Price of Being a Gay Couple." The New York Times (October 3). Online: http://www.nytimes.com/2009/10/03/your-money/03money.html.

Bernstein, Jared. 2012. "Why Trickle Down Economics Don't Work." *Christian Science Monitor* (January 13). Online: http://www.csmonitor.com/business/on-the-economy/2012/0113/why-trickle-down-economics-dont-work.

Bianchi, Suzanne. 1995. "Changing Economic Roles of Women and Men." In Reynolds Farley (Ed.), *State of the Union: America in the 1990s*, Vol. 1. New York: Russell Sage Foundation, pp. 107–154.

Bianchi, Suzanne M., and Lynn M. Casper. 2000. "American Families." *Population Bulletin* 55 (December): entire issue.

Bill and Melinda Gates Foundation. 2011. "Bill and Melinda Gates Applaud Progress Against Malaria While Urging Renewed Effort." (October 18).

Birnbaum, Michael. 2009. "Money-Hungry Schools Getting Down to Business." Commercial Alert.org (March 13). Online: http://www.commercialalert.org/news/archive/2009/03/money-hungry-schools-getting-down-to-business.

Blauner, Robert. 2001. *Still the Big News: Racial Oppression in America*. Philadelphia: Temple University Press.

Bleifuss, Joel. 2007. "Global Warming: Dim Bulbs, Bright Lights." *In These Times*. (April): 18–19.

Block, Pamela, Fabricio Balcazar, and Christopher Keys. 2001. "From Pathology to Power: Rethinking Race, Poverty, and Disability." *Journal of Disability Policy Studies* 12 (Summer):18–27, 39.

Block, Sandra. 2006. "Boomer Inheritances Shrink as Parents Live Longer, Health Costs Rise." *USA Today* (June 27):3B.

Blow, Charles M. 2009. "The Enemies Within." *New York Times* (April 18). Online: http://www.nytimes.com/2009/04/18/opinion/18blow.html?

Blumberg, Paul M., and P. W. Paul. 1975. "Continuities and Discontinuities in Upper-Class Marriage." *Journal of Marriage and the Family* 37 (February):63–78.

Blume, Howard. 2010. "Charter Schools' Growth Promoting Segregation, Studies Say." *Los Angeles Times* (February 5). Online: http://latimes.com/news/local/la-me-charters5-2010feb05,0,3300930.story.

Bobo, Lawrence D. 2009. "The Color Line, The Dilemma, and the Dream." In *Race and Ethnicity in Society*, Elizabeth Higginbotham and Margaret L. Anderson (eds.). Belmont, CA: Wadsworth Cengage Learning.

Bogdanich, Walt, and Eric Koli. 2003. "2 Paths of Bayer Drug in 80's: Riskier Type Went Overseas." *New York Times* (May 22). Online: http://www.nytimes.com/2003/05/22/business/22BLOO.html.

Bonacich, Edna. 1992. "Inequality in America: The Failure of the American System for People of Color." In Margaret L. Andersen and Patricia Hill Collins (Eds.), *Race, Class, and Gender*. Belmont, CA: Wadsworth, pp. 96–109.

Bonilla-Silva, Eduardo. 1996. "Rethinking Racism: Toward a Structural Interpretation," *American Sociological Review* 62 (June):465–480.

Bonilla-Silva, Eduardo. 2003. *Racism without Racists*. Lanham, MD: Rowman & Littlefield.

Bonilla-Silva, Eduardo. 2009. "Racism without Racists." In *The Matrix Reader*, Aby Ferber, Andrea O'Reilly Herrera, Christine M. Jimenez, and Dena R. Samuels (eds.). New York: McGraw-Hill.

Booher-Jennings, Jennifer. 2008. "Learning to Label: Socialization, Gender, and the Hidden Curriculum of High-Stakes Testing." *British Journal of Society and Education* 29, No. 2 (March):149–160.

Borenstein, Seth. 2012. "How Long Must You Fail to Earn as Much as This Man?" *Associated Press* (May 26).

Borosage, Robert L. 2001. "Forked-Tongue Budget." *Nation* (April 30):4–5.

Borosage, Robert L. 2010. "Common Sense on Budgets." *Progressive Populist* (March 1):12.

Boushey, Heather. 2007. "Values Begin at Home, But Who's Home?" *American Prospect* 18 (March):A2–A4.

Bowe, John. 2007. *Nobodies: Modern American Slave Labor and the Dark Side of the New Global Economy*. New York: Random House.

Boyle, D. Ellen, Nancy L. Marshall, and Wendy W. Robeson. 2003. "Gender at Play: Fourth-Grade Girls and Boys on the Playground." *The American Behavioral Scientist* 46(10):1326–1345.

Boyles, Saivnn. 2009. WebMD Health News (January 13). Online: www.americanheart.org/presenter.jhtml?identifier=3003499.

Brecher, Jeremy. 1998. "American Labor on the Eve of the Millennium: The Implications of the UPS Strike." *Z Magazine* 11 (October):25–28.

Bremer, Jason, Carl Houb, Marlene Lea, Mark Mather, and Eric Zuehlke. 2009. "World Population Highlights." *Population Bulletin* 64 (September).

Briggs, Xavier de Souza (Ed.). 2005. *The Geography of Opportunity: Race and Housing Choice in Metropolitan America*. Washington, DC: Brookings Institution Press.

Brisenden, S. 1986. "Independent Living and the Medical Model of Disability." *Disability, Handicap and Society* 1(2):173–178.

Brodkin, Karen. 2009. "How Did Jews Become White Folks." In Elizabeth Higginbotham and Margaret L. Andersen (Eds.), *Race and Ethnicity in Society*. Belmont, CA: Wadsworth Cengage Learning.

Brown, Jim. 2006. "Universities Continue Race-Based Admissions Despite Law." OneNewsNow.com. (December 22). Online: http://www.onenewsnow.com/2006/12/universities_continue_racebase.php.

Brown, Michael, and David Wellman. 2005. "Embedding the Color Line." *DuBois Review* 2:2:187–207.

Brown University. 2011. "Estimated Cost of Post-911-Wars: 225,000 Lives, up to \$4 Trillion." (June 29). Online: http://news.brown.edu/pressrelease/2011/06/warcosts.

Bruck, Connie. 2006. "Millions for Millions." *The New Yorker* (October 30):62–73.

Bruinius, Harry. 2010. "Megacities of the World: A Glimpse of How We'll Live Tomorrow." *Christian Science Monitor* (May 5). Online: http://www.csmonitor.com/world/global-issues/2010/05/05/megacities-of-the-world.html.

Bryan, Susan Montoya. 2012. "Average Farmer's Age Rising, Younger People Needed in Agriculture." *Huffington Post* (April 4). Online: http://huffingtonpost.com/2012/04/04/average-farmer-age-rising_n_1403542.html.

Budrys, Grace. 2012. *Our Unsystematic Health Care System*, 3rd Edition. Lansham, MD: Rowman and Littlefield.

Bullard, Robert D. 2000. *Dumping in Dixie: Race, Class, and Environmental Quality*, 3rd ed. Boulder, CO: Westview Press.

Bullard, Robert D. 2007. "Poverty and Pollution in the United States." In D. Stanley Eitzen and Janis E. Johnston (Eds.), *Inequality: Social Class and Its Consequences*. Boulder, CO: Paradigm Publishers, pp. 186–194.

Bullard, Robert D., and Beverly Wright. 2009. "The Color of Toxic Debris." *The American Prospect* 20 (March):A9–A11.

Bumiller, Elisabeth. 2010. "The War: A Trillion Can Be Cheap." *New York Times* (July 24). Online: http://www.nytimes.com/2010/07/25/weekinreview/25bumiller.html.

Bureau of Justice Statistics. 2007. "Drugs and Crime Facts: Enforcement." Online: http://www.ojp.usdoj.gov/bjs/dcf/enforce.htm.

Bureau of Justice Statistics (BJS). 2010. Online: http//bjs.ojp.usdoj.gov.

Bureau of Justice Statistics. 2012. Online: http://bjs.ojp.usdoj.gov.

Bureau of Labor Statistics. 2010. Online: http://www.bls.gov.

Buriel, Raymond, and Terri De Ment. 1997. "Immigration and Sociocultural Change in Mexican, Chinese, and Vietnamese American Families." In Alan Booth, Ann C. Crouter, and Nancy Landale (Eds.), *Immigration and the Family*. Mahwah, NJ: Erlbaum, pp. 165–200.

Burt, Keith B., and Jacqueline Scott. 2002. "Parent and Adolescent Gender Role Attitudes in 1990s Great Britain." *Sex Roles* 46 (7/8):239–245.

Burton, Linda, Eduardo Bonilla-Silva, Victor Ray, Rose Buckelew, and Elizabeth Hordge Freeman. 2010. "Critical Race Theories, Colorism, and the Decade's Research on Families of Color." *Journal of Marriage and Family* 72(3):440–459.

Bush, George W. 2001a. "Address to a Joint Session of Congress and the American People." Office of the Press Secretary, The White House (September 20). Online: http://www.whitehouse.gov/news/releases/2001/09/20010920-8.html.

Bush, George W. 2001b. "Address to the Nation." Office of the Press Secretary, The White House (September 11). Online: http://www.whitehouse.gov/news/releases/2001/09/20010911-16.html.

Business Week. 2002. "Crime Spree." (September 9):8.

Business Week. 2008. "Flying in for a Tune-Up Overseas." (April 21):26–27.

Butz, William P., and Barbara Boyle Torrey. 2006. "Some Frontiers in Social Science." *Science* 12 (June):1898–1899.

Bybee, Roger. 2010. "Which Side Are You On?" *In These Times* 34 (March):11.

Byne, William M. 1999. "Why We Cannot Conclude That Sexual Orientation Is Primarily a Biological Phenomenon." *Journal of Homosexuality* 34(1):73–80.

Byrnes, Nanette, and Christopher Palmeri. 2009. "Pensions Wade into Toxic Assets." *Business Week* (April 27):22.

Camarillo, Albert M. 2010. "Going Back to Compton: Real Estate, Racial Policies, and Black-Brown Relations." In Hazel Rose Marcus and Paula M.L. Moya (eds.), *Doing Race: 21 Essays for the 21st Century*. New York: W. W. Norton & Company, Inc., pp. 274–294.

The Campaign for Tobacco-Free Kids. 2012. Online: http://www.tobaccofreekids.org.

Campbell, Fiona Kumari. 2009. *Contours of Ableism: The Production of Disability and Ableness*. New York: Palgrave Macmillan.

Campbell, Frances A., Craig T. Ramey, E. P. Pungello, J. Sparling, and S. Miller-Johnson. 2002. "Early Childhood Education: Young Adult Outcomes from the Abecedarian Project." *Applied Developmental Science* (6):42–57.

Campenni, C. Estelle. 1999. "Gender Stereotyping of Children's Toys: A Comparison of Parents and Nonparents." *Sex Roles* 40 (1/2):121–138.

Carmichael, Mary. 2008. "New Era, New Worry." *Newsweek* (December 15):60.

Carmichael, Mary. 2010. "The Data Won't See You Now." *Newsweek* (March 8):46–47.

Carmichael, Stokely, and Charles V. Hamilton. 1967. *Black Power: The Politics of Liberation in America*. New York: Random House.

Carnahan, Kristin, and Chiara Coletti. 2006. "SAT Scores Hold Steady for College-Bound Seniors." *College Board*. Online: http://www.collegeboard.com/prod_downloads/about/news_info/cbsenior/yr2004/CBS2004Report.pdf.

Carney, Susan. 2007. "Advertising in Schools." Suite101.com. (August 24). Online: http://youthdevelopment.suite101.com/article.cfm/advertising_in_schools.

Carter, Michael J., and Susan Boslego Carter. 1981. "Women Get a Ticket to Ride after the Gravy Train Has Left the Station." *Feminist Studies* 7.477–504.

Carville, James. 1996. *We're Right, They're Wrong: A Handbook for Spirited Progressives*. New York: Random House.

Cary, Nathaniel. 2010. "Andre Bauer Equates 'Stray Animals' to People on Government Aid." GreenvilleOnline.com. (January 25). Online: http://greenvilleonline.com.

Cassidy, John. 1997. "The Melting Pot Myth." *The New Yorker* (July 14):40–43.

Cassidy, John. 2010. "The Tea Party U.S.A.: It's Still the Economy, Stupid!" *The New Yorker* (February 19). Online: http://www.commondreams.org/print/52997.

Castro, April. 2010. "Texas Board of Education Approves Resolution to Limit Islam References." *Huffington Post* (September 24). Online: http://www.huffingtonpost.com/2010/09/24/texas-board-of-education-islam-references_n_738930.html.

Catholic.com. 2004. "Homosexuality." Online: http://www.catholic.com/library/homosexuality.asp.

Cawthorne, Alexandra. 2011. "Canaries in the Coal Mine: Census Data Show Long-Term Financial Distress Among People of Color." *Poverty and Race Research Action Council*. PRRAC Research Briefs (September 19).

Cawthorne, Alexandra, and Stephanie Gross. 2008. "Equal Benefits for Women." Center for American Progress (December 9).

Online: http://www.americanprogress.org/issues/2008/12/equal_benefits.html.

Center for Neighborhood Technology. 2012. "National Index Reveals Combined Housing and Transportation Affordability Has Declined Since 2000." Online: http://www.cnt.org.

Center for Transit-Oriented Development. 2009. "Mixed-Income Housing Near Transit: Increasing Affordability with Location Efficiency." Online: http://www.reconnectingamerica.org/assets/uploads/091030ra201mixedhousefinal.pdf.

Center for Women in Politics. 2012. "Current Numbers of Women Office Holders." Online: http://www.cawp.rutgers.edu/fast_facts/levels_of_office/current_numbers.php.

Center on Social Welfare and Law. 1996. "Welfare Myths: Fact or Fiction?" Washington, DC: Author.

Centers for Disease Control and Prevention. n.d. "Prevalence of Disability Among Adults." Online: http://www.cdc.gov/ncbddd/disabilityandhealth/data.html.

Centers for Disease Control and Prevention. 2011. "Attention-Deficit/Hyperactivity Disorder." Online: http://www.cdc.gov/ncbddd/adhd/data.html.

Centers for Disease Control and Prevention. 2012. Online://www.cdc.gov.

Central Intelligence Agency. 2012. "The World Factbook." Online: http://www.cia.gov/library/publications/the-world-factbook-rankorder/2174rank.html.

Chafel, Judith A. 1997. "Societal Images of Poverty." *Youth and Society* 28 (June):432–463.

Chafetz, Janet Saltzman. 1997. "Feminist Theory and Sociology: Underutilized Contributions for Mainstream Theory." *Annual Review of Sociology* 23:97–120.

Chalk, Rosemary, Alison Gibbons, and Harriet J. Scarupa. 2002. "The Multiple Dimensions of Child Abuse and Neglect." Child Trends Research Brief. Online: http://www.childtrends.org/files/ChildAbuseRB.pdf.

Chang, Gordon H. 2010. "Eternally Foreign: Asian Americans, History, and Race," in Hazel Rose Marcus and Paula M.L. Moya (eds.), *Doing Race: 21 Essays for the 21st Century*. New York: W. W. Norton & Company, Inc., pp. 216–248.

Chapin, Laura. 2010. "Supreme Court Ruling Empowers Corporations More Than Labor Unions." *U.S. News & World Report* (January 22). Online: http://www.usnews.com/blogs/laura-chapin/2010/01/22.

Charles, Maria, and David B. Grusky. 2005. *Occupational Ghettos*. Palo Alto, CA: Stanford University Press.

Chen, Shaohua, and Martin Ravallion. 2012. "An Update to the World Bank and Estimates of Consumption Poverty in the Developing World." Briefing Note, Development Research Group, World Bank (March 1). Online: http://www.worldbank.org/intpovcalnet/resources/global_poverty_update_2012_02_19_12.pdf.

Cherlin, Andrew. 1981. *Marriage, Divorce, Remarriage*. Cambridge, MA: Harvard University Press.

Cherlin, Andrew. 1999. "Going to Extremes: Family Structure, Children's Well-Being and Social Science." *Demography* 36 (November):421–428.

Children's Defense Fund. 1997. *The State of America's Children: Yearbook 1997*. Washington, DC: Children's Defense Fund.

Children's Defense Fund. 2004. *The State of America's Children 2004*. Washington, DC: Children's Defense Fund.

Children's Defense Fund. 2005. *The State of America's Children 2005*. Online: http://www.childrensdefense.org/site/PageServer.

Children's Defense Fund. 2012. "Portrait of Inequality 2012: Black Children in America." Online: http://www.childrensdefense.org.

Clear Channel. 2012. "Media and Entertainment." Online: http://www.clearchannel.com/mediaandentertainment.

Cleveland, Harlan. 1992. "The Age of People Power." *Futurist* 26 (January/February):14–18.

Cloud, John. 2007. "Yep, They're Gay." *Time* (February 5):54.

CNN. 2012. "U.S. Sailor Is 3,000th Afghanistan War Death." CNN.com (May 25). Online: http://www.cnn.com/2012/05/25/us/afghanistan-war-deaths/index.html.

Cockburn, Andrew. 2009. "21st Century Slaves." In D. Stanley Eitzen and Maxine Baca Zinn (Eds.), *Globalization: The Transformation of Social Worlds*, 2nd ed. Belmont, CA: Wadsworth Cengage Learning.

Coffey, Laura T. 2011. "Home Disadvantage." *The American Prospect* (April):A12–A14.

Coker, Donna. 2005. "Shifting Power for Battered Woman Law, Material Resources and Poor Women of Color." In Natalie J. Sokoloff (Ed.), *Domestic Violence at the Margins: Readings on Race, Class, Gender, and Culture.* New Brunswick, NJ: Rutgers University Press, pp. 369–388.

Cole, Juan. 2012. "The Age of American Shadow Power." *The Nation* (April 30):25–27.

Cole, Wendy, and Christine Gorman. 1993. "The Shrinking Ten Percent." *Time* (April 26):27–29.

College Board. 2006. "College Board Announces Scores for New S.A.T. with Writing Section." Press Release (August 29). Online: http://www.collegeboard.com/press/releases/150054.html.

Collins, Chuck, Betsy Leondar-Wright, and Holly Sklar. 1999. *Shifting Fortunes. The Perils of the Growing American Wealth Gap.* Boston: United for a Fair Economy.

Collins, Patricia Hill. 1990. *Black Feminist Thought.* Cambridge, MA: Unwin Hyman.

Collins, Randall, and Scott Coltrane. 1995. *Sociology of Marriage and the Family,* 4th ed. Chicago: Nelson-Hall.

Colvin, Roddrick. 2004. "The Extent of Sexual Orientation Discrimination in Topeka, KS." Equal Justice Coalition and the National Gay and Lesbian Task Force Policy Institute. Online: http://www.thetaskforce.org/downloads/reports/reports/Topeka Discrimination.pdf.

Conason, Joe. 2007. *It Can Happen Here: Authoritarian Peril in the Age of Bush.* New York: Thomas Dunne Books.

Condon, Bernard, and Christina Rexrode. 2012. "Business Bosses Face Pay Backlash." Associated Press (May 26).

Connell, Robert W. 1992. "A Very Straight Gay: Masculinity, Homosexual Experience, and the Dynamics of Gender." *American Sociological Review* 57:735–751.

Connell, Robert W. 1998. "Masculinities and Globalization." *Men and Masculinities* 1 (July):3–23.

Conniff, Ruth. 2010. "The Disease of Inequality." *The Progressive* 74 (September):43.

Contemporary Sociology. 1995. "Symposium: The Bell Curve." 24 (March):149–161.

Cook, Bryan, and Young Kim. 2012. *The American College President 2012.* Washington, D.C.: American Council on Education.

Cook, Christopher D. 2002. "Drilling for Water." *The Progressive* 66 (October):19–23.

Coontz, Stephanie. 1992. *The Way We Never Were.* New York: Basic Books.

Coontz, Stephanie. 2005. *Marriage: A History.* New York: Viking.

Coontz, Stephanie. 2007. "New Census Report on Marriage." Council on Contemporary Families List Serve (September 18). Online: http://www.census.gov/population/www/socdemo/marr-div.html.

Copblock.org. 2011. "Human Trafficking." (August 5). Online: http://www.copblock.org/6446/human-trafficking.

Corbet, Barry. 2000. "Disabled Could Be King-Makers." *Denver Post* (September 27):9B.

Covey, Herbert C. 2007. *The Methamphetamine Crisis: Strategies to Save Addicts, Families, and Communities.* Westport, CT: Praeger Publishers.

Coy, Peter. 2012. "The Case for Way More Mandates." *Bloomberg Businessweek* (July 9):24–26.

Crabb, Peter, and Dawn Bielawski. 1994. "The Social Representation of Material Culture and Gender in Children's Books." *Sex Roles* 30 (1/2):69–79.

Crary, David. 2009. "American Market Fuels Drug Violence." The Associated Press (May 27).

Cronin, John, Michael Daklin, Deborah Adkins, and G. Gage Kingsbury. 2007. "The Proficiency Illusion." Thomas Fordham Institute. (October). Online: http://www.edexcellence.net/doc/The_Proficiency_Illusion.pdf.

Crooks, Robert, and Karla Baur. 1987. *Our Sexuality,* 3rd ed. Menlo Park, CA: Benjamin Cummings.

Cross, Merry. 1994. "Abuse." In L. Keith (Ed.), *Mustn't Grumble.* London: Women's Press.

Crowley, Sheila. 2002. "The National Low Income Housing Coalition." *Poverty and Race* 11 (January/February):24–26.

Curtin, Dave. 2001. "Report Blasts Teacher Prep." *Denver Post* (February 3):1B.

Curtis, John. 2011. "Persistent Inequity: Gender and Academic Employment." Presented at *New Voices in Pay Equity,* an event for Equal Pay Day (April 11). Available online: http://www.aaup.org/aaup/issues/women/resources.htm.

Daly, Clement. 2011. "Federal Investigation Finds Upper Big Branch Mine Disaster 'Entirely Preventable.'" *World Socialist* (December 13). Online: http://www.wsws.org/articles/2011/dec2011/msha-d13.shtml.

Danziger, Sheldon, and Peter Gottschalk. 1995. *America Unequal.* New York: Russell Sage Foundation.

Darling-Hammond, Linda. 2010. "Structured for Failure: Race, Resources, and Student Achievement." In Hazel Rose Marcus and Paula M.L. Moya (eds.), *Doing Race: 21 Essays for the 21st Century.* New York: W. W. Norton & Company, Inc., pp. 295–320.

David, Deborah S., and Robert Brannon. 1980. "The Male Sex Role." In Arlene S. Skolnick and Jerome H. Skolnick (Eds.), *Family in Transition,* 3rd ed. Boston: Little, Brown.

Davidson, Adam. 2012. "Making It in America." *The Atlantic* 309 (Jan/Feb):58–70.

Davidson, Kay. 2005. "Harvard President under Microscope: Female Scientists Debate Comments on Gender, Science." *San Francisco Chronicle* (January 31):4A.

Davidson, Paul. 2009. "Contract Workers Swelling Ranks." *USA Today* (December 7):1B.

Davis, Mike. 2006. "The Poor Man's Air Force." *Harper's Magazine* 313 (October):15–20.

Davis-Delano, Laurel R. 2009. Personal communication.

della Cava, Marco R. 2009. "Women Step Up as Men Lose Jobs." *USA Today* (March 19):D1–D2.

DeLollis, Barbara. 2012. "Regulation May Close Some Hotel Pools, Whirlpools." *USA Today* (March 14):1B.

del Pinal, Jorge, and Audrey Singer. 1997. "Generations of Diversity: Latinos in the United States." *Population Bulletin* 52 (October): entire issue.

DeNavas-Walt, Carmen, Bernadette D. Proctor, and Jessica C. Smith. 2011. "Income, Poverty, and Health Insurance Coverage in the United States: 2010." U.S. Census Bureau, *Current Population Reports,* P60–236.

DeParle, Jason. 2007. "The American Prison Nightmare." *New York Review of Books* (April 12). Online: http://www.nybooks.com/articles/20056.

Derysh, Igor. 2009. "Ties Between Government, Defense Contractors too Strong." *Congress Examiner* (June 8). Online: http://www.examiner.com/CP/CleanPrintProxy.aspx?1265473212400.

De Souza, Roge, John S. Williams, and Frederick A. B. Meyerson. 2003. "Critical Links: Population, Health, and the Environment." *Population Bulletin* 58 (September): entire issue.

De Vita, Carol J. 1996. "The United States at Mid-Decade." *Population Bulletin* 50 (March): entire issue.

Diamond, Marie, and Ian Millhiser. 2011. "2,000 Prisoners to Be Released to Rectify 'Fundamental Unfairness' of Past Drug Policy." *Think Progress* (July 1). Online: http://thinkprogress.org/justice/2011/07/01/258642/prisoners-released-rectify-unfairness-drug-policy/?mobile=nc.

Dickinson, Tim, and Jonathan Stein. 2006. "Chronicle of a War Foretold." *Mother Jones* 31 (September/October):61–69.

di Leonardo, Micaela. 1992. "Boyz in the Hood." *Nation* (August 17/24):178–186.

Dionne, E. J., Jr. 1996. *They Only Look Dead: Why Progressives Will Dominate the Next Political Era.* New York: Simon & Schuster.

Dokoupil, Tony. 2011. "Why Female Politicians Are More Effective." *Newsweek* (January 22). Online: http://www.newsweek.com.

Douglas, Susan J. 2010. "Enlightened Sexism: 'Women's Success' Means It's Fine to Resurrect—Even Celebrate—Sexist Stereotypes." *In These Times* (March 1). Online: http://www.AlterNet.org/story/145843.

Doyle, Jack, and Paul T. Schindler. 1974. "The Incoherent Society." Paper presented at the American Sociological Association, Montreal, Canada, August 25–29.

Draut, Tamara. 2008. "The Economic State of Young America." *Demos* (Spring).

Dreier, Peter. 2000. "Sprawl's Invisible Hand." *Nation* (February 21):6–7.

Dreier, Peter. 2012. "Scott Walker Spent 88% of the Money to Get 53% of the Vote." CommonDreams.org. (June 6). Online: http://www.commondreams.org.

Drucker, Peter F. 1993. *Post-Capitalist Society.* New York: HarperCollins.

Drug Enforcement Administration. 2012. Online: http://www.justice .gov/dea.

Drugsense.org. 2012. Online: http://www.drugsense.org.

Drugwarfacts.org. 2012. Online: http://www.drugwarfacts.org.

Drutman, Lee. 2003. "Corporate Crime Acts Like a Thief in the Night." *Los Angeles Times*.(November 4). Online: http://www.latimes.com/ news/opinion/commentary/la-oe-drutman4no.

Dubeck, Paula J., and Dana Dunn (Eds.). 2002. *Workplace/Women's Place: An Anthology*. Los Angeles: Roxbury.

Dunayer, Joan. 1995. "Sexist Words, Speciest Roots." In Carol J. Adams and Josephine Donovan (Eds.), *Animals and Women: Feminist Theoretical Exploration*. Durham, NC: Duke University Press, pp. 11–31.

Duncan, Margaret Carlisle. 2001. "The Sociology of Ability and Disability in Physical Activity." *Sociology of Sport Journal* 18(1):1–4.

Dunn, Andy. 2006. "The Other Domestic Spying." *Z Magazine* 19 (March):47–52.

Dunn, Dana. 1996. "Gender and Earnings." In Paula J. Dubeck and Kathryn Borman (Eds.), *Women and Work: A Handbook*. New York: Garland, pp. 61–63.

Dwyer, Paula. 2004. "The New Fat Cats." *Business Week* (April 12):32–35.

Dyer, Everett. 1979. *The American Family: Variety and Change*. New York: McGraw-Hill.

Early, Frances H. 1983. "The French-Canadian Family Economy and Standard of Living in Lowell, Massachusetts, 1870." In Michael Gordon (Ed.), *The American Family in Social Historical Perspective*, 3rd ed. New York: St. Martin's Press, pp. 482–503.

Eaton, Leslie. 2007. "In Mississippi, the Poor Lag in Hurricane Aid." *New York Times* (November 16). Online: http://www.nytimes .com/2007/n/16/us/16mississippi.html?

Economist. 2011. "Only and Lonely." (July 23):37–38.

Economist. 2012. "The Hands That Produce, the Wallets that Feed." (February 25):35–36.

Edelman, Marion Wright. 2009. "Promising Models for Reforming Juvenile Justice Systems." Children's Defense Fund (September 5). Online: http://www.childrensdefense.org/child-research-data-publications/data/marian-wright-edelman-child-watch-column/ promising-models-for-reforming.html.

Education News. 2011. "Report Finds Number of Schools Failing to Make AYP Rising." (May 2). Online: http://www.educationnews .org/ednews_today/155171.html.

Edwards, Renee, and Mark A. Hamilton. 2004. "You Need to Understand My Gender Role: An Empirical Test of Tannen's Model of Gender and Communication." *Sex Roles* 50(7/8):491–504.

Edwards, Richard C., Michael Reich, and Thomas E. Weisskopf. 1978. "Sexism." In R. C. Edwards, M. Reich, and T. E. Weisskopf (Eds.), *The Capitalist System*, 2nd ed. Upper Saddle River, NJ: Prentice Hall, pp. 331–341.

Eggen, Dan. 2009. "The Health Care Industry Operation." *Washington Post National Weekly Edition* (July 27):18.

Ehrenreich, Barbara. 2004. "Gouging the Poor." *Progressive* (68):12–13.

Ehrenreich, Barbara. 2006. "The High Cost of Being Poor." *AlterNet* (July 25). Online: http://www.AlterNet.org/story/39273.

Ehrenreich, Barbara, and Dedrick Muhammad. 2009. "The Recession's Racial Divide." *New York Times* (September 13):17.

Eilperin, Juliet. 2005. "Flooded Toxic Waste Sites Are Potential Health Threat." *Washington Post* (September 10):A15.

Eisenstein, Zillah. 1979. "Developing a Theory of Capitalist Patriarchy and Socialist Feminism." In Zillah Eisenstein (Ed.), *Capitalist Patriarchy and the Case for Socialist Feminism*. New York: Monthly Review Press, pp. 5–40.

Eisler, Peter. 2000. "Toxic Exposure Kept Secret." *USA Today* (September 6):1A–2A, 15A–18A.

Eisler, Peter. 2002. "Fallout Likely Caused 15,000 Deaths." *USA Today* (February 28):1A.

Eitzen, D. Stanley. 1984. "Teaching Social Problems: Implications of the Objectivist–Subjectivist Debate." *Society for the Study of Social Problems Newsletter* 16 (Fall):10–12.

Eitzen, D. Stanley. 2004. "The Atrophy of Social Life." *Society* 41 (September/October).

Eitzen, D. Stanley, and Maxine Baca Zinn. 1989. "The De-Athleticization of Women: The Naming and Gender Marking of Collegiate Sport Teams." *Sociology of Sport Journal* 6:362–370.

Eitzen, D. Stanley, and Maxine Baca Zinn. 1998. "The Shrinking Welfare State: The New Welfare Legislation and Families." Paper presented at the annual meeting of the American Sociological Association, San Francisco (August 21–25).

Eitzen, D. Stanley, and Maxine Baca Zinn. 2001. *In Conflict and Order: Understanding Society*, 9th ed. Boston: Allyn & Bacon.

Eitzen, D. Stanley, and Maxine Baca Zinn. 2012. *Globalization: The Transformation of Social Worlds*, 3rd ed. Belmont, CA: Wadsworth Cengage Learning.

Eitzen, D. Stanley, Maxine Baca Zinn, and Kelly Eitzen Smith. 2010. *In Conflict and Order: Understanding Society*, 12th ed. Boston: Pearson.

Eitzen, D. Stanley, Maxine Baca Zinn, and Kelly Eitzen Smith. 2013. *In Conflict and Order: Understanding Society*, 13th ed. Boston: Pearson.

Eitzen, D. Stanley, and Kelly Eitzen Smith (Eds.). 2003. *Experiencing Poverty: Voices from the Bottom*. Belmont, CA: Wadsworth.

Eitzen, D. Stanley, and George H. Sage (Eds.). 2007. *Solutions to Social Problems from the Top Down: The Role of Government*. Boston: Allyn & Bacon.

Eitzen, D. Stanley, and Kenneth L. Stewart (Eds.). 2007. *Solutions to Social Problems from the Bottom Up: Successful Social Movements*. Boston: Allyn & Bacon.

Elgin, Ben, and Keith Epstein. 2009. "It's a Bird, It's a Plane, It's Pork." *Business Week* (November 9): 46–48.

Elliot, James R., and Jeremy Pais. 2006. "Race, Class, and Hurricane Katrina: Social Differences in Human Responses to Disaster." *Social Science Research* 35:295–321.

El Nasser, Haya, and Lorrie Grant. 2005. "Immigration Causes Age, Race Split." *USA Today* (June 9):1A.

Engelhardt, Tom. 2007. "Rural America Pays the Price for War in Iraq." *AlterNet* (January 27). Online: http://www.AlterNet.org/ waroniraq/47235.

England, Paula. 2010. "The Gender Revolution: Uneven and Stalled." *Gender and Society* 24 (2):149–166.

Environmental Protection Agency. 2011a. "Food Waste." Online: http:// www.epa.gov/osw/conserve/materials/organics/food.

Environmental Protection Agency. 2011b. "Municipal Solid Waste Generation, Recycling, and Disposal in the United States: Facts and Figures for 2010." Online: http://www.epa.gov/osw/nonhaz/ municipal/pubs/msw_2010_factsheet.pdf.

Epstein, Cynthia Fuchs. 1970. *Woman's Place*. Berkeley, CA: University of California Press.

Ervin, Mike. 2011. "Exploring the 'Handicap Wage.' " *The Progressive* 75 (March):26–27.

Espiritu, Yen Le. 1996. "Asian American Panethnicity." In Karen E. Rosenblum and Toni-Michelle Travis (Eds.), *The Meaning of Difference*. New York: McGraw-Hill, pp. 51–61.

Everton, Terry. 2004. "Why School Sucks." *Z Magazine* (November):54–56.

Facing South. 2009. "Jena Six Case Comes to an End; Shone Light on Racism in Criminal Justice System." *The Institute for Southern Studies*. (June 30). Online: http://www.southernstudies.org/2009/06/ post-34.html.

Fahim, Kareem. 2003. "The Moving Target." *Amnesty Now* 29 (4) (Winter):6–9.

Faircloth, Susan C., and John W. Tippeconnie III. 2010. "The Dropout/ Graduation Rate Crisis Among American Indian and Alaska Native Students: Failure to Respond Places the Future of Native Peoples at Risk." *The Civil Rights Project/Proyecto Derechos Civiles at UCLA*. Los Angeles, CA. Online: http://www.civilrightsproject.ucla.edu.

Falk, Erika. 2008. "Cutting Women Out." *In These Times* (March):20–23.

Fallows, James. 2010. "How America Can Rise Again." *Atlantic* 305 (January/February):38–55.

Faludi, Susan. 1991. *Backlash: The Undeclared War against Women*. New York: Crown.

Farley, John E. and Gregory D. Squires. 2012. "Fences and Neighbors: Segregation in 21st Century America." In *Race and Ethnicity in Society*, Elizabeth Higginbotham and Margaret L. Andersen, eds. Wadsworth, Cengage Learning.

Farrell, Christopher. 2006. "Going Beyond Head Start." *Business Week* (October 23):108–110.

Faust, Kimberly A., and Jerome N. McKibben. 1999. In Marvin Sussman, Suzanne K. Steinmetz, and Gary W. Peterson (Eds.), *Handbook of Marriage and the Family*, 2nd ed. New York: Plenum Press, pp. 475–499.

Fausto-Sterling, Anne. 1992. *Myths of Gender: Biological Theories about Women and Men*. New York: Basic Books.

Feagin, Joe R. 2000. *Racist America*. New York: Routledge.

Feagin, Joe R. 2006. *Systemic Racism: A Theory of Oppression*. New York: Routledge.

Feagin, Joe R., Clairece Booher Feagin, and David V. Baker. 2006. *Social Problems: A Critical Power-Conflict Perspective*, 6th ed. Upper Saddle River, NJ: Prentice Hall.

Feagin, Joe, and Melvin P. Sikes. 1994. *Living with Racism: The Black Middle-Class Experience*. Boston: Beacon Press.

Federal Bureau of Investigation. 2012. "Crime in the United States 2010." Uniform Crime Reports. Online: http://www.fbi.gov.

Federal Interagency Forum on Aging-Related Statistics. 2010. "Older Americans 2010: Key Indicators of Well Being." Washington, DC: National Center on Health Statistics.

Feingold, Russ. 2001. "At the Debate of the Anti-Terrorism Bill, From the Senate Floor." (October 11). Online: http://feingold.senate.gov/~feingold/speeches/01/10/101101at.html.

Feldman, Marcus W. 2010. "The Biology of Ancestry: DNA, Genomic Variation, and Race." In Hazel Rose Marcus and Paula M.L. Moya (eds.), *Doing Race: 21 Essays for the 21st Century*. New York: W. W. Norton and Company, Inc., pp. 136–159.

Feldman, Noah. 2007. "Choosing a Sect." *New York Times* (March 4). Online: http://www.nytimes.com/2007/03/04/magazine/04wwInlede.t.html?ref=magazine&pagewanted.

Fernandez, Manny. 2012. "Perry Declares Texas' Rejection of Health Care Laws 'Intrusions.' " *New York Times* (July 10):A10.

Ferree, Myra Marx. 1991. "Feminism and Family Research." In Alan Booth (Ed.), *Contemporary Families: Looking Forward, Looking Back*. Minneapolis, MN: National Council on Family Relations, pp. 103–121.

Fields, Jason. 2004. "America's Families and Living Arrangements." *Current Population Reports*, P20–553. Washington, DC: U.S. Bureau of the Census.

Figueroa, Alyssa. 2012. "Wage Gap Between CEOs and Workers Continues to Grow." *Alternet* (June 20). Online: http://www.alternet.org/module/988597.

Filardo, Mary W., Jeffrey M. Vincent, Ping Sung, and Travis Stein. 2006. "Growth and Disparity: A Decade of U.S. Public School Construction." Building Educational Success Together (BEST). Online: http://www.21csf.org/csf-home/publications/BEST-Growth-Disparity-2006.pdf.

Fine, Mark A., Lawrence H. Ganong, and David H. Demo. 2005. "Divorce as a Family Stressor." In Patrick C. McKenry and Sharon J. Price (Eds.), *Families and Change: Coping with Stressful Events and Transitions*, 3rd ed. Thousand Oaks, CA: Sage, pp. 227–252.

Fineman, Howard. 2009. "On a Downtown Train." *Newsweek* (February 2):29.

Finklea, Kristin M. 2010. "Organized Crime in the United States: Trends and Issues for Congress." Congressional Research Service, CRS Report for Congress. R40525. Online: http://www.fas.org/sgp/crs/misc/R40525.pdf.

Fireside, Daniel. 2009. "Not Just Homeowners, But Renters Are Really Getting Screwed." *Dollars & Sense* (March 19). Online: http://www.alternet.org/story/131384.

Fischer, Claude S., Michael Hout, Martin Sanchez Jankowski, Samuel R. Lucas, Ann Swidler, and Kim Voss. 1996. *Inequality by Design: Cracking the Bell Curve Myth*. Princeton, NJ: Princeton University Press.

Fischman, Josh. 2007. "Unequal Treatment in the ER." *U.S. News & World Report* (February 12):82.

Fitzpatrick, Laura. 2009. "China's One-Child Policy." *Timeworld* (July 27). Online: http://www.time.com/time/world/article/0,8599,1912861,00.html.

Fletcher, Michael A. 2002. "When It Comes to Schools, Size Counts." *Washington Post National Weekly Edition* (April 22):34.

Flora, Cornelia Butler, Jan L. Flora, Jacqueline D. Spears, and Louis E. Swanson. 1992. *Rural Communities: Legacy and Change*. Boulder, CO: Westview Press.

Folbre, Nancy. 1985. "The Pauperization of Motherhood: Patriarchy and Social Policy in the U.S." *Review of Radical Political Economics* 16(4).

Folbre, Nancy. 2010. "The Declining Demand for Men." *New York Times* (December 13). Online: http://economix.blogs.nytimes.com/2010/12/13/the-declining-demand-for-men.

Folbre, Nancy, James Heintz, and the Center for Popular Economics. 2000. *The Ultimate Field Guide to the U.S. Economy*. New York: New Press.

Forbes. 2010. "The Forbes Global 2000." (May 10).

Forbes. 2011. "A Decade on Defense." (May 23):19.

Forbes. 2012. "Billionaires: The 1,226 Richest People on the Planet." Vol. 189 (March 26). Special Issue.

Forrest, Christopher B., and Ellen-Marie Whelan. 2000. "Primary Care Safety-Net Delivery Sites in the United States: A Comparison of Community Health Centers, Hospital Outpatient Departments, and Physicians Offices." *JAMA*, 284, No. 16 (October 25):2077–2083.

Fost, Dan. 1991. "American Indians in the Nineties." *American Demographics* 13 (December):26–34.

Fox, Greer Litton, Michael L. Benson, Alfred A. De Maris, and Judy Van Wyk. 2002. "Economic Distress and Intimate Violence: Testing Family Status and Resource Theories." *Journal of Marriage and Family* 64 (August):793–807.

Fox News Latino. 2012. "Alabama's Immigration Law to Cost State Millions in Lost Taxes." (February 1). Online: http://latino.foxnews.com/latino/politics/2012/02/01/alabamas-immigration-law-to-cost-state-millions.

Francis, David R. 2009. "Can Obama's Family-Planning Policies Help the Economy?" *Christian Science Monitor* (January 26).

Frank, Robert H. 2001. "Traffic and Tax Cuts." *New York Times* (May 11). Online: http://www.nytimes.com/2001/05/11/opinion/11FRAN.html.

Frankenburg, Ruth. 1993. *White Women, Race Matters: The Social Construction of Whiteness*. Minneapolis, MN: University of Minnesota Press.

Freeman, Jo. 1979. "The Women's Liberation Movement: Its Origins, Organizations, Activities, and Ideas." In J. Freeman (Ed.), *Women: A Feminist Perspective*, 2nd ed. Palo Alto, CA: Mayfield, pp. 557–574.

Freiberg, Peter. 1987. "The March on Washington." *Advocate* (November 10):11–22.

Friedman, Thomas L. 2005. *The World Is Flat*. New York: Farrar, Straus, and Giroux.

Fueleconomy.gov. nd. "Reduce Climate Change." Online: http://www.fueleconomy.gov/feg/climate.shtml.

Fuentes, Annette. 2007. "Segregation Is Back in Class." *USA Today* (March 14):11A.

Gallagher, Charles A. 2010. "Color Blind Privilege: The Social and Political Functions of Erasing the Color Line in Post Race America." In Margaret L. Andersen and Patricia Hill Collins (Eds.), *Race, Class, and Gender*, 7th ed. Belmont, CA: Wadsworth Cengage, pp. 95–97.

Gallagher, Charles A. 2012. "Color Blind Privilege: The Social and Political Functions of Erasing the Color Line in Post Race America." In *Race and Ethnicity in Society*, Elizabeth Higginbotham and Margaret L. Andersen, eds. Wadsworth Cengage Learning.

Gandel, Stephen. 2010. "The Teen Job Chop." *Time* (January 18):38–42.

Gandel, Stephen, and Paul J. Lim. 2008. "What Do I Do Now?" *Money* (November):89–91.

Gardner, David. 2009. "There's No Reason Only Poor People Should Get Malaria: The Moment Bill Gates Released a Jar of Mosquitos at Packed Conference." *Daily Mail* (February). Online: http://www.dailymail.co.uk/news/worldnews/article-1136463.

Garibaldi, Gerry. 2006. "How the Schools Shortchange Boys." *City Journal* (Summer). Online: http://www.city-journal.org/printable.php?id=2041.

Garrahy, Deborah A. 2001. "Three Third-Grade Teachers' Gender-Related Beliefs and Behavior." *The Elementary School Journal* 102(1):81–94.

Garrett-Peltier, Heidi. 2010. "Is Military Keynesianism the Solution?" *Dollars and Sense* 287 (March/April):7.

Gates. Gary J. 2011. "How Many People Are Lesbian, Gay, Bisexual, and Transgender?" The Williams Institute, UCLA School of Law. Online: http://williamsinstitute.law.ucla.edu/wp-content/uploads/Gates-How-Many-People-LGBT-Apr-2011.pdf.

Gates, Gary J. 2012. "Family Formation and Raising Children Among Same-Sex Couples." The Williams Institute. Online: http://williamsinstitute.law.ucla.edu.

Gawande, Atul, E. S. Fisher, J. Gruber, and M. B. Rosenthal. 2009. "Downwardly Mobile. The Accidental Case of Being Uninsured." *Archives of Surgery* 144(11):1006–1012.

Gay and Lesbian Victory Institute. 2012. Online: http://www.glli.org.

Gay, Lesbian, and Straight Education Network. 2010. "2009 National School Climate Survey." Online: http://www.glsen.org.

Gelles, Richard J. 1976. "Demythologizing Child Abuse." *Family Coordinator* 25 (April).

Gelles, Richard J. 1993. "Family Violence." In Robert L. Hampton, Thomas P. Gullota, Gerald R. Adams, Earl H. Potter, and Roger P. Weissberg (Eds.), *Family Violence: Prevention and Treatment.* Newbury Park, CA: Sage.

Gelles, Richard J. 1995. *Contemporary Families: A Sociological View.* Thousand Oaks, CA: Sage.

Gelles, Richard J., and Claire Pedrick Cornell. 1990. *Intimate Violence in Families,* 2nd ed. Newbury Park, CA: Sage.

Gelles, Richard J., and Murray A. Straus. 1979a. "Determinants of Violence in the Family." In Wesley R. Burr, Reuben Hill, F. Ivan Nye, and Ira L. Reiss (Eds.), *Contemporary Theories about the Family,* Vol. 1. New York: Free Press, pp. 549–581.

Gelles, Richard J., and Murray A. Straus. 1979b. "Domestic Violence and Sexual Abuse of Children." In Alan Booth (Ed.), *Contemporary Families: Looking Forward, Looking Back.* Minneapolis, MN: National Council on Family Relations, pp. 327–340.

Gelles, Richard J., and Murray A. Straus. 1988. *Intimate Violence.* New York: Simon & Schuster.

Genworth Financial. 2011. "Compare Cost of Care Across the United States." Online: http://www.genworth.com/content/products/long_term_care/Long_term_care/cost_of_care.html.

Gergen, David. 2001. "It's Not Can We, But Will We?" *U.S. News & World Report* (September 24):60.

Gerschick, Thomas J., and Adam Stephen Miller. 2001. "Coming to Terms: Masculinity and Physical Disability." In Michael S. Kimmel and Michael A. Messner (Eds.), *Men's Lives,* 5th ed. Boston: Allyn & Bacon, pp. 313–326.

Giddens, Anthony. 1991. *Introduction to Sociology.* New York: W. W. Norton.

Giele, Janet Z. 1988. "Gender and Sex Roles." In Neil J. Smelser (Ed.), *Handbook of Sociology.* Newbury Park, CA: Sage, pp. 291–323.

Gilman, Richard. 1971. "Where Did It All Go Wrong?" *Life* (August 13):40–55.

Gilson, Dave. 2012. "Politicians at Hourly Rates." *Mother Jones* (July/August):7.

Gilson, Stephen French, and Elizabeth Depoy. 2000. "Multiculturalism and Disability: A Critical Perspective." *Disability and Society* 15 (March):207–218.

Gitlin, Todd. 1995. *The Twilight of Common Dreams.* New York: Henry Holt.

Glasser, Ira. 2006. "Drug Busts = Jim Crow." *The Nation* (July 10):24–26.

Glasser, Ronald J. 2009. "'He Who Has the Gold Sets the Rules': How Managed Care Has Created an Unsustainable System for Doctors, Patients and Our Society." *Washington Post National Weekly Edition* (June 8):24.

Glaze, Lauren E. 2011. "Correctional Population in the United States, 2010." U.S. Department of Justice, Bureau of Justice Statistics. Online: http://www.bjs.gov.

Gleick, Elizabeth. 1995. "Rich Justice, Poor Justice." *Time* (June 19):40–47.

Goffman, Irving. 1963. *Stigma: Notes on the Management of Spoiled Identity.* Englewood Cliffs, NJ: Prentice Hall.

Golden, Daniel. 2006. *The Price of Admission: How America's Ruling Class Buys Its Way into Elite Colleges and Who Gets Left Outside the Gates.* New York: Crown Publishing/Random House, Inc.

Gonzalez, Antonio, and Stephanie Moore. 2003. "Wealthy Campaign Donors Stifle Minority Voices." *USA Today* (December 11):23A.

Goode, William J. 1983. "World Devolution in Family Patterns." In Arlene Skolnick and Jerome Skolnick (Eds.), *Family in Transition,* 4th ed. Boston: Little, Brown, pp. 43–52.

Goodman, David. 2009. "Data Minefield." *Mother Jones* 34 (September/October): 21–22.

Gopnik, Adam. 2012. "The Caging of America." *The New Yorker* (January 30):72–77.

Gordon, Beth Omansky, and Karen E. Rosenblum. 2001. "Bring Disability into the Sociological Frame: A Comparison of Disability with Race, Sex, and Sexual Orientation Statuses." *Disability and Society* 16 (January):5–19.

Gorman, Anna. 2007. "Immigrant Children Grow Fluent in English, Study Says." *Los Angeles Times* (November 30). Online: http://www.latimes.com/news/local/la-me-english30nov30,0,1163558.story?

Gould, Stephen Jay. 1994. "Curveball." *New Yorker* (November 28):139–149.

Gould, Stephen J. 1998. "The Sharp-Eyed Lynx, Outfoxed by Nature." *Natural History* (May):16–21, 70–72.

Gouldner, Alvin. 1962. "Anti-Minotaur: The Myth of Value-Free Sociology." *Social Problems* 9 (Winter).

Gray, Caroline. 2011. "Review of Fiona Kumari Campbell's *Contours of Ableism.*" *Contemporary Sociology* 40(6):694–695.

Green, Mark. 2002. *Selling Out: How Big Corporate Money Buys Elections, Rams Through Legislation, and Betrays Our Democracy.* New York: Regan Books.

Green, Mark. 2006. *Losing Our Democracy.* Naperville, IL: Sourcebooks, Inc.

Greene, Jay P., and Marcus A. Winters. 2006. "Leaving Boys Behind: Public High School Graduation Rates." *Civic Report* (April)(48). The Manhattan Institute for Policy Research. Online: http://www.manhattan-institute.org/html/cr_48.htm.

Greenhouse, Steven. 2005. "U.S. Meat Packing Industry Criticized on Human Rights Grounds." *New York Times* (January 25). Online: http://www.corpwatch.org/article.phpd=11806.

Greenhouse, Steven. 2009. *The Big Squeeze: Tough Times for the American Worker.* New York: Anchor Books.

Greenhouse, Steven. 2010. "Dangerous for Hispanic Laborers?" *New York Times* (August 27). Online: http://economy.blogs.nytimes.com/2010/08/27/are-working-conditions-dangerous-for-hispanic-laborers.

Greenwald, Glenn. 2010a. "The Sanctity of Military Spending." *Salon.com* (January 26). Online: http://www.commondreams.org/print/52079.

Greenwald, Glenn. 2010b. "Terrorism: The Most Meaningless and Manipulated Word." *Salon.com.* (February 19). Online: http://www.commondreams.org/print/529991.

Greider, William. 2004. "Under the Banner of the 'War' on Terror." *Nation* (June 21);11–14,18.

Greim, Lisa. 1998. "Working Women Protest Pay Gap." *Rocky Mountain News* (April 4):1B.

Griffis, Margaret. 2012. "The Human Cost of Occupation." Anti-War.com (February 11). Online: http://antiwar.com/casualties.

Grow, Brian. 2005. "Embracing Illegals." *Business Week* (July 18):56–64.

Guardian. 2009. "Nuclear Weapons: How Many Are There in 2009, and Who Has Them?" (September 6): Online: http://www.guardian.co.uk/news/datablog/2009/sep/06/nuclear-weapons.

Guastello, Denise D., and Stephen J. Guastello. 2003. "Androgyny, Gender Role Behavior, and Emotional Intelligence among College Students and Their Parents." *Sex Roles* 49 (1/2):663–673.

Guerino, Paul, Paige M. Harrison, and William J. Sabol. 2011. "Prisoners in 2010." Bureau of Justice Statistics, U.S. Department of Justice. Online: http://bjs.ojp.usdog.gov/content/pub/pdf/p10.pdf.

Gunther, Marc. 2006. "Queer Inc. How Corporate America Fell in Love with Gays and Lesbians. It's a Movement." *Fortune* (November 30). Online: http://money.cnn.com/magazines/fortune/fortune_archive/2006/12/11/8395465.

Guo, Guang, and Kathleen Mullan Harris, 2000. "The Mechanisms Mediating the Effects of Poverty on Children's Intellectual Development." *Demography* 37 (November):431–447.

Hacker, Andrew. 2003. *Mismatch: The Growing Gulf Between Women and Men.* New York: Scribners.

Hacker, Jacob S. 2006. *The Great Risk Shift.* New York: Oxford University Press.

Hagan, Frank E. 1994. *Introduction to Criminology,* 3rd ed. Chicago: Nelson-Hall.

Hagedorn, John. 1998. *People and Folks: Gangs, Crime and the Underclass in a Rustbelt City,* 2nd ed. Chicago: Lake View Press.

Hall, M. Ann. 1985. "Knowledge and Gender: Epistemological Questions in the Social Analysis of Sport." *Sociology of Sport Journal* 2:25–42.

Hamer, Dean, and Michael Rosbash. 2010. "Genetics and Proposition 8." LATimes.com. (February 23). Online: http://latimes.com/news/opinion/commentary/la-or-rosbash23-2010fed23,0,2291603.story.

Hanna, William J., and Elizabeth Rogovsky. 1991. "Women with Disabilities: Two Handicaps Plus." *Disability, Handicap and Society* 6 (1):55–56.

Hannon, Lance, and Donna Shai. 2003. "The Truly Disadvantaged and the Structural Covariates of Fire Death Rates." *The Social Science Journal* 40:129–136.

Hansen, Karen V. 2005. *Not-So-Nuclear Families: Class, Gender, and Networks of Care.* New Brunswick, NJ: Rutgers University Press.

Harden, Blaine. 2006. "America's Population Set to Top 300 Million." *Washington Post* (October 12):A1.

Harjo, Susan Shown. 1996. "Now and Then: Native Peoples in the United States." *Dissent* 43 (Summer):58–60.

Harkinson, Josh. 2010. "Fall Is Beautiful." *Mother Jones* 35 (May–June): 55–57.

Harnden, Toby. 2009. "Barack Obama Faces 30 Death Threats a Day, Stretching U.S. Secret Service." Telegraph (August 3). Online: http://www.telegraph.co.uk/news/worldnews/northamerica/usa/barakobama_faces_deaththreats.html.

Harrington, Michael. 1963. *The Other America: Poverty in the United States.* Baltimore: Penguin Books.

Harrington, Michael. 1985. *Taking Sides.* New York: Holt, Rinehart & Winston.

Hart, Gary. 2011. "Fighting the Next War." *The Atlantic* 307 (January/February):76–77.

Hartmann, Heidi I. 1976. "Capitalism, Patriarchy, and Job Segregation by Sex." *Signs* 1 (Spring):137–169.

Hartung, William. 2011. "Big 'Corporate' Brother: Is Lockheed Martin Shadowing You?" *CommonDreams.org* (January 11). Online: http://www.commondreams.org/64282.

Harwood, John. 2010. "Does Washington Need Fixing?" *New York Times* (February 19). Online: http://www.nytimes.com/2010/02/2/weekinreview/21Harwood.html?

Hastings Center. 2009. "A Conversation with David Himmelstein and Stiffie Woolhandler." *Health Care Cost Monitor* (August 27).

Hayes, Ashley. 2011. "Human Rights Watch Criticizes Alabama Immigration Law." *CNN.com.* (December 14). Online: http://articles.cnn.com/2011-12-14/us/us_alabama-immigration-report.

Haynes, V. Dion. 2009. "Young, Willing and Able—but Jobless." *Washington Post National Weekly Edition* (December 7):22.

Hazelden Foundation. 2003. "Rural America Rivals Big Cities in Drug Abuse" (June 2). Online: http://www.hazelden.org/servlet/hazelden/cma/ptt/hazl_alive_and_free.

Healy, Melissa, and Thomas H. Maugh II. 2011. "After 30 Years, the AIDS War Still Rages." *Los Angeles Times* (June 5). Online: http://www.latimes.com/health/la-the-aids-at-30-20110605,0,2300265.

Heatherington, E. Mavis. 2002. "Marriage and Divorce American Style." *American Prospect* (April 8):62–63.

Heckman, James J. 2006. "Skill Formation and the Economics of Investing in Disadvantaged Children." *Science* 312 (June):1900–1902.

Helliker, Kevin. 2011. "Hispanic College Enrollment Jumps." *Wall Street Journal* (August 26):A3.

Hellman, Chris. 2011. "The Real U.S. National Security Budget." Tomdispatch.com (March 1). Online: http://www.tomdispatch.com/post/17536.

Henderson, Nell. 2006. "Winners and Losers in the Short Run." *Washington Post National Weekly Edition* (April 24):21.

Henig, Jess. 2009. "Climategate." Factcheck.org. (December 10). Online: http://www.factcheck.org.

Herbert, Bob. 2001. "Fewer Students, Greater Gains." *New York Times* (March 12). Online: http://www.nytimes.com/2001/03/12/opinion/12HERB.html.

Herbert, Bob. 2003a. "Dancing with the Devil." *New York Times* (May 22). Online: http://www.nytimes.com/2003/05/22/opinion/22HERB.html.

Herbert, Bob. 2003b. "Locked Out at a Young Age." *New York Times* (October 20) Online: http://www.nytimes.com/2003/10/20/opinion/20HERB.html.

Herbert, Bob. 2006. "George Bush's Trillion-Dollar War." *New York Times* (March 23). Online: http://select.nytimes.com/2006/03/23/opinion23herbert.html?

Herbert, Bob. 2009. "A Scary Reality." *New York Times* (August 8). Online: http://www.nytimes.com/2009/08/11opinion/11herbert.html.

Herbert, Bob. 2010. "An Uneasy Feeling." *New York Times* (January 5). Online: http://www.commondreams.org/print/51238.

Herbert, Bob. 2011. "Losing Our Way." *New York Times* (March 29). Online: http://www.nytimes.com/2011/03/26/opinion/26herbert.html.

Herman, Edward S. 1994. "The New Racist Onslaught." *Z Magazine* 7 (December):24–26.

Herman, Edward S. 2006. "Torture, Moral Values, and Leadership of the Free World." *Z Magazine* 19 (November): 27–30.

Hernandez, Raymond, and David W. Chen. 2008. "Keeping Lawmakers Happy Through Gifts to Pet Charities." *New York Times* (October 19):1A, 19A.

Herrnstein, Richard. 1971. "I.Q." *Atlantic* 228 (September):43–64.

Herrnstein, Richard J. 1973. *I.Q. in the Meritocracy.* Boston: Little, Brown.

Herrnstein, Richard J., and Charles Murray. 1994. *The Bell Curve: Intelligence and Class Structure in American Life.* New York: Free Press.

Hershey, Laura. 2000. "Choosing Disability." In Estelle Disch (Ed.), *Reconstructing Gender: A Multicultural Anthology*, 2nd ed. Mountain View, CA: Mayfield, pp. 556–563.

Hewitt, Christopher. 2003. *Understanding Terrorism in America from the Klan to Al Queda.* New York: Routledge.

Higginbotham, Elizabeth. 1994. "Black Professional Women: Job Ceilings and Employment Sectors." In Maxine Baca Zinn and Bonnie Thornton Dill (Eds.), *Women of Color in U.S. Society.* Philadelphia: Temple University Press, pp. 113–131.

Higginbotham, Elizabeth, and Margaret L. Andersen. 2009. "Introduction, Race: Why It Matters." In Elizabeth Higginbotham and Margaret L. Andersen (Eds.), *Race and Ethnicity in Society.* Belmont, CA: Wadsworth Cengage Learning.

Higginbotham, Elizabeth, and Margaret L. Andersen. 2012. *Race and Ethnicity in Society*, 3rd ed. Belmont, CA: Wadsworth Cengage Learning.

Hightower, Jim. 2001. "Stand Up for your Democracy." *AlterNet* (September 19). Online: www.alternet.org/story.html?StoryID=11537.

Hightower, Jim. 2002a. "Looting the Treasury under Cover of the Flag." *The Hightower Lowdown* 4 (February):1–4.

Hightower, Jim. 2002b. "Stop the Corporate Takeover of Our Water." *The Hightower Lowdown* 4 (June):1–4.

Hightower, Jim. 2007. "Subprime Loans = Primetime for Vampire Lenders." *Hightower Lowdown* (August 22).

Hightower, Jim. 2010. "Is Death the Price of Having a Job?" *Alternet* (September 12). Online: http://www.alternet.org/module/148148.

Hill, M. 1994. "Getting Things Right." *Community Care Inside* 31 (March):7.

Hill, Shirley A., and Joey Sprague. 1999. "Parenting in Black and White Families: The Interaction of Gender with Race and Class." *Gender & Society* 13 (4):480–502.

Hockstader, Lee. 2002. "Dreams among the Poorest of the Poor." *Washington Post National Weekly Edition* (September 2–8):29.

Hole, Judith, and Ellen Levine. 1979. "The First Feminists." In Jo Freeman (Ed.), *Women: A Feminist Perspective.* Palo Alto, CA: Mayfield.

Holeywell, Ryan. 2011. "North Dakota's Oil Boom Is a Blessing and a Curse." *Governing the States and Localities* (August). Online: http://www.governing.com/topics/energy-env-north-dakotas-oil-boom-is-a-blessing-and-a-curse.

Holstein, James A., and Jay Gubrium. 1999. "What Is Family? Further Thoughts on a Social Constructionist Approach." *Marriage and Family Review* 28 (3/4):3–20.

Holzer, Harry J., Diane Whitmore Schanzenbach, Greg Duncan, and Jens Ludwig. 2007. "The Economic Costs of Poverty in the United States: Subsequent Effects of Children Growing Up Poor." *Center for American Progress.* Online: http://www.americanprogress.org/issues/2007/01/pdf/poverty_report.pdf.

Huffington, Arianna. 2012. "Roberts Saves Obamacare: How the Real Work of Reform Begins." *Huffington Post* (July 3). Online: http://www.huffingtonpost.com/arianna-huffington/roberts-obamacare_v_1646756.html.

Huffington Post. 2011. "10 Starting Statistics About Alabama's Immigration Law" (November 15). Online: http://www.huffingtonpost.com/2011/11/14alabamas-immigration-law.

Human Rights Campaign. 2011. Online: http://www.hrc.org.

Human Rights Watch. 2009. "Decades of Disparity: Drug Arrests and Race in the U.S." (March). Online: http://www.hrw.org.

Humes, Karen R., Nicholas A. Jones, and Roberto R. Ramirez. 2011. "Overview of Race and Hispanic Origin 2010." *2010 Census Briefs* C201BR (March). U.S. Census Bureau.

Huntington, Samuel P. 2004. *Who Are We? The Challenges to America's National Identity.* New York: Simon & Schuster.

Hutchins, Robert M. 1976. "Is Democracy Possible?" *Center Magazine* 9 (January/February):2–6.

Hyman, Rebecca. 2008. "America's Frightening Alzheimer's Epidemic." *AlterNet* (May 16). Online: http://www.alternet.org/story/85532.

Idle, Tracey, Eileen Wood, and Serge Desmarias. 1993. "Gender Role Socialization in Toy Play Situations: Mothers and Fathers with Their Sons and Daughters." *Sex Roles* 28 (11/12):679–691.

The Innocence Project. 2012. Online: http://www.innocenceproject.org.

Intelligence Report. 2001. "Reevaluating the Net." *The Southern Poverty Law Center* 102 (Summer):54–55.

Intergovernmental Panel on Climate Change, 2007. "IPCC Fourth Assessment Report: Climate Change 2007 (AR4)." Online: http://ipcc.ch/index.htm.

Isaacson, Walter. 2011. *Steve Jobs.* New York: Simon and Schuster.

ISR Newsletter. 1982. "Why Do Women Earn Less?" Ann Arbor, MI: University of Michigan, Institute for Social Research, Spring/Summer.

Ivins, Molly. 2003. "Bush Tax-Cut Plan Wrong in Oh So Very Many Ways." *Rocky Mountain News* (January 9):39A.

Iyengar, Shanto. 2010. "Race in the News: Stereotypes, Political Campaigns, and Market-Based Journalism." In Hazel Rose Marcus and Paula M.L. Moya (eds.), *Doing Race: 21 Essays for the 21st Century.* New York: W. W. Norton & Company, Inc., pp. 251–273.

Jackson, Derrick Z. 2010. "No More Concessions on Health Reform." *Boston Globe* (March 2). Online: http://www.commondreams.org/print/53345.

Jackson, Derrick Z. 2011. "U.S. Arms Sales at Odds with Words." *Boston Globe* (May 22). Online: http://www.article.boston.com/2011-05-21/bostonglobe/29569359_1_arma-sales-saudi-arabia-yemen-and-bahrain.

Jackson, Janine. 2000. "A Right, Not a Favor: Coverage of Disability Act Misses Historical Shift." Online: http://www.fair.org/extra-0011/ada.html.

Jackson, Jesse. 1998. "The Coming Collision." *Progressive Populist* 4 (August):19–20.

Jackson, Jesse. 2001. "Talking the Talk about the Poor." *Progressive Populist* (July 1):19.

Jackson, Jesse. 2006. "Healthcare Scandal Has Real Victims." *Progressive Populist* (November 15):14.

Jackson, Jesse. 2007. "Racially Biased Justice Still Infects American Courtrooms." *The Chicago Sun-Times* (September 18). Online: http://www.commondreams.org/archive/2007/09/18/3911.

Jackson, Jesse. 2010. "Mass Transit Too Crucial to Ignore." *Progressive Populist* (May 1):14.

Jackson, Jesse. 2011. "Thirty-Eight States Rig Voting Rules for GOP." *Progressive Populist* (October 15):14.

Jackson, Kenneth. 1985. *Crabgrass Frontier: The Suburbanization of the United States.* New York: Oxford University Press.

Jameson, Dave. 2011. "Upper Big Branch Report: Feds Release Devastating Findings on 'Preventable' Mine Disaster." *Huffington Post* (December 6).

Janus Report. 2011. "Don't Underestimate Your Life Expectancy." (Fall):4.

Jarrett, Robin, and Linda Burton. 1999. "Dynamic Dimensions of Family Structure in Low-Income African American Families." *Journal of Comparative Family Studies* 30 (Spring):177–187.

Jeffery, Clara. 2006. "Poor Losers: How the Poor Get Dinged at Every Turn." *Mother Jones* (July/August):20–21.

Jeffries, Sheila. 2008. "Keeping Women Down and Out: The Strip Club Boom and the Reinforcement of Male Dominance." *Signs: Journal of Women in Culture and Society* 34:151–173.

Jenkins, Philip. 1999. *Synthetic Panics: The Symbolic Politics of Designer Drugs.* New York: New York University Press.

Jensen, Arthur R. 1969. "How Much Can We Boost IQ and Scholastic Achievement?" *Harvard Educational Review* 39 (Winter):1–123.

Jensen, Arthur R. 1980. *Bias in Mental Testing.* New York: Free Press.

Johnson, Dirk. 2000. "Commandments Find Way into Schools." *Rocky Mountain News* (February 27):68A.

Johnson, Dirk. 2004. "Policing a Rural Plague." *Newsweek* (March 8):41.

Johnson, Dirk, and Vince Kuppig. 2004. "The Smell of Success." *Newsweek* (July 12):40.

Johnson, Harriet McBryde. 2003. "Should I Have Been Killed at Birth?" *New York Times Magazine* (February 16):50–55, 74, 78.

Johnson, Mark. 2009. "Inconvenient Truth: Reducing CO2 Emissions Will NOT Save the Planet." Global Warming Hoax.com (January 20). Online: http://www.globalwarminghoax.com/comment.php?comment.news.102.

Johnson, Michael P., and Kathleen J. Ferraro. 2000. "Research on Domestic Violence in the 1990s: Making Distinctions." *Journal of Marriage and Family* 60 (November):948–963.

Johnson, Robert. 2012. "You've Never Seen Anything Like This North Dakota Oil Boomtown." *Business Insider* (May 7). Online: http://www.businessinsider.com/youve-never-seen-anything-like-the-williston-oil-boom-2012-37op=1.

Johnston, L. D., P. M. O'Malley, J. G. Bachman, and J. E. Schulenberg. 2012. "Monitoring the Future National Results on Adolescent Drug Use: Overview of Key Findings, 2011." Ann Arbor: Institute for Social Research, University of Michigan. Online: http://monitoringthefuture.org/pubs/monographs/mtf-overview2011.pdf.

Jordan, Miriam. 2011. "Far Fewer Enter U.S. Illegally from Mexico." *Wall Street Journal* (December 13):1A–2A.

Judson, David. 1997. "Neglect of Kids 'No Less than Collective Sin.' " Gannett News Service (June).

Kalleberg, Arne L. 2009. "Precarious Work, Insecure Workers: Employment Relations in Transition." *American Sociological Review* 74 (February):11–22.

Kalof, Linda, Amy Fitzgerald, and Lori Baralt. 2004. "Animals, Women and Weapons: Blurred Sexual Boundaries in the Discourse of Sport Hunting." *Society and Animals* 12:3.

Kammeyer, Kenneth C. W., George Ritzer, and Norman R. Yetman. 1997. *Sociology,* 7th ed. Boston: Allyn & Bacon.

Kanter, Rosabeth Moss. 1977. *Men and Women of the Corporation.* New York: Basic Books.

Kaplan, David E. 2006. "Spies Among Us." *U.S. News & World Report* (May 8):40–49.

Kaplan, H. Roy. 2011. *The Myth of Post-Racial America: Searching for Equality in the Age of Materialism.* Lanham, MD: Rowman and Littlefield.

Katz-Fishman, Walda. 1990. "Higher Education in Crisis: The American Dream Denied." *Society for the Study of Social Problems Newsletter* 21 (Fall):22–23.

Kaul, Donald. 2010. "Next We'll Sell Senate Seats to Exxon Mobil and AT&T." *Progressive Populist* (March 1):23.

Kehrl, Brian H. 2004. "Don't Breathe Easy." *In These Times* (June 21):6–7.

Keillor, Garrison. 2005. "A Foul Tragedy: Democrats Fled in the Face of Danger." *In These Times* (November 21):26–27.

Keller, Bill. 2003. "The Thinkable." *New York Times Magazine* (May 5):48–53, 93–94.

Keller, Brennan. 2011. "Medical Expenses: Top Cause of Bankruptcy in the United States." *Giveforward.com* (October 13). Online: http://www.giveforward.com/blog/medical-expenses-top-cause-of-bankruptcy.

Kendall, Diana. 2001. *Sociology,* 3rd ed. Belmont, CA: Wadsworth.

Kennedy, David. 1996. "Can We Still Afford to Be a Nation of Immigrants?" *Atlantic Monthly* (November):51–80.

Kent, Mary M., Kelvin M. Pollard, John Haaga, and Mark Mather. 2001. "First Glimpses from the 2000 U.S. Census." *Population Bulletin* 56 (June): entire issue.

Kibria, Nazli. 1997. "The Concept of 'Bicultural Families' and Its Implications for Research on Immigrant and Ethnic Families." In Alan Booth, Ann C. Crouter, and Nancy Landale (Eds.), *Immigration and the Family.* Mahwah, NJ: Erlbaum, pp. 205–210.

Kids Count. 2011. "Children in Poverty—2010." Annie E. Casey Foundation. (September). Online: http://datacenter.kidscount.org/date/acrossstates/rankings.aspx?=end=43.

Kimmel, Michael. 1992. "Reading Men, Masculinity, and Publishing." *Contemporary Sociology* 21 (March):162–171.

Kimmel, Michael S. 2004. *The Gendered Society*, 2nd ed. New York: Oxford University Press.

Kimmel, Michael S., and Michael A. Messner (Eds.). 2007. *Men's Lives*, 7th ed. Boston: Allyn & Bacon.

Kirchhoff, Sue. 2005. "Minorities Depend on Subprime Loans." *USA Today* (March 17):4B.

Kirkham, Chris. 2011. "States Get Cash for Prisons." *The Progressive Populist* (March 15).

Klein, Joe. 2010. "Their Own Worst Enemy." *Time* (March 15):21.

Klein, Joe. 2012. "The Best News Out of Afghanistan." *Time* (June 4):25.

Klein, Naomi. 2011. "Capitalism vs. the Climate." *The Nation* (November 28):11–22.

Klinenberg, Eric. 2004. "Bourgeois Dystopias." *Nation* (June 28): 40–44.

Kluger, Jeffrey. 2009. "Big Tobacco's New Targets." *Time*. (July 27):50–51.

Kneebone, Elizabeth, Carey Nadeau, and Alan Berube. 2011. "The Re-Emergence of Concentrated Poverty: Metropolitan Trends in the 2000s." *Metropolitan Policy Program at Brookings*. (November).

Knickerbocker, Brad. 2006. "The Environmental Load of 300 Million: How Heavy?" *Christian Science Monitor* (September 26). Online: http://www.csmonitor.com/2006/0926/p01s01-usssc.htm.

Kocieniewski, David. 2010. "Taking Aim at the Mortgage Tax Break." *New York Times* (November 12). Online: http://www.nytimes.com/2010/11/13/business/economy/13mortgage.html.

Kocieniewski, David, and Robert Hanley. 2000. "Racial Profiling Routine, New Jersey Finds." *New York Times* (November 28). Online: http://www.nytimes.com/2001/11/28/nyregion/28TROOMet.html.

Kochhar, Rakesh, Richard Fry, and Paul Taylor. 2011. "Hispanic Household Wealth Fell by 66% from 2005 to 2008." *Pew Hispanic Center* (July 26). Online: http://www.pewhispanic.org/2011/07/26/the-toll-of-the-great-recession.

Kosberg, Jordan I. 1976. "Differences in Proprietary Institutions Caring for Affluent and Nonaffluent Elderly." In Cary S. Hart and Barbara B. Manard (Eds.), *Aging in America*. Port Washington, NY: Alfred.

Kotkin, Joel. 2010. "400 Million People Can't Be Wrong." *Newsweek* (April 16):44.

Kotz, Deborah. 2010. "Get Ready for the Age Wave." *U.S. News & World Report* (February):19–22.

Kozol, Jonathan. 2005. "Still Separate, Still Unequal: America's Educational Apartheid." *Harper's Magazine* (September):41–54.

Kristof, Nicholas D. 2003. "Gay at Birth?" *New York Times* (October 25):A19.

Kristof, Nicholas D. 2008. "Raising the World's IQ." *New York Times* (December 4). Online: http://www.nytimes.com/2008/12/04/opinion/04kristof.html.

Kroeger, Brook. 1994. "The Road Less Rewarded." *Working Woman* (July):50–55.

Krugman, Paul. 2008. "Grains Gone Wild." *New York Times* (April 7). Online: http://www.nytimes.com/2008/04/07/opinion/107krugman.html.

Krugman, Paul. 2009. "The Big Hate." *New York Times* (June 12). Online: http://www.nytimes.com/2009/06/12/opinion/12krugman.html.

Kulik, Liat. 2002. "Like-Sex versus Opposite-Sex Effects in Transmissions of Gender Role Ideology from Parents of Adolescents in Israel." *Journal of Youth and Adolescence* 31 (6):451–457.

Kurdek, Lawrence A. 2001. "Differences between Heterosexual-Nonparent Couples and Gay, Lesbian, and Heterosexual-Parent Couples." *Journal of Family Issues* 22(6):728–755.

Kurdek, Lawrence A. 2003. "Differences between Gay and Lesbian Cohabiting Couples." *Journal of Social and Personal Relationships* 20(4):411–436.

Kuttner, Robert. 1998. "Toward Universal Coverage." *Washington Post National Weekly Edition* (July 20):27.

Kuttner, Robert. 2012. "Tocqueville for Toffs." *American Prospect* 23 (January/February):40–46.

Ladika, Susan. 2012. "Personal Bankruptcies Rose 8 Percent in 2010." Creditcards.com. Online: http://www.creditcards.com/credit-card-news-bankruptcy-statistics-2010.

Ladner, Joyce A. 1971. *Tomorrow's Tomorrow*. New York: Doubleday.

Lakoff, Robin. 2003. "Language, Gender, and Politics: Putting 'Women' and 'Power' in the Same Sentence." In Janet Holmes and Miriam Meyerhoff (Eds.), *The Handbook of Language and Gender*. Malden, MA: Blackwell, pp. 161–178.

Lappe, Frances Moore, and Joseph Collins. 1979. *Food First: The Myth of Scarcity*. New York: Ballantine Books.

Lappe, Frances Moore, and Joseph Collins. 1986. *World Hunger: Twelve Myths*. New York: Grove Press.

Lauer, Nancy Cook. 2002. "Studies Show Women's Role in Media Shrinking." Online: http://www.equality2020.org/media.htm.

Laumann, Edward O., John H. Gagnon, and Stuart Michaels. 1994. *The Social Organization of Sexuality: Sexual Practices in the United States*. Chicago: University of Chicago Press.

Laurance, Jeremy. 2006. "Chemical Pollution 'Harms Children's Brains.'" *The Independent* (November 8). Online: http://news.independent.co.uk/uk/health_medical/article1962438.ece.

Lauzen, Martha M. 2011. "Boxed In: Employment of Behind-the-Scenes and On-Screen Women in the 2010–11 Prime-time Television Season." San Diego, CA: San Diego State University Center for the Study of Women in Television and Film. Online: http://womenintvfilm.sdsu.edu/research.html.

Lazare, Daniel. 2001. *America's Undeclared War: What's Killing Our Cities and How We Can Stop It*. New York: Harcourt.

Lederer, Edith M. 2012. "Human Trafficking Victims." *Huffington Post* (April 4). Online: http://www.huffingtonpost.com/2012/04/05/human-trafficking-victims.htm.

Ledger, Kate. 2009. "The Moynihan Report, a Retrospective." *Contexts* 8(4):48–52.

Lee, Jennifer, and Frank D. Bean. 2004. "America's Changing Color Lines: Immigration, Race/Ethnicity, and Multiracial Identification." *Annual Review of Sociology* 30:221–242.

Lee, Sharon M. 1998. "Asian Americans: Diverse and Growing." *Population Bulletin* 53 (June): entire issue.

Lee, Valerie E., and David T. Burkam. 2002. *Inequality at the Starting Gate*. Economic Policy Institute. Washington, DC. Online: http://www.epinet.org/books/starting_gate.html.

Lefkowitz, Bernard. 1998. *Our Guys*. New York: Random House Vintage.

Leinwand, Donna. 1999. "Debate Rages on Remedies for Women's Pay Gap." *Denver Post* (October 11):15A.

Lemann, Nicholas. 1986. "The Origins of the Underclass." Parts 1 and 2. *Atlantic Monthly* (June):31–55; (July):54–68.

Lendman, Stephen. 2010. "Global Sweatshop Wage Slavery." *Dissident Voice* (February 25). Online: http://dissidentvoice.org/2010/02/global-sweatshop-wage-slavery.

Leonard-Wright, Betsy, Meizhu Lui, Gloribell Mota, Dedrick Mohammad, and Mara Voukydis. 2005. *State of the Dream 2005: Disowned in the Ownership Society*. Boston: United for a Fair Economy.

Leslie, Jacques. 2008. "Can the World Survive China's Headlong Rush to Emulate the American Way of Life?" *Mother Jones* (Jan/Feb):29–39.

Lessig, Lawrence. 2010. "How to Get Our Democracy Back." *The Nation* (February 22):12–19.

Lever, Janet. 1976. "Sex Differences in the Games Children Play." *Social Problems* 23 (April):478–487.

Levin, Andy. 2004. "Speech." C-Span (September 6), AFL-CIO.

Levin, David C. 2004. "Me and My M.R.I." *New York Times* (July 6): Online: http://www.nytimes.com/2004/07/06/opinion/06LEVI.html.

Lewis, Amanda E., Maria Kryson, Sharon M. Collins, Korie Edwards, and Geoff Ward. 2004. "Institutional Patterns and Transformations: Race and Ethnicity in Housing, Education, Labor Markets, Religion, and Criminal Justice." In Maria Kryson and Amanda E. Lewis (Eds.), *The Changing Terrain of Race and Ethnicity*. New York: Russell Sage, pp. 67–122.

Lewis, Amanda E., Maria Kryson, and Nakisha Harris. 2004. "Introduction: Assessing Changes in the Meaning and Significance of Race and Ethnicity." In *The Changing Terrain of Race and Ethnicity*, Maria Krysan and Amanda Lewis (eds.). New York: Russell Sage Foundation, pp. 1–24.

Liazos, Alexander. 1972. "The Poverty of the Sociology of Deviance: Nuts, Sluts, and Preverts." *Social Problems* 20 (Summer):103–120.

Liazos, Alexander. 1982. *People First: An Introduction to Social Problems*. Boston: Allyn & Bacon.

Lichtenberg, Illya. 2006. "Examining Race as a Tool in the War on Drugs." *Police Practice and Research* 7 (March):49–60.

Lichtenberg, Judith. 1992. "Racism in the Head, Racism in the World." Report from the Institute for Philosophy and Public Policy. University of Maryland, Vol. 12 (Spring/Summer):3–5.

Lichter, Daniel T., and Zhenchao Qian. 2004. *Marriage and Family in a Multiracial Society*. Washington, DC: Russell Sage Foundation.

Lind, Michael. 2011. "The Cost of Free Trade." *American Prospect* (December):52–57.

Lindorff, Dane. 2010. "Your Tax Dollars at War." *Commondreams.org* (April 13). Online: http://www.commondreams.org/54890.

Lindsey, Rebecca. 2007. "Tropical Deforestation." Earth Observatory at NASA. Online: http://earthobservatory.nasa.gov/features/deforestation/deforestation_update.php.

Lingeman, Richard. 2010. "Noted." *Nation* (March 15):5.

Linton, Simi. 1998. *Claiming Disability: Knowledge and Identity*. New York: New York University Press.

Llewellyn, A., and K. Hogan. 2000. "The Use and Abuse of Modes of Disability." *Disability and Society* 15 (January): 157–165.

Lockheed, Marlaine. 1985. "Sex Equity in the Classroom Organization and Climate." In Susan S. Klein (Ed.), *Handbook for Achieving Sex Equity through Education*. Baltimore: Johns Hopkins University Press, pp. 189–217.

Longman, Phillip J. 2001. "American Gridlock." *U.S. News & World Report* (May 28):16–22.

Lopiano, Donna. 2008. "Pay Inequity in Athletics." Women's Sports Foundation. Online: http://www.womenssports-foundation.org/cgi-bin/iowa/issues/disc/article.html?record=118.

Lorber, Judith. 1994. *Paradoxes of Gender*. New Haven, CT: Yale University Press.

Lorber, Judith. 2005. *Gender Inequality: Feminist Theories and Politics*. Los Angeles: Roxbury.

Lorber, Judith. 2011. "Gendered and Sexed Brains." *Contemporary Sociology* 40(4):405–409.

Lott, Juanita Tamayo, and Judy C. Felt. 1991. "Studying the Pan Asian Community." *Population Today* 19 (April 1):6–8.

Loury, Glenn C. 2007. "Why Are So Many Americans in Prison?" *Boston Review* (September 1). Online: http://bostonreview.net/BR32.4/article_loury.php.

Love, Alice Ann. 1998. "Gender Wage Gap Shrinks Slightly." *USA Today* (June 10):1A.

Lucal, Betsy. 1996. "Oppression and Privilege: Toward a Relational Conceptualization of Race." *Teaching Sociology* 24 (July):245–255.

Lyons, Dan. 2011. "Who Needs Humans?" *Newsweek* (July 25):28.

Mabry, J. Beth, Roseann Giarrusso, and Vern L. Bengston. 2004. "Generations, the Life Course, and Family Change." In Jacqueline Scott, Judith Treas, and Martin Richards (Eds.), *The Blackwell Companion to the Sociology of Families*. Malden, MA: Blackwell, pp. 87–108.

MacDorman, Marian F. and T. J. Mathews. 2011. "Understanding Racial and Ethnic Disparities in U.S. Infant Mortality Rates." *Centers for Disease Control and Prevention*, NCHS Data Brief. No. 74 (September). Online: http://www.cdc.gov/nchs/data/databriefs.db74.htm.

MacGillis, Alec. 2009. "The Gang on the Hill." *Washington Post National Weekly Edition* (August 17):26–27.

Mach, Henry Jay. 1987. "Shrink, Shrank, Shrunk: The Stormy Relationship between Gays and Mental Health Experts." *Advocate* (October 13):43–49.

Mackinnon, Ian. 2009. " 'Ecstasy Oil' Factories Destroyed in Cambodian Rainforest." *The Guardian* (February 25). Online: http://www.guardian.co.uk/environment/2009/feb/25/ecstasy-cambodia.

Maddow, Rachel. 2012. *Drift: The Unmooring of American Military Power*. New York: Crown.

Mairs, Nancy. 1992. "On Being a Cripple." In L. McDowell and R. Pringle (Eds.), *Defining Women*. Cambridge: Polity.

Males, Mike. 1996. *The Scapegoat Generation: America's War on Adolescents*. Monroe, ME: Common Courage Press.

Malveaux, Julianne. 2011. "More Female Grads, But What About Pay?" *USA Today* (May 13):11A.

Mann, Coramae Rickey, Leon Pittiway, and Ralph Weisheit. (n.d.). "Drugs and the Rural Community." Online: http://www.asc41.com/taskreports/drugs&community.txt.

Marcus, Mary Brophy. 2010. "Minorities More Likely to Develop Alzheimer's." *USA Today* (March 9):4D.

Markee, Patrick. 2011. "The Unfathomable Cuts in Housing Aid." *The Nation* (December 14). Online: http://www.thenation.com/article/16516/unfathomable-cuts-housing-aid.

Marklein, Mary Beth. 2009. "SAT Scores Show Disparities by Race, Gender, Family Income." *USAToday.com*. (August 26). Online: http://www.usatoday.com/news/education/2009-08-25-SAT-scores_N.htm.

Marshall, Stephen. 2003. "Prime Time Payola." *In These Times* (May 5):23–24.

Marsiglio, William, Paul Amato, Ronald D. Day, and Michael E. Lamb. 2001. "Scholarship on Fatherhood in the 1990s and Beyond." In Robert M. Milardo (Ed.), *Understanding Families into the New Millennium: A Decade in Review*. Minneapolis: National Council on Family Relations, pp. 392–410.

Martin, Karen A. 2005. "William Wants a Doll: Can He Have One?" *Gender & Society* 19 (August):456–479.

Martin, Patricia Yancey. 2003. "Said and Done Versus Saying and Doing: Gendering Practices, Practicing Gender at Work." *Gender & Society* 17 (June):342–366.

Martin, Philip, and Elizabeth Midgley. 1999. "Immigration to the United States." *Population Bulletin* 54 (June): entire issue.

Martin, Philip, and Elizabeth Midgley. 2010. "Immigration in America 2010." *Population Bulleting Update*. Population Reference Bureau (June).

Massey, Douglas S. 1993. "Latino Poverty Research: An Agenda for the 1990s." *Items* (Social Science Research Council) 47 (March):7–11.

Massey, Douglas S. 1996. "Concentrating Poverty Breeds Violence." *Population Today* 24 (June/July):5.

Massey, Douglas S. 2006. "The Wall That Keeps Illegal Workers In." *New York Times* (April 4). Online: http://www.nytimes.com/2006/04/04/opinion/04massey.html.

Massey, Douglas S., and Nancy Denton. 1993. *American Apartheid: Segregation and the Making of the Underclass*. Cambridge, MA: Harvard University Press.

Matthews, Jay. 2006. "Study Casts Doubt on the 'Boy Crisis.' " *Washington Post* (June 26):A1.

Mauriello, Tracie. 2011. "$210 Million Settlement in Upper Branch Mine Explosion." *Pittsburgh Post-Gazette* (December 6). Online: http://www.post-gazette.com/pg/11340/1194962-100-0.stm.

Mazzetta, Jill, and Tillman Clark. 2010. "Fewer Guns! More Butter!" *Dollars and Sense* 287 (March/April):6.

McAdoo, John. 1988. "Changing Perspectives on the Role of the Black Father." In P. Bronstein and C. P. Cowan (Eds.), *Fatherhood Today, Men's Changing Role in the Family*. New York: Wiley, pp. 79–92.

McCabe, Janice, Emily Fairchild, Liz Graverholz, Bernice A. Pescosolido, and Daniel Trope. 2011. "Gender in Twentieth Century Children's Books: Patterns of Disparity in Titles and Central Characters." *Gender and Society* 25(2):197–226.

McCarthy, Michael. 2004. "Circulation Scandals Cast Shadow on Newspaper." *USA Today* (August 9):5B.

McClam, Erin. 2000. "Less Teens Smoked in '99, CDC Says." Associated Press (August 25).

McGinn, Daniel. 2009. "The Greenest Companies in America." *Newsweek* (September 28).

McGovern, Ray. 2012. "The Obama Team Just Doesn't Get It; U.S. Violence and Occupation Spark Terrorism." *Alternet* (May 3). Online: http://www.alternet.org/moedule/155246.

McIntosh, Peggy. 1992. "White Privilege and Male Privilege." In Margaret L. Andersen and Patricia Hill Collins (Eds.), *Race, Class, and Gender*. Belmont, CA: Wadsworth, pp. 70–81.

McKinley, Donald Gilbert. 1964. *Social Class and Family Life*. Glencoe, IL: Free Press.

McKinley, James C. 2010. "Texas Conservatives Win Curriculum Change." *The New York Times* (March 15). Online: http://www.nytimes.com/2010/03/13/education/13texas.html.

McLanahan, Sara, and Karen Booth. 1991. "Mother Only Families." In Alan Booth (Ed.), *Contemporary Families: Looking Forward, Looking Back*. Minneapolis: National Council of Family Relations, pp. 405–428.

Mead, Sara. 2006. "The Truth About Boys and Girls." Education Sector Report (June 27). Online: http://www.educationsector.org/analysis_show.htm?doc_id=378705.

Means, Marianne. 1996. "Blatant Bigotry in Name of Christ." *Rocky Mountain News* (June 15):56A.

Medical News Today. 2004. "Addicted Rats Have Same Compulsive Drive for Cocaine as Humans Do." (August 13). Online: http://www.medicalnewstoday.com/medicalnews.php?newsid=12032.

Messner, Michael A. 1992. *Power at Play: Sports and the Problem of Masculinity*. Boston: Beacon.

Messner, Michael A. 1996. "Studying Up on Sex." *Sociology of Sport Journal* 13:221–237.

Metcalf, Stephen. 2002. "Reading between the Lines." *Nation* (January 28):18–22.

Meyer, Philip. 2012. "Income Inequality Does Matter." *USA Today* (March 28):9A.

Meyerson, Harold. 2010. "The Politics of Industrial Renaissance." *American Prospect* 21 (January/February):A16–A18.

Meyerson, Harold. 2011. "Back from Church?" *American Prospect* (December):42–51.

Midwest Coalition for Human Rights. 2011. "Petition Demonstration Concern About Working Conditions in Meatpacking Plants." (December). Online: http://www.midwesthumanrights.org/petition-demonstration-growing-concern-about-working-conditions.

Mignon, Sylvia I., Calvin J. Larson, and William M. Holmes. 2002. *Family Abuse: Consequences, Theories, and Responses*. Boston: Allyn & Bacon. Online: http://www.feminist.com/fairpay.

Migoya, David. 2002. "Rejected Meat Resold by ConAgra." *Denver Post* (July 28):1A,11A.

Milburn, John. 2009. "State's Relationship with Military Means Big Bucks." *Hutchinson News* (December 7):A3.

Milchen, Jeff, and Jonathan Power. 2001. "Why Is Killing for Capital Not a Capital Crime?" *Progressive Populist* (July 15):9.

Miller, Casey, and Kate Swift. 1980. *The Handbook of Nonsexist Writing*. New York: Lippincott & Crowell.

Miller, David. 1991. "A Vision of Market Socialism." *Dissent* 38 (Summer):406–414.

Mills, C. Wright. 1959. *The Sociological Imagination*. Fair Lawn, NJ: Oxford University Press.

Mills, C. Wright. 1962. "The Big City: Private Troubles and Public Issues." In Irving Louis Horowitz (Ed.), *Power, Politics, and People: The Collected Essays of C. Wright Mills*. New York: Ballantine Books, pp. 395–402.

Mintz, Steven. 2012. "The Kids Are Moving Back After College? Smart Career Move." *Washington Post* (June 1). Online: http://washingtonpost.com.

Mitchell, Linda M., and Amy Buchele-Ash. 2000. "Abuse and Neglect of Individuals with Disabilities." *Journal of Disability Policy Studies* 10(2):225–243.

Mohan, Geoffrey, and Ann M. Simmons. 2004. "Diversity Spoken in 39 Languages." *Los Angeles Times* (June 16). Online: http://www.latimes.com/news/locak/la-me-multilingual16jun16,1,157.

Mokhiber, Russell. 2010. "The Monopolization of America." *Corporate Crime Reporter* (February 13). Online: http://www.commondreams.org/view/2010/02/13–1.

Montgomery, Mark R. 2009. "Urban Poverty and Health in Developing Countries." *Population Bulletin* 64 (June).

Moore, Joan W., and Raquel Pinderhughes (Eds.). 1994. *In the Barrios: Latinos and the Underclass Debate*. New York: Russell Sage Foundation.

Moore, Martha. 2006. "Episcopal Church Torn by Gay Issue as More Parishes Leave U.S. Branch." *USA Today* (March 3):1A.

Morantz, Alison D. 2011. "Coal Mine Safety: Do Unions Make a Difference?" *Social Science Research Network* (May 27). Online: http://papers.ssrn.com/sel13/papers.chapter?abstract_id=1846700.

Morris, Jenny. 1991. *Pride against Prejudice*. London: Women's Press.

Morton, Lois Wright. 2003. "Rural Health Policy." In David L. Brown and Louis E. Swanson (Eds.), *Challenges for Rural America in the Twenty-First Century*. University Park: The Pennsylvania State University Press, pp. 290–302.

Mosher, Clayton J. and Scott Akins. 2007. *Drugs and Drug Policy: The Control of Consciousness Alteration*. Thousand Oaks, CA: Sage.

Mothana, Ibrahim. 2012. "How Drones Help Al Qaeda." *CommonDreams.org* (June 14). Online: http://www.commondreams.org/view/2012/06/14–7.

Mouawad, Jad, and Simon Romero. 2005. "Unmentioned Energy Fix: A 55 M.P.H. Speed Limit." *New York Times* (May 1):24xt.

Moya, Paula M.L. and Hazel Rose Marcus. 2010. "An Introduction." In Hazel Rose Marcus and Paula M.L. Moya (eds.), *Doing Race: 21 Essays for the 21st Century*. New York: W. W. Norton & Company, Inc., pp. 1–103.

Moyers, Bill. 2012. "The Real Costs of War." *Truthout.org* (April). Online: http://truth-out.org/news/item/8238-the-real-cost-of-war.

Moyers, Bill, and Michael Winship. 2009. "Changing the Rules of the Blame Game." *CommonDreams.org* (April 8). Online: http://www.commondreams.org/print/40559.

Moyers, Bill, and Michael Winship. 2010. "What Are We Bid for American Justice?" CommonDreams.org (February 20). Online: http://www.commondreams.org/print/53016.

Moynihan, Daniel P. 1988. "Our Poorest Citizens—Children." *Focus* 11 (Spring):5–6.

Muhammad, Dedrick. 2009. *Challenges to Native American Advancement: The Recession and Native America*. New York: Institute for Policy Studies.

Mukhopadhyay, Carol, and Rosemary C. Henze. 2003. "How Real Is Race? Using Anthropology to Make Sense of Human Diversity." *Phi Delta Kappan* (May):669–678.

Murdoch, William M. 1980. *The Poverty of Nations: The Political Economy of Hunger and Population*. Baltimore: Johns Hopkins University Press.

Murray, Charles. 1984. *Losing Ground*. New York: Basic Books.

Muwakkil, Salim. 1994. "Dangerous Curve." *In These Times* (November 28):22–24.

Muwakkil, Salim. 1998a. "Movin' on Apart." *In These Times* (March 22):11–12.

Muwakkil, Salim. 1998b. "Real Minority, Media Majority: TV News Needs to Root Out Stereotypes about Blacks and Crime." *In These Times* (June 28):18–19.

Myrdal, Gunnar. 1944. *An American Dilemma*. New York: Pantheon Books.

NAACP. 2009. "End Campus Racism Campaign, 2009." Online: http://www.naacp.org/youth/college/endcampusracism/index.htm.

Naples, Nancy A. 1998. "Women's Community Activism and Feminist Action Research." In Nancy A. Naples (Ed.), *Community Activism and Feminist Politics*. New York: Routledge, pp. 1–27.

Nation. 1996. "In Fact. . . ." (January 1):5.

Nation. 2009. "Filibustering the Public." (December 14):3.

Nation. 2012. "Obama's Kill List." (June 25):3.

National Alliance to End Homelessness. 2012. "State of Homelessness in America 2012." (January 17). Online: http://www.endhomelessness.org.

National Association of College and University Business Officers (NACUBO). 2012. Online: http://www.nacubo.org.

National Center for Education Statistics. 2010. "Digest of Education Statistics: 2010." Online: http://nces.ed.gov.

National Center for Education Statistics. 2012. Online: http://nces.ed.gov.

National Center for Science Education. 2006. "Defending the Teaching of Evolution in the Public Schools." Online: http://www.ncseweb.org.

National Center for Science Education. 2007. "Evolution Returns to Kansas." (February 14). Online: http://www.ncseweb.org/resources/news/2007/KS/286_evolution_returns_to_Kansas_2_14_2007.asp.

National Center on Elder Abuse. 1998. *National Elder Abuse Incidence Study*. Washington, DC: American Public Health Services Association.

National Center on Family Homelessness. 2011. "1.6 Million Children Homeless in America." (December 13).

National Conference of State Legislatures. 2009. "Disparities in Health." (August) Online: http://www.ncsl.org/?tabid+14494#Life Expectancy.

National Council of La Raza. 1999. "The Mainstreaming of Hate: A Report on Latinos and Harassment, Hate Violence, and Law Enforcement Abuse in the '90s." (July). Washington, DC.

National Geographic. n.d. "The New Suburb." Online: http://www.nationalgeographic.com/features/00/earthpulse/sprawl/index_flash.html.

National Highway Traffic Safety Administration. 2012. "Impaired Driving." Online: http://www.nhtsa.gov/Impaired.

National Institute on Drug Abuse. 2012. Online: http://www.drugabuse.gov.

National Latino Congresso. 2011. "Wealth Gap Widens Between Whites, Minorities." (July 26). Online: http://www.latinocongresso.org.

National Low Income Housing Coalition. 2012. "Out of Reach 2012." Online: http://nlihc.org/oor/2012.

Navarrette, Ruben. 2009. "What Mexico's Drug War Means for U.S." CNN.com. (February 27). Online: http://www.cnn.com/2009/politics/02/27/navarrette.mexico/index.html.

Navarro, Lygia. 2011. "The Melting Pot." *The American Prospect* (April) A18–A20.

Navarro, Mireya. 2012. "For Many Latinos, Racial Identity Is More Culture Than Color." *New York Times* (January 13). Online: http://www.nytimes.com/2012/01/14/us/for-many-latinos-race-is-more-culture-than-color.html?pagewanted=all&_r=0.

Navarro, Vicente. 1991. "Class and Race: Life and Death Situations." *Monthly Review* 43 (September):1–13.

Neilson, Joyce McCarl. 1990. *Sex and Gender in Society*, 2nd ed. Prospect Heights, IL: Waveland Press.

New America Foundation. 2009. "School Finance." Online: http://febp.newamerica.net/background-analysis/school-finance.

New York Times. 2000. "A Fix for the Broadcast Giveaway." (October 11). Online: http://nytimes.com/2000/10/11/opinion/11WED2.html.

New York Times. 2002. "The Population Slowdown." (March 28). Online: http://www.nytimes.com/2002/03/28/opinion/_28THU2.html.

New York Times. 2006. "Money Down the Drain in Iraq." (October 26): Online: http://www.nytimes.com/2006/10/26/opinion/26thr1.html?pagewanted=print.

New York Times. 2010. "The Court's Blow to Democracy." (January 22). Online: http://www.nytimes.com/2010/01/22/opinion/22fri1.html.

New York Times. 2012. "Too Much Power for a President." (May 30). Online: http://www.nytimes.com/2012/05/30/opinion/too-much-power-for-a-president.

Newman, Katherine S. 1988. *Falling from Grace: The Experience of Downward Mobility in the American Middle Class*. New York: Free Press.

Newport, Frank. 2011. "Record-High 50% of Americans Favor Legalizing Marijuana Use." *Gallup*. (October 17). Online: http://www.gallup.com/poll/150149/Record-High-Americans-Favor-Legalizing-Marijuana.aspx.

Newsweek. 2007. "The Human Cost of War." (April 2):42–43.

Nichols, Michelle. 2006. "Conservative Jews OK Gay Rabbis." Reuters (December 6). Online: http://today.reuters.com/news/articlesnews.aspx?type=domesticNews&storyID=2006-12-06T2116492_01.

Nilges, Lynda M., and Albert F. Spencer. 2002. "The Pictorial Representation in Notable Children's Picture Books: 1995–1999." *Sex Roles* 45 (1/2):89–101.

Nordland, Rod. 2012. "Risks of Afghan War Shift from Soldiers to Contractors." *New York Times* (February 11). Online: http://www.nytimes.com/2012/02/12/world/asia/afghan-war-risks-are-shifting-from-soldiers-to-contractors.

Nore, Gordon W. E. 1991. "An Interview with Jonathan Kozol." *Progressive* 55 (December):34–36.

Nye, Joseph S. Jr. 2006. "Transformation Is Hard." *Time* (July 9). Online: Time.com/time/magazine/article/0,9171,1211591,00.html.

Nye, Joseph S. Jr. 2012. "When Women Lead." *Nation of Change*. Online: http://www.nationofchange.org/when-women-lead-1328971896.

Obama, Barack. 2006. "Growth and Disparity: A Decade of U.S. Public School Construction." Statement by Senator Barack Obama. Online: http://www.21csf.org/csf-home/publications/Obamastatement.pdf.

O'Brien, Rebecca Davis. 2008. "Who Gets U.S. Foreign Aid." *Parade* (December 14). Online: http://www.parade.com/news/intelligence-report/archive/who-gets-us-foreign-aid.

O'Donnell, Jayne. 2000. "Suffering in Silence." *USA Today* (April 3):1B–2B.

O'Hare, William P. 1992. "America's Minorities: The Demographics of Diversity." *Population Bulletin* 47 (December): entire issue.

O'Hare, William P. 1996. "A New Look at Poverty in America." *Population Bulletin* 51 (September): entire issue.

O'Kelly, Charlotte. 1980. *Women and Men in Society*. New York: Van Nostrand.

Oliver, Melvin L., and Thomas M. Shapiro. 1995. *Black Wealth/White Wealth: A New Perspective on Racial Equality*. New York: Routledge.

Oliver, Mike. 1996. "A Sociology of Disability or a Disablist Sociology?" In Len Barton (Ed.), *Disability and Society: Emerging Issues and Insights*. New York: Longman, pp. 18–42.

Oliver, Rachel. 2008. "Rich, Poor, and Climate Change." CNN.com (February 17). Online: http://edition.cnn.com/2008/business/02/17/eco.class.

Omi, Michael, and Howard Winant. 1986. *Racial Formation in the United States*. London: Routledge & Kegan Paul.

Omi, Michael, and Howard Winant. 1994. *Racial Formation in the United States*, 2nd ed. New York: Routledge & Kegan Paul.

OpenSecrets.org. 2012. "Lobbying Database." Washington DC, Center for Responsive Politics. Online: http://www.opensecrets.org/lobby.

Oppenheim, Jerrold, and Theo MacGregor. 2006. "The Economics of Poverty: How Investments to Eliminate Poverty Benefit All Americans." *Entergy Corporation* (June). Online: http://www.democracyandregulation.com/detail.cfm?artid=99.

Orenstein, J. B. 2001. "America's Hospital Emergency." *Washington Post National Weekly Edition* (April 30):21.

Orenstein, Peggy. 2008. "Girls Will Be Girls." *New York Times* (February 28). Online: http://www.nytimes.com/2008/02/10/magazine/10ww/n-1ede-t.html.

Orfield, Gary, Genevieve Siegel-Hawley, and John Kucsera. 2011. "Divided We Fail: Segregated and Unequal Schools in the Southland." University of California, Los Angeles, Civil Rights Project. Online: http://civilrightsproject.ucla.edu.

Orfield, Gary, and Chungmei Lee. 2012. "Historical Reversals, Accelerating Resegregation, and the Need for New Integration Strategies." In *Race and Ethnicity in Society*, Elizabeth Higginbotham and Margaret L. Andersen, eds. Belmont, CA: Wadsworth Cengage Learning.

Ortner, Sherry B. 1974. "Is Female to Male as Nature Is to Culture?" In Michelle Zimbalist Rosaldo and Louise Lamphere (Eds.), *Woman, Culture, and Society*. Stanford, CA: Stanford University Press, pp. 66–88.

Oskamp, Stuart, Karen Kaufman, and Lianna Atchison Wolterbeek. 1996. "Gender Role Portrayal in Preschool Books." *Journal of Social Behavior and Personality* 11(5):27–39.

Pace, David. 2005. "Blacks, Poor More Likely to Breathe Most Unhealthy Air." Associated Press (December 14).

Page, Susan. 2009. "In One Year, 24 Million Slide from 'Thriving' to 'Struggling.' " *USA Today* (March 10):1A–2A.

Painter, Kim. 2008. "Can Wealth Affect Health?" *USA Today* (March 24):4D.

Palmer, James. 2007. "Trauma Severe for Iraqi Children." *USA Today* (April 16):1A.

Parenti, Michael. 1978. *Power and the Powerless*, 2nd ed. New York: St. Martin's Press.

Parenti, Michael. 1980. *Democracy for the Few*, 3rd ed. New York: St. Martin's Press.

Parenti, Michael. 1988. *Democracy for the Few*, 5th ed. New York: St. Martin's Press.

Parenti, Michael. 1995. *Democracy for the Few*, 6th ed. New York: St. Martin's Press.

Parenti, Michael. 2008. *Democracy for the Few*, 8th ed. Boston: Thomson Higher Education.

Parrish, Geov. 2001. "Fanning the Flames of Terrorism." *AlterNet* (September 20). Online: www.alternet.org/story.html?StoryID=11547.

Parsons, Claudia. 2009. "Hate Goes Viral on Social Network Sites." Reuters (May 13). Online: http://www.reuters.com/assets/print?aid=USTRE54C4KW20090513.

Passel, Jeffrey and D'Vera Cohn. 2011. "Unauthorized Immigrant Population: National and State Trends, 2010." Pew Hispanic Center (February 1).

Patterson, Orlando. 2007. "The Root of the Problem." *Time* (May 7):58.

Paulson, Michael. 2000. "More Women Embracing the Study of Jewish Faith." *Boston Globe* (March 13):1B, 5B.

Paulson, Tom. 2008. "The Lowdown on Topsoil: It's Disappearing." *Seattle PI* (January 22). Online: http://www.seattlepi.com/local/348200_dirt22.html.

Pear, Robert. 2004. "Selling to the Poor, Stoves Bill U.S. for Top Prices." *New York Times* (June 6):1.

Pearce, Diana. 1978. "The Feminization of Poverty: Women, Work, and Welfare." *Urban Change Review* 2 (February): 24–36.

Pena, Charles V. 2010. "A Penny Saved Is a Dollar Spent on Defense." *Wichita Eagle* (May 18):9A.

Penalver, Eduardo M. 2008. "The End of Sprawl?" *Washington Post National Weekly Edition* (January 7):31.

Peplau, Letitia Anne, Rosemary C. Veniegas, and Susan Miller Campbell. 2004. "Gay and Lesbian Relationships." In Michael S. Kimmel and Rebecca F. Plante (Eds.), *Sexualities: Identities, Behaviors, and Society*. New York: Oxford University Press, pp. 200–215.

Perry, Susan. 2010. "Tobacco Industry Constantly Re-invents Its Marketing Efforts, a Minnesota Report Points Out." MinnesotaPost .com (February 11). Online: http://www.minnpost.com/ healthblog/2010/02/11/15845/tobacco_industry_constantly_ reinvents_its_marketing_efforts_report_points_out.

Peters, Peter J. 1992. *Intolerance of Discrimination against, and the Death Penalty for Homosexuals as Prescribed in the Bible*. LaPorte, CO: Scriptures for America.

Peterson, Linda, and Elaine Enarson. 1974. "Blaming the Victim in the Sociology of Women: On the Misuse of the Concept of Socialization." Paper presented at the Pacific Sociological Association, San Jose, California, March.

Peterson, Peter. 1999. "The Global Aging Crisis." *Denver Post* (February 7):1J–2J.

Pew Charitable Trusts. 2012. "Pursuing the American Dream: Economic Mobility Across Generations." The Economic Mobility Project. Online: http://www.pewstates.org.

Pew Research Center. 2011. "Twenty-to-One: Wealth Gaps Rise to Record Highs Between Whites, Blacks, and Hispanics." (July). Online: http://pewsocialtrends.org.

Pew Research Center. 2012. "The Rise of Asian Americans." (June 16). Online: http://www.pewsocialtrends.org.

Pierce, Neal. 2011. "It's Time to Return to a Robust Urbanism." *CommonDreams.org* (January 2). Online: http://www.commondreams .org/63992.

Pierre, Robert E. 2004. "Pockets of the Poor." *Washington Post National Weekly Edition* (July 26/August 1):30.

Pike, Jennifer J., and Nancy A. Jennings. 2005. "The Effects of Commercials on Children's Perceptions of Gender Appropriate Toy Use." *Sex Roles* 52 (1/2):83–91.

Pillard, Richard C. and J. Michael Bailey. 1998. "Human Sexual Orientation Has a Heritable Component." *Human Biology* 70, no. 2 (April):347–365.

Pillemer, Karl A. 1993. "Abuse Is Caused by the Deviance and Dependence of Abusive Caregivers." In Richard J. Gelles and Donileen R. Loseke (Eds.), *Current Controversies on Family Violence*. Newbury Park, CA: Sage, pp. 237–249.

Pipher, Mary. 1994. *Reviving Ophelia: Saving the Selves of Adolescent Girls*. New York: Ballantine Books.

Pittman, Genevra. 2011. "Social Environment Linked to Gay Teen Suicide Risk." *Reuters Health* (April 18).

Piven, Frances Fox. 1996. "Welfare and the Transformation of Electoral Politics." *Dissent* 43 (Fall):61–67.

Piven, Frances Fox, and Richard A. Cloward. 1971. *Regulating the Poor*. New York: Random House.

Pizzigati, Sam. 2012. "Will CEO Pay Excess Outlast Our 'Shareholder Spring'?" *Inequality.org* (May 14). Online: http://inequality.org/ can-pay-excess-outlast-shareholder-spring.

Pollard, Kelvin M., and William P. O'Hare. 1999. "America's Racial and Ethnic Minorities." *Population Bulletin* 54, No. 3 (September). Washington, DC: Population Reference Bureau.

Pollitt, Katha. 2010. "The Decade for Women: Forward, Backward, Sideways?" *The Nation* (January 15):10.

Population Reference Bureau. 2009. "2009 World Population Data Sheet." Washington, DC.

Population Reference Bureau. 2011. "2011 World Population Data Sheet." (July).

Portes, Alejandro, and Min Zhou. 1993. "The New Second Generation: Segmented Assimilation and Its Variants." *Annals of the American Academy of Political and Social Science* 530:74–96.

Portillo, Ely. 2006. "Costs of Teen Drinking Add Up to $62 Billion." *Wichita Eagle* (June 30):4A.

Potok, Mark. 2011. "The Year in Hate and Extremism, 2010." *Southern Poverty Law Center*, Intelligence Report. 141 (Spring).

Powell, Bill. 2006. "When Outlaws Get the Bomb." *Time* (October 23):32–37.

Powers, Kristen A. 2007. "Immigrants Become Target for All of Society's Ills." *USA Today* (August 29):13A.

Press, Eyal, and Jennifer Washburn. 2000. "Neglect for Sale." *American Prospect* (May 8):22–29.

Prewitt, Kenneth. 2003. *Politics and Science in Census Taking*. New York: Russell Sage Foundation.

Progressive. 2009. "Job Loss Is Pentagon's Gain." Vol. 73 (December):5.

Public Broadcasting System. 2009. "Frontline: The Failure and Future of the Private Insurance Industry." (March 31).

Public Citizen. 2003. "The Other Drug War." (June 23). Online: http:// www.citizen.org/pressroom/release.cfm?ID=1469.

Pugh, Tony. 2012. "Health Care Mandate Will Prove Limited." *McClatchy Newspapers* (July 2).

Pyke, Karen. 2004. "Immigrant Families in the U.S." In *The Blackwell Companion to the Sociology of Families*. Malden, MA: Blackwell, pp. 253–269.

Pyke, Karen. 2008. "Immigrant Families in the U.S." In Stephanie Coontz (ed.), *American Families: A Multicultural Reader*, 2nd ed. New York: Routledge, pp. 210–221.

Quindlen, Anna. 2007. "Killing the Consumer." *Newsweek* (October 1).

Quinney, Richard. 1970. *The Social Reality of Crime*. Boston: Little, Brown.

Radio-Television Digital News Association. 2012. "2011 Women and Minorities Data." Online: http://www.rtdna.org/pages/research/ women-and-minorities.php.

Rall, Ted. 2006. "End of the U.S. as a Civilized Nation." *Progressive Populist* (November 15):19.

Ramirez, Jessica. 2010. "You and Whose Army?" *Newsweek* (June 28/ July 5):84.

Rampell, Catherine. 2012. "College-Educated Workers Gaining Jobs, High School Grads Losing Them." *New York Times* (January 9). Online: http://economix.blogs.nytimes.com/2012/01/09/ college-educated-gaining-jobs-highschool-grads-losing-them.

Rapp, Rayna. 1982. "Family and Class in Contemporary America." In Barrie Thorne and Marilyn Yalom (Eds.), *Rethinking the Family: Some Feminist Questions*. New York: Longman, pp. 168–187.

Rashbaum, William K. 2010. "New York Police Manipulated Crime Data, Retired Officials Say." *New York Times*. (February 7):20.

Ratner, Lizzy. 2009. "Generation Recession." *The Nation* (November 23):23–25.

Raum, Tom. 2009. "Higher Jobless Rates Could Be a 'New Normal.'" Associated Press (October 20).

Rawlings, Steve. 1995. "Households and Families: Population Profile of the United States: 1995." *Current Population Reports*, Series P23–189. Washington, DC: U.S. Government Printing Office.

Re, Richard. 2002. "A Persisting Evil." *Harvard International Review* 23 (Winter):32–35.

Reed, Adolph, Jr. 1990. "The Underclass as Myth and Symbol: The Poverty of Discourse about Poverty." *Radical America* 24 (January/ March):21–40.

Reed, Adolph, Jr. 1994. "Looking Backward." *Nation* (November 28):654–662.

Reed, Betsy. 2009. "Unemployment Is Hitting Men Particularly Hard— and Both Sexes are Losing Out." *AlterNet* (April 8). Online: http:// www.alternet.org/story/135521.

Reeves, Jay. 2011. "Hispanic Children Bullied in Law's Wake." *The Boston Globe* (October 23):B6.

Reich, Robert B. 1989. "Yes: Blame Election Funds." *New York Times* (October 12):A29.

Reich, Robert B. 1998. "Broken Faith: Why We Need to Renew the Social Compact." *Nation* (February 16):11–17.

Reich, Robert B. 2000. "What's the Difference?" *American Prospect* (August 28):64.

Reich, Robert B. 2012. "Memorial Day Thoughts on National Defense Spending." *CommonDreams.org* (May 27). Online: http://www .commondreams.org.

Reid, T. R. 2009. *The Healing of America*. New York: Penguin Press.

Reiman, Jeffrey H. 2007. *The Rich Get Richer and the Poor Get Prison: Ideology, Class, and Criminal Justice*, 8th ed. Boston: Allyn & Bacon.

ReligiousTolerance.org. 2009. "Judeo-Christianity and Homosexuality." Online: http://www.religioustolerance.org/hom_bibl.htm.

Renzetti, Claire M., and Daniel J. Curran. 2003. *Women, Men, and Society*, 5th ed. Boston: Allyn & Bacon.

Reskin, Barbara F. 1999. "Occupational Segregation by Race and Ethnicity among Women Workers." In Irene Brown (Ed.), *Latinas and African American Women at Work: Race, Gender, and Economic Inequality*. New York: Russell Sage.

Reskin, Barbara F., and Patricia A. Roos. 1990. *Job Queues, Gender Queues*. Philadelphia: Temple University Press.

Reuss, Alejandro. 2001. "Cause of Death: Inequality." *Dollars & Sense*, No. 235 (May/June):10–12.

Richburg, Keith B. 2004. "A Smorgasbord of Cultures." *Washington Post National Weekly Edition* (November 107):17.

Richburg, Keith B. 2009. "When Locking 'Em Up Costs Too Much," *Washington Post National Weekly* (July 20–26): 33.

Richmond-Abbott, Marie. 1992. *Masculine and Feminine: Sex Roles over the Life Cycle*, 2nd ed. New York: McGraw-Hill.

Ricks, Thomas E. 2006. *Fiasco: The American Military Adventure in Iraq*. New York: Penguin.

Ricks, Thomas E. 2012. "Let's Draft Our Kids." *New York Times* (July 10):A19.

Ridgeway, Cecilia L. 1997. "Interaction and the Conservation of Gender Inequality: Considering Employment." *American Sociological Review* 62 (April):218–235.

Ridgeway, Cecilia L. 2011. *Framed by Gender*. New York: Oxford University Press.

Ridgeway, Cecilia L., and Lynn Smith-Lovin. 1999. "The Gender System and Interaction." *Annual Review of Sociology* 25:191–216.

Ritchie, Liesel A., Duane A. Gill, and J. Steven Picou. 2011. "The BP Disaster as an Exxon Valdez Rerun." *Contexts* 10(3):30–35.

Risman, Barbara J. 1998. *Gender Vertigo*. New Haven, CT: Yale University Press.

Risman, Barbara J., and Donald Tomaskovic-Devey. 1998. "Editors Note." *Contemporary Sociology* 27 (March):vii–viii.

Rivera, Amaced, Jeannette Hullga, Christina Kasica, and Dedrick Muhammad. 2009. *The Silent Depression: State of the Dream 2009*. Boston: United for a Fair Economy.

Roberts, Sam. 2005. "More Africans Enter U.S. than in Days of Slavery." *New York Times* (February 21):A1.

Roberts, Sam. 2008. "In a Generation, Minorities May Be the U.S. Majority." *New York Times* (August 14). Online: http://www.nytimes.com/2008/08/14/washington/14census.html.

Roberts, Sam. 2010. "Census Figures Challenge Views of Race and Ethnicity." *New York Times* (January 22).

Robinson, Eugene. 2007. "Pulling over for Prejudice." *Washington Post National Weekly Edition* (May 7):31.

Rodgers, Harrell R. 2006. *American Poverty in a New Era of Reform*, 2nd ed. Armonk, New York: M.E. Sharpe.

Rodriguez, Luis J. 2012. "Banned in Tucson." *The Progressive* 76 (April):16–17.

Roediger, David. 1991. *Wages of Whiteness: Race and the Making of the American Working Class*. New York: Verso.

Rogers, Heather. 2005. *Gone Tomorrow: The Hidden Life of Garbage*. New York: The New Press.

Rogers, Joel. 1998. "Turning to the Cities: A Metropolitan Agenda." *In These Times* (October 18):14–17.

Rogers, Simon, and Lisa Evans. 2011. "World Carbon Dioxide Emissions Data by Country: China Speeds Ahead of the Rest." *The Guardian* (January 31). Online: http://www.guardian.co.uk/news/datablog/2011/jan/31/world-carbon-dioxide-emissions-country-data-co2.

Rogers, Susan Carol. 1978. "Women's Place: A Critical Review of Anthropological Theory." *Comparative Studies in Society and History* 20(1):123–162.

Romaine, Suzanne. 1999. *Communicating Gender*. Mahwah, NJ: Erlbaum.

Romano, Andrew. 2011. "Jim Webb's Last Crusade." *Newsweek* (September 19):50–53.

Rosaldo, Michelle Zimbalist. 1974. "Women, Culture, and Society: A Theoretical Overview." In Michelle Zimbalist Rosaldo and L. Lamphere (Eds.), *Woman, Culture, and Society*. Stanford, CA: Stanford University Press, pp. 17–42.

Rosaldo, Michelle Zimbalist. 1980. "The Use and Abuse of Anthropology." *Signs* 5 (Spring):389–417.

Rosenbaum, David E. 2001. "Ruling on Disability Rights Is a Blow, Advocates Say." *New York Times* (February 22). Online: http://www.nytimes.com/2001/02/22/national/22REAC.html.

Rosenthal, Andrew. 2011. "Oppression Is Not a State's Right." *New York Times* (November 8). Online: http://loyalopposition.blogs.nytimes.com/2011/11/08/opression-is-not-a-states-right.

Rosenthal, Robert, and Lenore Jacobson. 1968. *Pygmalion in the Classroom: Teacher Expectations and Pupils' Intellectual Development*. New York: Holt, Rinehart & Winston.

Rothstein, Richard. 2007. "A Wider Lens on the Black–White Achievement Gap." In D. Stanley Eitzen and Janis E. Johnston (Eds.), *Inequality: Social Class and Its Consequences*. Boulder, CO: Paradigm Publishers, pp. 120–128.

Roughgarden, Joan. 2004. *E.olution's Rainbow: Diversity, Gender, and Sexuality in Nature and People*. Ewing, NJ: University of California Press.

Rubin, Lillian B. 2006. "What Am I Going to Do with the Rest of My Life?" *Dissent* (Fall):88–94.

Rubin, Rita. 2007. "Study: Women, Blacks Less Likely to Get Implantable Heart Devices." *USA Today* (October 3):6D.

Ruckelshaus, William. 2010. "A New Shade of Green." *The Wall Street Journal* (April 17).

Rugaber, Christopher S. 2009. "Number of Long-Term Jobless Grows." Associated Press (December 5).

Rugh, Jacob S. and Douglas S. Massey. 2010. "Racial Segregation and the American Foreclosure Crisis." *American Sociological Review* 75(5):629–651.

Rundle, David P. 2011. "Give Roles to Actors with Disabilities." *Wichita Eagle* (September 18):15A.

Rupp, Leila J. 2007. "Everyone's Queer." In Susan J. Bunting (Ed.) *Annual Editions: Human Sexuality*, 30th ed. Dubuque, IA: McGraw-Hill., pp. 55–58.

Russell, Jan Jarboe. 2003. "Religious Right 'Monkeying' with Our Kids' Textbooks Again." *San Antonio Express-News* (September 14):1H.

Russell, Marta. 1998. *Beyond Ramps: Disability at the End of the Social Contract*. Monroe, ME: Common Courage Press.

Russell, Marta. 2000. "The Political Economy of Disablement." *Dollars & Sense*, No. 231 (September/October):13–15, 48–49.

Ryan, William. 1976. *Blaming the Victim*, rev. ed. New York: Random House (Vintage).

Saad, Lydia. 2010. "Nearly 4 in 10 Americans Still Fear Walking Alone at Night." Gallup.com (November 5). Online: http://www.gallup.com/poll/144272/nearly-americans-fear-walking-alone-night.aspx.

Sacks, Karen. 1974. "Engels Revisited: Women, the Organization of Production, and Private Property." In Michelle Zimbalist Rosaldo and Louise Lamphere (Eds.), *Woman, Culture, and Society*. Stanford, CA: Stanford University Press, pp. 207–222.

Sadker, David. 2002. "An Educator's Primer on the Gender War." *Phi Delta Kappan* 84(3):235–244.

Sadker, Myra, and David Sadker. 1994. *Failing at Fairness. How America's Schools Cheat Girls*. New York: Scribner.

Saenz, Rogelio. 2004. *Latinos and the Changing Face of America*. New York: Russell Sage Foundation and the Population Reference Bureau.

Saenz, Rogelio. 2010. "Latinos in the U.S. 2010," *Population Bulletin Update*. (December).

Sage, George H., and D. Stanley Eitzen. 2013. *Sociology of North American Sport*. 9th ed. New York: Oxford University Press.

Sandels, Alexandra. 2010. "Iraq, Afghanistan: American Casualties Total 500,000, Counting Injury and Disease." *Los Angeles Times* (June 24). Online: http://latimesblogs.latimes.com/babylonbeyond/2010/06/iraqafghanistan.

Sanders, Bernard. 1994. "Whither American Democracy." *Los Angeles Times* (January 16):B1.

Sandler, Lauren. 2009. "Code Pink." *Mother Jones* 34 (September/October):73–75.

Sapiro, Virginia. 1999. *Women in American Society*, 4th ed. Mountain View, CA: Mayfield.

Saporito, Bill. 2005. "The e-Health Revolution." *Time* (June 27):55–57.

Sauter, Michael B., Ashley C. Allen, Lisa Nelson, and Alexander E.M. Hess. 2012. "The 10 Richest- and Poorest-School Districts in America." *24/7 Wall Street* (June 11). Online: http://www.alternet.org/story/155824.

Scahill, Jeremy. 2007. "Bush's Shadow Army." *Nation* (April 2):11–19.

Scahill, Jeremy. 2009. "283 Bases, 170,000 Pieces of Equipment, 140,000 Troops, and an Army of Mercenaries: The Logistical Nightmare in Iraq." *AlterNet* (March 30). Online: http://www.alternet.orgg/module/printversion/133676.

Schactman, Brian A. 2012. "The Downside of North Dakota's Oil Boom." *CNBC* (February 1). Online: http://www.cnbc.com/id/46205381.

Scheer, Robert. 2002. "Playing Population-Explosion Politics." *Los Angeles Times* (November 5): Online: http://www.latimes.com/news/opinion/commentary/laoe-scheer5nov05,0,5557144.column?cnl.

Schemo, Diana. 2007. "Failing Schools Strain to Meet U.S. Standard." *New York Times* (October 16). Online: http://www.nytimes.com/2007/10/16/education/16child.html.

Scher, Abby. 2001. "Access Denied: Immigrants and Health Care." *Dollars & Sense*, No. 235 (May/June):8.

Schlosser, Eric. 2001. "The Chain Never Stops." *Mother Jones* (July/August). Online: http://www.motherjones.com/news/feature/2006/07/meatpacking.html.

Schlosser, Eric. 2006. "Hog Hell." *Nation* (September 11):28–31.

Schmid, Randolph E. 2006. "Study: Having Brothers Raises Chance of Being Gay." *Arizona Daily Star* (June 27):3A.

Schmidt, Peter. 2007. "How to Get into Yale With a 'B' Average." *The Week* (October 19):14.

Schmit, Julie. 2004. "Drug Companies Dodge Ban from Medicare, Medicaid." *USA Today* (August 16):1D.

Schmit, Julie, and Barbara Hansen. 2011. "Declines in Income Hurt Affordability of Housing." *USA Today* (September 22):3B.

Schmitt, Mark. 2010. "The End of the Tea Party." *American Prospect* (February 22). Online: http://prospect.org/cs/articles?article=the-end-of-the-tea-party.

Schneider, David M., and Raymond T. Smith. 1973. *Class Differences and Sex Roles in American Family and Kinship Structure.* Upper Saddle River, NJ: Prentice Hall.

Schoettler, Gail. 2000. "You Can't Buy Human Decency." *Denver Post* (October 1):2L.

Schouten, Fredreka, and Paul Overberg. 2009. "Lobbyists Unlimited in Honoring Lawmakers." *USA Today* (June 8):1A, 5A.

Schouten, Fredreka, Christopher Schnaars, and Gregory Korte. 2012. "Super Donors Keep GOP Race Going." *USA Today* (March 22):4A.

Schumpeter, Joseph. 1950. *Capitalism, Socialism, and Democracy*, 3rd ed. New York: Harpers.

Schur, Edwin. 1971. *Labeling Deviant Behavior: Its Sociological Implications.* New York: Harper & Row.

Schwartz, John. 2004. "Always on the Job, Employees Pay with Health." *New York Times* (September 5):1, 23.

Schwartz, Moshe. 2009. "Department of Defense Contractors in Iraq and Afghanistan." *Congressional Research Service*, R40764 (December 14).

Schwartz, Pepper. 2007. "The Social Construction of Heterosexuality." In Michael S. Kimmel (Ed.), *The Sexual Self: The Construction of Sexual Scripts.* Nashville, TN: Vanderbilt University Press, pp. 80–92.

Science Daily. 2008. "Symmetry of Homosexual Brain Resembles that of Opposite Sex, Swedish Study Finds." Online: http://www.sciencedaily.com/releases/2008/06/080617151845.htm.

Scorecard. 2011. The Pollution Information Site. "Toxic Chemical Releases." Online: http://scorecard.goodguide.com/env-releases/us-map.tcl.

Seefeldt, Karen, Gordon Abner, Joe A. Bolinger, Lanlan Xu, and John D. Graham. 2012. *At Risk: America's Poor During and After the Great Recession.* Bloomington, Indiana: School of Public and Environmental Affairs, Indiana University.

Seelye, Katharine Q. 2010. "Pro or Con, Lobbying Thrived." *New York Times* (January 31):20.

S.E.I.U. Service Employees International Union, AFL-CIO, CLC. 2005. Online: http://www.seiu.org.

Sen, Amartya. 1999. *Development as Freedom.* New York: Knopf.

Sen, Amartya. 2000. "Population and Gender Equity." *Nation* (July 24):16–18.

Servicemembers Legal Defense Network. 2006. "Executive Summary: 10th Annual Report on 'Don't Ask, Don't Tell.'" Online: http://www.sldn.org/templates/press/record.html?section=3&record=1450.

Shadid, Anthony. 2007. "A Widening Rift: Sunni–Shiite Tension Is Spreading across the Arab World." *Washington Post National Weekly Edition* (February 19):6–7.

Shah, Anup. 2009. "U.S. and Foreign Aid Assistance." GlobalIssues.org. (April 13). Online: http://www.globalissues.orgg/article35/usa-and-foreignaid-assistance#M.

Shakespeare, Tom. 1996. "Power and Prejudice: Issues of Gender, Sexuality, and Disability." In Len Barton (Ed.), *Disability and Society: Emerging Issues and Insights.* New York: Longman, pp. 191–214.

Shakespeare, Tom. 2006. *Disability Rights and Wrongs.* London: Routledge.

Shane, Scott. 2012. "Executive Overreach." *New York Times* (April 13). Online: http://www.nytimes.com/2012/04/13/books/review/drift-by-rachel-maddow.html.

Shanker, Albert. 1995. "In Defense of Government." *New York Times* (November 5):E7.

Shanker, Thom, Michael S. Schmidt, and Robert F. Worth. 2011. "In Baghdad, Panetta Leads Uneasy Moment of Closure." *New York Times* (December 15). Online: http://www.nytimes.com/2011/12/16/world/middleeast/panetta-in-baghdad-leads-uneasy-moment-of-closure.

Shapiro, Judith. 1981. "Anthropology and the Study of Gender." In Elizabeth Langland and Walter Gove (Eds.), *A Feminist Perspective in the Academy.* Chicago: University of Chicago Press, pp. 110–129.

Shelden, Randall G. 2001. *Controlling the Dangerous Classes: A Critical Introduction to the History of Criminal Justice.* Boston: Allyn & Bacon.

Shelton, Hilary O. 2009. Foreword to "Critical Condition: African-American Youth in the Justice System," by Neelum Arya and Ian Augarten. Campaign for Youth Justice. Online: http://www.campaignforyouthjustice.org/documents/AfricanAmericanBrief.pdf.

Shierholz, Heidi. 2012. "The Long Term Unemployed Aren't Lazy, There Just Aren't Enough Jobs." *Economic Policy Institute* (February 14). Online: http://www.epi.org/publication/long-term-unemployed-arent-lazy-arent-jobs.

Shipler, David K. 2004. *The Working Poor: Invisible in America.* New York: Alfred A. Knopf.

Short, Kathleen. 2011. "The Research Supplemental Poverty Measure: 2010." U.S. Census Bureau, Current Population Reports. P60-241.

Shulman, Beth. 2007. "America's Low Wage Workers." In D. Stanley Eitzen and Janis E. Johnston (Eds.), *Inequality: Social Class and Its Consequences.* Boulder, CO: Paradigm Publishers, pp. 97–102.

Sidel, Robin. 2012. "ATMs Fall Short on Disability Rule." *Wall Street Journal* (March 8):C1.

Siegel, Michael. 2007. "Unsafe at Any Level." *New York Times* (January 28). Online: http://www.nytimes.com/2007/01/28/opinion/28Siegel.html.

Silvers, Anita. 1998. "Formal Justice." In Anita Silvers, David Wasserman, and Mary B. Mahowald (Eds.), *Disability, Difference, Discrimination.* Lanham, MD: Rowman & Littlefield, pp. 13–145.

Singer, Matt. 2006. "Overpaying for Jobs." *Progressive Populist* (August 1):6.

Singh, Robert. 2006. "The Bush Doctrine." In Mary Buckley and Robert Singh (Eds.), *The Bush Doctrine and the War on Terrorism.* London: Routledge, pp. 12–31.

Sklar, Holly. 1993. "The Upperclass and Mothers and the Hood." *Z Magazine* 6 (March):22–36.

Sklar, Holly. 2004. "Break That Glass Ceiling." *Progressive Populist* (June 15):16.

Sklar, Holly. 2009. "Medicare for All: Yes We Can." *Progressive Populist* (November 1):15.

Slevin, Peter. 2005. "The Anti-Evolution Revolution." *The Washington Post National Weekly Edition* (March 21–27):6.

Small, Maria Luis, David J. Harding, and Michele Lamont. 2010. "Reconsidering Culture and Poverty." *The Annals of the American Academy of Political and Social Sciences* 629(6):6–27.

Smith, John Robert and Alia Anderson. 2010. "Changing Federal Policy in the U.S. to Promote Livable Communities." *PTI* (September/October). Online: http://www.reconnectingamerica.org.

Smith, Maureen. 2001. "An Exploration of African American Preschool-Aged Children's Behavioral Regulation in Emotionally Arousing Situations." *Child Study Journal* 31(1):13–45.

Smith, Tom W. 2011. "Public Attitudes Toward Homosexuality." NORC/University of Chicago. Online: http://news.uchicago.edu/sites/all/file/attachments/Public%20Attitudes%20Toward%20Homosexuality.pdf.

Snipp, Matthew. 1996. "The First Americans: American Indians." In Silvia Pedraza and Ruben G. Rumbaut (Eds.), *Origins and Destinies: Immigration, Race, and Ethnicity in America*. Belmont, CA: Wadsworth, pp. 390–403.

Sokoloff, Natalie J., and Ida Dupont. 2005. "Domestic Violence: Examining the Intersection of Race, Class, and Gender: An Introduction." In Natalie J. Sokoloff (Ed.), *Domestic Violence at the Margins: Readings on Race, Class, Gender, and Culture*. New Brunswick, NJ: Rutgers University Press, pp. 1–13.

Solomon, Norman. 2010. "Don't Call It a 'Defense' Budget." CommonDreams.org (February 2). Online: http://www.commondreams.org/52374.

Solomon, Sondra E., Esther D. Rothblum, and Kimberly F. Balsam. 2005. "Money, Housework, Sex, and Conflict: Same-Sex Couples in Civil Unions, Those Not in Civil Unions, and Heterosexual Married Siblings," *Sex Roles* 52(9/10):561–575.

Somander, Tanya, and Zaid Gilani. 2011. "PTSD Awareness Day: Five Ways PTSD Hurts U.S. Soldiers." ThinkProgress.org. (June 27). Online: http://thinkprogress.org/security/2011/06/27/255231/ptsd-awareness-day.

Sommers, Christina Hoff. 2000. *The War Against Boys: How Misguided Feminism Is Harming Our Young Men*. New York: Simon and Schuster.

SourceWatch. 2008. "Government-Industry Revolving Door." (July 23). Online: http://www.sourcewatch.org/index.php?title-Government-industry-revolving.

Southern Poverty Law Center. 2006. "Immigration Fervor Fuels Racist Extremism." *SPLC Report* 36 (June):1.

Southern Poverty Law Center. 2007. "Hate Group Numbers Continue to Increase." *SPLC Report* 37 (Spring):1.

South Texas Colonia Initiative. 2010. "Who We Are." (January 9). Online: http://www.southtexascolonia.org.

Specter, Michael. 2011. "Getting a Fix." *The New Yorker* (October 17):36–45.

Spector, Malcolm, and John I. Kitsuse. 1987. *Constructing Social Problems*. Hawthorne, NY: Aldine de Gruyter.

Spencer, Porche, and E. Toleman. 2003. "We've Come a Long Way—Maybe: New Challenges for Gender Equity in Education." *Teachers College Record* 105(9):1774–1807.

SPLC Report. 2012. "Radical-Right Movement Explodes." (Spring):1,3.

Spong, John Shelby. 2005. *The Sins of Scripture*. New York: Harper San Francisco.

Stacey, Judith. 1990. *Brave New Families: Stories of Domestic Upheaval in Late Twentieth-Century America*. New York: Basic Books.

Stacey, Judith. 1991. "Backward toward the Postmodern Family: Reflections on Gender, Kinship, and Class in the Silicon Valley." In Alan Wolfe (Ed.), *America at Century's End*. Berkeley: University of California Press, pp. 17–34.

Stack, Carol B. 1990. "Different Voices, Different Visions: Gender, Culture, and Moral Reasoning." In Faye Ginsburg and Anna Lowenhaupt Tsing (Eds.), *Uncertain Terms: Negotiating Gender in American Culture*. Boston: Beacon Press, pp. 19–27.

Stack, Joseph. 2010. "Joseph Stack Manifesto." *Fox News* (February 18). Online: http://www.foxnews.com/printer-friendly-story/0,3566,586627,00.html.

Starr, Paul. 2012. "Supreme Surprise." *The America Prospect* (June 29). Online: http://prospect.org/article/supreme-surprise.

StateMaster. n.d. "Defense Contracts: Expenditures by State. Online: http://www.statemaster.com/graph/mil_def_con_exp-military-defense-contracts-expenditures.

Stein, Peter J., Judith Richman, and Natalie Hannon. 1977. *The Family: Functions, Conflicts, and Symbols*. Reading, MA: Addison-Wesley.

Stein, Rob. 2009. "Poor Memory: Researchers Say Chronic Stress Impairs the Thinking of Children Raised in Poverty." *The Washington Post National Weekly Edition* (April 13–19):37.

Steinberg, Jacques. 2001. "Gains Found for the Poor in Rigorous Preschool." *New York Times* (May 9). Online: http://www.nytimes.com/2001/05/09/national/09SCHO.html.

Stelter, Brian. 2009. "8 Hours a Day Spent on Screens, Study Finds." *The New York Times* (March 26). Online: http://www.nytimes.com/2009/03/27/business/media/27adco.html.

Sternberg, Steve. 2010. "'I Know' How to Rally Young Blacks." *USA Today* (March 4):7D.

Stockholm International Peace Research Institute (SIPRI). 2012. "17 April 2012: World Military Spending Levels Out After 13 Years of Increases." (April 17). Online: http://www.sipri.org/media/pressrelease/17-april-2012-world-military-spending-levels.html.

Stolberg, Sheryl Gay. 2002. "Minorities Got Inferior Care, Even If Insured, Study Finds." *New York Times* (March 21).

Stoller, Gary. 2011. "Report Says Congestion Costs Billions." *USA Today* (December 26):1B.

Story, Louise. 2007. "Anywhere the Eye Can See, It's Likely to See an Ad." *New York Times* (January 15). Online: http://www.nytimes.com/2007/01/15/business/media/15everywhere.html?_r=1.

Streitland, David. 2006. "Illegal—But Essential." *Los Angeles Times* (October 1). Online: http://www.latimes.com/business/la-fi-immigecon1oct01,0,2804532,print.story?coll-la-ho.

Stretesky, Paul B., Janis E. Johnston, and Jeremy Arney. 2003. "'Environmental Inequity': An Analysis of Large-Scale Hog Operations in 17 States, 1982–1997." *Rural Sociology* 68 (June):231–252.

Substance Abuse and Mental Health Services Administration (SAMHSA). 2012a. "Results from the 2010 National Survey on Drug Use and Health: Summary of National Findings." Office of Applied Studies. NSDUH Series H-41, HHS Publication NO. (SMA) 11-4658. Rockville, MD.

Substance Abuse and Mental Health Services Administration (SAMHSA). 2012b. "The Dawn Report." Drug Abuse Warning Network. (July 2). Online: http://www.samhsa.gov/data/2k12/DAWN096/SR096EDHighlights2010.pdf.

Suskind, Ron. 2006. *The One Percent Solution*. New York: Simon & Schuster.

Sussman, Aaron. 2007. "The Military Commissions Act." *Z Magazine* 20 (January):7–9.

Swain, John, Sally French, and Colin Cameron. 2003. *Controversial Issues in a Disabling Society*. Buckingham, UK: Open University Press.

Sweeney, Megan. 2002. "Remarriage and the Nature of Divorce." *Journal of Family Issues* 23:410–440.

Switzer, Jacqueline Vaughn. 2003. *Disabled Rights: American Disability Policy and the Fight for Equality*. Baltimore, MD: Georgetown University Press.

Symonds, William C. 2006. "Campus Revolutionary." *Business Week* (February 27):65–70.

Szasz, Thomas S. 1970. *The Manufacture of Madness*. New York: Delta Books.

Takaki, Ronald. 1993. *A Different Mirror: A History of Multicultural America*. Boston: Little, Brown.

Talvi, Silja J. A. 2005. "Breaking Rank: Former Seattle Police Chief Norm Stamper Takes on the Drug War." *In These Times* (November 21):27–28.

Taub, Diane E., and Patricia L. Fanflick. 2000. "The Inclusion of Disability in Introductory Sociology Textbooks." *Teaching Sociology* 28 (January):12–23.

Tavernise, Sabrina. 2010. "Grandparents Role Grows as the Economy Struggles." *New York Times* (November 10). Online: http://www.nytimes.com.

Taylor, Howard F. 2009. "Defining Race." In Elizabeth Higginbotham and Margaret L. Andersen (Eds.), *Race and Ethnicity in Society*. Belmont, CA: Wadsworth Cengage Learning.

Texas Health and Human Services Commission. 2003. "Colonias Initiative" (August). Online: http://www.hhsc.state.tax.us/hhst_projects/colonias/colonia_home.html.

Thomas, Karen. 2001. "Back to School for ADHD Drugs." *USA Today* (August 28):1D–2D.

Thomas, Oliver. 2007. "Having Faith in Women." *USA Today* (April 9):13A.

Thomma, Steven. 2009. "Obama Urges Longer School Hours, Extended School Year." McClatchy Newspapers (March 10). Online: http://www.mcclatchydc.com/2009/03/10/63663/obama-urges-longer-school-hours.html.

Thompson, Larry. 1995. "Search for a Gay Gene." *Time* (June 12):61–62.

Thompson, Mark. 2007. "Broken Down." *Time* (April 16):28–35.

Thompson, Mark, and Nancy Gibbs. 2012. "More U.S. Soldiers Have Killed Themselves Than Have Died in the Afghan War. Why Can't the Army Win the War on Suicide?" *Time* (July 23):23–31.

Thornburgh, Nathan. 2006. "Dropout Nation." *Time* (April 17):29–40.

Thorne, Barrie. 1993. *Gender Play: Girls and Boys in School.* New Brunswick, NJ: Rutgers University Press.

Thornton, Russell. 1996. "North American Indians and the Demography of Contact." In Silvia Pedraza and Ruben Rumbaut (Eds.), *Origins and Destinies: Immigration, Race, and Ethnicity in America.* Belmont, CA: Wadsworth, pp. 43–50.

Time. 2006. "Numbers." (March 13):17.

Timmer, Doug A., D. Stanley Eitzen, and Kathryn D. Talley. 1994. *Paths to Homelessness: Extreme Poverty and the Urban Housing Crisis.* Boulder, CO: Westview Press.

Tivnan, Edward. 1987. "Homosexuals and the Churches." *New York Times Magazine* (October 11):84–91.

Tjaden, P., and N. Thoennes. 2000. *Extent, Nature, and Consequences of Intimate Partner Violence.* Washington, DC: National Institute of Justice/ Centers for Disease Control and Prevention.

Toland, Bill. 2007. "Pitt Study Says Black Americans Exposed to More Tobacco Advertising." *Pittsburgh Post-Gazette.* (August 21). Online: http://www.post-gazette.com/pg/07233/810904-114.stm.

Traub, James. 2003. "City Slights." *New York Times Magazine* (May 4):17–18.

Trottman, Melanie. 2012. "U.S. Pushes Target for Hiring the Disabled." *Wall Street Journal* (February 29):1B–2B.

Truman, Jennifer L. 2011. *Criminal Victimization, 2010.* National Crime Victimization Survey. Washington, DC: U.S. Department of Justice, Bureau of Justice Statistics.

Tucker, Cynthia. 2010. "Immigrant Babies Will Remain in U.S." *Atlanta Journal Constitution* (August 15):A18.

Tullock, S. (Ed.). 1993. *The Reader's Digest Oxford Wordfinder.* Oxford: Clarendon Press.

Turk, Austin T. 2004. "Sociology of Terrorism." *Annual Review of Sociology* 30:271–286.

Tyson, Ann Scott. 2009. "The U.S. Military Easily Meets Its Recruiting Goals." *Washington Post National Weekly Edition* (October 19):35.

Ukman, Jason. 2011. "Arab World-Views of U.S., President Obama Increasing Negative." *Washington Post* (July 12). Online: http://www.washingtonpost.com/blogs/checkpoint-washington/post/arab-worlds-view-of-U.S.

Union of Concerned Scientists. 2007. "Smoke, Mirrors, and Hot Air: How ExxonMobil Uses Big Tobacco's Tactics to Manufacture Uncertainty on Climate Science." (January). Online: http://www.ucsusa.org/assets/documents/global_warming/exxon_report.pdf.

Union of the Physically Impaired against Segregation (UPIAS). 1976. *Fundamental Principles of Disability.* London: UPIAS.

United Nations. 2004. Online: http://www.un.org/esa/index.html.

Unknown News. 2010. "Casualties in Afghanistan and Iraq." (August 10). Online: http://www.unknownnews.org/casualties.html.

Unnithan, N. Prabha. 1994. "The Processing of Homicide Cases with Child Victims: Systemic and Situational Contingencies." *Journal of Criminal Justice* 22(1):41–50.

U.S. Bureau of Labor Statistics. 2009. Online: http://www.bls.gov/pub/mlr/2009/11/art5fall.pdf.

U.S. Bureau of Labor Statistics. 2012a. *Current Population Survey.* Online: http://www.bls.gov/cps/tables.htm#empstat.

U.S. Bureau of Labor Statistics. 2012b. "Women in the Labor Force: A Databook (2011 Edition)." Online: http://www.blsgov/cps/wlf-databook2011.htm.

U.S. Census Bureau. 2010. "American Community Survey: Households and Families." Online: http://factfinder2.census.gov.

U.S. Census Bureau. 2011a. "America's Families and Living Arrangements: 2011." Online: http://www.census.gov.

U.S. Census Bureau. 2011b. "Anniversary of Americans with Disabilities Act." *Census Bureau News* (July 26).

U.S. Department of Agriculture. 2012. "Geography of Poverty." Online: http://www.ers.usda.gov/topics/rural-economy-population/rural-poverty-well-being/geography-of-poverty.aspx.

U.S. Department of Defense. 2010. *Quadrennial Defense Review Report* (February). Washington, DC.

U.S. Department of Education, National Center for Educational Statistics. 2006. *Digest of Education Statistics.* (NCES 2006-030). Online: http://nces.ed.gov.

U.S. Department of Energy. n.d. "Reduce Climate Change." Online: http://www.fueleconomy.gov/feg/climate.shtml.

U.S. Department of Health and Human Services. 2008. "What Is Child Abuse and Neglect?" Child Welfare Information Gateway. Online: http://www.childwelfare.gov/pubs/factsheets/whatiscan.pdf.

U.S. Department of Health and Human Services. 2009. *Child Maltreatment 2007.* Washington, DC: U.S. Government Printing Office.

U.S. Department of Health and Human Services, Administration on Children, Youth, and Families. 2010. "Child Maltreatment 2008." Washington, D.C.:U.S. Government Printing Office. Online: http://www.acf.hhs.gov.

U.S. Department of Health and Human Services, Administration on Children, Youth, and Families. 2011. "Child Maltreatment 2010." Washington, D.C.:U.S. Government Printing Office. Online: http://www.acf.hhs.gov.

U.S. Department of Heath and Human Services, Office of Minority Health. 2012. Online: http://minorityhealth.hhs.gov.

U.S. Department of Housing and Urban Development. 2012. "Understanding Neighborhood Effects of Concentrated Poverty." *Evidence Matters* (Winter). Online: http://www.huduser.org.

U.S. Department of Labor. 1965. *The Negro Family: The Case for National Action.* Washington, DC: U.S. Government Printing Office.

U.S. Department of Labor. 2009. "Employment Situation: February 2009." Online: http://www.bls.gov/news.release/archives/emp-sit_03062009.pdf.

U.S. Department of Labor. 2010. "Metropolitan Area Employment and Unemployment—November 2009." *Bureau of Labor Statistics Economic News Release* (January 5).

U.S. Energy Information Administration. 2011. "Oil: Crude and Petroleum Products." (July 5). Online: http://www.eia.gov/energyexplained/index.efm?page=oil_home#tab2.

U.S. Equal Employment Opportunity Commission. 2009. "Notice Concerning the Americans with Disabilities Act Amendments Act of 2008." Online: http://www.eeoc.gov/laws/statutes/adaa-notice.cfm.

USA Today. 2005. "FBI May Be Checking on You, But You Have No Way of Knowing" (November 9):14A.

USA Today. 2007. "Secrecy Rises: Washington Gives Public Less and Less" (March 12):8A.

USA Today. 2010. "Don't Spare the Pentagon from the Budgeting Ax" (December 2):10A.

USA Today. 2012. "Long, Messy Afghanistan War Heads toward Uncertain Ending" (May 23):8A.

Usdansky, Margaret L. 1992. "Middle Class 'Pulling Apart' to Rich, Poor." *USA Today* (February 20):A1.

Valian, Virginia. 1998. "Running in Place." *Sciences* 38 (January/February):18–23.

Van Biema, David. 2004. "Rising above the Stained-Glass Ceiling." *Time* (June 28):59–61.

vanden Heuvel, Katrina. 2010. "No Holiday for Labor Unions." *Washington Post* (September 5).

Vecoli, Rudolph J. 1964. "Contadini in Chicago: A Critique of the Uprooted." *Journal of American History* 51:405–417.

Veiga, Alex. 2013. "Fewer U.S. Homes Repossessed by Banks in 2012." *Yahoo! News* (January 17). Online: News.yahoo.com/fewer-us-homes-repossessed-banks-050347401.html.

Villano, Matt. 2009. "Reading, Writing, and Recession." *Time* (February 23):54–55.

Visher, Emily B., John S. Visher, and Kay Pasley. 2003. "Remarriage, Families, and Stepparenting." In Froma Walsh (Ed.), *Normal Family Processes: Growing Diversity and Complexity,* 3rd ed. New York: Guilford Press, pp. 153–175.

Von Drehle, David. 2007. "The Boys Are All Right." *Time* (August 6):40–42.

Wage Gap. 2003. Online: http://www.infoplease.com/ipa10/7/6/1/7/a076317.phtml.

Wagner, Peter and Susan Edwards. 2007. "New Orleans by the Numbers," In D. Stanley Eitzen and Janis Johnston (Eds.), *Inequality: Social Class and Its Consequences*. Boulder, CO: Paradigm Publishers.

Walby, Sylvia. 2000. "Gender, Globalization, and Democracy." *Gender and Development* 8 (March):20–28.

Wali, Alakka. 1992. "Multiculturalism: An Anthropological Perspective." *Report from the Institute for Philosophy and Public Policy*. University of Maryland, 23 (Spring/Summer):6–8.

Wallerstein, Judith S. 2003. "Children of Divorce: A Society in Search of Policy." In Mary Ann Mason, Arlene Skolnick, and Stephen D. Sugarman (Eds.), *All Our Families*, 2nd ed. New York: Oxford University Press, pp. 66–95.

Wallis, Claudia, and Sonja Steptoe. 2006. "How to Bring Our Schools out of the 20th Century." *Time* (December 18):50–56.

Walsh, Bryan. 2009. "It Will Pay to Save the Planet." *Time* (May 25):47.

Wang, Feng. 2012. "China's One Child Policy at 30." Brookings Institute (March 13). Online: http://www.brookings.edu/opinions/2010/09/24_china_one_child_policy_at_30.

Wang, Sam. 2013. "The Great Gerrymander of 2012." *New York Times* (February 2). Online: http://www.nytimes.com/2013/02/03/opinion/sunday/the-great-gerrymander-of-2012.

Wardrip, Keith E. 2009. "Out of Reach 2009." *National Low Income Housing Coalition* (April).

Warren, Mark. 2011. "The White Fight." *The American Prospect* (April):A20–A21.

Warren, Patricia, Donald Tomosakovic-Devey, William Smith, Matthew Zingraff, and Marcinda Mason. 2006. "Driving While Black: Bias Processes and Racial Disparity in Police Stops." *Criminology* 44, no. 3:709–738.

Washington, Harriet A. 2006. *Medical Apartheid: The Dark History of Medical Experimentation on Black Americans from Colonial Times to the Present*. New York: Doubleday.

Washington Post. 2007. "U.S. Infant Mortality Rate Twice as High for Blacks." (May 2). Online: http://www.washingtonpost.com/wp-dyn/content/article/2007/05/02/AR2007050201436.html.

Washington Times. 2003. "Bush Signs Paper Allowing Nuclear Response." (January 31). Online: http://www.washtimes.com/archive/2003013111255020010.html.

Waters, Mary C. 1996. "Optional Ethnicities: For Whites Only?" In *Origins and Destinies: Immigration, Race, and Ethnicity in America*, Silvia Pedraza and Ruben G. Rumbaut (eds.). Belmont, CA: Wadsworth.

Weatherall, Ann. 2002. *Gender, Language, and Discourse*. New York: Routledge.

Weber, Lynn. 2010. *Understanding Race, Class, Gender, and Sexuality*, 2nd ed. New York: Oxford University Press.

Webster's New World Dictionary of American English, 3rd ed. 1991. Victoria Neufeldt and David B. Guralnik (Eds.). Cleveland, NY: Simon & Schuster.

Wedekind, Jennifer. 2009. "Dying for Work." *Multinational Monitor* 30 (May/June):7–8.

Weisberg, Jacob. 1996. *In Defense of Government*. New York: Scribner.

Weiss, Lawrence D. 1997. *Private Medicine and Public Health: Profit, Politics, and Prejudice in the American Health Care Enterprise*. Boulder, CO: Westview Press.

Weissbourd, Richard. 1994. "Divided Families, Whole Children." *American Prospect* 18 (Summer):66–72.

Weitz, Rose. 2004. *The Sociology of Health, Illness, and Health Care*, 3rd ed. Belmont, CA: Wadsworth.

Weitzman, Lenore J. 1985. *The Divorce Revolution: The Unexpected Social and Economic Consequences for Women and Children in America*. New York: Free Press.

Weitzman, Lenore J., Deborah Eifler, Elizabeth Hokada, and Catherine Ross. 1972. "Sex-Role Socialization in Picture Books for Preschool Children." *American Journal of Sociology* 77 (May):1125–1150.

Wellman, David T. 1977. *Portraits of White Racism*, 2nd ed. Cambridge: Cambridge University Press.

Wellstone, Paul. 1998. "A Time for Change." *On the Road with Paul Wellstone. Newsletter* (Summer):1–2.

Wenzl, Roy. 2007. "Are We Losing Our Boys?" *Wichita Eagle* (February 25):1A.

Werner, Erica. 2009. "AARP: Prescription Drug Prices Up." *Health News*. Online: http://www.myfoxla.com/dpp/health/dpg-AARP-Prescription-Drug-Prices-Up.

Wertheimer, Fred. 2012a. "Super PACs a Disaster for Democracy." CNN (February 15). Online: http://www.cnn.com/2012/02/15/opinion/wertheimer-super-pacs/index.

Wertheimer, Fred. 2012b. "Super PACs Can Be Thwarted." *Washington Post* (April 3). Online: www.washingtonpost.com/opinions/super-pacs-ca-be-thwarted-even-with-citizensunited/2012/04/03/g1QARqytS_story.html.

West, Candace, and Don Zimmerman. 1987. "Doing Gender." *Gender & Society* 1.125–151.

West, Darrel M. 2010. "7 Myths That Have Clouded the Immigration Debate." *USA Today* (September 1):9A.

Western Regional Advocacy Project. 2010. *Without Housing: Decades of Federal Housing Cutbacks, Massive Homelessness and Policy Failures: 2010 Update*. San Francisco. Online: http://www.wrap_without_housing.pdf.

Wharton, Tony. 1998. "Expect Hurricanes Because of Gays, Pat Robertson Says." *Denver Post* (June 10):14A.

Wheatcroft, Geoffrey. 2007. "Who Made Her Queen." *Washington Post National Weekly Edition* (October 15):27.

Wheeler, David L. 1992. "Studies Tying Homosexuality to Genes Draw Criticism from Researchers." *Chronicle of Higher Education* (February 5):A1–A2, A9.

White, Joseph B. 2011. "American Idle." *Wall Street Journal* (February 2):D1–D2.

The White House. 2002a. "Operation Enduring Freedom: One Year of Accomplishments." Online: http://www.whitehouse.gov/infocus/defense/enduringfreedom.html.

The White House. 2002b. "The National Security Strategy of the United States of America." Online: http://www.whitehouse.gov/nssc/nss/pdf.

Whitty, Julia. 2010. "The Last Labor." *Mother Jones* 35(May–June):25–43.

Wildmon, Donald E. 2007. "Ford Helps Sponsor Explicit, Sickening Homosexual Scene." American Family Association. (January 23). Online: http://www.afa.net/aa012307.asp.

Wilkinson, Richard and Kate Pickett. 2010. *The Spirit Level: Why Greater Equality Makes Societies Stronger*. New York: Bloomsburg Press.

Will, George. 2007. "Golly, What Did Jon Do?" *Newsweek* (January 29):72.

Williams, Christine. 1992. "The Class Escalator: Hidden Advantages for Men in the 'Female' Professions." *Social Problems* 39 (August):253–267.

Williams, Christine. 1995. *Still a Man's World: Men Who Do Women's Work*. Berkeley: University of California Press.

Williams, David R. 1990. "Socioeconomic Differentials in Health: A Review and Redirection." *Social Psychology Quarterly* 53 (June):81–99.

Willis, Ellen. 1998. "We Need a Radical Left." *Nation* (June 29):18–21.

Wills, Garry. 1995. "The New Revolutionaries." *New York Review* (August 10):50–55.

Wilson, William J. 1987. *The Truly Disadvantaged: The Inner City, the Underclass, and Public Policy*. Chicago: University of Chicago Press.

Wilson, William J. 1996. *When Work Disappears: The World of the New Urban Poor*. New York: Knopf.

Wilson, William J. 2010. *More Than Just Race: Being Black and Poor in the Inner City*. New York: W. W. Norton & Company, Inc.

Winant, Howard. 2009. "Just Do It: Notes on Politics and Race at the Dawn of the Obama Presidency." *DuBois Review* 6.1):49–70.

Witt, Susan. 1997. "Parental Influence on Children's Socialization to Gender Roles." *Adolescence* 32(126):253–259.

Wittner, Lawrence. 2012. "The Shame of Nations: A New Record Is Set for Spending on War." (April 23). Online: http://www.commondreams.org.

Woellert, Lorraine, and Dawn Kopecke. 2006. "The Snooping Goes Beyond Phone Calls." *Business Week* (May 29):38.

Wolf, Rosalie S. 2000. "The Nature and Scope of Elder Abuse." *Generations* 24 (Summer):6–12.

Wolfe, Alan. 1989. *Whose Keeper? Social Science and Moral Obligation*. Berkeley: University of California Press.

World Health Organization. 2011. "Air Quality and Health." (September). Online: http://www.who.int/mediacentre/factsheets/fs313/en/index.html.

World Hunger Education Service. 2011. "2012 World Hunger and Poverty Facts and Statistics." (December 4). Online: http://www.worldhunger.org/articles/learn/worldhungerfacts2012.htm.

Worldwatch Institute. 2012. "The State of Consumption Today." (January 19). Online: http://www.worldwatch.org/node/810.

World Water Assessment Programme. 2009. "Water in a Changing World." Online: http://www.unesco.org/new/en/natural-sciences/environment/water/wwap/wwdr/wwdr3-2009.

Wright, D. Brad. 2009. "The Price of Prescription Drugs Around the World." *Huffington Post* (March 2). Online: http://www.huffingtonpost.com/d-brad-wright/the-price-of-prescription-drugs.

Wright, David, and Bradley Blackburn. 2010. "Why Do Hispanics Outlive White and Black Americans?" *ABC News*. Online: http://www.abcnews.go.com/wn/us-hispanics-longer-life-expectancy-white-black-americans/story?id=11883156.

Yen, Hope. 2009. "Minority Kids in Majority by 2023." Associated Press (March 5).

Yen, Hope. 2011. "U.S. Rural Population Falls to Lowest Ever." Associated Press (July 28).

Yen, Hope. 2012. "Census Finds Low Growth in Suburbs." Associated Press (April 8).

Youssef, Nancy A. 2010. "Pentagon Redefines Military's Mission." *Wichita Eagle* (February 2):1A, 5A.

Z, Mickey. 2006. "Read This Before You Vote." *Z Magazine* 19 (November):6–7.

Zakaria, Fareed. 2012. "Romney Is Wrong on Tax Cuts." *Washington Post* (June 7). Online: http://www.washingtonpost.com/opinions/fareed-zakaria-romney-is-wrong-on-tax-cuts/2012/06/07/g1QAy1phLV_story.html.

Zaslow, Martha J., and Kathryn Tout. 2002. "Child-Care Quality Matters." *American Prospect* (April 8), p. 49.

Zeitlin, Maurice, Kenneth G. Lutterman, and James W. Russell. 1977. "Death in Vietnam: Class, Poverty, and the Risks of War." In Maurice Zeitlin (Ed.), *American Society, Inc.*, 2nd ed. Chicago: Rand McNally, pp. 143–155.

Zelizer, Gerald L. 2004. "Time to Break the Stained Glass Ceiling." *USA Today* (September 16):1A.

Zhou, Min. 1997. "Growing Up American: The Challenge Confronting Immigrant Children and Children of Immigrants." *Annual Review of Sociology* 23:63–95.

Zimmerman, Jonathan. 2008. "Poverty, Not Sex Ed, Key Factor in Teen Pregnancy." SFGate.com (September 4). Online: http://articles.sfgate.com/2008-09-04.

Zinn, Howard. 2005. "Against Discouragement." Commencement Address, Spelman College (May 15).

Zinn, Howard. 2008. "Memo to Obama, McCain: No One Wins in a War." *Boston Globe* (July 17). Reprinted in Commondreams.org. Online: http://www.commondreams.org/archive/2008/07/17/10427.

Zuckerman, Mortimer B. 2000. "A Bit of Straight Talk." *U.S. News & World Report* (October 2):76.

Zuckerman, Mortimer B. 2006. "A Little Sanity, Please." *U.S. News & World Report* (April 17):74.

CREDITS

TEXT

CHAPTER 2

page 35:   Borosage, Robert L. 2001. "Forked-Tongue Budget." *Nation* (April 30):4–5; Reich, Robert B. 2000. "What's the Difference?" *American Prospect* (August 28):64.

page 45:   Parenti, Michael. 1978. *Power and the Powerless*, 2nd ed. New York: St. Martin's Press.

page 51:   Gonzalez, Antonio, and Stephanie Moore. 2003. "Wealthy Campaign Donors Stifle Minority Voices." *USA Today* (December 11):23A.

CHAPTER 3

page 60:   Scheer, Robert. 2002. "Playing Politics with World Population." *Los Angeles Times* (November 5).

CHAPTER 4

pages 77–78:   Based on Knickerbocker, Brad. 2006. "The Environmental Load of 300 Million: How Heavy?" *Christian Science Monitor* (September 26). Online: http://www.csmonitor.com/2006/0926/p01s01-usssc.htm.

page 81:   Oliver, Rachel. 2008. "Rich, Poor, and Climate Change." CNN.com. (February 17). Available online: http://edition.cnn.com/2008/business/02/17/eco.class.

page 88:   Based on Henig, Jess. 2009. "Climategate." Factcheck.org. (December 10). Available online: http://www.factcheck.org.

CHAPTER 6

page 143:   Traub, James. 2003. "City Slights." *New York Times Magazine* (May 4):17–18.

page 147:   Hockstader, Lee. 2002. "Dreams among the Poorest of the Poor." *Washington Post National Weekly Edition* (September 2–8):29.

CHAPTER 7

page 167:   Ehrenreich, Barbara. 2006. "The High Cost of Being Poor." AlterNet (July 25). Available online: http://www.AlterNet.org/story/39273.

pages 170–171:   Beck, Joan. 1995. "Preschool Can Help Close the Poverty Gap." *Denver Post* (January 19):7B. Materials courtesy of The Denver Post.

page 171:   Cary, Nathaniel. 2010. "Andre Bauer Equates 'Stray Animals' to People on Government Aid." Greenville Online.com. (January 25). Available online: http://greenvilleonline.com.

page 176:   Oppenheim, Jerrold, and Theo MacGregor. 2006. "The Economics of Poverty: How Investments to Eliminate Poverty Benefit All Americans." Entergy Corporation (June). Available online: http://www.democracyandregulation.com/detail.cfm?artid=99; Children's Defense Fund. 2004a. *The State of America's Children 2004*. Washington, DC: Children's Defense Fund.

CHAPTER 8

page 188:   Richburg, Keith B. 2004. "A Smorgasbord of Cultures." *Washington Post National Weekly Edition* (November 107):17.

page 195:   Parenti, Michael. 1978. *Power and the Powerless*, 2nd ed. New York: St. Martin's Press.

page 201:   Darling Hammond, Linda. 2010. "Structured for Failure: Race, Resources, and Student Achievement." In *Doing Race: Essays for the 21st Century*. Hazel, Rose Marcus and Paula M. L. Moya, Eds. NY: W. W. Norton & Company, Inc. pp. 295–320.

page 208:   Wilson, William J. 2010. *More Than Just Race: Being Black and Poor in the Inner City*. NY: W. W. Norton & Company, Inc.

CHAPTER 9

page 223:   Peterson, Linda, and Elaine Enarson. 1974. "Blaming the Victim in the Sociology of Women: On the Misuse of the Concept of Socialization." Paper presented at the Pacific Sociological Association, San Jose, California, March.

page 233:   Sklar, Holly. 2004. "Break That Glass Ceiling." *Progressive Populist* (June 15):16.

CHAPTER 10

page 246:   Wheeler, David L. 1992. "Studies Tying Homosexuality to Genes Draw Criticism from Researchers." *Chronicle of Higher Education* (February 5):A1–A2, A9.

CHAPTER 11

pages 272–273:   Based on Russell, Marta. 1998. *Beyond Ramps: Disability at the End of the Social Contract*. Monroe, ME: Common Courage Press.

Russell, Marta. 2000. "The Political Economy of Disablement." *Dollars & Sense* (September/October):13–15;48–49.

pages 277 and 278:   Hershey, Laura. 2000. "Choosing Disability." In Estelle Disch (Ed.), *Reconstructing Gender: A Multicultural Anthology*, 2nd ed. Mountain View, CA: Mayfield, pp. 556–563.

page 282:   Johnson, Harriet McBryde. 2004. "Stairway to Justice." *New York Times Magazine* (May 30):11–12.

page 283:   Schoettler, Gail. 2000. "You Can't Buy Human Decency." *Denver Post* (October 1):2L.

CHAPTER 12

page 296:   O'Donnell, Jayne. 2000. "Suffering in Silence." *USA Today* (April 3):1B–2B.

page 303:   Jackson, Jesse. 2007. "Racially Biased Justice Still Infects American Courtrooms." *The Chicago Sun-Times* (September 18). Available online: http://www.commondreams.org/archive/2007/09/18/3911; Facing South. 2009. "Jena Six Case Comes to an End; Shone Light on Racism in Criminal Justice System." The Institute for Southern Studies. (June 30). Available online: http://www.southernstudies.org/2009/06/post-34.html.

page 308:   Edelman, Marion Wright. 2009. "Promising Models for Reforming Juvenile Justice Systems." Children's Defense Fund (September 5). Available online: http://www.childrensdefense.org/child-research-datapublications/data/marian-wright-edelman-child-watch-column/promising-models-for-reforming.html.

CHAPTER 13

page 333:   Glasser, Ira. 2006. "Drug Busts = Jim Crow." *The Nation* (July 10):24–26.

page 336:   Talvi, Silja J. A. 2005. "Breaking Rank: Former Seattle Police Chief Norm Stamper Takes on the Drug War." *In These Times* (November 21):27–28.

CHAPTER 15

page 389:   Moynihan, Daniel P., from The Institute for Research on Poverty, copyright © 1988, by the Board of Regents of the University of Wisconsin.

CHAPTER 16

pages 402, 427:   Everton, Terry. 2004. "Why School Sucks." *Z Magazine* (November):54–56.

pages 412–413:   Mead, Sara. 2006. "The Truth About Boys and Girls." *Education Sector Report* (June 27). Available online: http://www.educationsector.org/analysis_show.htm?doc_id=378705.

page 413:   Douglas, Susan J. 2010. "Enlightened Sexism: 'Women's Success' Means It's Fine to Resurrect—Even Celebrate—Sexist Stereotypes." *In These Times* (March 1). Available online: http://www.AlterNet.org/story/145843.

page 420:   Orfield, Gary, Genevieve Siegel-Hawley, and John Kucsera. 2011. "Divided We Fail: Segregated and Unequal Schools in the Southland." University of California, Los Angeles, Civil Rights Project/Proyecto de Derechos Civiles. Online: http://civilrightsproject.ucla.edu.

CHAPTER 17

pages 432–433, 435, 449–450:   From *The Healing of America* by T. R. Reid, copyright © 2009 T. R. Reid. Used by permission of The Penguin Press, a division of Penguin Group (USA) Inc.

page 437:   Glasser, Ronald J. 2009. "'He Who Has the Gold Sets the Rules': How Managed Care Has Created an Unsustainable System for Doctors, Patients and Our Society." *Washington Post National Weekly Edition* (June 8):24.

page 449:   Sternberg, Steve. 2010. "'I Know' How to Rally Young Blacks." *USA Today* (March 4):7D; Kuttner, Robert. 1998. "Toward Universal Coverage." *Washington Post National Weekly Edition* (July 20):27.

page 457:   Frank, Robert H. 2012. "Giving Health Care a Chance to Evolve." *New York Times* (June 30). www.nytimes.com/2012/07/01/business/health-care-ruling-lets-the-system-evolve-economic-view.html, para 25.

CHAPTER 18

page 468:   McVeigh. 1992. Letter to Union-Sun and Journal (Lockport, New York) (February 11).

page 469:   Cassidy, John. 2010. "The Tea Party U.S.A.: It's Still the Economy Stupid!" *The New Yorker* (February 19). Online: http://www.commondreams.org/print/52997; Southern Poverty Law Center. 2012. "Radical-Right Movement Explodes." (Spring):1,3.

page 482: Based on Herman, Edward S. 2006. "Torture, Moral Values, and Leadership of the Free World." *Z Magazine* 19 (November):27–30.

CHAPTER 19

page 491: Wellstone, Paul. 1998b. "A Time for Change." On the Road with Paul Wellstone. Newsletter (Summer):1–2.

page 492: Risman, Barbara J., and Donald Tomaskovic-Devey. 1998. "Editors Note." *Contemporary Sociology* 27 (March):vii–viii.

page 494: Kaul, Donald. 2010. "Next We'll Sell Senate Seats to Exxon Mobil and AT&T." *Progressive Populist* (March 1):23. Donald Kaul is an Otherworlds columnist. Otherworlds.org.

page 497: Belsky, Jay. 1990. "Infant Day Care, Child Development, and Family Policy." *Society* (July/August):10–12.

page 498: Judson, David. 1997. "Neglect of Kids 'No Less than Collective Sin.' " Gannett News Service (June).

page 500: Shanker, Albert. 1995. "In Defense of Government." *New York Times* (November 5):E7.

page 501: *Nation*. 1996. "In Fact. . . ." (January 1):5.

page 503: Reich, Robert B. 1998. "Broken Faith: Why We Need to Renew the Social Compact." *Nation* (February 16):11–17.

page 504: Cleveland, Harlan. 1992. "The Age of People Power." *Futurist* 26 (January/February):14–18.

PHOTOS

CHAPTER 1

page 2: FREDERIC J. BROWN/AFP/Getty Images
page 4: Marmaduke St. John/Alamy
page 13: bikeriderlondon/Shutterstock

CHAPTER 2

page 26: Jim Young/REUTERS/Landov
page 31: AP Images/Peter Cosgrove
page 42: Brian Snyder/Reuters/Landov
page 43: Justin Sullivan/Getty Images

CHAPTER 3

page 54: Peter Treanor/Alamy
page 60: Kaveh Kazemi/Hulton Archive/Getty Images
page 66: Andrew Biraj/Reuters/Landov

CHAPTER 4

page 75: Justin Stumberg/US Navy/DOD/Sipa Press/Newscom
page 79: Chad Ehlers/Alamy
page 80: Spencer Tirey/ZUMA Press
page 84: Trevor Collens/Photoshot/Newscom
page 85: Dan Lamont/Corbis
page 87: Collection10/GlowImages/Alamy
page 92: mikeledray/Shutterstock

CHAPTER 5

page 98: Dorothy Alexander/Alamy
page 107: Jim West/Alamy
page 113: Michael Scheer/Alamy

CHAPTER 6

page 128: Nickolay Vinokurov/Shutterstock
page 133: Peter Steiner/Alamy
page 145: William Campbell/Corbis

CHAPTER 7

page 155: Marc Jackson/Axiom/ZUMAPRESS.com/Newscom
page 160: David A. Barnes/Alamy
page 161: Gary C. Caskey/UPI/Landov
page 170: Scott J. Ferrell/Congressional Quarterly/Alamy
page 174: David Grossman/Alamy
page 179: Rick Friedman/Corbis

CHAPTER 8

page 182: picturescolourlibrary/Pictures Colour Library/Newscom
page 190: Melanie Stetson Freeman/The Christian Science Monitor/Getty Images

CHAPTER 9

page 205: M. Spencer Green/AP Images
page 206: Alan Zinn/Lookaround

CHAPTER 9

page 211: Skjold Photographs/PhotoEdit, Inc
page 221: Adam Burn/Getty Images
page 228: Kevin Lamarque/Reuters/Landov

CHAPTER 10

page 241: Marilyn Humphries/The Image Works
page 243 (top): Win Mcnamee/Reuters/Landov
page 243 (bottom): Matt Sayles/AP Images
page 245 (left): Library of Congress Prints and Photographs Division [LC-DIG-ppmsca-19754]
page 245 (right): John Decker/ZUMA Press/Newscom
page 252: Marilyn Humphries/The Image Works
page 255: Zuma/ZUMA Wire Service/Alamy
page 256: Marilyn Humphries/The Image Works
page 261: Randy Holmes/ABC/Getty Images

CHAPTER 11

page 264: WENN.com/Newscom
page 266: Charles Stirling/Alamy
page 279: Toby Talbot/AP Images

CHAPTER 12

page 285: Hans Gutknecht/ZUMAPRESS/Newscom
page 289: MarkAllenJohnson/ZUMAPRESS.com/Newscom
page 293: picture-alliance/Newscom
page 295: Louis Lanzano/AP Images
page 300: Sandra Baker/Alamy
page 304: Gaetano/Corbis/Flirt/Glow Images

CHAPTER 13

page 311: David McNew/Getty Images
page 313: SSPL/The Image Works
page 318: Chicago Sun-Times/Rich Hein/AP Images
page 322: HO/REUTERS/Landov
page 329: Ben Margot/AP Images

CHAPTER 14

page 339: Kin Cheung/AP Images
page 344: Maurizio Gambarini/Agentur/Newscom
page 350: rSnapshotPhotos/Shutterstock

CHAPTER 15

page 369: Lambert/Archive Photos/Getty Images
page 372: HALFDARK/FSTOP/Corbis
page 381: auremar/Shutterstock
page 386: Jupiterimages/Comstock/Getty Images/Thinkstock

CHAPTER 16

page 401: Ted Thai/Time Life Pictures/Getty Images
page 402: Michael Ventura/PhotoEdit, Inc.
page 405: David Grossman/Alamy
page 407: TIM SLOAN/AFP/Newscom
page 417: Jeff Damone/Alamy
page 424: DarkoZeljkovic/Shutterstock.com
page 427: Brad Nading/Garden City Telegram/AP Images

CHAPTER 17

page 430: Chris Maddaloni/Roll Call/Getty Images
page 440: Claudio Gallone/Tips RM/Glow Images
page 456: Roger L. Wollenberg—Pool via CNP/Newscom

CHAPTER 18

page 459: Haji Mujtaba/Reuters/Landov
page 473: SEAN ADAIR/Reuters/Landov
page 478: Brooks Kraft/Corbis
page 486: epa european pressphoto agency b.v./Alamy

CHAPTER 19

page 489: Jim West/The Image Works
page 495: Joe Ferrer/Shutterstock
page 505: AP Images

INDEX

THE DEMOGRAPHICS OF U.S. POVERTY

Selected Demographics of the Poverty Population, 2010

	Number in Poverty	Percent in Poverty
All people	46.2 million	15.1%
Race/Ethnicity		
White, not Hispanic	19.6 million	9.9%
Black	10.7 million	27.4%
Asian	1.7 million	12.1%
Hispanic	13.2 million	26.6%
Age		
Under 18 years	16.4 million	22.0%
Over 65	3.5 million	9.0%
Nativity		
Native born	38.6 million	14.4%
Foreign born	7.6 million	19.9%
Type of Family		
Married-couple	3.6 million	6.2%
Female-householder, no husband present	4.7 million	31.6%
Male-householder, no wife present	880,000	15.8%

Source: DeNavas-Walt, Carmen, Bernadette D. Proctor, and Jessica C. Smith. 2011. "Income, Poverty, and Health Insurance Coverage in the United States: 2010." U.S. Census Bureau, Current Population Reports, P60-239. U.S. Government Printing Office, Washington, D.C., table 4, pages 15–16.

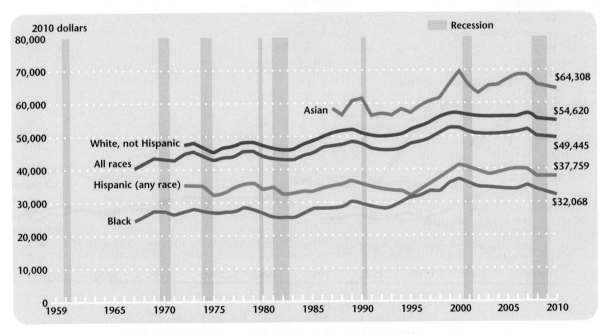

Real Median Household Income by Race and Hispanic Origin: 1967–2010

Note: Median household income data are not available prior to 1967.

Source: Carmen DeNavas-Walt, Bernadette D. Proctor, and Jessica C. Smith. 2011. U.S. Census Bureau, Current Population Reports, P60-239, *Income, Poverty, and Health Insurance Coverage in the United States: 2010*. Washington, DC: U.S. Government Printing Office, p. 8.

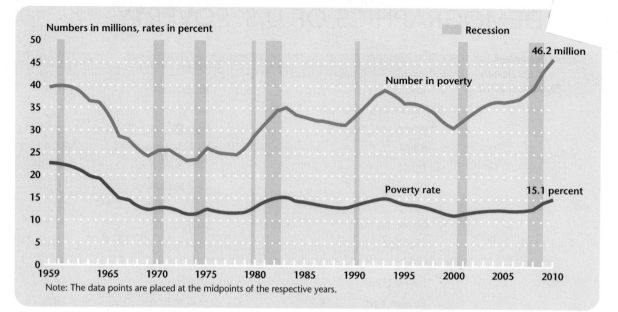

Number in Poverty and Poverty Rate: 1959 to 2010

Source: DeNavas-Walt, Carmen, Bernadette D. Proctor, and Jessica C. Smith. 2011. "Income, Poverty, and Health Insurance Coverage in the United States: 2010." U.S. Census Bureau, Current Population Reports, P60-239. U.S. Government Printing Office, Washington, D.C., [Figure 4, page 14].

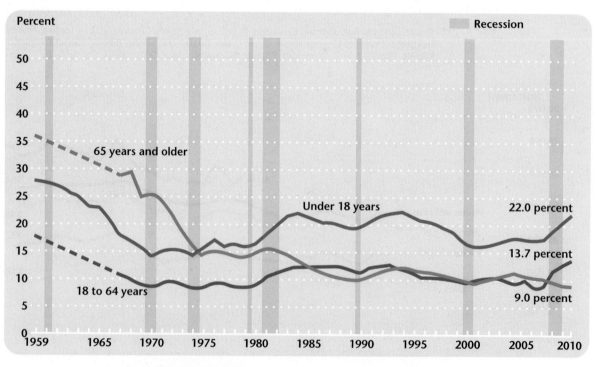

Poverty Rates by Age: 1959 to 2010

Source: Carmen DeNavas-Walt, Bernadette D. Proctor, and Jessica C. Smith. 2011. U.S. Census Bureau, Current Population Reports, P60, *Income, Poverty and Health Insurance Coverage in the United States: 2010*. U.S. Government Printing Office, Washington, DC, p. 17.